Assessment of Chil

WISC–IV and WPPSI–III Supplement

10/10/06

Jerome M. Sattler
San Diego State University

Ron Dumont
Fairleigh Dickinson University

Jerome M. Sattler, Publisher, Inc.
San Diego

Copyright © 2004 by Jerome M. Sattler, Publisher, Inc.
P.O. Box 3557, La Mesa, CA 91944-3557
Phone: 619-460-3667
Fax: 619-460-2489
www.sattlerpublisher.com

All rights reserved. No part of the material protected by this copyright notice may be reproduced or utilized in any form or by any means, electronic or mechanical, including photocopying, recording, or by any information storage and retrieval system, without written permission from the copyright owner.

Editorial Services: Sally Lifland, Lifland et al., Bookmakers
Interior Design: Jerome M. Sattler and Sally Lifland
Cover Design: Jerome M. Sattler
Proofreaders: Gail Magin, Jeanne Yost, Denise Throckmorton, Quica Ostrander, and David N. Sattler
Indexers: Ron Dumont and Jerome M. Sattler
Production Coordinators: Sally Lifland and Jerome M. Sattler
Compositor: Kadir Samuel
Cover Printer: Phoenix Color
Printer and Binder: Maple-Vail Book Manufacturing Group

This text was set in Times and Helvetica, printed on Bright White Tradebook, and Smyth sewn.

Cover: Timothy Nolan, _Shift_, 2004; Baking powder, baking soda, graphite and glitter sifted on concrete floor; 324 square feet; courtesy the artist, Timothy Nolan, and Newspace, Los Angeles; Photo credit: Joshua White

ISBN: 0-9702671-1-8

10   9   8   7   6   5   4

Printed in the United States of America

CONTENTS

LIST OF TABLES

LIST OF FIGURES

LIST OF EXHIBITS

PREFACE AND ACKNOWLEDGMENTS

Assessment of Children: WISC–IV and WPPSI–III Supplement is designed to be used by both students and professionals as a stand-alone text or in conjunction with *Assessment of Children: Cognitive Applications, Fourth Edition.* The text provides an in-depth analysis of two of the major instruments useful for the cognitive assessment of children. Some notable features of the text include the following:

1. A thorough discussion of the psychometric properties of each test.
2. An in-dept presentation of each subtest, including description, rationale, factor analytic findings, reliability and correlational highlights, administrative guidelines, and interpretive suggestions. Each administrative guidelines section includes a discussion of background considerations, starting considerations, reverse sequence, discontinue considerations, scoring guidelines, and the record form.
3. An extensive administrative checklist for the WISC–IV and for the WPPSI–III. The checklists are keyed to Chapters 2 and 3 (for the WISC–IV) and chapters 6 and 7 (for the WPPSI–III), where the points in the checklists are elaborated on.
4. Over 80 short-form combinations, along with the reliability, validity, and estimated IQs associated with each short-form combination.
5. Guidelines to assist in interpreting the individual Composites and Full Scale.
6. A sample WISC–IV report, including line-by-line analysis
7. Appendixes with confidence intervals, guidelines for interpreting subtests and Composites, relevant Cattell-Horn-Carroll abilities associated with each subtest, and much more.

The WISC–IV and the WPPSI–III are the latest of the Wechsler tests. David Wechsler gave the field of assessment a valuable tool—the Wechsler-Bellevue Intelligence Scale, Form I—over 65 years ago. The three Wechsler Scales now cover an age range of from 2 years, 6 months to 89 years.

Some critics have argued that it is inappropriate to measure preschool children's level of cognitive ability. However, we believe that such evaluations do contribute to our understanding of how children develop. Scores from reliable, valid, and well-standardized assessment instruments give us information useful for many different clinical and psychoeducational tasks. And assessment help us in obtaining needed services for children.

Edwin G. Boring said, "intelligence is whatever intelligence tests measure." Although this comment may have been facetious, it strikes a chord in the text authors. We wonder whether the revised structure of the WISC–IV and the WPPSI–III gives a more valid picture of the nature of intelligence or whether the former structure provided a more valid picture. The new editions will, of course, need to be investigated more extensively before a final judgment can be made about their value as assessments devices. Our field needs to study, in particular, how the new subtests contribute to our understanding of the cognitive functioning of both young children and school-age children.

We wish to acknowledge several individuals who generously gave their time to review parts of the manuscript. They are as follows:

Dr. Shawn K. Acheson, Western Carolina University
Carlea Alfieri, Fairleigh Dickinson University
Dr. Alan Brue, National Association of School Psychologists
Dr. Diane Coalson, The Psychological Corporation
Dr. Lisa Drozdick, The Psychological Corporation
Dr. Mary Evans, University of Guelph
Dr. Gail Gibson, Alabama A & M University
Steven Hardy-Braz, Psy.S., North Carolina School Psychology Association
Dr. Marsha Harman, Sam Houston State University
Dr. William A. Hillix, San Diego State University
Dr. Timothy Lionetti, Marywood University
Dr. David N. Sattler, Western Washington University
Dr. Anne Savage, Washington School of Professional Psychology at Argosy University
Dr. Cindy Simpson, Sam Houston State University
Dr. Janet V. Smith, Pittsburgh State University
Dr. John O. Willis, Rivier College
Dr. J. J. Zhu, The Psychological Corporation

Kadir Samuel, associate office manager at Jerome M. Sattler, Publisher, did an outstanding job of getting the manuscript ready for production. He not only typeset the entire text—including tables, figures, and exhibits—but also did the page layout. Thank you, Kadir, for your special talents, your patience, and your wisdom.

Sally Lifland and her staff at Lifland et al., including Gail Magin, Quica Ostrander, Denise Throckmorton, and Jeanne Yost, did an excellent job of editing and proofreading the text. Thank you all for your workmanship. We are fortunate in having such a great copy-editing and production house assist us in publishing this book.

We also are fortunate in having Roy Wallace, West Coast representative of Maple Vail Book Manufacturing, to work with us in getting the book printed and Sara Frank and David Bradley, from Phoenix Color, to assist us in getting the covers printed.

Thank you, Sharon Drum, office manager of Jerome M. Sattler, Publisher, for your help with managing the office during our long days of getting the manuscript ready for production.

We also wish to thank Maybeth and Kate Dumont and Geraldine Martinez for their patience and support during the project.

Note to Instructors: An *Instructor's Manual* accompanies *Assessment of Children: WISC–IV and WPPSI–III Supplement.* The manual contains multiple-choice questions useful for objective examinations. To instructors who have selected *Assessment of Children: WISC–IV and WPPSI–III Supplement* as a required text for their course, Jerome M. Sattler, Publisher, extends permission to photocopy the Administrative Checklists in Appendix D for use in their course. The Administrative Checklists cannot be reproduced in any form (including electronically) for any other purpose without the express permission of the publisher.

Jerome M. Sattler
San Diego State University

Ron Dumont
Fairleigh Dickinson University

June 2004

1

WECHSLER INTELLIGENCE SCALE FOR CHILDREN–IV (WISC–IV): DESCRIPTION

Mind is the great lever of all things; human thought is the process by which human ends are ultimately answered.

—Daniel Webster

Goals and Objectives

This chapter is designed to enable you to do the following:

- Evaluate the psychometric properties of the WISC–IV

- Competently and professionally administer the WISC–IV

- Evaluate short forms of the WISC–IV

- Compare the WISC–IV with other Wechsler tests

- Evaluate the assets and limitations of the WISC–IV

The Wechsler Intelligence Scale for Children–Fourth Edition (WISC–IV) is the latest version of the Wechsler scales for children 6 to 16 years old (Wechsler, 2003a; 2003b). The first edition was published in 1949 and was followed by a revision in 1974 (WISC–R) and another in 1991 (WISC–III). David Wechsler is cited as the author of the WISC–IV, even though he died in 1982. The staff of The Psychological Corporation prepared the last two revisions. The primary reasons for revising the test were to (a) improve its theoretical foundations, (b) improve its psychometric properties, (c) enhance its clinical utility, (d) increase developmental appropriateness, and (e) increase user friendliness.

Wechsler (1949) developed the WISC as a downward extension of the adult intelligence test, called the Wechsler–Bellevue Intelligence Scale (Wechsler, 1939). Other editions of the adult version of the scale were the Wechsler–Bellevue Intelligence Scale, Form II, published in 1946; the Wechsler Adult Intelligence Scale (WAIS), published in 1955; the WAIS–R, published in 1981; and the WAIS–III, published in 1997.

The WISC–IV contains 15 subtests divided into 10 core and 5 supplemental subtests (see Figure 1-1). The core and supplemental subtests form four Composites: Verbal Comprehension, Perceptual Reasoning, Working Memory, and Processing Speed.

- Verbal Comprehension comprises Similarities, Vocabulary, and Comprehension (three core subtests) and Information and Word Reasoning (two supplemental subtests).
- Perceptual Reasoning comprises Block Design, Picture Concepts, and Matrix Reasoning (three core subtests) and Picture Completion (one supplemental subtest).
- Working Memory comprises Digit Span and Letter–Number Sequencing (two core subtests) and Arithmetic (one supplemental subtest).
- Processing Speed comprises Coding and Symbol Search (two core subtests) and Cancellation (one supplemental subtest).

The WISC–IV also provides seven Process scores that are designed to provide additional information about cognitive abilities. These scores are Block Design No Time Bonus (BDN), Digit Span Forward (DSF), Digit Span Backward (DSB), Longest Digit Span Forward (LDSF), Longest Digit Span Backward (LDSB), Cancellation Random (CAR), and Cancellation Structured (CAS). *The Process scores should never be used*

to compute Composite scores on the Full Scale IQ.

Exhibit 1-1 shows items similar to those on the WISC–IV. The WISC–IV retains about 56% of the items used on the WISC–III, either in the original or in a slightly modified form. Picture Arrangement, Object Assembly, and Mazes have been omitted from the WISC–IV in order to reduce the number of subtests with time limits. Picture Concepts, Letter–Number Sequencing, Matrix Reasoning, Cancellation, and Word Reasoning are new subtests.

A NOTE ABOUT TERMINOLOGY

In this book we refer to the *WISC–IV Administration and Scoring Manual* as the Administration Manual and the *WISC–IV Technical and Interpretive Manual* as the Technical Manual. Also, the research studies cited in this chapter are from the Technical Manual, unless otherwise noted. Finally, the two manuals use different terms to describe children who are low functioning. The Administration Manual uses the term "intellectual deficiency" to classify children who may be low functioning, whereas the Technical Manual uses the term "extremely low" for children who have IQs of 69 and below. However, the American Psychiatric Association (2000) and the American Association on Mental Retardation (2002) use the term "mental retardation" to describe children whose IQ is below 70 and who have deficits in adaptive behavior. Finally, tables in the Appendix in this text are referred to with hyphens (e.g., A-1 or B-1) and those in the Administration Manual with periods (e.g., A.1 or B.1).

STANDARDIZATION

Except for Arithmetic, which was standardized on 1,100 children, the WISC–IV was standardized on 2,200 children who were selected to represent children in the United States. The demographic characteristics used to obtain a stratified sample were age, sex, race/ethnicity, geographic region, and parental education (used as a measure of socioeconomic status).

The standardization group contained 11 age groups, with children ranging in age from 6 to 16 years. There were 100 boys and 100 girls in each age group, except in the Arithmetic standardization group, where there

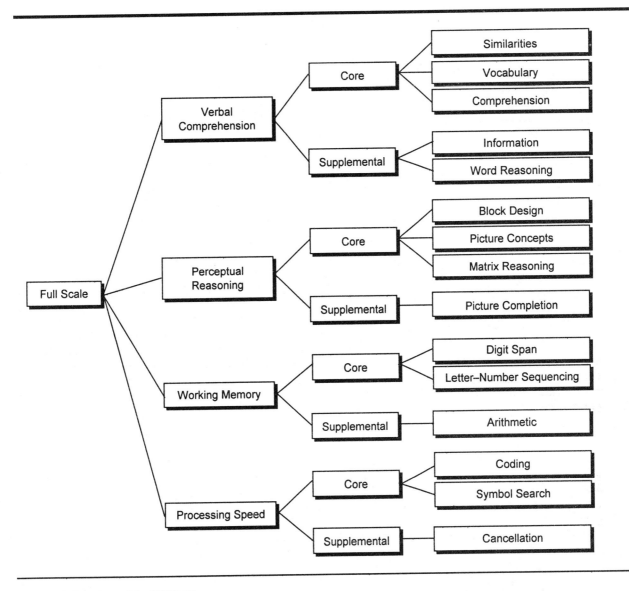

Figure 1-1. Structure of the WISC–IV.

were 50 boys and 50 girls in each age group. With respect to race/ethnic membership, children were from the following groups: Euro American, African American, Hispanic American, Asian American, or Other. The four geographical regions sampled were Northeast, South, Midwest, and West. Children were selected so that the composition of each age group matched as closely as possible the proportions found in the March 2000 U.S. Census with regard to race/ethnicity, geographic region, and parental education.

Table 1-1 shows the parental education and geographic region of the standardization sample by race/ethnic group. Parents in the Euro American, African American, and Asian American classifications had the most education—67.4% of the Euro American group, 53.1% of the African American group, and 60.5% of the Asian American group had at least some college education, while 24.9% of the Hispanic American group and 33.4% of the Other group had at least some college education. The majority of the Euro American and African American samples came from the Midwest and South. The majority of the Hispanic American sample came from the South and West, and over half of the Asian American sample came from the West. The Other sample came mostly from the South, Northeast, and West. The racial/ethnic proportions in the sample were 63.7% Euro American, 15.6% African American, 15.2% Hispanic American, 4.2% Asian American, and 1.3% Other. The sampling methodology was excellent.

Exhibit 1-1
Items Similar to Those on the WISC–IV

Similarities (23 items)
In what way are a pencil and a piece of chalk alike?
In what way are tea and coffee alike?
In what way are an inch and a mile alike?
In what way are binoculars and a microscope alike?

Vocabulary (36 items)
What is a ball?
What does *running* mean?
What is a poem?
What does *obstreperous* mean?

Comprehension (21 items)
Why do we wear shoes?
What is the thing to do if you see someone dropping a package?
In what two ways is a lamp better than a candle?
In the United States, why are we tried by a jury of our peers?

Information (33 items)
How many legs do you have?
What must you do to make water freeze?
Who developed the theory of relativity?
What is the capital of France?

Word Reasoning (24 items)
The task is to identify the common concept being described with a series of clues.
Clue 1: This has a motor . . .
Clue 2: . . . and it is used to cut grass.

Block Design (14 items)
The task is to reproduce stimulus designs using four or nine blocks (see below).

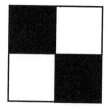

Picture Concepts (28 items)
The task is to choose one picture from each of two or three rows of pictures in such a way that all the pictures selected have a characteristic in common (see below).

Matrix Reasoning (35 items)
The task is to examine an incomplete matrix and select whichever of the five choices best completes the matrix (see below).

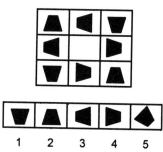

Picture Completion (38 items)
The task is to look at a picture—such as that of a car without a wheel, a scissors without a handle, or a telephone without numbers on the dial—and identify the essential missing part (see below).

Digit Span (16 items; 8 in Digit Span Forward, 8 in Digit Span Backward)
In the first part, the task is to repeat a string of numbers, ranging from 2 to 9 digits, in a forward direction (example: 1-8). In the second part, the task is to repeat a string of numbers, ranging from 2 to 8 digits, in reverse order (example: 6-4-9).

Letter–Number Sequencing (10 items, each with 3 trials)
The task is to listen to a combination of from 2 to 8 letters and digits (example: 1-b) and repeat the combination back with the numbers in ascending order followed by the letters in alphabetical order (example: e-6-d-9 would be repeated back as 6-9-d-e).

Arithmetic (34 items)
If I have one piece of candy and get another one, how many pieces will I have?
At 12 cents each, how much will 4 bars of soap cost?
If suits sell for ½ of the regular price, what is the cost of a $120 suit?

Exhibit 1-1 (*Continued*)

Coding (59 items in Coding A and 119 items in Coding B)
The task is to copy symbols from a key (see below).

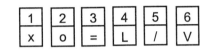

Cancellation (2 items, one Random and one Sequenced)
The task is to scan, within a specified time limit, both a random arrangement and a sequenced arrangement of pictures and mark target pictures (animals; see below).

Symbol Search (45 items in Part A and 60 items in Part B)
The task is to decide whether a stimulus figure (a symbol) appears in an array (see below).

Note. The items resemble those that appear on the WISC–IV but are not actually from the test. Chapter 2 describes the core subtests and Chapter 3 describes the supplemental subtests in more detail.

STANDARD SCORES, SCALED SCORES, AND TEST-AGE EQUIVALENTS

The WISC–IV, like the WPPSI–III and WAIS–III, uses standard scores ($M = 100$, $SD = 15$) for the four Index scores and for the Full Scale IQ, and scaled scores ($M = 10$, $SD = 3$) for the 15 subtests. Scaled scores are also used for five of the seven Process scores (BDN, DSF, DSB, CAR, CAS), while raw scores are used for the other two Process scores (LDSF, LDSB). The Full Scale IQ is computed by comparing the sum of the child's 10 core subtest scaled scores with the scores earned by a representative sample of the child's age group. After each subtest is scored, raw-score points are summed and converted to scaled scores within the child's own age group (in three-month intervals) through use of Table A.1 on pages 204 to 236 in the Administration Manual. Tables A.2 to A.6 in the Administration Manual (pp. 237–240) are used to obtain the Index scores and Full Scale IQs based on the 10 core subtests.

Prorating Procedure

If two of the three Verbal Comprehension core subtests are valid or if two of the three Perceptual Reasoning core subtests are valid, you can use Table A.7 on page 241 of the Administration Manual to prorate the sum of scaled scores. This table was constructed by multiplying the sum of the two scaled scores by 3/2. However, you cannot use proration for Working Memory or Processing Speed if only one of the two subtests is valid, because proration requires at least two valid subtests. Proration is similar to using a short form of the test.

Proration should be avoided whenever possible because it violates the standard test procedure and introduces unknown measurement error. If you do prorate, write "Estimate" by the Index scores and Full Scale IQ on the Record Form and in the psychological report. Later in the chapter we discuss how you can obtain estimated IQs for several short-form combinations using the Tellegen and Briggs (1967) procedure. We need research to determine which procedure—proration or the Tellegen and Briggs procedure—yields more valid IQs.

Table 1-1
Demographic Characteristics of WISC–IV Standardization Sample:
Parental Education and Geographic Region by Race/Ethnic Group

Demographic variable	Race/ethnic group (percent)				
	Euro American (N = 1402)	African American (N = 343)	Hispanic American (N = 335)	Asian American (N = 92)	Other[a] (N = 28)
Parental education					
Eight years or less	0.8	2.3	22.2	11.6	0.0
Some high school	4.8	13.8	24.8	7.0	33.3
High school graduate	27.0	30.8	28.1	20.9	33.3
Some college	35.6	31.4	19.0	23.3	26.7
College graduate	31.8	21.7	5.9	37.2	6.7
Total	100.0	100.0	100.0	100.0	100.0
Geographic region					
Northeast	19.6	19.4	7.2	19.5	23.1
South	31.4	52.9	30.8	12.2	38.5
Midwest	29.7	20.6	22.6	17.1	15.4
West	19.3	7.1	39.4	51.2	23.1
Total	100.0	100.0	100.0	100.0	100.0

Note. Race/ethnic distribution in total group (N = 2,200) was as follows: Euro American = 63.7%, African American = 15.6%, Hispanic American = 15.2%, Asian American = 4.2%, Other = 1.3%.
[a]*Other* represents the following groups: Native American, Eskimo, Aleut, and Pacific Islander.
Source: Adapted from Wechsler (2003b).

Test-Age Equivalents

When David Wechsler first developed the WISC, he believed that the mental-age concept was potentially misleading, and therefore he decided not to use it in calculating IQs. Wechsler rejected the notion that mental age represents an absolute level of mental capacity or that the same mental age in different children represents identical intelligence levels. Soon after the initial publication of the WISC, however, he recognized that mental-age equivalents or test-age equivalents could be useful. Therefore, in later printings of the WISC and in its subsequent revisions, test-age equivalents were provided (see Table A.9 on p. 253 in the Administration Manual). Test-age equivalents are essentially mental-age (MA) scores.

Test-age equivalents are obtained directly from the raw scores on each subtest. Because a scaled score of 10 represents the mean, the test-age equivalents of the raw scores reflect the average score for each specific age group. For example, at ages 6-0 to 6-3, a raw score of 13 on Block Design equals a scaled score of 10 (see p. 204 in the Administration Manual). Therefore, a raw score of 13 on Block Design is associated with a test age of 6-2 (see p. 253 in the Administration Manual). An average test-age equivalent is obtained by summing the individual subtest test ages and dividing the sum by the number of subtests. To obtain a median test age, rank the test ages from high to low and locate the middle-most test age. The median is a more appropriate description of the distribution of test ages than the mean because test ages do not have equal units.

The WISC–IV test-age equivalents can be compared with mental-age or test-age equivalents from other tests. Such comparisons may help parents, teachers, and others better understand a child's level of intellectual functioning. Research is needed to determine the validity of WISC–IV test-age equivalents.

RELIABILITY

The WISC–IV has good reliability. Internal consistency reliability coefficients for the 11 age groups range from .91 to .95 (M r_{xx} = .94) for Verbal Comprehension, from .91 to .93 (M r_{xx} = .92) for Perceptual Reasoning, from .90 to .93 (M r_{xx} = .92) for Working Memory, from .81 to .90 (M r_{xx} = .88) for Processing Speed, and from .96 to .97 (M r_{xx} = .97) for the Full Scale (see Table 1-2). The median individual Composite and Full Scale internal consistency reliability coefficients are similar for the 11 age groups (Mdn r_{xx} = .91 to .92 for the four individual Composites and Mdn r_{xx} = .96 to .97 for the Full Scale; see Table 1-3).

Subtest and Process Score Reliabilities

Two types of internal consistency reliability coefficients were used on the WISC–IV. The split-half method was used for 12 of the 15 subtests, while the test-retest stability coefficient was used for the other three subtests (Coding, Symbol Search, and Cancellation). For the Process scores, the split-half method was used for Block Design No Time Bonus, Digit Span Forward, and Digit Span Backward, while the test-retest stability coefficient was used for Cancellation Structured and Cancellation Random. Internal consistency reliabilities for the subtests and Process scores are lower than those for the Composites (see Table 1-2). This is to be expected, because there are fewer items in any one subtest than in a Composite composed of several subtests.

The 15 subtests have average internal consistency reliabilities that range from r_{xx} = .79 for Symbol Search and Cancellation to r_{xx} = .90 for Letter–Number Sequencing. The median subtest internal consistency reliability is lowest for 6-year-olds (Mdn r_{xx} = .83) and highest for 12-, 15-, and 16-year-olds (Mdn r_{xx} = .87; see Table 1-3).

The five Process scores for which reliability coefficients are provided have average internal consistency reliabilities that range from r_{xx} = .70 for Cancellation Random to r_{xx} = .84 for Block Design No Time Bonus (see Table 1-2). The median Process score internal consistency reliability is lowest for 8-year-olds (Mdn r_{xx} = .72) and highest for 12-, 14-, and 15-year-olds (Mdn r_{xx}

= .82; see Table 1-3). No reliability coefficients are reported for Longest Digit Span Forward and Longest Digit Span Backward.

Standard Errors of Measurement

The average standard errors of measurement (SEM) in standard-score points are 3.78 for Verbal Comprehension, 4.15 for Perceptual Reasoning, 4.27 for Working Memory, 5.21 for Processing Speed, and 2.68 for the Full Scale (see Table 1-2). You can place more confidence in the Full Scale than in any of the four individual Composites. In addition, you can place more confidence in Verbal Comprehension than in Perceptual Reasoning, Working Memory, or Processing Speed.

The average SEMs for the subtests in scaled-score points range from .97 for Letter–Number Sequencing to 1.38 for Cancellation. Within their respective Composites, Vocabulary has the smallest average SEM (1.00) and Word Reasoning has the largest (1.34), Matrix Reasoning has the smallest average SEM (.99) and Picture Concepts has the largest (1.29), Letter–Number Sequencing has the smallest average SEM (.97) and Digit Span has the largest (1.07), and Coding has the smallest average SEM (1.20) and Cancellation has the largest (1.38).

Test-Retest Reliability

The stability of the WISC–IV was assessed by retesting, after an interval of 13 to 63 days (M = 32 days), 18 to 27 children from each of the 11 age groups in the standardization sample, yielding a total of 243 children (Wechsler, 2003b). For statistical analysis, individual age groups were combined into five broad age groups: 6 to 7 years, 8 to 9 years, 10 to 11 years, 12 to 13 years, and 14 to 16 years.

The stability coefficients for the four individual Composites and the Full Scale in the five broad age groups ranged from .84 to .93 for Verbal Comprehension, from .81 to .87 for Perceptual Reasoning, from .74 to .90 for Working Memory, from .73 to .84 for Processing Speed, and from .85 to .92 for the Full Scale (see Table 1-2). For the total test-retest sample, the stability coefficients were .89 for Verbal Comprehension, .85 for Perceptual Reasoning, .85 for Working Memory, .79 for Processing Speed, and .89 for the Full Scale. The stability coefficients indicate that the WISC–IV generally provides stable Full Scale IQs. However, the stability

Table 1-2
Range of and Average Internal Consistency Reliabilities, Test-Retest Reliabilities, and Standard Errors of Measurement for 15 WISC–IV Subtests, Five Process Scores, and Five Composites

Subtest or Composite	Range of internal consistency reliabilities (r_{xx})	Average internal consistency reliability (r_{xx})	Range of test-retest reliabilities (r_{tt})	Average test-retest reliability (r_{tt})	Range of SEM	Average SEM
Verbal Comprehension						
Similarities	.82–.89	.86	.73–.87	.81	.99–1.27	1.13
Vocabulary	.82–.94	.89	.76–.91	.85	.73–1.27	1.00
Comprehension	.74–.86	.81	.55–.82	.72	1.12–1.53	1.31
Information	.78–.91	.86	.74–.91	.83	.90–1.41	1.16
Word Reasoning	.77–.84	.80	.65–.83	.75	1.20–1.44	1.34
Perceptual Reasoning						
Block Design	.83–.88	.86	.73–.88	.81	1.04–1.24	1.13
Picture Concepts	.76–.85	.82	.62–.82	.71	1.16–1.47	1.29
Matrix Reasoning	.86–.92	.89	.71–.85	.77	.85–1.12	0.99
Picture Completion	.81–.87	.84	.78–.85	.82	1.08–1.27	1.20
Working Memory						
Digit Span	.81–.92	.87	.61–.88	.81	.85–1.31	1.07
Letter–Number Sequencing	.85–.92	.90	.64–.81	.75	.85–1.16	0.97
Arithmetic	.84–.91	.88	.47–.84	.75	.90–1.20	1.05
Processing Speed						
Coding	.72–.89	.85	.74–.87	.81	.99–1.59	1.20
Symbol Search	.78–.82	.79	.57–.80	.68	1.27–1.41	1.36
Cancellation	.73–.84	.79	.69–.86	.78	1.20–1.56	1.38
Process Score[a]						
Block Design NTB	.79–.87	.84	.69–.84	.76	1.08–1.37	1.22
Digit Span Forward	.78–.88	.83	.56–.80	.72	1.04–1.41	1.24
Digit Span Backward	.68–.86	.80	.44–.77	.67	1.12–1.70	1.37
Cancellation Random	.65–.75	.70	.63–.76	.68	1.50–1.77	1.66
Cancellation Structured	.70–.80	.75	.68–.78	.73	1.34–1.64	1.51
Composite						
Verbal Comprehension	.91–.95	.94	.84–.93	.89	3.35–4.50	3.78
Perceptual Reasoning	.91–.93	.92	.81–.87	.85	3.97–4.50	4.15
Working Memory	.90–.93	.92	.74–.90	.85	3.97–4.74	4.27
Processing Speed	.81–.90	.88	.73–.84	.79	4.74–6.54	5.21
Full Scale	.96–.97	.97	.85–.92	.89	2.60–3.00	2.68

Note. Abbreviation: Block Design NTB = Block Design No Time Bonus. All reliability coefficients in table are uncorrected.
[a] There are no scaled scores for Longest Digit Span Forward and Longest Digit Span Backward.
Source: *Wechsler Intelligence Scale for Children: Fourth Edition.* Copyright © 2003 by The Psychological Corporation. Adapted and reproduced by permission. All rights reserved. *Wechsler Intelligence Scale for Children, WISC* and *WISC–IV* are trademarks of The Psychological Corporation registered in the United States of America and/or other jurisdictions.

coefficients are less than .80 at two broad ages (8 to 9 years and 12 to 13 years) for Processing Speed and are less than .80 at one broad age (8 to 9 years) for Working Memory.

In the total test-retest sample, average stability coefficients for the subtests ranged from a low of .68 for Symbol Search to a high of .85 for Vocabulary (see Table 1-2). Median internal consistency reliabilities are slightly higher than median test-retest reliabilities (*Mdn* r_{xx} = .85 versus *Mdn* r_{tt} = .83). Out of 75 stability coefficients for the 15 subtests at the five broad age groups, 43 stability coefficients are below .80 (12 coefficients at ages 6–7, 12 coefficients at ages 8–9, 6 coefficients at ages 10–11, 8 coefficients at ages 12–13, and 5 coefficients at ages 14–16). Thus, the subtests are less stable than the individual Composites or the Full Scale.

Changes in IQs. Table 1-4 shows the mean test-retest and change scores for Verbal Comprehension, Perceptual Reasoning, Working Memory, and Processing Speed and for the Full Scale for the five broad age groups and for the total test-retest sample. Mean increases from the first to the second testing were 2.1 points for Verbal Comprehension, 5.2 points for Perceptual Reasoning, 2.6 points for Working Memory, 7.1 points for Processing Speed, and 5.6 points for the Full Scale. Thus, prior exposure to items on Perceptual Reasoning and Processing Speed facilitates performance on retest more than prior exposure to items on Verbal Comprehension and Working Memory.

Higher retest scores after a short time interval are likely to be associated with practice effects, whereas those that occur after a long time interval may be associated with both practice effects and changes in ability.

Table 1-3
Range and Median Internal Consistency Reliabilities of WISC–IV Subtests, Process Scores, and Composites in Each of the 11 Age Groups plus Average

Age (in years)	Subtests		Process Scores		Composites		Full Scale
	Range of r_{xx}	Mdn r_{xx}	Range of r_{xx}	Mdn r_{xx}	Range of r_{xx}	Mdn r_{xx}	r_{xx}
6	.72–.92	.83	.70–.83	.79	.83–.91	.91	.96
7	.72–.91	.84	.69–.83	.75	.81–.92	.92	.96
8	.73–.92	.84	.68–.83	.72	.88–.93	.91	.97
9	.73–.92	.84	.70–.88	.77	.89–.94	.92	.97
10	.79–.90	.84	.72–.87	.77	.90–.94	.92	97
11	.78–.91	.84	.72–.86	.79	.90–.93	.92	97
12	.75–.92	.87	.67–.86	.82	.89–.95	.93	97
13	.75–.90	.85	.67–.85	.78	.89–.94	.92	97
14	.78–.91	.86	.65–.83	.82	.89–.95	.92	97
15	.77–.94	.87	.68–.87	.82	.90–.95	.92	97
16	.76–.92	.87	.65–.86	.80	.89–.95	.92	97
Average	.72–.92	.84	.70–.84	.80	.88–.94	.92	97

Source: *Wechsler Intelligence Scale for Children: Fourth Edition.* Copyright © 2003 by The Psychological Corporation. Adapted and reproduced by permission. All rights reserved. *Wechsler Intelligence Scale for Children, WISC* and *WISC–IV* are trademarks of The Psychological Corporation registered in the United States of America and/or other jurisdictions.

Table 1-4
Test-Retest WISC–IV Composite Scores for Five Age Groups and Total Group

Age (in years)	Composite	First testing		Second testing		Change	ES[a]
		Mean	SD	Mean	SD		
6–7 (N = 43)	Verbal Comprehension	96.1	11.3	99.5	10.8	3.4***	.31
	Perceptual Reasoning	99.3	13.5	105.7	14.1	6.4***	.46
	Working Memory	101.5	14.6	106.2	14.2	4.7***	.33
	Processing Speed	103.7	13.9	114.6	16.1	10.9***	.72
	Full Scale	99.9	13.0	108.2	13.8	8.3***	.62
8–9 (N = 51)	Verbal Comprehension	98.4	9.7	100.5	9.8	2.1**	.22
	Perceptual Reasoning	100.3	12.6	105.4	13.7	5.1***	.39
	Working Memory	99.1	11.8	101.5	10.8	2.4*	.21
	Processing Speed	101.2	12.4	109.9	14.6	8.7***	.64
	Full Scale	99.4	11.2	105.5	11.6	6.1***	.54
10–11 (N = 41)	Verbal Comprehension	99.2	11.2	101.4	12.0	2.2*	.19
	Perceptual Reasoning	101.2	11.3	104.5	11.8	3.3***	.29
	Working Memory	100.1	13.4	103.2	13.7	3.1*	.23
	Processing Speed	104.1	12.1	111.7	15.3	7.6***	.55
	Full Scale	100.9	10.4	106.5	11.1	5.6***	.52
12–13 (N = 49)	Verbal Comprehension	102.4	12.8	104.0	12.2	1.6*	.13
	Perceptual Reasoning	99.0	13.2	105.2	13.6	6.2***	.46
	Working Memory	97.6	13.3	99.0	13.6	1.4	.10
	Processing Speed	102.7	11.2	107.5	13.1	4.8***	.39
	Full Scale	101.4	11.1	105.6	11.6	4.2***	.37
14–16 (N = 59)	Verbal Comprehension	102.6	12.0	104.3	13.1	1.7**	.14
	Perceptual Reasoning	103.1	14.2	107.9	15.7	4.8***	.32
	Working Memory	100.8	12.7	102.5	13.7	1.7	.13
	Processing Speed	101.0	13.2	105.6	15.8	4.6***	.32
	Full Scale	103.1	12.6	107.4	14.1	4.3***	.32
Total (N = 243)	Verbal Comprehension	100.0	11.7	102.1	11.7	2.1**	.18
	Perceptual Reasoning	100.7	13.1	105.9	13.9	5.2***	.39
	Working Memory	99.8	13.1	102.4	13.3	2.6***	.20
	Processing Speed	102.4	12.6	109.5	15.2	7.1***	.51
	Full Scale	101.0	11.7	106.6	12.5	5.6***	.46

(Continued)

Table 1-4 (*Continued*)

Note. Test-retest intervals ranged from 13 to 63 days, with a mean retest interval of 32 days. The *N* for each age group was obtained from J. J. Zhu, Manager of Data Analysis Operations, The Psychological Corporation, December 2003.

The *t* test used to evaluate the mean changes on each Composite employed a repeated-measures formula:

$$t = \frac{M_1 - M_2}{\sqrt{\left(\frac{SD_1}{\sqrt{N_1}}\right)^2 + \left(\frac{SD_2}{\sqrt{N_2}}\right)^2 - 2r_{12}\left(\frac{SD_1}{\sqrt{N_1}}\right)\left(\frac{SD_2}{\sqrt{N_2}}\right)}}$$

[a] Effect size (ES) is the difference between two means divided by the square root of the pooled variance. Effect sizes are classified as small (ES = .20), medium (ES = .50), or large (ES = .80) (Cohen, 1988).

* *p* < .05.

** *p* < .01.

*** *p* < .001.

Source: Wechsler Intelligence Scale for Children: Fourth Edition. Copyright © 2003 by The Psychological Corporation. Adapted and reproduced by permission. All rights reserved. *Wechsler Intelligence Scale for Children, WISC* and *WISC–IV* are trademarks of The Psychological Corporation registered in the United States of America and/or other jurisdictions.

For example, the Processing Speed subtests may not be as novel on the repeated administration as they initially were. Carefully consider whether you want to use the WISC–IV again for repeated evaluations, especially if you plan to use the results obtained on the retest for placement, eligibility, or diagnostic decisions. If the time between tests is relatively short (e.g., less than 9 months), consider using another individually administered well-standardized test of cognitive ability for the reexamination.

Changes in subtest scaled scores. Table 1-5 shows the test-retest subtest scaled-score changes from the first to the second administration. Picture Completion showed the largest mean increase (1.8 points), while Comprehension showed the smallest mean increase (.2 point). Increases varied with age, depending on the subtest. For example, Arithmetic showed a small mean increase at ages 14 to 16 (.1 point) and a large mean increase at ages 6 to 7 (1.5 points). In contrast, Cancellation had the smallest increase at ages 6 to 7 (.1 point) and the largest at ages 14 to 16 (1.4 points).

Confidence Intervals

Table A-1 in Appendix A shows confidence intervals, based on the obtained score and the SEM, for the 68%, 85%, 90%, 95%, and 99% levels of confidence by age group and for the average of the standardization group

for Verbal Comprehension, Perceptual Reasoning, Working Memory, Processing Speed, and the Full Scale. We recommend that you use these confidence intervals rather than those in the Administration Manual, which are based on the estimated true score and the standard error of estimation (SE_E). The former method is preferred when a confidence interval is applied to a child's own individual score (see Sattler, 2001). *Use the child's specific age group—not the average of the 11 age groups—to obtain the most accurate confidence interval for any individual child.* At the 95% level of confidence, the confidence intervals range from ±7 to ±8 for Verbal Comprehension, from ±8 to ±9 for Perceptual Reasoning, from ±8 to ±10 for Working Memory, from ±10 to ±13 for Processing Speed, and from ±7 to ±8 for the Full Scale. The range is greatest for Processing Speed because this Composite is less reliable than the three other individual Composites and the Full Scale. Similar relationships hold for the other levels of confidence.

VALIDITY

Criterion Validity

Studies correlating the WISC–IV with the WISC–III, WPPSI–III, WAIS–III, WASI, and measures of achievement, memory, emotional intelligence, and adaptive behavior indicate that the WISC–IV has satisfactory

Table 1-5
Test-Retest Point Gains on WISC–IV Subtests for Five Age Groups and Total Group

Subtest	Age (in years)					Total	ES[a]
	6–7	8–9	10–11	12–13	14–16		
Block Design	1.2***	1.2***	0.9**	1.6***	1.1***	1.2***	.41
Similarities	0.9**	0.7**	0.6*	0.3	0.7**	0.6***	.24
Digit Span	0.4	0.8**	0.4	0.4	0.5*	0.5***	.18
Picture Concepts	1.4***	0.6*	0.3	0.8*	1.0**	0.8***	.29
Coding	2.1***	1.4***	1.7***	1.1***	1.1***	1.4***	.48
Vocabulary	0.2	0.5**	0.3	0.1	0.0	0.3***	.13
Letter–Number Sequencing	1.1***	0.3	0.2	0.2	0.1	0.4***	.16
Matrix Reasoning	0.6	0.7**	0.6**	0.8**	0.5	0.6***	.23
Comprehension	0.4	0.2	0.2	0.4	0.1	0.2	.08
Symbol Search	2.0***	1.5***	1.1**	0.6*	0.6*	1.1***	.41
Picture Completion	1.9***	1.8***	1.9***	1.7***	1.7***	1.8***	.60
Cancellation	0.1	1.2***	1.8***	1.3***	1.4***	1.1***	.37
Information	0.4	0.3	0.5**	0.6*	0.4*	0.4***	.16
Arithmetic	1.5***	0.6	0.4	0.5*	0.1	0.6***	.23
Word Reasoning	1.0**	0.7**	0.6	1.2***	0.4	0.8***	.31

Note. Test-retest intervals range from 13 to 63 days, with a mean retest interval of 32 days. The *t* test used to evaluate the mean changes on each subtest employed a repeated-measures formula:

$$t = \frac{M_1 - M_2}{\sqrt{\left(\frac{SD_1}{\sqrt{N_1}}\right)^2 + \left(\frac{SD_2}{\sqrt{N_2}}\right)^2 - 2r_{12}\left(\frac{SD_1}{\sqrt{N_1}}\right)\left(\frac{SD_2}{\sqrt{N_2}}\right)}}$$

[a] Effect size (ES) is for the total group only. Effect size is the difference between two means divided by the square root of the pooled variance. Effect sizes are classified as small (ES = .20), medium (ES = .50), or large (ES = .80) (Cohen, 1988).
  * $p < .05$.
 ** $p < .01$.
*** $p < .001$.
Source: Adapted from Wechsler (2003b).

criterion validity (see Table 1-6). The studies summarized in Table 1-6 are limited because they use only tests published by The Psychological Corporation. Criterion validity studies that use other individual tests of intelligence and achievement and measures of adaptive behavior are needed.

If you use the WISC–IV to retest children who were first tested with the WISC–III, WPPSI–III, or WAIS–III, bear in mind that the findings in the Technical Manual and those highlighted below came from children whose mean IQs were in the average range. Therefore, we do not know whether the findings are generalizable to children in the extreme ranges of intellectual ability or to children with special needs.

WISC–IV and WISC–III. As noted earlier, approximately 56% of the items on the WISC–III are also found on the WISC–IV. It seems plausible, therefore, that the research on the validity of the WISC–III generally applies to the WISC–IV. Studies of the validity of the WISC–III indicate that it had adequate construct, concurrent, and predictive validity for many types of children with or without disabilities in the age range covered by the test (Sattler, 2001).

A sample of 244 children 6 to 16 years of age were administered the WISC–IV and WISC–III in counterbalanced order within a 5- to 67-day period (*M* = 28 days). Correlations were .83 for Verbal Comprehension

Table 1-6
Summary of WISC–IV Criterion Validity Studies

Criterion	Composite					Criterion	Composite				
	VCI	PRI	WMI	PSI	FSIQ		VCI	PRI	WMI	PSI	FSIQ
WAIS–III						**CMS**					
VIQ	.84	—	—	—	—	Visual Immediate	.23	.29	.35	.17	.34
VCI	.84	—	—	—	—	Visual Delayed	.21	.30	.27	.16	.31
PIQ	—	.71	—	—	—	Verbal Immediate	.55	.36	.48	.18	.56
POI	—	.71	—	—	—	Verbal Delayed	.60	.46	.46	.34	.63
FDI	—	—	.78	—	—	General Memory	.54	.46	.52	.29	.61
PSI	—	—	—	.75	—	Attention/Conc.[a]	.58	.55	.74	.37	.72
FSIQ	—	—	—	—	.88	Learning	.42	.33	.49	.18	.51
						Delayed Recog.[b]	.51	.31	.32	.18	.48
WISC–III						**GRS–S**					
VIQ	.83	—	—	—	—	Intellectual Ability	.52	.48	.47	.37	.60
VCI	.85	—	—	—	—	Academic Ability	.53	.48	.46	.35	.60
PIQ	—	.73	—	—	—	Creativity	.45	.37	.35	.26	.48
POI	—	.70	—	—	—	Artistic Talent	.42	.41	.31	.35	.51
FDI	—	—	.74	—	—	Leadership	.28	.19	.29	.30	.35
PSI	—	—	—	.81	—	Motivation	.35	.36	.36	.36	.47
FSIQ	—	—	—	—	.87						
WPPSI–III						**BarOn EQ**					
VIQ	.76	—	—	—	—	Intrapersonal	.06	.12	.10	.16	.12
PIQ	—	.74	—	—	—	Interpersonal	.12	.19	.11	.17	.19
PSQ	—	—	—	.62	—	Stress Manage.[c]	.14	.23	.14	.10	.22
FSIQ	—	—	—	—	.89	Adaptability	.29	.31	.28	.25	.34
						Total EQ	.22	.29	.23	.24	.31
WASI						General Mood	.01	.09	.04	.16	.08
VIQ	.84	—	—	—	—	Positive Impress.[d]	–.01	.09	.00	.04	.04
PIQ	—	.78	—	—	—						
FSIQ–4	—	—	—	—	.86	**ABAS–II–P**					
FSIQ–2	—	—	—	—	.82	General Adaptive	.39	.30	.38	.23	.41
						Conceptual	.45	.37	.45	.25	.49
WIAT–II						Social	.36	.27	.35	.18	.35
Total	.80	.71	.71	.58	.87	Practical	.25	.16	.25	.18	.18
Reading	.74	.63	.66	.50	.78	**ABAS–II–T**					
Mathematics	.68	.67	.64	.53	.78	General Adaptive	.42	.39	.35	.34	.58
Written Language	.67	.61	.64	.55	.76	Conceptual	.44	.45	.34	.39	.63
Oral Language	.75	.63	.57	.49	.75	Social	.29	.26	.26	.26	.43
						Practical	.41	.35	.32	.27	.53

Note. Correlations are uncorrected with the Wechsler tests, and corrected with the other tests.

Abbreviations for Composites: VCI = Verbal Comprehension Index, PRI = Perceptual Reasoning Index, WMI = Working Memory Index, PSI = Processing Speed Index, FSIQ = Full Scale IQ, VIQ = Verbal IQ, PIQ = Performance IQ, POI = Perceptual Organization Index, FDI = Freedom from Distractibility Index.

Abbreviations for tests: WASI = Wechsler Abbreviated Scale Intelligence, WIAT–II = Wechsler Individual Achievement Test–II, CMS = Children's Memory Scale, GRS–S = GRS School Form, BarOn EQ = BarOn Emotional Quotient–Inventory, ABAS–II–P = Adaptive Behavior Assessment Scale–II–Parent, ABAS–II–T=

Adaptive Behavior Assessment Scale–II–Teacher.
[a] Attention/Conc. = Attention/Concentration.
[b] Delayed Recog. = Delayed Recognition.
[c] Stress Manage. = Stress Management
[d] Positive Impress. = Positive Impression.

Source: *Wechsler Intelligence Scale for Children: Fourth Edition.* Copyright © 2003 by The Psychological Corporation. Adapted and reproduced by permission. All rights reserved. *Wechsler Intelligence Scale for Children, WISC* and *WISC–IV* are trademarks of The Psychological Corporation registered in the United States of America and/or other jurisdictions.

and the Verbal Scale (and .85 for the two Verbal Comprehension Indexes), .73 for Perceptual Reasoning and the Performance Scale (and .70 for the Perceptual Reasoning Index and the Perceptual Organization Index), .74 for Working Memory and Freedom from Distractibility, .81 for the two Processing Speed Composites, and .87 for the two Full Scales. Mean Index scores were lower on the WISC–IV than on the WISC–III by from 1 to 5 points, and the mean WISC–IV Full Scale IQ was lower than the mean WISC–III Full Scale IQ by 2.5 points. Therefore, WISC–IV Full Scale IQs that are lower than WISC–III Full Scale IQs by about 3 points are simply a reflection of differences in the two tests. However, differences greater than 3 points may reflect meaningful changes in a child's ability; that is, such differences may reflect changes in ability that are beyond those associated with the new edition of the test.

WISC–IV and WPPSI–III.

Because the WISC–IV and WPPSI–III overlap for children ages 6-0 to 7-3, it is important to know the relationship between the two tests for this age group. A sample of 182 6-year-old children were administered the WISC–IV and WPPSI–III in counterbalanced order within a 9- to 62-day period ($M = 22$ days). Correlations were .76 for Verbal Comprehension and the Verbal Scale, .74 for Perceptual Reasoning and the Performance Scale, .62 for the two Processing Speed Composites, and .85 for the two Full Scales. Individual mean Composites on the two tests differed by 1.2 points or less, whereas the Full Scale IQs differed by .2 point.

The WISC–IV and WPPSI–III are not completely independent tests. There is an overlap of two items on Block Design, three items on Picture Completion, and three items on Information. It would be better if the two tests had no items in common to eliminate the possibility of direct practice effects.

WISC–IV and WAIS–III.

Because the WISC–IV and WAIS–III overlap for children ages 16-0 to 16-11, it is important to have information about the relationship between the two tests for this age group. The WISC–IV and the WAIS–III were administered in counterbalanced order within a 10- to 67-day period ($M = 22$ days) to a sample of 198 16-year-olds. Correlations were .84 for Verbal Comprehension and the Verbal Scale, .71 for Perceptual Reasoning and the Performance Scale, .78 for Working Memory and Freedom from Distractibility, .75 for the two Processing Speed Composites, and .88 for the two Full Scales. Means on Verbal Comprehen-

sion, Perceptual Reasoning, and Processing Speed were lower on the WISC–IV than on the WAIS–III by about 3 points, whereas the mean on Working Memory was 1 point higher on the WISC–IV than on the WAIS–III. The mean Full Scale IQ was 3.1 points lower on the WISC–IV than on the WAIS–III. Therefore, differences of about 3 points or less should be seen as a reflection of different tests, whereas differences larger than 3 points may reflect meaningful changes in a child's ability.

The WISC–IV and WAIS–III are not completely independent tests. There is an overlap of three items on Picture Completion and one item on Information. It would be better if the two tests had no items in common to eliminate the possibility of direct practice effects. However, there is no item overlap on the Composite scores if only the WISC–IV core subtests are used.

WISC–IV and WASI.

The Wechsler Abbreviated Scale of Intelligence (WASI) overlaps with the WISC–IV for children ages 6-0 to 16-11. The two tests were administered in counterbalanced order to a sample of 260 6- to 16-year-olds, with a test-retest interval ranging from 12 to 64 days ($M = 29$ days). Correlations were .84 between Verbal Comprehension and the Verbal Scale, .78 between Perceptual Reasoning and the Performance Scale, .82 between the WISC–IV Full Scale and the WASI Full Scale derived from two subtests, and .86 between the WISC–IV Full Scale and the WASI Full Scale derived from four subtests. The mean Full Scale IQ on the WISC–IV was lower than that on the two-subtest WASI by 1.8 points and lower than that on the four-subtest WASI by 3.4 points. The results suggest that the two tests are somewhat highly correlated but should not be used interchangeably.

Special group studies.

The Technical Manual presents 16 special group studies, summarized in Table 1-7. Highlights of Table 1-7 follow:

- *Intellectually gifted:* The sample obtained a mean Full Scale IQ of 123.5. The individual mean Composite scores ranged from 110.6 (Processing Speed) to 124.7 (Verbal Comprehension).
- *Mental retardation—mild:* The sample obtained a mean Full Scale IQ of 60.5. The individual mean Composite scores ranged from 65.5 (Perceptual Reasoning) to 73.0 (Processing Speed).
- *Mental retardation—moderate:* The sample obtained a mean Full Scale IQ of 46.4. The individual mean Composite scores ranged from 52.3 (Verbal Com-

prehension) to 58.2 (Processing Speed).

- *Reading disorder:* The sample obtained a mean Full Scale IQ of 89.1. The individual mean Composite scores ranged from 87.0 (Working Memory) to 94.4 (Perceptual Reasoning).
- *Reading and written expression disorders:* The sample obtained a mean Full Scale IQ of 92.5. The individual mean Composite scores ranged from 90.2 (Working Memory) to 98.0 (Perceptual Reasoning).
- *Mathematics disorder:* The sample obtained a mean Full Scale IQ of 88.7. The individual mean Composite scores ranged from 87.7 (Perceptual Reasoning) to 93.2 (Verbal Comprehension).
- *Reading, written expression, and mathematics disorders:* The sample obtained a mean Full Scale IQ of 87.6. The individual mean Composite scores ranged from 89.7 (Working Memory) to 90.5 (Processing Speed).
- *Learning disorder and attention-deficit/hyperactivity disorder:* The sample obtained a mean Full Scale IQ of 88.1. The individual mean Composite scores ranged from 88.2 (Processing Speed) to 92.7 (Verbal Comprehension and Perceptual Reasoning).
- *Attention-deficit/hyperactivity disorder:* The sample obtained a mean Full Scale IQ of 97.6. The individual mean Composite scores ranged from 93.4 (Processing Speed) to 100.1 (Perceptual Reasoning).
- *Expressive language disorder:* The sample obtained a mean Full Scale IQ of 83.0. The individual mean Composite scores ranged from 82.7 (Verbal Comprehension) to 91.6 (Perceptual Reasoning).
- *Mixed receptive-expressive language disorder:* The sample obtained a mean Full Scale IQ of 77.3. The individual mean Composite scores ranged from 78.2 (Verbal Comprehension) to 86.7 (Perceptual Reasoning).
- *Open head injury:* The sample obtained a mean Full Scale IQ of 92.4. The individual mean Composite scores ranged from 84.1 (Processing Speed) to 94.5 (Verbal Comprehension).
- *Closed head injury:* The sample obtained a mean Full Scale IQ of 90.0. The individual mean Composite scores ranged from 85.0 (Processing Speed) to 95.2 (Working Memory).
- *Autistic disorder:* The sample obtained a mean Full Scale IQ of 76.4. The individual mean Composite scores ranged from 70.2 (Processing Speed) to 85.7 (Perceptual Reasoning).
- *Asperger's disorder:* The sample obtained a mean Full Scale IQ of 99.2. The individual mean Composite scores ranged from 86.5 (Processing Speed) to 105.6 (Verbal Comprehension).
- *Motor impairment:* The sample obtained a mean Full Scale IQ of 85.7. The individual mean Composite scores ranged from 78.2 (Processing Speed) to 95.5 (Verbal Comprehension).

The range of individual mean Composite scores is greatest for the Asperger's disorder group (about 19 points), followed by the motor impairment group (about 17 points), the autistic disorder group (about 15 points), and the intellectually gifted group (about 14 points). The remaining 12 groups have an individual mean Composite score range no greater than about 10 points.

These special group studies are a welcome part of the Technical Manual. However, 8 of the 16 groups have fewer than 40 participants. We need additional research with special groups, including research on how children with special needs perform on the WISC–IV and the WISC–III.

Comment on criterion validity. The validity studies cited in the Technical Manual support the criterion validity of the WISC–IV. Additional research is needed on the relationship between the WISC–IV and other measures of ability and achievement.

Construct Validity

Studies reported in the Technical Manual and the results of our factor analysis presented later in the chapter indicate (a) that the WISC–IV is a good measure of general intelligence and (b) that it has group factors as well as specific factors.

INTERCORRELATIONS FOR SUBTESTS AND COMPOSITES

Intercorrelations between the 15 subtests range from a low of .10 to a high of .75. The highest correlations are between Vocabulary and Information (.75), Vocabulary and Similarities (.74), Similarities and Information (.70), Comprehension and Vocabulary (.68), Word Reasoning and Vocabulary (.66), Comprehension and Similarities (.62), Comprehension and Information (.62), Comprehension and Word Reasoning (.62), Word Reasoning and Similarities (.62), Word Reasoning and Information (.62), and Arithmetic and Information (.62).

The lowest correlations are between Cancellation and

Table 1-7
Summary of Special Group Studies with the WISC–IV

| Special group | N | Individual Composite | | | | | | | | | |
| | | Verbal Comprehension | | Perceptual Reasoning | | Working Memory | | Processing Speed | | Full Scale | |
		M	SD	M	SD	M	SD	M	SD	M	SD
Intellectually gifted	63	124.7	11.0	120.4	11.0	112.5	11.9	110.6	11.5	123.5	8.5
Mental retardation—mild	63	67.1	9.1	65.5	10.3	66.8	11.1	73.0	11.6	60.5	9.2
Mental retardation—moderate	57	52.3	7.5	52.5	9.2	57.0	9.5	58.2	11.0	46.4	8.5
Reading disorder	56	91.9	9.7	94.4	11.2	87.0	12.9	92.5	11.7	89.1	10.3
Reading and written expression dis.	35	94.8	11.1	98.0	11.4	90.2	13.2	90.6	13.3	92.5	11.1
Mathematics disorder	33	93.2	6.4	87.7	9.3	92.9	10.6	90.6	14.1	88.7	8.6
Reading, written expres., & math dis.	42	89.8	11.4	90.1	12.5	89.7	12.3	90.5	12.6	87.6	10.6
Learning disorder & ADHD	45	92.7	15.8	92.7	13.7	88.7	13.7	88.2	12.3	88.1	13.0
Attention-deficit/hyperactivity dis.	89	99.0	13.6	100.1	14.2	96.1	15.5	93.4	12.6	97.6	14.0
Expressive language disorder	27	82.7	11.7	91.6	12.9	85.6	12.2	87.7	11.9	83.0	11.1
Mixed receptive-expressive lan. dis.	41	78.2	11.4	86.7	15.8	83.1	12.3	79.3	12.8	77.3	12.6
Open head injury	16	94.5	16.4	93.8	14.9	93.3	17.8	84.1	20.3	92.4	17.8
Closed head injury	27	94.0	14.1	92.6	12.5	95.2	15.1	85.0	10.0	90.0	12.2
Autistic disorder	19	80.2	17.4	85.7	20.6	76.9	16.5	70.2	18.3	76.4	19.5
Asperger's disorder	27	105.6	18.5	101.2	18.5	95.4	17.8	86.5	17.1	99.2	17.7
Motor impairment	21	95.5	11.2	83.8	16.0	92.0	13.1	78.2	17.8	85.7	14.9

Note. Abbreviations: Reading and written expression dis. = Reading and written expression disorders, Reading, written expres., & math dis. = Reading, written expression, and mathematics disorders, Learning disorder & ADHD = Learning disorder and attention-deficit/hyperactivity disorder, Attention-deficit/hyperactivity dis. = Attention-deficit/hyperactivity disorder, Mixed receptive-expressive lan. dis. = Mixed receptive-expressive language disorder.
Source: Adapted from Wechsler (2003b).

Digit Span (.10), Cancellation and Information (.11), Cancellation and Comprehension (.11), Cancellation and Letter–Number Sequencing (.11), Cancellation and Word Reasoning (.13), Cancellation and Picture Concepts (.14), Cancellation and Vocabulary (.14), Cancellation and Matrix Reasoning (.14), Cancellation and Picture Completion (.14), Cancellation and Similarities (.16), Cancellation and Arithmetic (.17), and Cancellation and Block Design (.19).

In the total group, the Verbal Comprehension subtests correlate more highly with each other (*Mdn r* = .64) than do the Perceptual Reasoning subtests (*Mdn r* = .47), the Working Memory subtests (*Mdn r* = .47), or the Processing Speed subtests (*Mdn r* = .40). Average correlations range from .70 to .91 (*Mdn r* = .86) between the Verbal Comprehension subtests and the Verbal Comprehension Composite, from .57 to .84 (*Mdn r* = .79) between the Perceptual Reasoning subtests and the Perceptual Reasoning Composite, from .57 to .86 (*Mdn r* =

.86) between the Working Memory subtests and the Working Memory Composite, and from .41 to .88 (*Mdn r* = .87) between the Processing Speed subtests and the Processing Speed Composite.

Average correlations between each of the 15 individual subtests and the Full Scale range from .26 to .79 (*Mdn r* = .69; see Table 1-8). Vocabulary has the highest correlation with the Full Scale (.79), followed by Similarities (.77), Information (.73), Arithmetic (.72), Matrix Reasoning (.72), Comprehension (.71), Block Design (.70), Letter–Number Sequencing (.69), Symbol Search (.66), Word Reasoning (.65), Picture Concepts (.64), Digit Span (.62), Picture Completion (.60), Coding (.57), and Cancellation (.26). Within each Composite, the highest correlations between the subtest scores and their respective Index scores are for Vocabulary in Verbal Comprehension (.91), Matrix Reasoning in Perceptual Reasoning (.84), Digit Span and Letter–Number Sequencing in Working Memory (.86), and Coding in

Processing Speed (.88).

There is a strong positive relationship ($\rho = .91$, $p < .01$) between the extent to which subtests correlate with the Full Scale and their g loadings (see discussion later in the chapter). Thus, subtests that correlate highly with the Full Scale are likely to measure general intelligence better than subtests that have low correlations with the Full Scale.

Table 1-8
Average Correlations Between WISC–IV Subtests and Composites

	Composite				
Subtest	VCI	PRI	WMI	PSI	FSIQ
Verbal Comprehension					
Similarities	.89	.59	.50	.38	.77
Vocabulary	.91	.58	.53	.39	.79
Comprehension	.86	.49	.46	.37	.71
Information	.77	.57	.51	.39	.73
Word Reasoning	.70	.52	.45	.35	.65
Perceptual Reasoning					
Block Design	.50	.81	.42	.45	.70
Picture Concepts	.47	.77	.39	.36	.64
Matrix Reasoning	.52	.84	.46	.44	.72
Picture Completion	.55	.57	.35	.39	.60
Working Memory					
Digit Span	.44	.42	.86	.30	.62
Letter–Number Seq.[a]	.52	.48	.86	.40	.69
Arithmetic	.63	.62	.57	.45	.72
Processing Speed					
Coding	.34	.40	.30	.88	.57
Symbol Search	.42	.50	.40	.87	.66
Cancellation	.15	.20	.12	.41	.26

Note. Abbreviations: VCI = Verbal Comprehension Index, PRI = Perceptual Reasoning Index, WMI = Working Memory Index, PSI = Processing Speed Index, FSIQ = Full Scale IQ.
[a]Letter–Number Seq. = Letter–Number Sequencing.
Source: Wechsler Intelligence Scale for Children: Fourth Edition. Copyright © 2003 by The Psychological Corporation. Adapted and reproduced by permission. All rights reserved. *Wechsler Intelligence Scale for Children, WISC* and *WISC–IV* are trademarks of The Psychological Corporation registered in the United States of America and/or other jurisdictions.

DEMOGRAPHIC VARIABLES

Table 1-9 shows the means and standard deviations of the Index scores and the Full Scale IQ for the four demographic variables used to stratify the standardization sample. Highlights of Table 1-9 follow.

Sex

The mean Full Scale IQs of boys and girls were similar, as were their mean Index scores on Verbal Comprehension, Perceptual Reasoning, and Working Memory. However, the mean Index score on Processing Speed was about 5 points higher for boys than for girls.

Race/Ethnicity

The mean Full Scale IQ of Euro American children was about 11.5 points higher than that of African American children and about 10 points higher than that of Hispanic American children. However, the mean Full Scale IQ of Asian American children was about 3 points higher than that of Euro American children.

Although the four mean Index scores were essentially similar for Euro American children, the mean Index scores differed somewhat in the other three racial/ethnic groups.

1. *African American children.* The mean Index scores for Working Memory and Processing Speed were about 4 to 5 points higher than those for Verbal Comprehension and Perceptual Reasoning.

2. *Hispanic American children.* The mean Index scores for Perceptual Reasoning, Working Memory, and Processing Speed were about 3 to 6 points higher than that for Verbal Comprehension.

3. *Asian American children.* The mean Index scores for Perceptual Reasoning and Processing Speed were about 5 points higher than those for Verbal Comprehension and Working Memory.

Parental Education

The mean Full Scale IQ of children whose parents had graduated from college was about 20 points higher than that of children whose parents had an eighth-grade education or less. Similar trends were observed for the mean Index scores on Verbal Comprehension (about 22 points), Perceptual Reasoning (about 15 points), Working Memory (about 15 points), and Processing Speed (about 7 points).

Table 1-9
Relationship of WISC–IV IQs to Sex, Race/Ethnicity, Parental Education, and Geographic Region

Demographic variable	N	Composite									
		Verbal Comprehension		Perceptual Reasoning		Working Memory		Processing Speed		Full Scale	
		M	SD	M	SD	M	SD	M	SD	M	SD
Sex											
Boys	1100	98.69	15.02	99.56	14.92	99.65	14.38	102.48	14.57	100.24	15.27
Girls	1100	100.13	15.00	100.61	14.88	99.26	15.02	97.63	15.00	99.78	15.31
Race/Ethnicity											
Euro American	1402	102.92	13.80	102.77	14.36	101.26	14.55	101.41	14.70	103.24	14.52
African American	343	91.86	15.42	91.43	15.07	96.12	15.35	95.00	15.66	91.72	15.74
Hispanic American	335	91.51	14.45	95.67	12.96	94.24	13.75	97.67	13.43	93.09	12.64
Asian American	92	102.27	15.67	107.26	12.85	102.68	12.20	107.64	15.73	106.53	14.20
Other	28	101.11	15.92	101.00	11.82	101.39	10.60	97.68	14.21	101.04	12.70
Parental Education											
Eight years or less	108	86.47	12.06	92.59	12.46	89.49	12.76	97.54	14.54	88.71	12.21
Some high school	213	87.55	13.82	90.64	14.36	91.62	14.56	94.04	14.44	88.18	14.17
High school graduate	619	95.36	13.08	96.54	13.56	97.61	14.08	97.15	15.08	95.83	13.72
Some college	713	101.64	12.94	101.55	14.08	101.34	13.87	101.14	13.96	102.25	13.47
College graduate	547	108.25	14.23	107.34	14.21	104.10	14.41	104.76	14.87	108.65	14.28
Geographic Region											
Northeast	396	102.67	14.88	100.74	14.93	100.62	14.58	100.79	15.35	102.08	15.40
South	747	97.38	15.62	98.20	15.54	99.69	15.05	98.02	15.28	98.09	15.90
Midwest	528	101.75	13.51	102.57	13.99	100.02	14.10	102.37	14.57	102.61	14.16
West	529	97.48	14.98	99.77	14.52	97.69	14.79	100.07	14.32	98.57	14.91

Source: Wechsler Intelligence Scale for Children: Fourth Edition. Copyright © 2003 by The Psychological Corporation. Adapted and reproduced by permission. All rights reserved. *Wechsler Intelligence Scale for Children, WISC* and *WISC–IV* are trademarks of The Psychological Corporation registered in the United States of America and/or other jurisdictions.

Geographic Region

The mean Full Scale IQ of children from the Northeast and Midwest was about 4 points higher than that of children from the South and West. Similar trends were observed for the mean Index scores on Verbal Comprehension (about 4 to 5 points), Perceptual Reasoning (about 2 to 3 points), Working Memory (about 1 to 2 points), and Processing Speed (about 3 to 4 points).

FACTOR ANALYSIS

We performed a principal axis factor analysis (oblimin rotation with four factors specified and two iterations) using the correlation matrices in the Administration Manual for each of the 11 age groups in the standardization sample and for the total group. The results, which indicated that the following four-factor model holds overall (but not at all ages; see discussion below), generally agreed with the results of the factor analysis reported in the Technical Manual (see Table 1-10).

- *Verbal Comprehension:* Similarities, Vocabulary, Comprehension, Information, and Word Reasoning
- *Perceptual Reasoning:* Block Design, Picture Concepts, Matrix Reasoning, and Picture Completion
- *Working Memory:* Digit Span, Letter–Number Sequencing, and Arithmetic
- *Processing Speed:* Coding, Symbol Search, and Cancellation

Table 1-10
Factor Loadings of WISC–IV Subtests for 11 Age Groups and Total Group Following Principal Axis Factor Analysis (Oblimin Rotation and Two Iterations)

Subtest	Age (in years)											Total
	6	7	8	9	10	11	12	13	14	15	16	
Verbal Comprehension												
Similarities	.47	.66	.49	.79	.79	.69	.77	.58	.83	.69	.80	.73
Vocabulary	.72	.82	.55	.77	.81	.89	.98	.72	.93	.78	.88	.90
Comprehension	.72	.73	.42	.84	.74	.74	.83	.74	.73	.76	.77	.77
Information	.35	.70	.25	.77	.72	.86	.81	.62	.83	.76	.66	.74
Word Reasoning	.56	.78	.36	.66	.83	.65	.59	.62	.79	.86	.59	.71
Block Design	.07	.11	−.11	−.02	.02	−.05	.16	−.12	.06	−.01	.00	−.02
Picture Concepts	.21	.26	.15	.27	.07	.05	.11	.08	.08	.24	.05	.15
Matrix Reasoning	.07	.09	−.13	.08	−.03	.15	.12	.07	.42	.05	.04	.00
Picture Completion	.17	.34	.12	.21	.34	.36	.31	.20	−.06	.25	.37	.37
Digit Span	.10	.01	.06	.23	.22	.04	.02	−.02	.23	−.04	.07	.08
Letter–Number Sequencing	−.02	.25	−.10	.24	.32	.23	.13	.07	.43	.24	.10	.18
Arithmetic	.11	.10	.14	.27	.48	.34	.12	.30	.20	.24	.12	.22
Coding	−.17	−.08	−.17	.00	.08	.19	.09	.23	.02	−.03	.09	.01
Symbol Search	.02	.04	−.05	−.16	.02	.09	.02	.05	.13	.01	.07	.00
Cancellation	.24	.02	.05	.04	−.05	−.13	−.02	−.09	−.04	.02	−.08	−.01
Perceptual Reasoning												
Similarities	.30	−.05	.24	.12	.11	.13	.07	.31	.03	.12	.02	.09
Vocabulary	−.01	−.02	.15	.10	.15	−.05	−.05	.02	−.04	.00	−.08	.02
Comprehension	.07	.07	.11	−.06	−.02	−.02	−.13	.04	−.01	.06	−.10	−.11
Information	.16	.14	.02	−.01	.10	.00	.06	.09	.07	.15	.22	.04
Word Reasoning	.14	−.02	.39	.17	−.11	.13	.21	.25	−.04	−.07	.23	.05
Block Design	.46	.50	.75	.71	.74	.82	.46	.60	.75	.75	.64	.70
Picture Concepts	.30	.00	.57	.43	.50	.50	.40	.48	.48	.22	.51	.35
Matrix Reasoning	.67	.20	.70	.59	.85	.42	.44	.53	.29	.67	.63	.57
Picture Completion	.48	.45	.72	.68	.46	.55	.33	.64	.70	.39	.40	.51
Digit Span	−.18	−.08	.03	.20	.17	.18	.12	.11	.30	.19	.06	.06
Letter–Number Sequencing	.08	.09	.03	.19	.12	−.05	.07	.09	.12	−.08	.04	.04
Arithmetic	.41	.28	.36	−.03	.03	.42	.74	−.09	.56	.52	.34	.24
Coding	.14	.22	.14	.22	.11	−.06	−.20	−.06	.22	.01	.06	.03
Symbol Search	.28	.30	.32	.41	.38	.20	.14	.10	.20	.00	.08	.19
Cancellation	−.13	−.07	−.05	−.08	−.03	.02	.06	.05	−.13	.03	−.04	−.05

(Continued)

Table 1-10 (Continued)

Subtest	Age (in years)											
	6	7	8	9	10	11	12	13	14	15	16	Total
Working Memory												
Similarities	.12	.25	**.36**	−.07	.02	.03	−.07	.06	−.11	.10	.06	.04
Vocabulary	.14	.08	**.39**	.09	.03	.01	−.01	.25	.03	.11	.11	−.02
Comprehension	.01	−.03	.14	−.02	.04	.08	.12	−.02	.12	.09	.09	.08
Information	**.35**	.12	**.74**	.21	.14	.00	−.01	.26	−.08	.03	.03	.11
Word Reasoning	.09	−.05	.10	.04	−.04	.06	.01	−.03	.04	−.09	−.05	.00
Block Design	.04	.22	.08	.10	−.02	.13	.16	.24	−.25	−.06	.13	.08
Picture Concepts	.08	**.38**	−.04	−.16	.10	.05	.21	.03	.07	.09	.05	.13
Matrix Reasoning	.05	**.53**	.15	.10	.09	**.31**	.24	.15	−.31	.14	.11	.23
Picture Completion	−.01	−.11	−.13	−.05	−.21	−.30	−.05	−.07	.03	−.01	−.13	−.20
Digit Span	**.70**	**.67**	**.57**	.25	**.49**	**.56**	**.58**	**.51**	**.33**	**.61**	**.65**	**.55**
Letter–Number Sequencing	**.58**	**.44**	**.69**	**.39**	.29	**.56**	**.62**	**.70**	**.35**	**.62**	**.70**	**.52**
Arithmetic	**.54**	**.64**	.23	**.52**	**.35**	.20	.11	**.65**	.19	.18	**.54**	**.40**
Coding	.07	.11	.25	.06	−.11	.03	.24	.02	.15	.11	−.05	.07
Symbol Search	.18	.22	.23	.29	.04	.16	.26	**.32**	−.01	.10	−.09	.15
Cancellation	−.03	−.06	−.05	−.03	.05	−.04	−.16	−.05	−.05	−.11	.09	−.07
Processing Speed												
Similarities	−.01	.08	−.07	.11	−.07	.07	.03	.01	.03	.03	.00	.01
Vocabulary	.02	−.07	.03	.05	−.10	.06	−.02	.00	−.01	.10	.00	−.01
Comprehension	.00	.04	.25	.02	.03	.00	.00	.08	.06	−.04	.09	.05
Information	.05	−.15	−.05	.02	−.07	.00	−.02	.00	−.08	.00	−.06	−.02
Word Reasoning	.06	.04	.16	−.08	.11	−.10	.00	.03	.02	.01	.02	.01
Block Design	.24	−.03	−.04	.02	.03	.02	.19	.20	.10	.14	.06	.08
Picture Concepts	.07	.16	.02	.09	.09	.06	.17	−.01	−.01	.23	.14	.07
Matrix Reasoning	−.03	.14	−.06	.09	−.03	.13	.08	.02	−.01	.02	.01	.04
Picture Completion	.10	.09	.06	−.05	.10	.04	.26	.03	.07	.15	.05	.04
Digit Span	.09	−.05	.00	−.02	−.04	−.02	−.03	.00	.07	.03	−.01	.01
Letter–Number Sequencing	−.03	−.01	.13	−.04	.15	.17	.06	−.04	.10	.10	.08	.07
Arithmetic	−.05	−.09	.09	.26	**.31**	.03	−.13	.15	−.12	−.04	.08	.07
Coding	**.64**	**.41**	**.47**	**.61**	**.71**	**.74**	**.64**	**.65**	**.62**	**.77**	**.72**	**.68**
Symbol Search	**.47**	.22	**.34**	**.36**	**.36**	**.49**	**.54**	**.45**	**.63**	**.75**	**.75**	**.53**
Cancellation	**.58**	**.54**	**.48**	**.62**	**.68**	**.66**	**.68**	**.59**	**.61**	**.51**	**.51**	**.58**

Note. Factor loadings at or above .30 are in bold.

Description of the Four Factors

Following is a description of the four factors.

- The term *Verbal Comprehension* describes a hypothesized verbal-related ability underlying the Composite for both item content (verbal) and mental process (comprehension). Verbal Comprehension measures verbal knowledge and understanding obtained through both informal and formal education and reflects the application of verbal skills to new situations. Similarities, Vocabulary, Comprehension, Information, and Word Reasoning have high loadings on Verbal Comprehension, followed by Picture Completion, which has a moderate loading. Verbal mediation, perhaps, may be involved in performance on Picture Completion.
- The term *Perceptual Reasoning* describes a hypothesized performance-related ability underlying the Composite for both item content (perceptual) and mental process (reasoning). Perceptual Reasoning measures the ability to interpret and organize visually perceived material and to generate and test hypotheses related to problem solutions. Block Design, Matrix Reasoning, and Picture Completion have high loadings on Perceptual Reasoning, followed by Picture Concepts, which has a moderate loading.
- The term *Working Memory* describes a hypothesized memory-related ability underlying the Composite. Working Memory measures immediate memory and the ability to sustain attention, concentrate, and exert mental control. Digit Span, Letter–Number Sequencing, and Arithmetic have high loadings on Working Memory.
- The term *Processing Speed* describes a hypothesized processing speed ability underlying the Composite. Processing Speed measures the ability to process visually perceived nonverbal information quickly, with concentration and rapid eye-hand coordination being important components. Coding, Symbol Search, and Cancellation have high loadings on Processing Speed.

The factor analytic results give empirical support to interpretation of the four individual Composites as separately functioning entities in the WISC–IV. The factor structure of the WISC–IV into verbal comprehension, perceptual reasoning, working memory, and processing speed components closely agrees with the organization of the test.

Factor Analytic Findings Related to Age

Our factor analytic findings show a diverse pattern with age (see Table 1-11). It is difficult to explain why the factor loadings vary at different ages. The varied loadings may be a function of (a) the fact that all subtests are differentially related to *g*, (b) measurement error, or (c) developmental trends.

1. *Verbal Comprehension.* The five Verbal Comprehension subtests—Similarities, Vocabulary, Comprehension, Information, and Word Reasoning—have loadings above .30 on Verbal Comprehension at 10 of the 11 ages. The one exception is Information, which has a loading of .25 at age 8. Picture Completion, Matrix Reasoning, Letter–Number Sequencing, and Arithmetic, subtests associated with other Composites, also have loadings above .30 on Verbal Comprehension at various ages.

2. *Perceptual Reasoning.* The four Perceptual Reasoning subtests—Block Design, Picture Concepts, Matrix Reasoning, and Picture Completion—have loadings above .30 on Perceptual Reasoning at 8 of the 11 ages. The four exceptions are Picture Concepts, which has loadings of .00 and .22 at ages 7 and 15, respectively, and Matrix Reasoning, which has loadings of .20 and .29 at ages 7 and 14, respectively. Similarities, Word Reasoning, Arithmetic, and Symbol Search, subtests associated with other Composites, have loadings above .30 on Perceptual Reasoning at various ages.

3. *Working Memory.* The three Working Memory subtests—Digit Span, Letter–Number Sequencing, and Arithmetic—have loadings above .30 on Working Memory at 4 of the 11 ages. The seven exceptions are Digit Span, which has a loading of .25 at age 9; Letter–Number Sequencing, which has a loading of .29 at age 10; and Arithmetic, which has loadings of .23, .20, .11, .19, and .18 at ages 8, 11, 12, 14, and 15, respectively. Similarities, Vocabulary, Information, Picture Concepts, Matrix Reasoning, and Symbol Search, subtests associated with other Composites, have loadings above .30 on Working Memory at various ages.

4. *Processing Speed.* The three Processing Speed subtests—Coding, Symbol Search, and Cancellation—have loadings above .30 at 10 of the 11 ages. The one exception is Symbol Search, which has a loading of .22 at age 7. Arithmetic, a subtest associated with another Composite, has a loading above .30 on Processing Speed at age 10.

Table 1-11
Summary of Major Trends of Principal Axis Factor Analysis on WISC–IV, by Age Level and for the Total Group

Age (in years)	Subtests with loadings of .30 or higher on Verbal Comprehension	Subtests with loadings of .30 or higher on Perceptual Reasoning	Subtests with loadings of .30 or higher on Working Memory	Subtests with loadings of .30 or higher on Processing Speed
6	SI, VC, CO, IN, WR	BD, PCn, MR, PCm, SI, AR	IN, DS, LN, AR	CD, SS, CA
7	SI, VC, CO, IN, WR, PCm	BD, PCm, SS	PCn, MR, DS, LN, AR	CD, CA
8	SI, VC, CO, WR	BD, PCn, MR, PCm, WR, AR, SS	SI, VC, IN, DS, LN	CD, SS, CA
9	SI, VC, CO, IN, WR	BD, PCn, MR, PCm, SS	LN, AR	CD, SS, CA
10	SI, VC, CO, IN, WR, PCm, LN, AR	BD, PCn, MR, PCm, SS	DS, AR	CD, SS, CA, AR
11	SI, VC, CO, IN, WR, PCm, AR	BD, PCn, MR, PCm, AR	DS, LN	CD, SS, CA
12	SI, VC, CO, IN, WR, PCm	BD, PCn, MR, PCm, AR	DS, LN	CD, SS, CA
13	SI, VC, CO, IN, WR, AR	BD, PCn, MR, PCm, SI	DS, LN, AR, SS	CD, SS, CA
14	SI, VC, CO, IN, WR, MR, LN	BD, PCn, PCm, DS, AR	DS, LN	CD, SS, CA
15	SI, VC, CO, IN, WR	BD, MR, PCm, AR	DS, LN	CD, SS, CA
16	SI, VC, CO, IN, WR, PCm	BD, PCn, MR, PCm, AR	DS, LN, AR	CD, SS, CA
Total	SI, VC, CO, IN, WR, PCm	BD, PCn, MR, PCm	DS, LN, AR	CD, SS, CA

Note. Abbreviations: BD = Block Design, SI = Similarities, DS = Digit Span, PCn = Picture Concepts, CD = Coding, VC = Vocabulary, LN = Letter–Number Sequencing, MR = Matrix Reasoning, CO = Comprehension, SS = Symbol Search, PCm = Picture Completion, CA = Cancellation, IN = Information, AR = Arithmetic, WR = Word Reasoning.

Subtests as Measure of *g*

The loadings on the first unrotated factor provide information about *g*, or general intelligence. The WISC–IV subtests form three *g*-related clusters (see Table 1-12):

- Vocabulary, Information, Similarities, Arithmetic, Word Reasoning, and Comprehension are good measures of *g*.
- Block Design, Matrix Reasoning, Picture Completion, Letter–Number Sequencing, Symbol Search, Picture Concepts, Digit Span, and Coding are fair measures of *g*.
- Cancellation is a poor measure of *g*.

The Verbal Comprehension subtests have the highest *g* loadings in the test. On average, the proportion of variance attributed to *g* is 62% for the Verbal Comprehension subtests, 45% for the Perceptual Reasoning subtests, 43% for the Working Memory subtests, and 23% for the Processing Speed subtests. Subtests with the highest proportion of variance attributed to *g* are (a) Vocabulary, Information, Similarities, Word Reasoning, and Comprehension in Verbal Comprehension and (b)

Arithmetic in Working Memory. None of the Perceptual Reasoning or Processing Speed subtests are good measures of *g*.

Subtest Specificity

Subtest specificity refers to the proportion of a subtest's variance that is both reliable (i.e., not related to error of measurement) and distinctive to the subtest (see Chapter 4 in Sattler, 2001, for further information about subtest specificity). Although the individual subtests on the WISC–IV overlap in their measurement properties (i.e., the majority of the reliable variance for most subtests is common factor variance), many possess sufficient specificity at some ages to justify interpretation of specific subtest functions.

Block Design, Picture Concepts, Matrix Reasoning, Digit Span, Letter–Number Sequencing, Coding, Symbol Search, and Cancellation have ample specificity at all ages (see Table 1-13). In addition, Picture Completion has ample specificity at 10 of the 11 ages, and Arithmetic has ample specificity at 6 of the 11 ages. Each of the five remaining subtests—Similarities, Vo-

Table 1-12
WISC–IV Subtests as Measures of *g*

Good measure of *g*			Fair measure of *g*			Poor measure of *g*		
Subtest	Average loading of *g*	Proportion of variance attributed to *g* (%)	Subtest	Average loading of *g*	Proportion of variance attributed to *g* (%)	Subtest	Average loading of *g*	Proportion of variance attributed to *g* (%)
Vocabulary	.83	69	Block Design	.70	49	Cancellation	.27	7
Information	.81	66	Matrix Reasoning	.70	49			
Similarities	.81	66	Picture Completion	.66	44			
Arithmetic	.77	59	Letter–Number Seq.[a]	.66	43			
Word Reasoning	.73	54	Symbol Search	.61	37			
Comprehension	.73	53	Picture Concepts	.61	37			
			Digit Span	.57	32			
			Coding	.51	26			

Note. A three-place decimal average loading of *g* was squared to obtain the proportion of variance attributed to *g*.
[a] Letter–Number Seq. = Letter–Number Sequencing.

cabulary, Comprehension, Information, and Word Reasoning—shows a unique pattern of specificity; that is, the ages at which each has ample, adequate, or inadequate specificity differ.

Converting Core Subtest Scaled Scores to Index Scores and Full Scale IQs

The following tables in the Administration Manual are used to convert core subtest scores to Index scores and Full Scale IQs:

- Table A.2 (p. 237) for Verbal Comprehension (Similarities, Vocabulary, and Comprehension)
- Table A.3 (p. 237) for Perceptual Reasoning (Block Design, Picture Concepts, and Matrix Reasoning)
- Table A.4 (p. 238) for Working Memory (Digit Span and Letter–Number Sequencing)
- Table A.5 (p. 238) for Processing Speed (Coding and Symbol Search)
- Table A.6 (pp. 239–240) for the Full Scale (10 core subtests)

There are no similar tables in the Administration Manual that were derived using core and supplemental subtests.

RANGE OF SUBTEST AND PROCESS SCORE SCALED SCORES

Subtest Scaled Scores

The range of scaled scores from 1 to 19 is available for most subtests at each age (see Table 1-14). The three exceptions are Similarities (range of 2 to 19 at ages 6-0 to 6-11), Letter–Number Sequencing (range of 2 to 19 at ages 6-0 to 6-11), and Word Reasoning (range of 1 to 18 at ages 14-4 to 15-11 and 1 to 17 at ages 16-0 to 16-11). Children receive credit even when they obtain a raw score of 0 on all items of a subtest. The generally uniform subtest scaled-score range helps in the interpretation process.

Process Score Scaled Scores

Cancellation Random and Cancellation Structured have a range of scaled scores from 1 to 19 at every age, but the other three Process scores with scaled scores do not. Block Design No Time Bonus has a major restriction of range at several ages (range of 1 to 18 at ages 9-8 to 10-3, 1 to 17 at ages 10-4 to 10-11, 1 to 16 at ages 11-0 to 12-11, 1 to 15 at ages 13-0 to 13-11, and 1 to 14 at ages 14-0 to 16-11). Digit Span Forward has a minor restriction of range (range of 1 to 18 at ages 15-0 to 16-11).

Table 1-13
Amount of Specificity in WISC–IV Subtests for 11 Ages and Total Group

Subtest	Ages for which subtest has ample specificity	Ages for which subtest has adequate specificity	Ages for which subtest has inadequate specificity
Similarities	6, 12	7, 10–11, 14–16, Total	8–9, 13
Vocabulary	6	7, 11, 13–16, Total	8–10, 12
Comprehension	6, 8, 14, 16, Total	9, 10–13	7, 15
Information	6	12–16, Total	7–11
Word Reasoning	6–8, 14–15, Total	9, 11, 13	10, 12, 16
Block Design	6–16, Total	—	—
Picture Concepts	6–16, Total	—	—
Matrix Reasoning	6–16, Total	—	—
Picture Completion	6–8, 10–16, Total	9	—
Digit Span	6–16, Total	—	—
Letter–Number Sequencing	6–16, Total	—	—
Arithmetic	7–9, 12, 14–15, Total	6, 10–11, 13, 16	—
Coding	6–16, Total	—	—
Symbol Search	6–16, Total	—	—
Cancellation	6–16, Total	—	—

Note. Kaufman's (1975) rule of thumb was used to classify the amount of specificity in each subtest. Subtests with ample specificity have specific variance that (a) reflects 25% or more of the subtest's total variance (100%) and (b) exceeds the subtest's error variance. Subtests with adequate specificity have specific variance that (a) reflects between 15% and 24% of the subtest's total variance and (b) exceeds the subtest's error variance. Subtests with inadequate specificity have specific variance that either (a) is less than 15% of the subtest's total variance or (b) is equal to or less than the subtest's error variance.

Specific variance is obtained by subtracting the squared multiple correlation (from the maximum-likelihood factor analysis with varimax rotation) from the subtest's reliability (r_{xx} – SMC) (A. Silverstein, personal communication, October 1991). Error variance is obtained by subtracting the subtest's reliability from 1.00 ($1 - r_{xx}$).

Similarly, Digit Span Backward has a minor restriction of range (range of 3 to 19 at ages 6-0 to 6-11 and 2 to 19 at ages 7-0 to 7-11). Of the five Process scores with scaled scores, those on Block Design No Time Bonus are the ones that are primarily restricted.

RANGE OF FULL SCALE IQS

The range of WISC–IV Full Scale IQs is 40 to 160 and is available at all ages of the test. This range is insufficient for children who are extremely low functioning or extremely high functioning. Even the lowest possible score on the test does not reflect the extent of a child's cognitive ability because, as noted previously, standard-score points are awarded even when a child receives 0 points on every item on a subtest. For example, a 6-year-old who obtains raw scores of 0 on the 10 core subtests receives 12 scaled-score points and a corresponding Full Scale IQ of 40.

Recognizing that awarding scaled-score points for no successes might be a problem, the Administration Manual provides the following guidelines for computing scores in the event that a child has raw scores of 0.

- The Verbal Comprehension Index should be computed *only* when the child obtains a raw score greater than 0 on at least *two of the three subtests* in the Composite.

Table 1-14
WISC–IV Subtest and Process Score Scaled-Score Ranges by Age

Subtest or Process score	Scaled-score range	Age
Verbal Comprehension		
Similarities	2–19	6-0 to 6-11
	1–19	7-0 to 16-11
Vocabulary	1–19	6-0 to 16-11
Comprehension	1–19	6-0 to 16-11
Information	1–19	6-0 to 16-11
Word Reasoning	1–19	6-0 to 14-3
	1–18	14-4 to 15-11
	1–17	16-0 to 16-11
Perceptual Reasoning		
Block Design	1–19	6-0 to 16-11
Picture Concepts	1–19	6-0 to 16-11
Matrix Reasoning	1–19	6-0 to 16-11
Picture Completion	1–19	6-0 to 16-11
Working Memory		
Digit Span	1–19	6-0 to 16-11
Letter–Number Sequencing	2–19	6-0 to 16-11
	1–19	7-0 to 16-11
Arithmetic	1–19	6-0 to 16-11
Processing Speed		
Coding	1–19	6-0 to 16-11
Symbol Search	1–19	6-0 to 16-11
Cancellation	1–19	6-0 to 16-11
Process Score		
Block Design No Time Bonus	1–19	6-0 to 9-7
	1–18	9-8 to 10-3
	1–17	10-4 to 10-11
	1–16	11-0 to 12-11
	1–15	13-0 to 13-11
	1–14	14-0 to 16-11
Digit Span Forward	1–19	6-0 to 14-11
	1–18	15-0 to 16-11
Digit Span Backward	3–19	6-0 to 6-11
	2–19	7-0 to 7-11
	1–19	8-0 to 16-11
Cancellation Random	1–19	6-0 to 16-11
Cancellation Structured	1–19	6-0 to 16-11

Note. There are no scaled scores for Longest Digit Span Forward and Longest Digit Span Backward.
Source: Adapted from Wechsler (2003a).

- The Perceptual Reasoning Index should be computed *only* when the child obtains a raw score greater than 0 on at least *two of the three subtests* in the Composite.
- The Working Memory Index should be computed *only* when the child obtains a raw score greater than 0 on at least *one of the two subtests* in the Composite.
- The Processing Speed Index should be computed *only* when the child obtains a raw score greater than 0 on at least *one of the two subtests* in the Composite.
- The Full Scale IQ should be computed *only* when the child obtains raw scores greater than 0 on at least (a) *two of the three subtests* in Verbal Comprehension, (b) *two of the three subtests* in Perceptual Reasoning, (c) *one of the two subtests* in Working Memory, and (d) *one of the two subtests* in Processing Speed.

Neither the Administration Manual nor the Technical Manual provides any empirical basis (e.g., psychometric or research evidence) for these rules. Although they appear to have some merit, we need research to determine whether these rules are valid or whether other rules would be equally or more valid for computing Index scores and IQs.

If The Psychological Corporation's recommended procedure is followed, the lowest possible IQ that a 6-year-old child can receive is 41, arrived at in the following way: The child obtains raw scores of 1 on Vocabulary, Comprehension, Block Design, Matrix Reasoning, Digit Span, and Letter–Number Sequencing and raw scores of 0 on the remaining four subtests. The resulting Index scores and IQ are as follows: Verbal Comprehension Index = 50 (5 scaled-score points), Perceptual Reasoning Index = 51 (6 scaled-score points), Working Memory Index = 52 (3 scaled-score points), Processing Speed Index = 50 (2 scaled-score points), and Full Scale IQ = 41 (16 scaled-score points). Six 1-point raw scores thus yield a Full Scale IQ of 41. Therefore, the WISC–IV may not provide accurate IQs for young children who are functioning at three or more standard deviations below the mean of the test. In other words, the WISC–IV does not appear to sample a sufficient range of cognitive abilities for children who are extremely low functioning.

Table A.6 (FSIQ Equivalents of Sums of Scaled Scores) in the Administration Manual does not give any Full Scale IQs for sums of scaled scores below 10. In addition, sums of scaled scores of 10, 11, 12, 13, 14, and 15 points all convert to the same Full Scale IQ of 40.

COMPARISON OF THE WISC–IV AND WISC–III

Although similar in some ways, the WISC–IV and WISC–III have considerably different structures. Among the differences are variations in the composition of the Full Scale, the composition of the individual Composites, and the number of supplemental subtests (see Tables 1-15, 1-16, and 1-17).

Composition of the Core Subtests on the Full Scale

The WISC–IV Full Scale is composed of three core subtests assessing verbal comprehension (Similarities, Vocabulary, and Comprehension), three core subtests assessing nonverbal perceptual reasoning (Block Design, Picture Concepts, and Matrix Reasoning), two core subtests assessing short-term auditory rote memory for nonmeaningful material (Digit Span and Letter–Number Sequencing), and two core subtests assessing visuomotor processing speed (Coding and Symbol Search).

The WISC–III Full Scale is composed of four core subtests assessing verbal comprehension (Information, Comprehension, Similarities, and Vocabulary), four core subtests assessing nonverbal perceptual reasoning (Picture Arrangement, Block Design, Picture Completion, and Object Assembly), one core subtest assessing working memory and quantitative knowledge (Arithmetic), and one core subtest assessing visuomotor processing speed (Coding).

Composition of the Individual Composites

Verbal Comprehension. The WISC–IV Verbal Comprehension Composite has three core subtests, while the WISC–III Verbal Scale has five core subtests. Similarities, Vocabulary, and Comprehension are core subtests in both tests. The two other WISC–III Verbal Scale core subtests are supplemental subtests in the WISC–IV (Information in Verbal Comprehension and Arithmetic in Working Memory).

The Verbal Comprehension Index in the WISC–IV is similar to the Verbal Comprehension Index in the WISC–III. However, the WISC–IV Verbal Comprehension Index is composed of Similarities, Vocabulary, and Comprehension, while the WISC–III Verbal Comprehension Index is composed of Information, Similarities, Vocabulary, and Comprehension.

Note that both the Administration Manual and the Technical Manual indicate that the WISC–IV Verbal Comprehension Index can serve as a substitute for the WISC–III Verbal Scale IQ in clinical decision making and in other situations where the Verbal Scale IQ was previously used. However, we recommend that this be done with caution, because the correlation between the two composite scores is only .83 and the two composite scores have 69% of the variance in common.

Perceptual Reasoning. The WISC–IV Perceptual Reasoning Composite has three core subtests, while the WISC–III Performance Scale has five core subtests. Block Design is a core subtest in both tests. The two other WISC–IV core subtests are new (Picture Concepts and Matrix Reasoning). Of the four other WISC–III Performance Scale core subtests, Coding is a core Processing Speed subtest in the WISC–IV, Picture Completion is a supplemental Perceptual Reasoning subtest in the WISC–IV, and Picture Arrangement and Object Assembly are not included in the WISC–IV.

The Perceptual Reasoning Composite in the WISC–IV is similar to the Perceptual Organization Index in the WISC–III. However, the WISC–IV Perceptual Reasoning Composite is composed of Block Design, Picture Concepts, and Matrix Reasoning, while the WISC–III Perceptual Organization Index is composed of Picture Completion, Picture Arrangement, Block Design, and Object Assembly.

Note that both the Administration Manual and the Technical Manual indicate that the WISC–IV Perceptual Reasoning Index can serve as a substitute for the WISC–III Performance Scale IQ in clinical decision making and in other situations where the Performance Scale IQ was previously used. However, we recommend that this be done with caution, because the correlation between the two composite scores is only .73 and the two composite scores have 53% of the variance in common.

Working Memory. The WISC–IV Working Memory Composite has one core subtest that is a supplemental subtest in the WISC–III Verbal Scale (Digit Span); the other WISC–IV core subtest is new (Letter–Number Sequencing).

The Working Memory Composite in the WISC–IV is similar to the Freedom from Distractibility Index in the WISC–III. However, the WISC–IV Working Memory Composite is composed of Digit Span and Letter–Number Sequencing, while the WISC–III Freedom from Distractibility Index is composed of Arithmetic and Digit Span.

Table 1-15
Comparison of Numbers of Items on the WISC–IV and the WISC–III

Subtest or Composite	Number of items		% increase in items	WISC–IV			
				Items retained[g]		New items[h]	
	WISC–III	WISC–IV		N	%	N	%
Verbal Comprehension							
Similarities	19	23	21.1	12	52.2	11	47.8
Vocabulary	30	36	20.0	27	75.0	9	25.0
Comprehension	18	21	16.7	10	47.6	11	52.4
Information	30	33	10.0	22	66.7	11	33.3
Word Reasoning	—	24	—	—	—	24	100.0
Perceptual Reasoning[a]							
Block Design	12	14	16.7	11	78.6	3	21.4
Picture Concepts	—	28	—	—	—	28	100.0
Matrix Reasoning	—	35	—	—	—	35	100.0
Picture Completion	30	38	26.7	25	65.8	13	34.2
Picture Arrangement	14	—	—	—	—	—	—
Object Assembly	5	—	—	—	—	—	—
Mazes[b]	10	—	—	—	—	—	—
Working Memory[c]							
Digit Span	15	16	6.7	10	62.5	6	37.5
Letter–Number Sequencing	—	10	—	—	—	10	100.0
Arithmetic	24	34	41.7	12	35.3	22	64.7
Processing Speed							
Coding[d]							
Part A/Form A	59	59	0.0	59	100.0	0	0.0
Part B/Form B	119	119	0.0	119	100.0	0	0.0
Symbol Search[d]							
Part A/Form A	45	45	0.0	45	100.0	0	0.0
Part B/Form B	45	60	33.0	45	75.0	15	25.0
Cancellation	—	2	—	—	—	2	100.0
Composite							
Verbal Comprehension	97	137	41.2	71	51.8	66	48.2
Perceptual Reasoning[a]	61	115	88.5	36	31.3	79	68.7
Working Memory[c, f]	39	60	53.8	22	36.7	38	63.3
Processing Speed[d, e]							
Part A/Form A	104	106	1.9	104	98.1	2	1.8
Part B/Form B	164	181	10.4	164	90.6	17	9.4
Full Scale[d]							
with Part A/Form A	301	418	38.8	233	55.7	185	44.3
with Part B/Form B	361	493	36.6	293	59.4	200	40.6

[a] Referred to as Perceptual Organization Index in WISC–III.
[b] Not part of Perceptual Organization Index in WISC–III.
[c] Referred to as Freedom from Distractibility Index in WISC–III.
[d] The WISC–III uses the terms Part A and Part B, while the WISC–IV uses the terms Form A and Form B.
[e] For the WISC–III, refers to Part A or Part B on Symbol Search and Coding; for the WISC–IV, refers to Form A or Form B on Symbol Search and Coding plus Cancellation.
[f] For the WISC–III, refers to Digit Span and Arithmetic; for the WISC–IV, refers to Digit Span, Letter–Number Sequencing, and Arithmetic.
[g] Essentially the same as they were in the WISC–III.
[h] Newly written or worded differently than in the WISC–III.

Table 1-16
Highlights of Characteristics of the WISC–IV

Area	Characteristics of the WISC–IV
Age range	Continues to cover ages from 6-0 to 16-11.
Standardization	2000 U.S. Census data used to stratify a sample of 2,200 children, except in the case of Arithmetic, where 1,100 children were used.
Stratification variables	Generally similar to those of the WISC–III.
Number of subtests	15 instead of 13 (as on the WISC–III).
Number of items	More than on comparable WISC–III subtests (e.g., 14 vs. 12 on Block Design, 16 vs. 15 on Digit Span, 21 vs. 18 on Comprehension, 33 vs. 30 on Information, 34 vs. 24 on Arithmetic, 36 vs. 30 on Vocabulary, 23 vs. 19 on Similarities, 38 vs. 30 on Picture Completion, and 60 vs. 45 on Symbol Search B).
New subtests	Picture Concepts, Matrix Reasoning, Letter–Number Sequencing, Cancellation, and Word Reasoning.
Deleted subtests	Picture Arrangement, Object Assembly, and Mazes.
Manipulative materials	Fewer than on the WISC–III (e.g., Picture Arrangement, Object Assembly, and Mazes are deleted).
Core subtests	Block Design, Similarities, Digit Span, Picture Concepts, Coding, Vocabulary, Letter–Number Sequencing, Matrix Reasoning, Comprehension, and Symbol Search.
Supplemental subtests	Picture Completion, Cancellation, Information, Arithmetic, and Word Reasoning.
Process scores	Five new ones: Block Design No Time Bonus, Digit Span Forward, Digit Span Backward, Cancellation Random, and Cancellation Structured.
Reliability	Generally similar to that of the WISC–III.
Validity	Generally similar to that of the WISC–III.
Scoring examples	Generally similar to those of the WISC–III.
General administration	Changes in order of administering subtests, item order, start-point items, discontinue criteria, and bonus-point allotment. Sample items, easier items, and more difficult items added.
Administration time	Longer than that of the WISC–III (e.g., 65 to 80 minutes vs. 50 to 70 minutes).
Time to respond	Longer than that of the WISC–III (suggests that examiners wait 10 to 30 seconds for child to respond before going to the next item vs. 15 to 20 seconds for the WISC–III).
Time bonuses	Fewer than on the WISC–III (e.g., Arithmetic has no time bonuses, Block Design awards time bonuses only beginning with item 9, Picture Arrangement is deleted, and Object Assembly is deleted).
Discontinue criteria	On some subtests, more consecutive failures required to discontinue than on comparable WISC–III subtests (e.g., 3 vs. 2 on Block Design, 4 vs. 3 on Similarities, 5 vs. 4 on Vocabulary, 4 vs. 3 on Comprehension, 6 vs. 5 on Picture Completion, and 4 vs. 3 on Arithmetic).

(Continued)

Table 1-16 (*Continued*)

Area	Characteristics of the WISC–IV
Computation of IQ	Based on 10 core subtests (3 from Verbal Comprehension, 3 from Perceptual Reasoning, 2 from Working Memory, and 2 from Processing Speed). Four Indexes computed with the following restrictions: (a) at least two raw scores greater than 0 on Verbal Comprehension, (b) at least two raw scores greater than 0 on Perceptual Reasoning, (c) at least one raw score greater than 0 on Working Memory, and (d) at least one raw score greater than 0 on Processing Speed. Full Scale IQ computed only when the four Indexes can be computed (minimum of 6 raw scores of more than 0).
Intelligence classification	IQs below 70 classified as "Extremely Low" instead of "Intellectually Deficient" (as on the WISC–III).
Record Form	Greatly expanded. First page contains sections for profiles for subtests and Composites, identifying information, raw score to scaled score conversions, scaled score to Composite score conversions. Second page is a discrepancy analysis page with sections for determining subtest strengths and weaknesses and process analysis. Information about start points, reversals, time limits, prompts, and discontinue criteria is included on subtest pages. Last page contains sections for demographic information and behavioral observations. More space is provided to write responses.
Record Booklet	Two Record Booklets instead of one (as on the WISC–III). One Record Booklet contains Coding A, Coding B, Symbol Search A, and Symbol Search B, and the other contains Cancellation.
Types of scores	Provides a FSIQ ($M = 100$, $SD = 15$), four Index scores ($M = 100$, $SD = 15$), percentile ranks, subtest scaled scores ($M = 10$, $SD = 3$), and Process scores ($M = 10$, $SD = 3$).
Confidence intervals	Based on the estimated true score.
Factor structure	A four-factor model, consisting of Verbal Comprehension, Perceptual Reasoning, Working Memory, and Processing Speed, that differs slightly from the model on the WISC–III.
g loading	About the same as that of the WISC–III.
Art work	Updated to look more attractive and more contemporary.
Test-retest changes	Generally comparable to those of the WISC–III.
Range of Full Scale IQs	Same as on the WISC–III (40 to 160).
Range of subtest scaled scores	More subtests have a range of 1 to 19 scaled-score points than in the WISC–III.

Processing Speed. The WISC–IV Processing Speed Composite has one core subtest that is also a core subtest in the WISC–III Performance Scale (Coding); the other WISC–IV core subtest is a supplemental subtest in the WISC–III (Symbol Search).

The Processing Speed Composite in the WISC–IV is similar to the Processing Speed Index in the WISC–III in that both are composed of Coding and Symbol Search.

Supplemental Subtests

The WISC–IV has five supplemental subtests, whereas the WISC–III has three supplemental subtests. Informa-

tion, Arithmetic, and Picture Completion, core subtests in the WISC–III, are supplemental subtests in the WISC–IV. Arithmetic, a core Verbal Scale subtest in the WISC–III, is a supplemental Working Memory subtest in the WISC–IV. Symbol Search, a core Processing Speed subtest in the WISC–IV, is a supplemental subtest in the WISC–III. Mazes, a supplemental subtest in the WISC–III, is not included in the WISC–IV. Cancellation in the Processing Speed Composite and Word Reasoning in the Verbal Comprehension Composite are two new WISC–IV supplemental subtests. Supplemental subtests in both tests can be used as substitutes for the core subtests (with special rules).

Other Differences

Other differences between the WISC–IV and WISC–III include the following. The WISC–IV eliminates the terms "Verbal Scale" and "Performance Scale" and, as noted previously, has four individual Composites in addition to the Full Scale. Scoring guidelines and administrative procedures have been modified. For example, changes have been made in item content, the order in which subtests are administered, the order of items, start points, discontinue criteria, timing, allotment of bonus points, and querying and scoring guidelines. The WISC–IV deemphasizes speed of performance on tasks outside of Processing Speed. Finally, the number of items has been increased on most subtests.

Comment on Comparison of the WISC–IV and WISC–III

The cumulative effects of these changes are particularly evident in the WISC–IV Full Scale. Of the core subtests in the WISC–IV Full Scale, 50% are not core subtests in the WISC–III Full Scale. The new WISC–IV core subtests are Digit Span, Picture Concepts, Letter–Number Sequencing, Matrix Reasoning, and Symbol Search. The core subtests assessing nonmeaningful auditory rote memory represent 20% of the WISC–IV Full Scale, versus 0% of the WISC–III Full Scale. (We do not consider Arithmetic, which is a core WISC–III subtest, to be a measure of nonmeaningful rote memory, as it involves quantitative knowledge and fluid reasoning in addition

Table 1-17
Highlights of Changes in the WISC–IV Subtests

Subtest	Changes from the WISC–III
Block Design	Contains 14 instead of 12 items, with 11 retained and 3 new items. Changes in bonus-point allotment and discontinue criterion.
Similarities	Contains 23 instead of 19 items, with 12 retained and 11 new items. Changes in start points, discontinue criterion, and scoring.
Digit Span	Contains 16 instead of 15 sets of digits, with one 2-digit set added to Digit Span Backward. Is now a core rather than a supplemental subtest. Norms by age group are provided for Digit Span Forward and Digit Span Backward. Critical value and base rate tables are provided for Digit Span Forward minus Digit Span Backward.
Picture Concepts	New subtest with 28 items.
Coding	Instructions have been shortened.
Vocabulary	Contains 36 instead of 30 items, with 27 retained and 9 new items, 4 of which are picture items. Changes in discontinue criterion and scoring.
Letter–Number Sequencing	New subtest with 10 sets of number-letter combinations.
Matrix Reasoning	New subtest with 35 items.
Comprehension	Contains 21 instead of 18 items, with 10 retained and 11 new items. Changes in start points, discontinue criterion, and scoring.
Symbol Search	Retains Form A with no changes and expands Form B to 60 items. Instructions have been shortened.
Picture Completion	Contains 38 instead of 30 items, with 25 retained and 13 new items. Now a supplemental subtest. Changes in discontinue criterion and scoring, and a time change on one item.
Cancellation	New subtest with 2 items.
Information	Contains 33 instead of 30 items, with 22 retained and 11 new items. Now a supplemental subtest. Changes in discontinue criterion and scoring.
Arithmetic	Contains 34 instead of 24 items, with 12 items retained and 22 new items. Changes in discontinue criterion, and bonus points have been eliminated.
Word Reasoning	New subtest with 24 items.

to working memory.) The core subtests assessing visuomotor processing speed represent 20% of the WISC–IV Full Scale, versus 10% of the WISC–III Full Scale. Consequently, 60% of the core subtests in the WISC–IV Full Scale measure crystallized knowledge and fluid reasoning ability, while 40% measure immediate auditory rote memory and visuomotor processing speed. In contrast, 90% of the core subtests in the WISC–III Full Scale measure crystallized knowledge and fluid reasoning ability, while 10% measure visuomotor processing speed. In addition, Digit Span and Symbol Search, which were supplemental subtests in the WISC–III, are core subtests in the WISC–IV.

The tasks that measure crystallized knowledge and fluid reasoning ability involve complex transformations and mental manipulations and require reasoning, problem solving, concept formation, and solving figural analogies. One must consciously manipulate the input in order to arrive at the correct output. In contrast, the tasks that measure immediate auditory rote memory and visuomotor processing speed involve little transformation of the input; a high degree of correspondence exists between the form of stimulus input and the form of response output. These tasks require either (a) rote memory and some mental transformations or (b) scanning and visual matching.

You will need to take into account the different structures of the WISC–IV and WISC–III when comparing test-retest scores from the two tests. For example, a child with cognitive strengths in working memory and processing speed and relative weaknesses in verbal and nonverbal reasoning would probably have a higher Full Scale IQ on the WISC–IV than on the WISC–III, whereas a child with cognitive strengths in verbal and nonverbal reasoning and relative weaknesses in working memory and processing speed would probably have a higher Full Scale IQ on the WISC–III than on the WISC–IV. In evaluating test-retest scores, you also will need to consider other factors, such as practice effects, changes in the child's health, changes in the child's home environment, changes in the school setting, and changes in examiners (see Sattler, 2001, for further information about test-retest changes). As noted previously, Full Scale IQs are likely to be lower on the WISC–IV than on the WISC–III by about 3 points. A study of the pattern of subtest scores on the two tests, taking into account the different structures of the two tests, and the case history will guide you in interpreting test-retest changes from the WISC–III to the WISC–IV.

ADMINISTERING THE WISC–IV

To become proficient in administering the WISC–IV, you must master the procedures described in the Administration Manual. Be careful not to confuse the administration procedures for the WISC–III, WPPSI–III, or WAIS–III with those for the WISC–IV. Confusion could occur because some subtests with the same name have different instructions and time limits. The administration guidelines discussed in the next two chapters (Chapter 2 for the core subtests and Chapter 3 for the supplemental subtests) complement those in the Administration Manual. Table C-8 in Appendix C presents special procedures for administering the WISC–IV Perceptual Reasoning subtests to children with hearing impairments. Chapters 2 and 3, along with the suggestions in Exhibit 1-2 and the checklist in Table D-1 in Appendix D, will help you become proficient in administering the WISC–IV. By mastering the administrative procedures early in your testing career, you will be better able to focus on the equally important tasks of learning how to establish rapport, observe the child, and interpret the test results. (The procedures for administering psychological tests, discussed in Chapter 7 of Sattler, 2001, also are helpful in administering the WISC–IV.)

General Guidelines for Test Administration

As you read about the subtests in Chapters 2 and 3, you will find questions to guide you in your test administration and in your evaluation and interpretation of the child's performance. The quality of the child's responses and the pattern of successes and failures, along with the child's scores and behavior, are important parts of the evaluation. Recording the child's responses verbatim, along with pertinent behavioral observations, will help you evaluate the test results, especially when you review your scoring, testify at an administrative hearing or in court, share the evaluation with other professionals, or reevaluate the child. Make an entry on the Record Form for every item that you administer.

As you administer the test, use the exact wording of the directions, questions, or items. Do not add explanations, use synonyms, or ad lib. Sometimes, however, you can use your own wording, except for the subtest questions, and these instances are noted in the Administration Manual. Common sense may dictate that you occa-

Exhibit 1-2
Supplementary Instructions for Administering the WISC–IV

SUPPLEMENTARY INSTRUCTIONS FOR ADMINISTERING THE WISC–IV

Preparing to Administer the WISC–IV

1. Study the instructions in the Administration Manual, and practice administering the test before you give it to a child. It is a good idea to take the test yourself before you study it.
2. Organize your test materials before the child comes into the room. Make sure that all test materials—including the Stimulus Book, blocks, Record Form, Response Booklets, stopwatch, and pencils—are in the kit. Have extra blank paper on which to take notes, if necessary.
3. Keep anything not needed for the test off the table (e.g., soda cans, pocketbook, keys).
4. Complete the top of the first page of the Record Form (child's name and examiner's name).
5. Complete the "Calculation of Child's Age" section. Enter the date of testing and the child's date of birth and then compute the child's age at testing (i.e., chronological age). Months are considered to have 30 days for testing purposes. Check the child's chronological age by adding the child's chronological age to the date of birth to obtain the date of testing.

Administering the WISC–IV

6. Administer the subtests in the order presented in the Administration Manual or on the Record Form, except in rare circumstances. Do not change the wording on any subtest. Read the directions exactly as shown in the Administration Manual. Do not ad lib.
7. Start with the appropriate item on each subtest and follow both the reverse rule and the discontinue criteria. You must be thoroughly familiar with the scoring criteria *before* you give the test.
8. Write down verbatim all of the child's responses that are pertinent to the test, the testing situation, and the referral question or that are otherwise helpful in understanding the child. Write clearly, and do not use unusual abbreviations. Record time accurately in the spaces provided on the Record Form. Use a stopwatch (or a wristwatch with a digital timer) to administer the timed WISC–IV subtests.
9. Clearly and accurately complete the Record Form. A clearly written and accurate Record Form will (a) give you an opportunity to review your scoring after the test is completed, (b) provide a record for qualitative analysis, and (c) provide a document in case of litigation.
10. Question all incomplete, vague, or unclear responses, writing "(Q)" after each questionable response. Question all responses followed by "(Q)" in the Administration Manual.
11. Introduce the test by using the introduction on page 59 of the Administration Manual. Make eye contact with the child from time to time, and use the child's first name when possible. Watch for signs that the child

needs a break (e.g., a stretch, a drink, or a trip to the bathroom). If needed, between subtests say something like "Now we'll do something different." At the end of the test, thank the child for coming and for being cooperative (if appropriate).
12. Complete the last page of Response Booklet 1 by entering the child's name, the examiner's name, the date, and the child's age.
13. If you administer Cancellation, complete the first page of Response Booklet 2 by entering the child's name, the examiner's name, the date, and the child's age.

Scoring

14. Be prepared to spend more time scoring the subtests in the Verbal Comprehension Composite because they are generally more difficult to score than subtests in the other Composites.
15. Recheck your scoring when the test is finished. If you failed to question a response when you should have and the response is obviously not a 0-point response, give the child the most appropriate score based on the child's actual response.
16. If a subtest was spoiled, write "spoiled" by the subtest total score and on the first page of the Record Form next to the name of the subtest. If the subtest was not administered, write "NA" in the margin of the Record Form next to the subtest name and on the first page of the Record Form.
17. Add the raw scores for each subtest carefully.
18. Make sure that you give credit for all items below the first two items with perfect scores (even those with 0 points).
19. Make sure that you do not give credit for items above the last discontinue-point item (even those with perfect scores).

Record Form

20. Transfer subtest scores from the inside pages of the Record Form to the first page of the Record Form in the section labeled "Total Raw Score to Scaled Score Conversions." After transferring the raw scores to the first page of the Record Form, check to see that you copied them correctly.
21. Transform raw scores into scaled scores by using Table A.1 on pages 204 to 236 of the Administration Manual. Be sure to use the page of Table A.1 that is appropriate for the child's age and the correct column for each transformation. For example, to convert a raw score on Block Design (the first subtest administered) to a scaled score, you must use the column labeled BD in Table A.1. Find the entry for your raw score and the corresponding scaled score in the first column (labeled "Scaled Score").

(Continued)

Exhibit 1-2 (*Continued*)

22. Add the scaled scores for the three core Verbal Comprehension subtests to compute the sum of the scaled scores. Do not use Information or Word Reasoning unless you have substituted one for another Verbal Comprehension subtest. Compute the Verbal Comprehension Index only when the child has raw scores greater than 0 on at least two of the three subtests in the Composite.

23. Add the scaled scores for the three core Perceptual Reasoning subtests. Do not use Picture Completion unless you have substituted it for another Perceptual Reasoning subtest. Compute the Perceptual Reasoning Index only when the child has raw scores greater than 0 on at least two of the three subtests in the Composite.

24. Add the scaled scores for the two core Working Memory subtests. Do not use Arithmetic unless you have substituted it for another Working Memory subtest. Compute the Working Memory Index only when the child has a raw score greater than 0 on at least one of the two subtests in the Composite.

25. Add the scaled scores for the two core Processing Speed subtests. Do not use Cancellation unless you have substituted it for another Processing Speed subtest. Compute the Processing Speed Index only when the child has a raw score greater than 0 on at least one of the two subtests in the Composite.

26. Add the Verbal Comprehension, Perceptual Reasoning, Working Memory, and Processing Speed subtest scaled scores to obtain the sum for the Full Scale. Double check all of your additions. Compute the Full Scale IQ only when the child has raw scores greater than 0 on at least (a) two of the three subtests in both the Verbal Comprehension and the Perceptual Reasoning Composite and (b) one of the two subtests in both the Working Memory and the Processing Speed Composites (i.e., a total of six raw-score points greater than 0).

27. Convert the sums of scaled scores for the Verbal Comprehension, Perceptual Reasoning, Working Memory, and Processing Speed Composites and for the Full Scale by using the appropriate conversion tables in Appendix A in the Administration Manual. Use Table A.2 for the Verbal Comprehension Index (p. 237), Table A.3 for the Perceptual Reasoning Index (p. 237), Table A.4 for the Working Memory Index (p. 238), Table A.5 for the Processing Speed Index (p. 238), and Table A.6 for the Full Scale IQ (pp. 239–240). Be sure to use the correct table for the appropriate Composite. Record the Indexes and Full Scale IQ in the appropriate boxes on the first page of the Record Form.

28. We recommend that you not compute either Index scores or the Full Scale IQ if a supplementary subtest has been substituted for a core subtest because the norms were derived from the core subtests only. This recommendation is especially important in situations in which precise scores will be used for decision-making purposes (i.e., diagnostic classifications, eligibility decisions, etc.).

29. Recheck all of your work. If the IQ was obtained by use of a short form, write "SF" beside the appropriate IQ. If IQs were prorated, write "PRO" beside each appropriate IQ.

30. Make a profile of the child's scaled scores on the first page of the Record Form by plotting the scores on the graph provided.

31. Look up the confidence interval for the Full Scale in Table A-1 in Appendix A of this text. Use the confidence interval appropriate for the child's age. Write the confidence interval on the first page of the Record Form in the space provided. It is not necessary to obtain the confidence interval for any Index.

32. Look up the percentile ranks for the Indexes and Full Scale IQ by using Table C-10 in Appendix C in this text or Tables A.2 to A.6 (pp. 237–240) in the Administration Manual. Use Table C-11 in Appendix C in this text or Table 6.3 (p. 101) in the Technical Manual to obtain the classification of the IQ.

33. If you want to obtain test-age equivalents, use Table A.9 (p. 253) in the Administration Manual. The equivalents can be placed (in parentheses) in the right margin of the box that contains the scaled scores on the first page of the Record Form. For test-age equivalents *above* those in the table, use the highest test-age equivalent and a plus sign. For test-age equivalents *below* those in the table, use the lowest test-age equivalent and a minus sign.

34. If you want to, complete the Analysis Page, which is page 2 of the Record Form. Table A.8 (pp. 242–252) in the Administration Manual provides the raw score to scaled score equivalents for the five Process scores.

35. Complete the last page of the Record Form. Enter the identifying information requested and complete the Behavioral Observations section.

Miscellaneous Information and Suggestions

36. Appendix B in the Administration Manual (pp. 256–270) contains 10 tables that provide statistical information about the Indexes and subtest comparisons, including base rates and critical differences.

37. Appendixes A and C in this text contain several tables to assist you in interpreting the WISC–IV and in obtaining IQs associated with short forms.

38. Be sure to check the scores you enter into any computer program you use to assist you in writing a report.

Summary

39. In summary, read the directions verbatim, pronounce words clearly, query and prompt at the appropriate times, start with the appropriate item, place items properly before the child, use correct timing, score appropriately, discontinue at the proper place, follow the specific guidelines in the Administration Manual for administering the test, and complete the Record Form appropriately.

sionally say something that is not in the Administration Manual, such as "Tell me when you're finished." Overall, the aim is to administer the test in a standardized manner.

When you compute the Full Scale IQ or Index scores, never include scores from spoiled subtests (e.g., subtests spoiled through improper timing, interruptions, or mistakes in administration) or from supplemental subtests that were administered in addition to the core subtests.

When a child says "I don't know," consider what this response might mean and how you want to respond to it. It could mean, for example, that the child (a) does not know the answer, (b) is not confident of the answer and is unwilling to take a risk, (c) is being uncooperative and doesn't want to answer the question, or (d) has been inattentive and therefore doesn't know what the question is. If you decide that the response reflects a motivational issue, encourage the child to answer. If the subtest directions permit you to do so, consider repeating the question or asking it again at some later point, especially if the child says "I don't know" to easy questions.

Better yet, the first time a child says "I don't know," say something like "I want you to try your hardest on each question. Try your best to answer each question. If you are not sure, go ahead and take your best guess." You can also say, "It is OK to answer even if you are not sure." Give the child credit if the question is answered correctly.

Estimating the Time Required to Administer the WISC–IV Core Battery

According to the Administration Manual, the times required to administer the WISC–IV core battery to three groups were as follows:

- Standardization sample: 50% completed the test in 67 minutes or less, 75% in 80 minutes or less, 90% in 94 minutes or less, and 95% in 102 minutes or less.
- Intellectually gifted sample: 50% in 79 minutes or less, 75% in 90 minutes or less, 90% in 104 minutes or less, and 95% in 106 minutes or less.
- Sample with mental retardation: 50% in 50 minutes or less, 75% in 62 minutes or less, 90% in 73 minutes or less, and 95% in 79 minutes or less.

Thus, the core battery can usually be administered in approximately 1 to 1½ hours, and the time required seldom exceeds 2 hours. The time tends to increase with

increasing intellectual levels.

At the Beginning

At the beginning of a testing session, make sure that the room is well lit, has comfortable size-appropriate furniture for the child, and is free from distractions. Appropriate lighting is especially necessary when you are using the Record Form because several subtests are printed in light blue ink in order to prevent the items or correct answers from being photocopied. However, the Record Form has other subtests with correct answers not printed in light blue ink. Position the child away from any windows and sit directly across from the child. If a parent is present, ask the parent to remain in the background and sit quietly out of the child's view. (Some of the material in this section is adapted from Wechsler, 2003a.)

Prepare for the session by making sure that the test materials are in order. During testing, keep the test kit out of the child's view. As you establish rapport, tell the child that breaks are OK and to let you know if a break is needed. Position the Administration Manual and the Record Form so that the child cannot read the questions or answers. After you establish rapport, begin the test. Do not prolong the getting-acquainted period, overstimulate the child, or entertain the child excessively. Introduce the test by reading the instructions on page 59 in the Administration Manual; avoid using the term "intelligence" during the introduction. Respond truthfully to any questions that the child has about the purpose of testing.

Subtest Sequence

Administer the subtests in the order specified in the Administration Manual (see p. 25) unless you have a compelling reason to use another order, such as to motivate a bored or frustrated child or to administer subtests that are appropriate for the child's disability (e.g., verbal subtests for a child with a visual impairment). By following the standard sequence of administration you use an order that (a) can serve as a baseline for evaluating children whom you may test in the future, (b) is comparable to that used by other examiners, and (c) alternates nonverbal and verbal subtests.

The subtest order was designed to increase the child's interest in the test, to maintain a variety of activities throughout the session, and to minimize fatigue effects. Block Design, which is the first subtest adminis-tered, provides a nonverbal introduction to the test. Core subtests are administered first and are followed by sup-plemental subtests, if any are administered. *Deviations from the specified subtest order should be based on clinical considerations and not on your own personal preference.* Note the reasons for any deviations from the specified subtest order on the Record Form and in the psychological report.

Attend to the child's behavior throughout the test, but especially at the beginning of the session. Do not as-sume that the order of the subtests will automatically reduce a child's level of anxiety or help a child feel re-laxed. We need research on how the order of the sub-tests affects children's anxiety level and performance in general.

Queries

The rules that cover queries vary among subtests (see p. 38 of the Administration Manual for a general discus-sion of queries). Queries allow you to evaluate more thoroughly the extent of the child's knowledge. You will need to query any responses followed by a "(Q)" in the Administration Manual, as well as any other responses that you judge to be unclear, vague, or incomplete. However, you should not query a clear 0-point or 1-point answer in order to elicit a better answer unless the answer is listed in the Administration Manual. You also should not query obviously wrong answers or obviously right answers. Excessive queries prolong the test unnec-essarily and may invalidate the test results.

Prompts

Prompts are used to help the child follow the subtest instructions. For example, if the child says that there are two correct answers for a Picture Concepts item, you should tell the child to give only the one best answer. The General Directions in the Administration Manual for each subtest discuss the use of prompts. Record a "P" on the Record Form for each prompt that you give.

Start Point

On several subtests, the item with which you start de-pends on the child's age and ability level. For example, on the Vocabulary subtest you start with item 5 for chil-dren 6 to 8 years of age, item 7 for children 9 to 11 years

of age, and item 9 for children 12 to 16 years of age. In the Administration Manual, in the Record Form, and in this text, any ages expressed only in years are inclusive ages—that is, 6 to 8 years of age means 6-0 to 8-11, 9 to 11 years of age means 9-0 to 11-11, and 12 to 16 years of age means 12-0 to 16-11.

The different start points on Similarities, Vocabulary, Comprehension, and Picture Completion mean that some children will be exposed to fewer teaching items than others. For example, on the Similarities subtest, children beginning with item 1 are given two items (1 and 2) plus the sample for which a correct response is modeled by the examiner to help the child establish a response set. In contrast, those beginning with a higher start-point item are exposed to only the sample item, and if they fail the start-point item and the subsequent item, they are given only one teaching item (the sample), unless the examiner goes back to items 2 and 1.

If you suspect that a child has an intellectual defi-ciency, regardless of the child's chronological age, be-gin at the start point for a 6-year-old child on all sub-tests, with the exception of Coding and Symbol Search. On these two subtests, use the appropriate form (Form A or B) for the child's chronological age, regardless of the child's estimated level of intellectual ability.

Reverse Sequence

Block Design, Similarities, Picture Concepts, Vocabu-lary, Matrix Reasoning, Comprehension, Picture Com-pletion, Information, Arithmetic, and Word Reasoning have a reverse sequence, whereas Digit Span, Coding, Letter–Number Sequencing, Symbol Search, and Can-cellation do not. Thus, all Verbal Comprehension and Perceptual Reasoning subtests and one Working Mem-ory subtest have a reverse sequence, while none of the Processing Speed subtests have a reverse sequence.

Use a reverse sequence when the child (a) does not obtain a perfect score on the first start-point item (except when item 1 is the start-point item) or (b) obtains a per-fect score on the first start-point item but not on the sub-sequent item (again, except when item 1 is the start-point item). Sometimes you may reach item 1 and the child still does not have (a) two consecutive items with perfect scores or (b) the number of consecutive scores of 0 specified in the discontinue criterion (i.e., three, four, or five scores of 0 or four scores of 0 on five consecu-tive items). In either case, continue to administer items after the start-point item or subsequent item until the discontinue criterion has been met. If the discontinue criterion is met during a reversal, continue administering items in reverse order until the child has two consecutive perfect scores or until item 1 has been administered before discontinuing the subtest.

Let's look at some examples of how the reverse sequence is carried out. First, let's consider the Similarities subtest.

No Perfect Score on Item 5

If you start with item 5 and the child does not obtain a perfect score on item 5, administer items 4, 3, 2, and 1 in reverse sequence, as needed. If the child obtains two consecutive perfect scores, stop the reverse sequence and continue with item 6. If you reach item 1 and the child has neither two consecutive perfect scores nor five consecutive scores of 0, continue with item 6 and discontinue when the child meets the discontinue criterion for the Similarities subtest.

A Perfect Score on Item 5 but Not on Item 6

If you start with item 5 and the child obtains a perfect score on item 5 but not on item 6, administer items 4, 3, 2, and 1 in reverse sequence, as needed. If the child obtains two consecutive perfect scores, stop the reverse sequence and continue with item 7. If you reach item 1 and the child has neither two consecutive perfect scores nor five consecutive scores of 0, continue with item 7 and discontinue when the child meets the discontinue criterion for the Similarities subtest.

Now let's look at the reverse sequence on the Matrix Reasoning subtest.

No Perfect Score on Item 4

If you start with item 4 and the child does not obtain a perfect score on item 4, administer items 3, 2, and 1 in reverse sequence, as needed. If the child obtains two consecutive perfect scores, stop the reverse sequence and continue with item 5. If you reach item 1 and the child has neither two consecutive perfect scores nor four consecutive scores of 0, continue with item 5 and discontinue when the child meets the discontinue criterion for the Matrix Reasoning subtest.

A Perfect Score on Item 4 but Not on Item 5

If you start with item 4 and the child obtains a perfect score on item 4 but not on item 5, administer items 3, 2, and 1 in reverse sequence, as needed. If the child obtains two consecutive perfect scores, stop the reverse sequence and continue with item 6. If you reach item 1 and the child does not have two consecutive perfect scores, four consecutive scores of 0, or four scores of 0

on five consecutive items, continue with item 6 and discontinue when the child meets the discontinue criterion for the Matrix Reasoning subtest.

No Perfect Score on Item 7

If you start with item 7 and the child does not obtain a perfect score on item 7, administer items 6, 5, 4, 3, 2, and 1 in reverse sequence, as needed. If the child obtains two consecutive perfect scores, stop the reverse sequence and continue with item 8. If you reach item 1 and the child does not have two consecutive perfect scores, four consecutive scores of 0, or four scores of 0 on five consecutive items, continue with item 8 and discontinue when the child meets the discontinue criterion for the Matrix Reasoning subtest.

A Perfect Score on Item 7 but Not on Item 8

If you start with item 7 and the child obtains a perfect score on item 7 but not on item 8, administer items 6, 5, 4, 3, 2, and 1 in reverse sequence, as needed. If the child obtains two consecutive perfect scores, stop the reverse sequence and continue with item 9. If you reach item 1 and the child does not have two consecutive perfect scores, four consecutive scores of 0, or four scores of 0 on five consecutive items, continue with item 9 and discontinue when the child meets the discontinue criterion for the Matrix Reasoning subtest.

Start-Point Scoring Rule

The start-point scoring rule states that the child receives full credit for all items located below the start-point item and subsequent item on which perfect scores were obtained. This rule applies to both administered and unadministered items, regardless of the child's scores on any items that were administered. The start-point scoring rule also applies in a reverse sequence to any items below two consecutive perfect scores.

Here is an example of the application of the start-point scoring rule. You administer items 5 and 6 on the Comprehension subtest to a 12-year-old child who obtains a perfect score on item 5 and a score of 0 on item 6. You then reverse the order of administration and give items 4 and 3, on each of which the child clearly obtains 0 points. You administer items 2 and 1, on each of which the child clearly obtains a perfect score. You then continue the subtest with item 7 because the discontinue criterion was not reached. After the examination, you review your scoring and decide that the child did indeed obtain a perfect score on item 6. The start-point scoring rule requires that you give full credit for items 3 and 4, even though the child obtained 0 points on these items, because items 3 and 4 are below the start-point item and subsequent item on which perfect scores were obtained.

The start-point scoring rule ensures that you do not penalize the child for obtaining 0 points on items that, as it turned out, you did not have to administer. The start-point scoring rule is an attempt to maintain standardized scoring procedures.

Discontinue-Point Scoring Rule

The discontinue-point scoring rule states that the child does not receive credit for any items above the last discontinue-point item. This rule applies to both administered and unadministered items, regardless of the child's scores on any items that were administered.

Here is an example of the application of the discontinue-point scoring rule. You administer the first 14 items of the Vocabulary subtest, but are uncertain about how to score the child's responses to items 10 to 14. You then administer additional items. The child receives perfect scores on items 15 and 16 and 0 points on items 17 to 21. You therefore discontinue the subtest after item 21. After the test is over, you check your scoring and decide that the child should receive 0 points for items 10 to 14. The discontinue-point scoring rule requires that you not give credit for items 15 and 16, even though the child's definitions were correct, because these items were administered after the discontinue criterion was met.

The discontinue-point scoring rule ensures that you do not give credit for items that, as it turned out, you did not have to administer. The rule is another attempt to maintain standardized scoring procedures.

Perfect Scores

Perfect scores are not the same on all subtests, and even within the same subtest items may have different perfect scores. Table 1-18 shows that Picture Concepts, Coding, Matrix Reasoning, Symbol Search, Picture Completion, Cancellation (on which each target marked correctly is counted as a perfect score of 1), Information, Arithmetic, and Word Reasoning have a perfect score of 1 on all items. Digit Span and Comprehension have a perfect score of 2 on all items (on Digit Span, both trials must be passed to obtain a raw score of 2). Letter–Number Sequencing has a perfect score of 3 on all items (all three trials must be passed to obtain a raw score of 3).

The remaining subtests have variable perfect scores.

Points for Unadministered Items

As you have recently read, the child receives points for unadministered items that *precede* perfect scores on (a) the age-appropriate start-point item and subsequent item or (b) the first two consecutive items below the age-appropriate start-point item if a reverse sequence was used. The number of additional points you award for the unadministered items depends on the subtest. For example, if you start with item 3 on Block Design and the child receives a perfect score on items 3 and 4, you award 4 points (2 points each for items 1 and 2). If you start with item 7 on Picture Concepts and the child obtains 0 points on items 7 and 6 but obtains a perfect score on items 5 and 4, you award 3 points (1 point each for items 1, 2, and 3). The Administration Manual (see p. 29) recommends that you record the points for the unadministered items by putting a slash mark in the Score column on the Record Form over the item preceding the first two perfect scores and writing below the slash mark the number of points awarded.

You also award points for unadministered items when a reverse sequence is used. Thus, if you begin a subtest with item 7 and the child obtains 0 points on the item, administer item 6 and then items 5, 4, 3, 2, and 1, as needed. If the child obtains 0 points on item 6 but obtains a perfect score on items 5 and 4, do not administer items 3, 2, and 1; however, give the child full credit for these three items. If the perfect score on each item is 1 point, you would initially give, in this example, 5 points—1 point each for passing items 5 and 4 and 1 point for each of the three unadministered items (3, 2, and 1)—in addition to any points obtained on later items.

Repeating Instructions

An introductory statement is used to begin Block Design, Similarities, Digit Span, Vocabulary, Letter–Number Sequencing, Comprehension, Picture Completion, Information, and Arithmetic. The introductory statement can be repeated as often as requested by the child or whenever you think that repetition is needed. In contrast, Picture Concepts, Coding, Matrix Reasoning, Symbol Search, Cancellation, and Word Reasoning do not begin with an introductory statement, but rather with a sample item.

Table 1-18
Perfect Scores on WISC–IV Subtests

Subtest	Perfect score
Block Design	2 points on items 1 to 3, 4 points on items 4 to 8, and 7 points on items 9 to 14 (2 points are given only on trial 1 of items 1 to 3)
Similarities	1 point on items 1 and 2 and 2 points on items 3 to 23
Digit Span	2 points on all items (reverse sequence does not apply)
Picture Concepts	1 point on all items
Coding	1 point on all items (reverse sequence does not apply)
Vocabulary	1 point on items 1 to 4 and 2 points on items 5 to 36
Letter–Number Sequencing	3 points on all items (reverse sequence does not apply)
Matrix Reasoning	1 point on all items
Comprehension	2 points on all items
Symbol Search	1 point on all items (reverse sequence does not apply)
Picture Completion	1 point on all items
Cancellation	1 point for each target (reverse sequence does not apply)
Information	1 point on all items
Arithmetic	1 point on all items
Word Reasoning	1 point on all items

Source: Adapted from Wechsler (2003a).

Repeating Items

On Similarities, Picture Concepts, Vocabulary, Matrix Reasoning, Comprehension, and Information, you are permitted to repeat items if (a) the child requests repetition, (b) you believe that the child misheard, misunderstood, or forgot the item, or (c) you need to administer the item again (e.g., if the child has not responded within 5 to 10 seconds, you will need to repeat the item unless it is clear that the child is thinking about a response). Record the repetition with an "R" on the Record Form. Additionally, on these six subtests, if a child responds to one or more earlier items with "I don't know" but then receives points on more difficult items, readminister the earlier items if you believe the child might pass them (see p. 39 of the Administration Manual).

You are not permitted to repeat items on Digit Span, Letter–Number Sequencing, Block Design, Coding, Symbol Search, Picture Completion, and Cancellation. On Arithmetic you are permitted to repeat items once only, and on Word Reasoning you need to follow the specific directions for repeating items.

The following statement on page 39 in the first printing of the Administration Manual is misleading if read out of context: "The Arithmetic and Word Reasoning subtests provide specific directions for the repetition of items. All other subtests allow for repetition of instructions and items **as often as requested** by the child." The statement belongs in the paragraph above it in the Administration Manual, which states that Digit Span and Letter–Number Sequencing do not allow for repetition of items (Lisa Drozdick, Research Director, The Psychological Corporation, personal communication, February 2004). In addition, once the time limit has expired for an item or for the entire subtest, you are not allowed to repeat items on Block Design, Coding, Symbol Search, Picture Completion, and Cancellation. For guidelines about repeating items, follow the General Directions section in the Administration Manual for each subtest.

Additional Help

For each subtest, do not give additional help beyond that noted in the Administration Manual. This means that you should not spell, define, or explain any words that are in the directions, questions, or items or give any other kind of help unless it is specified in the Administration Manual. If a child asks for the meaning of a word, simply say, "Do the best you can" or something similar.

Waiting Time

For the Similarities, Picture Concepts, Vocabulary, Matrix Reasoning, Comprehension, and Information subtests, wait about 30 seconds before going to the next item if the child makes no response, except when the child has been doing well and seems to need the additional time to solve a difficult item. However, use your judgment about when to move to the next item. For children who are clearly beyond their ability, 30 seconds may be a long time to wait, especially if it is the third or fourth 30-second wait. This might be the case for children who seem bored, who shrug their shoulders, or who look around the room after a few seconds and do not look at the items. On all subtests, when you proceed to another item, you may say, "Let's try another one."

Discontinue Criterion

Every subtest has a discontinue criterion—either a specific number of consecutive scores of 0 or a time limit. The discontinue criterion is noted in the Administration Manual as well as on the Record Form. Carefully study the discontinue criterion for each subtest. Coding, Symbol Search, and Cancellation are discontinued after a specified time limit, unless the child finishes before the time limit is reached.

The discontinue criterion has one exception: *In a reverse sequence, continue to administer items even after the discontinue criterion has been met until you reach item 1 or until the child has perfect scores on two consecutive items.* This exception is illustrated in Figure 2.6 on page 33 of the Administration Manual. Figure 2.6 shows that Picture Concepts was started with item 7 and then a reverse sequence was followed because the child obtained a perfect score on item 7 but not on item 8. The child then obtained scores of 0 on items 6, 5, 4, 3, and 2 and therefore met the discontinue criterion (5 consecutive scores of 0 points). However, item 1 was still ad-

ministered. Otherwise, once the discontinue criterion has been met, do not give additional items.

Scoring

Scoring the Similarities, Vocabulary, Comprehension, and Word Reasoning subtests may be especially challenging. Carefully study the scoring criteria, scoring guidelines, and scoring examples in the Administration Manual. Recognize that the scoring guidelines and sample responses for these four subtests do not cover all possible responses that children may give or cover every response contingency. For this reason, you must use judgment in scoring responses. As you study the scoring guidelines and the sample responses, try to understand the rationale underlying the guidelines.

Score the best response when a child gives multiple acceptable responses. If a child gives both a correct and an incorrect response and it is not clear which is the intended answer, ask, "Now, which one is it?" and then base your score on the answer. Do the best job possible with the scoring guidelines given in the Administration Manual. However, whenever you have any doubt about the scoring of a response, consult a colleague. In scoring queried responses, either those followed by a "(Q)" in the Administration Manual or those in response to your own queries, consider the child's entire response—the initial answer plus the answer to the query—in arriving at a score.

Some examiners are more lenient than others in giving credit, and even the same examiner may not consistently follow his or her own (relative) standards. For example, the examiner may be strict on some occasions and lenient on others or strict with some children and lenient with others. Studies with other editions of the WISC or other Wechsler tests have reported differences in the scoring standards of examiners (see Sattler, 2001). We need research about how examiners score WISC–IV responses.

Spoiled Responses

A spoiled response is one that was on the right path to obtain credit but was spoiled by the child's incorrect elaboration on the initial response—the elaboration revealed a fundamental misconception. A response may be spoiled when it contains multiple elements, some of which are correct and others incorrect. For example, if a child says that *clock* means "Goes tick-tock" and then spontaneously or in response to your query says, "It's the engine on a motorcycle," he or she has spoiled the response. The child's elaboration reveals a misconception about the meaning of the word *clock*, and hence the response receives a score of 0.

If a child adds additional irrelevant information that is not contrary to fact, the correct initial response is not spoiled, despite the fact that the information by itself might be given 0 points. For example, suppose a child defines *cow* as "an animal" and adds "My aunt has cows on her farm. Some cows have spots. I like cows; they have ears." The response is given a perfect score because the elaboration does not reveal a fundamental misconception about the word *cow*. Sometimes it may be difficult to distinguish a spoiled response from a poor response.

Testing-of-Limits

Testing-of-limits is an informal, nonstandardized procedure designed to provide additional information about a child's cognitive abilities and processing skills. *Conduct testing-of-limits only after you have administered the entire test following standard procedures.* If you conduct testing-of-limits before you have administered the entire test, you will violate standard procedures, and the cues you give the child may lead to higher scores and to an invalid assessment. Research with previous editions of the Wechsler tests has shown that children may obtain higher scores when they receive extra help during the test (see Sattler, 2001).

Testing-of-limits is useful for (a) following up leads about the child's abilities, (b) testing clinical hypotheses, and (c) evaluating whether additional cues, strategies, or extra time helps the child solve problems. *Testing-of-limits may invalidate repeated evaluations and should be used cautiously.* In school settings, you may not want to use testing-of-limits if you think that the child may be reevaluated within a 3-year period. Any procedures used to test limits should be clearly described in the report. Scores derived from testing-of-limits procedures should be clearly differentiated from scores obtained under standardized conditions.

A multiple-choice testing-of-limits procedure may provide information about whether the child has a word retrieval deficit or a word knowledge deficit (see, for example, the discussion of testing-of-limits for the Similarities subtest in Chapter 2). Testing-of-limits allows you to generate hypotheses. However, you should not draw conclusions about a child's abilities or processing skills based on a few testing-of-limits multiple-choice questions. Follow up any hypotheses by testing the child

with a psychometrically sound instrument.

Subtest Substitution

According to the Administration Manual, the following substitutions are acceptable:

- Information or Word Reasoning may be substituted for a core Verbal Comprehension subtest.
- Picture Completion may be substituted for a core Perceptual Reasoning subtest.
- Arithmetic may be substituted for a core Working Memory subtest.
- Cancellation may be substituted for a core Processing Speed subtest.

Substitutions should be based on clinical need or a similar appropriate reason, not your own preferences or convenience. For example, you may substitute Cancellation for Coding or Picture Completion for Block Design for a child with fine-motor difficulties, or you may substitute Arithmetic for Digit Span when Digit Span is invalidated (e.g., interrupted by a fire drill or because the child had a seizure).

Further, only one substitution is allowed for each Composite. For example, if Information is substituted for one of the three Verbal Comprehension core subtests, Word Reasoning cannot be substituted for another Verbal Comprehension core subtest. Although *one* substitution is permitted for each Composite (resulting in four permissible substitutions), only *two* substitutions are allowed for the Full Scale. Maintain the standard order of administration (described on the first page of the Record Form) when you substitute a supplemental subtest for a core subtest or when you administer a supplemental subtest in addition to the 10 core subtests.

Neither the Administration Manual nor the Technical Manual discusses how the previous guidelines were developed or presents descriptive statistics for Composites composed of both core and supplemental subtests. Consider the following questions:

1. How can the norms based only on the core subtests be used when supplemental subtests, which have psychometric properties that differ from those of the core subtests, are substituted for core subtests?
2. What are the reliability and validity of the Index scores and Full Scale IQ when a substitution is made?
3. What confidence intervals can be used for the Index scores and Full Scale IQ when a substitution is

made?

4. Why are only two substitutions permitted for the Full Scale?

5. Why is only one substitution permitted for each Composite?

6. What evidence is there that Full Scale IQs are less reliable and valid when three, four, or five substitutions are made?

The Administration Manual (see p. 10) advises that supplemental subtests may be substituted for core subtests in a reevaluation conducted after a short time interval. Also, the directions for the Letter–Number Sequencing subtest state that if the child fails either of the qualifying items, the examiner should administer the Arithmetic subtest as a substitute in order to compute the Working Memory Index and the Full Scale IQ. We question whether there is a reasonable clinical need to substitute a supplemental subtest (a) in a reevaluation conducted after a short time period or (b) when a child fails a qualifying item on the Letter–Number Sequencing subtest. Substitutions breach an important principle underlying standardized testing: to give the same set of items to all children administered the test, if at all possible.

We advise that substitutions be avoided whenever a specific IQ or Index score needs to be used for decision-making purposes. Our reasons follow. There are a total of seven Verbal Comprehension subtest combinations, four Perceptual Reasoning subtest combinations, and three subtest combinations each for Working Memory and Processing Speed. These possible combinations allow for extreme latitude in deriving Index scores and Full Scale IQs. There are, in fact, over 50 different possible subtest combinations when supplemental subtests are substituted for core subtests. *Because the Full Scale IQ tables are based on the 10 core subtests only, scores derived using one or two supplemental subtests have an unknown degree of additional measurement error.* Even a difference of 1 point may be critical for some decision-making purposes. If you do report Index scores or IQs based on the substitution of one or more supplemental subtests, write "Estimated" before the scores.

The supplemental and core subtests differ with regard to their reliability, correlations with the Composite and with the Full Scale, and g loadings. Let's compare the supplemental subtests with the core subtests on one of these dimensions—correlations with the Index score.

First, with the Verbal Comprehension Index, Information and Word Reasoning have correlations of .77 and .70, respectively, whereas Similarities, Vocabulary,

and Comprehension have correlations of .89, .91, and .86, respectively.

Second, with the Perceptual Reasoning Index, Picture Completion has a correlation of .57, whereas Block Design, Matrix Reasoning, and Picture Concepts have correlations of .81, .77, and .84, respectively.

Third, with the Working Memory Index, Arithmetic has a correlation of .57, whereas Digit Span and Letter–Number Sequencing each have a correlation of .86.

Fourth, with the Processing Speed Index, Cancellation has a correlation of .26, whereas Coding and Symbol Search have correlations of .88 and .87, respectively.

The Psychological Corporation provided us with the following information about substitutions (Lisa Drozdick, Research Director, The Psychological Corporation, personal communication, February 2004).

There is not an explicit paragraph in either of the manuals about the increase in measurement error introduced by substitution. It is explicitly described for prorating but not for substitution. Page 12 of the Technical Manual states that the decision to substitute should be based on clinical need and appropriateness, rather than on examiner preference. In addition, on page 21 of the Administration Manual, it clearly states that any deviation from the standard procedures should be noted on the Record Form and considered carefully when interpreting test scores. Substitution, while allowed, is a deviation from the standard administration and should be noted in the Record Form and taken into consideration in interpretation.

While substitutions are available to avoid invalidating a Composite score due to a single invalidated subtest, they should be used sparingly. Substitutions should only be used when a subtest is invalidated due to an administration error or a non-test-related event (e.g., child becomes ill), or if the subtest is likely to be invalidated for a clinical reason (e.g., a motor impaired child is more likely to invalidate Block Design than Picture Completion). Therefore, substitutions should only be used when the validity of a subtest is in question.

It is important to note that each substitution used in the derivation of the FSIQ introduces measurement error into the FSIQ. Classical test theory states that every obtained score is composed of the individual's true score and measurement error. The greater the measurement error, the further the obtained score is from the true score. Thus each substitution yields a score that is slightly further from the true FSIQ than a score obtained with the core subtests. In order to minimize measurement error and maintain the reliability and validity of the FSIQ, only two substitutions are allowed when deriving the FSIQ.

The case that follows illustrates how you can get different Index scores and Full Scale IQs depending on which subtests you select to form the individual Composites and Full Scale (Jean Elbert, personal communication, February 2004).

CASE STUDY

MA is a 14-year, 5-month-old adolescent who obtained the following subtest scaled scores on the WISC–IV (Word Reasoning was not administered).

Subtest	Scaled Score
Block Design	10
Similarities	11
Digit Span	12
Picture Concepts	12
Coding	9
Vocabulary	10
Letter–Number Sequencing	12
Matrix Reasoning	15
Comprehension	16
Symbol Search	9
Picture Completion	17
Cancellation	13
Information	16
Arithmetic	11

Let's now compare the Index scores and Full Scale IQs for the core subtests only and for one combination of core and supplemental subtests.

Verbal Comprehension

Core subtests: Similarities (11) + Vocabulary (10) + Comprehension (16) = 37; VCI = 112

Core with substitute subtest: Similarities (11) + Comprehension (16) + Information (16) = 43; VCI = 126

Perceptual Reasoning

Core subtests: Block Design (10) + Picture Concepts (12) + Matrix Reasoning (15) = 37; PRI = 115

Core with substitute subtest: Picture Concepts (12) + Matrix Reasoning (15) + Picture Completion (17) = 44; PRI = 129

Working Memory

Core subtests: Digit Span (12) + Letter–Number Sequencing (12) = 24; WMI = 110

Core with substitute subtest: Letter–Number Sequencing (12) + Arithmetic (11) = 23; WMI = 107

Processing Speed

Core subtests: Coding (9) + Symbol Search (9) = 18; PSI = 94

Core with substitute subtest: Coding (9) + Cancellation (13) = 22; PSI = 106

Full Scale

Core subtests: Block Design (10) + Similarities (11) + Digit Span (12) + Picture Concepts (12) + Coding (9) + Vocabulary (10) + Letter–Number Sequencing (12) + Matrix Reasoning (15) + Comprehension (16) + Symbol Search (9) = 116; FSIQ = 112

Core with two substitute subtests: Similarities (11) + Digit Span (12) + Picture Concepts (12) + Coding (9) + Letter–Number Sequencing (12) + Matrix Reasoning (15) + Comprehension (16) + Symbol Search (9) + Information (16) + Picture Completion (17) = 129; FSIQ = 122

The results indicate that, depending on the combination of subtests chosen, MA's Index scores could differ by as much as 14 points and his Full Scale IQ by as much as 10 points. Because such drastic differences are possible, we advise using supplemental subtests only to obtain additional information about the child's cognitive abilities. It would be a poor assessment practice to administer all 15 subtests and then select the combination of subtests that best served your purpose. And you are on shaky ground when you report Index scores and Full Scale IQs for which there are no descriptive statistics.

Qualifying Items

Only one subtest on the WISC–IV, Letter–Number Sequencing, uses two qualifying items as a requisite for administering the formal subtest items. If the child cannot both count to three and say the first three letters of the alphabet, the subtest is not administered, and the Arithmetic subtest (a supplemental subtest) is substituted for it. The use of these two qualifying items introduces a new element on the WISC–IV and raises several issues, such as why Letter–Number Sequencing is the only subtest with qualifying items and why other subtests are not discontinued when children fail the sample items. Although the requisite skills needed to take one or more of the WISC–IV subtests include adequate hearing, vision, speech, fine-motor control, and understanding of English, there are no qualifying items to assess these skills.

We believe that if qualifying items are used on a test, some qualifying items should evaluate children's understanding of terms used in the subtest instructions and sample items. On the WISC–IV, however, children who do not understand words or phrases such as *alike, half, backward, go together,* and *shape* are still administered subtests that contain these terms in the instructions or sample items.

Finally, Symbol Search requires the child to mark boxes labeled YES or NO, yet there is no qualifying item that evaluates reading. We wonder (a) what the probability is that children who cannot count to three on the Letter–Number Sequencing subtest will pass any of the Arithmetic items and (b) what the validity will be of the scores obtained by children who do not understand the subtest instructions or sample items. The Technical Manual provides no information about these issues, and they deserve to be investigated.

Potential Problems in Administering the WISC–IV

Let's look at some potential problems examiners may have.

Problems Related to Establishing Rapport
1. Failing to establish rapport.
2. Interrogating the child as you try to establish rapport.
3. Taking excessive time to establish rapport.
4. Failing to clarify the child's expectations for the assessment.
5. Failing to be sensitive to the child's need for a break.
6. Rushing the child.
7. Showing impatience or frustration with the child.

Problems Related to Speech
8. Reading questions too quickly or too slowly.
9. Failing to speak clearly or making mistakes in pronunciation.
10. Failing to recognize that a child whose first language is not English may have difficulty understanding English.
11. Failing to recognize that the child may have some physical impairments that affect the assessment (e.g., hearing or visual loss).

Problems Related to Layout of Test Materials
12. Failing to position the Record Form so that the child cannot observe the correct answers.
13. Failing to position the Administration Manual so that the child cannot observe the correct answers.
14. Leaving unessential materials on the table.

15. Failing to have all needed materials nearby.

Problems Related to Test Administration
16. Failing to record responses verbatim.
17. Focusing too much on the Administration Manual, thus making little eye contact and paying little attention to the child.
18. Prolonging the test because of unfamiliarity with scoring or with the test materials.
19. Violating standard procedures by defining or explaining words or giving other kinds of hints.
20. Ad-libbing or failing to read instructions and items exactly as written in the Administration Manual.
21. Providing nonverbal cues.
22. Calculating chronological age incorrectly.
23. Querying incorrectly.
24. Prompting incorrectly.
25. Giving second trials incorrectly.
26. Failing to give second trials when needed.
27. Giving instructions incorrectly.
28. Ignoring time limits.
29. Failing to begin timing correctly.
30. Failing to stop timing when the child has obviously finished.
31. Failing to stop the subtest when the time limit has been reached.
32. Stopping timing prematurely when the child is still working on a response.
33. Questioning unnecessarily.
34. Failing to follow the start item with the appropriate item.
35. Failing to adhere to the discontinue criterion.
36. Conducting testing-of-limits during the subtest proper.
37. Repeating items incorrectly.
38. Allowing the child to use paper and pencil when standard procedure forbids it.
39. Failing to administer the reverse sequence appropriately.

Problems Related to Scoring
40. Failing to credit responses.
41. Failing to score a subtest.
42. Failing to use the scoring guidelines appropriately.
43. Failing to give full credit for unadministered items or for items with 0 points that are below the first two items with perfect scores.
44. Counting in the final score items above the discontinue point that were answered correctly.
45. Giving time-bonus credits incorrectly.
46. Failing to give a score of 0 to an incorrect response.

47. Adding raw scores incorrectly.
48. Incorrectly transferring raw scores to the front page of the Record Form.
49. Incorrectly converting raw scores to scaled scores.
50. Using inappropriate norms.
51. Adding scaled scores incorrectly.
52. Incorrectly converting scaled scores to IQs.
53. Prorating incorrectly.
54. Counting a supplemental subtest, in addition to the 10 core subtests, in computing a Full Scale IQ.

Several studies have demonstrated that examiners make errors in administering and scoring the Wechsler tests (Alfonso, Johnson, Patinella, & Rader, 1998; Klassen & Kishor, 1996; Levenson, Golden-Scaduto, Aiosa-Karpas, & Ward, 1988; Slate & Hunnicutt, 1988; Slate, Jones, Coulter, & Covert, 1992; Wagoner, 1988). For example, Klassen and Kishor (1996) reported that seven master's-level psychologists made clerical errors on 42% of the 75 to 105 WISC–III protocols that each examiner administered. Only one of the seven examiners made no errors. The most common errors were in the addition of raw scores, transformation of raw scores to scaled scores, addition of scaled scores, and transformation of scaled scores to IQs. Wagoner (1988) found that examiners made an average of 8.4 errors per WISC–R protocol, including errors in 34% of the Full Scale IQs.

Another study found that 15 graduate students, who administered 60 WISC–III tests, committed a total of 468 errors, with 7.8 errors per protocol (range of 1 to 37 errors; Alfonso et al., 1998). Most of the errors involved failure to (a) query, (b) record responses verbatim, (c) report Full Scale IQs correctly, (d) report Verbal Scale IQs correctly, or (e) add individual subtest scores correctly.

Reasons examiners commit scoring errors include (a) poor training in test administration, (b) ambiguous scoring criteria in the Administration Manual, (c) carelessness, (d) a poor relationship with the child, (e) personal stress or fatigue, and (f) boredom with administering the test (Slate & Hunnicutt, 1988). To avoid scoring and administration errors, carefully review how you administer and score each subtest. Assign tentative scores as you administer the test, but always rescore each item after the test is completed. If you are unsure of how to score a response as you administer a subtest, continue to administer items until you are confident of the scoring; it is better to err on the side of safety.

Following are examples of situations in which examiners were not sensitive to the child's needs or influenced the child's performance inappropriately (adapted, in part, from Teglasi & Freeman, 1983).

Example 1. Failure to recognize nonverbal cues. Before administering the test, the examiner discussed with the child issues connected with the child's stealing. Later, when given an item about finding someone's wallet, the child looked distressed, but the examiner did not recognize the distress. *Comment:* Be sensitive to nonverbal and verbal cues. An alert examiner would have said something like "Now, this question has nothing to do with our previous discussion. This is one of the questions I ask everyone." Or the examiner could have waited to discuss the potentially emotionally arousing "stealing" issue until after the child had completed the test. Always consider how any discussion prior to the test administration may affect rapport and how the child responds to the test questions.

Example 2. Failure to recognize and stifle incongruent comments. The examiner tried to be supportive after the child obtained a low score on the Digit Span subtest. The examiner said, "Are you aware that you have a very good memory?" The child said, "No, I have a lousy one. I forget things all the time" and became somewhat upset. *Comment:* Be sure that any reinforcing comments you make are congruent with the child's performance or case history and given at appropriate times. Also, praise the child's efforts, not the child's performance.

Example 3. Failure to follow standard procedures. The examiner watched a 10-year-old assemble block designs. The child was unable to assemble several of the designs within the designated time limits, and the examiner gave the child an additional 30 seconds on each incorrectly assembled design, allowing the child to eventually solve several items. On later items, perhaps benefiting from the additional practice, the child assembled the blocks correctly. *Comment:* Follow the guidelines specified in the Administration Manual, because violations of the guidelines might invalidate the test results.

Example 4. Failure to be neutral. When the child answered correctly, the examiner nodded or said, "Good"; when the child missed an item, the examiner was silent. The child soon caught on. *Comment:* Do not give verbal or nonverbal cues that may alert children to how well they are doing.

Example 5. Failure to follow directions. The examiner, noting that a child had misplaced only one block in a complicated block design, said, "Be sure to check your answer." *Comment:* Do not give a prompt in an attempt to help the child get a better score unless that prompt is specified in the directions in the Administration Manual.

Example 6. Failure to probe correctly. Instead of saying "Tell me more about it," the examiner repeated a part of the child's response and asked the child to clarify that part. *Comment:* Do not emphasize a part of the child's response; ask only for further clarification of the entire response. Emphasizing part of a response may give clues to the child.

We recommend that when you review the test results, you make a mental checklist of possible inconsistencies, such as the following:

- "How is it possible that this 8-year-old child has a scaled score of 5 on Block Design when each item was successfully completed in the required time?"
- "How is it possible to have a Verbal Comprehension score of 109 with no Verbal Comprehension subtest scaled scores exceeding 9, unless I added incorrectly, misread the table, or added in a supplemental subtest?"
- "Is it possible that I made scoring errors during this examination because I was tired today? If so, I need to go back and recheck all of the calculations again."
- "How is it possible that the child received scaled scores of 12 or above on 9 of the 10 core subtests and a scaled score of 2 on the remaining one?"

Overall Guidelines for Test Administration

Maintain good rapport by being friendly and courteous, showing a reasonable amount of flexibility, being alert to the child's moods, and never badgering the child. Handle behavior problems appropriately as they arise.

Administer the test in a professional, unhurried manner; be well organized; and follow the recommended order for administering the subtests, altering it only on the basis of clinical need. Maintain a steady pace, and make smooth transitions from subtest to subtest. Place the test materials not currently in use out of the child's sight but within your easy reach. Avoid conspicuous efforts to conceal the materials. However, shield from the child's view the Record Form and the pages in the Administration Manual that have the correct answers. Also shield your writing because children may monitor it (particularly the scores you enter on the Record Form).

Take short breaks at the end of subtests, as needed, and not in the middle of subtests. Allow a fidgety child to take a break at the end of a subtest and walk around the room, if necessary. A hesitant child needs to be encouraged to try to answer the questions. Praise the child's effort (but not successes) by saying, for example, "I appreciate your efforts" or "You are working hard and that is good." Do not say "good" or "right" after a correct response unless these words are part of the instructions. Show empathy when the child is aware of performing poorly. Some children may need additional assurance if they are anxious about how they might perform. Encourage them to try their best, and remind them that some items will be easy and others hard. However, do not provide additional help beyond the instructions, such as by giving additional practice items, asking leading questions, spelling words, or defining words.

Record a "Q" for queried responses and a "P" for prompted responses. Repeat the instructions upon request, unless the directions prohibit repetition. On untimed subtests, when the child says "I don't know" to easy items but then responds correctly to more difficult items, readminister the early items.

Also, on untimed subtests, use good judgment in deciding how much time to give the child to solve each item. Score each item after the child answers so that you know when to use a reverse procedure and when to discontinue the subtest. Be careful in scoring responses. Also, recheck your scoring when the test is finished. Make an entry in the Record Form for every item administered.

Always award full credit for all items preceding the first two items with perfect scores, regardless of the child's performance on the preceding items. Do this by putting a slash mark in the Score column over the item preceding the two items with perfect scores and writing the additional points. Never give credit for items passed above the last discontinue item or after the time limit. Record any deviations from the standard order for administering the subtests. The standard order is shown on the Record Form and on page 25 of the Administration Manual. Make every effort to administer the entire test in one session. If you cannot, try to complete the test within a 1-week period.

Overall, administer the subtests in the recommended order, start each subtest with the appropriate item, follow the instructions in the Administration Manual for administering each subtest, score each item, follow the reverse procedure if needed, follow the discontinue criterion, add the item scores for each subtest, complete the Record Form, and check all of your work.

It is valuable during training to make a videotape of one or more of your test administrations. Review the tape yourself, and have a fellow student review it as well. Making a videotape might also be a class assignment. Complete the Administrative Checklist for the WISC–IV (see Table D-1 in Appendix D) after each administration, and have a fellow student also complete it after reviewing your tape. Your teacher or teaching assistant also might review your videotape or observe your test administration through a one-way mirror and then complete the Administrative Checklist. In order to administer the WISC–IV efficiently and correctly, become thoroughly familiar with the administrative and scoring guidelines in the Administration Manual and in this text, be alert to any covert and overt sources of error in your test administration, and learn from your own mistakes and from the feedback you receive from others.

SHORT FORMS

Short forms of the WISC–IV may be used for (a) screening purposes, when the short form may be followed by administration of the rest of the test, (b) research purposes, or (c) obtaining an estimate of the child's intellectual status when a precise IQ is not required. Ideally, the short form you select should (a) have acceptable reliability and validity, (b) be able to answer the referral question and provide clinically useful information, (c) be suited to the child's physical capabilities, and (d) be administered when the full battery of 10 core subtests cannot be administered or is not needed. Short forms greatly magnify the effect of any administrative errors and give much weight to each subtest used in the short form. *If you need a classification for a clinical or psychoeducational purpose or need information for programming decisions, do not use a short form.* In addition, whenever you report IQs based on short forms, write "Estimated" by the IQ on the Record Form and in the psychological report.

Table A-7 in Appendix A lists the 10 most valid short-form combinations of two, three, four, and five WISC–IV subtests, plus other short forms that may serve various purposes (e.g., to evaluate a child with a hearing impairment). The reliability and validity coefficients shown in Table A-7 in Appendix A were calculated using the standardization data and the Tellegen and Briggs (1967) procedure, which takes into account the reliabilities of the subtests used in the short form. Exhibit 8-4 (pp. 256–257) in *Assessment of Children: Cognitive Applications* (Sattler, 2001) shows the formulas used to compute the reliability and validity of the short-form combinations.

An inspection of the coefficients in Table A-7 in Appendix A indicates that the 10 best four- and five-subtest short-form combinations have validity coefficients of .93 or higher. The best three-subtest short-form combinations (e.g., Vocabulary, Symbol Search, and Arithmetic; Vocabulary, Matrix Reasoning, and Arithmetic; Block Design, Vocabulary, and Arithmetic) have validity coefficients of .90 or higher, while the best two-subtest short-form combinations (e.g., Vocabulary and Arithmetic; Block Design and Vocabulary; Similarities and Arithmetic) have validity coefficients of .86 to .88. Overall, for the combinations shown in Table A-7 in Appendix A, the more subtests used in the short form, the higher the reliability and validity of the estimated IQ.

Because the reliabilities and validities of the various short forms are high, clinical considerations also should guide you in selecting a short form. For example, if you want to use a four-subtest short form, consider selecting a combination that includes one subtest from each Composite (e.g., Similarities, Block Design, Digit Span, and Coding) so that each area measured by the test (verbal comprehension, perceptual reasoning, working memory, and processing speed) is represented.

A child's physical capabilities also may guide you in selecting a short form. Children with marked visual impairment or severe motor dysfunction of the upper extremities will have difficulty with some Perceptual Reasoning or Processing Speed subtests. In such cases, the core Verbal Comprehension subtests serve as a useful short form. For children with hearing impairments, the core Perceptual Reasoning subtests alone comprise a useful short form. Administer these short forms by using the child's preferred mode of communication and, if possible, supplement your evaluation by using other tests designed to accommodate the special physical abilities of the child (see Sattler, 2001).

Converting Short-Form Scores into IQs

After you administer the short form, you will need to convert the scaled scores to a Full Scale IQ estimate. Simple proration and regression procedures are not applicable in this case because they do not deal adequately with the problem of subtest reliability (Tellegen & Briggs, 1967). The more acceptable procedure is to transform the short-form scores into an IQ, which has a mean of 100 and a standard deviation of 15. Exhibit 8-4 in *Assessment of Children: Cognitive Applications* (Sattler, 2001) also shows the procedure for converting the short-form scores into IQs. This procedure holds for all

Wechsler tests. Although this approach does not eliminate the many problems associated with short forms, it is statistically appropriate for computing Full Scale IQs.

We used the Tellegen and Briggs (1967) procedure to obtain estimated WISC–IV IQs for all the short-form combinations shown in Table A-7 in Appendix A. Tables A-9 to A-12 show the estimated IQs for two-, three-, four-, and five-subtest short-form combinations. In addition, Table A-13 shows the estimated IQs for one six-subtest short-form combination consisting of the three core Verbal Comprehension subtests and three core Perceptual Reasoning subtests.

A two-subtest combination that is popular as a short-form screening instrument is Block Design plus Vocabulary. These two subtests have good reliability, correlate highly with the Full Scale, and are good or fair measures of *g*. If this combination is chosen, Table A-9 in Appendix A can be used to convert the sum of scaled scores directly into an estimated Full Scale IQ. The composite has satisfactory reliability and validity ($r_{xx} = .92$ and $r = .87$).

Short-Form Subtest Scatter

Table A-8 in Appendix A shows whether the observed scatter (the highest scaled score minus the lowest scaled score) on all the short forms in Table A-7 in Appendix A (a) represents a reliable scaled-score range and (b) is unusual. Table A-8 indicates that for the two-subtest short form composed of Block Design and Vocabulary, a range of 3 points between the two scores represents a reliable scaled-score range (i.e., a range of 3 or greater represents nonchance difference at the .05 level). A range of 6 (or more) occurs in less than 10% of the population and should be considered unusual. Less credence can be placed in the estimated short-form IQ when the scatter is larger than expected.

CHOOSING BETWEEN THE WISC–IV AND THE WPPSI–III AND BETWEEN THE WISC–IV AND THE WAIS–III

The WISC–IV and WPPSI–III and the WISC–IV and WAIS–III overlap at ages 6-0 to 7-3 and ages 16-0 to 16-11, respectively. At the overlapping ages you have a choice about which test to administer, and you also have an alternative test to administer in retest situations. In order to determine which test to recommend at the overlapping ages, we compared the tests on several criteria, including mean subtest reliability, Full Scale reliability, mean subtest floor (mean number of raw-score points needed to obtain a scaled score of 1), mean subtest ceiling (mean number of raw-score points needed to obtain the highest scaled score), item gradients (number of raw-score points needed to go from the floor to the mean and from the mean to the ceiling and the relationship of raw-score points to scaled-score points), Full Scale floor, Full Scale ceiling, and breadth of coverage.

WISC–IV vs. WPPSI–III

The WISC–IV and WPPSI–III generally have similar psychometric properties at the overlapping ages. The primary advantage of the WISC–IV over the WPPSI–III is in its breadth of coverage. The WISC–IV has in its core battery 10 subtests that fall into four Composite areas, while the WPPSI–III has in its core battery seven subtests that fall into two Composite areas.

Because of its breadth of coverage, we recommend the following:

* *The WISC–IV should be used with children 6-0 to 7-3 years of age at all ability levels.*

This recommendation differs somewhat from those in the Administration Manual, which advises that (a) the WPPSI–III be used for children suspected of below-average cognitive ability, (b) the WISC–IV be used for children suspected of above-average cognitive ability, and (c) clinical judgment be used to select the test for children suspected of average ability.

WISC–IV vs. WAIS–III

The WISC–IV and WAIS–III generally have similar psychometric properties at the overlapping ages. However, the item gradients between scaled scores of 1 and 10 are less steep on the WISC–IV than on the WAIS–III—that is, the WISC–IV requires more raw-score points to go from a scaled score of 1 to a scaled score of 10 than does the WAIS–III. In contrast, the item gradients between scaled scores of 11 and 19 are, in most cases, less steep on the WAIS–III than on the WISC–IV—that is, the WAIS–III requires more raw-score points than the WISC–IV to go from a scaled score of 11 to a scaled score of 19. However, while the ceiling scaled score is 19 on all WISC–IV subtests, the ceiling scaled scores are 17 and 18 on two WAIS–III subtests.

The two tests differ in other ways. The WISC–IV has norms in 4-month age intervals for 16-year-olds, whereas the WAIS–III combines 16- and 17-year-olds into one normative table. The WISC–IV Full Scale is composed of subtests that differ from those in the WAIS–III Full Scale. For example, the WAIS–III includes in its core battery four subtests (Information, Picture Completion, Arithmetic, and Picture Arrangement) that are not included in the WISC–IV core battery. In addition, Block Design on the WAIS–III places more emphasis on speed than does Block Design on the WISC–IV.

We recommend the following:

- The WISC–IV should be used for children 16-0 to 16-11 years of age suspected of below-average cognitive ability.
- Either the WISC–IV or the WAIS–III should be used for children 16-0 to 16-11 years of age suspected of average or above-average cognitive ability.

These recommendations differ somewhat from those in the Administration Manual, which advises that (a) the WISC–IV be used for children suspected of below-average cognitive ability, (b) the WAIS–III be used for children suspected of above-average cognitive ability, and (c) clinical judgment be used to select the test for children suspected of average cognitive ability.

ADMINISTERING THE WISC–IV TO CHILDREN WITH DISABILITIES

You will need to evaluate the sensory-motor abilities of children with disabilities before you administer the WISC–IV. If you find that a child has a visual, hearing, attentional, or motor problem that may interfere with his or her ability to take one or more of the subtests, do not use these subtests in computing Index scores or a Full Scale IQ. Examine closely the supplemental subtests and evaluate whether or not they offer the type of task that is most relevant to your evaluation. For example, you will not be able to administer any subtests requiring vision to children who are seriously visually impaired. Verbal subtests usually are extremely difficult to administer to children with hearing impairments; obviously, if you give the directions aloud, the child must be able to hear what you say. Table C-8 in Appendix C shows modified instructions for administering the WISC–IV Perceptual Reasoning subtests to examinees with hearing impairments. Table C-9 in Appendix C shows the physical abilities needed for the WISC–IV.

If you administer the WISC–IV to a child with a physical disability, you should not provide special cues. If your modifications go beyond simply permitting the child to respond in his or her preferred mode of communication or using alternative procedures to present the items, the results may be invalid. The Administration Manual (see pp. 12 to 18) provides information about administering the WISC–IV to children with hearing impairments.

Verbal Comprehension

You can administer all of the Verbal Comprehension subtests to a child whose hearing is intact. If the child cannot hear but can read, you can type the Similarities, Vocabulary, Comprehension, Information, and Word Reasoning questions on cards and show the cards to the child one at a time. If the child cannot speak, you can accept written replies, replies typed on a keyboard, or replies made by pointing to letters on an alphabet sheet. Administering the test in American Sign Language may provide unintended cues, but it may be the only alternative for assessing the child's verbal abilities.

Perceptual Reasoning

Adaptations of the Perceptual Reasoning subtests center on the child's method of responding. You can give Picture Concepts, Matrix Reasoning, and Picture Completion to a child who has adequate vision and who can say, write, or type the answer or point to the answer, if appropriate. On subtests where a pointing response is acceptable, provide the child with a small, pointed stick that is soft and dull enough not to mar the pictures. You cannot easily adapt Block Design for a child whose arm-hand use is severely impaired. The Perceptual Reasoning subtests can be administered with few, if any, modifications to a child with a hearing impairment. However, because you will still need to convey the instructions in some manner, a child with a hearing impairment may be at a disadvantage. When you are reading the directions and items or giving prompts and queries, the child cannot look at the sample items or subtest items at the same time that he or she attends to your signs, cues, or lips.

Working Memory

You can administer the Working Memory subtests in the standard way to a child whose hearing is intact. If the child cannot hear but can read, you can present the Digit Span, Letter–Number Sequencing, and Arithmetic items visually. However, visual presentation poses difficulties because of the time limits involved in the Arithmetic subtest and because visual presentation is quite different from oral presentation for the Digit Span and Letter–Number Sequencing items and, to some extent, the Arithmetic items. Therefore, you may have to omit Digit Span and Letter–Number Sequencing when you test children with a hearing impairment. If you do omit these subtests, make a note of it in your report.

Processing Speed

You can adapt the Coding, Symbol Search, and Cancellation subtests by pointing to each item and having the child say, type, point to, or indicate by head movements the response (e.g., which symbol goes in the empty box or whether the symbol is or is not in the array).

Advantages of Separate Composites

The division of the WISC–IV into the four individual Composites and the availability of supplemental subtests are helpful in testing children with disabilities. You can usually administer the Verbal Comprehension and Working Memory subtests to a child with a visual impairment or to a child with severe motor disabilities. And you can administer the Perceptual Reasoning and Processing Speed subtests to a child with a hearing impairment or to a child with little or no speech. If you also administer the Verbal Comprehension subtests to a child with a hearing impairment, you can compare the child's performance on Verbal Comprehension with that on Perceptual Reasoning to evaluate whether there are any verbal deficits.

Unknown Effects of Modifications

Without empirical findings, there is no way of knowing whether modifications affect the reliability and validity of the test scores. Yet, when you cannot follow standard procedures because disabilities prevent the child from comprehending the instructions or manipulating the test materials, modifications are needed. *When you use modifications, consider the resulting score only as a rough estimate of the score that the child might obtain under standardized procedures.* Be sure to note any modifications on the Record Form and in the psycho-

logical report.

You might want to consider a test other than the WISC–IV for evaluating a child with a disability. Examples include the Leiter International Performance Scale–R, the Universal Nonverbal Intelligence Test, and the Test of Nonverbal Intelligence. (See Chapter 16 in Sattler 2001, *Assessment of Children: Cognitive Applications*, for reviews of these and other tests.)

ASSETS

The WISC–IV has several assets.

1. *Excellent standardization.* The standardization procedures were excellent, sampling four geographical regions, both sexes, the four major ethnic groups (Euro American, African American, Hispanic American, and Asian American), and the entire socioeconomic status range. The standardization group well represents the nation as a whole for the age groups covered by the test.

2. *Good overall psychometric properties.* The Verbal Comprehension, Perceptual Reasoning, Working Memory, and Processing Speed Composites and the Full Scale have good reliability, and the Full Scale has adequate validity.

3. *Useful diagnostic information.* The WISC–IV provides diagnostic information useful for the assessment of cognitive abilities of elementary- and high-school-age children who are functioning within three standard deviations from the mean (±3 *SD*). It also provides data likely to be helpful in planning special school programs, perhaps tapping important developmental or maturational factors needed for school success, especially in the lower grades. The Verbal Comprehension, Perceptual Reasoning, Working Memory, and Processing Speed Composites are helpful in clinical and psychoeducational evaluations and aid in the assessment of brain-behavior relationships.

4. *Inclusion of Process scores.* Process scores add potentially valuable diagnostic information, particularly in clinical situations.

5. *Generally good administrative procedures.* The examiner actively probes the child's responses to evaluate the breadth of the child's knowledge and to determine whether the child really knows the answer. On items that require two reasons for maximum credit, examiners ask the child for another reason if the child gives only one correct reason. These procedures ensure that the test does not penalize the child for failing to

understand the subtest requirements. The emphasis on probing questions and queries is extremely desirable.

6. *Good manuals and interesting test materials.* The Administration Manual is relatively easy to use, with clear directions and tables in most cases. Examiners are aided by instructions printed in a color that differs from that of other test materials. The Technical Manual presents useful information about the test and is well written. The test materials are interesting to children.

7. *Generally helpful scoring criteria.* Scoring guidelines for the Similarities and Vocabulary subtests detail the rationale for 2-, 1-, and 0-point scores. Several examples demonstrate the application of the scoring principles for items on the Similarities, Vocabulary, and Comprehension subtests. In addition, the guidelines for each Comprehension item provide the general rationale for the correct answer.

8. *Usefulness for children with some disabilities.* You can administer subtests on Verbal Comprehension and Working Memory to children who have visual or motor impairments and subtests on Perceptual Reasoning and Processing Speed to children who are hearing impaired if they can understand the directions.

9. *Extensive research and clinical literature with prior versions of the test.* Because most of the WISC–IV subtests are from earlier versions of the test or from other Wechsler tests, the prior research and clinical base provide a solid basis for interpretation.

LIMITATIONS

The WISC–IV also has several limitations.

1. *Failure to provide conversion tables for computing Index scores and Full Scale IQs when supplemental subtests are substituted for core subtests.* Not only are these conversion tables absent, but the Technical Manual does not give any descriptive statistics for distributions using substitute subtests. (Thus, you should substitute a supplemental subtest for a core subtest only in unusual circumstances and label the results "Estimated" when you report the test results.)

2. *Failure to provide the psychometric basis for the requirement that a child must obtain six raw scores of 1 in order for a Full Scale IQ to be computed.* What is the justification for the requirement that a child must obtain raw scores of 1 on at least two Verbal Comprehension subtests, two Perceptual Reasoning subtests, one Working Memory subtest, and one Processing Speed subtest

in order for a Full Scale IQ to be computed? How do we know that another rule would not be equally valid or that this rule provides valid IQs? Although we advise you to follow this rule, it would have been helpful had The Psychological Corporation provided the psychometric justification for it.

3. *Use of 1,100 children instead of 2,200 children to standardize Arithmetic.* We believe that it is poor psychometric practice to have 14 subtests standardized on 2,200 children and one subtest standardized on 1,100 children. The Psychological Corporation should have made every effort to have the same number of children in the standardization group for all subtests.

4. *Limited range of scores for children who are extremely low functioning or children who are extremely high functioning.* The cognitive ability of children who are functioning below or above three standard deviations from the mean is not adequately assessed by the WISC–IV.

5. *Limited criterion validity studies.* We believe that it is poor practice to base information about the criterion validity of the WISC–IV only on tests published by The Psychological Corporation. The failure to provide information about the relationship between the WISC–IV and tests of cognitive ability and achievement available from other publishers limits our understanding of the WISC–IV.

6. *Possible difficulties in scoring responses.* Work with previous editions indicated that Similarities, Vocabulary, and Comprehension may be difficult to score. The Technical Manual presents a study indicating high agreement among four examiners' scores. Although these results are encouraging, additional studies are needed, particularly with diversified samples of children and both student and professional examiners. We recommend that you consult a colleague whenever you are uncertain about scoring responses.

7. *Somewhat large practice effects.* Perceptual Reasoning and Processing Speed have practice effects of about 5 and 7 points, respectively, for retest intervals of less than 9 weeks. Research is needed to determine practice effects over a longer period of time and with special populations. (See Chapter 4 in Sattler, 2001, *Assessment of Children: Cognitive Applications*, for more information about practice effects or repeated evaluations.) Because of the potentially confounding practice effects, carefully consider whether you want to use the WISC–IV for a retest when you have previously given the test to the child.

8. *Poor quality of some test materials.* The templates on the Coding and Symbol Search subtests are poorly

constructed and may rip. The Cancellation scoring template is especially thin and can rip or tear easily.

9. *Occasional confusing guidelines.* The directions for subtests that have sample items fail to mention that all children should be given the sample items. Placing several different sample responses on one line separated by semicolons hinders scanning. Directions for scoring multiple responses could be improved. One scoring criterion for Arithmetic—giving credit for responses even when they contain incorrect units—seems inappropriate. The Administration Manual fails to give the rationale for the correct answers on Picture Concepts, although it does do so for the Comprehension subtest. In addition, some subtests have correct answers not acknowledged in the Administration Manual.

CONCLUDING COMMENT

The WISC–IV has good standardization, reliability, and concurrent and construct validity and generally useful administrative and scoring guidelines. The Administration Manual and Technical Manual are good, and much thought and preparation have gone into the revision. The WISC–IV will likely serve as a valuable instrument in the assessment of children's intelligence for many years to come. However, we need research to evaluate how the changed structure of the WISC–IV will affect how children are classified, particularly children who are intellectually gifted, children with learning disabilities, and children with mental retardation.

You can obtain answers to frequently asked questions by going to the WISC–IV page of The Psychological Corporation's Web site. You can go to

http://www.WISC–IV.com

and then click on the link called "WISC–IV Frequently Asked Questions."

THINKING THROUGH THE ISSUES

1. Why do you think previous editions of the Wechsler tests were so successful?
2. Under what circumstances would you use a supplemental subtest as a substitute for a core subtest?
3. How does having at least 50 different combinations of subtests for computing Full Scale IQs create the potential for abuse? Discuss your answer.
4. When would you use the Process scores? How might they contribute to the assessment process?
5. Why do you think Verbal Comprehension and Perceptual Reasoning are better measures of *g* than are Working Memory and Processing Speed?
6. What can you do to develop skill at properly administering the WISC–IV?
7. What limitations of the WISC–IV might affect its clinical and psychoeducational usefulness?
8. Do you believe that the WISC–IV is a good measure of intelligence? Discuss your answer.
9. What other kinds of subtests would you like to see in an intelligence test?
10. Is the WISC–IV culturally biased or culturally fair? Discuss your answer.

SUMMARY

1. The WISC–IV was published in 2003, 12 years after the previous edition, called the WISC–III.
2. There are 10 core and 5 supplemental subtests in the WISC–IV.
3. Verbal Comprehension comprises Similarities, Vocabulary, and Comprehension (three core subtests) and Information and Word Reasoning (two supplemental subtests).
4. Perceptual Reasoning comprises Block Design, Picture Concepts, and Matrix Reasoning (three core subtests) and Picture Completion (one supplemental subtest).
5. Working Memory comprises Digit Span and Letter–Number Sequencing (two core subtests) and Arithmetic (one supplemental subtest).
6. Processing Speed comprises Coding and Symbol Search (two core subtests) and Cancellation (one supplemental subtest).
7. The WISC–IV also provides seven Process scores: Block Design No Time Bonus (BDN), Digit Span Forward (DSF), Digit Span Backward (DSB), Longest Digit Span Forward (LDSF), Longest Digit Span Backward (LDSB), Cancellation Random (CAR), and Cancellation Structured (CAS).

Standardization

8. Except for Arithmetic, which was standardized on 1,100 children, the WISC–IV was standardized on 2,200 children who were selected to represent children in the United States.

Standard Scores, Scaled Scores, and Test-Age Equivalents

9. The WISC–IV, like the WPPSI–III and WAIS–III, uses standard scores ($M = 100$, $SD = 15$) for the four Index scores and for the Full Scale IQ, and scaled scores ($M = 10$, $SD = 3$) for the 15 subtests. Scaled scores are also used for five of the seven Process scores (BDN, DSF, DSB, CAR, CAS), and raw scores are used for the other two Process scores (LDSF, LDSB).

10. Although you can prorate Verbal Comprehension and Perceptual Reasoning if two of the three subtests in each Composite are valid, avoid proration if at all possible because it introduces unknown measurement error.

11. Test-age equivalents are obtained directly from the raw scores on each subtest.

Reliability

12. The WISC–IV has good reliability. For example, the four Composites and the Full Scale have internal consistency reliability coefficients of .81 or above over the entire age range covered in the standardization group.

13. Average internal consistency reliabilities are .94 for Verbal Comprehension, .92 for both Perceptual Reasoning and Working Memory, .88 for Processing Speed, and .97 for the Full Scale.

14. Average internal consistency reliabilities for the subtests range from .79 for Symbol Search and Cancellation to .90 for Letter–Number Sequencing.

15. Average internal consistency reliabilities for the five Process scores for which reliabilities are reported range from .70 for Cancellation Random to .84 for Block Design No Time Bonus.

16. The average standard errors of measurement (SEM) in standard-score points are 3.78 for Verbal Comprehension, 4.15 for Perceptual Reasoning, 4.27 for Working Memory, 5.21 for Processing Speed, and 2.68 for the Full Scale.

17. The average standard errors of measurement (SEM) in scaled-score points range from .97 for Letter–Number Sequencing to 1.38 for Cancellation.

18. Test-retest reliability coefficients indicate that the WISC–IV generally provides stable Index scores and Full Scale IQs.

19. In the total test-retest sample, average stability coefficients for the subtests ranged from a low of .68 for Symbol Search to a high of .85 for Vocabulary. The subtests are less stable than the four individual Composites and the Full Scale.

20. Mean increases from the first to the second testing were 2.1 points for Verbal Comprehension, 5.2 points for Perceptual Reasoning, 2.6 points for Working Memory, 7.1 points for Processing Speed, and 5.6 points for the Full Scale.

21. When tested a second time, children are likely to have greater gains on Perceptual Reasoning and Processing Speed than on Verbal Comprehension and Working Memory.

22. From first to second administration, Picture Completion showed the largest increase (1.8 points), while Comprehension showed the smallest increase (.2 point).

23. Use the child's specific age group—not the average of the 11 age groups—to obtain the most accurate confidence interval.

Validity

24. Studies correlating the WISC–IV with the WISC–III, WPPSI–III, WAIS–III, WASI, and measures of achievement, memory, emotional intelligence, and adaptive behavior indicate that the WISC–IV has satisfactory criterion validity.

25. Mean WISC–IV Full Scale IQs are lower than mean WISC–III Full Scale IQs by about 2.5 points.

26. Mean WISC–IV and WPPSI–III Full Scale IQs differed by .2 point.

27. Mean WISC–IV Full Scale IQs are lower than mean WAIS–III Full Scale IQs by 3.1 points.

28. The mean Full Scale IQ on the WISC–IV was lower than that on the two-subtest WASI by 1.8 points and lower than that on the four-subtest WASI by 3.4 points.

Intercorrelations for Subtests and Composites

29. Intercorrelations between the 15 subtests range from a low of .10 (Cancellation and Digit Span) to a high of .75 (Vocabulary and Information).

30. In the total group, the Verbal Comprehension subtests correlate more highly with each other ($Mdn\ r = .64$) than do the Perceptual Reasoning subtests ($Mdn\ r = .47$), the Working Memory subtests ($Mdn\ r = .47$), or the Processing Speed subtests ($Mdn\ r = .40$).

Demographic Variables

31. The mean Full Scale IQs of boys and girls were similar, as were their mean Index scores on Verbal Comprehension, Perceptual Reasoning, and Working Memory. However, the mean Index score on

Processing Speed was about 5 points higher for boys than for girls.

32. The mean Full Scale IQ of Euro American children was about 11.5 points higher than that of African American children and about 10 points higher than that of Hispanic American children. However, the mean Full Scale IQ of Asian American children was about 3 points higher than that of Euro American children.

33. The mean Full Scale IQ of children whose parents had graduated from college was about 22 points higher than that of children whose parents had an eighth-grade education or less.

34. The mean Full Scale IQ of children from the Northeast and Midwest was about 4 points higher than that of children from the South and West.

Factor Analysis

35. The results of a factor analysis indicated that a four-factor model best describes the WISC–IV: Verbal Comprehension (Similarities, Vocabulary, Comprehension, Information, and Word Reasoning), Perceptual Reasoning (Block Design, Picture Concepts, Matrix Reasoning, and Picture Completion), Working Memory (Digit Span, Letter–Number Sequencing, and Arithmetic), and Processing Speed (Coding, Symbol Search, and Cancellation).

36. The term *Verbal Comprehension* describes a hypothesized verbal-related ability underlying the Composite for both item content (verbal) and mental processes (comprehension). Verbal Comprehension measures verbal knowledge and understanding obtained through both informal and formal education and reflects the application of verbal skills to new situations.

37. The term *Perceptual Reasoning* describes a hypothesized performance-related ability underlying the Composite for both item content (perceptual) and mental processes (reasoning). Perceptual Reasoning measures the ability to interpret and organize visually perceived material and to generate and test hypotheses related to problem solutions.

38. The term *Working Memory* describes a hypothesized memory-related ability underlying the Composite. Working Memory measures immediate memory and the ability to sustain attention, concentrate, and exert mental control.

39. The term *Processing Speed* describes a hypothesized processing speed ability underlying the Composite. Processing Speed measures the ability to process visually perceived nonverbal information

quickly, with concentration and rapid eye-hand coordination being important components.

40. The factor analytic findings show different patterns of loadings at different ages.

41. The WISC–IV subtests form three clusters with respect to the measurement of *g*: (a) Vocabulary, Information, Similarities, Arithmetic, Word Reasoning, and Comprehension are good measures of *g*; (b) Block Design, Matrix Reasoning, Picture Completion, Letter–Number Sequencing, Symbol Search, Picture Concepts, Digit Span, and Coding are fair measures of *g*; and (c) Cancellation is a poor measure of *g*.

42. Many subtests possess sufficient specificity at some ages to justify interpretation of specific subtest functions.

Range of Subtest and Process Score Scaled Scores

43. The range of scaled scores from 1 to 19 is available for most subtests at each age group.

44. The range of scaled scores from 1 to 19 is not available for three of the five Process scores.

Range of Full Scale IQS

45. The range of WISC–IV Full Scale IQs is 40 to 160 and is available at all ages of the test. This range is insufficient for children who are extremely low functioning or extremely high functioning.

46. Compute the Full Scale IQ only when the child obtains raw scores greater than 0 on at least (a) two of the three Verbal Comprehension subtests, (b) two of the three Perceptual Reasoning subtests, (c) one of the two Working Memory subtests, and (d) one of the two Processing Speed subtests.

Comparison of the WISC–IV and WISC–III

47. Although similar in some ways, the WISC–IV and WISC–III have considerably different structures. Among the differences are variations in the composition of the Full Scale, the composition of the individual Composites, and the number of supplemental subtests.

48. Of the core subtests in the WISC–IV Full Scale, 50% are not core subtests in the WISC–III Full Scale.

49. In the WISC–IV, 60% of the core subtests in the Full Scale measure crystallized knowledge and fluid reasoning ability, while 40% measure immediate auditory rote memory and visuomotor processing speed. In contrast, in the WISC–III, 90% of the core

subtests in the Full Scale measure crystallized knowledge and fluid reasoning, while 10% measure visuomotor processing speed.

50. A study of the pattern of subtest scores on the two tests, taking into account the different structures of the two tests, and the case history will guide you in interpreting test-retest changes from the WISC–III to the WISC–IV.

Administering the WISC–IV

51. To become proficient in administering the WISC–IV, you must master the procedures described in the Administration Manual.

52. Areas on which you will need to focus are preparing for the session, following the subtest sequence, using queries and prompts, starting at the appropriate place, using a reverse sequence, following the start-point scoring rule, following the discontinue-point scoring rule, awarding perfect scores, awarding points for unadministered items, repeating instructions and items, giving additional help, determining how long to wait for a child's response, following discontinue criteria, following appropriate scoring procedures, scoring spoiled responses, using testing-of-limits, making subtest substitutions, and using qualifying items.

53. The start-point scoring rule states that the child receives full credit for all items located below the start-point item and subsequent item on which perfect scores were obtained.

54. The discontinue-point scoring rule states that the child does not receive credit for any items above the last discontinue-point item.

55. In a reverse sequence, continue to administer items even after the discontinue criterion has been met until you reach item 1 or until the child has perfect scores on two consecutive items.

56. Conduct testing-of-limits only after you have administered the entire test following standard procedures.

57. Testing-of-limits may invalidate repeated evaluations and should be used cautiously.

58. Substitutions should be based on clinical need or a similar appropriate reason, not your own preferences or convenience.

59. We advise that substitutions be avoided whenever a specific IQ or Composite score needs to be used for decision-making purposes.

60. Because the Full Scale IQ tables are based on the core subtests only, scores derived using one or two supplemental subtests have an unknown degree of additional measurement error.

61. Reasons examiners commit scoring errors include (a) poor training in test administration, (b) ambiguous scoring criteria in the Administration Manual, (c) carelessness, (d) a poor relationship with the child, (e) personal stress or fatigue, and (f) boredom with administering the test.

62. Overall, administer the subtests in the recommended order, start each subtest with the appropriate item, follow the instructions in the Administration Manual for administering each subtest, score each item, follow the reverse procedure if needed, follow the discontinue criterion, add the item scores for each subtest, complete the Record Form, and check all of your work.

Short Forms

63. Short forms of the WISC–IV may be used for (a) screening purposes, when the short form may be followed by administration of the rest of the test, (b) research purposes, or (c) obtaining an estimate of the child's intellectual status when a precise IQ is not required.

64. If you need a classification for a clinical or psychoeducational purpose or need information for programming decisions, do not use a short form.

Choosing Between the WISC–IV and the WPPSI–R and Between the WISC–IV and the WAIS–III

65. Because of its breadth of coverage, we recommend that at the overlapping ages (6-0 to 7-3), the WISC–IV be used instead of the WPPSI–III with children at all ability levels.

66. We recommend that at the overlapping ages, the WISC–IV be used with children with below-average ability and that either the WISC–IV or the WAIS–III be used with children with average or above-average ability.

Administering the WISC–IV to Children with Disabilities

67. You will need to evaluate the sensory-motor abilities of children with disabilities before you administer the WISC–IV. If you find that a child has a visual, hearing, attentional, or motor problem that may interfere with his or her ability to take one or more of the subtests, do not use these subtests in computing Index scores or a Full Scale IQ.

68. If you administer the WISC–IV to a child with a physical disability, you should not provide special cues. If your modifications go beyond simply per-

mitting the child to respond in his or her preferred mode of communication or using alternative procedures to present the items, the results may be invalid.

69. When you use modifications, consider the resulting score only as a rough estimate of the score that the child might obtain under standardized procedures.

Assets

70. The assets of the WISC–IV include its excellent standardization, good overall psychometric properties, useful diagnostic information, inclusion of Process scores, generally good administrative procedures, good manuals and interesting test materials, generally helpful scoring criteria, usefulness for children with some disabilities, and extensive research and clinical literature with prior versions of the test.

Limitations

71. The limitations of the WISC–IV include failure to provide conversion tables for computing Index scores and Full Scale IQs when supplemental subtests are substituted for core subtests, failure to provide the psychometric basis for the requirement that a child must obtain six raw scores of 1 in order for a Full Scale IQ to be computed, use of 1,100 children instead of 2,200 children to standardize Arithmetic, limited range of scores for children who are extremely high or low functioning, limited criterion validity studies, possible difficulties in scoring responses, somewhat large practice effects, poor quality of some test materials, and occasional confusing guidelines.

Concluding Comment

72. The WISC–IV will likely serve as a valuable instrument in the assessment of children's intelligence for many years to come, although we need research to evaluate how the changed structure of the WISC–IV will affect how children are classified.

KEY TERMS, CONCEPTS, AND NAMES

STUDY QUESTIONS

1. Discuss the WISC–IV. Include in your discussion the following issues: standardization, types of scores, test-age equivalents, reliability, and validity.
2. Describe and interpret the intercorrelations between WISC–IV subtests and Composites.
3. Discuss demographic characteristics of the WISC–IV standardization sample.
4. Describe and interpret WISC–IV factor analytic findings.
5. Discuss the range of subtest scaled scores and Full Scale IQs on the WISC–IV.
6. Compare the WISC–III and WISC–IV.
7. Discuss administrative considerations for the WISC–IV.
8. Identify common administrative and scoring errors on the WISC–IV, and describe what measures you could take to minimize and avoid these errors.
9. Discuss the substitution of supplemental subtests for core subtests.
10. Discuss WISC–IV short forms, including their value and limitations.
11. For the overlapping ages, explain how you would go about choosing between the WISC–IV and the WPPSI–III, and between the WISC–IV and the WAIS-III. What recommendations would you make regarding which test to choose?
12. Identify the most important factors to consider in administering the WISC–IV to children with disabilities.
13. Discuss the strengths and limitations of the WISC–IV.

2

WISC–IV CORE SUBTESTS

The knowledge of words is the gate to scholarship.
—Woodrow Wilson

Wit is brushwood, judgment is timber. The first makes the brightest flame, but the other gives the most lasting heat.
—Hebrew proverb

Block Design

Similarities

Digit Span

Picture Concepts

Coding

Vocabulary

Letter–Number Sequencing

Matrix Reasoning

Comprehension

Symbol Search

Thinking Through the Issues

Summary

Key Terms, Concepts, and Names

Study Questions

Goals and Objectives

This chapter is designed to enable you to do the following:

- Critically evaluate the 10 WISC–IV core subtests

- Describe the rationales, factor analytic findings, reliability and correlational highlights, and administrative and interpretive considerations for the 10 WISC–IV core subtests

This is the first of two chapters that provide information to help you administer, score, and interpret the WISC–IV subtests. This chapter covers the 10 WISC–IV core subtests, while the next chapter covers the five WISC–IV supplemental subtests. Included in each of these chapters are the rationale, factor analytic findings, reliability and correlational highlights, administrative guidelines, and interpretive suggestions for each subtest covered. The factor analytic findings discussed in the two chapters are based on a principal factor analysis that we conducted based on the data presented in the Technical Manual (also see Chapter 1). The reliability and correlational findings reported in the two chapters are also based on the Technical Manual. Reliabilities for the Coding, Symbol Search, and Cancellation subtests are test-retest correlations, whereas those for the remaining 12 subtests are split-half correlations corrected by the Spearman-Brown formula. The suggestions for administration are based on the Administration Manual, while the interpretive suggestions are based on clinical considerations.

Table C-2 in Appendix C summarizes (a) the abilities purportedly measured by each WISC–IV subtest (along with the abilities in the Cattell-Horn-Carroll [CHC] model), (b) background factors influencing performance, (c) implications of high and low subtest scaled scores, and (d) instructional implications. Table C-2 deserves careful study because it is especially useful for report writing. Also see Tables C-3 and C-4 in Appendix C, which describe the Wechsler subtests associated with the CHC model.

Recognize that the standard administration of all WISC–IV subtests requires the child to hear, pay attention, listen, understand directions, and retain the directions while solving problems. Several subtests (Block Design, Picture Concepts, Coding, Vocabulary, Matrix Reasoning, Symbol Search, Picture Completion, and Cancellation) also require the child to have adequate vision. In addition, Block Design, Coding, Symbol Search, and Cancellation require the child to have adequate fine-motor skills.

Many of the WISC–IV subtests have enough subtest specificity (i.e., ample or adequate) at most ages (see Table 1-13 in Chapter 1) to provide reliable estimates of specific abilities—or at least to permit development of hypotheses about the underlying cognitive functions that the subtests may measure.

The best estimates of abilities are provided by the Full Scale, followed by the Verbal Comprehension, Perceptual Reasoning, Working Memory, and Processing Speed Composites, other combinations of subtests, and, finally, individual subtests. For example, the Full Scale IQ, derived from a combination of 10 subtests, provides the best estimate of general ability. The Verbal Comprehension Composite, derived from a combination of three core Verbal subtests (Similarities, Vocabulary, and Comprehension), yields more accurate information about a child's verbal skills than does any single Verbal Comprehension subtest. Similarly, the Perceptual Reasoning Composite, derived from a combination of the three Perceptual Reasoning subtests (Block Design, Picture Concepts, and Matrix Reasoning), yields more accurate information about a child's nonverbal reasoning skills than does any single Perceptual Reasoning subtest. Finally, the Working Memory Composite (Digit Span and Letter–Number Sequencing) and the Processing Speed Composite (Coding and Symbol Search) provide more information about each area than does either of the two component subtests in each composite.

As noted in Chapter 1, Table D-1 in Appendix D is a useful checklist that will help in learning to administer the WISC–IV. The Administrative Guidelines provided for each subtest in this and the following chapter are related to Table D-1 in Appendix D. The Administrative Guidelines represent an extended version of the brief checklist in Table D-1 in Appendix D.

Note that the reverse sequence rule discussed in this and the following chapter applies only when the subtest is started with an item higher than item 1.

On the Record Form, record a "(Q)" when you query a response and record a "(P)" when you prompt for an additional response.

Note that in the first printing of the Behavioral Observations page (back page) of the Record Form, the percentile ranks under the normal curve are standard scores, not percentile ranks. The correct percentile ranks (P_{xx}) for the standard-score ranges are as follows: $\leq 69 = P_2$; $70–79 = P_2–P_8$; $80–89 = P_9–P_{23}$; $90–109 = P_{25}–P_{73}$; $110–119 = P_{75}–P_{90}$; $120–129 = P_{91}–P_{97}$; $\geq 130 = \geq P_{98}$.

As you read about each subtest, you will encounter questions posed to guide you in your test administration. Answering these questions will help you evaluate and interpret the child's performance. In addition to the child's scores, consider the quality of the child's responses, style of responding, problem-solving approach, fine-motor skills, and pattern of successes and failures.

If you conduct testing-of-limits, remember that the results are to be used to guide your understanding of the child's abilities and not for computing scores obtained under standard administration. If there is a need to retest using the WISC–IV within a 3-year period, testing-of-limits is not advisable.

BLOCK DESIGN

Block Design, a core Perceptual Reasoning subtest, requires the child to reproduce designs, using blocks that have red surfaces, white surfaces, and surfaces divided diagonally into half red and half white. The subtest contains 14 items and is timed. The child uses blocks to assemble a design identical to a model constructed by the examiner (items 1 to 3) or to a picture of a two-dimensional, red-and-white design (items 3 to 14). For item 3, the model is disassembled prior to the child's constructing the design—the child constructs the design while viewing the picture only. The subtest is somewhat difficult to administer and score.

Rationale

Block Design requires that the child perceive and analyze forms by breaking down a whole (the design) into its parts and then assembling the components into a design identical to the one shown in the model or the picture. This process is called analysis and synthesis. To succeed, the child must use visual organization and visual-motor coordination. Success also involves the application of logic and reasoning to spatial relationship problems. Consequently, you can consider Block Design to be a nonverbal concept-formation task requiring perceptual organization, spatial visualization, and abstract conceptualization. It also can be viewed as a constructional task involving spatial relations and figure-ground separation.

Different strategies can be used to assemble the blocks (Rozencwajg, 1991; Rozencwajg & Corroyer, 2002). One is a *global strategy* in which the design is viewed as a whole and not differentiated into units. The child assembles blocks in a stepwise trial-and-error procedure; with this strategy, the child does not analyze the components of the model. The order of placing the blocks is independent of the pattern. Children look frequently at the design to make the pattern.

A second is an *analytical strategy* in which the child forms a representation of the model and then decomposes the design into the appropriate number of blocks. Once the blocks have been separated, the child selects and orients them before placing them in the design. The order of placing the blocks is independent of the pattern. Children look frequently at the design to make the pattern.

A third is a *synthetic strategy* in which the placement of the blocks is dependent on the pattern in the design. In this strategy, the gestalts in the block patterns govern the child's placement of blocks. "A gestalt is a form or structure that cannot be reduced to the mere juxtaposition of elements; it has a specific quality that is not found in any of its constituents" (Rozencwajg & Corroyer, 2002, p. 3). The blocks are placed in an order that reflects the gestalts in the design. Children may not need to look frequently at the design to make the pattern.

A child's performance on Block Design may be affected by motor skill and vision. Do not interpret inadequate performance as direct evidence of inadequate visual form and pattern perception, because the ability to discriminate block designs (i.e., to perceive the designs accurately at a recognition level) may be intact even when the ability to reproduce the designs is impaired.

Factor Analytic Findings

Block Design is a fair measure of g (49% of its variance can be attributed to g). It contributes substantially to the Perceptual Reasoning Index (average loading = .65). Specificity is ample at all ages.

Reliability and Correlational Highlights

Block Design is a reliable subtest (r_{xx} = .86), with reliability coefficients above .83 at each age (range of .83 to .88). It correlates better with Matrix Reasoning and Arithmetic (r = .55) than with any of the other subtests. It has a moderately high correlation with the Full Scale IQ (r = .70), a moderate correlation with the Verbal Comprehension Index (r = .50), a high correlation with the Perceptual Reasoning Index (r = .81), and moderately low correlations with the Working Memory Index (r = .42) and Processing Speed Index (r = .45).

Administrative Guidelines

The following administrative guidelines for the Block Design subtest must be followed carefully.

Background Considerations

1. Clear the area on your desk that you use to administer Block Design.
2. Read the directions verbatim.
3. Read the directions clearly.
4. Use a stopwatch quietly, if possible.
5. Keep the stopwatch on the table, if needed, but out of the child's reach, and handle it unobtrusively.
6. Repeat the instructions if the child asks or has not responded within 5 to 10 seconds, unless it is clear that the child is considering a response.

7. On items 5 to 10, if the child clearly understands the task, shorten the instructions, if desired.

8. When explaining the task, only clarify the instructions by pointing to the model or picture as you speak to the child. Do not explain the construction to the child.

9. Make sure that the child is seated directly in front of the table.

10. Show the different sides of the block as you read the instructions.

11. Give the child only the number of blocks needed for each item (two blocks for item 1, four blocks for items 2 to 10, and nine blocks for items 11 to 14).

12. Disassemble the models as noted in the Administration Manual.

13. Place the intact model or Stimulus Book and blocks properly.

a. When demonstrating a design, place the intact model or Stimulus Book about 7 inches from the edge of the table closest to the child.

b. For a right-handed child, place the intact model or Stimulus Book slightly to the left of the child's midline.

c. For a left-handed child, place the intact model or Stimulus Book slightly to the right of the child's midline.

d. If unable to determine whether the child is right- or left-handed, place the intact model or Stimulus Book directly in front of the child.

e. Place the coil-bound edge of the Stimulus Book facing the child for items 3 to 14 so that the book is completely flat when it is opened, and then open it to the appropriate page.

f. When placing or scrambling the blocks for items 2 to 10, be sure that only one block has a red-and-white side facing up.

g. When placing or scrambling the blocks for items 11 to 14, be sure that only two blocks have a red-and-white side facing up.

14. Turn the pages of the Stimulus Book toward the child as you administer the items.

15. Use only blocks as models on items 1 and 2, use blocks *and* a picture as models on item 3, and use *only* pictures as models on items 4 to 14.

16. On items 1 and 2, leave the model intact as the child constructs the designs.

17. On items 1 and 2, give appropriate caution if the child attempts to duplicate sides of the model.

18. Follow the appropriate procedure for item 3. Place the Stimulus Book toward the child, with the item 3 picture exposed. After building the model for item 3, disassemble it, scramble the blocks, place the

blocks in front of the child, and leave the picture facing the child.

19. Scramble the blocks between designs.

20. Remove all unnecessary blocks from the child's view.

21. Do not permit the child to rotate the Stimulus Book.

22. Time correctly.

a. Begin timing after you read the last word of the instructions.

b. Use the following time limits: 30 seconds maximum for item 1; 45 seconds maximum for items 2 to 5; 75 seconds maximum for items 6 to 10; and 120 seconds maximum for items 11 to 14.

c. When in doubt as to whether the child is finished with the task, say, "Tell me when you have finished." Note that this instruction is not in the Administration Manual.

d. Stop timing when the child is obviously finished with an item, when the child indicates with gestures that the item is completed, or when the time limit is reached.

e. Allow a few additional seconds after the time limit if the child is nearing completion of the design.

f. Do not stop timing once timing has begun, even to clarify instructions.

23. Give appropriate prompts.

a. One time only, if the child rotates or reverses a design on any item, say, "See, it goes this way" and correct the child's design.

b. On items 1 and 2, if the child tries to duplicate both the top and the sides of a model, say something like "Match only the tops of the blocks" or "Only the tops of the blocks need to be the same."

24. Administer the trials correctly.

a. When demonstrating trials 1 and 2 on items 1, 2, and 3, put the blocks together slowly. Be careful not to cover the blocks with your hand; the child needs to see what you are doing. Make the designs so that they are in the appropriate direction for the child. This means that you will be making the designs upside down. Do not make a design right side up and then turn it around to face the child.

b. Administer a second trial on items 1, 2, and 3 if the child makes an incorrect construction on the first trial.

c. Do not give a second trial on items 4 to 14.

Starting Considerations

25. Start with the appropriate item.

a. The ages listed under "Start" on page 60 of the Administration Manual are always intended to be inclusive; thus, ages 6–7 means children 6-0 to 7-11 years of age and ages 8–16 means children 8-0 to 16-11 years of age.

b. The starting ages on the Record Form are also inclusive.

c. Children 6 to 7 years of age (and older children suspected of having intellectual deficiency) start with item 1.

d. Children 8 to 16 years of age (not suspected of having intellectual deficiency) start with item 3.

Reverse Sequence

26. If necessary, administer the items in reverse sequence as directed in the Administration Manual.

a. The instructions on page 60 of the Administration Manual under the heading "Reverse" pertain to children who begin the subtest with item 3.

b. If the child (a) does not obtain full credit on the start-point item or (b) obtains full credit on the start-point item and a score of 0 on the next item, administer the items in reverse sequence. In addition, if the child starts with item 3, trial 1, and then makes an incorrect construction on trial 1 followed by either a correct *or* an incorrect construction on trial 2, administer the items in reverse sequence.

c. Continue the reverse sequence until the child has perfect scores on two consecutive items or until item 1 has been administered, even if the discontinue criterion is met.

d. When there is a reverse sequence, the discontinue criterion is not met, and either there are two consecutive items with perfect scores or item 1 is administered, continue administration with the item after the last start-point item.

e. The reverse rule for children 8 to 16 years of age that is printed on the Record Form should say, "Score of **0** or **1** on item 3 or score of **0** on item 4, administer preceding items in reverse order until two consecutive perfect scores are obtained."

Discontinue Considerations

27. Count items administered in reverse sequence toward the discontinue criterion.

28. Discontinue the subtest when three consecutive scores of 0 are obtained, unless the consecutive 0's are obtained during a reverse sequence and (a) item 1 has not been reached or (b) the child has not obtained perfect scores on two consecutive items.

29. Once the subtest is completed, remove the Stimulus Book and blocks from the child's view.

Scoring Guidelines

30. Score the items using the following guidelines.

a. Items 1 to 3 are scored 0 (incorrect constructions on trials 1 and 2), 1 (correct construction on trial 2), or 2 (correct construction on trial 1).

b. Items 4 to 8 are scored 0 or 4.

c. Items 9 to 14 are scored 0, 4, 5, 6, or 7.

d. For all items, do not give the child credit if there are rotations of 30° or more in the designs, even when the designs are assembled correctly.

e. When the child earns perfect scores on the first two items at the start point or in a reversal, award full credit for all preceding items, regardless of the child's performance on these items if they have been administered.

f. Award no points for any items beyond the last score of 0 required for the discontinue criterion to be met, regardless of the child's performance on these items if they have been administered.

g. Do not award credit for any items completed after the time limit has expired.

h. To compute the Block Design No Time Bonus (BDN) total raw score, score items 1 to 3 as 0, 1, or 2 and score items 4 to 14 as 0 or 4.

Record Form

31. For each item (and for each trial on items 1 to 3), record the completion time in seconds in the Completion Time column. To assist you in recording the times for the two trials on items 1 to 3, draw a horizontal line dividing the three Completion Time boxes in half. Label the upper half of the box "Trial 1" and the lower half "Trial 2."

32. Note or sketch the incorrect design arrangements in the Constructed Design column, if desired.

33. When the design is correct, make a check mark over the picture of the blocks in the Constructed Design column, if desired.

34. Note rotations with an arrow and the amount of rotation (in degrees) in the Constructed Design column, if desired.

35. Circle Y or N in the Correct Design column. Circle Y for items that are correctly assembled even if they are (a) correctly completed after the time limit or (b) rotated but completed within the time limit. Circle N for items that are incorrectly assembled.

36. Circle 0, 1, 2, 4, 5, 6, or 7 in the Score column.

a. For items 1 to 3, circle 0 in the Score column when the child makes incorrect constructions on both trials.

b. For items 1 to 3, circle 1 in the Score column when the child makes a correct construction on the second trial.

c. For items 1 to 3, circle 2 in the Score column when the child makes a correct construction on the first trial.

d. For items 4 to 8, circle 0 in the Score column when the child makes an incorrect construction.

e. For items 4 to 8, circle 4 in the Score column when the child makes a correct construction.

f. For items 9 to 14, circle 0 in the Score column when the child makes an incorrect construction.

g. For items 9 to 14, circle 4, 5, 6, or 7 in the Score column when the child makes a correct construction within the specific time limits.

h. For all items, circle 0 in the Score column for a correct construction assembled after the time limit.

i. For all items, circle 0 in the Score column for rotations of 30° or more.

37. To note the points awarded for items not administered below the first two items with perfect scores, put a slash mark in the Score column over the item preceding the first two items with perfect scores and write the numerals for these points.

38. Add the points, including the points for correct answers and the points for items not administered before the first two perfect scores, but not for items administered after the last discontinue item or for items completed after the time limit.

39. Enter the Total Raw Score in the shaded box.

40. Enter the Block Design No Time Bonus (BDN) total raw score in the shaded box at the bottom right-hand corner on page 3 of the Record Form.

Interpretive Suggestions

The following questions are useful to guide your observation of the child's performance on the Block Design subtest.

- Is the child hasty and impulsive or deliberate and careful?
- Does the child slowly and methodically check each block with the design or rarely check?
- Does the child quit easily or become frustrated when faced with possible failure, or does the child persist and keep on working even after the time limit is reached?
- Does the child use only one approach to make the designs, or does the child alter the approach as the need arises?
- Does the child use a slow approach or a rapid trial-and-error approach to make the designs?
- Is the child excessively concerned with aligning the blocks precisely?
- Does the child study the designs first, before attempting to construct them?
- Does the child appear to have a plan when assembling the blocks?

- Does the child understand the principle of using individual blocks to construct the designs?
- Does the child try to place the blocks on the picture of the design on items 3 to 14?
- Does the child express concerns about differences between blocks?
- Does the child interpret white portions of the design card as open spaces in the assembled designs?
- Does the child use a solid red or solid white block surface for a red-and-white surface?
- Does the child say that the constructed designs are correct when, in fact, they are not?
- Are the child's designs correct but rotated? If so, how much are the designs usually rotated?
- Does the child rotate single blocks? If so, how many degrees are the individual blocks usually rotated?
- Does the child rotate a row of blocks at the bottom when the blocks are in the wrong direction, or does the child start the entire design over again?
- Does the child show any indications of fine-motor difficulties such as tremor or clumsiness?
- Does the child tend to construct the designs using a sequential, block-by-block approach or a more random, haphazard approach?
- Does the child use a left-to-right approach or the less common right-to-left or bottom-to-top approach?
- Does the child make internal detail errors or loss of configuration errors?
- Does the child make errors when the grid lines are removed from the stimulus pictures? Note that items 3 to 5 have grid lines while items 6 to 14 do not (item 14 additionally lacks outside boundary lines).
- Does the child assist you by shuffling the blocks or turning the pages of the Stimulus Book?
- Does the child describe what he or she is doing with the blocks?
- Is the child overly concerned with speed or accuracy?
- Does the child try to begin before being told to do so or change blocks after saying that the designs are done?
- Does the child offer to put the blocks back in the box after the task is completed?

Excessive fumbling or failure to check the pattern may indicate anxiety. Visuosensory difficulties may be indicated if the child moves or twists to improve perspective on the design or if the child leaves space between the blocks in the assembled design. Try to differentiate between excessive cautiousness as a personality style and excessive slowness as a possible indication of depression or boredom. Children who continually recheck their work with the model may be revealing insecurities or obsessive tendencies.

As we noted in the Scoring Guidelines, the WISC–IV provides a Process Score for the Block Design subtest—Block Design No Time Bonus (BDN). This score is based on the total raw score without time-bonus points. After you calculate the BDN raw score, convert it to a scaled score ($M = 10$ and $SD = 3$) by using Table A.8 in the Administration Manual (pp. 242–252). Table B.9 (p. 269) provides the critical values needed for a significant difference between the Block Design scaled score and the BDN scaled score, while Table B.10 (p. 270) provides the frequency of observed discrepancies. The comparison of Block Design with time bonuses versus BDN gives you information about the effect of speed on performance. However, we need research to evaluate what BDN and the BD–BDN discrepancy mean clinically.

High scores on the Block Design subtest may indicate good spatial orientation in conjunction with speed, accuracy, and persistence; good visual-motor-spatial integration; good conceptualizing, analyzing, and synthesizing skills; good nonverbal reasoning ability; good use of trial-and-error methods to solve problems; good hand-eye coordination; good ability to evaluate a problem quickly and accurately; good attention to detail; or good motivation.

Low scores on the Block Design subtest may indicate poor visual-motor-spatial integration, visual-perceptual problems, poor spatial orientation, poor analyzing and synthesizing ability, poor nonverbal reasoning ability, poor ability to evaluate a problem, poor attention to detail, poor hand-eye coordination, difficulty working under time pressure, slow performance, poor motivation, or impulsivity.

One useful testing-of-limits procedure is to select an item that the child has incorrectly constructed, assemble the incorrect reproduction, and ask the child if the reproduction is the same as or different from the original design. If the child recognizes that the design is incorrect and can relate the specific errors (e.g., "A red-and-white block goes here, not a white block"), the child may have a visual-motor execution problem rather than a visual-motor recognition problem. In such cases, it may be useful to ask the child to make the recognized correction or corrections by saying "Go ahead and make it look the way it should look."

Another testing-of-limits procedure involves showing the child a design that the child failed. As you give the directions again, place one row or block in its correct position. Say, "Let's try some of these again. I'm going to put together some of the blocks. I'll make the top row [or arrange the first block]. Now you go ahead and finish it. Make one like this. Tell me when you have finished." If the child fails with this first cue, arrange additional blocks. Record the amount of help the child needs to reproduce the design accurately. A child who needs many cues to reproduce the design may have weaker spatial reasoning ability than a child who needs only one or a few cues. In some cases, the additional cues may not help the child reproduce the design.

Other testing-of-limits procedures are also possible. One is to show the child three different arrangements, only one of which is correct. Then ask the child to point to the arrangement that is the same as the model. Be sure to vary the placement of the correct design. Another procedure is to ask the child to tell you how the designs were constructed. You may also provide the child with a transparent overlay with grid lines and ask the child to construct the designs on the grid. You can also place an overlay over the Stimulus Book and see if that helps the child break up the stimulus. Additionally, you may ask the child to make the 9-block designs inside the block box.

The consistent full range of scaled scores from 1 to 19 at all ages aids in profile analysis. Profile analysis is discussed in Chapter 4.

SIMILARITIES

Similarities, a core Verbal Comprehension subtest, requires the child to answer questions about how two common objects or concepts are alike. The child is asked to state the similarity between the two items in each pair. The subtest contains 23 pairs of words and one sample and is not timed. It is relatively easy to administer but difficult to score.

Rationale

On the Similarities subtest, the child must perceive the common elements of the paired terms and then bring the common elements together into a meaningful concept. Thus, the subtest appears to measure verbal concept formation—the ability to place objects and events together into a meaningful group. To do this, the child may need to find relationships that are not at first obvious, a process of abstraction. Although concept formation can be a voluntary, effortful process, it also can reflect well-automatized verbal conventions. Performance on the subtest may be related to cultural opportunities and interest patterns. Memory is also involved. Success initially depends on the child's ability to comprehend the meaning of the task—that is, to find the common element of the paired items even though some of the paired items may be opposites. If the child does understand the task, in order to receive credit the child still needs to know the concept that reflects the common element in the paired items.

Factor Analytic Findings

Similarities is a good measure of g (66% of its variance can be attributed to g). It ties with Information as the second best measure of g in the scale. It contributes substantially to the Verbal Comprehension Index (average loading = .69). Specificity is ample or adequate at ages 6, 7, 10 to 12, and 14 to 16 and inadequate at ages 8, 9, and 13 years.

Reliability and Correlational Highlights

Similarities is a reliable subtest (r_{xx} = .86), with reliability coefficients at or above .82 at all 11 age groups (range of .82 to .89). It correlates better with Vocabulary (r = .74) than with any of the other subtests. It has a moderately high correlation with the Full Scale IQ (r = .77), a high correlation with the Verbal Comprehension Index (r = .89), moderate correlations with the Perceptual Reasoning Index (r = .59) and Working Memory Index (r = .50), and a moderately low correlation with the Processing Speed Index (r = .38).

Administrative Guidelines

The following administrative guidelines for the Similarities subtest must be followed carefully.

Background Considerations

1. Read the instructions verbatim.
2. Read the instructions clearly.
3. Read the items verbatim.
4. Read the items clearly.
5. Repeat the instructions if the child asks or has not responded within 5 to 10 seconds, unless it is clear that the child is considering a response.
6. Repeat each item as often as necessary.
7. Query unclear or vague responses, as well as the sample responses marked by a "(Q)" in the Administration Manual. *This includes all the responses separated by semicolons on a line that has a "(Q)" at the end.* Do not query responses that are clearly wrong or responses that are clearly correct.
8. If the child makes an incorrect response, give the child correct answers to the sample and to items 1

and 2.
9. For items 3 to 23, do not give the child the correct answers.
10. If the child fails to respond and has been performing poorly, wait about 30 seconds before going to the next item and say, "Let's try another one." However, use your judgment about moving to the next item sooner. For children who are clearly beyond their ability, 30 seconds may be a long time to wait, especially if it is the third or fourth 30-second wait. For example, this would be the case for children who seem to be bored, who are shrugging their shoulders, or who are looking around the room after a few seconds and not looking at the item.
11. If the child fails to respond but has been performing successfully and appears to be working on a response, give the child the necessary time to respond before going to the next item.

Starting Considerations

12. Start with the appropriate item.
   a. The ages listed under "Start" on page 69 of the Administration Manual are always intended to be inclusive; thus, ages 6–8 means children 6-0 to 8-11 years of age, ages 9–11 means children 9-0 to 11-11 years of age, and ages 12–16 means children 12-0 to 16-11 years of age.
   b. The starting ages on the Record Form are also inclusive.
   c. Children 6 to 8 years of age (and older children suspected of having intellectual deficiency) start with the sample and then item 1.
   d. Children 9 to 11 years of age (not suspected of having intellectual deficiency) start with the sample and then item 3.
   e. Children 12 to 16 years of age (not suspected of having intellectual deficiency) start with the sample and then item 5.

Reverse Sequence

13. If necessary, administer the items in reverse sequence as directed in the Administration Manual.
   a. The instructions on page 69 of the Administration Manual under the heading "Reverse" pertain to children who begin the subtest with the sample and then with item 3.
   b. If the child (a) does not obtain full credit on the start-point item or (b) obtains full credit on the start-point item and a score of 0 on the next item, administer the items in reverse sequence.
   c. Continue the reverse sequence until the child has perfect scores on two consecutive items or until

item 1 has been administered, even if the discontinue criterion is met.

d. When there is a reverse sequence, the discontinue criterion is not met, and either there are two consecutive items with perfect scores or item 1 is administered, continue administration with the item after the last start-point item.

Discontinue Considerations

14. Count items administered in reverse sequence toward the discontinue criterion.
15. Discontinue the subtest when five consecutive scores of 0 are obtained, unless the consecutive 0's are obtained during a reverse sequence and (a) item 1 has not been reached or (b) the child has not obtained perfect scores on two consecutive items.

Scoring Guidelines

16. Score the responses using the following guidelines.
   a. When a child gives multiple acceptable responses for an item, score the best response.
   b. The scoring examples are not an exhaustive list of correct and incorrect responses.
   c. A careful study of the sample responses will help you become more proficient in scoring Similarities responses.
   d. Study—and master—the General Principles, which clarify the rationales for scores of 0, 1, and 2.
   e. Note that the General Principles do not literally pertain to items 1 and 2. This is because items 1 and 2 can be scored only 0 or 1.
   f. When parts of the response vary in quality but none spoil the entire response, score the best response.
   g. Score the response without considering extraneous parts of the response.
   h. Give a score of 0 to the entire response if it has been spoiled or if it is not pertinent to both objects (or terms), is too general, or reflects a difference in the objects (or terms).
   i. Give a score of 1 on items 1 and 2 for any response that reflects a major classification, a minor classification, or a specific property of the objects (or terms) or on items 3 to 23 for any response that reflects a concrete response (i.e., a specific property common to both objects or terms) or that reflects a less major classification.
   j. Give a score of 2 on items 3 to 23 for any response that reflects a conceptual response, such as a major classification.
   k. When the child earns perfect scores on the first two items at the start point or in a reversal, award full credit for all preceding items, regardless of the

child's performance on these items if they have been administered.

l. Award no points for any items beyond the last score of 0 required for the discontinue criterion to be met, regardless of the child's performance on these items if they have been administered.

Record Form

17. Record the child's responses verbatim in the Response column.
18. Circle 0 or 1 in the Score column for items 1 and 2 and circle 0, 1, or 2 in the Score column for items 3 to 23.
19. To note the points awarded for items not administered below the first two items with perfect scores, put a slash mark in the Score column over the item preceding the first two items with perfect scores and write the numerals for these points.
20. Add the points, including the points for correct answers and the points for items not administered before the first two perfect scores, but not for items administered after the last discontinue item.
21. Enter the Total Raw Score in the shaded box.

Interpretive Suggestions

The following questions are useful to guide your observation of the child's performance on the Similarities subtest.

- Does the child seem to understand the task?
- How many 0-point, 1-point, and 2-point responses does the child have?
- Is the pattern of scores consistent or variable?
- Is the child thinking through the questions, responding impulsively, or simply guessing?
- Does the child appear confident or hesitant when responding?
- Does the child give peculiar responses? If so, in what way? What might these responses suggest?
- Does the child frequently say, "I know this answer, but I can't think of it" or "I don't know"?
- Are the child's answers precise, imprecise, or vague?
- Are the child's answers close to the correct answer or completely wrong?
- Are the child's answers overinclusive (see below)?
- Does the child give overly verbose responses or short, succinct responses?
- Does the child frequently give phonetic similarities between the words (e.g., says that both words end in *ing* or both words start with *p*)?
- Are there frequent self-corrections?

- Does the child seem to be inhibited in making responses?
- What is the pattern of the child's successes and failures?

The subtest requires knowing what the two words in each pair mean; therefore, a child who does not know the meaning of each word in the pair is likely to fail that item. If several items are failed because of vocabulary difficulties, the child's performance probably is related to vocabulary deficiency rather than to categorization ability deficiency.

Observing the child's typical level of conceptualization will help you understand the child's thinking style. Consider whether the answers are concrete, functional, or abstract. *Concrete answers* typically refer to qualities of the objects (or stimuli) that can be seen or touched (apple-banana: "Both have a skin"). *Functional answers* typically concern a function or use of the objects (apple-banana: "You eat them"). Finally, *abstract answers* typically refer to a more universal property or to a common classification of the objects (apple-banana: "Both are fruits").

You can tell, in part, whether the child's response style is concrete, functional, or abstract by the numbers of 0-, 1-, and 2-point responses. Zero- and 1-point responses suggest a more concrete and functional conceptualization style, while 2-point responses suggest a more abstract conceptualization style. However, a 2-point response does not necessarily reflect abstract thinking ability and may simply be an overlearned response. For example, there may be a difference between the 2-point response "Both fruits" for apple-banana and the 2-point response "Artistic expressions" for painting-statue. Although "Both fruits" receives 2 points, it may be an overlearned response, whereas "Artistic expressions" may reflect a more abstract level of conceptual ability.

Furthermore, if the child earns 1 point on several items but has few 2-point scores, the child may have a good breadth of knowledge but not depth. If the child earns 2 points on several items but has few 1-point scores, the child may have a good depth of knowledge but less breadth.

Failures on easy items coupled with successes on more difficult ones may suggest poor motivation, anxiety, temporary inefficiency, boredom, or an inconsistent environment. Alternatively, this pattern may indicate a problem with lower-level conceptual responses.

Overinclusive responses are so general that several objects are included in the concept. For example, the reply "Both contain molecules" to a question asking for the similarity between an apple and a banana is overinclusive because it does not delimit the particular characteristics of these two objects.

A pattern of either overinclusive responses or responses filled with numerous similarities may suggest perfectionistic tendencies. Alternatively, responses with an excessive number of similarities may simply reflect the child's desire to impress you. Consider the child's entire test performance, plus other relevant information, when you interpret *overinclusive responses*. Excessive overinclusive responses may be a subtle indication of unusual thinking.

Observe how the child handles any frustration induced by the subtest questions. For example, when the child has difficulty answering the questions, does the child become negativistic and uncooperative or continue to try to answer the questions? A child who responds with "They are not alike" may be displaying negativism, avoidance of the task demands, suspiciousness, a coping mechanism, or deficient knowledge. To determine which of these may account for the child's response, compare the child's style of responding to the Similarities questions with the style of responding to questions on other subtests; also refer to the interview and to other sources of information to develop and confirm hypotheses.

High scores on the Similarities subtest may indicate good conceptual thinking, good ability to see relationships, good ability to use logical and abstract thinking, good ability to discriminate fundamental from superficial relationships, good ability to select and verbalize appropriate relationships between two objects or concepts, or flexibility of thought processes.

Low scores on the Similarities subtest may indicate poor conceptual thinking, difficulty in seeing relationships, difficulty in selecting and verbalizing appropriate relationships between two objects or concepts, an overly concrete mode of thinking, poor vocabulary knowledge, rigidity of thought processes, or negativism.

If you suspect word-retrieval problems, use a multiple-choice testing-of-limits procedure. This procedure may help distinguish deficits associated with word-retrieval difficulties from those associated with deficient knowledge. After completing the *entire test*, go back to the item (or items) with which the child had difficulty and give the child three answers from which to choose. For example, follow an item like "In what way are radio and television alike?" with "Choose one of the following: Because you read them, listen to news on them, or watch cartoons on them. What is your answer?" Be sure to randomly vary the position of the correct answer in the series (i.e., put the correct answer sometimes in first, sometimes in second, and sometimes in third position). If the child answers the multiple-choice questions correctly, the child may have a word-retrieval difficulty rather than deficient knowledge. However, the multiple-choice procedure should not be used to calculate an IQ.

The consistent full range of scaled scores from 1 to 19 for children 7 to 16 years of age aids in profile analysis. The restricted range of scaled scores from 2 to 19 for children 6 years of age somewhat limits profile analysis.

DIGIT SPAN

Digit Span, a core Working Memory subtest, requires the child to repeat a series of digits that you read aloud. The subtest has two parts: Digit Span Forward, which contains series ranging in length from two to nine digits, and Digit Span Backward, which contains series ranging in length from two to eight digits. On Digit Span Forward, the child is asked to repeat the numbers as given. On Digit Span Backward, the child is asked to repeat numbers in reverse order (or backwards). There are two series of digits for each sequence length. For all children, administer Digit Span Forward first and then Digit Span Backward. The subtest is not timed and is relatively easy to administer and score.

Rationale

Digit Span is a measure of the child's short-term auditory memory and attention. The child's performance on the Digit Span subtest may be affected by ability to relax, as a child who is calm and relaxed may achieve a higher score than one who is excessively anxious. The task assesses the child's ability to retain several elements that have no logical relationship to one another. Because the child must recall auditory information and repeat the information aloud in proper sequence, the task also involves sequencing.

Digit Span Forward primarily involves rote learning and memory, whereas Digit Span Backward requires transformation of the stimulus input prior to responding. On Digit Span Backward, the child not only must hold the mental image of the numerical sequence longer (usually) than on Digit Span Forward, but also must manipulate the sequence before restating it. High scores on Digit Span Backward may indicate flexibility, tolerance for stress, and excellent concentration. Digit Span Backward involves more complex cognitive processing than does Digit Span Forward.

Digit Span Forward appears to involve primarily sequential processing and short-term memory, whereas Digit Span Backward appears to involve both planning ability and sequential processing and may provide some insight into working memory. Additionally, Digit Span Backward may involve the ability to (a) form mental images and (b) scan an internal visual display formed from an auditory stimulus. However, we need more research to support the hypothesis about the role of visualization in Digit Span Backward performance.

Because of the differences between the two tasks, it is useful to consider Digit Span Forward and Digit Span Backward separately. The WISC–IV provides several Process Scores for the Digit Span subtest. These include (a) Digit Span Forward based on raw scores, (b) Digit Span Backward based on raw scores, (c) Longest Digit Span Forward based on the number of digits recalled correctly on the last trial awarded points, and (d) Longest Digit Span Backward based on the number of digits recalled correctly on the last trial awarded points. Digit Span Forward and Digit Span Backward raw scores are converted to scaled scores ($M = 10$ and $SD = 3$) by using Table A.8 (pp. 242–252) in the Administration Manual. Table B.9 (p. 269) in the Administration Manual provides the critical values needed for a significant difference between the Digit Span Forward and Digit Span Backward scaled scores, while Table B.10 (p. 270) in the Administration Manual provides the frequency of observed discrepancies. Base rates for raw scores for both Longest Digit Span Forward and Longest Digit Span Backward are provided in Table B.7 (p. 267) in the Administration Manual, and base rates for differences between the two (the Longest Digit Span Forward minus the Longest Digit Span Backward) are provided in Table B.8 (p. 268) in the Administration Manual.

Factor Analytic Findings

Digit Span is a fair measure of g (32% of its variance can be attributed to g). It contributes substantially to the Working Memory Index (average loading = .54). Specificity is ample at all ages.

Reliability and Correlational Highlights

Digit Span is a reliable subtest ($r_{xx} = .87$), with reliability coefficients above .81 at each age (range of .81 to .92). It correlates better with Letter–Number Sequencing ($r = .49$) than with any of the other subtests. It has a moderate correlation with the Full Scale IQ ($r = .62$), moderately low correlations with the Verbal Comprehension Index ($r = .44$), the Perceptual Reasoning Index ($r = .42$), and the Processing Speed Index ($r = .30$), and a high correlation with the Working Memory Index ($r = .86$).

Administrative Guidelines

The following administrative guidelines for the Digit Span subtest must be followed carefully.

Background Considerations

1. Read the directions verbatim.
2. Read the directions clearly.
3. Repeat the instructions if the child asks or has not responded within 5 to 10 seconds, unless it is clear that the child is considering a response.
4. Be sure that the child cannot see the digits in the Administration Manual or on the Record Form.
5. Read the digits clearly at the rate of one digit per second, and drop your voice inflection on the last digit in the series. Also, do not break up the digits into groups by unintentionally pausing between sets of digits as you read them. Doing so may provide the child with a mnemonic device—chunking—that may make recall of the digits easier. Finally, practice the speed of reading the digits with a stopwatch.
6. Always administer both trials of each series and provide correct feedback on Digit Span Backward, as noted in the Administration Manual. On Digit Span Backward, if the child passes the first sample two-digit series (on either the first or the second trial), go to the second sample two-digit series in the subtest proper. If the child fails either of the sample series, read the specific directions in the Administration Manual that explain how to repeat the series (p. 89). This is the only assistance allowed on this subtest.
7. Do not repeat any trial of any item except for failures on the two trials of the Digit Span Backward sample. If asked to repeat an item, say, "Just take your best guess."

Starting Considerations

8. Start with the appropriate item.
a. The ages listed under "Start" on page 69 of the Administration Manual are always intended to be inclusive; thus, ages 6–16 means children 6-0 to 6-11 years of age.

b. The starting ages on the Record Form are also inclusive.
c. All children begin Digit Span Forward with item 1 and begin Digit Span Backward with the sample and then item 1. There is no Reverse Sequence on the Digit Span subtest.

Discontinue Considerations

9. Digit Span Forward and Digit Span Backward are both discontinued after scores of 0 on both trials of an item.

Scoring Guidelines

10. Score the items using the following guidelines.
a. Score all trials as 0 or 1.
b. The item score is the sum of the scores from the individual trials.
c. Digit Span Forward Total Raw Score is the sum of the scores for all of the Digit Span Forward items administered (i.e., 1 point for each trial administered).
d. Digit Span Backward Total Raw Score is the sum of the scores for all of the Digit Span Backward items administered (i.e., 1 point for each trial administered).
e. Sum the scores for Digit Span Forward and for Digit Span Backward to obtain the total raw score.
f. The Digit Span Forward process score and the Digit Span Backward process score are based on the raw scores for the items in Digit Span Forward and Digit Span Backward, respectively.
g. The Longest Digit Span Forward process score and Longest Digit Span Backward process score are based on the number of digits recalled on the last trial scored as correct for Digit Span Forward and Digit Span Backward, respectively.

Record Form

11. Record the child's responses verbatim in the Response column.
12. Circle 0 or 1 in the Trial Score column for each trial administered.
13. Circle 0, 1, or 2 in the Item Score column for each item administered.
14. Enter the Total Raw Score for Digit Span Forward, the Total Raw Score for Digit Span Backward, and the Total Raw Score in the appropriate boxes.
15. Enter the Longest Digit Span Forward score.
16. Enter the Longest Digit Span Backward score.

To record the digits recalled in each series, place in the Record Form either a mark designating a correct answer above each digit correctly recalled or a mark designating an incorrect answer on each digit missed. An even better procedure is to record the exact sequence given by the child in the available space. A good record can help you evaluate the child's performance.

Interpretive Suggestions

The following questions are useful to guide your observation of the child's performance on the Digit Span subtest.

- Is the child's performance effortless, or does the child seem to use considerable concentration?
- Does the child respond quickly, right after the item is read, or does the child consider the response prior to responding?
- Does the child view the task as interesting, boring, or difficult?
- Does the child notice errors, or does the child think that his or her answers are always correct?
- Does the child understand the difference between Digit Span Backward and Digit Span Forward?
- Are the errors made by the child on Digit Span Backward similar to or different from those made on Digit Span Forward (e.g., omitting numbers, recalling numbers correctly but in the wrong sequence)?
- What is the child's reaction as the Digit Span Backward series proceeds? For example, does the child become stimulated and encouraged or tense, anxious, and frustrated?
- Does the child do much better on Digit Span Forward than on Digit Span Backward?
- Does the child make more errors on Digit Span Forward than on Digit Span Backward?
- What strategy does the child use to recall the digits?

Observe whether the child's failures involve omitting one or more digits, transposing digits, interjecting incorrect digits, producing more digits than were given, or giving a series of digits in numerical order (e.g., 6-7-8-9). The child who recalls the correct digits but in an incorrect sequence is more likely to have a deficit in auditory sequential memory than in auditory memory. The child who fails the first trial but passes the second trial may be displaying a learning-to-learn pattern or a need for a warm-up to achieve success.

The child who consistently misses the last digit in the first series and then successfully completes the second series differs from one who fails to recall any of the digits in the first series but successfully completes the second. Similarly, the child who responds to the sequence 3-4-1-7 with "3-1-4-7" has better short-term memory than the child who says "9-8-5-6." The scoring system does not distinguish between these or other failure patterns.

To learn what method was used to recall the digits, ask the child what strategy was used. Strategies include simply repeating what was heard, rehearsing the digits, visualizing the digits by closing the eyes, using a finger to write the digits on the table, and grouping the digits. Some grouping techniques introduce meaning into the task, as separate digits become numbers grouped into hundreds, tens, or other units (e.g., 3-1-7 becomes three hundred seventeen). If the child uses grouping, the function underlying the task may be changed from one of attention to one of concentration. Record the child's response.

Whenever you have any doubt about the child's auditory acuity, request an audiological examination. Because this subtest contains no contextual cues (i.e., you only present several random series of digits), children who are hearing impaired may be especially prone to failure.

The Administration Manual provides separate scaled scores for Digit Span Forward and Digit Span Backward (Table A.8, pp. 242–252). Table B.9 (p. 269) shows that differences of approximately 4 points between Digit Span Forward and Digit Span Backward are at the .05 level of significance. Table B.10 (p. 270) shows the extent to which children's scaled scores were higher for Digit Span Forward than for Digit Span Backward and vice versa. The median difference between Digit Span Forward and Digit Span Backward (regardless of direction) was 2 points. Less than 10% of the standardization sample obtained Digit Span Forward scaled scores that were 5 or more points higher than Digit Span Backward scaled scores.

Table B.7 (p. 267) shows the longest Digit Span Forward span and the longest Digit Span Backward span recalled by children. Across all age groups, children had a median Digit Span Forward span of 6 (range of 5 to 7) and a median Digit Span Backward span of 4 (range of 3 to 5).

Table B.8 (p. 268) shows the extent to which the Digit Span Forward number strings recalled by children were longer than the Digit Span Backward number strings and vice versa. In all age groups and in the total sample, children recalled more digits forward than backward (*Mdn* difference = 2 at each of the 11 age groups and in the total sample). Thus, consider as noteworthy raw score differences of 3 points or more between Longest Digit Span Forward and Longest Digit

Span Backward. The percentage of children in the standardization group who recalled more digits backward than forward ranged from .5% at ages 6-0 to 7-11 to 5.5% at ages 14-0 to 14-11.

Digit Span Forward appears to be a measure of short-term memory span, while Digit Span Backward appears to be a measure of working memory. A significantly higher score on Digit Span Forward than Digit Span Backward suggests that the child has better short-term memory than ability to hold information in memory and manipulate it. In addition, the more complex operations required on Digit Span Backward may induce anxiety in the child.

A significantly higher score on Digit Span Backward than Digit Span Forward suggests that the child may view Digit Span Backward as more of a challenge and therefore mobilize more resources, such as added concentration and attention, to cope with the more demanding Digit Span Backward task.

High scores on the Digit Span subtest may indicate strength in auditory sequential processing, good short-term auditory memory, good rote memory, good immediate recall, good attention and concentration, flexibility in shifting tasks, or cooperativeness.

Low scores on the Digit Span subtest may indicate difficulty in auditory sequential processing, poor short-term auditory memory, poor rote memory, poor immediate recall, inattention, distractibility, difficulty in shifting tasks, a possible learning deficit, negativism, boredom, or anxiety.

The consistent full range of scaled scores from 1 to 19 at all ages aids in profile analysis.

PICTURE CONCEPTS

Picture Concepts, a core Perceptual Reasoning subtest, requires the child to look at two or three rows of pictures and then select from each row one picture that best goes together with the other selection(s) to form a concept. The task is to find a common element in the pictures that forms a category, concept, or classification. The subtest has 28 items and is not timed. It is relatively easy to administer and score.

Rationale

Picture Concepts appears to measure abstract, categorical reasoning based on perceptual recognition processes. The task is to scan an array of pictures and determine which pictures have a common characteristic. The child

first must recognize or identify each picture and then determine a quality that a picture in one row shares with a picture in another row. The quality might represent a category (e.g., animals), an appearance (e.g., round), a function (e.g., bounce), or a use (e.g., for eating).

The correct answers are limited in that they do not recognize all possible logical classifications. Because the child only has to point to the answer, there is no way of knowing the basis for the answer. If two animals were selected, there is no way to know, for example, whether the child knows (a) the names of the animals, (b) that the pictures are of animals, (c) or that the pictures represent any category at all. The child's response could be based simply on the fact that the two pictures look similar (visual matching), have something in common like feet or a menacing look (conceptual reasoning), look different from the other pictures (visual discrimination), or look nice (personal decision that may have no cognitive component).

Factor Analytic Findings

Picture Concepts is a fair measure of g (37% of its variance can be attributed to g). It contributes moderately to the Perceptual Reasoning Index (average loading = .40). Specificity is ample at all ages.

Reliability and Correlational Highlights

Picture Concepts is a reliable subtest (r_{xx} = .82), with reliability coefficients at or above .76 at each of the 11 age groups (range of .76 to .85). It correlates better with Matrix Reasoning (r = .47) than with any of the other subtests. It has a moderate correlation with the Full Scale IQ (r = .64), a moderately high correlation with the Perceptual Reasoning Index (r = .77), and a moderately low correlation with the Verbal Comprehension Index (r = .47), the Working Memory Index (r = .39), and the Processing Speed Index (r = .36).

Administrative Guidelines

The following administrative guidelines for the Picture Concepts subtest must be followed carefully.

Background Considerations

1. Read the directions verbatim.
2. Read the directions clearly.

3. Repeat the instructions if the child asks or has not responded within 5 to 10 seconds, unless it is clear that the child is considering a response.

4. Place the closed Stimulus Book with the coil-bound edge facing the child so that the book is completely flat when it is opened.

5. Position the Stimulus Book close enough so that the child can easily point to the desired response.

6. As the directions are read, point across the first and second rows for samples A and B and items 1 to 12 and across the first, second, and third rows for items 13 to 28.

7. Turn the pages of the Stimulus Book toward the child and show the items one at a time.

8. On items 2 to 12 and 14 to 28, when the child understands the task, shorten or eliminate the instructions, if desired.

9. If the child fails to select a picture in each row, selects more than one picture in a row, or offers more than one combination of selected pictures, give the prompts noted on page 91 of the Administration Manual as often as necessary.

10. If you are asked, tell the child the name of any picture.

11. Ask the child to point to the picture if his or her verbal response is not clear. Say, "Point to the picture you mean."

12. Ask, "Why do they go together?" when the child gives the correct response to sample A or B.

13. If the child passes sample A or B but does not say the correct reason, give the correct reason for the answer.

14. If the child gives an incorrect answer to either sample A or sample B, give the correct answer, point to the correct objects, and then give the reason for the answer.

15. Do not give the child the correct answer or explain the correct answer on subtest items.

16. If the child fails to respond and has been performing poorly, wait about 30 seconds before going to the next item and say, "Let's try another one." However, use your judgment about moving to the next item sooner. For children who are clearly beyond their ability, 30 seconds may be a long time to wait, especially if it is the third or fourth 30-second wait. For example, this would be the case for children who seem to be bored, who are shrugging their shoulders, or who are looking around the room after a few seconds and not looking at the item.

17. If the child fails to respond but has been performing successfully and appears to be working on a response, give the child the necessary time to respond before going to the next item.

Starting Considerations

18. Start with the appropriate item.

a. The ages listed under "Start" on page 90 of the Administration Manual are always intended to be inclusive; thus, ages 6–8 means children 6-0 to 8-11 years of age, ages 9–11 means children 9-0 to 11-11 years of age, and ages 12–16 means children 12-0 to 16-11 years of age.

b. The starting ages on the Record Form are also inclusive.

c. Children 6 to 8 years of age (and older children suspected of having intellectual deficiency) start with samples A and B and then item 1.

d. Children 9 to 11 years of age (not suspected of having intellectual deficiency) start with samples A and B and then item 5.

e. Children 12 to 16 years of age (not suspected of having intellectual deficiency) start with samples A and B and then item 7.

f. Even if the child fails the two samples, proceed to the start-point item.

Reverse Sequence

19. If necessary, administer the items in reverse sequence as directed in the Administration Manual.

a. The instructions on page 90 of the Administration Manual under the heading "Reverse" pertain to children who begin the subtest with the samples and then with item 5 or higher.

b. If the child (a) does not obtain full credit on the start-point item or (b) obtains full credit on the start-point item and a score of 0 on the next item, administer the items in reverse sequence.

c. Continue the reverse sequence until the child has perfect scores on two consecutive items or until item 1 has been administered, even if the discontinue criterion is met.

d. When there is a reverse sequence, the discontinue criterion is not met, and either there are two consecutive items with perfect scores or item 1 is administered, continue administration with the item after the last start-point item.

Discontinue Considerations

20. Count items administered in reverse sequence toward the discontinue criterion.

21. Discontinue the subtest when five consecutive scores of 0 are obtained, unless the consecutive 0's are obtained during a reverse sequence and (a) item 1 has not been reached or (b) the child has not obtained perfect scores on two consecutive items.

22. Once the subtest is completed, remove the Stimulus Book from the child's view.

Scoring Guidelines

23. Score the items using the following guidelines.
    a. All responses are scored 0 or 1.
    b. To receive a score of 1 on an item, the child must select the one correct picture from each of two rows (items 1 to 12) or the one correct picture from each of three rows (items 13 to 28).
    c. Give credit if the child points to or names the pictures or says the numbers of the chosen pictures.
    d. When the child earns perfect scores on the first two items at the start point or in a reversal, award full credit for all preceding items, regardless of the child's performance on these items if they have been administered.
    e. Award no points for any items beyond the last score of 0 required for the discontinue criterion to be met, regardless of the child's performance on these items if they have been administered.
    f. Although there appear to be two correct answers for item 27, follow the scoring guidelines in the Administration Manual.

Record Form

24. Circle the response number or DK (don't know) for each item administered.
25. Circle DK when the child does not respond or says that the answer is unknown.
26. Circle 0 or 1 in the Score column for each item administered.
27. To note the points awarded for items not administered below the first two items with perfect scores, put a slash mark in the Score column over the item preceding the first two items with perfect scores and write the numerals for these points.
28. Add the points, including the points for correct answers and the points for items not administered before the first two perfect scores, but not for items administered after the last discontinue item.
29. Enter the Total Raw Score in the shaded box.

Interpretive Suggestions

The following questions are useful to guide your observation of the child's performance on the Picture Concepts subtest.

- What is the tempo of the child's responses (e.g., fast, slow, deliberate, impulsive, careful)?

- Are there any signs of a response set (e.g., child points to the same numbered choice or position on the page for each item)?
- What might the reasons be for any long response times?
- How does the child's pattern of responding on Picture Concepts compare with responses on other subtests?
- How does the child respond to prompts?
- Are there any indications of visual difficulties that might impede the child's performance (e.g., visual acuity difficulties, color blindness)?
- Are there any signs of negativism or uncooperative behavior? If so, what are the signs?

A useful testing-of-limits procedure is to ask the child the reasons for the chosen responses: "Tell me the reason why these two [three] pictures go together."

High scores on the Picture Concepts subtest may indicate good conceptual thinking, good ability to see relationships, good logical and abstract thinking ability, good ability to discriminate fundamental from superficial relationships, good ability to select appropriate relationships between two objects or concepts, or flexibility of thought processes.

Low scores on the Picture Concepts subtest may indicate poor conceptual thinking, difficulty in seeing relationships, poor logical and abstract thinking ability, difficulty in discriminating fundamental from superficial relationships, difficulty in selecting appropriate relationships between two objects or concepts, or rigidity of thought processes.

In some cases, low scores might be associated with bright children whose categorizations differ from those of the test constructor. To explore this hypothesis, ask the child to give you the reasons for the chosen responses.

The consistent full range of scaled scores from 1 to 19 at all ages aids in profile analysis.

CODING

Coding, a core Processing Speed subtest, requires that the child copy symbols paired with other symbols. The subtest consists of two separate and distinct parts. Each part uses a sample, or key.

In Coding A, which is given to children ages 6 to 7, the sample (or key) consists of five shapes (e.g., star, circle). Within each sample shape, there is a special mark (e.g., a vertical line, two horizontal lines). The child must place within each test shape (which is empty) the mark that is within the sample shape. There are 5 practice shapes, followed by 59 shapes in the subtest proper. Follow the directions on page 95 of the Administration Manual for children who are left-handed.

In Coding B, which is given to children ages 8 to 16, the sample (or key) consists of boxes containing a numeral from 1 to 9 in the upper part and a symbol in the lower part. Each number is paired with a different symbol. The test stimuli are boxes containing a number in the upper part and an empty space in the lower part. The child must write in the empty space the symbol that is paired with the number in the sample. There are 7 practice boxes, followed by 119 boxes in the subtest proper.

The subtest is timed and is relatively easy to administer and score.

Rationale

Coding assesses the child's ability to learn an unfamiliar task. The subtest involves the speed and accuracy of visual-motor coordination (or psychomotor speed), speed of mental operation (processing speed), attentional skills, visual acuity, visual scanning and tracking (repeated visual scanning between the code key and answer spaces), short-term memory for new learning (paired-associate learning of an unfamiliar code), cognitive flexibility (in shifting rapidly from one pair to another), handwriting speed, and, possibly, motivation. Success depends not only on comprehension of the task but also on fine-motor pencil-and-paper skills. The subtest is sensitive to visuosensory difficulties.

Coding also may involve a verbal-encoding process if the child attaches verbal descriptions to the symbols. For example, a child may label the = symbol as an "equal sign" or the 0 as a "circle" or "zero." Performance may be improved if the child uses verbal labels to code the symbols. Consequently, Coding can be described in part as measuring the ability to learn combinations of symbols and shapes and the ability to make associations quickly and accurately. The task requires the child to identify the shape (either verbally or nonverbally), go to the proper shape in the key, code the information, and carry this information in short-term memory long enough to reproduce the symbol in the space. Thus, Coding can be conceptualized as an information-processing task involving the discrimination and memory of visual pattern symbols.

Factor Analytic Findings

Coding is a fair measure of g (26% of its variance can be attributed to g). It contributes substantially to the Processing Speed Index (average loading = .63). Specificity is ample at all ages.

Reliability and Correlational Highlights

Coding is a reliable subtest (r_{xx} = .85), with reliability coefficients at or above .83 at 9 out of 11 age groups (range of .72 to .89). It correlates better with Symbol Search (r = .53) than with any of the other subtests. It has a moderate correlation with the Full Scale IQ (r = .57), moderately low correlations with the Verbal Comprehension Index (r = .34), the Perceptual Reasoning Index (r = .40), and the Working Memory Index (r = .30), and a high correlation with the Processing Speed Index (r = .88).

Administrative Guidelines

The following administrative guidelines for the Coding subtest must be followed carefully.

Background Considerations

1. Provide a smooth working surface by placing the Response Booklet over a piece of cardboard, if needed.
2. Read the instructions verbatim.
3. Read the instructions clearly.
4. Repeat the instructions if the child asks or has not responded within 5 to 10 seconds, unless it is clear that the child is considering a response.
5. Point to the key as you read the instructions.
6. Wait until the child understands the task before proceeding with items.
7. Use a stopwatch quietly, if possible.
8. Keep the stopwatch on the table, if needed, but out of the child's reach, and handle it unobtrusively.
9. Both Coding A and Coding B have a 120-second time limit; however, practice items are not timed. Begin timing after the last word of instructions. Once timing has begun, do not stop timing to clarify instructions.
10. Note the child's handedness and write it in the space provided for Notes on the Behavioral Observations page of the Record Form.
11. Coding may penalize a left-handed child if the way the child writes causes him or her to cover the key immediately above the line of writing. If this is the case, the child will have to lift her or his hand repeatedly during the task to view the key. If the child is left-handed, place a second Response Booklet to the right of the first Response Booklet so that the key in the second Response Booklet for the sample and subtest items is aligned with the key in the first Response Booklet.
12. Demonstrate the sample.

13. Give the child a number 2 pencil without an eraser. Both you and the child should use pencils without erasers.
14. Does not provide or allow for the use of an eraser.
15. Give instructions verbatim, including the word "Go," even if explanations are not necessary.
16. Give further explanations, if necessary, before saying "Go."
17. If the child asks about a mistake, say, "That's OK. Just keep working as fast as you can" (see p. 95 of the Administration Manual). If the child omits an item, begins to complete a row in reverse order, or skips a complete row, say, "Do them in order. Don't skip any," and then point to the first omitted item and say, "Do this one next." These are new instructions authorized by The Psychological Corporation (personal communication, November 2003, Diane Coalson, Senior Research Director, The Psychological Corporation). Give this prompt as often as needed within the time limit, even though the Administration Manual says, "Give no further assistance . . . ." (personal communication, November 2003, Diane Coalson, Senior Research Director, The Psychological Corporation). If the child stops prematurely, say, "Keep working until I tell you to stop" (or something similar).
18. Count the time taken to give prompts as part of the 120-second time limit.
19. Allow the child to make spontaneous corrections unless the corrections are done repeatedly or impede the child's performance. When the child does so repeatedly, say something like "Try not to make so many corrections" or "Work as fast as you can without making mistakes."

Starting Considerations

20. Start with the appropriate item.
  a. The ages listed under "Start" on page 94 of the Administration Manual are always intended to be inclusive; thus, ages 6–7 means children 6-0 to 7-11 years of age and ages 8–16 means children 8-0 to 16-11 years of age.
  b. The starting ages on the Record Form are also inclusive.
  c. Children 6 to 7 years of age are given Coding A, and children 8 to 16 years of age are given Coding B.
  d. Coding A is located on page 1 in Response Booklet 1, while Coding B is located on page 2 in Response Booklet 1.
  e. When you administer the practice items, correct the child's mistakes immediately.

  f. Do not start the subtest until the child clearly understands the task.
  g. There is no reverse sequence on the Coding subtest.

Discontinue Considerations

21. Discontinue the subtest (a) if the child still does not understand the task after instructions have been given and further explanation provided, (b) after 120 seconds, or (c) when the child finishes before the time limit.
22. Stop timing if the child finishes before 120 seconds.
23. After 120 seconds, say, "Stop" and discontinue the subtest.
24. Once the subtest is completed, close the Response Booklet and remove it from the child's view.

Scoring Guidelines

25. Score the subtest using the following guidelines.
  a. Use the template to score the subtest.
  b. Score only items completed within the allotted 120 seconds. Do not give credit for any items completed after 120 seconds.
  c. On Coding A, give 1 point for each correct item, and give as many as 6 additional time-bonus points for a perfect score. On Coding B, give 1 point for each correct item, but do *not* give time-bonus points.
  d. Do not include the responses to the practice items in scoring the subtest.
  e. Give credit for any symbol identifiable as a keyed symbol and distinguishable from other symbols; therefore, do not penalize the child for imperfectly drawn symbols.
  f. Give credit for symbols that are spontaneously corrected within the time limit, including a spontaneously drawn correct symbol near an incorrectly drawn symbol.
  g. Use the appropriate side of the Coding Scoring Key to score the subtest, and align the key properly.
  h. Do not count any item that was *not* attempted (i.e., either skipped or not reached before the time elapsed).
  i. To prolong the life of the Scoring Key, which has the cumulative number of symbols at the end of each row, you may want to laminate the template.

Response Booklet

26. Enter the child's name, examiner's name, date, and child's age on Response Booklet 1.

Record Form

27. Record the time in seconds in the Completion Time box.
28. On Coding A, if the child has a perfect score (59 points) and finishes before 116 seconds, circle the appropriate time-bonus points.
29. Add the points.
30. Enter the Total Raw Score in the shaded box.

Interpretive Suggestions

The following questions are useful to guide your observation of the child's performance on the Coding subtest.

- Does the child understand the task?
- Does the child understand and proceed correctly after you give an explanation?
- Does the child use one hand to hold the paper in place and the other hand to draw the symbols?
- Is the child impulsive?
- Is the child meticulous?
- Does the child seem overly anxious?
- Does the child display tremor?
- Does the child's speed increase or decrease as the subtest proceeds?
- Are the child's symbol marks well executed, barely recognizable, or incorrect?
- Do the child's symbol marks show any distortions, such as reversals? If so, do the distortions appear only once, occasionally, or each time the child draws the symbol mark? How many different symbols are distorted?
- Are there any noticeable differences in the quality of symbols drawn early and late in the task?
- Does the child draw the same symbol repeatedly even though the shapes/numbers change (perseveration)?
- Is the child penalized for slowness, inaccuracy, or both?
- Are the child's failures associated with inadequate form perception or with poor attention?
- Does the child check each symbol with the sample, or does the child seem to remember the symbols (e.g., not look up at the code at the top of the page)?
- Does the child recheck every symbol before moving on to the next one?
- Does the child try to pick one shape/number only and skip the others?
- Is the child's work smooth and orderly, or does the child seem confused at times and have difficulty finding the place?
- Is the child aware of any errors?
- Do the child's errors occur in some regular manner?
- How does the child react to errors?
- Is the child persistent?
- Does the child need urging to continue the task?
- Does the child appear bored with the task?
- Does the child hold the pencil in an appropriate or inappropriate way?
- Is the child's hand steady or shaking?
- Does the child try to use an eraser from another pencil or another source? If so, does the child seem to realize that an eraser is not supposed to be used?
- Does the child stop in the middle of the task, stretch, sigh, look around, or talk?
- Does the child talk, sing, or hum while working?

Answers to the above questions will provide information about the child's attention span, method of working, and other behaviors. If the child makes many errors, consider whether the errors might be related to impulsivity, poor self-monitoring, poor self-correction, or visual-motor difficulties. An increase in speed, coupled with correct copying of symbols, suggests that the child is adjusting well to the task. A decrease in speed, coupled with incorrect copying of symbols, suggests that the child may be showing fatigue. And a decrease in speed, coupled with correct copying of symbols, suggests that the child may be bored, distracted, or fatigued.

Coding is particularly useful for evaluating a child's attention when you suspect attentional difficulties, such as in cases of attention-deficit/hyperactivity disorder, anxiety, or a traumatic brain injury. If other tests indicate that the child has adequate response speed and visual acuity, then poor scores on Coding are likely to be associated with attentional deficits and not visuosensory difficulties per se. A slow and deliberate approach may suggest depressive features.

Distortion of forms may mean that the child has perceptual difficulties. To discern whether the symbol has some symbolic meaning to the child, ask the child about any symbol that was written peculiarly. Perseveration may suggest neurological difficulties that should be investigated further. Boredom might be present with a bright child who is not challenged by the task.

High scores on the Coding subtest may indicate good visual sequential processing ability, good visual-motor dexterity, good attention and concentration, good ability to learn new material associatively and reproduce it with speed and accuracy, sustained energy or persistence, motivation, or desire for achievement.

Low scores on the Coding subtest may indicate poor visual sequential processing ability, poor visual-motor dexterity, poor attention and concentration, difficulty in learning new material associatively and reproducing it with speed and accuracy, lethargy or boredom, limited motivation, distractibility, anxiety, poor pencil control, perfectionism (e.g., excessive concern for detail in reproducing symbols), difficulty in working under time pressure, or impulsivity.

After the *entire test* is completed, you can go back to the Coding subtest and ask the child about how the symbol-shape/number combinations were remembered. This testing-of-limits procedure may give you insight about the strategies the child used on the task. You also may want to review each symbol that was copied incorrectly and ask the child to tell you whether it looks like the symbol in the key.

The consistent full range of scaled scores from 1 to 19 at all ages aids in profile analysis.

VOCABULARY

Vocabulary, a core Verbal subtest, requires the child to look at pictures and give the names of the objects (items 1 to 4) or to define words you have read aloud (items 5 to 36). The subtest contains 36 items (4 picture items and 32 word items). The child is asked to give names (e.g., "What is this?") for items 1 to 4 and to explain the meaning of words ("What is a ____?" or "What does ____ mean?") for items 5 to 36. The two different item types—naming pictures and defining words—measure different types of lexical knowledge. Vocabulary is relatively easy to administer and difficult to score.

Rationale

Vocabulary, a test of word knowledge, assesses several cognitive factors—such as the child's learning ability, fund of information, richness of ideas, memory, concept formation, and language development—that may be closely related to the child's home environment and, to some extent, educational experiences. Since a well-developed vocabulary is a reflection of the child's ability to learn and to accumulate information, the subtest provides an excellent estimate of intellectual ability. Performance on the subtest is stable over time and relatively resistant to neurological deficit and psychological disturbance. Scores on the Vocabulary subtest provide a useful index of the child's general mental ability.

Factor Analytic Findings

Vocabulary is a good measure of g (69% of its variance can be attributed to g). It is the best measure of g in the scale. It contributes substantially to the Verbal Comprehension Index (average loading = .80). Specificity is ample at age 6, adequate at ages 7, 11, and 13 to 16, and inadequate at ages 8 to 10 and 12.

Reliability and Correlational Highlights

Vocabulary is a reliable subtest ($r_{xx} = .89$), with reliability coefficients above .82 at each age (range of .82 to .94). It correlates better with Information ($r = .75$) than with any of the other subtests. It has a moderately high correlation with the Full Scale IQ ($r = .79$), a high correlation with the Verbal Comprehension Index ($r = .91$), moderate correlations with the Perceptual Reasoning Index ($r = .58$) and the Working Memory Index ($r = .53$), and a moderately low correlation with the Processing Speed Index ($r = .39$).

Administrative Guidelines

The following administrative guidelines for the Vocabulary subtest must be followed carefully.

Background Considerations

1. Read the directions verbatim.
2. Read the directions clearly.
3. Pronounce each word clearly and correctly, especially for children 6 to 8 years of age, because you are not allowed to show the words to children in this age group or to spell the words. For children 9 to 16 years of age, you also must pronounce the words carefully, but the children see the words in the Stimulus Book in addition to hearing the words. Use the local pronunciation of each word or the pronunciation that might be familiar to the child.
4. Repeat the instructions if the child asks or has not responded within 5 to 10 seconds, unless it is clear that the child is considering a response.
5. You can repeat each item as often as necessary, but do not change the wording in any way. If the child's response suggests that a word was misunderstood, repeat the question with emphasis on the particular word.
6. If you suspect that the child has not heard a word correctly, say, "Listen carefully, what does ____ mean?" or use similar neutral wording.
7. Place the closed Stimulus Book with the coil-bound edge facing the child so that the book is completely

flat when it is opened, and then open it to the appropriate page.

8. For items 1 to 4, open the Stimulus Book, point to the picture, and say, "What is this?"

9. For items 5 to 36, point to each word in the Stimulus Book as you pronounce it. Use the Stimulus Book for items 5 to 36 only for children between 9 and 16 years of age.

10. Turn the pages of the Stimulus Book toward the child.

11. On items 1 to 4 (the picture items), query marginal responses, generalized responses, functional responses, and hand gesture responses as often as necessary. The Administration Manual (see pp. 100 and 101) gives suggested wording for such queries. However, on all items, query unclear or vague responses, as well as the sample responses marked by a "(Q)" in the Administration Manual. *This includes all the responses separated by semicolons on a line that has a "(Q)" at the end.* Do not query clearly wrong responses, personalized responses, or responses that are clearly correct. On items 11, 23, 32, and 33 (word items), use the specific query noted in the Administration Manual (see pp. 109, 117, 123, and 124). When you have any doubt about the acceptability of a response, ask the child for further elaboration or another meaning of the word, using the queries on page 101 of the Administration Manual.

12. When a perfect score (2) is not obtained on item 5 or 6, tell the child the correct answer.

13. On items 1 to 4 and 7 to 36, do not give the child the correct answer.

14. If the child fails to respond and has been performing poorly, wait about 30 seconds before going to the next item and say, "Let's try another one." However, use your judgment about moving to the next item sooner. For children who are clearly beyond their ability, 30 seconds may be a long time to wait, especially if it is the third or fourth 30-second wait. For example, this would be the case for children who seem to be bored, who are shrugging their shoulders, or who are looking around the room after a few seconds and not looking at the item.

15. If the child fails to respond but has been performing successfully and appears to be working on a response, give the child the necessary time to respond before going to the next item.

Starting Considerations

16. Start with the appropriate item.
   a. The ages listed under "Start" on page 100 of the Administration Manual are always intended to be in-

clusive; thus, ages 6–8 means children 6-0 to 8-11 years of age, ages 9–11 means children 9-0 to 11-11 years of age, and ages 12–16 means children 12-0 to 16-11 years of age.
   b. The starting ages on the Record Form are also inclusive.
   c. Children 6 to 8 years of age (and older children suspected of having intellectual deficiency) start with item 5.
   d. Children 9 to 11 years of age (not suspected of having intellectual deficiency) start with item 7.
   e. Children 12 to 16 years of age (not suspected of having intellectual deficiency) start with item 9.

Reverse Sequence

17. If necessary, administer the items in reverse sequence as directed in the Administration Manual.
   a. The instructions on page 100 of the Administration Manual under the heading "Reverse" pertain to all children.
   b. If the child (a) does not obtain full credit on the start-point item or (b) obtains full credit on the start-point item and a score of 0 on the next item, administer the items in reverse sequence.
   c. Continue the reverse sequence until the child has perfect scores on two consecutive items or until item 1 has been administered, even if the discontinue criterion is met.
   d. When there is a reverse sequence, the discontinue criterion is not met, and either there are two consecutive items with perfect scores or item 1 is administered, continue administration with the item after the last start-point item.

Discontinue Considerations

18. Count items administered in reverse sequence toward the discontinue criterion.

19. Discontinue the subtest when five consecutive scores of 0 are obtained, unless the consecutive 0's are obtained during a reverse sequence and (a) item 1 has not been reached or (b) the child has not obtained perfect scores on two consecutive items.

20. Once the subtest is completed or once the picture items have been administered, remove the Stimulus Book from the child's view.

Scoring Guidelines

21. Score the responses using the following guidelines.
   a. Study the General Scoring Principles on page 103 of the Administration Manual and use the sample responses as guidelines to help you score responses.

b. Items 1 to 4 (the four picture items) are scored 0 or 1.

c. Items 5 to 36 (the word items) are scored 0, 1, or 2.

d. On items 1 to 4, give 0 points for inappropriate marginal, generalized, or functional responses, for hand gestures, or for personalized responses.

e. On items 5 to 36, give 0 points for obviously incorrect answers; responses to queries that show no real understanding; demonstrations without elaboration in words; responses that are vague, trivial, or lacking in content; and regionalisms and slang not recognized in dictionaries.

f. On all items, give 0 points for a multiple response that has both correct and incorrect definitions, with the incorrect portion of the answer revealing a fundamental misunderstanding of the item; this is a spoiled response.

g. On items 5 to 36, award 1 point for minimal content responses, vague synonyms, less pertinent synonyms, minor uses, a less definitive feature, an unelaborated example using the word itself, a definition of a related word, or an unelaborated concrete interpretation of the word.

h. On items 5 to 36, award 2 points for appropriate synonyms, major uses, general classifications, a primary feature, several less definitive but correct descriptive features, or a definitive example (for verbs).

i. In scoring the responses, do not consider the child's elegance of expression.

j. Do not penalize the child for articulation problems or for faulty pronunciation. Use your judgment in deciding, based on the response, whether the child knows what the word means, despite an inability to pronounce the word clearly.

k. Give credit for all meanings recognized by standard dictionaries.

l. Score the entire response, including the response to the query.

m. When parts of the response vary in quality but none spoil the entire response, score the best response.

n. Score the response without considering extraneous parts of the response.

o. Inquiring about borderline responses and carefully studying the scoring guidelines may help you resolve some scoring problems.

p. When you have any doubt about the acceptability of a response, ask the child for another meaning of the word.

q. When the child earns perfect scores on the first two items at the start point or in a reversal, award full credit for all preceding items, regardless of the child's performance on these items if they have been administered.

r. Award no points for any items beyond the last score of 0 required for the discontinue criterion to be met, regardless of the child's performance on these items if they have been administered.

Record Form

22. For each item administered, record the child's responses verbatim in the Response column.

23. Circle 0 or 1 in the Score column for items 1 to 4 and circle 0, 1, or 2 for items 5 to 36.

24. To note the points awarded for items not administered below the first two items with perfect scores, put a slash mark in the Score column over the item preceding the first two items with perfect scores and write the numerals for these points.

25. Add the points, including the points for correct answers and the points for items not administered before the first two perfect scores, but not for items administered after the last discontinue item.

26. Enter the Total Raw Score in the shaded box.

The Vocabulary subtest is administered in two different ways, depending on the child's age. For children 9 years of age and older, the examiner presents the items visually as well as verbally, whereas for children younger than 9 years of age, the examiner presents the items verbally only. This means that children 9 years of age and older who can read are given more assistance than younger children because they not only hear the words, but see them as well. This procedure is likely to be useful, especially if the examiner speaks with an accent or has some difficulty pronouncing words or if children have a hearing problem or attention difficulties. Children less than 9 years of age who can read are also not given the aid of the printed words.

Scoring Vocabulary items is difficult because the scoring criteria are often subtle. The Administration Manual (p. 103) notes that "several less definitive but correct descriptive features that cumulatively indicate understanding of the word" receive 2 points. However, it is difficult to determine precisely what constitute "several less definitive but correct descriptive features" for each stimulus word.

Interpretive Suggestions

The following questions are useful to guide your observation of the child's performance on the Vocabulary subtest.

- Is the child definitely familiar with the word or only vaguely familiar with it?
- What is the quality of the child's definitions (e.g., precise and brief, indirect and vague, or verbose and lengthy)?
- Are the child's responses objective or subjective (i.e., do they relate to impersonal or personal experiences)?
- Does the child confuse the word with another one that sounds like it?
- Does the child guess if the meaning of a word is not known?
- Does the child readily say, "I don't know" and shake off further inquiries, or does the child pause, ponder, or think aloud about the item?
- Does the child show signs of a possible hearing difficulty? If so, what are the signs (e.g., hears words with some distortion)?
- Does the child easily express the meaning of a word, or does the child struggle to define the words?
- Does the child have mechanical difficulties with pronouncing words properly? If so, what are these difficulties?
- Does the child seem uncertain about how best to express thoughts?
- Does the child use gestures to illustrate responses or even depend on gestures exclusively?
- Are the child's responses synonyms for the stimulus word (e.g., thief: "A burglar"), or do they describe an action (e.g., thief: "Takes stuff")?
- Does the child describe a particular feature of the object (e.g., donkey: "It has four legs") or try to fit it into some category (e.g., donkey: "A living creature that is kept in a barn")?
- Does the child respond with any non-English words?
- Are 2-point responses given freely, or do they require query?
- Does the child's response pattern vary, or is it fairly consistent across items?
- Are there any emotional overtones or references to personal experiences in the child's responses (e.g., alphabet: "I hate to write")? If so, what are the emotional overtones?

Children's responses to the Vocabulary subtest may reveal something about their language skills, background, cultural milieu, social development, life experiences, responses to frustration, and thought processes. Try to determine the basis for incorrect responses, and distinguish among guesses, clang associations (i.e., responses that appear to be based on the sound of the stimulus word rather than on its meaning), and idiosyn-

cratic associations or bizarre associations. Whenever a child gives peculiar responses, mispronounces words, or has peculiar inflections, inquire further. Occasionally, you can identify language disturbances in the word definitions of children with a pervasive developmental disorder.

High scores on the Vocabulary subtest may indicate good word knowledge, good verbal comprehension, good verbal skills, good language development, good ability to conceptualize, intellectual striving, an enriched family or cultural background, or meaningful preschooling or schooling.

Low scores on the Vocabulary subtest may indicate poor word knowledge, poor verbal comprehension, poor verbal skills, poor language development, or poor ability to conceptualize. Low scores may also reflect a limited educational background, a home environment in which verbalization was not encouraged, or that English is the child's second language.

If you suspect word-retrieval problems, use a multiple-choice testing-of-limits procedure. This procedure may help you differentiate deficits associated with word-retrieval difficulties from those associated with deficient knowledge. After completing the *entire test*, go back to the item (or items) with which the child had difficulty and give the child three answers from which to choose. You might ask, for example, "Which one of the following does *pen* mean—something to eat, something to take to bed, or something to write with? Which one is it?" Be sure to randomly vary the position of the correct answer in the series (i.e., put the correct answer sometimes in first, sometimes in second, and sometimes in third position). If the child answers the multiple-choice questions correctly, the child has a word-retrieval difficulty and not deficient knowledge. However, the multiple-choice procedure should not be used to calculate an IQ.

If the child gave any responses during the subtest that are possibly indicative of a thought disorder, you may want to inquire about these responses. You might say, "When I asked you to tell me the meaning of _____, you said _____. Tell me more about your answer."

The consistent full range of scaled scores from 1 to 19 at all ages aids in profile analysis.

LETTER–NUMBER SEQUENCING

Letter–Number Sequencing, a core Working Memory subtest, contains 10 items, each consisting of three trials.

Each trial requires the child to order sequentially a series of numbers and letters that are orally presented in a specified random order. Children 6 and 7 years of age must pass two "Qualifying Items" that demonstrate their ability to count to 3 and to recite the alphabet correctly through at least the letter C. The subtest is not timed and is relatively easy to administer and score.

Rationale

To complete the Letter–Number Sequencing subtest successfully, the child must (a) simultaneously track letters and numbers, (b) arrange the numbers in ascending order, (c) arrange the letters in alphabetical order following the numbers, and (d) perform both mental operations without forgetting any part of the series. The Letter–Number Sequencing subtest involves attention, short-term auditory memory, and information processing. The subtest measures working memory—the ability to maintain information actively in conscious awareness, perform some operation or manipulation with it, and produce a result (Wechsler, 2003b).

Letter–Number Sequencing is a measure of the child's short-term auditory working memory, sequencing, mental manipulation, visual-spatial imaging, and attention. The child's performance on the Letter–Number Sequencing subtest may be affected by an ability to relax, as a child who is calm and relaxed may achieve a higher score than one who is excessively anxious. Because the child must recall auditory information and repeat the information aloud in proper sequence, the task also involves sequencing.

Factor Analytic Findings

Letter–Number Sequencing is a fair measure of g (43% of its variance can be attributed to g). It contributes moderately to the Working Memory Index (average loading = .54). Specificity is ample at all ages.

Reliability and Correlational Highlights

Letter–Number Sequencing is a reliable subtest (r_{xx} = .90), with reliability coefficients at or above .85 at each age (range of .85 to .92). It correlates better with Arithmetic ($r = .51$) than with any of the other subtests. It has moderate correlations with the Full Scale IQ ($r = .69$) and the Verbal Comprehension Index ($r = .52$), moderately low correlations with the Perceptual Reasoning Index ($r = .48$) and the Processing Speed Index ($r = .40$),

and a high correlation with the Working Memory Index ($r = .86$).

Administrative Guidelines

The following administrative guidelines for the Letter–Number Sequencing subtest must be followed carefully.

Background Considerations

1. Read the directions verbatim.
2. Read the directions clearly.
3. Repeat the instructions if the child asks or has not responded within 5 to 10 seconds, unless it is clear that the child is considering a response.
4. Be sure that the child cannot see the digits and letters in the Administration Manual or on the Record Form.
5. Administer the first qualifying item, and then give the second one if the child passes the first one.
6. Administer the two trials of the sample, regardless of the child's response on the first trial.
7. If the child makes an incorrect response on trial 1 of the sample, correct the child and readminister trial 1.
8. If the child makes an incorrect response on trial 2 of the sample, correct the child and readminister trial 2.
9. Proceed with the subtest even if the child makes incorrect responses on both trials of the sample.
10. Administer item 1 after the sample.
11. Read the digits and letters singly and distinctly, at the rate of one number or letter per second without chunking—that is, do not break up the digits or letters into groups by unintentionally pausing between sets of digits as you read them. Doing so may provide the child with a mnemonic device—chunking—that may make recall of the digits and letters easier. Practice reading speed with a stopwatch.
12. Drop your voice slightly on the last digit or letter in a sequence.
13. Always administer all three trials of each item.
14. Pause after each sequence to allow the child to respond.
15. Never repeat any of the digits or letters on any trial of a series during the subtest proper.
16. If the child asks you to repeat a trial, say, "Just take your best guess."
17. Correct the child using the appropriate wording if the child does not (a) state the number first on trial 1 of item 1, (b) reorder the letters on trial 2 of item 4, or (c) reorder the numbers on trial 1 of item 5. The third bullet under the General Directions heading on

page 126 of the Administration Manual should read, "On specific trials of items 1, 4, and 5, certain responses require prompts. Trials requiring a specific prompt are identified with an asterisk (*) in this Manual. Provide the prompt only for those responses indicated" (personal communication, November 2003, Diane Coalson, Senior Research Director, The Psychological Corporation).

18. Say nothing if the child makes a mistake on items 2, 3, and 6 to 10 or on trials 2 and 3 of item 1, trials 1 and 3 of item 4, and trials 2 and 3 of item 5.

Starting Considerations

19. Start with the appropriate item.
   a. The ages listed under "Start" on page 126 of the Administration Manual are always intended to be inclusive; thus, ages 6–7 means children 6-0 to 7-11 years of age and ages 8–16 means children 8-0 to 16-11 years of age.
   b. The starting ages on the Record Form are also inclusive.
   c. Children 6 to 7 years of age (and older children suspected of having intellectual deficiency) start with the counting qualifying item.
   d. Children 8 to 16 years of age (not suspected of having intellectual deficiency) start with the sample and then item 1. There is no reverse sequence on the Letter–Number Sequencing subtest.
   e. If children 6 to 7 years of age (or older children suspected of having intellectual deficiency) pass the counting qualifying item, administer the alphabet qualifying item.
   f. If children 6 to 7 years of age (or older children suspected of having intellectual deficiency) pass the alphabet qualifying item, administer the sample and then item 1.

Discontinue Considerations

20. Discontinue the subtest after failure on *either* of the qualifying items or after failure on all three trials of an item.

Scoring Guidelines

21. Score the items using the following guidelines.
   a. Do not count the two qualifying items in the final score.
   b. Items 1 to 10 are scored 0, 1, 2, or 3.
   c. The second bullet under the Score heading on page 127 of the Administration Manual should read, "If the indicated prompt is necessary for Item 1, Item 4, or Item 5, place a **P** on the Record Form to indicate that a prompt was given. For Item 1, the prompted

response is scored 1 point. The prompted responses for Items 4 and 5 are scored 0 points" (personal communication, November 2003, Diane Coalson, Senior Research Director, The Psychological Corporation).
   d. Give the child credit for each trial passed. Also give credit for any response in which the letters and numbers are in the correct sequence, regardless of whether the numbers or the letters are said first. Thus, for example, for item 1, trial 1, give credit for the response "L-2." Award no credit for responses given after a prompt.
   e. The item score is the sum of the scores on the three trials.

Record Form

22. Circle Y or N (Yes or No) in the Correct column, as appropriate.
23. Record the number of digits and letters correctly recalled in each trial by recording the exact sequence given by the child in the Verbatim Response column in the Record Form. A less desirable, but permissible, procedure is to record the letters and numbers correctly recalled in each series, either by placing a check mark above each letter or number correctly recalled or by putting a mark designating an incorrect answer on each letter or number missed.
24. Circle 0 or 1 in the Trial Score column for each item administered.
25. Circle 0, 1, 2, or 3 in the Item Score column for each item administered.
26. Add the points.
27. Enter the Total Raw Score in the shaded box.

Interpretive Suggestions

The following questions are useful to guide your observation of the child's performance on the Letter–Number Sequencing subtest.

- Is the child's performance effortless, or does the child seem to use much concentration?
- Does the child view the task as interesting, boring, or difficult?
- Does the child notice errors made when responding, or does the child think that the given responses are always correct?
- Does the child say the numbers first or the letters first?
- What strategy does the child use to recall the numbers and letters?

- What types of errors does the child make?
- Does the child respond immediately, or is there a long latency between the item presentation and the response?
- Does the child chunk digits or letters in the response?
- Does the child respond appropriately to prompts?

Because this subtest contains no cues (i.e., only a random series of letters and numbers is presented), children with hearing impairments may be especially prone to failure.

A good record can help you evaluate the child's performance. For example, a child who consistently fails to recall the last item in a letter-number series (e.g., for T-9-A-3 the child says, "3-9-A") is different from a child who says an incorrect letter (e.g., for T-9-A-3, the child says, "3-9-A-D"). Failing to recall a letter or number may reflect poor attention or concentration, whereas mistaking T for D may reflect an auditory discrimination problem. Unfortunately, the scoring system does not distinguish among failure patterns. For example, a child who places one letter out of sequence in a six-item series obtains the same score as a child who misses all six items, even though the second child's performance is less efficient than the first child's. Finally, although the child who gives the letters first and then the numbers receives credit, the response demonstrates poor understanding of the directions or inability to follow the directions. *Note that a child who gives the letters first and then the numbers in the correct order is not penalized.* This scoring rule is confusing, because the directions stress the importance of saying the numbers first, followed by the letters. Nevertheless, you must follow this scoring rule.

Strategies used to recall the numbers and letters include simply repeating what is heard, rehearsing the numbers and letters before saying them, visualizing the numbers and letters, chunking, and using a finger to write the numbers and letters.

Types of errors include omission errors (leaving one number or letter out of the correct sequence), addition errors (adding one or more numbers or letters to the correct sequence), perseveration errors (repeating one or more numbers or letters), sequential errors (giving the correct numbers and letters but in the wrong sequence), sequence reversal errors (giving the correct numbers and letters but reversing two or more of them), and auditory discrimination errors (e.g., saying the letter D instead of T).

High scores on the Letter–Number Sequencing subtest may indicate good auditory sequential processing, good short-term auditory memory, good working memory, good attention and concentration, or persistence.

Low scores on the Letter–Number Sequencing subtest may indicate poor auditory sequential processing, poor short-term auditory memory, poor working memory, inattention, distractibility, anxiety, impulsivity, or negativism.

The consistent full range of scaled scores from 1 to 19 for children 7 to 16 years of age aids in profile analysis. The restricted range of scaled scores from 2 to 19 for children 6 years of age somewhat limits profile analysis.

MATRIX REASONING

Matrix Reasoning, a core Perceptual Reasoning subtest, consists of individually presented colored matrices, each of which has a part missing. The child is asked to select the one pattern from an array of four or five choices that best completes the matrix. The subtest is composed of three samples and 35 subtest items and is not timed. It is relatively easy to administer and score.

Rationale

The Matrix Reasoning subtest involves perceptual reasoning ability without a speed component. Perceptual matching, attention to detail, concentration, classification, analogic reasoning, and serial reasoning are required for successful performance; spatial ability also may be involved for some children. Matrix Reasoning can be considered a measure of nonverbal fluid reasoning ability. Experience with part-whole relationships and pattern completion may be helpful, as may a willingness to respond when uncertain. Matrix Reasoning may also have a verbal mediation component and visuosensory and visuospatial construction skill components, but research is needed to determine whether this hypothesis holds for young children (cf. Dugbartey, Sanchez, Rosenbaum, Mahurin, Davis, & Townes, 1999).

Factor Analytic Findings

Matrix Reasoning is a fair measure of *g* (49% of its variance can be attributed to *g*). It contributes substantially to the Perceptual Reasoning Index (average loading = .54). Specificity is ample at all ages.

Reliability and Correlational Highlights

Matrix Reasoning is a reliable subtest (r_{xx} = .89), with reliability coefficients at or above .86 at all 11 age groups (range of .86 to .92). It correlates better with Block Design (r = .55) than with any of the other subtests. It has a moderately high correlation with the Full Scale IQ (r = .72), a moderate correlation with the Verbal Comprehension Index (r = .52), a high correlation with the Perceptual Reasoning Index (r = .84), and moderately low correlations with the Working Memory Index (r = .46) and the Processing Speed Index (r = .44).

Administrative Guidelines

The following administrative guidelines for the Matrix Reasoning subtest must be followed carefully.

Background Considerations

1. Read the directions verbatim.
2. Read the directions clearly.
3. Place the closed Stimulus Book with the coil-bound edge facing the child so that the book is completely flat when it is opened, and then open it to the appropriate page.
4. Position the Stimulus Book close to the child so that pointing to a response is easily accomplished. Also, if children rotate their bodies around the table, ask them to remain in their chairs during the test administration, and note this behavior in "Other Notes" on the back page of the Record Form and in the report if appropriate (personal communication, November 2003, Diane Coalson, Senior Research Director, The Psychological Corporation).
5. Turn the pages of the Stimulus Book toward the child during the subtest administration. Allow the child to rotate the Stimulus Book if he or she wants to do so (personal communication, February 5, 2004, Lisa Drozdick, Research Director, The Psychological Corporation).
6. If necessary, clarify the instructions by pointing across the response options and to the box with the question mark as the instructions and items are read.
7. If any sample is failed, demonstrate the correct way to solve the problem.
8. Repeat the instructions if the child asks or has not responded within 5 to 10 seconds, unless it is clear that the child is considering a response.
9. If the child names the picture or says other types of things, other than pointing to the response option or saying the number of the response, say, "Show me." If the child points to or says the name of more than one box, say, "There is only one correct answer to each problem. Just choose the best one."
10. Provide feedback only on the three samples.
11. If the child fails to respond and has been performing poorly, wait about 30 seconds before going to the next item and say, "Let's try another one." However, use your judgment about moving to the next item sooner. For children who are clearly beyond their ability, 30 seconds may be a long time to wait, especially if it is the third or fourth 30-second wait. For example, this would be the case for children who seem to be bored, who are shrugging their shoulders, or who are looking around the room after a few seconds and not looking at the item.
12. If the child fails to respond but has been performing successfully and appears to be working on a response, give the child the necessary time to respond before going to the next item.

Starting Considerations

13. Start with the appropriate item.
   a. The ages listed under "Start" on page 131 of the Administration Manual are always intended to be inclusive; thus, ages 6–8 means children 6-0 to 8-11 years of age, ages 9-11 means children 9-0 to 11-11 years of age, and ages 12–16 means children 12-0 to 16-11 years of age.
   b. The starting ages on the Record Form are also inclusive.
   c. All children are given the three samples. These items are intended to help them understand the instructions.
   d. Children 6 to 8 years of age (and older children suspected of having intellectual deficiency) begin with the three samples and then item 4.
   e. Children 9 to 11 years of age (not suspected of having intellectual deficiency) begin with the three samples and then item 7.
   f. Children 12 to 16 years of age (not suspected of having intellectual deficiency) begin with the three samples and then item 11.
   g. If the child fails the three samples, proceed to the appropriate start-point item.

Reverse Sequence

14. If necessary, administer the items in reverse sequence as directed in the Administration Manual.
   a. The instructions on page 131 of the Administration Manual under the heading "Reverse" pertain to all children.
   b. If the child (a) does not obtain full credit on the start-point item or (b) obtains full credit on the start-

point item and a score of 0 on the next item, administer the items in reverse sequence.

c. Continue the reverse sequence until the child has perfect scores on two consecutive items or until item 1 has been administered, even if the discontinue criterion is met.

d. When there is a reverse sequence, the discontinue criterion is not met, and either there are two consecutive items with perfect scores or item 1 is administered, continue administration with the item after the last start-point item.

Discontinue Considerations

15. Count items administered in reverse sequence toward the discontinue criterion.
16. Discontinue the subtest when four consecutive or four of five consecutive scores of 0 are obtained, unless the consecutive 0's are obtained during a reverse sequence and (a) item 1 has not been reached or (b) the child has not obtained perfect scores on two consecutive items.
17. Once the subtest is completed, remove the Stimulus Book from the child's view.

Scoring Guidelines

18. Score the items using the following guidelines.
a. All items are scored 0 or 1.
b. When the child earns perfect scores on the first two items at the start point or in a reversal, award full credit for all preceding items, regardless of the child's performance on these items if they have been administered.
c. Award no points for any items beyond the last score of 0 required for the discontinue criterion to be met, regardless of the child's performance on these items if they have been administered.
d. Although there appear to be two correct answers for item 26, follow the scoring guidelines in the Administration Manual.

Record Form

19. Circle the response number or DK (don't know) for all sample and subtest items administered.
20. Circle 0 or 1 in the Score column for each item administered.
21. To note the points awarded for items not administered below the first two items with perfect scores, put a slash mark in the Score column over the item preceding the first two items with perfect scores and write the numerals for these points.

22. Add the points, including the points for correct answers and the points for items not administered before the first two perfect scores, but not for items administered after the last discontinue item.
23. Enter the Total Raw Score in the shaded box.

Interpretive Suggestions

The following questions are useful to guide your observation of the child's performance on the Matrix Reasoning subtest.

- What is the tempo of the child's responses (e.g., fast, slow, deliberate, impulsive, careful)?
- Are there any signs of a response set (i.e., child points to the same numbered choice for each item)?
- If the child takes a long time to respond, what might the reasons be for the long response time (e.g., depression, thoughtfulness, inability to make a decision, anxiety, hope that the right answer will somehow come to her or him)?
- How does the pattern of responding on Matrix Reasoning compare with the child's pattern of responding on other subtests?
- Are there any indications of visual difficulties that might impede the child's performance (e.g., visual acuity difficulties, color blindness)?
- On what types of items does the child have difficulty (e.g., pattern recognition)?
- Does the child point or trace items to assist in responding?
- Are there signs of negativism or uncooperative behavior? If so, what are the signs?
- Does the child talk, sing, or hum while working?

After you administer the *entire test*, you can ask the child about strategies used to solve the problems. The reply may provide insight about the child's problem-solving strategies.

High scores on the Matrix Reasoning subtest may indicate good perceptual organization ability, good reasoning ability, good attention to detail, good concentration, good vision, and persistence.

Low scores on the Matrix Reasoning subtest may indicate poor perceptual organization ability, poor reasoning ability, poor attention to detail, poor concentration, visual problems, limited motivation, or impulsivity.

The consistent full range of scaled scores from 1 to 19 at all ages aids in profile analysis.

COMPREHENSION

Comprehension, a core Verbal Comprehension subtest, requires the child to explain situations, actions, or activities that relate to events familiar to most children. The questions cover several content areas, including survival skills, health practices, knowledge of one's body, interpersonal relations, and social mores. The subtest contains 21 questions and is not timed. It is somewhat difficult to administer and score.

Rationale

On the Comprehension subtest, the child must understand given situations and provide answers to specific problems. Success depends on the child's possession of practical information, plus an ability to make use of previous experiences. Responses may reflect the child's knowledge of conventional societal customs and behaviors and the extensiveness of cultural opportunities, particularly exposure to middle-class mores and customs. Success suggests that the child has common sense, social judgment, and a grasp of social conventionality. These characteristics imply an ability to use facts in a pertinent, meaningful, and emotionally appropriate manner. Success is also based on the child's ability to verbalize acceptable reasons for why certain things are done in our culture.

Factor Analytic Findings

Comprehension is a good measure of g (53% of its variance can be attributed to g). It contributes substantially to the Verbal Comprehension Index (average loading = .73). Specificity is ample at ages 6, 8, 14, and 16, adequate at ages 9 and 10 to 13, and inadequate at ages 7 and 15.

Reliability and Correlational Highlights

Comprehension is a reliable subtest (r_{xx} = .81), with reliability coefficients at or above .74 at each age (range of .74 to .86). It correlates better with Vocabulary (r = .68) than with any of the other subtests. It has a moderately high correlation with the Full Scale IQ (r = .71), a high correlation with the Verbal Comprehension Index (r = .86), and moderately low correlations with the Perceptual Reasoning Index (r = .49), the Working Memory Index (r = .46), and the Processing Speed Index (r = .37).

Administrative Guidelines

The following administrative guidelines for the Comprehension subtest must be followed carefully.

Background Considerations

1. Read the instructions verbatim.
2. Read the instructions clearly.
3. Read the items verbatim.
4. Read the items clearly.
5. Repeat the instructions if the child asks or has not responded within 5 to 10 seconds, unless it is clear that the child is considering a response.
6. Repeat items correctly.
7. If the child is hesitant, say, "Yes" or "Go ahead" or another suitable statement. However, do not define words or give any other help not specifically indicated in the Administration Manual.
8. If the child gives a 0- or 1-point response to item 1, give the correct 2-point answer.
9. For items 2 to 21, do not tell the child the correct answers.
10. Query unclear or vague responses, as well as the sample responses marked by a "(Q)" in the Administration Manual. *This includes all the responses separated by semicolons on a line that has a "(Q)" at the end.* Do not query clearly wrong responses or responses that are clearly correct. For the nine items noted by an asterisk, prompt the child for a second response when the child's initial response reflects only one correct general concept. For these nine items, also prompt the child for a third response when the child's second response, given either spontaneously or as a result of a former query, reflects the same general concept as the child's first response.
11. If the child fails to respond and has been performing poorly, wait about 30 seconds before going to the next item and say, "Let's try another one." However, use your judgment about moving to the next item sooner. For children who are clearly beyond their ability, 30 seconds may be a long time to wait, especially if it is the third or fourth 30-second wait. For example, this would be the case for children who seem to be bored, who are shrugging their shoulders, or who are looking around the room after a few seconds and not looking at the item.
12. If the child fails to respond but has been performing successfully and appears to be working on a response, give the child the necessary time to respond before going to the next item.

Starting Considerations

13. Start with the appropriate item.
    a. The ages listed under "Start" on page 134 of the Administration Manual are always intended to be inclusive; thus, ages 6–8 means children 6-0 to 8-11 years of age, ages 9–11 means children 9-0 to 11-11 years of age, and ages 12–16 means children 12-0 to 16-11 years of age.
    b. The starting ages on the Record Form are also inclusive.
    c. Children 6 to 8 years of age (and older children suspected of having intellectual deficiency) start with item 1.
    d. Children 9 to 11 years of age (not suspected of having intellectual deficiency) start with item 3.
    e. Children 12 to 16 years of age (not suspected of having intellectual deficiency) start with item 5.

Reverse Sequence

14. If necessary, administer the items in reverse sequence as directed in the Administration Manual.
    a. The instructions on page 134 of the Administration Manual under the heading "Reverse" pertain to children who begin the subtest with item 3 or higher.
    b. If the child (a) does not obtain full credit on the start-point item or (b) obtains full credit on the start-point item and a score of 0 on the next item, administer the items in reverse sequence.
    c. Continue the reverse sequence until the child has perfect scores on two consecutive items or until item 1 has been administered, even if the discontinue criterion is met.
    d. When there is a reverse sequence, the discontinue criterion is not met, and either there are two consecutive items with perfect scores or item 1 is administered, continue administration with the item after the last start-point item.

Discontinue Considerations

15. Count items administered in reverse sequence toward the discontinue criterion.
16. Discontinue the subtest when four consecutive scores of 0 are obtained, unless the consecutive 0's are obtained during a reverse sequence and (a) item 1 has not been reached or (b) the child has not obtained perfect scores on two consecutive items.

Scoring Guidelines

17. Score the items using the following guidelines.

    a. Study carefully the general scoring principle for each item. The Comprehension subtest is difficult to score, and children may give responses that differ from those provided in the Administration Manual.
    b. To score the child's response, use the general rule noted for each item.
    c. All items are scored 0, 1, or 2. The most complete or best response receives a score of 2; a less adequate response, 1; and an incorrect response, 0.
    d. For multiple responses, score the entire response given, rather than just the initial response.
    e. Added remarks that do not spoil an answer do not affect the score.
    f. If a child gives a response that has multiple parts, none of which spoils the entire response, and these parts could be scored separately as 0, 1, or 2, score the best response.
    g. Give 0 points for a multiple response that has both correct and incorrect concepts, with the incorrect portion of the answer revealing a fundamental misunderstanding of the item; this is a spoiled response.
    h. The scoring guidelines for Comprehension items 6, 8, 10, 14, 15, 16, 20, and 21 should say "or" instead of "and" in the last phrase of the guideline (personal communication, November 2003, Diane Coalson, Senior Research Director, The Psychological Corporation).
    i. When the child earns perfect scores on the first two items at the start point or in a reversal, award full credit for all preceding items, regardless of the child's performance on these items if they have been administered.
    j. Award no points for any items beyond the last score of 0 required for the discontinue criterion to be met, regardless of the child's performance on these items if they have been administered.

Record Form

18. Record the child's responses verbatim in the Response column.
19. Circle 0, 1, or 2 in the Score column for each item administered.
20. To note the points awarded for items not administered below the first two items with perfect scores, put a slash mark in the Score column over the item preceding the first two items with perfect scores and write the numerals for these points.
21. Add the points, including the points for correct answers and the points for items not administered before the first two perfect scores, but not for items administered after the last discontinue item.
22. Enter the Total Raw Score in the shaded box.

Interpretive Suggestions

The following questions are useful to guide your observation of the child's performance on the Comprehension subtest.

- Do the child's failures indicate misunderstanding of the meaning of a word or the implications of a particular phrase?
- Does the child provide a complete answer or just part of one?
- Does the child respond to the entire question or only to a part of it?
- Does the child seem to be objective, seeing various possibilities and choosing the best possible response?
- Is the child indecisive, unable to give firm answers?
- Are the child's responses too quick, indicating failure to consider the questions in their entirety?
- Does the child recognize when answers were sufficient or insufficient?
- How does the child respond when asked to explain his or her answer (e.g., becomes impatient, flustered, challenged by the request)?
- Are any of the child's responses unusual? If so, how?

Responses to the Comprehension questions may provide information about the child's personality style, ethical values, and social and cultural background. Unlike the Information questions, which usually elicit precise answers, the Comprehension questions may elicit more complex and idiosyncratic replies. Because the questions may involve judgment of social situations, the answers may reflect the child's social attitudes. Some responses may reveal understanding and acceptance of social mores, whereas others may reveal understanding but not acceptance of social mores. A child may know the right answers but not always act properly.

A child's replies may reveal initiative, self-reliance, independence, self-confidence, helplessness, indecisiveness, inflexibility, manipulative tendencies, naive perceptions of problems, cooperative solutions, hostility, aggression, or other traits. For example, a child with a dependent personality style might describe seeking help from others when faced with a problem situation.

Because Comprehension requires considerable verbal expression, the subtest may be sensitive to mild language impairments and to disordered thought processes. Be alert to language deficits (such as word-retrieval difficulties), circumstantial or tangential speech, or other expressive difficulties.

High scores on the Comprehension subtest may indicate skill in forming social judgments and in using common sense, skill in recognizing when practical judgment and common sense are necessary, skill in knowing the rules of conventional behavior, skill in organizing knowledge, skill in verbalizing, maturity, or having had wide experiences.

Low scores on the Comprehension subtest may indicate difficulty in forming social judgments and in using common sense, difficulty in recognizing when practical judgment and common sense are necessary, difficulty in knowing the rules of conventional behavior, difficulty in organizing knowledge, difficulty in verbalizing, immaturity, or having had limited experiences. In some cases, low scores may reflect either creativity in looking for unusual solutions or negativism.

If you suspect word-retrieval problems, use a multiple-choice testing-of-limits procedure. This procedure may help you distinguish between deficits associated with word-retrieval difficulties and those associated with deficient knowledge. After completing the *entire test*, go back to the item (or items) with which the child had difficulty and give the child three answers from which to choose. For example, say, "Why do we wear shoes—because shoes are hard to find, because shoes keep our feet dry when it rains, or because the heels wear out? Which one is it?" Be sure to randomly vary the position of the correct answer in the series (i.e., put the correct answer sometimes in first, sometimes in second, and sometimes in third position). If the child answers the multiple-choice questions correctly, the child may have a word-retrieval difficulty and not deficient knowledge. However, the multiple-choice procedure should not be used to calculate an IQ. Another testing-of-limits procedure is to ask the child to explain any unusual responses after the test is completed.

The consistent full range of scaled scores from 1 to 19 at all ages aids in profile analysis.

SYMBOL SEARCH

Symbol Search, a core Processing Speed subtest, requires the child to look at a symbol and then decide whether the symbol is present in an array of symbols. In Symbol Search A, which is given to children 6-0 to 7-11 years of age, there is one target symbol and three symbols in the array. The child is instructed to draw a slash (/) through the box labeled YES if the target symbol is also in the array. The child is instructed to draw a slash (/) through the box labeled NO if the target symbol is not in the array. The target symbols usually are nonsense shapes and designs, as are the symbols in the array. There are two demonstration (sample) items and two practice items. Part A contains 45 items, in addition to the two sample and two practice items.

In Symbol Search B, which is given to children 8-0 to 16-11 years of age, there are two target symbols and five symbols in the array. The child is instructed to draw a slash (/) through the box labeled YES if either of the target symbols is also in the array. The child is instructed to draw a slash (/) through the box labeled NO if neither of the target symbols is in the array. The target symbols, like those in Part A, are usually nonsense shapes and designs, as are the symbols in the array. There are two demonstration (sample) items and two practice items. Part B contains 60 items, in addition to the two sample and two practice items. Some symbols in Part A and Part B are the same. Each part has a 120-second time limit. Both parts of the subtest are relatively easy to administer and score.

Rationale

On the Symbol Search subtest, the child looks at a stimulus figure (target stimulus), scans an array, and decides whether the stimulus figure appears in the array. The task involves perceptual discrimination, speed and accuracy, visual scanning, attention and concentration, short-term memory, and cognitive flexibility (in shifting rapidly from one array to the next). Visual-motor coordination plays a role, although minor, because the only motor movement is that of drawing a slash. Part B is more complex than Part A because there are two target stimulus figures instead of one and five symbols in the array instead of three.

Most of the symbols used in the Symbol Search subtest will be difficult to encode verbally. However, the child may verbally encode some symbols to which verbal descriptions can be attached. These include, for example, ± (plus or minus), ∟ (L shape), > (greater than), ∩ (inverted U), and ⊢ (a T on its side). We need research to learn whether children verbally encode these or other symbols and whether the encoding affects their performance.

As in the Coding subtest, the speed and accuracy with which the child performs the Symbol Search task are measures of the child's intellectual ability. For each item, the child must inspect the target stimulus, go to the array, view the array items and determine whether the target stimulus is present, and then mark the appropriate box (YES or NO) once the decision is made. You can thus conceptualize Symbol Search as a task involving visual discrimination and visuosensory scanning.

Factor Analytic Findings

Symbol Search is a fair measure of g (37% of its variance can be attributed to g). It contributes moderately to the Processing Speed Index (average loading = .49). Specificity is ample at all ages.

Reliability and Correlational Highlights

Symbol Search is a relatively reliable subtest (r_{xx} = .79), with reliability coefficients at or above .78 at nine out of the 11 age groups (range of .78 to .82). It correlates better with Coding (r = .53) than with any of the other subtests. It has moderate correlations with the Full Scale IQ (r = .66) and the Perceptual Reasoning Index (r = .50), moderately low correlations with the Verbal Comprehension Index (r = .42) and the Working Memory Index (r = .40), and a high correlation with the Processing Speed Index (r = .87).

Administrative Guidelines

The following administrative guidelines for the Symbol Search subtest must be followed carefully.

Background Considerations

1. Provide a smooth working surface by placing the Record Booklet over a piece of cardboard, if needed.
2. Read the directions verbatim.
3. Read the directions clearly.
4. Repeat the instructions if the child asks or has not responded within 5 to 10 seconds, unless it is clear that the child is considering a response.
5. Use a stopwatch quietly, if possible.
6. Keep the stopwatch on the table, if needed, but out of the child's reach, and handle it unobtrusively.
7. During the sample and practice items, make sure that the child sees only the sample page of Response Booklet 1 (Symbol Search A on p. 3 for children 6 to 7 years of age and Symbol Search B on p. 7 for children 8 to 16 years of age).
8. Give the child a number 2 pencil without an eraser. Both you and the child should use pencils without erasers.
9. Open Response Booklet 1 to the appropriate page (p. 3 or p. 7).
10. Point to the target symbol and search groups for the samples as you read the instructions.

11. Draw a diagonal line through the correct YES or NO box for the samples.
12. Point to the target symbol and search groups for the practice items, and give appropriate instructions.
13. If the child makes the correct response on the first practice item, say, "Yes" or "Right."
14. If the child makes an error on the practice items, correct the error immediately by following the instructions on page 160 of the Administration Manual.
15. If the child does not understand the instructions or appears confused when doing the practice items, explain the instructions and demonstrate the task using the practice items.
16. Do not proceed to subtest items unless the child understands the task.
17. After the child understands the task and completes the practice items, open Response Booklet 1 to page 4 (Symbol Search A) or to page 8 (Symbol Search B).
18. Give the instructions verbatim, including the word "Go," even if explanations are not necessary.
19. If necessary, give further explanations before saying "Go."
20. After you say the last word of the instructions, begin timing immediately.
21. If the child reaches the end of the page and stops working, turn each page of Response Booklet 1 for the child.
22. Give the following appropriate prompts.
   a. If the child stops working after an item or after he or she reaches the end of a page before 120 seconds, say, "Keep working as fast as you can."
   b. If the child asks what to do about a mistake or asks for an eraser, say, "Keep working until I tell you to stop."
   c. If the child skips an item, omits an item, or begins to complete a page in reverse order, say, "Do them in order. Don't skip any." Point to the item that should be completed and say, "Do this one next."
23. Count the time taken to give prompts as part of the 120-second time limit.
24. Do not discourage the child from making spontaneous corrections unless the corrections impede performance. When the child does so repeatedly, say something like "Try not to make so many corrections" or "Work as fast as you can without making mistakes."

Starting Considerations

25. Start with the appropriate item.

   a. The ages listed under "Start" on page 157 of the Administration Manual are always intended to be inclusive; thus, ages 6–7 means ages 6-0 to 7-11 years and ages 8–16 means ages 8-0 to 16-11 years.
   b. The starting ages on the Record Form are also inclusive.
   c. Children 6-0 to 7-11 years of age are administered Symbol Search A. Start with the samples, then go to the practice items, and then go to the subtest items on page 4.
   d. Children 8-0 to 16-11 years of age are administered Symbol Search B. Start with the samples, then go to the practice items, and then go to the subtest items on page 8.
   e. Based on their chronological age, children suspected of having an intellectual deficiency are given either Symbol Search A or Symbol Search B.
   f. There is no reverse sequence on the Symbol Search subtest.

Discontinue Considerations

26. Discontinue the subtest (a) if the child still does not understand the task after instructions have been given and further explanation provided, (b) after 120 seconds, or (c) when the child finishes before the time limit.
27. If the child finishes before 120 seconds, stop timing.
28. After 120 seconds, say, "Stop" and discontinue the subtest.
29. After the child completes the subtest, close Response Booklet 1 and remove it from the child's view.

Scoring Guidelines

30. Score the subtest using the following guidelines.
   a. Use the template to score the subtest.
   b. Score only items completed within the allotted 120 seconds. Do not give credit for any items completed after 120 seconds.
   c. Align the scoring template properly by using the appropriate side of the Symbol Search Scoring Key.
   d. Record a + (plus) or a – (minus) sign next to each item in the Response Booklet.
   e. If both YES and NO are marked and there is no clear indication of self-correction, count the item as incorrect.
   f. If there is a clear indication of self-correction, score the final response.
   g. Do not count skipped items, items that have not been reached, or sample and practice items.

h. There are no time-bonus credits for either Part A or Part B.

Response Booklet

31. If Coding was not administered, enter the child's name and age, the date, and your name at the top of Response Booklet 1.
32. Enter the number of correct responses in the appropriate space at the bottom of each page of the Response Booklet.
33. Enter the number of incorrect responses in the appropriate space at the bottom of each page of the Response Booklet.

Record Form

34. Record the completion time in seconds in the Completion Time box.
35. Add the number of correct items (C) from the bottom of each page of Response Booklet 1, and enter the sum in the Number Correct box on the Record Form.
36. Add the number of incorrect items (I) from the bottom of each page of Response Booklet 1, and enter the sum in the Number Incorrect box on the Record Form.
37. Subtract the number of incorrect items from the number of correct items (not from the total number of items completed), and enter the score in the Total Raw Score box on the Record Form.
38. If the total raw score is equal to or less than 0 points, enter a 0.

Note that Symbol Search A contains two samples, two practice items, and 45 subtest items, while Symbol Search B contains two samples, two practice items, and 60 subtest items. Symbol Search A contains one target symbol and three symbols in the search group, while Symbol Search B contains two target symbols and five symbols in the search group. The sample and practice items are not timed, nor are they counted as part of the time limit.

Interpretive Suggestions

The following are useful questions to guide your observation of the child's performance on the Symbol Search subtest.

- Does the child use one hand to hold the paper in place and the other hand to draw the diagonal lines?
- How does the child approach the task (e.g., is the child impulsive, meticulous, overly anxious)?
- Does the child display tremor?
- As the subtest proceeds, does the child's speed increase or decrease?
- Are the child's diagonal lines (/) well executed, or are they barely recognizable?
- Does the child draw the diagonal lines slowly or quickly?
- Does the child make errors? If so, note the kinds of errors made, the manner in which they are made, the child's awareness of making errors, and the child's reaction to the errors. For example, does the child mark NO when there is a match for the stimulus figure or mark YES when there is not a match for the stimulus figure?
- How long does it take for the child to understand the task?
- Is there any pattern to the child's successes and failures? For example, does the child tend to succeed on items in which the target symbol is displayed in the search group but fail items in which the target symbol is not displayed in the search group?
- Does the child lose points for inaccuracy?
- Does the child recheck every item before moving on to the next one?
- Does the child frequently look back and forth between the target symbol or symbols and the search group?
- Is the child's work smooth and orderly, or does the child seem confused at times and have difficulty finding his or her place?
- Is the child persistent?
- Does the child need repeated urging to continue the task?
- Is the child bored with the task?
- Does the child hold the pencil in an appropriate way?
- Does the child try to use an eraser from another pencil or another source? If so, does the child seem to realize that an eraser is not supposed to be used?
- Does the child stop in the middle of the task, stretch, sigh, look around, or talk?
- Does the child talk, sing, or hum while working?
- Does the child work so slowly that the task is not completed within the allotted time? If so, what might account for this performance?
- Does the child put a premium on speed or accuracy (i.e., is the final score a result of the child's going too fast at the expense of making mistakes or going too slow at the expense of completing too few items)?

Answers to these questions (and similar ones) may give you information about the child's attention, persistence, impulsive tendencies, compulsive tendencies, and depressive tendencies. An increase in speed, coupled with success on items, suggests that the child is adjusting well to the task. A decrease in speed, coupled with failure on items, suggests that the child may be showing fatigue.

It may be of interest to compare children who obtain the same score in varying ways. For example, suppose two children each get a raw score of 25, but one child completes 25 items and has 25 correct and 0 incorrect items and the other child completes 45 items and has 35 correct and 10 incorrect items. These two children display different styles of working. The first child is slower than the second child but careful in approaching the task. Perhaps this first child is a meticulous worker who carries out tasks steadily and methodically. In contrast, the second child works faster, but makes errors. Perhaps this second child is somewhat careless and impulsive. To support your hypotheses, you will need to examine scores from other WISC–IV subtests, scores from other tests, and information from observations, interviews, and the case history.

Children may be penalized on the Symbol Search subtest if they (a) respond extremely slowly and carefully, (b) are compulsive and constantly check the target symbol against those in the search group, (c) are impulsive and fail to check the search group symbols against the target symbol, or (d) have trouble discriminating symbols. Again, look at the child's entire performance on the subtest (and all other sources of information) for possible hypotheses that might account for the child's performance on the Symbol Search subtest.

High scores on the Symbol Search subtest may indicate good processing speed ability, good perceptual discrimination ability, good attention and concentration, good short-term visual memory, sustained energy or persistence, motivation, or desire for achievement.

Low scores on the Symbol Search subtest may indicate poor processing speed ability, poor perceptual discrimination ability, poor attention and concentration, poor short-term visual memory, lethargy or boredom, limited motivation, limited desire to achieve, anxiety, difficulty in working under time pressure, or impulsivity.

For children who make many errors, one testing-of-limits procedure that can be carried out after the *entire test* is completed is to go over each item on which an error occurred. You can point to the items on which an error occurred and say, "Tell me about your answer" or "Tell me about why you marked that one." Another testing-of-limits procedure for highly distractible children is

to see whether their performance improves when they are provided with a ruler or a piece of paper with which to cover all the rows except the one to be completed.

The consistent full range of scaled scores from 1 to 19 at all ages aids in profile analysis.

THINKING THROUGH THE ISSUES

1. Why is it important to follow standard procedures in administering the WISC–IV?
2. When might you use testing-of-limits?
3. Do you believe that three subtests provide an adequate measure of a specific cognitive area?
4. How are the four composite scores related?
5. When would a composite score be more valid than the Full Scale IQ?

SUMMARY

1. This chapter provides information about the rationale, factor analytic findings, reliability and correlational highlights, administrative guidelines, and interpretive suggestions for the 10 WISC–IV core subtests.
2. Many of the WISC–IV subtests have enough subtest specificity (i.e., ample or adequate) at most ages to provide reliable estimates of specific abilities or at least to permit development of hypotheses about the underlying cognitive functions that the subtests may measure.
3. The best estimates of abilities are provided by the Full Scale IQ, followed by the Verbal Comprehension, Perceptual Reasoning, Working Memory, and Processing Speed Factors, the other combinations of subtests, and, finally, individual subtests.
4. In evaluating and interpreting the child's performance, always consider, in addition to the child's scores, the quality of the child's responses and the pattern of the successes and failures.

Block Design

5. Block Design measures nonverbal concept formation and requires perceptual organization, spatial visualization, and abstract conceptualization. The subtest is a fair measure of *g* and contributes substantially to the Perceptual Reasoning Index. Specificity is ample. Block Design is a reliable subtest

(r_{xx} = .86). It is somewhat difficult to administer and score.

Similarities

6. Similarities measures verbal concept formation. The subtest is a good measure of g and contributes substantially to the Verbal Comprehension Index. Specificity is ample, adequate, or inadequate, depending on the age level. Similarities is a reliable subtest (r_{xx} = .86). It is relatively easy to administer, but difficult to score.

Digit Span

7. Digit Span measures short-term auditory memory and attention. The subtest is a fair measure of g and contributes substantially to the Working Memory Index. Specificity is ample. Digit Span is a reliable subtest (r_{xx} = .87). It is relatively easy to administer and score.

Picture Concepts

8. Picture Concepts measures abstract, categorical reasoning based on perceptual recognition processes. The subtest is a fair measure of g and contributes moderately to the Perceptual Reasoning Index. Specificity is ample. Picture Concepts is a reliable subtest (r_{xx} = .82). It is relatively easy to administer and score.

Coding

9. Coding measures the speed and accuracy of visual-motor coordination, speed of mental operation, attentional skills, visual acuity, visual scanning and tracking, short-term memory, cognitive flexibility, handwriting speed, and, possibly, motivation. The subtest is a fair measure of g and contributes substantially to the Processing Speed Index. Specificity is ample. Coding is a reliable subtest (r_{xx} = .85). It is relatively easy to administer and score.

Vocabulary

10. Vocabulary measures learning ability, fund of information, richness of ideas, memory, concept formation, and language development. The subtest is a good measure of g and contributes substantially to the Verbal Comprehension Index. Specificity is ample, adequate, or inadequate, depending on the age level. Vocabulary is a reliable subtest (r_{xx} = .89). It is relatively easy to administer, but difficult to score.

Letter–Number Sequencing

11. Letter–Number Sequencing measures short-term auditory working memory, sequencing, mental manipulation, visual-spatial imaging, and attention. The subtest is a fair measure of g and contributes moderately to the Working Memory Index. Specificity is ample. Letter–Number Sequencing is a reliable subtest (r_{xx} = .90). It is relatively easy to administer and score.

Matrix Reasoning

12. Matrix Reasoning involves perceptual reasoning ability without a speed component. Perceptual matching, attention to detail, concentration, analogic reasoning, and serial reasoning are required for successful performance. Matrix Reasoning is a fair measure of g and contributes substantially to the Perceptual Reasoning Index. Specificity is ample. Matrix Reasoning is a reliable subtest (r_{xx} = .89). It is relatively easy to administer and score.

Comprehension

13. Comprehension measures common sense, social judgment, and a grasp of social conventionality. The subtest is a good measure of g and contributes substantially to the Verbal Comprehension Index. Specificity is ample, adequate, or inadequate, depending on the age level. Comprehension is a reliable subtest (r_{xx} = .81). It is somewhat difficult to administer and score.

Symbol Search

14. Symbol Search measures perceptual discrimination, speed and accuracy, attention and concentration, short-term memory, and cognitive flexibility. The subtest is a fair measure of g and contributes moderately to the Processing Speed Index. Specificity is ample. Symbol Search is a relatively reliable subtest (r_{xx} = .79). It is relatively easy to administer and score.

KEY TERMS, CONCEPTS, AND NAMES

STUDY QUESTIONS

1. Discuss the rationale for each of the 10 WISC–IV core subtests.

2. Describe the factor analytic findings for each of the 10 WISC–IV core subtests. In your description, compare and contrast the major factor analytic findings among the 10 subtests.

3. Discuss the reliability and correlational highlights for each of the 10 WISC–IV core subtests. In your discussion, compare and contrast the reliability and correlational highlights among the 10 subtests.

4. List some major administrative guidelines for each of the 10 WISC–IV core subtests.

5. Describe the interpretive suggestions for each of the 10 WISC–IV core subtests.

6. Which two of the 10 WISC–IV core subtests are the best measures of intelligence? Give the reasons for your answer.

3

WISC–IV SUPPLEMENTAL SUBTESTS

The true art of memory is the art of attention.
—Samuel Johnson

Goals and Objectives

This chapter is designed to enable you to do the following:

- Critically evaluate the five WISC–IV supplemental subtests

- Describe the rationales, factor analytic findings, reliability and correlational highlights, and administrative and interpretive considerations for the five WISC–IV supplemental subtests

This chapter covers the five WISC–IV supplemental subtests. As noted in Chapter 1, (a) Information and Word Reasoning can substitute for Similarities, Vocabulary, or Comprehension, (b) Picture Completion can substitute for Block Design, Picture Concepts, or Matrix Reasoning, (c) Arithmetic can substitute for Digit Span or Letter–Number Sequencing, and (d) Cancellation can substitute for Coding or Symbol Search. However, substitutions introduce unknown degrees of measurement error because the norm tables for the index scores and IQs do not take into account the substitution of supplemental subtests for core subtests.

PICTURE COMPLETION

Picture Completion, a supplemental Perceptual Reasoning subtest, requires the child to identify the single most important missing detail in 38 drawings of common objects, animals, and people—such as a bicycle, a dog, or a man. The child's task is to name or point to the essential missing portion of the incomplete picture within the 20-second time limit. The subtest is relatively easy to administer and score.

Rationale

On the Picture Completion subtest, the child must recognize the object depicted in the picture, appreciate its incompleteness, and determine the missing part. It is a test of visual discrimination—the ability to differentiate between essential and non-essential details. Picture Completion requires concentration, reasoning (or visual alertness), attention to detail, visual organization, and long-term visual memory (as many of the items require a child to have stored information from previous experience and to retrieve the information to determine what is incomplete about the figure).

Picture Completion also may measure the perceptual and conceptual abilities involved in visual recognition and identification of familiar objects. Perception, cognition, judgment, and delay of impulse all may influence performance. The time limit on the subtest places additional demands on the child. The richness of the child's life experiences also may affect her or his performance on the subtest.

Factor Analytic Findings

Picture Completion is a fair measure of g (44% of its variance can be attributed to g). It contributes substantially to the Perceptual Reasoning Index (average loading = .53). Specificity is ample at all ages except age 9, where it is adequate.

Reliability and Correlational Highlights

Picture Completion is a reliable subtest (r_{xx} = .84), with reliability coefficients at or above .81 at each of the 11 age groups (range of .81 to .87). It correlates better with Block Design (r = .54) than with any of the other subtests. It has a moderate correlation with the Full Scale IQ (r = .60), as well as with the Verbal Comprehension Index (r = .55) and the Perceptual Reasoning Index (r = .57), and a moderately low correlation with the Working Memory Index (r = .35) and the Processing Speed Index (r = .39).

Administrative Guidelines

The following administrative guidelines for the Picture Completion subtest must be followed carefully.

Background Considerations

1. Read the instructions verbatim.
2. Read the instructions clearly.
3. Read the items verbatim.
4. Read the items clearly.
5. Repeat the instructions if the child asks or has not responded within 5 to 10 seconds.
6. Place the closed Stimulus Book with the coil-bound edge facing and close to the child so that the book is completely flat when it is opened.
7. Open the Stimulus Book to the sample, and turn the pages one at a time to show consecutive pictures.
8. Allow 20 seconds for each item.
9. On items 3 to 38, if the child clearly understands the task, shorten or eliminate the instructions, if desired.
10. Begin timing after the last word of the instructions. Count any prompts as part of the 20-second time limit.
11. Stop timing when the child answers or after 20 seconds. Allow the child additional time after the time limit to complete his or her answer, if needed, but do not score as correct any response after the 20-second time limit.

12. Repeat the child's correct answer on the sample.

13. If the child gives an incorrect response (or no response) to the sample or to item 1 or 2, give the child the correct answer.

14. For items 3 to 38, do not give the child the correct answers.

15. Use each of the following prompts or queries *only once* during the subtest if the child (a) names the object instead of the missing part, (b) names a part that is off the picture, or (c) mentions an unessential missing part. Use the specific queries noted on page 164 of the Administration Manual.

16. After an ambiguous or incomplete response, say, "Show me where you mean" as often as needed.

17. If the child gives one of the responses noted in the right-hand column of pages 166 to 169 in the Administration Manual, say, "Show me where you mean." On item 29, one response requires a specific query.

Starting Considerations

18. Start with the appropriate item.
   a. The ages listed under "Start" on page 163 of the Administration Manual are always intended to be inclusive; thus, ages 6–8 means children 6-0 to 8-11 years of age, ages 9–11 means children 9-0 to 11-11 years of age, and ages 12–16 means children 12-0 to 16-11 years of age.
   b. The starting ages on the Record Form are also inclusive.
   c. Children 6 to 8 years of age (and older children suspected of having intellectual deficiency) start with the sample and then item 1.
   d. Children 9 to 11 years of age (not suspected of having intellectual deficiency) start with the sample and then item 5.
   e. Children 12 to 16 years of age (not suspected of having intellectual deficiency) start with the sample and then item 10.

Reverse Sequence

19. If necessary, administer the items in reverse sequence as directed in the Administration Manual.
   a. The instructions on page 163 of the Administration Manual under the heading "Reverse" pertain to the children who begin the subtest with the sample and then with item 5 or 10.
   b. If the child (a) does not obtain full credit on the start-point item or (b) obtains full credit on the start-point item and a score of 0 on the next item, administer the items in reverse sequence.

   c. Continue the reverse sequence until the child has perfect scores on two consecutive items or until item 1 has been administered, even if the discontinue criterion is met.
   d. When there is a reverse sequence, the discontinue criterion is not met, and either there are two consecutive items with perfect scores or item 1 is administered, continue administration with the item after the last start-point item.

Discontinue Considerations

20. Count items administered in reverse sequence toward the discontinue criterion.

21. Discontinue the subtest when six consecutive scores of 0 are obtained, unless the consecutive 0's are obtained during a reverse sequence and (a) item 1 has not been reached or (b) the child has not obtained perfect scores on two consecutive items.

22. Once the subtest is completed, remove the Stimulus Book from the child's view.

Scoring Guidelines

23. Score the items using the following guidelines.
   a. All items are scored 0 or 1.
   b. Give 0 points for an incorrect response, a spoiled response (e.g., a correct pointing response accompanied by an incorrect verbal response), or a correct response given after the 20-second time limit.
   c. Give 1 point for any reasonable response; the response does not have to be the exact name of the missing part. Therefore, give 1 point for a correct verbal *or* pointing response (including any verbal *or* pointing response listed in the *second column* on pages 166 to 169 of the Administration Manual), a synonym for the missing part, a description of the missing part, or a verbal response listed in the *third column* on pages 166 to 169 of the Administration Manual that is accompanied by a correct pointing response.
   d. After a query, score the best response.
   e. When the child earns perfect scores on the first two items at the start point or in a reversal, award full credit for all preceding items, regardless of the child's performance on these items if they have been administered.
   f. Award no points for any items beyond the last score of 0 required for the discontinue criterion to be met, regardless of the child's performance on these items if they have been administered.

Record Form

24. Record the child's responses verbatim in the Response column. As an optional procedure, you can also record the completion time in seconds in the Response column.
25. Use PC to record a correct pointing response.
26. Use PX to record an incorrect pointing response.
27. Circle 0 or 1 in the Score column for each item administered.
28. To note the points awarded for items not administered below the first two items with perfect scores, put a slash mark in the Score column over the item preceding the first two items with perfect scores and write the numerals for these points.
29. Add the points, including the points for correct answers and the points for items not administered before the first two perfect scores, but not for items administered after the last discontinue item.
30. Enter the Total Raw Score in the shaded box.

Interpretive Suggestions

The following questions are useful to guide your observation of the child's performance on the Picture Completion subtest.

- Does the child understand the task?
- Does the child respond with a word, with a description of the missing detail, or by pointing?
- Does the child give mainly verbal responses or pointing responses?
- Does the child respond impulsively, saying anything that comes to mind, or does the child search for the right answer?
- How does the child respond when the missing part is not identified (e.g., accepts the failure or finds fault with himself or herself or with the picture)?
- Does the child benefit from any queries listed on page 164 of the Administration Manual?
- What is the child's rate of response (e.g., quick and impulsive or slow and deliberate)?
- Is the child fearful of making an error, hesitant, or suspicious?
- Is the child aware of being timed? If so, does the timing make the child anxious or prompt the child to change the pace of responding?
- Does the child frequently use nondescriptive speech, such as "It's that thing there"?
- Does the child give roundabout descriptions of words (sometimes called *circumlocutions* or *paraphasic language*)?

- Does the child have trouble producing the right word?
- Does the child repeatedly say that nothing is missing?
- Does the child hold the Stimulus Book near or move close to it?
- Does child make a story about the picture while forming or giving a response?
- Is the child's response pattern consistent?
- Does the child have problems identifying specific items (e.g., does he or she ask what the picture is)?
- Does the child consistently miss items in which the missing part is in a specific area of the page (e.g., visual neglect)?
- How frequently does the child give correct answers after the time limit?
- Does the child attempt to turn pages of the Stimulus Book (showing impatience or a desire to control the testing situation)?

If the child's performance leaves any doubt as to whether he or she has normal vision, request a visual examination.

The child who usually responds in less than 5 seconds may be more impulsive, more confident, and, if correct, more skilled than the child who takes more time. The child who responds correctly after the time limit (for which no credit is received) may be more skilled than the child who fails the item even with additional time. Because the pass-fail scoring does not make provisions for such qualitative factors, carefully evaluate individual variations in each case and discuss these qualitative factors in the written report. Correct responses made slightly before or slightly after 20 seconds may suggest temporary inefficiency, insecurity, depression, or simply a slow and diligent approach, whereas extremely quick but incorrect responses may reflect impulsivity.

Circumlocutions, as well as difficulty producing the right word, suggest that the child has word-retrieval difficulties. Word-retrieval difficulties may be related to dysnomia (i.e., nominal aphasia), a form of aphasia in which the child has difficulty naming objects. A child who repeatedly says that nothing is missing may be revealing negativism. A child who holds the Stimulus Book close to his or her face or puts his or her face close to the Stimulus Book may have visual difficulties.

High scores on the Picture Completion subtest may indicate good perception and concentration, good alertness to details, good ability to differentiate between essential and nonessential details, or good ability to establish a learning set quickly.

Low scores on the Picture Completion subtest may indicate poor perception and concentration, poor alertness to details, difficulty in differentiating between essential and nonessential details, difficulty in establishing a learning set quickly, preoccupation with irrelevant details, anxiety, or negativism.

After you administer the subtest, you can inquire about the child's perceptions of the task: "How did you go about coming up with the answer?" or "How did you decide when to give an answer?" Inquire about any noteworthy or unclear answers. Children's behavior during this subtest may provide insight into their reaction to time pressure. As a testing-of-limits procedure, ask the child to look again at the pictures that were missed. Say, "Look at this picture again. Before, you said that ____ was missing. That's not the part that's missing. Look for something else." In some cases, it may be appropriate to ask the child to describe or name the picture, especially when many items are missed.

The consistent full range of scaled scores from 1 to 19 at all ages aids in profile analysis.

CANCELLATION

Cancellation, a supplemental Processing Speed subtest, contains two items: a random arrangement of pictures (item 1) and a structured arrangement of pictures (item 2). The child must scan the arrangements and mark each target picture (an animal) within a 45-second period. "Random arrangement" and "structured arrangement" refer to the layout of the pictures on the page. In item 1, the layout is haphazard, whereas in item 2, the layout is in neat rows and columns. To assist in the scoring, the template is divided into four quadrants. The placement of the 16 target animals in each quadrant is the same for each item. Two process scores—Cancellation Random (CAR) and Cancellation Structured (CAS)—are derived. The subtest is relatively easy to administer but somewhat difficult to score.

Rationale

On the Cancellation subtest, the child scans a page of relatively small, colorful pictures. The pictures include many types of animals (e.g., cow, bear, dog, fish) and objects (e.g., hat, umbrella, flashlight, saw). The child must examine each picture (or scan a part of the page) as quickly as possible and mark each picture that looks like an animal. The task involves perceptual discrimination, perceptual recognition ability, speed and accuracy, perceptual scanning ability, attention and concentration, short-term memory (i.e., remembering that only animals

are to be marked), persistence, and the ability to remain focused (i.e., not become distracted). Visual-motor coordination plays a role, although minor, because the only motor movement is that of drawing a line through the picture of an animal.

As in the Coding and Symbol Search subtests, the speed and accuracy with which the child performs the task are a measure of the child's intellectual ability. Thus, Cancellation can be conceptualized as a task involving visual recognition and visuosensory scanning.

Factor Analytic Findings

Cancellation is the poorest measure of g in the scale (7% of its variance can be attributed to g). It contributes substantially to the Processing Speed Index (average loading = .59). Specificity is ample at all ages.

Reliability and Correlational Highlights

Cancellation is a relatively reliable subtest (r_{xx} = .79), with reliability coefficients at or above .73 at each age (range of .73 to .84). It correlates better with Coding (r = .40) than with any of the other subtests. It has low correlations with the Full Scale IQ (r = .26), the Verbal Comprehension Index (r = .15), the Perceptual Reasoning Index (r = .20), and the Working Memory Index (r = .12), and a moderately low correlation with the Processing Speed Index (r = .41).

Administrative Guidelines

The following administrative guidelines for the Cancellation subtest must be followed carefully.

Background Considerations

1. Read the directions verbatim.
2. Read the directions clearly.
3. Repeat the instructions if the child asks or has not responded within 5 to 10 seconds, unless it is clear that the child is considering a response. If the child fails to understand the task, demonstrate the task again using the practice items.
4. Provide a smooth working surface by placing Response Booklet 2 over a piece of cardboard, if needed.

5. When you begin the subtest, show only the cover page of Response Booklet 2 to the child.
6. Use only a red pencil without an eraser, and do not provide the child with an eraser. (The Psychological Corporation chose red pencil so that the child's marks would contrast with the animals and be easier for the examiner to see. If the examiner has difficulty seeing red pencil, another color may be used. However, the pencil should always lack an eraser [personal communication, January 2004, Lisa Drozdick, Research Director, The Psychological Corporation].)
7. Use a stopwatch quietly, if possible.
8. Keep the stopwatch on the table, if needed, but out of the child's reach, and handle it unobtrusively.
9. When you administer the sample, direct the child's attention to the animals at the top of the page.
10. Point to the row of animals with a sweeping motion, left to right from the child's perspective.
11. Draw a line through the two animal pictures in the samples.
12. Point to the practice items while reading the instructions.
13. Say, "Yes" or "Right" for each animal correctly marked by the child on the practice item. If the child makes correct responses on all four practice items, say, "That's right. Now you know how to do them."
14. On the practice items, if the child marks fewer than four animals or marks a nonanimal, correct errors immediately, using the appropriate instructions.
15. If the child asks about what should be done if he or she makes a mistake, say, "That's OK. Just keep working as fast as you can" (see p. 171 of the Administration Manual). If the child stops prematurely, say, "Keep working until I tell you to stop" (or something similar).
16. Count the time taken to give prompts as part of the 45-second time limit for each item.
17. Allow spontaneous corrections unless the child does them repeatedly or they impede the child's performance. When the child does so repeatedly, say something like "Try not to make so many corrections" or "Work as fast as you can without making mistakes."
18. Proceed to item 1 only after you have administered the sample and practice items and the child understands the task. If the child appears confused or does not understand the task, repeat the explanation and demonstrate the task again using the practice items.
19. After the child completes the sample and practice items, open Response Booklet 2 so that the child sees both pages of item 1.
20. Give the instructions verbatim for item 1, including the word "Go," even if explanations are not necessary.
21. Before saying "Go," give further explanations for item 1, if necessary,
22. Begin timing item 1 after the last word of the instructions.
23. If the child completes item 1 in less than 45 seconds, record the time and administer item 2.
24. After 45 seconds on item 1, say, "Stop" and administer item 2.
25. After the child completes item 1, turn Response Booklet 2 to the blank page on the back of the booklet. Open the booklet so that the child sees both pages of item 2.
26. Give the instructions verbatim for item 2, including the word "Go," even if explanations are not necessary.
27. Before saying "Go," give further explanations for item 2, if necessary.
28. Begin timing item 2 after the last word of the instructions.

Starting Considerations

29. Start all children with the sample, followed by the practice item and then items 1 and 2.

Discontinue Considerations

30. Discontinue the subtest (a) if the child still does not understand the task after instructions have been given and further explanations provided, (b) after 45 seconds on item 2, or (c) when the child finishes before the time limit on item 2.
31. If the child completes item 2 in less than 45 seconds, record the time and discontinue the subtest.
32. After 45 seconds on item 2, say, "Stop" and discontinue the subtest.
33. After the subtest is completed, close Response Booklet 2 and remove it from the child's view.

Scoring Guidelines

34. Score the subtest using the following guidelines.
  a. Use the template to score the subtest. To make the semi-opaque template more durable and easier to use, photocopy the template on two overhead transparencies, first inserting a blank paper inside the folded template to prevent copying of both sides at once (suggestion courtesy of Judy Newcomb).

b. Align the template on the Response Booklet, making sure that the item number is clearly visible in the small box located in the upper left-hand corner of the template.

c. Give 1 point for each target item correctly marked.

d. Do not score the sample or practice items, skipped items, or items not reached before the time limit.

e. Consider objects marked only if it is clear that the child intended to mark them.

f. If two objects are marked with a single line, count only the original object, unless it is clear that the child intended to mark the adjacent object as well.

g. If a blank area near an object is marked, the object closest to the mark should be judged as marked. If the closest object is not clear, no object should be judged as marked.

h. If multiple objects are marked with a single line, score marks through target objects as correct and score marks through nontarget objects as incorrect.

i. If you want to record the number of correct and incorrect objects marked by quadrant, write the following on the front page of Response Booklet 2: q1, c = ___, i = ___ ; q2, c = ___, i = ___ ; q3, c = ___, i = ___ ; q4, c = ___, i = ___. Then enter the appropriate numbers for each of the four quadrants.

Response Booklet

35. At the top of Response Booklet 2, enter the child's name and age, the date, and your name.

Record Form

36. Enter the time in seconds in the Completion Time box for each item.

37. For items 1 and 2, enter the number of correct objects marked in the Number Correct column.

38. For items 1 and 2, enter the number of incorrect objects marked in the Number Incorrect column.

39. For each item, subtract the Number Incorrect from the Number Correct, and enter the result in the Difference column.

40. If the Difference is equal to or greater than 60 and the child has completed item 1 or item 2 in less than 45 seconds, enter the appropriate number of time-bonus points (1, 2, 3, or 4) for that item in the Bonus Points column. If there are no bonus points, enter a score of 0 in the Bonus Points column.

41. Add the Difference and the Bonus Points to obtain the total raw score for each item, and enter this number in the column headed "Total Raw Score." (The "Total Raw Score" label at the bottom of the last column refers to the sum of the total raw scores

on items 1 and 2, which is entered in the shaded box.)

42. Enter the Total Raw Score in the shaded box by summing the Total Raw Score points for items 1 and 2. If the Total Raw Score is less than or equal to 0, enter a 0.

Interpretive Suggestions

The following questions are useful to guide your observation of the child's performance on the Cancellation subtest.

- Does the child understand the task?
- After you give an explanation, does the child proceed correctly?
- What is the child's approach to the task (e.g., smooth and orderly, impulsive, marking objects haphazardly, overly anxious, persistent, distractible, giving up easily)?
- Does the child seem confused at times and have difficulty knowing how to proceed?
- Is the child aware of any errors?
- Does the child need urging to continue the task?
- Does the child appear bored with the task?
- Does the child hold the pencil in an appropriate or in an inappropriate way?
- Is the child's hand steady or shaking?
- Does the child try to use an eraser from another pencil or another source? If so, does the child seem to realize that an eraser is not supposed to be used?
- As the subtest progresses, how does the child's performance change?
- Does the child ignore any area of the pages (e.g., visual neglect)?
- What kind of search pattern does the child follow (e.g., organized or random)?
- Does the child consistently skip over a certain animal or mark a specific nonanimal?

Answers to the above questions will provide information about the child's attention span, problem-solving strategies, and other behaviors. If the child makes many errors, consider whether the errors might be due to impulsivity, poor self-monitoring, or visual-motor difficulties. If the child has worked in an orderly manner from the top to the bottom of the page, determine whether there was an increase or decrease in the number of correct and incorrect objects marked. An increase may indicate growing confidence in the strategy being used to complete the task, while a decrease may indicate boredom, anxiety, or fatigue.

Cancellation may be particularly useful for evaluating a child's attention when you suspect attentional difficulties, such as in cases of attention-deficit/hyperactivity disorder, anxiety, or a traumatic brain injury. If other tests indicate that the child has adequate response speed and visual acuity, then poor scores on Cancellation are likely to be associated with attentional deficits and not visuosensory difficulties per se.

The Administration Manual (Table A.8, pp. 242–252) provides separate scaled scores for Cancellation Random (item 1) and Cancellation Structured (item 2). Table B.9 (p. 269 of the Administration Manual) shows that a difference of 4.40 scaled-score points between scores on Cancellation Random and Cancellation Structured is significant at the .05 level of confidence. Table B.10 (p. 270 of the Administration Manual) shows the extent to which children's scaled scores were higher for Cancellation Random than for Cancellation Structured and vice versa. The median difference between the Cancellation Random and Cancellation Structured scaled scores (regardless of direction) was 2 points, while less than 8% of the standardization sample had differences of 4 or more points.

The process score may give you information about a child's ability to perform a processing speed task in a structured versus a less structured situation. However, in comparing a child's performance on the two items, you should also consider practice effects as a possible reason for any differences. We need research to see whether the process score is clinically useful. Perhaps children with certain types of disabilities (e.g., some forms of brain injury) may have more difficulty on the random task than on the structured task.

High scores on the Cancellation subtest may indicate good processing speed, good perceptual scanning ability, good perceptual recognition ability, good attention and concentration, good short-term memory, sustained energy, persistence, desire for achievement, or high motivation.

Low scores on the Cancellation subtest may indicate poor processing speed, poor perceptual scanning ability, poor perceptual recognition ability, poor attention and concentration, poor short-term memory, visual difficulties (including visual neglect), lethargy and boredom, limited desire for achievement, limited motivation, anxiety, difficulty in working under time pressure, or impulsivity.

The consistent full range of scaled scores from 1 to 19 at all ages aids in profile analysis.

INFORMATION

Information, a supplemental Verbal Comprehension subtest, requires the child to answer questions dealing with various types of content, including body parts, calendar information, historical figures, and science and geographical facts. Children need only show that they know facts; they need not find relationships between these facts. The subtest has 33 items and is not timed. It is easy to administer and score.

Rationale

The amount of knowledge a child has acquired may depend on (a) natural endowment, (b) cultural opportunities, experiences, and interests, and (c) both formal and informal education. The Information subtest samples the knowledge that average children with average opportunities should have acquired through typical home and school experiences in the American culture. The child's responses and comments provide clues about range of information, alertness to the environment, social or cultural background, and attitudes toward school and school-like tasks. For example, a 6-year-old child may say, "Those questions are hard, just like the ones my teacher asks."

High scores may not necessarily indicate cognitive competence; children may have acquired isolated facts but may not know how to use the facts appropriately or effectively. Additionally, intellectual drive may contribute to higher scores. Successful performance on the Information subtest requires memory for habitual, over-learned material (i.e., repeated exposure), especially in school-aged children. Thus, Information provides clues about the child's ability to store and retrieve acquired knowledge (i.e., long-term memory).

Factor Analytic Findings

Information is a good measure of g (66% of its variance can be attributed to g). It ties with Similarities as the second best measure of g in the scale. It contributes substantially to the Verbal Comprehension Index (average loading = .67). Specificity is ample at age 6, adequate at ages 12 to 16, but inadequate at ages 7 to 11.

Reliability and Correlational Highlights

Information is a reliable subtest (r_{xx} = .86), with reliability coefficients at or above .78 at all 11 age groups (range of .78 to .91). It correlates better with Vocabulary ($r = .75$) than with any of the other subtests. It has moderately high correlations with the Full Scale IQ ($r = .73$) and the Verbal Comprehension Index ($r = .77$), moderate correlations with the Perceptual Reasoning Index ($r = .57$) and the Working Memory Index ($r = .51$), and a moderately low correlation with the Processing Speed Index ($r = .39$).

Administrative Guidelines

The following administrative guidelines for the Information subtest must be followed carefully.

Background Considerations

1. Read the directions verbatim.
2. Read the directions clearly.
3. Read the items verbatim.
4. Read the items clearly.
5. You can repeat an item as often as necessary, but do not change the wording in any way.
6. Repeat the instructions if the child asks or has not responded within 5 to 10 seconds, unless it is clear that the child is considering a response.
7. Query unclear or vague responses, as well as the sample responses marked by a "(Q)" in the Administration Manual. *This includes all the responses separated by semicolons on a line that has a "(Q)" at the end.* Query specific responses noted by an asterisk (*) in the Administration Manual. (These are for items 4, 7, 8, 11, 12, 14, 15, 18, 20, 22, 27, 31 and 33.) However, do not query clearly wrong responses or responses that are clearly correct. If the child gives a correct verbal response along with an incorrect nonverbal response or vice versa, say, "What do you mean?" If the child's response suggests that a word was misunderstood, repeat the item with emphasis on the particular word.
8. For items 1 and 2, give correct answers if the child obtains a score of 0.
9. Do not give correct answers for items 3 to 33.
10. If the child fails to respond and has been performing poorly, wait about 30 seconds before going to the next item and say, "Let's try another one." However, use your judgment about moving to the next item sooner. For children who are clearly beyond their ability, 30 seconds may be a long time to wait, especially if it is the third or fourth 30-second wait. For example, this would be the case for children who seem to be bored, who are shrugging their shoulders, or who are looking around the room after a few seconds and not looking at the item.
11. If the child fails to respond but has been performing successfully and appears to be working on a response, give the child the necessary time to respond before going to the next item.

Starting Considerations

12. Start with the appropriate item.
    a. The ages listed under "Start" on page 175 of the Administration Manual are always intended to be inclusive; thus, ages 6–8 means children 6-0 to 8-11 years of age, ages 9–11 means children 9-0 to 11-11 years of age, and ages 12–16 means children 12-0 to 16-11 years of age.
    b. The starting ages on the Record Form are also inclusive.
    c. Children 6 to 8 years of age (and older children suspected of having intellectual deficiency) start with item 5.
    d. Children 9 to 11 years of age (not suspected of having intellectual deficiency) start with item 10.
    e. Children 12 to 16 years of age (not suspected of having intellectual deficiency) start with item 12.

Reverse Sequence

13. If necessary, administer the items in reverse sequence as directed in the Administration Manual.
    a. The instructions on page 175 of the Administration Manual under the heading "Reverse" pertain to all children.
    b. If the child (a) does not obtain full credit on the start-point item or (b) obtains full credit on the start-point item and a score of 0 on the next item, administer the items in reverse sequence.
    c. Continue the reverse sequence until the child has perfect scores on two consecutive items or until item 1 has been administered, even if the discontinue criterion is met.
    d. When there is a reverse sequence, the discontinue criterion is not met, and either there are two consecutive items with perfect scores or item 1 is administered, continue administration with the item after the last start-point item.

Discontinue Considerations

14. Count items administered in reverse sequence toward the discontinue criterion.
15. Discontinue the subtest when five consecutive scores of 0 are obtained, unless the consecutive 0's are obtained during a reverse sequence and (a) item 1 has not been reached or (b) the child has not obtained perfect scores on two consecutive items.

Scoring Guidelines

16. Score the items using the following guidelines.
   a. Scoring is straightforward: A correct response receives 1 point, and an incorrect response, 0 points.
   b. Give credit for responses that are of the same caliber as those listed in the Administration Manual.
   c. When two or more answers to an item vary greatly in quality and none reflect a fundamental misconception (a spoiled response), score the best answer given.
   d. When two or more answers are given to an item, one of which reflects a fundamental misconception (a spoiled response), give the response a score of 0.
   e. Superfluous remarks, in addition to the answer, do not affect the score.
   f. Give credit for a correct touching, pointing, or other nonverbal response on item 1.
   g. When the child earns perfect scores on the first two items at the start point or in a reversal, award full credit for all preceding items, regardless of the child's performance on these items if they have been administered.
   h. Award no points for any items beyond the last score of 0 required for the discontinue criterion to be met, regardless of the child's performance on these items if they have been administered.

Record Form

17. For each item administered, record the child's response verbatim.
18. Circle 0 or 1 in the Score column for each item administered.
19. To note the points awarded for items not administered below the first two items with perfect scores, put a slash mark in the Score column over the item preceding the first two items with perfect scores and write the numerals for these points.
20. Add the points, including the points for correct answers and the points for items not administered before the first two perfect scores, but not for items administered after the last discontinue item.
21. Enter the Total Raw Score in the shaded box.

Interpretive Suggestions

The following questions are useful to guide your observation of the child's performance on the Information subtest.

- Is the child thinking through the questions, responding impulsively, or simply guessing?
- When responding, does the child appear confident or hesitant?
- Does the child give peculiar responses? What does your inquiry reveal?
- Does the child frequently say, "I know this answer, but I can't think of it" or "I don't know"?
- Are the child's answers precise, imprecise, or vague?
- Are the child's answers close to the correct answer or completely wrong?
- Are the child's answers wordy?
- Does the child seem to be inhibited in making responses?
- What is the pattern of the child's successes and failures?

Failures on easy items, coupled with successes on more difficult ones, may suggest poor motivation, anxiety, temporary inefficiency, boredom, or an inconsistent environment. Alternatively, this pattern may indicate a problem with retrieval of information from long-term memory. When you suspect such a problem, analyze the content of the failed items. Content analysis may provide clues about the child's interests, areas about which you might want to inquire after you complete the WISC–IV, or areas that need remediation.

Difficulty in giving precise answers, such as saying, "When it is hot" instead of "Summer" or "When it is cold" instead of "Winter," may suggest word-retrieval difficulties. Overly long responses or responses filled with extraneous information may suggest an obsessive-compulsive orientation—a child with this orientation sometimes feels compelled to prove how much he or she knows. Alternatively, responses with excessive details may simply reflect the style of responding of a gifted child or the child's desire to impress you. Consider the child's entire test performance, plus other relevant information, when you interpret overly long responses.

Inability to recall an answer may suggest that the question is associated with conflict-laden material. For example, a child may not be able to recall the number of legs on a dog because of an earlier traumatic experience with dogs. If possible, explore hypotheses during an interview with the child and his or her parents (see Sattler, 2002).

High scores on the Information subtest may indicate a wide range of factual knowledge, knowledge of the cultural and educational environment, good memory, an enriched background, alertness and interest in the environment, intellectual ambitiousness, intellectual curiosity, an urge to collect knowledge, or interest in a school-type task.

Low scores on the Information subtest may indicate a limited range of factual knowledge, limited knowledge of the cultural and educational environment, poor memory, a limited background, limited alertness and interest in the environment, limited intellectual ambitiousness, limited intellectual curiosity, a limited urge to collect knowledge, hostility to a school-type task, or having English as a second language.

If you suspect word-retrieval problems, use a multiple-choice testing-of-limits procedure. This procedure may help you distinguish between deficits associated with word-retrieval difficulties and those associated with deficient knowledge. After completing the *entire test*, go back to the item (or items) with which the child had difficulty and give the child three answers from which to choose. For example, say, "How many ears does a cat have—one, three, or two? Which one is it?" Be sure to randomly vary the position of the correct answer in the series (i.e., put the correct answer sometimes in first, sometimes in second, and sometimes in third position). If the child answers the multiple-choice questions correctly, the child may have a word-retrieval difficulty and not deficient knowledge. However, scores from the multiple-choice procedure should not be used to calculate an IQ.

The consistent full range of scaled scores from 1 to 19 at all ages aids in profile analysis.

ARITHMETIC

Arithmetic, a supplemental Working Memory subtest, requires the child to answer simple to complex problems involving arithmetical concepts and numerical reasoning. The subtest contains 34 items, with 5 presented on picture cards and 29 presented orally. The first five items are in the Stimulus Book. Many of the arithmetic problems are similar to those commonly encountered by children in school, although the child cannot use paper and pencil to solve the problems.

Items on the Arithmetic subtest test various skills. Items 1, 2, 3, and 4 require direct counting of discrete objects. Item 5 requires subtraction using objects as the stimuli. Items 6 to 14 require simple addition or subtraction. Items 15 through 34 require the use of automatized number facts and subtle mathematical reasoning operations, such as identifying relevant relationships at a glance, understanding task requirements, and understanding probability. These later items also often require the child to perform multiple steps in order to arrive at the correct answer. The subtest is timed and is relatively easy to administer and score.

Rationale

The items on the Arithmetic subtest require the child to hear, comprehend, and follow verbal directions; concentrate on selected parts of questions; and use numerical operations. The child may need knowledge of addition, subtraction, multiplication, and division operations, depending on the item. The emphasis of the items is not on mathematical knowledge per se, but on mental computation and concentration. Working memory is especially important for the more complex items.

The Arithmetic subtest measures numerical reasoning—the ability to solve arithmetical problems. It requires the use of concentration and attention in conjunction with knowledge of numerical operations. Success on the subtest is influenced by education, interests, fluctuations of attention, and transient emotional reactions such as anxiety. Like the Vocabulary and Information subtests, Arithmetic taps memory and prior learning; however, it also requires concentration and the active application of select skills to new and unique situations.

Information-processing strategies, as well as mathematical skills, may underlie performance on the Arithmetic subtest. These strategies may include (a) rehearsal (to remember the information presented in the task) and (b) recognition of an appropriate response (e.g., to change a strategy that leads to failure). The mathematical skills include the ability to comprehend and integrate verbal information presented in a mathematical context, together with numerical ability.

Factor Analytic Findings

Arithmetic is a good measure of g (59% of its variance can be attributed to g). It contributes moderately to the Working Memory Index (average loading = .38). Specificity is ample at ages 7 to 9, 12, 14, and 15 and adequate at ages 6, 10, 11, 13, and 16.

Reliability and Correlational Highlights

Arithmetic is a reliable subtest (r_{xx} = .88), with reliability coefficients above .84 at each age (range of .84 to .91). It correlates better with Information (r = .62) than with any of the other subtests. It has a moderately high correlation with the Full Scale IQ (r = .72), moderate correlations with the Verbal Comprehension Index (r = .63), the Perceptual Reasoning Index (r = .62), and the Working Memory Index (r = .57), and a moderately low correlation with the Processing Speed Index (r = .45).

Administrative Guidelines

The following administrative guidelines for the Arithmetic subtest must be followed carefully.

Background Considerations

1. Read the directions verbatim.
2. Read the directions clearly.
3. Repeat the instructions if the child asks or has not responded within 5 to 10 seconds, unless it is clear that the child is considering a response.
4. Repeat an item only once if the child fails to understand the item or if the child requests to have it repeated, but do not stop timing.
5. Place the closed Stimulus Book with the coil-bound edge facing the child so that the book is completely flat when it is opened for items 1 to 5, and then open it to the appropriate page.
6. During the subtest administration, turn the pages of the Stimulus Book toward the child.
7. Time correctly: (a) Allow 30 seconds for each item. (b) Begin timing after the last word of the instructions. (c) Continue timing even when the instructions are clarified. (d) Stop timing the item when the child responds or after 30 seconds. (e) If the child seems to be on the verge of solving the problem, allow the child additional time after the time limit to complete the problem, but score only answers given within the 30-second time limit.
8. For items 1, 2, and 3, provide appropriate feedback on incorrect responses.
9. For items 4 to 34, do not give answers.
10. Do not allow the child to use pencil and paper.
11. Allow the child to use a finger to "write" on the table.
12. When it is not clear which response is the final choice, ask the child to select one of two responses; say, "You said _____ and you said _____. Which one do you mean?"

Starting Considerations

13. Start with the appropriate item.
   a. The ages listed under "Start" on page 190 of the Administration Manual are always intended to be inclusive; thus, ages 6–7 means children 6-0 to 7-11 years of age, ages 8–9 means children 8-0 to 9-11 years of age, and ages 10–16 means children 10-0 to 16-11 years of age.
   b. The starting ages on the Record Form are also inclusive.

   c. Children 6 to 7 years of age (and older children suspected of having intellectual deficiency) start with item 3.
   d. Children 8 to 9 years of age (not suspected of having intellectual deficiency) start with item 9.
   e. Children 10 to 16 years of age (not suspected of having intellectual deficiency) start with item 12.

Reverse Sequence

14. If necessary, administer the items in reverse sequence as directed in the Administration Manual.
   a. The instructions on page 190 of the Administration Manual under the heading "Reverse" pertain to all children.
   b. If the child (a) does not obtain full credit on the start-point item or (b) obtains full credit on the start-point item and a score of 0 on the next item, administer the items in reverse sequence.
   c. Continue the reverse sequence until the child has perfect scores on two consecutive items or until item 1 has been administered, even if the discontinue criterion is met.
   d. When there is a reverse sequence, the discontinue criterion is not met, and either there are two consecutive items with perfect scores or item 1 is administered, continue administration with the item after the last start-point item.

Discontinue Considerations

15. Count items administered in reverse sequence toward the discontinue criterion.
16. Discontinue the subtest when four consecutive scores of 0 are obtained, unless the consecutive 0's are obtained during a reverse sequence and (a) item 1 has not been reached or (b) the child has not obtained perfect scores on two consecutive items.
17. Once the subtest is completed, remove the Stimulus Book from the child's view.

Scoring Guidelines

18. Score the items using the following guidelines.
   a. A numerically correct response is considered correct even if the child incorrectly states or does not state the units. (We have strong reservations about this scoring procedure. A child who gives a correct number together with an incorrect unit [e.g., the child says, "three cents" when the correct answer is "three dollars"] is showing poor understanding of the application of arithmetical skills to practical

situations and hence doesn't deserve the same credit as the child whose answer is completely correct.) According to Lisa Drozdick, Research Director, The Psychological Corporation (personal communication, February 2004), giving credit for responses showing an understanding of the correct numerical operation, but not an understanding of the arithmetic concept, is an attempt to highlight the working memory component of the Arithmetic subtest. Further, she observed that "getting the units incorrect may reflect numerous issues other than working memory and the ability to mentally perform calculations."

b. For items in which the units are units of time or money (e.g., hours, dollars), an otherwise satisfactory alternative numerical response is acceptable only when accompanied by the correct unit. For example, if the correct numerical answer to a question involving hours is "three," give a score of 1 to "three," "three hours," "three seconds," or "180 minutes." However, give a score of 0 to "180 seconds" because in the latter case the numerical answer is invalidated by the mistake in units.

c. Items 1, 2, and 3 require the child to count objects correctly, not simply provide a final result. For example, for item 1 the child must correctly count to 3 rather than simply saying "three."

d. If the child spontaneously changes a response within the 30-second time limit, accept and score the new response.

e. Do not give credit for a correct response made after the time limit.

f. When the child earns perfect scores on the first two items at the start point or in a reversal, award full credit for all preceding items, regardless of the child's performance on these items if they have been administered.

g. Award no points for any items beyond the last score of 0 required for the discontinue criterion to be met, regardless of the child's performance on these items if they have been administered.

Record Form

19. Record the child's responses verbatim in the Response column.

20. Circle 0 or 1 in the Score column for each item administered.

21. To note the points awarded for items not administered below the first two items with perfect scores, put a slash mark in the Score column over the item preceding the first two items with perfect scores and write the numerals for these points.

22. Add the points, including the points for correct answers and the points for items not administered before the first two perfect scores, but not for items administered after the last discontinue item.

23. Enter the Total Raw Score in the shaded box.

Interpretive Suggestions

The following questions are useful to guide your observation of the child's performance on the Arithmetic subtest.

- Is the child anxious (e.g., seems to be in a state of panic at the thought of doing math problems)?
- What approach does the child use to solve problems (e.g., counting on fingers, drawing with a finger on the table, closing eyes and imagining the numbers in his or her head, talking out loud)?
- Does the child show temporary inefficiencies? If so, of what type?
- Does the child recognize failures?
- Does the child attempt to correct perceived errors?
- How frequently does the child ask to have questions repeated?
- Does the child show a misunderstanding of the mathematical operation (e.g., adds when the problem requires subtraction)?
- Even if the answer is incorrect, does the child show an understanding of the process required to solve the problem (e.g., is able to estimate the correct answer)?
- Does the child have frequent self-corrections?
- What is the quality of the child's responses (e.g., quick or effortful)?

High scores on the Arithmetic subtest may indicate good ability in mental arithmetic, good ability to apply reasoning skills in the solution of mathematical problems, good ability to apply arithmetical skills in personal and social problem-solving situations, good concentration and attention, good short-term memory, good ability to convert word problems into mathematical calculations, good ability to engage in complex thought patterns (holds mainly for upper-level items), or good interest in school achievement.

Low scores on the Arithmetic subtest may indicate inadequate ability in mental arithmetic, difficulty in applying reasoning skills in the solution of mathematical problems, difficulty in applying arithmetical skills in personal and social problem-solving situations, poor concentration and attention, poor short-term memory, problems converting word problems into mathematical calculations, difficulty in engaging in complex thought patterns (holds mainly for upper-level items), anxiety (e.g., over a school-like task or personal problems), blocking toward mathematical tasks, fear of asking for repetition (i.e., social anxiety), or limited interest in school achievement.

As a testing-of-limits procedure, you might want to learn about the reasons for the child's failure. After the *entire test* is administered, ask about the child's performance. Perhaps say, "Let's try this one again. Tell me how you solved the problem." If necessary, tell the child to think aloud. This may help determine how the child went about solving the problem. The child may have failed because of poor knowledge of arithmetical operations, inadequate conceptualization of the problem, temporary inefficiency or anxiety, poor concentration, or carelessness.

Another testing-of-limits procedure may help to differentiate inadequate conceptualization of the problem from poor mastery of mathematical operations. For example, if the child fails a word problem such as "If Matthew has one cookie and his mom gives him three more, how many cookies does he have altogether?" you can say, "How much is 1 plus 3?"

Allowing the child to use paper and pencil is another testing-of-limits procedure that may help determine whether the child has poor arithmetical knowledge or attention and concentration difficulties. If the child can solve the problems with pencil and paper, the failure is not associated with poor arithmetical knowledge; rather, the errors may be associated with attention or concentration difficulties that inhibit mental computation. If the child fails the items in both situations, the failures more likely reflect difficulties with arithmetical knowledge, although attention and concentration difficulties also may interfere with the child's ability to solve written arithmetic problems. Inspect the written work to see whether the child misaligns numbers, sequences computational steps incorrectly, or has poor mastery of basic arithmetical operations. A child who misaligns numbers while working may have spatial difficulties.

The information obtained from testing-of-limits may help distinguish between failures associated with temporary inefficiency and those associated with limited knowledge. Successful delayed performance, for example, may indicate temporary inefficiency or a slow, painstaking approach to problem solving. During testing-of-limits, note whether the child passes or fails the items. Of course, do not give the child credit for any correct answers given during testing-of-limits.

The consistent full range of scaled scores from 1 to 19 at all ages aids in profile analysis.

WORD REASONING

Word Reasoning, a supplemental Verbal Comprehension subtest, requires the child to identify the common object or concept described by an increasingly specific series of one to three clues. The subtest contains two samples and 24 subtest items. It is not timed and is somewhat awkward to administer and difficult to score. Administration is awkward because both the Record Form and the Administration Manual are needed, as the items are listed in the Record Form but not in the Administration Manual.

Rationale

Word Reasoning involves verbal reasoning, deductive reasoning, verbal comprehension, verbal abstraction, synthesizing ability, and the ability to generate alternative concepts (Wechsler, 2003b).

Factor Analytic Findings

Word Reasoning is a good measure of g (54% of its variance can be attributed to g). It contributes substantially to the Verbal Comprehension Index (average loading = .66). Specificity is ample at ages 6 to 8, 14, and 15, adequate at ages 9, 11, and 13, and inadequate at ages 10, 12, and 16.

Reliability and Correlational Highlights

Word Reasoning is a reliable subtest (r_{xx} = .80), with reliability coefficients at or above .77 at all 11 age groups (range of .77 to .84). It correlates better with Vocabulary (r = .66) than with any of the other subtests. It has a moderate correlation with the Full Scale IQ (r = .65) and the Perceptual Reasoning Index (r = .52), a moderately high correlation with the Verbal Comprehension Index (r = .70), and moderately low correlations with the Working Memory Index (r = .45) and the Processing Speed Index (r = .35).

Administrative Guidelines

The following administrative guidelines for the Word Reasoning subtest must be followed carefully.

Background Considerations

1. Read the items verbatim.
2. Read the items clearly.
3. Introduce each item by saying "Let's try another one."
4. After you give each clue, allow the child about 5 seconds to answer.
5. If requested by the child or if the child delays 5 seconds before responding, repeat each clue one time only.
6. After each repetition of the clues, allow the child an additional 5 seconds to make a response.
7. As you add more clues, restate the preceding clues. For example, for items with two clues, restate the first clue before giving the second clue. For items with three clues, restate the first and second clues before giving the third clue. The instructions to "restate the preceding clues" on page 197 of the Administration Manual mean to repeat clues, not to rephrase them.
8. If the child gets an item correct before all clues have been presented, administer the next item.

Starting Considerations

9. Start with the appropriate item.
   a. The ages listed under "Start" on page 196 of the Administration Manual are always intended to be inclusive; thus, ages 6–9 means children 6-0 to 9-11 years of age and ages 10–16 means children 10-0 to 16-11 years of age.
   b. The starting ages on the Record Form are also inclusive.
   c. Children 6 to 9 years of age (and older children suspected of having intellectual deficiency) start with samples A and B and then item 1.
   d. Children 10 to 16 years of age (not suspected of intellectual deficiency) start with samples A and B and then item 5.

Reverse Sequence

10. If necessary, administer the items in reverse sequence as directed in the Administration Manual.
    a. The instructions on page 196 of the Administration Manual under the heading "Reverse" pertain to children who begin the subtest with the sample and then with item 5.
    b. If the child (a) does not obtain full credit on the start-point item or (b) obtains full credit on the start-point item and a score of 0 on the next item, administer the items in reverse sequence.
    c. Continue the reverse sequence until the child has perfect scores on two consecutive items or until

item 1 has been administered, even if the discontinue criterion is met.
    d. When there is a reverse sequence, the discontinue criterion is not met, and either there are two consecutive items with perfect scores or item 1 is administered, continue administration with the item after the last start-point item.

Discontinue Considerations

11. Count items administered in reverse sequence toward the discontinue criterion.
12. Discontinue the subtest when five consecutive scores of 0 are obtained, unless the consecutive 0's are obtained during a reverse sequence and (a) item 1 has not been reached or (b) the child has not obtained perfect scores on two consecutive items.

Scoring Guidelines

13. Score responses using the following guidelines.
    a. A correct response on each item receives a score of 1, regardless of whether the child receives one, two, or three clues.
    b. An incorrect response receives a score of 0.
    c. Give credit for responses that are of the same caliber—such as synonyms, specific brands, or objects—as those listed on pages 200 to 202 in the Administration Manual.
    d. Although the subtest is not timed, the instructions in the Administration Manual say that, if you repeat a clue, you should allow another 5 seconds for the child to respond and then, if the child answers incorrectly or does not respond, give the next clue or item. The instructions also state that you give credit for correct responses made after 5 seconds.
    e. When the child earns perfect scores on the first two items at the start point or in a reversal, award full credit for all preceding items, regardless of the child's performance on these items if they have been administered.
    f. Award no points for any items beyond the last score of 0 required for the discontinue criterion to be met, regardless of the child's performance on these items if they have been administered.

Record Form

14. Record the child's responses verbatim in the Response column.
15. If a clue is repeated, record an R.
16. Circle Y or N for each clue administered.
17. Circle 0 or 1 for each item administered.
18. To note the points awarded for items not administered below the first two items with perfect scores,

put a slash mark in the Score column over the item preceding the first two items with perfect scores and write the numerals for these points.

19. Add the points, including the points for unadministered items, but not for items administered after the last discontinue item.

20. Enter the Total Raw Score in the shaded box.

Interpretive Suggestions

The following questions are useful to guide your observation of the child's performance on the Word Reasoning subtest.

- Is the child thinking through the questions, responding impulsively, or simply guessing?
- When responding, does the child appear confident or hesitant?
- Does the child give peculiar responses? What does your inquiry reveal?
- Does the child frequently say, "I know this answer, but I can't think of it" or "I don't know"?
- Are the child's answers precise or imprecise?
- How many clues does the child need to solve items 16 to 24?
- Is there a pattern of needing fewer clues on some items and more clues on other ones? If so, what is the pattern? What might the pattern suggest?
- Does the child synthesize clues or give separate responses to each clue?
- Does the child have problems beginning with item 1 (first one-clue item), beginning with item 7 (first two-clue item), or beginning with item 16 (first three-clue item)?

High scores on the Word Reasoning subtest may indicate good analogic reasoning ability or deductive reasoning ability, good ability to integrate and synthesize, good ability to generate alternative concepts, good ability to see relationships, good short-term memory, good vocabulary, good attention, or good achievement orientation.

Low scores on the Word Reasoning subtest may indicate poor analogic reasoning ability or deductive reasoning ability, difficulty in integrating and synthesizing, difficulty in generating alternative concepts, difficulty in seeing relationships, poor short-term memory, poor vocabulary, attention difficulties, low achievement orientation, or having English as a second language.

If you suspect word-retrieval problems, use a multiple-choice testing-of-limits procedure. This procedure may help you distinguish between deficits associated with word-retrieval difficulties and those associated with deficient knowledge. After completing the *entire test*, go back to the item (or items) with which the child had difficulty and give the child three answers from which to choose. For example, for a sample-like item say, "This is an animal that goes meow. Is it a dog, a cat, or a bird?" Be sure to randomly vary the position of the correct answer in the series (i.e., put the correct answer sometimes in first, sometimes in second, and sometimes in third position). If the child answers the multiple-choice questions correctly, the child may have a word-retrieval difficulty and not deficient knowledge. However, the multiple-choice procedure should not be used to calculate an IQ.

The consistent full range of scaled scores from 1 to 19 for children 6 to 13 years of age aids in profile analysis. The restricted ranges of scaled scores from 1 to 18 for children 14 to 15 years of age and from 1 to 17 for children 16 years of age somewhat limit profile analysis.

THINKING THROUGH THE ISSUES

1. Under what set of circumstances should a supplemental subtest replace a core subtest?
2. When might you administer a supplemental subtest in addition to the core subtests?
3. How do you weigh the cost of additional time required versus information gained in administering additional subtests?
4. Should substitutions of supplemental for core subtests be decided on before the test is administered or after the test has started? What is the reason for your answer?

SUMMARY

Picture Completion

1. Picture Completion measures visual discrimination (i.e., the ability to distinguish between essential and nonessential details) and requires concentration, reasoning, visual organization, and long-term visual memory. The subtest is a fair measure of *g* and contributes substantially to the Perceptual Reasoning Index. Specificity is ample at all ages except 9 years. Picture Completion is a reliable subtest ($r_{xx} = .84$). It is relatively easy to administer and score.

Cancellation

2. Cancellation involves perceptual discrimination, recognition ability, speed and accuracy, attention and concentration, short-term memory, persistence, and the ability to remain focused. The subtest is a poor measure of g, but contributes substantially to the Processing Speed Index. Specificity is ample. Cancellation is a relatively reliable subtest (r_{xx} = .79). It is relatively easy to administer but somewhat difficult to score.

Information

3. Information measures the child's store of available information acquired as a result of natural endowment, cultural opportunities, experiences, interests, and both formal and informal education. Long-term memory is an important aspect of performance on the subtest. The subtest is a good measure of g and contributes substantially to the Verbal Comprehension Index. Specificity is ample, adequate, or inadequate, depending on the age level. Information is a reliable subtest (r_{xx} = .86). It is easy to administer and score.

Arithmetic

4. Arithmetic measures numerical reasoning—the ability to solve arithmetical problems. It requires the use of noncognitive functions (concentration and attention) in conjunction with cognitive functions (knowledge of numerical operations). The subtest is a good measure of g and contributes moderately to the Working Memory Index. Specificity is either ample or adequate, depending on the age level. Arithmetic is a reliable subtest (r_{xx} = .88). It is relatively easy to administer and score.

Word Reasoning

5. Word Reasoning involves verbal reasoning, deductive reasoning, verbal comprehension, verbal abstraction, synthesizing ability, and ability to gener-

ate alternative concepts. The subtest is a good measure of g and contributes substantially to the Verbal Comprehension Index. Specificity is ample, adequate, or inadequate, depending on the age level. Word Reasoning is a reliable subtest (r_{xx} = .80). It is somewhat difficult to administer and score.

KEY TERMS, CONCEPTS, AND NAMES

WISC–IV Picture Completion (p. 96)
Circumlocutions (p. 98)
Paraphasic language (p. 98)
WISC–IV Cancellation (p. 99)
WISC–IV Information (p. 102)
WISC–IV Arithmetic (p. 105)
WISC–IV Word Reasoning (p. 108)

STUDY QUESTIONS

1. Discuss the rationale for each of the five WISC–IV supplemental subtests.
2. Describe the factor analytic findings for each of the five WISC–IV supplemental subtests. In your description, compare and contrast the major factor analytic findings among the five supplemental subtests.
3. Discuss the reliability and correlational highlights for each of the five WISC–IV supplemental subtests. In your discussion, compare and contrast the reliability and correlational highlights among the five supplemental subtests.
4. List some major administrative guidelines for each of the five WISC–IV supplemental subtests.
5. Describe the interpretive suggestions for each of the five WISC–IV supplemental subtests.
6. Which two of the five WISC–IV supplemental subtests are the best measures of intelligence? Give the reasons for your answer.

4

INTERPRETING THE WISC–IV

The gifts of nature are infinite in their variety, and mind differs from mind almost as much as body from body.
—Quintilian

Goals and Objectives

This chapter is designed to enable you to do the following:

* Describe profile analysis for the WISC–IV

* Analyze and evaluate WISC–IV scores from multiple perspectives

* Develop hypotheses about WISC–IV scores and responses

* Report WISC–IV findings to parents and others

This chapter will help you (a) perform a profile analysis, (b) determine whether the four Index scores differ significantly from each other, (c) determine whether the subtest scaled scores differ significantly from each other, (d) obtain the base rates for differences between the Index scores, (e) obtain the base rates for differences between some of the subtest scaled scores, (f) determine base rates for intersubtest scatter, and (g) develop hypotheses and interpretations. Because the Full Scale IQ and Index scores have a mean of 100 and standard deviation of 15 and because subtest scaled scores have a mean of 10 and standard deviation of 3, you can statistically evaluate profiles across the Indexes and across the subtests.

After you statistically evaluate the Index score discrepancies, subtest discrepancies, and the profile of subtest scaled scores, you will need to interpret the findings. This chapter, along with the information presented in Chapters 1, 2, and 3 and Appendixes A and C, will help you accomplish this goal. Table C-7 in Appendix C provides useful suggestions for describing the Composite scores and subtest scores to the referral source, to the parents, and in your report. In addition, your interpretation will benefit if you know about theories of intelligence and intellectual functioning (see Chapters 5 and 6 in Sattler, 2001), normal child development, and child psychopathology and exceptional children (see Sattler, 2002).

PROFILE ANALYSIS

Profile analysis (sometimes referred to as scatter analysis) is a procedure for analyzing a child's pattern of subtest scaled scores and Composite standard scores. Some profiles show extreme variability of subtest scaled scores (e.g., from 1 to 19); others, moderate variability (e.g., from 5 to 15); and still others, minimal variability (e.g., from 8 to 12). Profiles of the four Index scores also can show extreme variability (e.g., standard scores from 70 to 130); others, moderate variability (e.g., standard scores from 80 to 120); and still others, minimal variability (e.g., standard scores from 90 to 110). You can examine the pattern of subtest scaled scores within each of the four individual Composites and within the entire test. You can also examine the relationship among the four Index scores and among the subtest scaled scores.

In the early days of the Wechsler and Wechsler-type scales, psychologists hoped that profile analysis would increase diagnostic precision. They attempted not only to examine the pattern of Index and subtest scores, but also to discern profiles that would help to diagnose children's disabilities and learning styles. These efforts did not yield the clinical results hoped for. *Thus, profile analysis with the WISC–IV cannot be used to arrive at a diagnostic label.* Profile analysis is problematic because the subtest scaled scores are not as reliable as the Index scores and because neither the subtests nor the individual Composites measure unique cognitive processes. Still, profile analysis can provide information about a child's cognitive strengths and weaknesses and can help in developing hypotheses about the child's cognitive functioning.

Aim of Profile Analysis

The Full Scale IQ, although a valuable measure of general intellectual ability, by itself tells us little about the underlying abilities on which it is based. For example, a Full Scale IQ of 100 may reflect subtest scaled scores that range between (a) 8 and 12, (b) 5 and 15, or (c) 1 and 19. And the same range in two or more profiles may be based on high and low scores on different subtests. Profile analysis therefore attempts to describe the child's unique ability pattern and, in so doing, to go beyond the information contained solely in the Full Scale IQ or Index scores. Knowledge of ability patterns also can help in formulating teaching strategies and other types of interventions.

The following are examples of profile types.

1. A flat profile with all subtest scaled scores much above average (e.g., from 14 to 16) suggests that the child is gifted intellectually and may profit from instruction that capitalizes on the child's exceptional intellectual skills.
2. A flat profile with subtest scaled scores all much below average (e.g., from 2 to 4) suggests that the child has limited intellectual ability and needs specialized instruction appropriate for the child's level of functioning.
3. A profile with highly variable subtest scaled scores (e.g., scaled scores from 3 to 16) suggests special strengths and weaknesses and may help generate hypotheses for possible interventions.
4. A profile of subtest scaled scores within normal limits (e.g., 8 to 12) suggests average ability without any exceptionality.

The goal of profile analysis is to generate hypotheses about the child's abilities. The hypotheses generated need to be checked against other information about the child. Hypotheses can be used to clarify the functional nature of a child's learning problems and can be the basis for recommendations regarding treatment, educational programs, or vocational placement.

Intersubtest variability (i.e., variability among subtests) may result, for example, from special aptitudes or weaknesses, temporary inefficiencies, motivational difficulties, vision or hearing problems, concentration difficulties, rebelliousness, learning disabilities, uneven school experiences, or disturbed home experiences. You will need to determine which, if any, of these interpretations (or others) is appropriate. In each case, you will have to seek the best explanation of the child's profile, using information obtained from the test and other relevant sources. *Even variability that is outside of "normal limits" may not indicate the presence of psychopathology or exceptionality; rather, variability may simply reflect the child's cognitive strengths and weaknesses.*

You can analyze profiles from two frames of reference. One compares the child's scores to the norm group—an *interindividual comparison.* The other compares the child's scores to his or her own unique profile—an *intraindividual comparison.* In either case, you use scaled scores based on the norm group.

All strengths or weaknesses are relative to some standard or frame of reference, either the performance of the child's age peers or the child's own pattern of abilities. In your written or oral psychological or psychoeducational report, clearly indicate which standard or frame of reference you are using when you discuss the child's abilities.

Interindividual Comparison

The simplest way to approach a subtest profile analysis is to evaluate the scores in reference to the norm group. A mean of 10 (coupled with a standard deviation of 3) serves as the reference point for the norm group. You can describe subtest scaled scores using a three-category approach (see Table 4-1) or a more refined five-category approach (see Table 4-2). In either approach,

- Subtest scaled scores of 13 to 19 *always* indicate a strength (one to three standard deviations above the mean).
- Subtest scaled scores of 8 to 12 *always* indicate average ability (within one standard deviation of the mean).

- Subtest scaled scores of 1 to 7 *always* indicate a weakness (one to three standard deviations below the mean).

Whether you use the three- or five-category system to describe subtest scaled scores is a matter of preference. You may prefer one system for some reports and the other system for others. Overall, the five-category system is generally preferable to the three-category system because it allows for greater detail in describing scores, especially scores at the low and high ends. As you study Tables 4-1 and 4-2, notice that if all of the subtest scaled

**Table 4-1
A Three-Category Approach to Describing WISC–IV Subtest Scaled Scores**

Scaled score	Description	Percentile rank
1 to 7	Weakness or below average	1st to 16th
8 to 12	Average	25th to 75th
13 to 19	Strength or above average	84th to 99th

Note. The range of subtest scaled scores from 1 to 19 does not allow for any finer discriminations between percentile ranks; thus, there are gaps in the percentile ranks between scaled scores of 7 and 8 and 12 and 13.

**Table 4-2
A Five-Category Approach to Describing WISC–IV Subtest Scaled Scores**

Scaled score	Description	Percentile rank
1 to 4	Exceptional weakness or very poorly developed or far below average	1st to 2nd
5 to 7	Weakness or poorly developed or below average	5th to 16th
8 to 12	Average	25th to 75th
13 to 15	Strength or well developed or above average	84th to 95th
16 to 19	Exceptional strength or very well developed or superior	98th to 99th

Note. The range of subtest scaled scores from 1 to 19 does not allow for any finer discriminations between percentile ranks; thus, there are gaps in the percentile ranks between scaled scores of 4 and 5, 7 and 8, 12 and 13, and 15 and 16.

scores are 8 or above, the child has no weaknesses relative to his or her age peers. If all subtest scaled scores are 7 or below, the child has no strengths relative to his or her age peers. *Remember, however, that the child may have cognitive strengths or weaknesses in areas not measured by the test.*

After you describe the subtest scaled scores and the abilities with which they are associated, you might also note their percentile ranks (see Table C-1 in Appendix C). The percentile ranks provide a more precise description of the child's level of functioning, and you are encouraged to include percentile ranks in your reports.

Here are some illustrations of how to describe scaled scores:

- "She has strengths in abstract reasoning (91st percentile) and vocabulary knowledge (84th percentile)."
- "His weaknesses are in spatial visualization organization (5th percentile) and sustained attention for auditory information (9th percentile)."
- "She has average ability in all of the verbal comprehension subtests; all scores were between the 25th and 75th percentiles."
- "His abilities in . . . are above average (in the 84th to 95th percentiles)."
- "Within the verbal comprehension domain, her skills range from the 16th percentile to the 63rd percentile. Her vocabulary knowledge and understanding of social mores and customs are below average, while her concept formation ability is average."

Intraindividual Comparison

When you describe a child's cognitive abilities in relation to his or her own level of performance, you are making an *intraindividual comparison* (or using an *ipsative approach*). With the intraindividual approach, as with the interindividual approach, subtest scaled scores of 13 to 19 are always strengths; subtest scaled scores of 8 to 12 are always average; and subtest scaled scores of 1 to 7 are always weaknesses.

Avoid reporting that subtest scaled scores of 8 or higher reflect a weakness or that subtest scaled scores of 7 or lower reflect a strength. For example, if 9 of the 10 subtest scaled scores in a profile are 18 and 19, and one is 13, 13 still represents a strength (it is at the 84th percentile rank), even though it is the lowest score in the profile. You do not want to imply that a subtest scaled score of 13 indicates limited ability or a weakness or a deficit. It is the absolute score (in this case, a subtest scaled score of 13), not a comparison with any other of

the child's scores, that reflects the child's level of ability. However, in interpreting this profile you can report that a subtest scaled score of 13 indicates a strength in the ability measured by that particular subtest, but that ability is not as well developed as the child's other abilities.

Following are key phrases to use in an intraindividual comparison:

- Relative to John's own level of ability
- Within Jill's average level of functioning
- Reflects a better developed ability
- Relatively more developed
- Relative strength
- Strength
- Reflects a less developed ability
- Relatively less developed
- Relative weakness
- Weakness

Here are some examples of how such phrases might be used in describing various profiles:

Example 1. This statement was based on subtest scaled scores of 3 to 7 in the Verbal Comprehension Composite: "Relative to John's own level of verbal ability, his social comprehension is better developed, but still is at a below-average level (16th percentile)." The key phrase "relative to John's own level of verbal ability" reflects a comparison based on the child's individual profile. Note, however, that the absolute values of the subtest scaled scores are still used for an intraindividual profile analysis. His subtest scaled score of 7 does not indicate a strength, even though it is the highest score in the profile. Also note that the phrase "but still is at a below-average level" helps the reader understand that, although social comprehension is the child's best ability, it is still below average in comparison to the norm group.

Example 2. This statement was based on Wechsler subtest scaled scores of 7 to 15 over the 10 core subtests and a Full Scale IQ of 113: "Within Mary's overall above-average level of functioning, her command of word knowledge is a considerable strength (95th percentile)." The key phrase "within Mary's overall above-average level of functioning" prepares the reader for some comment related to the child's individual profile.

Example 3. In a profile with nine Wechsler subtest scaled scores below 4 and one subtest scaled score of 9, you could report that the subtest scaled score of 9, at the 37th percentile, "reflects an ability that is better developed than Jose's other abilities." (In this example, 9 of the 10 scores reflect weaknesses relative to the child's age group.)

Example 4. In a profile with nine Wechsler subtest scaled scores above 16 and one subtest scaled score of 10, you could report that the score of 10, "albeit average at the 50th percentile, is less well developed than Katika's other abilities." (In this example, one score is average and the rest are above average relative to the child's age group.)

Establishing Significant Differences

To be able to say that one score is meaningfully (i.e., statistically significantly) higher than another score, you must first determine that the difference between the two scores does not represent chance variation—you cannot simply look at two scores and say that one is meaningfully (or statistically significantly) higher or lower than the other. Two numerically different scores may not reflect a meaningful difference because they are based on subtests (or Indexes) that are not perfectly reliable. A statistically significant difference reflects a high probability that the skill levels measured by the two subtest scaled scores are different. In other words, the differences are greater than those that might be expected to occur simply by chance.

One approach to profile analysis is to determine whether certain scores differ significantly from each other; this is called the *significant difference approach.* For example, you may want to compare the Verbal Comprehension Index and the Perceptual Reasoning Index or compare certain subtests, such as Vocabulary and Similarities. To make these comparisons, you will need to answer questions like the following:

- Do the Indexes of interest differ significantly from each other?
- Do the subtest scaled scores of interest differ significantly from the means of their respective Composites?
- Do the subtest scaled scores of interest differ from one another?

Whatever comparisons you opt to make—between Indexes, between scores, or between scores and the means of their respective Composites—you must find out whether the differences are significant. The information that follows describes how to do these comparisons. First, let's look at how base rates can also help with profile analysis.

Base Rates

A second approach to profile analysis is to determine the frequency with which the differences between scores in the child's profile occurred in the standardization sample; this is called the *base rate approach* or the *probability-of-occurrence approach.* The following tables in the Administration Manual will give you base rate information:

- Table B.2 for differences between the four Index scores
- Table B.4 for differences associated with seven pairs of subtests
- Table B.5 for differences between individual subtest scaled scores and the mean subtest scaled score for the three core Verbal Comprehension subtests, the three core Perceptual Reasoning subtests, the two core Processing Speed subtests, and the 10 core Full Scale subtests
- Table B.6 for intersubtest scatter for three, four, and five Verbal Comprehension subtests, three and four Perceptual Reasoning subtests, and 10, 11, 12, 13, 14, and 15 Full Scale subtests

Table A-3 in Appendix A in this text also provides information about the probabilities associated with differences between Indexes.

Primary Methods of Profile Analysis

The primary methods of profile analysis are the following:

Method 1. Compare the Verbal Comprehension Index, Perceptual Reasoning Index, Working Memory Index, and Processing Speed Index.

Method 2. Compare each Verbal Comprehension subtest scaled score with the mean Verbal Comprehension Index scaled score.

Method 3. Compare each Perceptual Reasoning subtest scaled score with the mean Perceptual Reasoning Index scaled score.

Method 4. Compare each Working Memory subtest scaled score with the mean Working Memory Index scaled score.

Method 5. Compare each Processing Speed subtest scaled score with the mean Processing Speed Index scaled score.

Method 6. Compare each subtest scaled score with the mean subtest scaled score based on the 10 core subtests and based on all 15 subtests.

Method 7. Compare sets of individual subtest scaled scores.

Method 8. Compare the range of subtest scaled scores with that found in the standardization sample.

Method 9. Compare sets of individual Process scaled scores.

Method 10. Compare the range of Process scaled scores with that found in the standardization sample.

Method 1: Compare the Verbal Comprehension Index, Perceptual Reasoning Index, Working Memory Index, and Processing Speed Index.

Table A-2 in Appendix A provides the critical values for comparing the four Indexes for the 11 WISC–IV age groups and for the average. These values range from 11 to 16 at the .05 level and from 14 to 21 at the .01 level. You should not use an average critical value based on the entire standardization group, because this value may be misleading for some ages. Rather, use the values for a specific age group to evaluate differences between the Indexes.

Exhibit 4-1 describes the procedure that was used to obtain the critical values shown in Table A-2 in Appendix A. You can use this procedure to determine the needed critical values for any comparison involving two Indexes or two subtests. The values in Table A-2 in Appendix A differ in two ways from those in Table B.1 in the Administration Manual. First, the values in Table A-2 in Appendix A are whole numbers instead of decimals. A child's standard scores are always whole numbers without decimals. Second, the values in Table A-2 in Appendix A are for the .05 and .01 significance levels instead of the .15 and .05 significance levels. We recommend using either the .05 significance level or the .01 significance level; the .15 significance level is not traditionally used.

Table A-3 in Appendix A shows the probabilities associated with various differences between the four Indexes. This table provides an estimate of the probability of obtaining a given or greater discrepancy by chance. It shows probabilities from .001 (1 in 1,000) to .50 (50 in 100, or 1 out of 2). Thus, at age 6 years, there is a 1 in 1,000 chance that a difference of 21.00 points will be found between the Verbal Comprehension Index and the Perceptual Reasoning Index. On the other hand, at this

same age, there is a 50% chance that a difference of 4.30 points will be found between the Verbal Comprehension Index and the Perceptual Reasoning Index.

Table B.2 (p. 257) in the Administration Manual shows the cumulative percentages in the standardization sample that obtained various Index score discrepancies for the overall sample as well as for five ability levels (Full Scale IQs for 79 and below, 80 to 89, 90 to 109, 110 to 119, and 120 and above). In the segment of the overall sample that had a higher Verbal Comprehension Index than Perceptual Reasoning Index, the mean difference was 10.8 points, whereas in the segment that had a higher Perceptual Reasoning Index than Verbal Comprehension Index, the mean difference was 10.4 points. The Verbal Comprehension Index was higher than the Perceptual Reasoning Index by 15 points (one standard deviation) in 14.5% of the sample, whereas the Verbal Comprehension Index was lower than the Perceptual Reasoning Index by 15 points (one standard deviation) in 12.0% of the sample.

The cumulative percentages for the six Index comparisons shown in Table B.2 differ at the five ability levels. For example, the base rate for a 15-point discrepancy for the Perceptual Reasoning Index > Processing Speed Index comparison is 16.5% in the overall sample, but it ranges from 9.5% to 26.8% at the five ability levels: 14.0% at FSIQ 79 and below, 9.5% at FSIQ 80 to 89, 16.1% at FSIQ 90 to 109, 19.9% at FSIQ 110 to 119, and 26.8% at FSIQ 120 and above. Use the child's Full Scale IQ to obtain the most accurate base rates for these comparisons.

Developing hypotheses based on a significant difference. A significant difference between any two Index scores may indicate the following:

- Interest patterns
- Cognitive style
- Deficiencies or strengths in processing information
- Deficiencies or strengths in modes of expression
- Deficiencies or strengths in the ability to work under time pressure (such as the time constraints on Perceptual Reasoning subtests)
- Sensory deficiencies
- Brain injury
- Psychopathology
- Behavioral problems, such as limited motivation or rebelliousness or anxiety
- A home or school environment in which language or materials differ from those commonly used in the wider culture

Exhibit 4-1
Procedure Used to Determine Whether Two Scores in a Profile Are Significantly Different

In order to establish whether differences between scores in a profile are reliable, it is necessary to apply statistical procedures to the profile. As always, we cannot be 100% certain that the difference between any two subtest scores is reliable. A confidence level must therefore be selected, such as a 95% level of certainty that the differences are significant. In order to determine whether the difference between two Composites or subtests or tests is reliable, the following formula can be used:

$$\text{Difference Score} = z\sqrt{\text{SEM}_A^2 + \text{SEM}_B^2}$$

The Difference Score refers to the magnitude of the difference between scales or subtests A and B. The *z* refers to the normal curve value associated with the desired confidence level. If we select the 95% level, the associated *z* value is 1.96. The terms under the square root sign refer to the SEM (standard error of measurement) associated with each scale or subtest or test. Many test manuals provide these SEMs.

The following example illustrates how to determine whether there is a significant difference between two scaled scores. Suppose that we are interested in determining the value needed to represent a significant difference between the WISC–IV Verbal Comprehension Composite and Perceptual Reasoning Composite for children in the standardization group. The average SEMs associated with these two Composites are 3.78 and 4.15, respectively, as indicated in the WISC–IV Technical Manual. We know from a normal curve table that, at the 95% confidence level, the *z* value is 1.96. Substituting these values into the formula yields the following:

$$\text{Difference Score} = 1.96\sqrt{3.78^2 + 4.15^2} = 12$$

Thus, differences of 12 or more points between these two scales are significant at the 95% level of confidence. A larger difference (15) is needed for the 99% confidence level. These values appear in the lower right-hand corner of Table A-2 in Appendix A. All values in Tables A-2 and B-2 in Appendixes A and B were obtained by following the above procedure. For the 99% confidence level, a *z* value of 2.58 is used in the equation.

You will need to evaluate the child's entire performance, clinical history, and background information to arrive at the most reasonable hypothesis to account for a significant difference between Index scores. Always formulate hypotheses about Index score differences in relationship to the child's *absolute* score in each area and in relationship to the Full Scale IQ, and only when the differences are significant. This means, for example, that you would not say that a child with a Verbal Comprehension Index of 150 and a Perceptual Reasoning Index of 125 had a perceptual reasoning deficit (or performance deficit or nonverbal deficit), even though the Perceptual Reasoning Index is significantly lower than the Verbal Comprehension Index. In this case, both abilities are well developed; verbal comprehension skills are simply better developed than perceptual reasoning skills. Similarly, you should view a child with a Verbal Comprehension Index of 68 and a Perceptual Reasoning Index of 50 as having both a verbal comprehension deficit and a perceptual reasoning deficit (or performance deficit or nonverbal deficit), even though the Verbal Comprehension Index is significantly higher than the Perceptual Reasoning Index. As noted previously, the Verbal Comprehension Index of 68 may reflect a relative strength for this child, but it is not an absolute one.

Discrepancies between Index scores may be used to generate hypotheses about a child's cognitive functioning but should not be used to diagnose or classify a child or to conclude that a child has a disability. *For example, a discrepancy between two or more Index scores should never be used as the sole criterion for making a diagnosis of learning disability, brain injury, or mental retardation.* Table 4-3 shows suggested major abilities and background factors associated with the four individual Composites.

Examples of hypotheses for Index scores. Examples of hypotheses for all Index scores comparisons follow.

ILLUSTRATIVE HYPOTHESES FOR
VERBAL COMPREHENSION > PERCEPTUAL REASONING

1. Verbal comprehension skills are better developed than perceptual reasoning skills.
2. Verbal processing is better developed than visual-spatial processing.
3. Auditory-vocal processing is better developed than visual-perceptual processing.
4. Knowledge acquired through accumulated experience is better developed than knowledge needed to solve nonverbal problems.
5. Retrieval of verbal information from long-term memory is better developed than nonverbal reasoning.

Table 4-3
Suggested Major Abilities and Background Factors Associated with
WISC–IV Composites

Verbal Comprehension (VC)	Perceptual Reasoning (PR)	Working Memory (WM)	Processing Speed (PS)	Full Scale (FS)	Major abilities and background factors
VC	PR	WM	PS	FS	Attention
		WM		FS	Auditory acuity and discrimination
VC				FS	Auditory-vocal processing
	PR	WM	PS	FS	Concentration
		WM		FS	Crystallized knowledge
VC				FS	Cultural opportunity
VC				FS	Extent of outside reading
	PR			FS	Fluid reasoning ability
	PR			FS	Immediate problem solving
VC				FS	Interests and reading patterns
VC				FS	Language development
VC				FS	Lexical knowledge
	PR			FS	Nonverbal reasoning
	PR			FS	Perceptual reasoning
			PS	FS	Processing speed
VC				FS	Retrieval of material from long-term memory
			PS	FS	Scanning ability
		WM		FS	Short-term auditory memory
		WM	PS	FS	Short-term memory
			PS	FS	Short-term visual memory
			PS	FS	Speed of mental operation
		WM		FS	Use of encoding strategies
		WM		FS	Use of rehearsal strategies
VC				FS	Verbal comprehension
	PR		PS	FS	Visual acuity and discrimination
			PS	FS	Visual-motor coordination
			PS	FS	Visual-motor discrimination
	PR		PS	FS	Visual-perceptual discrimination
	PR			FS	Visual-perceptual reasoning
	PR			FS	Visual-spatial ability
VC				FS	Vocabulary
		WM		FS	Working memory

6. Crystallized knowledge is better developed than fluid reasoning ability.

ILLUSTRATIVE HYPOTHESES FOR
PERCEPTUAL REASONING > VERBAL COMPREHENSION

1. Perceptual reasoning skills are better developed than verbal comprehension skills.
2. Visual-spatial processing is better developed than verbal processing.
3. Visual-discrimination processing is better developed than auditory-vocal processing.
4. Knowledge needed to solve nonverbal problems is better developed than knowledge acquired through accumulated experience.
5. Nonverbal problem solving is better developed than retrieval of verbal information from long-term memory.
6. Fluid reasoning ability is better developed than crystallized knowledge.

ILLUSTRATIVE HYPOTHESES FOR
VERBAL COMPREHENSION > WORKING MEMORY

1. Verbal comprehension is better developed than working memory.
2. Verbal processing is better developed than short-term auditory memory.
3. Auditory-vocal processing is better developed than use of encoding strategies.
4. Long-term verbal memory is better developed than short-term auditory memory.
5. Retrieval of verbal information from long-term memory is better developed than retrieval of information from short-term memory.
6. Crystallized knowledge is better developed than short-term auditory memory.

ILLUSTRATIVE HYPOTHESES FOR
WORKING MEMORY > VERBAL COMPREHENSION

1. Working memory is better developed than verbal comprehension.
2. Short-term auditory memory is better developed than verbal processing.
3. Use of encoding strategies is better developed than auditory-vocal processing.
4. Short-term auditory memory is better developed than long-term verbal memory.
5. Retrieval of information from short-term memory is better developed than retrieval of verbal information from long-term memory.
6. Short-term auditory memory is better developed than crystallized knowledge.

ILLUSTRATIVE HYPOTHESES FOR
VERBAL COMPREHENSION > PROCESSING SPEED

1. Verbal comprehension is better developed than processing speed.
2. Verbal processing is better developed than speed of mental operation.
3. Auditory-vocal processing is better developed than visual-motor coordination.
4. Processing of verbal stimuli is better developed than processing of nonverbal stimuli.
5. Long-term verbal memory is better developed than short-term visual memory.
6. Crystallized knowledge is better developed than processing speed.

ILLUSTRATIVE HYPOTHESES FOR
PROCESSING SPEED > VERBAL COMPREHENSION

1. Processing speed is better developed than verbal comprehension.
2. Speed of mental operation is better developed than verbal processing.
3. Visual-motor processing is better developed than auditory-vocal processing.
4. Processing of nonverbal stimuli is better developed than processing of verbal stimuli.
5. Short-term visual memory is better developed than long-term verbal memory.
6. Processing speed is better developed than crystallized knowledge.

ILLUSTRATIVE HYPOTHESES FOR
PERCEPTUAL REASONING > WORKING MEMORY

1. Perceptual reasoning is better developed than working memory.
2. Visual-spatial processing is better developed than short-term auditory memory.
3. Immediate problem solving ability is better developed than use of encoding strategies.
4. Fluid reasoning ability is better developed than short-term auditory memory.

ILLUSTRATIVE HYPOTHESES FOR
WORKING MEMORY > PERCEPTUAL REASONING

1. Working memory is better developed than perceptual reasoning.
2. Short-term auditory memory is better developed than visual-spatial processing.
3. Use of encoding strategies is better developed than immediate problem solving ability.
4. Short-term auditory memory is better developed than fluid reasoning ability.

**ILLUSTRATIVE HYPOTHESES FOR
PERCEPTUAL REASONING > PROCESSING SPEED**

1. Perceptual reasoning is better developed than processing speed.
2. Visual-spatial processing is better developed than speed of mental operation.
3. Immediate problem solving is better developed than visual-motor coordination.
4. Fluid reasoning ability is better developed than speed of processing nonverbal stimuli.

**ILLUSTRATIVE HYPOTHESES FOR
PROCESSING SPEED > PERCEPTUAL REASONING**

1. Processing speed is better developed than perceptual reasoning.
2. Speed of mental operation is better developed than visual-spatial processing.
3. Visual-motor coordination is better developed than immediate problem-solving.
4. Speed of processing nonverbal stimuli is better developed than fluid reasoning ability.

**ILLUSTRATIVE HYPOTHESES FOR
WORKING MEMORY > PROCESSING SPEED**

1. Working memory is better developed than processing speed.
2. Short-term memory is better developed than speed of mental operation.
3. Ability to use rehearsal strategies is better developed than visual-motor coordination.
4. Ability to sustain attention is better developed for tasks requiring processing of verbal stimuli than for tasks requiring processing of nonverbal stimuli.
5. Short-term auditory memory is better developed than short-term visual memory.

**ILLUSTRATIVE HYPOTHESES FOR
PROCESSING SPEED > WORKING MEMORY**

1. Processing speed is better developed than working memory.
2. Speed of mental operation is better developed than short-term memory.
3. Visual-motor coordination is better developed than the ability to use rehearsal strategies.
4. Ability to sustain attention is better developed for tasks requiring processing of nonverbal stimuli than for tasks requiring processing of verbal stimuli.
5. Short-term visual memory is better developed than short-term auditory memory.

Formulate hypotheses about Index scores only when they are significantly different from each other (see Table A-2 in Appendix A). Table A-3 in Appendix A shows the estimates of the probability of obtaining designated differences between WISC–IV Composite scores by chance. For example, at the 6-year age level, the probability of obtaining a difference of 10.47 between Verbal Comprehension and Perceptual Reasoning is 10%. You can find a summary of interpretive rationales for Composite scores in Table C-5 in Appendix C. In all cases, to determine the best explanation of a child's Index score, carefully analyze the child's entire performance on the WISC–IV and on other tests and the child's case history information.

When the subtest scaled scores that comprise an Index score are in a similar direction (e.g., all above average or all below average), you are on firm ground in interpreting the Index score. However, when the subtest scaled scores that comprise an Index differ in direction (e.g., some above average and some below average), the mean Index score should be interpreted in light of the variability of its component subtest scores.

For example, let's consider two cases. In one case, the child has a Digit Span scaled score of 15 and a Letter–Number Sequencing scaled score of 5. In the other case, the child has a Digit Span scaled score of 10 and a Letter–Number Sequencing scaled score of 10. In both cases the mean scaled score is 10. However, in the first case, the mean reflects two discrepant subtest scaled scores—one high and one low. In the other case, the mean represents two similar subtest scaled scores—both average. In reporting on the first case, you must point out that the overall average score is based on above-average immediate memory ability for digits and below-average immediate memory ability for digits and letters. The reader must be informed that the child's working memory ability (as measured by these two WISC–IV subtests) is variable. In the second case, you need simply point out that short-term memory ability is average. Apply this same rationale when you evaluate all of the Index scores.

Method 2: Compare each Verbal Comprehension subtest scaled score with the mean Verbal Comprehension Index scaled score.

Table A-4 in Appendix A provides the critical values for comparing each of the Verbal Comprehension subtests with the mean of (a) the three core Verbal Comprehension subtests, (b) the three core Verbal Comprehension subtests plus the Information supplemental subtest, (c) the three core Verbal Reasoning subtests plus the Word Reasoning supplemental subtest, and (d) the three core Verbal Comprehension subtests plus the Information and Word Reasoning supplemental subtests for each of the 11 WISC–IV age groups and the total group. For example, critical values for 6-year-old children on the three core Verbal Comprehension subtests range from 2.50 to 2.57 at the .05 level and from 3.07 to 3.15 at the .01 level. We recommend that you use each individual age group to get the most accurate critical value.

Table B.5 (p. 265) in the Administration Manual gives similar values, but only for (a) the overall sample, (b) the .15 and .05 significance levels, and (c) the core subtests. In contrast, Table A-4 in Appendix A in this text gives values for each individual age group as well as for the total group, provides values at the .05 and .01 significance levels, and provides values for all core and supplemental subtest combinations for the Verbal Comprehension Composite.

Table B.5 in the Administration Manual also gives the base rates for differences obtained by various percentages of the standardization sample between a subtest scaled score and the child's mean on the core subtests. The table shows, for example, that a difference of 3.67 points between the subtest scaled score on Similarities and the mean Verbal Comprehension Index (derived for the three core Verbal Comprehension subtests) was obtained by 1% of the standardization sample. The base rates are independent of the significance levels. Further, a significant difference of 2.23 for Similarities at the .05 level occurred in between 10% and 25% of the standardization sample.

Method 3: Compare each Perceptual Reasoning subtest scaled score with the mean Perceptual Reasoning Index scaled score. Table A-4 in Appendix A provides the critical values for comparing each of the Perceptual Reasoning subtests with the mean of (a) the three core Perceptual Reasoning subtests and (b) the three core Perceptual Reasoning subtests plus the Picture Completion supplemental subtest for each of the 11 WISC–IV age groups and the total group. For example, critical values for 6-year-old children on the three core Perceptual Reasoning subtests range from 2.09 to 2.33 at the .05 level and from 2.57 to 2.86 at the .01 level. We recommend that you use each individual age group to get the most accurate critical value.

Table B.5 (p. 265) in the Administration Manual gives similar values, but only for (a) the overall sample, (b) the .15 and .05 significance levels, and (c) the core subtests. In contrast, Table A-4 in Appendix A in this text gives values for each individual age group as well as for the overall group, provides values at the .05 and .01 significance levels, and provides values for all core and supplemental subtest combinations for the Perceptual Reasoning Composite.

Table B.5 in the Administration Manual also gives the base rates for differences obtained by various percentages of the standardization sample between a subtest scaled score and the child's mean on the core subtests. The table shows, for example, that a difference of 4.33 points between the subtest scaled score on Block Design and the mean Perceptual Reasoning Index (derived for the three core Perceptual Reasoning subtests) was obtained by 1% of the standardization sample. The base rates are independent of the significance levels. Further, a significant difference of 2.22 for Block Design at the .05 level occurred in between 10% and 25% of the standardization sample.

Method 4: Compare each Working Memory subtest scaled score with the mean Working Memory Index scaled score. Table A-4 in Appendix A provides the critical values for comparing the mean of (a) the two core Working Memory subtests and (b) the two core Working Memory subtests plus the Arithmetic supplemental subtest for each of the 11 WISC–IV age groups and the total group. For example, critical values for 6-year-old children on the two core Working Memory subtests are 1.38 at the .05 level and 1.81 at the .01 level. We recommend that you use each individual age group to get the most accurate critical values.

Table B.5 (p. 265) in the Administration Manual does not provide any values for Working Memory, including base rates. However, they are shown in Tables B.3 (for comparisons between Digit Span and Letter–Number Sequencing) and B.4 (for base rates of differences between Digit Span and Letter–Number Sequencing). Table B.4 shows that the Digit Span score was 7 points lower than the Letter–Number Sequencing score in .9% of the standardization sample. The base rates are independent of the significance levels. Further, a significant difference of 3 points between Digit Span and Letter–Number Sequencing (in favor of Letter–Number Sequencing) occurred in 19.8% of the population.

Method 5: Compare each Processing Speed subtest scaled score with the mean Processing Speed Index scaled score.

Table A-4 in Appendix A provides the critical values for comparing each of the Processing Speed subtests with the mean of (a) the two core Processing Speed subtests and (b) the two core Processing Speed subtests plus the Cancellation subtest for each of the 11 WISC–IV age groups and the total group. For example, critical values for 6-year-old children on the two core Processing Speed subtests are 2.06 at the .05 level and 2.71 at the .01 level. We recommend that you use each individual age group to get the most accurate critical value.

Table B.5 (p. 265) in the Administration Manual does not provide any values for Processing Speed, including base rates. However, they are shown in Tables B.3 (for comparisons between Coding and Symbol Search) and B.4 (for base rates of differences between Coding and Symbol Search). Table B.4 shows that the Coding score was 7 points lower than the Symbol Search score in 1% of the standardization sample. The base rates are independent of the significance levels. Further, a significant difference of 4 points between Coding and Symbol Search (in favor of Symbol Search) occurred in 10.5% of the population.

Method 6: Compare each subtest scaled score with the mean subtest scaled score based on the 10 core subtests and based on all 15 subtests.

Table A-4 in Appendix A provides critical values for each of the 11 age groups and the total group for the 10 core subtests and for the 15 core and supplemental subtests. For example, critical values for 6-year-old children for the 10 core subtests range from 2.40 to 4.15 at the .05 level and from 2.82 to 4.87 at the .01 level. We recommend that you use each individual age group to get the most accurate critical value.

Table B.5 in the Administration Manual also gives the base rates for differences obtained by various percentages of the standardization sample between a subtest scaled score and the child's mean on the 10 core subtests (but not on the 15 subtests). The table shows, for example, that a difference of 5.50 points between the subtest scaled score on Block Design and the mean of the 10 core subtests was obtained by 1% of the standardization sample. The base rates are independent of the significance levels. Further, a significant difference of 3.01 for Block Design at the .05 level occurred in between 10% and 25% of the standardization sample.

Method 7: Compare sets of individual subtest scaled scores.

Table A-2 in Appendix A provides critical values for comparing sets of subtest scaled scores for each of the 11 age groups and for the total group. For example, at age 6 the critical values for comparing Block Design and Similarities are 4 points at the .05 level and 5 points at the .01 level. The values in Table A-2 in Appendix A and Table B.3 in the Administration Manual are overly liberal (i.e., they often lead to significant differences that may not be true differences) when more than one comparison is made. They are most accurate when you plan to make specific comparisons before you administer the test—for example, when you plan to compare Similarities with Vocabulary or Digit Span with Letter–Number Sequencing.

Table B.3 in the Administration Manual gives similar values in decimal form, but only for the overall sample and the .15 and .05 significance levels. In contrast, Table A-2 in Appendix A in this text gives values for each individual age group as well as for the total group, provides values at the .05 and .01 significance levels, and provides whole numbers instead of decimals (a child's subtest scaled scores are always whole numbers without decimals).

Before making multiple comparisons among the 10 core subtests, determine the difference between the highest and lowest subtest scaled scores. If this difference is 5 or more scaled-score points, a significant difference at the .05 level is indicated. Differences of 5 or more scaled-score points between subtests can then be interpreted. If the difference between the highest and lowest subtest scaled scores is less than 5 scaled-score points, multiple comparisons should not be made between individual subtest scaled scores. (The Note to Table A-2 in Appendix A shows the formula that was used to compute the significant difference. The formula considers the average standard error of measurement for each of the 10 core subtests and the Studentized range statistic.)

Comparisons between subtests. If you find significant differences between subtest scaled scores (see Table A-2 in Appendix A), you will need to interpret the findings. Several parts of this text will help you do so. First, study Table C-1 in Appendix C, which presents the percentile ranks and qualitative descriptions associated with the subtest scaled scores. Second, study Table C-2 in Appendix C and Table 4-4 in this chapter, which show suggested abilities associated with the 15 WISC–IV subtests. Third, review the three preceding chapters,

Table 4-4
Suggested Abilities or Background Factors Associated with WISC–IV Subtests

Block Design (BD)	Similarities (SI)	Digit Span (DS)	Picture Concepts (PCn)	Coding (CD)	Vocabulary (VC)	Letter-Number Seq. (LN)	Matrix Reasoning (MR)	Comprehension (CO)	Symbol Search (SS)	Picture Completion (PCm)	Cancellation (CA)	Information (IN)	Arithmetic (AR)	Word Reasoning (WR)	M	Abilities or background factors
		DS		CD		LN	MR		SS	PCm	CA		AR	WR	___	Attention
		DS				LN							AR		___	Auditory acuity
		DS				LN							AR		___	Auditory sequential processing
	SI		PCn	CD					SS		CA			WR	___	Cognitive flexibility
BD		DS		CD		LN	MR		SS	PCm	CA		AR		___	Concentration
BD	SI		PCn		VC									WR	___	Conceptual thinking
	SI		PCn		VC			CO				IN	AR		___	Crystallized knowledge
	SI				VC			CO				IN		WR	___	Cultural opportunities
	SI		PCn		VC							IN		WR	___	Extent of outside reading
BD				CD					SS		CA				___	Fine-motor coordination
			PCn				MR							WR	___	Fluid reasoning ability
					VC			CO				IN	AR		___	Fund of information
			PCn		VC							IN		WR	___	Intellectual curiosity
	SI		PCn		VC							IN		WR	___	Interest and reading patterns
	SI				VC			CO						WR	___	Language development
	SI				VC									WR	___	Lexical knowledge
	SI				VC			CO		PCm		IN	AR	WR	___	Long-term memory
BD				CD			MR		SS		CA				___	Motivation and persistence
BD			PCn				MR			PCm					___	Nonverbal reasoning
		DS		CD		LN							AR		___	Numerical ability
			PCn							PCm					___	Perception of meaningful stimuli
				CD					SS		CA				___	Processing speed
	SI		PCn		VC			CO				IN	AR	WR	___	Quality of schooling
BD	SI		PCn				MR	CO		PCm			AR	WR	___	Reasoning
				CD					SS	PCm	CA				___	Scanning ability
		DS		CD		LN			SS		CA		AR	WR	___	Short-term memory
BD							MR			PCm					___	Spatial perception
BD				CD					SS	PCm	CA				___	Speed of mental processing
	SI				VC			CO				IN		WR	___	Verbal comprehension
BD			PCn	CD			MR		SS	PCm	CA				___	Visual acuity
				CD					SS	PCm					___	Visual memory
BD				CD					SS		CA				___	Visual-motor coordination
BD			PCn	CD			MR		SS	PCm	CA				___	Visual-perceptual discrimination
BD			PCn				MR		SS	PCm					___	Visual-perceptual organization
BD			PCn	CD			MR		SS	PCm	CA				___	Visual-perceptual processing
BD			PCn				MR			PCm					___	Visual-perceptual reasoning
BD							MR								___	Visual-spatial ability
	SI				VC			CO						WR	___	Vocabulary
		DS				LN							AR		___	Working memory

Note. M = mean of the subtest scaled scores for the ability or background factor. For additional suggested abilities or factors, **see** Chapters 2 and 3 and Table C-2 in Appendix C.

because much of the material in these chapters is relevant to interpreting subtest scaled scores. Fourth, study the examples below, which are designed to help you make subtest comparisons.

Treat all hypotheses developed from subtest comparisons as tentative. Develop your hypotheses based on both significant differences between subtest scaled scores and the absolute values of the subtest scaled scores. Thus, remember that *subtest scaled scores of 10 or higher should be described as reflecting average or above-average ability and never as absolute weaknesses, whereas subtest scaled scores of 7 or lower should be described as reflecting below-average ability and never as absolute strengths. Any hypotheses about subtest scaled scores should be developed through study of the child's entire test performance and clinical history.*

Interpretation of subtest comparisons. Let's first look at subtests that are in the same Composite and then look at subtests across Composites.

COMPARISON OF VERBAL COMPREHENSION SUBTESTS

1. *Similarities (SI) and Comprehension (CO).* Similarities and Comprehension both involve conceptualizing skills. Similarities usually requires a response expressing one primary idea, while Comprehension requires an extended response. In addition, Similarities also measures verbal concept formation, whereas Comprehension measures factual knowledge and social judgment.

- SI > CO: This pattern may suggest that verbal concept formation is better developed than factual knowledge and social judgment.
- CO > SI: This pattern may suggest that factual knowledge and social judgment are better developed than verbal concept formation.

2. *Vocabulary (VC) and Similarities (SI).* Both Vocabulary and Similarities measure abstract thinking ability and ability to form concepts, but Similarities is a better measure of these abilities.

- SI > VC: This pattern may suggest that the ability to categorize is better developed than the ability to understand or express the meaning of individual words.
- VC > SI: This pattern may suggest that the ability to understand or express the meaning of individual words is better developed than the ability to categorize.

3. *Similarities (SI) and Word Reasoning (WR).* Both Similarities and Word Reasoning measure verbal comprehension and verbal abstraction. However, Similarities is a better measure of verbal concept formation, while Word Reasoning is a better measure of verbal reasoning and deductive reasoning.

- SI > WR: This pattern may suggest that the ability to categorize is better developed than the ability to reason deductively.
- WR > SI: This pattern may suggest that the ability to reason deductively is better developed than the ability to categorize.

4. *Information (IN) and Comprehension (CO).* This comparison relates the amount of information retained (Information) to the ability to use information (Comprehension). Information requires factual knowledge, while Comprehension requires both factual knowledge and social judgment.

- IN > CO: This pattern may suggest that the child's fund of information is better developed than his or her social judgment.
- CO > IN: This pattern may suggest that the child's social judgment is better developed than his or her fund of information.

5. *Information (IN) and Similarities (SI).* This comparison relates the amount of information retained (Information) to the ability to engage in conceptual thinking (Similarities).

- SI > IN: This pattern may suggest that the child's conceptual reasoning ability is better developed than his or her fund of information.
- IN > SI: This pattern may suggest that the child's fund of information is better developed than his or her conceptual reasoning ability.

6. *Information (IN) and Word Reasoning (WR).* This comparison relates the amount of information retained (Information) to the ability to reason deductively (Word Reasoning).

- IN > WR: This pattern may suggest that the child's fund of information is better developed than his or her ability to reason deductively.
- WR > IN: This pattern may suggest that the child's ability to reason deductively is better developed than his or her fund of information.

7. *Vocabulary (VC) and Word Reasoning (WR)*. Both Vocabulary and Word Reasoning measure abstract thinking ability and ability to form concepts, but Word Reasoning is a better measure of verbal reasoning and deductive reasoning.

- VC > WR: This pattern may suggest that the ability to understand or express the meaning of individual words is better developed than the ability to reason deductively.
- WR > VC: This pattern may suggest that the ability to reason deductively is better developed than the ability to understand or express the meaning of individual words.

8. *Vocabulary (VC), Comprehension (CO), and Information (IN)*. All three subtests involve verbal processing, but in different contexts.

- VC, IN > CO: This pattern may suggest that verbal ability and fund of information are better developed than social judgment.
- CO > VC, IN: This pattern may suggest that social judgment is better developed than verbal ability and fund of information.
- VC, CO > IN: This pattern may suggest that verbal ability and social judgment are better developed than fund of information.
- IN > VC, CO: This pattern may suggest that fund of information is better developed than verbal ability and social judgment.

COMPARISON OF PERCEPTUAL REASONING SUBTESTS

1. *Matrix Reasoning (MR) and Block Design (BD)*. This comparison relates two subtests that measure nonverbal reasoning ability. Matrix Reasoning requires analogic perceptual reasoning and has no time limits, whereas Block Design requires analysis and synthesis and has time limits.

- MR > BD: This pattern may suggest that analogic perceptual reasoning is better developed than perceptual analysis and synthesis skills when working under time pressure.
- BD > MR: This pattern may suggest that perceptual analysis and synthesis skills when working under time pressure are better developed than analogic perceptual reasoning.

2. *Matrix Reasoning (MR) and Picture Concepts (PCn)*. This comparison relates two subtests that meas-

ure perceptual reasoning. However, Matrix Reasoning also measures spatial ability and perceptual organization, whereas Picture Concepts also measures conceptual thinking.

- MR > PCn: This pattern may suggest that analogic perceptual reasoning is better developed than conceptual thinking in a perceptual task.
- PCn > MR: This pattern may suggest that conceptual thinking in a perceptual task is better developed than analogic perceptual reasoning.

3. *Picture Completion (PCm) and Block Design (BD)*. This comparison relates nonspatial visual perceptual ability (Picture Completion) to spatial visualization ability (Block Design).

- PCm > BD: This pattern may suggest that nonspatial visual perceptual ability is better developed than spatial visualization ability.
- BD > PCm: This pattern may suggest that spatial visualization ability is better developed than nonspatial visual perceptual ability.

4. *Matrix Reasoning (MR) and Picture Completion (PCm)*. This comparison relates analogic perceptual reasoning (Matrix Reasoning) to nonspatial visual perceptual ability (Picture Completion).

- MR > PCm: This pattern may suggest that analogic perceptual reasoning is better developed than nonspatial visual perceptual ability.
- PCm > MR: This pattern may suggest that nonspatial visual perceptual ability is better developed than analogic perceptual reasoning.

5. *Picture Completion (PCm) and Picture Concepts (PCn)*. This comparison relates two subtests that measure perceptual reasoning ability and perceptual recognition ability. However, Picture Completion also measures the ability to distinguish essential from nonessential details, whereas Picture Concepts also measures conceptual thinking.

- PCm > PCn: This pattern may suggest that the ability to distinguish essential from nonessential details is better developed than conceptual thinking in a perceptual task.
- PCn > PCm: This pattern may suggest that conceptual thinking in a perceptual task is better developed than the ability to distinguish essential from nonessential details.

6. *Block Design (BD) and Matrix Reasoning (MR) vs. Picture Concepts (PCn) and Picture Completion (PCm)*. Block Design, Matrix Reasoning, Picture Concepts, and Picture Completion all require perceptual reasoning, attention to detail, and concentration. In addition, both Matrix Reasoning and Block Design may involve spatial ability.

- BD, MR > PCn, PCm: This pattern may suggest that spatial reasoning ability is better developed than nonspatial reasoning ability.
- PCn, PCm > MR, BD: This pattern may suggest that nonspatial reasoning ability is better developed than spatial reasoning ability.

COMPARISON OF WORKING MEMORY SUBTESTS

1. *Digit Span (DS) and Letter–Number Sequencing (LN)*. This comparison relates two subtests that measure short-term rote auditory memory. In Digit Span the stimuli are numbers only, whereas in Letter–Number Sequencing the stimuli are both numbers and letters, and Letter–Number Sequencing involves a greater degree of information processing.

- DS > LN: This pattern may suggest that short-term auditory memory for tasks that require rote memorization with minimal information processing is better developed than short-term auditory memory for tasks that require rote memorization and information processing.
- LN > DS: This pattern may suggest that short-term auditory memory for tasks that require rote memorization and information processing is better developed than short-term auditory memory for tasks that require rote memorization with minimal information processing.

2. *Digit Span (DS) and Arithmetic (AR)*. Both Digit Span and Arithmetic require auditory memory and facility with numbers, but Digit Span is a better measure of auditory rote memory and Arithmetic is a better measure of numerical ability.

- DS > AR: This pattern may suggest that auditory rote memory is better developed than numerical ability.
- AR > DS: This pattern may suggest that numerical ability is better developed than auditory rote memory.

3. *Digit Span Forward (DSF) and Digit Span Backward (DSB)*. Digit Span Forward and Digit Span Backward involve auditory short-term memory and attention.

Digit Span Backward, however, involves more complex attentional processes.

- DSF > DSB: This pattern may suggest that auditory short-term rote memory is better developed than auditory short-term rote memory requiring some transformation.
- DSB > DSF: This pattern may suggest that auditory short-term rote memory requiring some transformation is better developed than auditory short-term rote memory.

COMPARISON OF PROCESSING SPEED SUBTESTS

1. *Coding (CD) and Symbol Search (SS)*. Both Coding and Symbol Search involve processing speed, perceptual discrimination, accuracy, attention, and concentration. However, Coding requires perceptual symbol-associative skills to a greater degree than Symbol Search, whereas Symbol Search requires perceptual discrimination skills to a greater extent than Coding.

- CD > SS: This pattern may suggest that perceptual symbol-associative skills are better developed than perceptual discrimination skills that do not involve association.
- SS > CD: This pattern may suggest that perceptual discrimination skills that do not involve association are better developed than perceptual symbol-associative skills.

2. *Coding (CD) and Cancellation (CA)*. Both Coding and Cancellation involve processing speed, perceptual discrimination, accuracy, attention, and concentration. However, Coding requires perceptual symbol-associative skills, whereas Cancellation requires perceptual recognition ability.

- CD > CA: This pattern may suggest that perceptual symbol-associative skills are better developed than perceptual recognition ability.
- CA > CD: This pattern may suggest that perceptual recognition ability is better developed than perceptual symbol-associative skills.

COMPARISON OF VERBAL COMPREHENSION AND PERCEPTUAL REASONING SUBTESTS

1. *Similarities (SI) and Block Design (BD)*. Similarities and Block Design both reflect abstract reasoning ability. The subtests require the abstraction of relations among stimulus items. However, Similarities involves verbal material and requires a verbal response, whereas

Block Design involves nonverbal material and requires a motor response.

- SI > BD: This pattern may suggest that abstract reasoning ability with verbal stimuli is better developed than abstract reasoning ability with nonverbal stimuli.
- BD > SI: This pattern may suggest that abstract reasoning ability with nonverbal stimuli is better developed than abstract reasoning ability with verbal stimuli.

2. *Similarities (SI) and Picture Concepts (PCn).* Similarities and Picture Concepts both reflect abstract reasoning ability involving conceptualization and categorization. They require the abstraction of relations among stimulus items. However, Similarities involves verbal stimuli and requires a verbal response, whereas Picture Concepts involves visual stimuli and requires either a pointing or a verbal response. In addition, Picture Concepts does not require the child to express verbally the categorical concept.

- SI > PCn: This pattern may suggest that abstract reasoning ability with verbal stimuli is better developed than abstract reasoning ability with visual stimuli.
- PCn > SI: This pattern may suggest that abstract reasoning ability with visual stimuli is better developed than abstract reasoning ability with verbal stimuli.

3. *Similarities (SI) and Matrix Reasoning (MR).* This comparison relates the ability to engage in verbal conceptual reasoning (Similarities) to analogic nonverbal reasoning ability (Matrix Reasoning).

- SI > MR: This pattern may suggest that verbal conceptual reasoning is better developed than analogic nonverbal reasoning ability.
- MR > SI: This pattern may suggest that analogic nonverbal reasoning ability is better developed than verbal conceptual reasoning.

4. *Comprehension (CO) and Matrix Reasoning (MR).* This comparison relates social judgment (Comprehension) to analogic nonverbal reasoning ability (Matrix Reasoning).

- CO > MR: This pattern may suggest that social judgment is better developed than analogic nonverbal reasoning ability.
- MR > CO: This pattern may suggest that analogic

nonverbal reasoning ability is better developed than social judgment.

5. *Vocabulary (VC) and Matrix Reasoning (MR).* This comparison relates the ability to understand or express the meanings of individual words (Vocabulary) to analogic nonverbal reasoning ability (Matrix Reasoning).

- VC > MR: This pattern may suggest that the ability to understand or express the meanings of individual words is better developed than analogic nonverbal reasoning ability.
- MR > VC: This pattern may suggest that analogic nonverbal reasoning ability is better developed than the ability to understand or express the meanings of individual words.

6. *Word Reasoning (WR) and Picture Concepts (PCn).* Word Reasoning and Picture Concepts both reflect abstract reasoning ability involving conceptualization and categorization. They require the abstraction of relations among stimulus items. However, Word Reasoning involves verbal stimuli and requires a verbal response, whereas Picture Concepts involves visual stimuli and requires either a pointing or a verbal response. In addition, Picture Concepts does not require the child to express verbally the categorical concept.

- WR > PCn: This pattern may suggest that abstract reasoning ability with verbal stimuli is better developed than abstract reasoning ability with visual stimuli.
- PCn > WR: This pattern may suggest that abstract reasoning ability with visual stimuli is better developed than abstract reasoning ability with verbal stimuli.

7. *Vocabulary (VC) and Information (IN) vs. Block Design (BD) and Matrix Reasoning (MR).* This is a comparison of two subtests that reflect the extent of previously learned and stored verbal material and crystallized knowledge (Vocabulary and Information) versus two subtests that reflect perceptual reasoning and fluid reasoning ability (Block Design and Matrix Reasoning).

- VC, IN > BD, MR: This pattern may suggest that abilities dependent on well-learned verbal facts and relationships are better developed than spatial reasoning ability and novel problem-solving ability.

- BD, MR > VC, IN: This pattern may suggest that spatial reasoning ability and novel problem-solving ability are better developed than abilities dependent on well-learned verbal facts and relationships.

COMPARISON OF VERBAL COMPREHENSION AND WORKING MEMORY SUBTESTS

1. *Comprehension (CO) and Arithmetic (AR).* Comprehension and Arithmetic both require reasoning ability, such as the ability to analyze a given set of materials and then to recognize the elements needed for the solution of the specified problem. However, Comprehension involves social situations, whereas Arithmetic involves the manipulation of numbers.

- CO > AR: This pattern may suggest that reasoning ability in social situations is better developed than reasoning ability in mathematical tasks.
- AR > CO: This pattern may suggest that reasoning ability in mathematical tasks is better developed than reasoning ability in social settings.

2. *Similarities (SI) and Arithmetic (AR).* Similarities and Arithmetic both require conceptual thinking, one with verbal symbols and the other with numerical symbols.

- SI > AR: This pattern may suggest that conceptual thinking is better developed with verbal material than with numerical symbols.
- AR > SI: This pattern may suggest that conceptual thinking is better developed with numerical symbols than with verbal material.

COMPARISON OF PERCEPTUAL REASONING AND WORKING MEMORY SUBTESTS

1. *Picture Completion (PCm) and Arithmetic (AR).* Picture Completion and Arithmetic both involve concentration. On Picture Completion, however, the child concentrates on an externalized form—a visual stimulus—while on Arithmetic the child concentrates on an internalized stimulus—a memory trace.

- PCm > AR: This pattern may suggest that concentration on visual details is better developed than concentration on mathematical problems.
- AR > PCm: This pattern may suggest that concentration on mathematical problems is better developed than concentration on visual details.

COMPARISON OF PERCEPTUAL REASONING AND PROCESSING SPEED SUBTESTS

1. *Matrix Reasoning (MR) and Coding (CD).* This comparison relates analogic nonverbal reasoning ability (Matrix Reasoning) to processing speed (Coding).

- MR > CD: This pattern may suggest that analogic perceptual reasoning is better developed than processing speed.
- CD > MR: This pattern may suggest that processing speed is better developed than analogic perceptual reasoning.

2. *Matrix Reasoning (MR) and Symbol Search (SS).* This comparison relates analogic nonverbal reasoning ability (Matrix Reasoning) to processing speed (Symbol Search).

- MR > SS: This pattern may suggest that analogic perceptual reasoning is better developed than processing speed.
- SS > MR: This pattern may suggest that processing speed is better developed than analogic perceptual reasoning.

3. *Block Design (BD), Matrix Reasoning (MR), and Picture Concepts (PCn) vs. Coding (CD) and Symbol Search (SS).* This is a comparison of sequential processing versus simultaneous processing.

- BD, MR, PCn > CD, SS: This pattern may suggest that sequential processing is better developed than simultaneous processing.
- CD, SS > BD, MR, PCn: This pattern may suggest that simultaneous processing is better developed than sequential processing.

COMPARISON OF WORKING MEMORY AND PROCESSING SPEED SUBTESTS

1. *Digit Span (DS) and Letter–Number Sequencing (LN) vs. Coding (CD) and Symbol Search (SS).* Digit Span and Letter–Number Sequencing require short-term auditory memory and attention and concentration, whereas Coding and Symbol Search require short-term visual memory and attention and concentration.

- DS, LN > CD, SS: This pattern may suggest that short-term auditory memory is better developed than short-term visual memory.
- CD, SS > DS, LN: This pattern may suggest that short-term visual memory is better developed than short-term auditory memory.

Method 8: Compare the range of subtest scaled scores with that found in the standardization sample. The subtest scaled-score range provides information about the variability (or scatter) in a child's WISC–IV profile. The scaled-score range is the distance between the two most extreme subtest scaled scores. It is obtained by subtracting the lowest subtest scaled score from the highest subtest scaled score. For example, in a profile where the highest subtest scaled score is 15 and the lowest subtest scaled score is 3, the range is 12, since $15 - 3 = 12$. If the highest score in the profile is 10 and the lowest score is 5, the range is 5, since $10 - 5 = 5$.

Note that the scaled-score range is based on only two scores and therefore fails to take into account the variability among all subtest scaled scores used in the comparison. The base rate scaled-score range is still useful, however, because it provides information about what occurred in the standardization sample. It also is a relatively simple measure of variability that can be compared with more complex indices of variability, such as the standard deviation of the subtests. Let's look at two ways to evaluate intersubtest scatter by using data from the standardization sample.

1. *Overall scaled-score range.* One method is to compare the child's scaled-score range to the range found in the standardization sample for the 10 core subtests. Table B.6 in the Administration Manual shows that the median scaled-score range was 7 points for the 10 core subtests. Table B.6 also shows scatter for other combinations of subtests (4 and 5 Verbal Comprehension subtests, 4 Perceptual Reasoning subtests, and 11, 12, 13, 14, and 15 subtests).

2. *Scaled-score range based on specific subtest scaled scores.* Table B.6 shows that the median scaled-score range was 3 points for the three core Verbal Comprehension subtests and 3 points for the three core Perceptual Reasoning subtests. Table B.4 shows that the median scaled-score range was 2 points in either direction on Digit Span vs. Letter–Number Sequencing, Coding vs. Symbol Search, Similarities vs. Picture Concepts, Digit Span vs. Arithmetic, and Letter–Number Sequencing vs. Arithmetic. The median scaled-score range was 2 points on Coding < Cancellation and 3 points on Coding > Cancellation, and 3 points in either direction on Symbol Search vs. Cancellation.

Method 9: Compare sets of individual Process scaled scores. Table A-5 in Appendix A provides critical values for comparing sets of Process scaled scores for each of the 11 age groups and for the total group. For example, at age 6, the critical values for comparing Block Design and Block Design No Time Bonus are 4 points at the .05 level and 5 points at the .01 level. Notice that there are three sets of comparisons in Table A-5, and each set represents scores from the same area (i.e., Block Design, Digit Span, and Cancellation). Two of the three sets are pairs of Process scores (Digit Span Backward and Digit Span Forward; Cancellation Structured and Cancellation Random), while the other set compares a subtest scaled score with a Process scaled score (Block Design and Block Design No Time Bonus).

Table B.9 in the Administration Manual gives similar values in decimal form, but only for the overall sample and the .15 and .05 significance levels. In contrast, Table A-2 in Appendix A in this text gives values for each individual age group as well as the total group, provides values at the .05 and .01 significance levels, and provides values in whole numbers instead of decimals (a child's scaled scores are always whole numbers without decimals).

Because we need research to investigate what the comparisons of the three sets of Process scores mean clinically, the following discussion is best viewed as tentative. The Digit Span Forward vs. Digit Span Backward comparison relates two short-term auditory memory tasks, one requiring no transformation and the other requiring transformation. As noted in Chapter 2, Digit Span Forward involves primarily rote learning and memory, whereas Digit Span Backward requires transformation of the stimulus input prior to responding. A higher score on Digit Span Forward than on Digit Span Backward suggests that the child's auditory short-term memory is better when small bits of information need to be recalled than when small bits of information need to be transformed. In contrast, a higher score on Digit Span Backward than on Digit Span Forward suggests that short-term auditory memory is better when the task is challenging than when the task simply requires repetition.

The Block Design vs. Block Design No Time Bonus comparison gives you information about the effect of speed on performance of a spatial visualization task without and with time limits. A higher score on Block Design No Time Bonus than on Block Design suggests that the child does better on a spatial visualization task when speed is not required. A higher score on Block Design than on Block Design No Time Bonus suggests that the child works well under a time limit. Two similar scores suggest that the child does not benefit from the bonus points associated with speed.

The Cancellation Random vs. Cancellation Structured comparison reflects how the child performs in a less structured and a more structured processing speed task. A lower score on Cancellation Structured than on Cancellation Random suggests that the child does not benefit from practice, that fatigue might have set in, or that structure is not helpful. A higher score on Cancellation Structured than on Cancellation Random suggests that the child benefits from practice, that fatigue did not set in, or that structure is helpful.

Method 10: Compare the range of Process scaled scores with that found in the standardization sample.

The Process scaled-score range provides information about the variability (or scatter) in a child's WISC–IV profile. Table B.10 in the Administration Manual shows that the median Process scaled-score range was 1 point for Block Design vs. Block Design No Time Bonus, 2 points for Digit Span Forward vs. Digit Span Backward, and 2 points for Cancellation Structured vs. Cancellation Random.

Statistically Reliable vs. Empirically Observed IQ Differences

We have seen that there are two types of complementary measures that can assist in profile analysis—statistically reliable differences and empirically observed base rates. Table A-2 in Appendix A presents the differences required between the four Indexes for statistical significance. Table B.2 in the Administration Manual gives the actual (i.e., empirically observed) base rates of the frequencies of differences between the Index scores for the standardization sample.

Whether an occurrence is "unusual" (i.e., low base rate) depends on how one defines the term. A difference that occurs in 15% or 20% of the population may be considered unusual by some, whereas others may consider a difference unusual only if it occurs in no more than 5% or 10% of the population. We believe that all statistically significant differences between scores are "unusual," regardless of the base rate, and deserve consideration in evaluating a child's profile of abilities. We also suggest that a low base rate is one that occurs in 10% to 15% or less of the standardization sample. In fact, all of the significant differences between the six sets of Composite comparisons in Table B.2 in the Administration Manual (Verbal Comprehension Index vs. Perceptual Reasoning Index, Verbal Comprehension Index vs. Working Memory Index, Verbal Comprehension Index vs. Processing Speed Index, Perceptual Reasoning Index vs. Working Memory Index, Perceptual Reasoning Index vs. Processing Speed Index, Working Memory Index vs. Processing Speed Index) also occur in less than 16% of the overall sample.

Let's look at an example. A 6-year-old child with a Full Scale IQ of 110 has a Verbal Comprehension Index that is 13 points higher than the Perceptual Reasoning Index. This difference is statistically significant at the .05 level. This is a reliable difference that is unlikely to be the result of measurement error (i.e., chance). Differences that are greater than chance may reflect differential functioning in the abilities measured by Verbal Comprehension and Perceptual Reasoning. From Table B.2 in the Administration Manual (p. 261) we find that a difference of 13 points (VCI > PRI) occurred in 12.9% of the standardization sample. This 13-point difference, therefore, is statistically significant and occurs in less than 15% of the standardization sample. Whether the 13-point difference is clinically meaningful is, of course, an empirical question.

Clinical acumen, the child's medical history, behavioral observations, and the results of other tests that the child has taken will help you interpret differences between the Index scores. The magnitude and direction of the Index score discrepancies and subtest scaled-score discrepancies can be influenced by several variables, such as the child's educational level and cultural and linguistic background. For example, on average, children who are in honors programs in school or in advanced placement classes may have higher scores on Verbal Comprehension than on Perceptual Reasoning, whereas children with a non-English or limited English linguistic background may have lower scores on Verbal Comprehension than on Perceptual Reasoning.

Procedure to Follow in Determining Whether Subtest Scaled Scores Are Significantly Different from the Mean

The following procedure will help you determine whether a subtest scaled score is significantly different from the mean of its respective Composite (based on 2, 3, 4, or 5 subtests) or the mean based on 10 or 15 subtests.

Step 1. Write the names of the subtests and their respective scaled scores on a sheet of paper.

VERBAL COMPREHENSION

Step 2. Sum the three, four, or five Verbal Comprehension subtest scaled scores.

Step 3. Compute the mean of the Verbal Comprehension subtests by dividing the sum of the Verbal Comprehension subtest scaled scores by the total number of Verbal Comprehension subtests administered (3, 4, or 5).

Step 4. Calculate the deviation from the mean for each Verbal Comprehension subtest by subtracting the Verbal Comprehension mean from each Verbal Comprehension subtest scaled score. Enter these deviations, with a negative sign if appropriate (–), opposite the subtest scaled scores.

PERCEPTUAL REASONING

Step 5. Sum the three or four Perceptual Reasoning subtest scaled scores.

Step 6. Compute the mean of the Perceptual Reasoning subtests by dividing the sum of the Perceptual Reasoning subtest scaled scores by the total number of Perceptual Reasoning subtests administered (3 or 4).

Step 7. Calculate the deviation from the mean for each Perceptual Reasoning subtest by subtracting the Perceptual Reasoning mean from each Perceptual Reasoning subtest scaled score. Enter these deviations, with a negative sign if appropriate (–), opposite the subtest scaled scores.

WORKING MEMORY

Step 8. Sum the two or three Working Memory subtest scaled scores.

Step 9. Compute the mean of the Working Memory subtests by dividing the sum of the Working Memory subtests by the total number of Working Memory subtests administered (2 or 3).

Step 10. Calculate the deviation from the mean for each Working Memory subtest by subtracting the Working Memory mean from each Working Memory subtest scaled score. Enter these deviations, with a negative sign if appropriate (–), opposite the subtest scaled scores.

PROCESSING SPEED

Step 11. Sum the two or three Processing Speed subtest scaled scores.

Step 12. Compute the mean of the Processing Speed subtests by dividing the sum of the Processing Speed subtests by the total number of Processing Speed subtests administered (2 or 3).

Step 13. Calculate the deviation from the mean for each Processing Speed subtest by subtracting the Processing Speed mean from each Processing Speed subtest scaled score. Enter these deviations, with a negative sign if appropriate (–), opposite the subtest scaled scores.

FULL SCALE

Step 14. Sum all of the subtest scaled scores.

Step 15. Compute the mean of the Full Scale by dividing the sum of the subtest scaled scores by the total number of subtests administered.

Step 16. Calculate the deviation from the Full Scale mean for each subtest scaled score by subtracting the Full Scale mean from each subtest scaled score. Enter these deviations, with a negative sign if appropriate (–), opposite the subtest scaled scores.

DETERMINING SIGNIFICANT DIFFERENCES

Step 17. Determine whether the deviations are significant by using Table A-4 in Appendix A. The values in Table A-4 reflect significant differences at the .05 and .01 levels of probability by age group. Be sure to use the appropriate column in Table A-4 to obtain the significant deviations.

Step 18. Place an asterisk next to each subtest deviation that is significant.

Step 19. After each asterisk, write S for a *strength* (interindividual comparison), RS for a *relative strength* (intraindividual comparison), W for a *weakness* (interindividual comparison), or RW for a *relative weakness* (intraindividual comparison).

Table 4-5 illustrates these steps and shows whether the subtest scaled scores differ significantly from the mean of (a) the Verbal Comprehension scaled scores, (b) the Perceptual Reasoning scaled scores, (c) the Working Memory scaled scores, (d) the Processing Speed scaled scores, and (e) all Full Scale scaled scores for a 6-year-old child who was administered all 15 subtests. The comparisons in Table 4-5 show the following:

- Information was the only subtest whose score was significantly lower than the Verbal Comprehension mean.
- Matrix Reasoning was the only subtest whose score was significantly lower than the Perceptual Reasoning mean.
- The Digit Span score was significantly higher than the Working Memory mean.
- No subtest score differed significantly from the Processing Speed mean.
- Matrix Reasoning, Letter–Number Sequencing, and Arithmetic subtest scaled scores were significantly lower than the Full Scale mean.

In determining whether a subtest scaled score is significantly different from the mean, disregard any minus signs in Table 4-5. You may now infer that the differences between the Information, Matrix Reasoning, and Digit Span subtest scaled scores and the child's respective Composite mean scaled scores are not chance differences. The results suggest that, for this child, the abilities reflected by the Digit Span subtest scaled score are strengths, and the abilities reflected by the Information and Matrix Reasoning subtest scaled scores are weaknesses.

The critical values used in the preparation of Table 4-5 are based on the assumption that the scores on all subtests in a scale are to be compared with the mean score for that scale. Therefore, use only one significance level (either .05 or .01) to determine the critical values. *Do not mix levels of significance for this type of comparison.*

Table 4-5
An Example of Profile Analysis on the WISC–IV: Comparing Each Subtest Scaled Score to the Mean Individual Composite Scaled Score and the Mean Full Scale Scaled Score

| | | | Deviation from | |
			Individual Composite mean	Full Scale mean
Composite	Subtest	Scaled score		
Verbal Comprehension	Similarities	11	0.8	1.6
	Vocabulary	11	0.8	1.6
	Comprehension	13	2.8	3.6
	Information	7	−3.2*W	−2.4
	Word Reasoning	9	−1.2	−0.4
	Mean	10.2		
Perceptual Reasoning	Block Design	11	1.7	1.6
	Picture Concepts	11	1.7	1.6
	Matrix Reasoning	5	−4.3*W	−4.4*W
	Picture Completion	10	0.7	0.6
	Mean	9.3		
Working Memory	Digit Span	10	2.7*S	0.6
	Letter–Number Sequencing	6	−1.3	−3.4*W
	Arithmetic	6	−1.3	−3.4*W
	Mean	7.3		
Processing Speed	Coding	8	−2.3	−1.4
	Symbol Search	11	0.7	1.6
	Cancellation	12	1.7	2.6
	Mean	10.3		
Overall	Mean	9.4		

Note. S = strength, W = weakness. See Table A-4 in Appendix A to obtain deviations that are significant.
*$p < .05$.

As noted earlier, when evaluating the difference between Index scores, you should determine whether the difference is likely to have occurred by chance—this is known as the *reliability-of-difference approach*. Differences that are not significant do not warrant your attention, because they are likely to have occurred by chance. Index score differences may be significant yet occur with some frequency in the population. Thus, the discrepancy may be reliable but not occur infrequently. Whether a significant difference has practical significance is open to question. Statistically significant differences probably have diagnostic relevance (i.e., the difference tells you something about the child's abilities) even if they occur frequently in the population. Therefore, given a significant difference only, you can still formulate hypotheses about the child's cognitive strengths and weaknesses.

The standard error of measurement of each Composite is used in the reliability-of-difference approach, and the correlation between two Composites is used in the probability-of-occurrence approach. Both approaches assist in clinical judgment; however, neither should be used in a mechanical fashion or as a replacement for clinical judgment.

Comment on Profile Analysis

When a difference between two subtests or a difference between two Composites is statistically significant, it is large enough that it likely cannot be attributed to chance (i.e., measurement error). The Administration Manual lists the .15 level of significance as the minimum level for determining whether there are significant differences between subtest scaled scores or between Index scores. In contrast, we recommend that you use the .05 level of significance as the minimum level because it is traditionally used.

Do not use scores on individual subtests to attempt precise descriptions of specific cognitive skills; rather, use them to generate hypotheses about the child's abilities. You can derive more reliable estimates of specific abilities from each Index than from individual subtest scaled scores. The Index scores also provide more reliable information about abilities than do individual subtest scaled scores. In fact, of the 165 separate reliability coefficients for the 15 subtests at the 11 age groups of the test, 85% (139) are .80 or above. Of these, 24 are .90 or above. The remaining 26 reliability coefficients are

below .80 and are not sufficiently reliable for decision-making or classification purposes (see Table 4.1 on page 34 of the Technical Manual). However, reliability coefficients of .70 or above on subtests are useful for generating hypotheses.

The difference between a child's subtest scaled score and the mean scaled score is a statistically more accurate measure than the difference between pairs of subtest scaled scores. Use of the mean scaled score has the additional advantage of reducing the accumulation of errors associated with multiple comparisons.

What might account for a certain profile of scores? To attempt to answer this question, you must consider both stable factors (also referred to as trait characteristics or long-term factors) and transient conditions (also referred to as state characteristics or short-term factors). *Stable factors* include the child's cognitive skill development, age, sex, cultural group, socioeconomic status, education, special training, social and physical environment, family background, ethnicity, temperament, personality, and psychopathology. *Transient conditions* include the child's current health status (e.g., short-term illnesses), the amount of sleep the child had the previous night, the degree of tension in the home, any acute trauma that the child has faced (with possible post-traumatic stress disorder reactions), test anxiety, and adverse (or unexpected) drug reactions. Variability of subtest scores may even be simply a reflection of the unreliability of the subtest scaled scores, factors associated with the characteristics of the examiner, or factors associated with the assessment situation.

Profile analysis is a useful tool for evaluating intraindividual variability in various ability and achievement areas. Variability of scores, however, may represent only uneven skill development and is not a sufficient basis for making decisions about psychopathology. Again, you should view profile analysis as a clinical tool to be used *together with* other assessment strategies in developing hypotheses about the child's abilities.

A SUCCESSIVE-LEVEL APPROACH TO TEST INTERPRETATION

The following six-level approach to test interpretation can help you better understand a child's performance on the WISC–IV (see Figure 4-1).

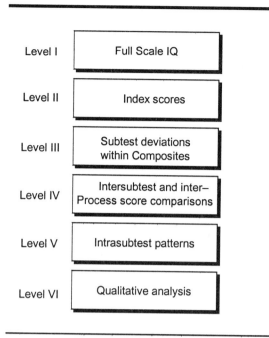

Level I	Full Scale IQ
Level II	Index scores
Level III	Subtest deviations within Composites
Level IV	Intersubtest and inter–Process score comparisons
Level V	Intrasubtest patterns
Level VI	Qualitative analysis

Figure 4-1. A successive-level approach to interpreting the WISC–IV.

Level I: Full Scale IQ. The first level focuses on the Full Scale IQ. In most cases, the Full Scale IQ is the most reliable and valid estimate of the child's intellectual ability provided by the test. It is the primary numerical and quantitative index, providing information about the child's relative standing in the general population (as represented by the standardization group). The Full Scale IQ is a global estimate of the child's level of cognitive ability; it assesses verbal comprehension, perceptual reasoning, working memory, and processing speed. The Full Scale IQ is usually used to obtain the descriptive classification of the child's IQ level (e.g., Very Superior, Superior, High Average, Average, Low Average, Borderline, and Extremely Low). Converting the Full Scale IQ to a percentile rank will help you interpret this score for individuals who are not familiar with standard scores.

The Full Scale IQ is also "the most parsimonious and powerful predictor of academic achievement obtainable from the Wechsler scales" (Glutting, Youngstrom, Ward, Ward, & Hale, 1997, p. 300). We therefore recommend that the Full Scale IQ be used in a regression formula to determine whether a severe discrepancy exists between ability and achievement in establishing a diagnosis of learning disability (see Chapter 12 in Sattler, 2002), unless there is a compelling reason to use either the Verbal Comprehension Index or the Perceptual Reasoning Index (e.g., if the child has a sensory

deficit—such as a visual, auditory, or motor deficit—that interferes with her or his ability to take some subtests).

Level II: Index scores. The second level focuses on the four Index scores and the extent to which there is a significant difference between them. Verbal Comprehension provides information about verbal comprehension skills and crystallized knowledge. Perceptual Reasoning covers perceptual reasoning skills and fluid reasoning ability. Working Memory provides information about short-term memory and working memory. Processing Speed provides information about processing speed and rate of test taking.

Level III: Subtest deviations within Composites. The third level focuses on deviations of subtests from their respective Composite mean: (a) Verbal Comprehension subtest scaled scores from their mean, (b) Perceptual Reasoning subtest scaled scores from their mean, (c) Working Memory subtest scaled scores from their mean, and (d) Processing Speed subtest scaled scores from their mean. You can develop hypotheses about strengths and weaknesses from these analyses.

Level IV: Intersubtest and inter–Process score comparisons. The fourth level focuses on comparisons between sets of subtest scaled scores, between sets of Process scores, or among clusters of subtest scaled scores. Although these comparisons are open to the errors associated with multiple comparisons, they are valuable for generating hypotheses about the child's intellectual abilities.

Level V: Intrasubtest patterns. The fifth level focuses on the pattern of raw scores within each subtest. Within a subtest, the items are arranged in order of difficulty, which will help you to evaluate the pattern of successes and failures. Here are two examples:

1. A child who passes the first item, fails the next four, passes the next one, fails the next four, and overall passes a total of four items shows a different pattern from a child who passes the first four items and fails the remainder, although both children receive 4 raw-score points (assuming each item is worth 1 raw-score point). The child with the markedly uneven pattern may have cognitive or attentional inefficiencies that need to be explored further.

2. A pattern of missing easy items and succeeding on

more difficult items may occur among bright children who are bored by the easy items and thus give careless or even nonsense replies, only to become challenged by more difficult items that allow them to demonstrate their skills. This pattern is sometimes evident, for example, on the Digit Span subtest, where a child may be observed to perform better on the more demanding backward task. This pattern also may suggest inconsistent attention or effort resulting from anxiety or other factors.

Level VI: Qualitative analysis. The sixth level focuses on specific item failures and the content of the responses, or what is called "qualitative analysis." Inspecting responses to specific items can aid in understanding the child's knowledge of specific information. The child's unique or idiosyncratic responses also may help you in formulating hypotheses about his or her functioning. For example, querulous, distrustful, or legalistic responses (e.g., "I'm being tricked," "Why are you writing everything down?" "Are you going to use my answers against me?") will require further investigation, as will slow, hesitant, and blocked responses, interspersed with self-deprecatory remarks (e.g., "I'm worthless," "These things are tiring," "I've never been good at this," "Sure takes a lot of energy to do this puzzle"). Also consider nonverbal responses that accompany verbal responses, such as grimaces, laughter, crying, tone of voice, and motor movements.

STEPS IN ANALYZING A PROTOCOL

Use the following steps in analyzing a WISC–IV protocol.

RELIABILITY AND VALIDITY

Step 1. Evaluate the reliability of the test scores.
Step 2. Evaluate the validity of the test scores.

COMPOSITES

Step 3. Examine the Full Scale IQ and its percentile rank, and evaluate the implications of this score.
Step 4. Examine the Verbal Comprehension Index and its percentile rank, and evaluate the implications of this score.
Step 5. Examine the Perceptual Reasoning Index and its percentile rank, and evaluate the implications of this score.

Step 6. Examine the Working Memory Index and its percentile rank, and evaluate the implications of this score.
Step 7. Examine the Processing Speed Index and its percentile rank, and evaluate the implications of this score.

SIGNIFICANT DIFFERENCES

Step 8. Determine whether there are any significant discrepancies among the Index scores. If so, which ones are discrepant? Note which Index score is higher or lower than the others and the absolute level of each Index score. What are the implications of any significant discrepancies?
Step 9. Determine whether any of the subtest scaled scores in a Composite differ significantly from the mean of that Composite. If there are significant differences, are these subtest scaled scores lower or higher than the mean? What are the base rates for the discrepancies? Note the absolute level of each subtest scaled score that differs significantly from its respective mean score. What are the implications of any significant discrepancies?
Step 10. Determine whether there are subtest scaled scores of interest that differ significantly from each other. If so, which ones? What are the implications of each discrepancy? Note which subtest scaled score is higher or lower than the other and the absolute level of each subtest scaled score. What are the implications of any significant discrepancies?
Step 11. Determine whether the two Process score scaled scores in a set differ significantly from each other. If so, which ones are discrepant? What are the implications of each discrepancy? Note which Process scaled score is higher or lower than the other and the absolute level of each Process scaled score.

QUALITATIVE FEATURES

Step 12. Note any noteworthy qualitative features of the child's performance. What are the implications of any noteworthy features by themselves and in relation to the Full Scale IQ, the Index scores, the subtest scaled scores, and the referral question and case history?

THE COMPOSITES

When you develop hypotheses about a child's performance on the Full Scale and the four individual Composites, the hypotheses are based primarily on the individual subtests that make up the respective Composite. However, some general observations about the Composites still can be made. To help guide your interpretations of the five Composites (Full Scale IQ and four Index scores), Table C-5 in Appendix C presents for each Composite a summary of (a) interpretive rationales, (b) possible implications of high scores, (c) possible implications of low scores, and (d) instructional implications.

Items on the Full Scale and the four individual Composites can be solved by the use of verbal strategies, nonverbal strategies, or a combination of the two. For example, items on Digit Span, Letter–Number Sequencing, and Arithmetic in the Working Memory Composite can be solved in part by verbal processing as well as by nonverbal processing, including visualization strategies. Items on Coding, Symbol Search, and Cancellation in the Processing Speed Composite can be solved by either nonverbal strategies (e.g., primarily visual scanning) or verbal strategies (e.g., language activity in the form of overt verbal responses or mediating symbolic activity). Indeed, there may be no *pure* measures of verbal comprehension, perceptual reasoning, working memory, or processing speed on the WISC–IV.

Verbal Comprehension

Verbal Comprehension tasks draw on the child's accumulated experience. The child is asked to respond verbally with what is likely learned information. The questions (input) are presented orally, and the child responds (output) orally. The Verbal Comprehension Composite measures verbal comprehension, application of verbal skills and information to the solution of new problems, verbal ability, ability to process verbal information, ability to think with words, and crystallized knowledge.

Perceptual Reasoning

Perceptual Reasoning tasks require immediate problem-solving ability. The child uses previously acquired skills to solve a novel set of problems. The stimuli (input) are nonverbal (aside from the directions), and most are presented visually. The child's solutions (output) require motor responses and, to a lesser extent, verbal responses. The Perceptual Reasoning Composite measures perceptual reasoning; ability to think in terms of visual images and manipulate them with fluency, flexibility, and relative speed; ability to interpret or organize visually perceived material within a time limit; nonverbal ability; ability to form relatively abstract concepts and relationships without the use of words; and fluid reasoning ability.

Let's examine more closely the subtests on Perceptual Reasoning for possible influences of verbal abilities on the child's performance.

- Block Design depends on the ability to visualize configurations in space and therefore may not depend heavily on verbal processing. However, verbal strategies, such as thinking about the placement of the blocks or what the appropriate positions of the blocks should be, may accompany efforts to solve the problems.
- Picture Concepts depends on the ability to identify pictures, an ability that involves visual processing and may also involve verbal processing to categorize the pictures into logical groups.
- Matrix Reasoning depends on the ability to process information visually and may also involve verbal processing to solve the matrix.
- Picture Completion depends on the ability to know "the way the world is," and this knowledge may be imparted by verbal means.

Working Memory

Working Memory tasks require the child to attend to information presented by the examiner and then repeat the information from memory (two subtests: Digit Span and Letter–Number Sequencing) or solve mathematical problems (one subtest: Arithmetic). Digit Span is a nonmeaningful rote memory task, Letter–Number Sequencing is a nonmeaningful rote memory task with additional processing components, and Arithmetic is a meaningful memory task centering on arithmetical ability and use of past learnings. Digit Span and Letter–Number Sequencing involve nonmeaningful material because the items are simply numbers or letters. All three subtests provide information about memory span and working memory skills. The Working Memory Composite measures working memory, the ability to sustain attention, short-term memory, numerical ability, encoding ability, ability to use rehearsal strategies, auditory processing skills, ability to shift mental operations on symbolic material, and ability to self-monitor.

Processing Speed

Processing Speed tasks require the child to carry out instructions given by the examiner quickly and efficiently. The tasks rely heavily on visual processing and less on fine-motor skills. The Processing Speed Composite measures perceptual discrimination, speed of mental operation, psychomotor speed, attention, concentration, short-term visual memory, visual-motor coordination, and cognitive flexibility.

Let's examine more closely the subtests on Processing Speed for possible influences of verbal abilities on the child's performance.

- Coding B depends on the ability to learn associations between digits and symbols that can be encoded verbally.
- Symbol Search depends on the ability to scan symbols rapidly, an ability that may be facilitated by attaching verbal descriptions to symbols.
- Cancellation depends on the ability to scan pictures rapidly, choosing those that are in a particular category (animals) while ignoring pictures from other categories. The task may be facilitated by attaching verbal descriptions to the pictures.

ESTIMATED PERCENTILE RANKS AND TEST-AGE EQUIVALENTS FOR RAW SCORES

When you explain the test results to teachers, parents, physicians, attorneys, or other people involved in the assessment, it is helpful to use the percentile ranks associated with the Full Scale IQ, Index scores, and subtest scaled scores. Tables A.2, A.3, A.4, A.5, and A.6 in the Administration Manual show the percentile ranks for the Verbal Comprehension Index, Perceptual Reasoning Index, Working Memory Index, Processing Speed Index, and Full Scale IQ, respectively. The qualitative descriptions for Composite score ranges are as follows (Wechsler, 2003b):

130 and above:	Very Superior
120–129:	Superior
110–119:	High Average
90–109:	Average
80–89:	Low Average
70–79:	Borderline
69 and below:	Extremely Low

Table C-1 in Appendix C gives the estimated percentile ranks and qualitative descriptions for each WISC–IV subtest scaled score. *You should never estimate an IQ based on only one subtest scaled score.*

Occasionally, you may want to use test-age equivalents. Table A.9 (p. 253) in the Administration Manual gives the test-age equivalents for raw scores on each subtest. The test-age equivalents provide approximate developmental levels for the child's achievement on a subtest. For example, a raw score of 9 on Similarities is roughly equivalent to a developmental age level of 6-6 years. Because test-age equivalents have several drawbacks, we do not recommend their routine use (see Chapter 4 in Sattler, 2001). The exception is for discussions with parents and others who may more easily understand test-age equivalents than standard scores.

ILLUSTRATION OF A PORTION OF A PSYCHOLOGICAL REPORT

The following portion of a psychological report illustrates how quantitative and qualitative information can be woven into a report and how a child's profile can be discussed. The report, only parts of which are shown below, was based on the administration of the WISC–IV to Kate, a female who was 8 years, 2 months old. Kate's scores were as follows:

PSYCHOLOGICAL REPORT

Block Design	11
Similarities	11
Digit Span	10
(Digit Span Forward)	(12)
(Digit Span Backward)	(4)
Picture Concepts	11
Coding	7
Vocabulary	11
Letter–Number Sequencing	6
Matrix Reasoning	5
Comprehension	13
Symbol Search	11
(Picture Completion)	(10)
(Cancellation)	(12)
(Information)	(7)
(Arithmetic)	(6)
(Word Reasoning)	(9)
Verbal Comprehension Index	108
Perceptual Reasoning Index	94

Working Memory Index	88
Processing Speed Index	94
Full Scale IQ	97

Kate's short-term auditory sequential working memory is relatively less well developed than her verbal skills. The subtests measuring short-term auditory sequential memory involve repeating a sequence of digits from immediate memory, reversing digits, repeating back numbers and letters in ascending and alphabetical order, and doing math problems without the use of paper and pencil. Although her weakness in short-term auditory sequential working memory may be related to temporary inefficiency caused by anxiety or inattention, neither anxiety nor inattention appeared to affect her performance on other subtests. Therefore, it is more likely that her weakness in short-term auditory sequential working memory for digit sequences reversed, Letter–Number sequences, and arithmetical skills indicates difficulty with forming in memory an adequate mental image of the correct series. For example, Kate was often able to recall the correct digits forward, but when asked to manipulate the series by repeating the numbers in reverse order, she often included all the numbers but in the wrong sequence, indicating a specific weakness in auditory sequential working memory rather than in general auditory memory per se.

Kate's ability to deduce the answer to matrices missing one part is relatively less well developed than her other nonverbal reasoning skills. Kate's average attention to visual detail, coupled with her below-average fluid reasoning ability, indicates that although her perception of visual details is adequate, her ability to organize and manipulate these details is poor. Moreover, Kate's abilities on a subtest measuring graphomotor speed were less well developed than those on subtests assessing mental-processing speed. It is unclear how Kate's weakness in auditory working memory and graphomotor speed has affected her academic performance at school; this needs to be investigated. However, her overall average skills indicate that she has the ability to perform adequately in school.

COMMENT ON INTERPRETING THE WISC–IV

Sometimes children have difficulty completing tasks. For example, tasks requiring speed and quick execution, such as Coding, Symbol Search, or Cancellation, may be taxing for depressed children. Although depressed children's performance on these tasks may not reflect their level of cognitive ability, the tasks are still valuable because they provide information not readily obtained from interviews or observations conducted in natural settings. Coding, for example, can give you clues about the child's ability to follow a complex set of instructions, visual scanning processes, and learning ability. Symbol Search gives you clues about visual scanning and ability to shift rapidly. Cancellation may give you clues about visual scanning and how the child works in structured and unstructured situations. You may not want to report a score for these subtests for children who are depressed, but you can use the results to develop hypotheses to guide your clinical judgments.

When a significant split occurs between the Index scores, the Full Scale IQ may be only a forced average of rather disparate primary skills. What meaning, for example, can we attach to a Full Scale IQ of 100 and a Verbal Comprehension Index of 130, a Perceptual Reasoning Index of 70, a Working Memory Index of 130, and a Processing Speed Index of 70? Although the IQ of 100 may be the best overall estimate of the child's cognitive level, the child is not likely to be average in situations calling for verbal reasoning, nonverbal reasoning, working memory, and processing speed. Unfortunately, there is little research that can help us understand how children with large Index discrepancies function outside the test situation.

To a lesser extent, a similar problem exists in interpreting an Index score when there is an exceptionally large amount of variability among the subtests within the Index. Consider a child who obtains a score of 10 on each of the three core Verbal Comprehension subtests and comes out with a Verbal Comprehension Index of 100. Then consider another child who obtains scores of 1, 10, and 19 on the three core Verbal Comprehension subtests and a resulting Verbal Comprehension Index of 100. What is the meaning of the 100 Index score in each case? Obviously, these two children differ in their pattern of ability. How should we interpret the Verbal Comprehension Index in each case? You will need to point out the variability and its possible implications (e.g., that the subtests comprising the Index have variable scores and that the ability measured by the Index is not pure).

In situations requiring the reporting of one number (e.g., in the determination of mental retardation or when a discrepancy formula is involved in cases of learning disability), we need to report a Full Scale IQ, regardless of whether it is obtained from a profile with minimal variability or one with extensive variability. Unfortunately, there is little research to guide us in determining whether the Full Scale IQ becomes invalid when the subtest scores are variable.

Subtest scaled scores, Index scores, and Full Scale IQs are multidetermined. This means that any one subtest or Composite likely measures several abilities. Consequently, a high score or a low score does not indicate which particular functions measured by the subtest or Composite are well developed or not well developed. This information will come only from a sifting of all WISC–IV scores, scores obtained on other tests, qualitative information, testing-of-limits, and the child's clinical history. As noted in Chapter 1, the WISC–IV may not be the instrument of choice for evaluating the cognitive abilities of children who function at either an extremely low or an extremely high cognitive level. In both cases, there may be too few items on the test—that is, not enough easy items for low-functioning children and not enough challenging ones for high-functioning children.

Interpreting the WISC–IV is a challenging activity. The WISC–IV gives an estimate of the child's level of intellectual functioning. We need to emphasize the word *estimate*. The WISC–IV provides useful—but not complete—information about the range, depth, and real-world applications of a child's intellectual ability.

The WISC–IV should not be used to evaluate personality and temperament, to diagnose psychopathology, or to determine brain lateralization. Instead, the WISC–IV should be used to learn about the child's intellectual ability and to generate hypotheses to account for the child's functioning on the test. There is a world of difference between reporting that the child performed in an impulsive manner and reporting that the WISC–IV test results indicate that the child has ADHD. Once we go beyond the confines of the Full Scale IQ, Index scores, and subtest scores, the ground becomes loose and wobbly. Interpretations become more impressionistic and less reliable and valid. When on this ground, step carefully, continually getting your bearings from research findings, other sources of information, and clinical experience. There are no WISC–IV profiles that are known to reliably distinguish clinical groups from normal groups.

REPORT WRITING GUIDELINES

The following guidelines will help you in writing the psychological report. For further information about report writing, see Chapter 21 in *Assessment of Children: Cognitive Applications* (Sattler, 2001).

FOCUS OF THE REPORT

1. The primary focus of the report should be on the Full Scale IQ, followed by the Index scores and then the subtest scores.

2. In most cases, let the Full Scale IQ guide you in evaluating the child's overall cognitive skills.

3. The intersubtest comparisons of interest should be made only after each subtest has been compared with the mean of its respective Index.

4. Remember to look at the pattern of raw scores within each subtest and the qualitative features of the child's performance.

STYLE OF THE REPORT

5. Stress what the child did do, not what he or she did not do.

6. Report the Full Scale IQ without qualifying terms, such as "approximate" (e.g., do not write "She obtained an approximate IQ of 105").

7. Report significant differences without qualifying terms, such as "appears" (e.g., do not write "There appears to be a significant difference").

8. Do not use colloquial or potentially misleading terms, such as "respectable," "retarded," or "decent," to describe the child's scores.

9. Do not present too much technical information in the report. For example, it is not necessary to include the possible range of scaled scores, the number of children in the norm group, the child's raw scores, the number of items with perfect scores or scores of 0, or the standard deviation of the subtest, Index scores, and Full Scale IQ.

10. Attach a precision range primarily to the Full Scale IQ (e.g., ± 9), and use only one classification for it (e.g., Average, Above Average, or Below Average). You will confuse the reader if you present more than one classification.

INTERPRETATIONS

11. In interpreting the child's performance, consider all sources of information, including the child's educational history, previous assessment results, other current assessment results, developmental history, cultural and linguistic background, family environment, health history, and temporary situational factors.

12. If the Full Scale IQ does not appear to be a valid estimate of the child's ability, consider one or more of the Index scores as possible substitutes; in this case, also consider following up with another intelligence test.

13. Never delete a subtest simply because the child obtained a low score.

14. Always delete a subtest when it is spoiled during the

administration or when the child has a physical disability that interferes with the administration of the subtest.

15. Base your descriptions of the child's strengths, weaknesses, or average abilities on the Full Scale IQ, Index scores, and subtest scaled scores.

16. In interpreting the child's scores, also examine the quality of the child's performance, such as language, behavior, affect, attention, motivation, persistence, approach to the tasks, and relationship to the examiner.

17. Evaluate the child's problem-solving strategies, such as self-verbalizations, checking solutions, repeating key elements of problems, recognizing when solutions were correct or incorrect, finding alternative ways of solving problems, and formulating plans to solve problems.

18. Do not conclude that a subtest is spoiled or invalid because a child's score is lower or higher than the child's score on another subtest. A subtest is spoiled, for example, when it is improperly administered, when the child does not attend to the task, or when an external event interrupts the test administration.

19. The inferences you draw from the child's performance should be directed primarily to cognitive abilities. Thus, if you want to evaluate reading skill, give a reading proficiency examination. If you want to evaluate personality, give an appropriate test of personality.

20. Be cautious in extrapolating from the test situation to how the child may behave outside of the test situation. For example, the level of energy displayed during the test may or may not reflect what the child does in another setting.

21. On a retest, describe any changes in the child's ability, and then try to account for any changes in performance by studying the entire case history. Test-retest changes may be associated with practice effects, maturational changes, growth spurts, changes in item content, motivation, situational variables, environmental changes, or changes in norms.

22. Be careful about the use of the term "lack" when referring to a child's cognitive abilities because of its implications. Most children do not completely "lack" an ability.

23. Being persistent or trying hard is not a good explanation for why a child obtains high scores. Persistence may help a child in solving various tasks, but unless it is coupled with the requisite abilities, the child cannot obtain high scores.

24. Intelligence test scores, in and of themselves, should never be used as a basis for establishing a learning disability diagnosis. No pattern of Index scores or subtest scores necessarily indicates a learning disability. Also, accurate documentation of academic achievement, among other things, is necessary for a diagnosis of learning disability.

25. Test results provide information about current functioning, not capacity. Therefore, it is better not to use the term "capacity" in a report.

26. There is no one-to-one correspondence between verbal knowledge, as revealed by high Verbal Comprehension subtest scores, and expressive skills. For example, there are children with average or above-average Verbal Comprehension scores who may have expressive difficulties, either in writing or in speech.

27. The WISC–IV provides information about cognitive functioning; it does not provide direct information about school performance. There is no one-to-one correspondence between performance on an intelligence test and performance in school; many different factors are associated with both.

28. A scaled score of 10 is in the Average range and should not be considered "poor."

29. Children who have maturationally average visual-motor skills may still obtain high scores or low scores on Perceptual Reasoning subtests, because these subtests call primarily for cognitive skills.

30. Children may obtain high scores on Comprehension but still not have above-average social or interpersonal skills. Similarly, low scores on Comprehension do not imply emotional disturbance.

31. Intrasubtest variability indicates an uneven pattern of performance, not a lack of persistence.

32. Verbal Comprehension subtests do not simply require automatic responding; they also require judgment, problem solving, conceptualization, and attention.

33. Discuss the abilities measured by the Index scores and subtests, rather than simply mentioning their names.

34. All areas of an intelligence test are related in some degree to the individual's life experiences, social-educational exposure, and learning. It is misleading to isolate one area of the test and say that it is the only one related to these factors.

35. It is preferable not to use the term "scatter" in the report; if you use it, be sure to explain it. The term "variability" is preferred.

PSYCHOLOGICAL EVALUATION

The psychological evaluation in Exhibit 4-2 illustrates how the WISC–IV can contribute to the assessment of a youngster with emotional difficulties. For illustrative purposes the report focuses on only the WISC–IV. In practice, of course, several assessment procedures would be used for a thorough assessment.

Exhibit 4-2
Analysis of and Line-by-Line Notations on a Psychological Evaluation of an Emotionally Disturbed 7-Year-Old Examined with the WISC–IV

PSYCHOLOGICAL EVALUATION

INTRODUCTORY REMARKS

The following pages contain a case study of an emotionally disturbed child. Jim, a 7-year-old boy referred for evaluation because of antisocial behavior, was administered the WISC–IV. His Full Scale IQ of 108 is classified in the Average range of intelligence. There were significant differences between the Processing Speed Index and the other Indexes. Table A-2 in Appendix A gives the differences that are significant between the Index scores. Most subtest scores were average or above average, with the exception of scores on two Processing Speed subtests (Coding and Symbol Search), which were below average. These results suggest that his verbal comprehension, perceptual reasoning, and working memory skills may be better developed than his processing speed skills. Note that several of his answers were related to his antisocial behavior pattern. This case illustrates that emotional disturbance may not necessarily affect cognitive functioning.

OVERVIEW OF THE REPORT

Identifying Data
The report begins with the traditional identification data. In an actual report, the child's last name would be included.

Test Administered
This part of the report cites the name(s) of the test(s) administered and the test scores. It is optional, because the name of the test and major WISC–IV scores (Verbal Comprehension, Perceptual Organization, Working Memory, Processing Speed, and Full Scale) can be included in the body of the report. Often the subtest scores are not included in the report.

Reason for Referral
This section, which usually begins the narrative portion of the report, explains the reason for the evaluation. It documents what the examiner perceives as the purpose for the evaluation and helps to develop the focus of the recommendations. It also may contain information about the child that is related to the referral question.

Background Information
This section describes portions of Jim's background that might be pertinent to the issues under consideration. The first paragraph sets the stage for a historical understanding of the problem and provides information as to possible resources available within the family for remediation. The second paragraph cites in more detail the behaviors that led to Jim's referral. The third paragraph focuses on school behavior and recent changes in problem behaviors.

Behavioral Observations
This section describes Jim's behavior during the examination, with particular emphasis on his approach to the test and behavior reflective of his unique style.

Assessment Results and Clinical Impressions
This section begins with a description of Jim's overall test performance. Normative data and confidence levels are then reported. The confidence bands for IQs are found in Table A-1 in Appendix A.

The second paragraph discusses the discrepancy between his Index scores. Table A-4 in Appendix A gives values that indicate significant differences between individual subtest scores and their respective mean scaled scores.

The third paragraph describes Jim's strengths and weaknesses based on his subtest scores. Table C-1 in Appendix C gives the percentile ranks for each subtest scaled score. Jim's range of knowledge and language usage are well developed, as suggested by his scores on Similarities, Vocabulary, and Comprehension. Equally developed are his perceptual reasoning abilities, as suggested by his scores on Block Design, Picture Concepts, and Matrix Reasoning. Short-term memory is adequate, as indicated by his scores on Digit Span and Letter–Number Sequencing. Less adequate are his visual-motor coordination and psychomotor speed, as indicated by his scores on Coding and Symbol Search. Table C-2 in Appendix C provides a summary of the skills associated with the individual WISC–IV subtests.

The fourth paragraph describes some idiosyncratic responses that may reflect Jim's behavior problem. Finally, the last paragraph provides a brief summary of Jim's overall level of functioning.

Recommendations
Recommendations are made before the final summary. Note that because the evaluation did not include personality tests, the recommendations call for further testing and evaluation.

Summary
The final section of the report summarizes the major findings and recommendations.

(Continued)

Exhibit 4-2 (*Continued*)

THE REPORT WITH LINE-BY-LINE NOTATIONS

Name: Jim
Date of birth: July 17, 1996
Chronological age: 7-4

Date of examination: November 20, 2003
Date of report: November 21, 2003
Grade: Second

Test Administered
Wechsler Intelligence Scale for Children–IV

VERBAL COMPREHENSION		PERCEPTUAL REASONING	
Similarities	12	Block Design	14
Vocabulary	13	Picture Concepts	13
Comprehension	12	Matrix Reasoning	10

WORKING MEMORY		PROCESSING SPEED	
Digit Span	11	Coding	6
Letter–Number Sequencing	12	Symbol Search	7

Verbal Comprehension Index = 112
Perceptual Reasoning Index = 115
Working Memory Index = 107
Processing Speed Index = 80
Full Scale IQ = 108 ± 5 at the 95% confidence level

Reason for Referral

1 Jim, a 7-year, 4-month-old boy, was referred to the clinic
2 by his aunt for evaluation because of involuntary
3 defecation, fecal smearing, enuresis, and stealing.

Background Information

4 According to his aunt, Jim was born to a single mother and
5 never knew his natural father. He was separated from his
6 mother at 6 months of age, when she developed leukemia
7 from which she died a year later. Since that time, Jim has
8 lived with a paternal aunt and her three children, who
9 range in age from 8 to 18 years. The aunt has been di-
10 vorced twice. Jim calls his aunt "mother" and thought of
11 her first husband as his father. This man, who had been in
12 the family as long as Jim, has not been involved with the
13 family since he divorced the aunt. Jim was 2½ years old at
14 the time of the divorce. His aunt described having made
15 incomplete and ineffective attempts at toilet training during
16 this period of turmoil. Last year Jim's aunt remarried. Dur-
17 ing the 6 months that the marriage lasted, Jim formed no
18 attachment to his second step-uncle.
19   Jim's aunt reported that he has bowel movements in
20 the bathtub; he smears feces on the walls or leaves them
21 in trash cans around the house. He also soils himself
22 frequently. He wanders around the house at night and
23 sometimes vanishes for hours while in the park or on his
24 way home from school. His aunt stated that he stole a
25 stopwatch from the principal's office, and food and money
26 from other places. Apparently, he makes an effort to be
27 discovered when he steals.

Notations

1–2 who was referred and who made the referral
2–3 specific behavior leading to the referral

4–7 early infancy and family background

8–10 family constellation

10–11 attachment to parental figures

12–14 time of early separation from parental figure

14–16 past parental behaviors that may relate to Jim's current problems
16 recent family changes
17–18 Jim's relationship to new family member

19–22 encopresis

22–24 wandering behavior

24–27 stealing behavior

(*Continued*)

Exhibit 4-2 (*Continued*)

28 Jim is an excellent student, although he is difficult to	28–29 level of academic achievement and deviant
29 manage because of his opposition and defiance. His	classroom behavior
30 behavior in the past three months has been changing.	29–33 recent changes in behavior
31 There has been a decrease in encopresis and fecal	
32 smearing and an increase in stealing and aggressive	
33 behavior.	

Behavioral Observations

34 Jim is a small, thinly built, energetic child. He was	34 appearance
35 cooperative and friendly during the evaluation. His test	35 overall response to being tested
36 behavior was characterized by competitiveness, tenacity,	35–39 response to test materials
37 and anxiety. He seemed to want to answer all of the	
38 questions correctly and was reluctant to admit he could not	
39 answer any question. On the Comprehension subtest, he	39–44 example of response to a test question
40 responded to a question about the thing to do if he saw	
41 smoke coming from the window of a neighbor's house with	
42 "Call 911," but could not generate another action. He had	
43 to be encouraged to proceed to the next question, and	
44 three questions later he spontaneously returned to the	44–46 style of relating to examiner
45 smoke question, adding "I would also try to warn them."	
46 Jim seemed to need continual assurance from the	46–48 example of test behavior
47 examiner that he was answering the items correctly. He	
48 often asked, "Have I gotten them all right?"	

Assessment Results and Clinical Impressions

49 With a chronological age of 7-4, Jim achieved a Verbal	49 chronological age
50 Comprehension score of 112, a Perceptual Reasoning	49–52 Index scores
51 score of 115, a Working Memory score of 107, a	
52 Processing Speed score of 80, and a Full Scale IQ of 108	52–53 Full Scale IQ and confidence band
53 ± 5 on the WISC–IV. His overall performance is classified	
54 in the Average range and is equal to or higher than that of	54 normative classification based on Full Scale IQ
55 70% of the children his age (70th percentile). The chances	55–56 percentile rank and confidence range of IQ
56 that the range of scores from 103 to 113 includes his true	
57 IQ are about 95 out of 100. The present measure of his	57–58 validity of test result
58 level of intellectual functioning appears to be valid.	
59 Although there were significant differences between the	59 discrepancy between Indexes
60 four Index scores, the differences were associated primarily	60–61 variability noted in Processing Speed area
61 with his low scores on the two Processing Speed subtests.	
62 Whereas his verbal, visual-spatial reasoning, and memory	62–63 description of verbal, reasoning, and memory skills
63 skills are uniformly well developed, his visual-motor	63–64 description of processing speed skills
64 coordination and psychomotor speed skills are less well	
65 developed. Overall (with the exception of Coding and	65–67 summary of performance on WISC–IV
66 Symbol Search), Jim consistently demonstrated average	
67 and above-average skills as assessed by the WISC–IV.	
68 Within the verbal comprehension area, his range of	68–71 verbal skill strengths
69 knowledge and language usage are excellent. Social	
70 comprehension and concept formation abilities are also	
71 strong. Within the perceptual reasoning area, his analytic	71–72 visual-spatial reasoning skill strengths
72 and synthetic abilities, as well as his visual concept	
73 formation, are all well developed. Also, his short-term	73–74 memory skill strengths
74 memory for auditory information is well developed. Less	
75 adequate are skills associated with visual-motor	75–76 processing speed skill weaknesses
76 coordination and with psychomotor speed. It is difficult to	76–78 relation of weaknesses to overall ability
77 account for his lower scores on these two subtests in light	
78 of his overall average ability. Perhaps the scores reflect	78–81 possible reasons for low scores
79 temporary inefficiency due to fatigue, or perhaps they	
80 simply indicate that his abilities in these areas are not well	
81 developed.	

(*Continued*)

Exhibit 4-2 (*Continued*)

82 The test results suggest that Jim's behavioral	82–84 effect of behavior problems on cognitive functioning
83 problems, for the most part, have not interfered with his	
84 intellectual functioning. His psychomotor speed and	84–86 weaknesses
85 visual-motor coordination are less adequately developed	
86 than his other abilities, but his overall functioning is in the	86–87 level of overall functioning
87 average range. There were suggestions of preoccupation	87–88 relation of specific responses to behavior problems
88 with stealing, but it is difficult to determine the extent of this	88–89 limits of interpretation
89 preoccupation.	

Recommendations

90 On the basis of the present limited evaluation, it is	90 limitations of current testing
91 recommended that a personality evaluation be conducted.	91 recommendation for personality testing
92 Furthermore, the seriousness of his behavioral	92–94 therapeutic interventions
93 disturbance suggests that therapy should be initiated for	
94 both Jim and his aunt. Every attempt should be made to	94–97 needed additional information about home environment
95 obtain further information about his home environment and	
96 to determine which factors in the home may be reinforcing	
97 his deviant behavior pattern. His aunt should be actively	97–98 suggested intervention
98 engaged in the development of a treatment program.	

Summary

99 Jim, with a chronological age of 7-4, achieved an IQ of 108	99 chronological age
100 ± 5 on the WISC–IV. This IQ is at the 70th percentile and	99–100 IQ and name of test
101 in the Average range. The chances that the range of	99–100 percentile rank and normative classification of IQ
102 scores from 103 to 113 includes his true IQ are about 95	101–102 confidence limits associated with IQ
103 out of 100. The test results appear to give a valid	103–104 validity of test results
104 indication of his present level of intellectual functioning.	104–106 verbal, visual-spatial reasoning, and memory skills
105 Jim's verbal, visual-spatial reasoning, and memory skills	
106 were uniformly well developed, but there was some	
107 variability in his processing speed skills. The findings	107 variability of nonverbal skills
108 suggest that his behavioral problems are not significantly	108–109 possible effects of behavior problems on intellectual functioning
109 interfering with his cognitive skills. A personality evaluation	
110 was recommended, along with a treatment program that	
111 would involve Jim and his aunt.	109–111 recommendations

(Signature)

Jo Lynn Mack, M.A.

TEST YOUR SKILL

Exhibit 4-3 presents four sets of exercises designed to sharpen your skill in interpreting the WISC–IV. Each sentence illustrates one or more inadequacies of description or interpretation. Find the mistakes in each sentence. After you have completed your analysis, compare your evaluations with those shown in the Comment section of each exercise set.

THINKING THROUGH THE ISSUES

1. In interpreting the WISC–IV, you can use various procedures. How does profile analysis help in evaluating a child's WISC–IV performance? What problems are associated with profile analysis?

2. The successive-level approach to test interpretation is based on a hierarchical model. What is the logic underlying the hierarchy?

3. How might a child function if he had a Verbal Comprehension Index of 120 and a Perceptual Reasoning Index of 80?

4. How might a child function if she had a Verbal Comprehension Index of 80 and a Perceptual Reasoning Index of 120?

5. How might a child function if he had a Working Memory Index of 120 and a Processing Speed Index of 80?

Exhibit 4-3
Test-Your-Skill Exercises for the WISC–IV

Directions: Read each item to determine why it is inadequate. Then compare your evaluations with those in the Comment section that follows each part.

Part 1. Unnecessary Technical Information
1. On the Comprehension subtest, Bill scored 18; 10 is average and 19 is the ceiling.
2. On Block Design, she failed items 3, 4, and 5.
3. Bill scored 5 points on the Similarities subtest.
4. The Cancellation subtest is an optional subtest and was not used in computing the IQ.
5. On the WISC–IV, the majority of her scores hovered around a scaled score of 12.
6. A total scaled score of 31 yielded a Perceptual Reasoning standard score of 102.
7. On the Information subtest, she earned a scaled score of 13, which is 1 standard deviation above the mean of 10.
8. A review of Glenda's Verbal Comprehension scores indicates significance at the .05 level in her Vocabulary and Comprehension tests.
9. Her score on Coding was 4 points lower than her score on Block Design and 5 points lower than her score on Matrix Reasoning.
10. Intersubtest scatter was minimal.

Comment on Part 1
1. It is not necessary to report this technical information. *Suggestion:* "Bill's social reasoning and verbal comprehension are well developed."
2. Delete this sentence from the report unless there is some significance to the pattern of missed items. If there is, discuss the significance of the pattern.
3. The reference to "5 points" is potentially misleading. The reader does not know whether the 5 points refers to a raw score or a standard score. This sentence should be rewritten to convey the child's knowledge of what is required on the Similarities subtest. *Suggestion:* If his score is below average (scaled score of 7 or below) and significantly below his Verbal Scale mean, you could say, "Bill's conceptual thinking ability is less well developed (at the 16th percentile) than are his other verbal skills."
4. This sentence provides unnecessary technical information and should be deleted.
5. It is preferable to discuss percentile ranks rather than scaled scores, because they are more easily understood by parents and teachers.
6. It is not necessary to report the total scaled score.
7. Standard deviation is a technical concept and should not be used in the report. The scaled scores should be interpreted rather than cited. *Suggestion:* "Her range of knowledge is above average."
8. This is a poorly written sentence that fails to communicate useful information. It does not tell whether the abilities measured by these subtests are well or poorly developed. Also, it is not necessary to present the significance level. Finally, Vocabulary and Comprehension should be re-

ferred to as subtests, not tests. *Suggestion:* Assuming that her Comprehension score was significantly higher than her Vocabulary score, you could say, "In the verbal area, Glenda's social reasoning ability is better developed than her word knowledge."
9. This sentence fails to present useful information. The reader does not know whether these scores reflect strengths or weaknesses. *Suggestion:* "Her sequencing and visual memory abilities are weaker than her spatial and perceptual organization abilities."
10. This sentence will have little meaning to the average reader. *Suggestion:* If all Verbal Comprehension subtest scaled scores are between 9 and 11, you could say, "On verbal comprehension tasks, his performance was consistently within the Average range."

Part 2. Poor Writing
11. His score on the WISC–IV was equivalent to an IQ of approximately 98.
12. Her Verbal Comprehension abilities ranged from average to very superior when compared to those of other children in her chronological age group.
13. Average abilities were indicated in Pat's attention and concentration and how well they are used in conjunction with solving basic arithmetic problems, and in her auditory vocal sequencing memory.
14. All of Mary's scores were respectable and adequate, with the exception of Digit Span, where she received a 7.
15. Bill has better mental than nonverbal abilities.
16. Statistical factors and the tenor of his test performance indicate an excellent chance (95%) that his test performance would fall consistently (other things being equal) within the range of 117 to 129.
17. Her verbal subtest scores appear to be within the average range.
18. The accuracy of his intrasubtest scores were intermittent on many of his subtests. He missed items in such proportions that he was able to complete all of the subtests.
19. In reviewing her Perceptual Reasoning subtest scores, there appears to be a significance at the .05 level between her Matrix Reasoning and Block Design.
20. She showed a retarded score on the ability to see spatial relationships.

Comment on Part 2
11. The IQ achieved by a child is a specific number. You do not have to write "approximately 98." The notion of "approximately" is handled by the confidence interval or precision range. *Suggestion:* "He obtained a Full Scale IQ of 98 ± 6 on the WISC–IV. This score is in the Average classification."
12. It is redundant to write "when compared to those of other children of her chronological age group." Including this phrase every time a child's ability is discussed would unnecessarily lengthen the report. The phrase should be deleted.

Exhibit 4-3 (*Continued*)

13. This sentence is poorly constructed and redundant in places. *Suggestion:* "She has average short-term memory ability and mathematical skills."
14. The term "respectable" is not appropriate for describing a test score. It implies that some scores are "not respectable." Also, the reference to a score of 7, without some explanation, is not informative. *Suggestion:* "All of Mary's abilities appear to be developed at an average level, with the exception of short-term memory for digits, which is relatively weak."
15. The WISC–IV measures "mental" abilities. The writer may have meant to write "verbal" instead of "mental."
16. The term "statistical factors" is too general, and the phrase "tenor of his performance" is vague. *Suggestion:* "Joe obtained an IQ of 123 ± 6. The chances that the range of scores from 117 to 129 includes his true IQ are about 95 out of 100."
17. This sentence is too tentative. If the scores are in fact in the Average range (9 to 11 on Verbal Comprehension), say so: "Her Verbal Comprehension subtest scores are in the Average range."
18. The wording of these two sentences is awkward and is likely to confuse most readers. Also, the first sentence is grammatically incorrect because the singular subject of the sentence ("accuracy") requires a singular verb ("was"). *Suggestion:* "On many subtests he failed easy items but passed more difficult ones."
19. This sentence is poorly constructed. Also, it is not necessary to state probability levels in the report. *Suggestion:* Assuming that the score on Block Design was significantly higher than the score on Matrix Reasoning, the sentence could read, "On nonverbal tasks, her spatial reasoning skills are stronger than her analogic reasoning skills."
20. The score itself is not retarded, although it may reflect a weakness or poorly developed skill in a specific area. *Suggestion:* If the score on Block Design is low, it is preferable to say, "Her spatial visualization skills are not well developed, as indicated by her weak performance in re-creating designs with three-dimensional blocks."

Part 3. Technical Errors
21. A lower score on Information (scaled score 9) shows poor range of knowledge.
22. Henry scored in the average intellectual range on the WISC–IV, with a mental age of 7-2 and a chronological age of 7-6.
23. The 10-point difference between Brandon's Verbal Comprehension Index and Perceptual Reasoning Index approaches significance at the 5% level, suggesting that his verbal skill development is somewhat ahead of his nonverbal reasoning development.
24. Her Full Scale IQ of 109 ± 6 just barely reaches the Above Average classification.
25. The Picture Completion score was significantly lower than the Block Design score. Because these two subtests are somewhat similar in the testing of detail, reasoning ability, and perceptual organization, the Picture Completion sub-

test may have been spoiled.
26. Bill's IQ of 114 ± 7 classifies him in a range from average, high average, to superior intellectual functioning.
27. On the basis of a range of subtest scaled scores from 12 to 19 (Verbal Comprehension = 142, Perceptual Reasoning = 131, Working Memory = 125, Processing Speed = 129, Full Scale IQ = 140), the following statement was made: His subtest scores show great variability, indicating he has definite strengths and weaknesses.
28. Bill achieved a Verbal Comprehension score of 39, a Perceptual Reasoning score of 38, a Working Memory score of 26, a Processing Speed score of 25, and a Full Scale IQ of 121.
29. Her scaled score of 3 on Information places her in the Mentally Retarded range.
30. The following statement was made on the basis of a Verbal Comprehension score of 108 and a Perceptual Reasoning score of 112: Her Perceptual Reasoning abilities are higher than her Verbal Comprehension abilities.

Comment on Part 3
21. Scaled scores of 9 or higher do not indicate "poor" ability. A scaled score of 9 is only one-third of a standard deviation below the mean scaled score of 10; it is within the Average range.
22. The WISC–IV does not use mental ages, but it provides test-age equivalents for the 15 subtests. These test ages should be used cautiously. Mental ages usually are not given in a report.
23. It is not necessary to put in the report the technical information contained in this sentence ("approaches significance at the 5% level"). Because the 10-point difference is not significant, it is not appropriate to infer that verbal development is better than nonverbal reasoning development. This inference should be made only when there is a significant discrepancy between the Verbal Comprehension Index and the Perceptual Reasoning Index.
24. A Full Scale IQ of 109 receives an Average classification, not an Above Average classification. *Suggestion:* "Her Full Scale IQ of 109 ± 6 is classified in the Average range." If there is reason to suspect a higher level of functioning than the test scores indicate, discuss your concerns in the report.
25. It is not appropriate to conclude that a subtest may be "spoiled" or invalid because the score is lower than the score on another subtest. A subtest is spoiled when it is improperly administered or when the child does not attend to the task, not when a child's score on it is low. Focus on the implications of the findings (strengths and weaknesses) rather than on the procedures used to arrive at the implications. Any interpretations of the discrepancy between the two subtest scores should relate to characteristics of the child—for example, "Although Tom's visual perception and attention to detail skills are strong, his spatial reasoning skills are less well developed."

(*Continued*)

Exhibit 4-3 (*Continued*)

26. Although a precision range is attached to the IQ (in this case, ±7), cite only one classification for the obtained IQ. In this case, an IQ of 114 falls into the High Average classification. Presenting more than one classification is confusing.

27. There are no weaknesses in this profile. The sentence might be rephrased to reflect relative strengths. *Suggestion:* "All of his scores were above average. However, there were areas that reflect special strengths relative to his own level of functioning." This statement should be followed with a discussion of the child's relative strengths.

28. This sentence mixes up sums of scaled scores and IQs. Report Index standard scores, not total scaled scores—for example, "Bill achieved a Verbal Comprehension score of 116, a Perceptual Reasoning score of 117, a Working Memory score of 116, a Processing Speed score of 115, and a Full Scale IQ of 121." Then add a precision range.

29. Classifications should be used primarily for the Full Scale IQ. *Suggestion:* A phrase such as "considerably below average" or "represents a weakness" can be used to describe a scaled score of 3. Or you might say, "Her knowledge of factual information is limited and at the 1st percentile rank."

30. Although this statement is literally correct, it should be deleted because the 4-point difference is not statistically significant. *Suggestion:* "Her verbal and nonverbal reasoning skills are not significantly different from each other, being at the 70th and 79th percentiles, respectively."

Part 4. Inaccurate or Incomplete Interpretations
31. His low functioning on Coding may relate to his apparently weak background in school-related tasks.
32. A high Matrix Reasoning subtest score and a low Coding subtest score may predict difficulty in reading.
33. Bill scored high on Matrix Reasoning because he was persistent in his attempt to figure out the problems.
34. The 15-point discrepancy between Mary's Verbal Comprehension and Perceptual Reasoning Index scores indicates that she has a learning disability.
35. The following statement was based on a Similarities scaled score of 15 and a Digit Span scaled score of 10: She has good conceptualizing ability and poor rote memory for digits.
36. The 40-point difference between Greg's Verbal Comprehension and Perceptual Reasoning Index scores can probably be accounted for by the fact that at age 6, Greg has not yet developed the visual-motor skills he needs to do his best on the nonverbal part of the WISC–IV.
37. The intrasubtest scatter may indicate a lack of persistence.
38. Her verbal skills appear significantly better developed than her reasoning skills, suggesting that her ability to respond automatically with what is already known may be more developed than her ability to use past experiences and previously acquired skills to solve new problems.
39. A review of her Verbal Comprehension subtests does not appear to indicate any areas of significance.

40. The following statement was based on a Verbal Comprehension Index of 98, Perceptual Reasoning Index of 135, Working Memory Index of 102, Processing Speed Index of 126, and Full Scale IQ of 120: The discrepancy between her verbal and nonverbal scores is significant and may suggest that she is compensating for her lack of verbal abilities with her superior performance abilities to achieve good grades in school. In addition, Ellen is very strong in areas where using one's hands is important.

Comment on Part 4
31. Low functioning on the Coding subtest may be associated with several factors, and the reason given in the sentence seems to be inappropriate.
32. Reading involves many different skills, and only a reliable and valid reading test should be used to evaluate reading proficiency.
33. Persistence may help a child in solving various tasks, but unless it is coupled with adequate cognitive ability, the child's performance is not likely to be successful. *Suggestion*: "In completing the matrix items, Bill was persistent and worked quickly and accurately. His high score in this area reflects his strong abilities in understanding spatial relationships and in perceptual organization."
34. Intelligence test scores in and of themselves should never be used as a basis for establishing the presence of a learning disability. *Suggestion*: "The 15-point discrepancy between Mary's Verbal Comprehension and Perceptual Reasoning scores indicates that her verbal abilities are better developed than her nonverbal reasoning abilities."
35. A scaled score of 10 is in the Average range and should not be considered "poor." The sentence should be rewritten. *Suggestion*: "She has excellent concept formation skills and average rote memory ability."
36. The explanation offered for the child's Verbal Comprehension–Perceptual Reasoning discrepancy is probably incorrect. The items on the WISC–IV Perceptual Reasoning Index call for cognitive skills primarily. Although visual-motor skills are necessary for some items, they are not the major determinant of success on the Perceptual Reasoning items. Indeed, if the writer's reasoning were correct, there would be no way for children who were maturationally average to obtain superior nonverbal scores. Additionally, scaled scores are normed in reference to children of the same age as the child being tested; therefore, lower scores indicate abilities that are less well developed than those of other children of the same age.
37. Intrasubtest variability indicates an uneven pattern of performance. It is a great leap, and likely an improper one, to infer "lack of persistence" solely on the basis of intrasubtest variability. Furthermore, "intrasubtest scatter" is a technical concept that is better left out of the report. *Suggestion*: "There were many failures on easy items and successes on more difficult ones." Then offer an interpretation of this pattern.
38. This interpretation is misleading. Verbal subtests do not simply require automatic responding; they also require

(Continued)

Exhibit 4-3 (Continued)

judgment, problem solving, conceptualization, and attention.

39. This sentence fails to present the child's level of performance. Also, the term "significance," as used here, is vague. The sentence should be deleted and replaced with a discussion of the child's test performance.

40. These interpretations are problematic. First, the child does not "lack" verbal abilities. Her scores suggest that some abilities are better developed than others. Her good performance in school should not be attributed to compensation for average verbal skills. The logic of this inference is not clear. Second, the Perceptual Reasoning Index and the Processing Speed Index do not measure fine or gross

motor skills, as is implied in this statement. Rather, they measure cognitive skills and visual-motor coordination and integration. It is the integration of cognitive and motor skills that is required for success on these Composites. *Suggestion:* "Ellen's excellent nonverbal reasoning and processing speed skills (99th and 96th percentile rank, respectively) are considerably better developed than are her verbal comprehension and working memory skills (45th and 55th percentile rank, respectively)." This statement can then be followed with a discussion of specific subtest scores.

---

6. How might a child function if she had a Working Memory Index of 80 and a Processing Speed Index of 120?

7. How might a child function if he had a Verbal Comprehension Index of 120, a Working Memory Index of 120, a Perceptual Reasoning Index of 80, and a Processing Speed Index of 80?

8. How might a child function if she had a Verbal Comprehension Index of 80, a Working Memory Index of 80, a Perceptual Reasoning Index of 120, and a Processing Speed Index of 120?

9. What would you do to improve the WISC–IV?

10. How would you answer a parent who asked, "What is my child's potential?" after learning how the child did on the WISC–IV?

SUMMARY

Profile Analysis

1. Profile analysis (sometimes referred to as scatter analysis) is a procedure for analyzing a child's pattern of subtest scaled scores and Composite standard scores.

2. Profile analysis with the WISC–IV cannot be used to arrive at a diagnostic label.

3. The Full Scale IQ, although a valuable measure of general intellectual ability, by itself tells us little about the underlying abilities on which it is based.

4. The goal of profile analysis is to generate hypotheses about the child's abilities.

5. Variability that is outside of "normal limits" may not indicate the presence of psychopathology or exceptionality; rather, variability may simply reflect the child's cognitive strengths and weaknesses.

6. The simplest way to approach a subtest profile analysis is to evaluate the scores in reference to the norm group—an interindividual comparison.

7. Subtest scaled scores of 13 to 19 always indicate a strength; subtest scaled scores of 8 to 12 always indicate average ability; and subtest scaled scores of 1 to 7 always indicate a weakness.

8. When you describe the child's cognitive abilities in relation to his or her own level of performance, you are making an intraindividual comparison.

9. To be able to say that one score is meaningfully (i.e., statistically significantly) higher than another score, you must first determine that the difference between the two scores does not represent chance variation—you cannot simply look at two scores and say that one is meaningfully (or statistically significantly) higher or lower than the other.

10. One approach to profile analysis is to determine whether certain scores differ significantly from each other; this is called the significant difference approach.

11. A second approach to profile analysis is to determine the frequency with which the differences between scores in the child's profile occurred in the standardization sample; this is called the base rate approach or the probability-of-occurrence approach.

12. The primary methods of profile analysis are evaluating the four Index scores, the subtest scaled scores, and the range of subtest scaled scores (or intersubtest scatter).

13. Both statistically reliable differences and empirically observed base rates can assist in profile analysis.

14. You will need to evaluate the child's entire performance, clinical history, and background information to arrive at the most reasonable hypothesis to account for a significant difference between Index scores.

15. A discrepancy between two or more Index scores should never be used as the sole criterion for making a diagnosis of learning disability, brain injury, or mental retardation.

16. Any hypotheses about subtest scaled scores should be developed through study of the child's entire test performance and clinical history.

17. Subtest scaled scores of 10 or higher should be described as reflecting average or above-average ability and never as absolute weaknesses, whereas subtest scaled scores of 7 or lower should be described as reflecting below-average ability and never as absolute strengths.

18. All statistically significant differences between scores are "unusual," regardless of the base rate, and deserve consideration in evaluating a child's profile of abilities.

19. We suggest that a low base rate is one that occurs in 10% to 15% or less of the standardization sample.

20. Clinical acumen, the child's medical history, behavioral observations, and the results of other tests that the child has taken will help you interpret differences between the Index scores.

21. Neither the reliability-of-difference approach nor the probability-of-occurrence approach should be used in a mechanical fashion or as a replacement for clinical judgment.

22. You can derive more reliable estimates of specific abilities from each Index score than from individual subtest scaled scores.

23. When a difference between two subtests or a difference between two Composites is statistically significant, it is large enough that it cannot be attributed to chance (i.e., measurement error).

24. Do not use scores on individual subtests to attempt precise descriptions of specific cognitive skills; rather, use them to generate hypotheses about the child's abilities.

25. Variability of scores may represent only uneven skill development and is not a sufficient basis for making decisions about psychopathology.

A Successive-Level Approach to Test Interpretation

26. A successive-level approach to test interpretation can help you better understand a child's performance. The six levels of the approach are (a) Full Scale IQ, (b) Index scores, (c) subtests within each Composite, (d) subtest scaled score differences and Process score differences, (e) intrasubtest variability, and (f) qualitative analysis.

Steps in Analyzing a Protocol

27. A 12-step procedure is useful for analyzing a WISC–IV protocol. The steps focus on evaluating the reliability and validity of the test scores, examining the five Composite scores, determining significant differences between the scores, and evaluating qualitative features of the child's performance.

The Composites

28. When you develop hypotheses about a child's performance on the Full Scale and the four individual Composites, the hypotheses are based primarily on the individual subtests that make up the respective Composite.

29. Verbal Comprehension draws on the child's accumulated experience, Perceptual Reasoning requires immediate problem-solving ability, Working Memory measures short-term auditory memory and arithmetical ability, and Processing Speed relies on visual processing.

Estimated Percentile Ranks and Test-Age Equivalents for Raw Scores

30. When you explain the test results to parents or others involved in the assessment, it is helpful to use the percentile ranks associated with the Full Scale IQ, Index scores, and subtest scaled scores.

31. Occasionally, you may want to use test-age equivalents in your explanations.

Illustration of a Portion of a Psychological Report

32. A portion of a psychological report illustrates how quantitative information can be woven into a report and how a child's profile can be discussed.

Comment on Interpreting the WISC–IV

33. When a significant split occurs between the Index scores, the Full Scale IQ may be only a forced average of rather disparate primary skills.

34. Subtest scaled scores, Index scores, and Full Scale IQs are multidetermined.

35. The WISC–IV gives an estimate of the child's level of intellectual functioning and provides useful— but not complete—information about the range, depth, and real-world applications of a child's intellectual ability.

36. The WISC–IV should not be used to evaluate personality and temperament, to diagnose psychopathology, or to determine brain lateralization.

Report Writing Guidelines

37. The primary focus of the report should be on the Full Scale IQ, followed by the Index scores and then the subtest scores.

38. Stress what the child did do, not what he or she did not do.

39. In interpreting the child's performance, consider all sources of information, including the child's educational history, previous assessment results, other current assessment results, developmental history, cultural and linguistic background, family environment, health history, and temporary situational factors.

40. Intelligence test scores, in and of themselves, should never be used as a basis for establishing a learning disability diagnosis.

Psychological Evaluation

41. The psychological evaluation in Exhibit 4-2 illustrates how the WISC–IV can contribute to the assessment of a youngster with emotional difficulties.

KEY TERMS, CONCEPTS, AND NAMES

Profile analysis (p. 114)
Interindividual comparison (p. 115)
Intraindividual comparison (p. 116)
Ipsative approach (p. 116)
Significant difference approach (p. 117)
Base rate approach (p. 117)
Probability-of-occurrence approach (p. 117)
Primary methods of profile analysis (p. 117)
Reliability-of-difference approach (p. 135)
Successive-level approach to test interpretation (p. 135)
Steps in analyzing a protocol (p. 137)
Estimated percentile ranks (p. 139)
Test-age equivalents (p. 139)

STUDY QUESTIONS

1. Discuss the intent of profile analysis, methods of profile analysis, and approaches to profile analysis on the WISC–IV.
2. Describe the successive-level approach to interpreting the WISC–IV.
3. Describe the steps used to analyze a WISC–IV protocol.
4. Discuss how to interpret differences between the WISC–IV Index scores.
5. Discuss how to interpret differences between WISC–IV subtests. Cite at least seven subtest comparisons.
6. What are some general considerations in interpreting the WISC–IV?
7. Present 10 useful guidelines for report writing.

5

WECHSLER PRESCHOOL AND PRIMARY SCALE OF INTELLIGENCE–III (WPPSI–III): DESCRIPTION

From the child of five to myself is but a step. But from the new-born to the child of five is an appalling distance.

— Leo Tolstoy

A Note About Terminology

Standardization

Standard Scores, Scaled Scores, and Test-Age Equivalents

Reliability

Validity

Intercorrelations for Subtests and Composites

Demographic Variables

Factor Analysis

Range of Subtest Scaled Scores

Range of Full Scale IQs

Comparison of the WPPSI–III and WPPSI–R

Administering the WPPSI–III

Short Forms

Choosing Between the WPPSI–III and the WISC–IV and Between the WPPSI–III and the BSID–II

Administering the WPPSI–III to Children with Disabilities

Assets

Limitations

Concluding Comment

Thinking Through the Issues

Summary

Key Terms, Concepts, and Names

Study Questions

Goals and Objectives

This chapter is designed to enable you to do the following:

- Evaluate the psychometric properties of the WPPSI–III

- Learn how to administer the WPPSI–III

- Select useful WPPSI–III short forms

- Choose between the WPPSI–III and the WISC–III in the overlapping ages

- Choose between the WPPSI–III and the Bayley Scales of Infant Development in the overlapping ages

The Wechsler Preschool and Primary Scale of Intelligence–III (WPPSI–III; Wechsler, 2002a, b) is the 2002 edition of an intelligence test first published in 1967 and previously revised in 1989 (WPPSI–R). It is a derivative of the original 1939 scale called the Wechsler-Bellevue Intelligence Scale, Form I (Wechsler, 1939) and named after David Wechsler and Bellevue Hospital in New York City, where Wechsler served as chief psychologist.

The WPPSI–III is divided into two broad age groups: ages 2-6 to 3-11 and ages 4-0 to 7-3. Subtests are designated as one of three types:

- *Core subtests* are used in the computation of the Verbal, Performance, and Full Scale IQ.
- *Supplemental subtests* are used as replacements for the core subtests or to obtain additional information about cognitive functioning.
- *Optional subtests* are used to obtain additional useful information about cognitive functioning, but are not used as replacements for core subtests.

The age group from 2-6 to 3-11 has four core subtests and one supplemental subtest, but no optional subtests (see Figure 5-1). The four core subtests are Receptive Vocabulary and Information, which form the Verbal Composite, and Block Design and Object Assembly, which form the Performance Composite. These four core subtests form the Full Scale. The one supplemental subtest is Picture Naming, which can be substituted for Receptive Vocabulary and, if administered, forms, with Receptive Vocabulary, the General Language Composite.

The age group from 4-0 to 7-3 has seven core subtests, five supplemental subtests, and two optional subtests (see Figure 5-2). The seven core subtests are (a) Information, Vocabulary, and Word Reasoning, which form the Verbal Composite, (b) Block Design, Matrix Reasoning, and Picture Concepts, which form the Performance Composite, and (c) Coding, which is in neither the Verbal nor the Performance Composite. The Supplemental subtests are Similarities, Comprehension, Object Assembly, Picture Completion, and Symbol Search. Symbol Search, if administered, combines with Coding to form the Processing Speed Composite. The optional subtests, Receptive Vocabulary and Picture Naming, cannot be used as substitutes for any subtests at ages 4-0 to 7-3; however, if administered, they form the General Language Composite.

Note that some subtests may be designated as core, supplemental, or optional depending on their placement in one of the two broad age groups. Thus, Block Design

and Information are core subtests in both age groups. Receptive Vocabulary is a core subtest at ages 2-6 to 3-11 but an optional subtest at ages 4-0 to 7-3. Object Assembly is a core subtest at ages 2-6 to 3-11 but a supplemental subtest at ages 4-0 to 7-3. Finally, Picture Naming is a supplemental subtest at ages 2-6 to 3-11 but an optional subtest at ages 4-0 to 7-3.

A NOTE ABOUT TERMINOLOGY

In this section of the book, we refer to the *WPPSI–III Administration and Scoring Manual* as the Administration Manual and the *WPPSI–III Technical and Interpretive Manual* as the Technical Manual. Also, the research studies cited in this chapter are from the Technical Manual, unless otherwise noted. Finally, the two manuals use different terms to describe children who are low functioning. The Administration Manual uses the term "intellectual deficiency" to classify children who may be low functioning, whereas the Technical Manual uses the term "extremely low" for children who have IQs of 69 and below. However, the term "mental retardation" is used by the American Psychiatric Association (2000) and by the American Association on Mental Retardation (2002) to describe children whose IQ is below 70 and who have deficits in adaptive behavior. Finally, tables in the Appendix in this text are referred to with hyphens (e.g., A-1 or B-1) and those in the Administration Manual with periods (e.g., A.1 or B.1).

STANDARDIZATION

The WPPSI–III was standardized on 1,700 children who were selected to represent children in the United States. The demographic characteristics used to obtain a stratified sample were age, sex, race/ethnicity, geographic region, and parental education (used as a measure of socioeconomic status).

The standardization group contained nine age groups, with children ranging from ages 2-6 to 7-3. There were 100 boys and 100 girls in each age group, except at the ages 7-0 to 7-3, where there were 50 boys and 50 girls. With respect to race/ethnic membership, children were from the following groups: Euro American, African American, Hispanic American, Asian American, or Other (refers to other racial groups). The four geographical regions sampled were Northeast, South, Midwest, and West. Children were selected so that the composition of each age group matched as closely as possi-

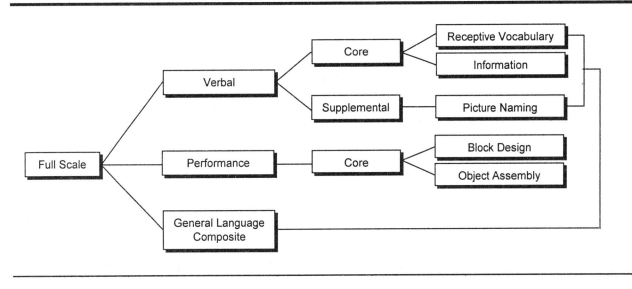

Figure 5-1. Structure of the WPPSI–III at ages 2-6 to 3-11.

ble the proportions found in the 2000 U.S. Census with regard to race/ethnicity, geographic region, and parental education.

Table 5-1 shows the parental education and geographic region of the standardization sample by race/ethnic group. Parents in the Asian American, Euro American, and Other classifications had the most education—73.6% of the Asian American group, 71.0% of the Euro American group, and 65.0% of the Other group had some college education or graduated from college, while 46.8% of the African American group and 31.6% of the Hispanic American group had some college education or graduated from college. The majority of the Euro American and African American samples came from the Midwest and South. The majority of the Hispanic American and Other samples came from the South. Most of the Asian American sample came from the West and Midwest. The racial/ethnic proportions in the sample were 60.9% Euro American, 15.6% African American, 18.1% Hispanic American, 4.2% Asian American, and 1.2% Other. The Euro American sample was more evenly distributed across geographic regions than the other racial/ethnic groups.

The WPPSI–III sampling procedure is more refined than the one used on the WPPSI–R—the WPPSI–III has a separate classification for Asian Americans, whereas the WPPSI–R included Asian Americans in the "Other" category. However, the WPPSI–III uses parental education level as the only measure of socioeconomic status, whereas the WPPSI–R used both parental education level and parent occupation. Overall, the sampling

methodology was excellent.

A comparison of the percentages of persons in each of 10 occupational categories in the standardization sample and in the corresponding United States noninstitutionalized civilian population shows some discrepancies between the sample and the population. For example, 3.2% of those in the standardization sample were managers, while 6.9% of those in the U.S. population were so classified; 8.6% of those in the standardization sample were administrative support and clerical specialists, while 16.7% of the population was in this category. These discrepancies should not detract from the representativeness of the standardization sample, however.

STANDARD SCORES, SCALED SCORES, AND TEST-AGE EQUIVALENTS

The WPPSI–III, like the WISC–IV and WAIS–III, uses standard scores ($M = 100$, $SD = 15$) for the Verbal IQ, Performance IQ, Full Scale IQ, Processing Speed Quotient, and General Language Composite, and scaled scores ($M = 10$, $SD = 3$) for the 14 subtests. The Full Scale IQ is computed by comparing the sum of the child's core subtest scaled scores (four core subtests at ages 2-6 to 3-11 and seven core subtests at ages 4-0 to 7-3) with the scores earned by a representative sample of the child's age group. After each subtest is scored,

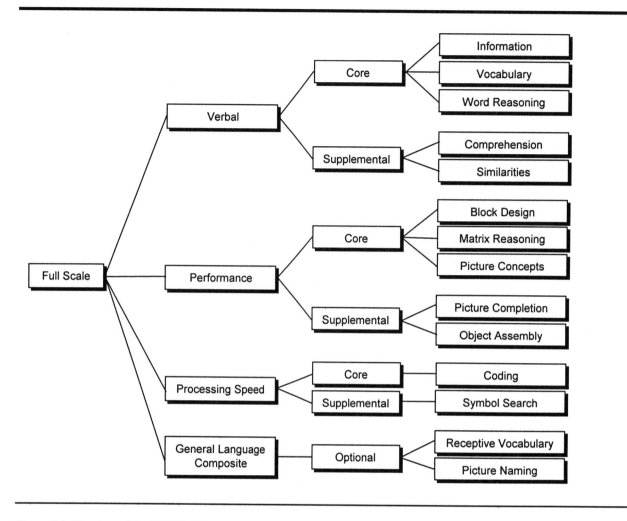

Figure 5-2. Structure of the WPPSI–III at ages 4-0 to 7-3.

raw-score points are summed and converted to scaled scores within the child's own age group (in three-month intervals) through use of Table A.1 on pages 216 to 230 in the Administration Manual. Table A.1 is in 3-month intervals at ages 2-6 to 5-11 and in 4-month intervals at ages 6-0 to 7-3. Tables A.2, A.3, A.4, and A.5 in the Administration Manual (pp. 231–234) are used to obtain the individual Composite scores and Full Scale IQs based on the core subtests at ages 2-6 to 3-11, whereas Tables A.6, A.7, A.8, A.9, and A.10 (pp. 235–240) are used to obtain the individual Composite scores and Full Scale IQs based on the core subtests at ages 4-0 to 7-3.

Prorating Procedure

For children ages 2-6 to 3-11, if three subtests are valid, you can use Table A.11 on page 241 of the Administra-

tion Manual to prorate the sum of scaled scores to obtain a Full Scale IQ. This part of the table was constructed by multiplying the sum of the three scaled scores by 4/3. For children ages 4-0 to 7-3, if six subtests are valid, you can use Table A.11 to prorate the sum of scaled scores to obtain a Full Scale IQ. This part of the table was constructed by multiplying the sum of the six scaled scores by 7/3. However, for children ages 2-6 to 3-11, you cannot use proration to obtain a Verbal IQ or Performance IQ if only one of the two subtests in each IQ is valid, because proration requires at least two valid subtests. Proration is similar to using a short form of the test.

Proration should be avoided whenever possible because it violates the standard test procedure and introduces unknown measurement error. If you do prorate, write "Estimate" by the Composite scores and Full Scale IQ on the Record Form and in the psychological report. Later in the chapter we discuss how you can obtain es-

Table 5-1
**Demographic Characteristics of WPPSI–III Standardization Sample:
Parental Education and Geographic Region by Race/Ethnic Group**

Demographic variable	Race/ethnic group (percent)				
	Euro American (N = 1036)	African American (N = 265)	Hispanic American (N = 307)	Asian American (N = 72)	Other[a] (N = 20)
Parental education					
Eight years or less	1.0	2.3	16.0	1.4	0.0
Some high school	3.8	15.1	23.8	12.5	10.0
High school graduate	24.2	35.8	28.6	12.5	25.0
Some college	35.5	33.2	22.8	27.8	40.0
College graduate	35.5	13.6	8.8	45.8	25.0
Total	100.0	100.0	100.0	100.0	100.0
Geographic region					
Northeast	18.5	12.8	8.1	15.3	5.0
South	33.2	44.9	51.8	16.7	55.5
Midwest	27.8	35.5	4.6	22.2	15.0
West	20.5	6.8	35.5	45.8	25.0
Total	100.0	100.0	100.0	100.0	100.0

Note. Race/ethnic distribution in total group (*N* = 1,700) was as follows: Euro American = 60.9%, African American = 15.6%, Hispanic American = 18.1%, Asian American = 4.2%, Other = 1.2%.
[a]*Other* represents the following groups: Native American, Eskimo, Aleut, and Pacific Islander.
Source: Adapted from Wechsler (2002b).

timated IQs for several short-form combinations using the Tellegen and Briggs (1967) procedure. We need research to determine which procedure—proration or the Tellegen and Briggs procedure—yields more valid IQs.

Test-Age Equivalents

Test-age equivalents are provided in Table A.12 (p. 242) in the Administration Manual. Test-age equivalents, which are essentially mental-age (MA) scores, are obtained directly from the raw scores on each subtest. Because a scaled score of 10 represents the mean, the test-age equivalents of the raw scores reflect the average score for each specific age group. For example, at 4 years of age, a raw score of 20 on Block Design equals a scaled score of 10 (see p. 219 in the Administration Manual). Therefore, a raw score of 20 on Block Design is equal to a test-age equivalent of 4-1. An average test-age equivalent is obtained by summing the individual subtest test ages and dividing the sum by the number of subtests. To obtain a median test age, rank the test ages from high to low and locate the middle-most test age. The median is a more appropriate description of the distribution of test ages than the mean because test ages do not have equal units.

The WPPSI–III test-age equivalents can be compared with mental-age or test-age equivalents from other tests. Such comparisons may help parents, teachers, and others better understand a child's level of intellectual functioning. Research is needed to determine the validity of WPPSI–III test-age equivalents.

RELIABILITY

The WPPSI–III has good reliability. Internal consistency reliability coefficients for the nine age groups range from .94 to .96 ($M\ r_{xx} = .95$) for the Verbal IQ, from .89 to .95 ($M\ r_{xx} = .93$) for the Performance IQ, and from .95 to .97 ($M\ r_{xx} = .96$) for the Full Scale IQ (see Table 5-2). Internal consistency reliability coefficients range from .86 to .92 ($M\ r_{xx} = .89$) for the Processing Speed Quotient at ages 4-0 to 7-3; subtests comprising the Processing Speed Quotient are not administered at ages 2-6 to 3-11. The median individual Composites and Full Scale internal consistency reliability coefficients are similar for the nine age groups ($Mdn\ r_{xx} = .86$ to .96 for the three individual Composites and $Mdn\ r_{xx} = .95$ to .97 for the Full Scale, see Table 5-3).

Subtest Reliabilities

Two types of internal consistency reliability coefficients were used on the WPPSI–III. The split-half method was used for 12 of the 14 subtests, while the test-retest stability coefficient was used for the other two subtests (Coding and Symbol Search). Internal consistency reliabilities for the subtest scores are lower than those for the IQs and Processing Speed Quotient (see Table 5-2). This is to be expected, because there are fewer items in any one subtest than in an IQ composed of two or more subtests.

The 14 subtests have average internal consistency reliabilities that range from a low of $r_{xx} = .83$ for Symbol Search to a high of .95 for Similarities. The median subtest internal consistency reliability is lowest at ages 2-6

Table 5-2
Range of and Average Internal Consistency Reliabilities, Test-Retest Reliabilities, and Standard Errors of Measurement for 14 WPPSI–III Subtests and Five Composites

Subtest or Composite	Range of internal consistency reliabilities (r_{xx})	Average internal consistency reliability (r_{xx})	Range of test-retest reliabilities (r_{tt})	Average test-retest reliability (r_{tt})	Range of SEM	Average SEM
Block Design	.75–.91	.84	.69–.80	.74	.90–1.50	1.20
Information	.83–.93	.88	.72–.90	.83	.79–1.24	1.05
Matrix Reasoning	.88–.90	.90	.59–.80	.71	.90–1.04	.96
Vocabulary	.86–.92	.89	.68–.73	.71	.85–1.12	1.01
Picture Concepts	.89–.93	.91	.54–.67	.61	.85–.99	.91
Symbol Search	.80–.86	.83	.75–.81	.78	1.12–1.34	1.23
Word Reasoning	.89–.93	.91	.72–.78	.75	.79–.99	.88
Coding	.79–.88	.84	.78–.82	.80	1.04–1.37	1.22
Comprehension	.87–.90	.88	.74–.80	.77	.95–1.12	1.03
Picture Completion	.87–.92	.90	.70–.77	.74	.85–1.08	.96
Similarities	.91–.96	.95	.75–.90	.84	.60–.90	.69
Receptive Vocabulary	.82–.91	.88	.68–.80	.77	.90–1.27	1.04
Object Assembly	.78–.90	.85	.68–.72	.70	.95–1.41	1.18
Picture Naming	.84–.90	.88	.82–.89	.85	.95–1.20	1.05
Verbal	.94–.96	.95	.85–.88	.87	3.00–3.67	3.35
Performance	.89–.95	.93	.75–.84	.81	3.35–4.97	4.15
Processing Speed	.86–.92	.89	.84–.88	.86	4.24–5.61	4.94
Full Scale	.95–.97	.96	.80–.90	.86	2.60–3.35	2.92
General Language	.90–.94	.93	—	—	3.67–4.50	4.03

Note. All reliability coefficients are uncorrected.
Source: WPPSI–III Technical and Interpretive Manual. Copyright © 2002 by The Psychological Corporation. Reproduced by permission. All rights reserved. "Wechsler Preschool and Primary Scale of Intelligence–Third Edition" is a registered trademark of The Psychological Corporation.

Table 5-3
**Range and Median Internal Consistency Reliabilities of WPPSI–III Subtests
for Ages 2-6 to 7-3**

	Subtests		Individual Composites		Full Scale
Age	Range of r_{xx}	Mdn r_{xx}	Range of r_{xx}	Mdn r_{xx}	r_{xx}
2-6 to 2-11	.84–.92	.87	.89–.95	.94	.95
3-0 to 3-5	.85–.91	.90	.89–.95	.94	.95
3-6 to 3-11	.85–.93	.90	.91–.95	.94	.96
Average[a]	.84–.93	.90	.90–.95	.94	.95
4-0 to 4-5	.75–.95	.89	.91–.95	.93	.96
4-6 to 4-11	.84–.96	.88	.91–.95	.93	.97
5-0 to 5-5	.82–.95	.90	.92–.96	.93	.97
5-6 to 5-11	.79–.96	.88	.87–.95	.93	.97
6-0 to 6-11	.78–.91	.87	.87–.94	.92	.96
7-0 to 7-3	.79–.95	.88	.86–.95	.93	.97
Average[b]	.78–.96	.88	.89–.95	.93	.97

[a]For ages 2-6 to 3-11.
[b]For ages 4-0 to 7-3.
Source: Adapted from Wechsler (2002b).

to 2-11 and ages 6-0 to 6-11 (*Mdn* r_{xx} = .87) and highest at ages 3-0 to 3-11 and ages 5-0 to 5-5 (*Mdn* r_{xx} = .90; see Table 5-3).

Standard Errors of Measurement

The average standard errors of measurement (SEM) in standard-score points are 3.35 for the Verbal IQ, 4.15 for the Performance IQ, 4.94 for the Processing Speed Quotient, and 2.92 for the Full Scale IQ (see Table 5-2). You can place more confidence in the Full Scale than in the other IQs. In addition, you can place more confidence in the Verbal IQ than in the Performance IQ or Processing Speed Quotient.

The average SEMs for the subtests in scaled-score points range from .69 for Similarities to 1.23 for Symbol Search (see Table 5-2). Within their respective Composites, Word Reasoning has the smallest average SEM (.88) of the Verbal subtests and Information has the largest (1.05), Picture Concepts has the smallest average SEM (.91) of the Performance subtests and Block Design has the largest (1.20), and the Processing Speed subtests Coding and Symbol Search have similar average SEMs (1.22 and 1.23, respectively).

Test-Retest Reliability

The stability of the WPPSI–III was assessed by retesting, after an interval of 14 to 50 days (*M* = 26 days; Wechsler, 2002b), 157 children; 13 to 27 came from each of the nine age groups in the standardization sample. For statistical analysis, individual age groups were combined into three broad age groups: ages 2-6 to 3-11, ages 4-0 to 5-5, and ages 5-6 to 7-3.

The stability coefficients for the three individual Composites and the Full Scale in the three age groups ranged from .85 to .88 for the Verbal IQ, from .75 to .84 for the Performance IQ, from .84 to .88 for the Processing Speed Quotient, and from .80 to .90 for the Full Scale (see Table 5-2). For the total test-retest sample, the stability coefficients were .87 for the Verbal IQ, .81 for the Performance IQ, .86 for the Processing Speed Quotient, and .86 for the Full Scale. The stability coefficients indicate that the WPPSI–III generally provides stable Full Scale IQs. However, the stability coefficients are less than .80 at one broad age (4-0 to 5-5) for the Performance IQ.

In the total test-retest sample, average stability coefficients for the subtests ranged from a low of .61 for

Picture Concepts to a high of .85 for Picture Naming (see Table 5-2). Median internal consistency reliabilities are higher than median test-retest reliabilities (*Mdn* r_{xx} = .88 versus *Mdn* r_{tt} = .76). Out of the 33 stability coefficients for the 14 subtests at the three broad age groups, 20 stability coefficients are below .80 (1 coefficient at ages 2-6 to 3-11, 11 coefficients at ages 4-0 to 5-5, and 8 coefficients at ages 5-6 to 7-3). Thus, the subtests are less stable than the individual Composites and the Full Scale.

Changes in IQs. Table 5-4 shows the mean test-retest and change scores for the Verbal IQ, Performance IQ, Processing Speed Quotient, and Full Scale IQ for the three broad age groups and for the total test-retest sample. For the total test-retest sample, mean increases from the first to the second testing were 2.8 points for the Verbal IQ, 5.0 points for the Performance IQ, 6.2 points for the Processing Speed Quotient, and 5.2 points for the Full Scale. Thus, prior exposure to Performance and Processing Speed items facilitates performance on retest

Table 5-4
Test-Retest WPPSI–III IQs for Three Age Groups and Total Group

Age	Composite	First testing		Second testing		Change	ES[a]
		Mean	SD	Mean	SD		
2-6 to 3-11	Verbal	100.0	13.9	101.6	13.1	1.6	.12
(N = 41)	Performance	98.0	14.8	102.2	14.0	4.2*	.29
	Full Scale	99.0	14.7	102.4	13.7	3.4*	.24
4-0 to 5-5	Verbal	104.7	10.6	109.7	10.2	5.0*	.48
(N = 34)	Performance	102.1	11.0	106.9	10.3	4.8*	.45
	Processing Speed	99.6	11.7	105.6	13.5	6.0*	.47
	Full Scale	103.4	9.5	109.8	9.2	6.4*	.68
5-6 to 7-3	Verbal	99.3	12.9	101.7	12.7	2.4*	.19
(N = 82)	Performance	99.3	13.1	105.0	13.4	5.7*	.43
	Processing Speed	98.9	14.3	105.2	15.5	6.3*	.42
	Full Scale	99.0	12.7	104.5	13.5	5.5*	.42
Total	Verbal	100.6	12.8	103.4	12.7	2.8*	.22
(N = 157)	Performance	99.6	13.2	104.6	13.0	5.0*	.38
	Processing Speed	99.1	13.6	105.3	14.9	6.2*	.43
	Full Scale	99.9	12.7	105.1	12.9	5.2*	.41

Note. Test-retest intervals ranged from 14 to 50 days, with a median retest interval of 26 days. The *N* for each age group was obtained from J. J. Zhu, Manager of Data Analysis Operations, The Psychological Corporation, December 2003.

The *t* test used to evaluate the mean changes on each Composite employed a repeated-measures formula:

$$t = \frac{M_1 - M_2}{\sqrt{\left(\frac{SD_1}{\sqrt{N_1}}\right)^2 + \left(\frac{SD_2}{\sqrt{N_2}}\right)^2 - 2r_{12}\left(\frac{SD_1}{\sqrt{N_1}}\right)\left(\frac{SD_2}{\sqrt{N_2}}\right)}}$$

[a] Effect size (ES) is the difference between two means divided by the square root of the pooled variance. Effect sizes are classified as small (ES = .20), medium (ES = .50), or large (ES = .80) (Cohen, 1988).
* *p* < .001.
Source: WPPSI–III Technical and Interpretive Manual. Copyright © 2002 by The Psychological Corporation. Reproduced by permission. All rights reserved. "Wechsler Preschool and Primary Scale of Intelligence–Third Edition" is a registered trademark of The Psychological Corporation.

more than prior exposure to Verbal items.

Higher retest scores after a short time interval are likely to be associated with practice effects, whereas those that occur after a long time interval may be associated with both practice effects and changes in ability. For example, items on the Performance Composite and items on Processing Speed subtests may not be as novel on the repeated administration as they initially were. Carefully consider whether you want to use the WPPSI–III again for repeated evaluations, especially if you plan to use the results obtained on the retest for placement, eligibility, or diagnostic decisions. If the time between tests is relatively short (e.g., less than 9 months), consider using another individually administered well-standardized test of cognitive ability for the reexamination.

Changes in subtest scaled scores. Table 5-5 shows the test-retest subtest scaled-score changes from the first to the second administration. Picture Completion showed the largest mean increase (1.4 points), while Vocabulary showed the smallest mean increase (.3 point). Increases varied with age, depending on the subtest. For example, Receptive Vocabulary showed a small mean increase at ages 5-6 to 7-3 (.3 point) and a large mean increase at ages 4-0 to 5-5 (1.0 point).

Confidence Intervals

Table B-1 in Appendix B shows confidence intervals, based on the obtained score and the SEM, for the 68%, 85%, 90%, 95%, and 99% levels of confidence by age group and for the average of the standardization group for Verbal IQ, Performance IQ, Processing Speed Quotient, and Full Scale IQ. We recommend that you use these confidence intervals rather than those in the Administration Manual, which are based on the estimated true score and the standard error of estimation (SE$_E$). The former method is preferred when a confidence interval is applied to a child's own individual score (see Sattler, 2001). *Use the child's specific age group—not the average of the nine age groups—to obtain the most accurate confidence interval for any individual child.* At the 95% level of confidence, the confidence intervals range from ±6 to ±8 for the Verbal Composite, from ±7 to ±10 for the Performance Composite, from ±9 to ±11 for the Processing Speed Quotient, and from ±6 to ±7 for the Full Scale. The range is greatest for Processing Speed because this Quotient is less reliable than the other ones. Similar relationships hold for the other levels of confidence.

VALIDITY

Criterion Validity

Studies correlating the WPPSI–III with the WPPSI–R, WISC–III, WISC–IV, and other measures of intelligence, achievement, memory, emotional intelligence, and adaptive behavior indicate that the WPPSI–III has satisfactory criterion validity (see Table 5-6). The studies summarized in Table 5-6 are limited because they use only tests published by The Psychological Corporation. Criterion validity studies that use other individual tests of intelligence and achievement and measures of adaptive behavior are needed.

If you use the WPPSI–III to retest children who were first tested with the WPPSI–R, bear in mind that the findings in the Technical Manual and those highlighted below came from children whose mean IQs were in the average range. Therefore, we do not know whether the findings are generalizable to children in the extreme ranges of intellectual ability or to children with special needs.

WPPSI–III and WPPSI–R. A sample of 176 children ages 3-0 to 7-3 were administered the WPPSI–III and WPPSI–R in counterbalanced order within an 8- to 58-day period (*M* = 28 days). Correlations were .83 for the Verbal Composites, .68 for the Performance Composites, and .82 for the Full Scales. Mean Verbal and Performance IQs were lower on the WPPSI–III than on the WPPSI–R by about .5 to 3 points, and the mean WPPSI–III Full Scale IQ was lower than the mean WPPSI–R Full Scale IQ by .6 point. Research studies conducted with the WPPSI–R are probably not applicable to the WPPSI–III because of the changes in the structure of the test.

WPPSI–III and WISC–III. A sample of 96 children ages 6-0 to 7-3 were administered the WPPSI–III and WISC–III in counterbalanced order within an 8- to 49-day period (*M* = 24 days). Correlations were .78 for the Verbal Composites, .78 for the Verbal IQ and Verbal Comprehension Index, .74 for the Performance Scales, .79 for the Performance IQ and Perceptual Organization Index, .71 for the Processing Speed Composites, and .85 for the Full Scales. Mean Verbal and Performance IQs were lower on the WPPSI–III than on the WISC–III by about 3 to 8 points, and the mean WPPSI–III Full Scale IQ was lower than the mean WISC–III Full Scale IQ by 4.9 points.

Table 5-5
Test-Retest Point Gains on WPPSI–III Subtests
for Three Age Groups and Total Group

	Age				
Subtest	2-6 to 3-11	4-0 to 5-5	5-6 to 7-3	Total	ES[a]
Block Design	.90**	.50	.60**	0.70***	.26
Information	.30	.90**	.30	.40**	.15
Matrix Reasoning	—	1.10**	1.30***	1.20***	.44
Vocabulary	—	.60*	.20	.30*	.12
Picture Concepts	—	.60	.80***	.70***	.28
Symbol Search	—	1.10***	1.00***	1.10***	.39
Word Reasoning	—	1.00**	.80***	.90***	.33
Coding	—	1.10***	1.10***	1.20***	.39
Comprehension	—	.80**	.30	.40***	.15
Picture Completion	—	1.50***	1.40***	1.40***	.53
Similarities	—	.30	.90***	.70***	.28
Receptive Vocabulary	.50	1.00**	.30	.50***	.18
Object Assembly	.50	1.10**	.80**	.70***	.25
Picture Naming	.70***	.90***	.30	.50***	.19

Note. Test-retest intervals range from 14 to 50 days, with a mean retest interval of 26 days. The *t* test used to evaluate the mean changes on each subtest employed a repeated-measures formula:

$$t = \frac{M_1 - M_2}{\sqrt{\left(\frac{SD_1}{\sqrt{N_1}}\right)^2 + \left(\frac{SD_2}{\sqrt{N_2}}\right)^2 - 2r_{12}\left(\frac{SD_1}{\sqrt{N_1}}\right)\left(\frac{SD_2}{\sqrt{N_2}}\right)}}$$

[a] Effect size (ES) is for the total group only. Effect size (ES) is the difference between two means divided by the square root of the pooled variance. Effect sizes are classified as small (ES = .20), medium (ES = .50), or large (ES = .80) (Cohen, 1988).
  * $p < .05$.
 ** $p < .01$.
*** $p < .001$.
Source: Adapted from Wechsler (2002b).

WPPSI–III and WISC–IV. Because the WPPSI–III and WISC–IV overlap for children ages 6-0 to 7-3, it is important to know the relationship between the two tests for this age group. A sample of 182 6-year-old children were administered the WPPSI–III and WISC–IV in counterbalanced order within a 9- to 62-day period (*M* = 22 days; Wechsler, 2003b). Correlations were .76 for the Verbal Composite and Verbal Comprehension, .74 for the Performance Composite and Perceptual Reason-

ing, .62 for the two Processing Speed Composites, and .85 for the two Full Scales. Individual mean Composites on the two tests differed by 1.2 points or less whereas the Full Scale IQs differed by .2 point.

The WPPSI–III and WISC–IV are not completely independent tests. There is an overlap of two items on Block Design, three items on Picture Completion, and three items on Information. It would be better if the two tests had no items in common to eliminate the possibility

Table 5-6
Summary of WPPSI–III Criterion Validity Studies

Criterion	Composite				
	VIQ	PIQ	PSQ	FSIQ	GLC
WPPSI–R					
VIQ	.83	—	—	—	—
PIQ	—	.68	—	—	—
FSIQ	—	—	—	.82	—
WISC–III					
VIQ	.78	—	—	—	—
VCI	.78	—	—	—	—
PIQ	—	.74	—	—	—
POI	—	.79	—	—	—
PSI	—	—	.71	—	—
FSIQ	—	—	—	.85	—
WISC–IV					
VCI	.76	—	—	—	—
PRI	—	.74	—	—	—
PSI	—	—	.62	—	—
FSIQ	—	—	—	.85	—
BSID–II					
Mental	.73	.61	—	.80	.69
Motor	.33	.48	—	.47	.32
DAS					
Verbal	.78	.54	.40	.74	.74
Nonverbal Reasoning	.56	.76	.47	.75	.42
Spatial	.48	.49	.56	.58	.38
GCA	.81	.74	.56	.87	.74
WIAT–II					
Total	.77	.55	.36	.78	.76
Reading	.60	.44	.31	.66	.65
Mathematics	.56	.60	.55	.77	.55
Written Language	.59	.36	.41	.39	.36
Oral Language	.72	.44	.39	.67	.67
CMS					
Visual Immediate	.25	.45	.23	.38	.34
Visual Delayed	.09	.14	.07	.10	.10
Verbal Immediate	.67	.38	.37	.63	.56
Verbal Delayed	.50	.25	.13	.43	.38
General Memory	.51	.41	.27	.52	.47
Attention/Concentration	.73	.68	.42	.79	.68
Learning	.54	.46	.32	.58	.48
Delayed Recognition	.62	.45	.49	.63	.57

Note. Correlations are uncorrected with the Wechsler tests, and corrected with the other tests.

Abbreviation for Composites: VIQ = Verbal IQ, PIQ = Performance IQ, PSQ = Processing Speed Quotient, FSIQ = Full Scale IQ, GLC = General Language Composite.

Abbreviations for tests: WPPSI–R = Wechsler Preschool and Primary Scale of Intelligence–Revised, WISC–III = Wechsler Intelligence Scale for Children–III, WISC–IV = Wechsler Intelligence Scale for Children–IV, BSID–II = Bayley Scales of Infant Development–II, DAS = Differential Ability Scales, WIAT–II = Wechsler Individual Achievement Test–II, CMS = Children's Memory Scale.

Source: Adapted from Wechsler (2002b).

of direct practice effects.

WPPSI–III and BSID–II. A sample of 84 children ages 2-6 to 3-6 were administered the WPPSI–III and BSID–II in counterbalanced order within a 7- to 42-day period ($M = 14$ days). The WPPSI–III FSIQ correlated more highly with the BSID–II Mental Composite (.80) than with the Motor Composite (.47). The mean WPPSI–III FSIQ was .9 point lower than the mean BSID–II Mental Composite.

WPPSI–III and DAS. A sample of 164 children ages 2-6 to 7-3 were administered the WPPSI–III and DAS in counterbalanced order within a 0- to 59-day period ($M = 28$ days). Correlations were .78 for the Verbal Composites, .76 for the Performance Composite and Nonverbal Reasoning Composite, and .87 for the Full Scale and GCA. Individual mean Composites on the two tests differed by 1 to 2 points, while the WPPSI–III Full Scale IQ was 1.6 points lower than the DAS GCA.

Special group studies. The Technical Manual presents 11 special group studies, summarized in Table 5-7. Highlights of Table 5-7 follow:

- *Intellectually gifted:* The sample obtained a mean Full Scale IQ of 126.2. The individual mean Composite scores ranged from 113.4 (Processing Speed) to 125.8 (Verbal).
- *Mild mental retardation:* The sample obtained a mean Full Scale IQ of 62.1. The individual mean Composite scores ranged from 65.6 (Performance) to 69.5 (General Language).
- *Moderate mental retardation:* The sample obtained a mean Full Scale IQ of 53.1. The individual mean Composite scores ranged from 57.1 (Performance) to 58.3 (Processing Speed).
- *Developmental delay:* The sample obtained a mean Full Scale IQ of 81.8. The individual mean Composite scores ranged from 82.8 (Verbal) to 86.1 (Performance).
- *Developmental risk factors:* The sample obtained a mean Full Scale IQ of 85.7. The individual mean Composite scores ranged from 85.7 (Performance) to 90.1 (Processing Speed).
- *Autistic disorder:* The sample obtained a mean Full Scale IQ of 76.6. The individual mean Composite scores ranged from 70.6 (Verbal) to 88.2 (Performance).
- *Expressive language disorder:* The sample obtained a mean Full Scale IQ of 90.1. The individual mean

Composite scores ranged from 90.6 (Verbal) to 94.7 (General Language).

- *Mixed receptive-expressive language disorder:* The sample obtained a mean Full Scale IQ of 81.9. The individual mean Composite scores ranged from 82.7 (Processing Speed) to 86.7 (General Language).
- *Limited English proficiency:* The sample obtained a mean Full Scale IQ of 87.0. The individual mean Composite scores ranged from 79.2 (General Language) to 100.1 (Processing Speed).
- *Attention-deficit/hyperactivity disorder:* The sample obtained a mean Full Scale IQ of 94.3. The individual mean Composite scores ranged from 93.8 (Verbal) to 97.4 (Performance).
- *Motor impairment:* The sample obtained a mean Full Scale IQ of 94.2. The individual mean Composite scores ranged from 87.7 (Performance) to 105.8 (General Language)

The range of individual mean Composite scores is greatest for the limited English proficiency group (about 21 points), followed by the motor impairment group and autistic disorder groups (about 18 points) and the intellectually gifted group (about 12 points). The remaining seven groups have an individual mean Composite score range no greater than about 5 points.

These special group studies are a welcome part of the Technical Manual. However, 6 of the 11 groups have fewer than 40 participants. We need additional research with special groups, including research on how children with special needs perform on the WPPSI–III and the WPPSI–R.

Comment on criterion validity. The validity studies cited in the Technical Manual support the criterion validity of the WPPSI–III. Additional research is needed on the relationship between the WPPSI–III and other measures of ability and achievement.

Construct Validity

Studies reported in the Technical Manual and the results of our factor analysis presented later in the chapter indicate (a) that the WPPSI–III is a good measure of general intelligence and (b) that it has group factors as well as specific factors.

Table 5-7
Summary of Special Group Studies with the WPPSI–III

| | | Individual Composite | | | | | | | | | |
| | | Verbal IQ | | Performance IQ | | Processing Speed Quotient | | General Language Composite | | Full Scale IQ | |
Special group	N	M	SD	M	SD	M	SD	M	SD	M	SD
Intellectually gifted	70	125.8	11.6	123.1	10.7	113.4	13.3	120.9	11.4	126.2	8.7
Mild mental retardation	40	65.7	9.7	65.6	9.6	66.6	13.4	69.5	10.8	62.1	10.1
Moderate mental retardation	19	58.1	7.9	57.1	8.0	58.3	8.9	57.9	10.7	53.1	7.5
Developmental delay	62	82.8	14.5	86.1	14.6	83.1	16.3	85.2	13.6	81.8	14.3
Developmental risk factors	32	88.6	14.9	85.7	10.9	90.1	16.7	86.7	13.5	85.7	13.3
Autistic disorder	21	70.6	16.7	88.2	21.7	82.5	19.1	84.7	17.6	76.6	20.2
Expressive language disorder	23	90.6	11.5	92.9	12.6	94.1	11.5	94.7	10.2	90.1	11.5
Mixed receptive-expressive lan. dis.	27	83.1	9.8	85.2	16.0	82.7	14.5	86.7	13.0	81.9	12.9
Limited English proficiency	44	80.2	9.9	95.0	14.1	100.1	13.2	79.2	10.4	87.0	10.2
Attention-deficit/hyperactivity dis.	41	93.8	12.6	97.4	14.5	95.4	16.1	96.0	13.2	94.3	12.4
Motor impairment	16	102.2	8.8	87.7	11.7	89.0	17.9	105.8	12.9	94.2	8.8

Note. Abbreviations: Mixed receptive-expressive lan. dis. = Mixed receptive-expressive language disorder, Attention-deficit/hyperactivity dis. = Attention-deficit/hyperactivity disorder.
Source: Adapted from Wechsler (2002b).

INTERCORRELATIONS FOR SUBTESTS AND COMPOSITES

Ages 2-0 to 3-11

Intercorrelations between the five subtests range from a low of .36 to a high of .74 (*Mdn r* = .43). The highest correlations are between Information and Picture Naming (.74), Information and Receptive Vocabulary (.71), and Receptive Vocabulary and Picture Naming (.71). The lowest correlations are between Block Design and Receptive Vocabulary (.36), Receptive Vocabulary and Object Assembly (.41), and Block Design and Object Assembly (.41). The Verbal subtests have higher intercorrelations (*Mdn r* = .71) than do the Performance subtests (*Mdn r* = .41).

Average correlations between each of the five individual subtests and the Full Scale range from .71 to .83 (*Mdn r* = .74; see Table 5-8). Information has the highest correlation with the Full Scale (.83), followed by Receptive Vocabulary (.81), Picture Naming (.74), Object Assembly (.73), and Block Design (.71). Overall, the Verbal subtests have higher correlations with the Full Scale (*Mdn r* = .81) than do the Performance subtests (*Mdn r* = .73). The average correlation between scores on the two core Verbal subtests and the Verbal IQ is .92, whereas the average correlation between scores on the two core Performance subtests and the Performance IQ is .84. Thus, the Verbal Composite subtests have more in common with each other than do the Performance Composite subtests.

There is a strong positive relationship (ρ = .90, *p* < .05) between the extent to which subtests correlate with the Full Scale and their *g* loadings (see discussion later in the chapter). Thus, subtests that correlate highly with the Full Scale are likely to measure general intelligence better than subtests that have low correlations with the Full Scale.

Ages 4-0 to 7-3

Intercorrelations between the 14 subtests range from a low of .27 to a high of .74 (*Mdn r* = .49). The highest correlations are between Information and Word Reasoning (.74), Information and Picture Naming (.73), Vocabulary and Word Reasoning (.71), Word Reasoning and Comprehension (.70), and Word Reasoning and Picture Naming (.70). The lowest correlations are bet-

Table 5-8
Average Correlations Between WPPSI–III Subtests and Composites for Ages 2-6 to 3-11

Subtest	Composite			
	Verbal[a]	Performance[b]	Full Scale[c]	General Language[d]
BD	.42	.84	.71	.39
IN	.92	.52	.83	.78
RV	.92	.46	.81	.93
OA	.46	.84	.73	.47
PN	.78	.48	.74	.92

Note. Abbreviations: BD = Block Design, IN = Information, RV = Receptive Vocabulary, OA = Object Assembly, PN = Picture Naming.
[a]Consists of Receptive Vocabulary and Information.
[b]Consists of Block Design and Object Assembly.
[c]Consists of Receptive Vocabulary, Information, Block Design, and Object Assembly.
[d]Consists of Receptive Vocabulary and Picture Naming.
Source: WPPSI–III Technical and Interpretive Manual. Copyright © 2002 by The Psychological Corporation. Reproduced by permission. All rights reserved. "Wechsler Preschool and Primary Scale of Intelligence–Third Edition" is a registered trademark of The Psychological Corporation.

ween Coding and Picture Naming (.27), Comprehension and Coding (.28), Similarities and Coding (.28), and Vocabulary and Coding (.29). The core and supplemental Verbal subtests have higher intercorrelations (*Mdn r* = .69) than do the core and supplemental Performance subtests (*Mdn r* = .47).

Average correlations between each of the 14 individual subtests and the Full Scale range from .55 to .82 (*Mdn r* = .71; see Table 5-9). Information has the highest correlation with the Full Scale (.82), followed by Word Reasoning (.81), Vocabulary (.78), Matrix Reasoning (.74), Similarities (.73), Block Design (.72), Picture Concepts (.71), Comprehension (.71), Picture Naming (.70), Receptive Vocabulary (.69), Picture Completion (.66), Symbol Search (.64), and Object Assembly (.55). Thus, three Verbal subtests (Information, Word Reasoning, and Vocabulary) correlate more highly with the Full Scale than do the other subtests (see Table 5-9). Word Reasoning has the highest correlation with the Verbal Composite (.91), and Matrix Reasoning has the highest correlation with the Performance Composite (.82).

Table 5-9
Average Correlations Between WPPSI–III Subtests and Composites for Ages 4-0 to 7-3

Subtest	Composite				
	Verbal[a]	Performance[b]	Full Scale[c]	Processing Speed[d]	General Language[e]
Block Design	.52	.80	.72	.50	.48
Information	.90	.63	.82	.41	.75
Matrix Reasoning	.55	.82	.74	.48	.50
Vocabulary	.89	.57	.78	.39	.67
Picture Concepts	.54	.79	.71	.44	.47
Symbol Search	.46	.60	.64	.89	.41
Word Reasoning	.91	.60	.81	.41	.74
Coding	.34	.46	.59	.89	.31
Comprehension	.76	.55	.71	.38	.62
Picture Completion	.59	.59	.66	.46	.57
Similarities	.75	.60	.73	.39	.63
Receptive Vocabulary	.70	.58	.69	.40	.91
Object Assembly	.43	.56	.55	.42	.41
Picture Naming	.76	.53	.70	.34	.92

[a]Consists of Information, Vocabulary, and Word Reasoning.
[b]Consists of Block Design, Matrix Reasoning, and Picture Concepts.
[c]Consists of Information, Vocabulary, Word Reasoning, Block Design, Matrix Reasoning, Picture Concepts, and Coding.
[d]Consists of Coding and Symbol Search.

[e]Consists of Receptive Vocabulary and Picture Naming.
Source: WPPSI–III Technical and Interpretive Manual. Copyright © 2002 by The Psychological Corporation. Reproduced by permission. All rights reserved. "Wechsler Preschool and Primary Scale of Intelligence–Third Edition" is a registered trademark of The Psychological Corporation.

Average correlations between each of the three core Verbal Composite subtests and the Verbal Composite range from .89 to .91 (*Mdn r* = .89); those between each of the three core Performance Composite subtests and the Performance Composite range from .79 to .82 (*Mdn r* = .80). Thus, the Verbal Composite subtests have more in common with each other than do the Performance Composite subtests.

There is a strong positive relationship (ρ = .91, *p* < .01) between the extent to which subtests correlate with the Full Scale and their *g* loadings (see discussion later in the chapter). Thus, subtests that correlate highly with the Full Scale are likely to measure general intelligence better than subtests that have low correlations with the Full Scale.

DEMOGRAPHIC VARIABLES

Table 5-10 shows the means and standard deviations of the Composite scores and the Full Scale IQ for the four demographic variables used to stratify the standardization sample. Highlights of Table 5-10 follow.

Sex

The mean Full Scale IQ was 3.22 points higher for girls than for boys. The most pronounced difference was on Processing Speed, where the mean Quotient was 6.38 points higher for girls than for boys. Girls also had a higher Performance IQ than boys by 2.79 points and a higher Verbal IQ than boys by 1.57 points.

Table 5-10
Relationship of WPPSI–III IQs and Composite Scores to Sex, Race/Ethnicity, Parental Education, and Geographic Region

| Demographic variable | N | Composite | | | | | | | | | | |
| | | Verbal | | Performance | | Processing Speed | | General Language | | Full Scale | |
		M	SD	M	SD	M	SD	M	SD	M	SD
Sex											
Boys	850	99.25	15.32	98.75	14.97	96.94	14.03	99.66	15.05	98.57	15.04
Girls	850	100.82	15.38	101.54	15.41	103.32	15.68	100.70	15.05	101.79	15.51
Race/Ethnicity											
Euro American	1037	104.41	14.34	102.68	14.98	101.11	15.54	104.96	13.69	103.93	14.77
African American	265	93.80	13.80	94.27	15.11	96.31	14.55	92.26	13.07	93.60	14.62
Hispanic American	306	89.92	12.79	95.50	12.96	99.54	14.35	90.23	12.68	92.21	12.20
Asian American	72	103.60	16.92	106.90	15.90	105.22	13.71	103.44	16.70	105.79	16.05
Other	20	97.60	16.02	93.40	19.02	89.00	8.82	97.35	16.27	94.25	18.18
Parental Education											
Eight years or less	66	82.96	12.58	90.86	12.51	96.44	11.07	83.23	11.57	85.82	11.12
Some high school	163	88.67	12.24	93.20	13.27	95.41	13.93	88.10	11.92	89.91	12.56
High school graduate	448	95.98	12.91	97.42	14.16	98.82	15.12	97.00	12.85	96.38	13.31
Some college	554	101.48	14.75	100.41	15.65	99.02	15.05	101.15	14.41	101.11	15.32
College graduate	469	108.55	13.77	106.16	14.45	104.91	15.34	108.64	13.32	108.29	13.84
Geographic Region											
Northeast	263	102.96	14.93	101.79	15.32	103.57	14.08	102.63	15.44	103.08	14.94
South	645	97.33	15.35	98.54	14.88	98.82	15.58	98.13	15.08	97.65	15.09
Midwest	415	102.24	15.25	101.47	16.27	98.96	16.94	101.77	15.14	102.16	16.28
West	377	100.19	15.08	100.29	14.45	100.78	13.10	100.22	14.20	100.29	14.39

Source: WPPSI–III Technical and Interpretive Manual. Copyright © 2002 by The Psychological Corporation. Adapted and reproduced by permission. All rights reserved. "Wechsler Preschool and Primary Scale of Intelligence–Third Edition" is a registered trademark of The Psychological Corporation

Race/Ethnicity

The mean Full Scale IQ of Euro American children was about 10.33 points higher than that of African American children and 11.72 points higher than that of Hispanic American children. However, the mean Full Scale IQ of Asian American children was 1.86 points higher than that of Euro American children.

The three individual mean Composite scores differed somewhat for each racial/ethnic group.

1. *Euro American children.* The mean Verbal Composite and General Language Composite scores were about 2 to 3 points higher than those for the Performance Composite and Processing Speed Composite.

2. *African American children.* The mean Processing Speed Composite score was about 3 to 4 points higher than those for the Verbal Composite and General Language Composite and about 2 points higher than that for the Performance Composite.

3. *Hispanic American children.* The mean Processing Speed Composite score was about 4 to 10 points higher than those for the Verbal Composite, General Language Composite, and Performance Composite.

4. *Asian American children.* The mean Performance Composite score was about 3 points higher than that for the Verbal Composite and General Language Composite and about 2 points higher than that for the Processing Speed Composite.

Parental Education

The mean Full Scale IQ of children whose parents had graduated from college was about 22 points higher than that of children whose parents had an eighth-grade education or less. Similar trends were observed for the mean scores on the Verbal Composite (about 26 points), Performance Composite (about 15 points), Processing Speed Composite (about 8 points), and General Language Composite (about 25 points).

Geographic Region

The mean Full Scale IQ of children from the Northeast was about 1 to 5 points higher than those of children from other regions. Similar trends were observed for the mean scores on the Verbal Composite (about 1 to 5 points), Performance Composite (about 0 to 3 points), Processing Speed Composite (about 3 to 5 points), and General Language Composite (1 to 5 points).

FACTOR ANALYSIS

We performed one principal axis factor analysis (oblimin rotation with two factors specified and two iterations) at ages 2-6 to 3-11 and used the correlation matrices in the Technical Manual for each of the three age groups in the standardization sample and for the total group. We performed another principal axis factor analysis (oblimin rotation with three factors specified and two iterations) at ages 4-0 to 7-3 and used the correlation matrices in the Technical Manual for each of the six age groups in the standardization sample and for the total group. In both analyses, we included both the core and supplemental subtests but did not include the optional subtests.

Factor Analytic Model at Ages 2-6 to 3-11

The results, which indicated that the following two-factor model holds at all ages from 2-6 to 3-11, gener-

ally agreed with the results of the factor analysis reported in the Technical Manual (see Table 5-11).

- *Verbal factor:* Information, Receptive Vocabulary, and Picture Naming
- *Performance factor:* Block Design and Object Assembly

Following is a description of the two factors at ages 2-6 to 3-11.

- The *Verbal factor* describes a hypothesized verbal-related ability underlying the Composite. The Verbal factor measures verbal knowledge and understanding obtained primarily through informal education and reflects the application of verbal skills to new situations. Information, Receptive Vocabulary, and Picture Naming have high loadings on the Verbal factor.
- The *Performance factor* describes a hypothesized performance-related ability underlying the Composite. The Performance factor measures the ability to

Table 5-11
Factor Loadings of WPPSI–III Subtests for Ages 2-6 to 3-11 Following Principal Axis Factor Analysis (Oblimin Rotation and Two Iterations)

Subtest	Age			
	2-6 to 2-11	*3-0 to 3-5*	*3-6 to 3-11*	*Total*
Verbal				
IN	.83	.76	.78	.80
RV	.87	.86	.74	.85
PN	.77	.84	.96	.85
BD	.00	−.04	−.03	−.03
OA	.01	.12	.09	.05
Performance				
IN	.00	.14	.10	.07
RV	−.05	−.03	.06	−.04
PN	.09	−.03	−.08	.00
BD	.61	.60	.66	.61
OA	.61	.51	.59	.59

Note. Abbreviations: IN = Information, RV = Receptive Vocabulary, PN = Picture Naming, BD = Block Design, OA = Object Assembly. Factor loadings at or above .30 are in bold.

interpret and organize visually perceived material and to generate and test hypotheses related to problem solutions. Block Design and Object Assembly have high loadings on the Performance factor.

Factor Analytic Model at Ages 4-0 to 7-3

The results, which indicated that the following three-factor model holds at all age groups from 4-0 to 7-3, generally agreed with the results of the factor analysis reported in the Technical Manual (see Table 5-12).

- *Verbal factor:* Information, Vocabulary, Word Reasoning, Similarities, and Comprehension
- *Performance factor:* Block Design, Matrix Reasoning, Picture Completion, and Object Assembly
- *Processing Speed factor:* Coding and Symbol Search

Following is a description of the factors at ages 4-0 to 7-3.

- The *Verbal factor* describes a hypothesized verbal-related ability underlying the Composite. The Verbal factor measures verbal knowledge and understanding obtained primarily through informal education and reflects the application of verbal skills to new situations. Information, Vocabulary, Word Reasoning, Similarities, and Comprehension have high loadings on the Verbal factor, followed by Picture Concepts, which has a moderate loading (but only at four age levels and for the total group). Verbal mediation, perhaps, may be involved in performance on Picture Concepts.
- The *Performance factor* describes a hypothesized performance-related ability underlying the Composite. The Performance factor measures the ability to interpret and organize visually perceived material and to generate and test hypotheses related to problem solutions. Block Design, Matrix Reasoning, Picture Completion, and Object Assembly have high loadings on the Performance factor. Coding and Symbol Search also have moderate to high loadings on the Performance factor at ages 4-6 to 4-11. Picture Concepts, which is placed in the Performance Composite, has loadings below .30 at three age levels (4-0 to 4-5, 5-0 to 5-5, and 7-0 to 7-3) and for the total group.
- The *Processing Speed factor* describes a hypothesized processing speed ability underlying the Composite. Processing Speed measures the ability to process visually perceived nonverbal information quickly, with concentration and rapid eye-hand coor-

dination being important components. Coding and Symbol Search have high loadings on Processing Speed at every age and for the total group, except at ages 4-6 to 4-11, where the loadings are negative.

The factor analytic results give empirical support to interpretation of the two individual Composites at ages 2-6 to 3-11 as separately functioning entities in the WPPSI–III. However, there is less empirical support for interpretation of the three individual Composites at ages 4-0 to 7-3. Picture Concepts is most questionable because of its minimal loadings at several ages on the Performance factor.

The factor structure of the WPPSI–III at ages 2-6 to 3-11 into verbal and performance components closely agrees with the organization of the test. At ages 4-0 to 7-3, the factor structure into verbal, performance, and processing speed components partially agrees with the organization of the test.

Factor Analytic Subtest Findings at Ages 2-6 to 3-11

Our factor analytic findings show a diverse pattern for the three age groups (see Table 5-13). It is difficult to explain why the factor loadings vary at different ages. The varied loadings may be a function of (a) the fact that all subtests are differentially related to *g*, (b) measurement error, or (c) developmental trends. The characteristics of the two factors at ages 2-6 to 3-11 follow:

1. *Verbal factor.* The three Verbal subtests—Information, Receptive Vocabulary, and Picture Naming—have loadings above .30 on the Verbal factor at the three ages. The two Performance subtests do not have loadings above .30 on the Verbal factor at any of the three ages.

2. *Performance factor.* The two Performance subtests—Block Design and Object Assembly—have loadings above .30 on the Performance factor at the three ages. The two Verbal subtests do not have loadings above .30 on the Performance factor at any of the three ages.

Factor Analytic Subtest Findings at Ages 4-0 to 7-3

Our factor analytic findings show a diverse pattern for the six age groups (see Table 5-13). It is difficult to explain why the factor loadings vary at different ages. The

Table 5-12
Factor Loadings of WPPSI–III Subtests for Ages 4-0 to 7-3 Following Principal Axis Factor Analysis (Oblimin Rotation and Two Iterations)

Subtest	Age						Total
	4-0 to 4-5	4-6 to 4-11	5-0 to 5-5	5-6 to 5-11	6-0 to 6-11	7-0 to 7-3	
Verbal							
Information	.73	.82	.76	.74	.76	.59	.76
Vocabulary	.77	.73	.88	.93	.88	.85	.88
Word Reasoning	.91	.85	.87	.65	.76	.83	.83
Similarities	.84	.83	.85	.83	.80	.79	.84
Comprehension	.75	.55	.81	.69	.76	.62	.75
Block Design	.01	.04	.02	.18	.00	−.04	.05
Matrix Reasoning	.12	.26	.10	.17	.15	.25	.23
Picture Concepts	.51	.10	.31	.03	.33	.73	.34
Picture Completion	.35	.27	.35	.20	.08	.57	.27
Object Assembly	−.05	−.03	−.02	−.07	−.05	−.01	−.05
Coding	.08	.05	.02	.14	.02	.36	.07
Symbol Search	.03	−.05	−.02	−.04	.04	−.03	−.06
Performance							
Information	.34	.11	.09	.23	.04	.37	.17
Vocabulary	−.04	−.01	−.08	−.09	−.09	.05	−.08
Word Reasoning	−.05	.04	.13	.34	.12	.02	.06
Similarities	−.12	−.02	−.10	−.12	.01	.01	−.08
Comprehension	−.01	−.03	−.02	.16	.01	.32	.04
Block Design	.29	.67	.66	.47	.76	.83	.62
Matrix Reasoning	.32	.23	.12	.51	.68	.60	.38
Picture Concepts	.12	.30	.27	.57	.31	−.07	.22
Picture Completion	.54	.61	.42	.57	.58	.02	.47
Object Assembly	.59	.74	.78	.68	.62	.64	.72
Coding	−.04	.41	.20	.06	.29	.12	.00
Symbol Search	.03	.63	−.07	.10	−.03	.08	.02
Processing Speed							
Information	−.13	.10	.04	−.13	.03	−.09	−.07
Vocabulary	.02	−.08	.09	.06	.06	−.14	.03
Word Reasoning	.03	.03	−.13	−.10	−.06	.06	−.03
Similarities	.10	.03	.03	.16	−.04	−.03	.05
Comprehension	−.02	−.34	.02	.06	.09	−.16	.02
Block Design	.38	.03	.19	.17	.06	.09	.11
Matrix Reasoning	.28	−.44	.57	.12	−.10	−.07	.16
Picture Concepts	.14	−.45	.22	.19	−.02	.08	.17
Picture Completion	−.02	.10	.06	.02	.14	.18	.04
Object Assembly	.19	.01	.01	.03	.06	.08	.00
Coding	.82	−.35	.61	.70	.59	.51	.76
Symbol Search	.73	−.15	.81	.69	.73	.67	.71

Note. Factor loadings at or above .30 are in bold.

Table 5-13
Summary of Major Trends of Principal Axis Factor Analysis on WPPSI–III, by Age Level and for the Total Group

Age	Subtests with loadings of .30 or higher on Verbal	Subtests with loadings of .30 or higher on Performance	Subtests with loadings of .30 or higher on Processing Speed
2-6 to 2-11	IN, RV, PN	BD, OA	—
3-0 to 3-5	IN, RV, PN	BD, OA	—
3-6 to 3-11	IN, RV, PN	BD, OA	—
Total (2-6 to 3-11)	IN, RV, PN	BD, OA	—
4-0 to 4-5	IN, VC, WR, SI, CO, PCn, PCm	MR, PCm, OA, IN	CD, SS, BD
4-6 to 4-11	IN, VC, WR, SI, CO	BD, PCn, PCm, OA, CD, SS	—
5-0 to 5-5	IN, VC, WR, SI, CO, PCn, PCm	BD, PCm, OA	CD, SS, MR
5-6 to 5-11	IN, VC, WR, SI, CO	BD, MR, PCn, PCm, OA, WR	CD, SS
6-0 to 6-11	IN, VC, WR, SI, CO, PCn	BD, MR, PCn, PCm, OA	CD, SS
7-0 to 7-3	IN, VC, WR, SI, CO, PCn, PCm, CD	BD, MR, OA, CO	CD, SS
Total (4-0 to 7-3)	IN, VC, WR, SI, CO, PCn	BD, MR, PCm, OA	CD, SS

Note. Abbreviations: BD = Block Design, IN = Information, MR = Matrix Reasoning, VC = Vocabulary, PCn = Picture Concepts, SS = Symbol Search, WR = Word Reasoning, CD = Coding, CO = Comprehension, PCm = Picture Completion, SI = Similarities, RV = Receptive Vocabulary, OA = Object Assembly, PN = Picture Naming.

varied loadings may be a function of (a) the fact that all subtests are differentially related to g, (b) measurement error, or (c) developmental trends. The characteristics of the three factors at ages 4-0 to 7-3 follow:

1. *Verbal factor.* The five Verbal subtests—Information, Vocabulary, Word Reasoning, Similarities, and Comprehension—have loadings above .30 on the Verbal factor at the six ages. Picture Concepts and Picture Completion, subtests associated with the Performance Composite, have loadings above .30 on the Verbal factor at various ages.

2. *Performance factor.* The five Performance subtests—Block Design, Matrix Reasoning, Picture Concepts, Picture Completion, and Object Assembly—have loadings above .30 on the Performance factor at most of the six ages. Information at ages 4-0 to 4-5 and Coding and Symbol Search at ages 4-6 to 4-11, subtests associated with the other Composites, have loadings above .30 on the Performance factor.

3. *Processing Speed factor.* The two Processing Speed subtests—Coding and Symbol Search—have loadings above .30 at five of the six ages. At age 4-6 to 4-11, the loadings are −.35 and −.15 for Coding and Symbol Search, respectively. Block Design at ages 4-0 to 4-5 and Matrix Reasoning at ages 5-0 to 5-5, subtests associated with the Performance Composite, have loadings above .30 on Processing Speed.

Subtests as Measure of *g* at Ages 2-6 to 3-11

The loadings on the first unrotated factor provide information about g, or general intelligence. The WPPSI–III subtests form two g-related clusters at ages 2-6 to 3-11 (see Table 5-14):

- Information, Picture Naming, and Receptive Vocabulary are good measures of g.
- Object Assembly and Block Design are fair measures of g.

The Verbal subtests have the highest g loadings in the test at ages 2-6 to 3-11. On average, the proportion of variance attributed to g is 70% for the Verbal subtests and 28% for the Performance subtests. Subtests with the highest proportion of variance attributed to g are Information, Picture Naming, and Receptive Vocabulary. Neither of the Performance subtests is a good measure of g.

Table 5-14
WPPSI–III Subtests as Measures of *g*

Ages 2-6 to 3-11						Ages 4-0 to 7-3					
Good measure of *g*			Fair measure of *g*			Good measure of *g*			Fair measure of *g*		
Subtest	Average loading of *g*	*g* proportion[a] (%)	Subtest	Average loading of *g*	*g* proportion[a] (%)	Subtest	Average loading of *g*	*g* proportion[a] (%)	Subtest	Average loading of *g*	*g* proportion[a] (%)
IN	.85	72	OA	.56	31	WR	.82	67	PCm	.69	48
PN	.84	71	BD	.51	26	IN	.81	66	MR	.67	45
RV	.81	66				VC	.78	61	BD	.66	44
						SI	.76	58	SS	.65	42
						CO	.75	56	PCn	.64	41
									OA	.58	34
									CD	.50	25

Note. Abbreviations: BD = Block Design, IN = Information, MR = Matrix Reasoning, VC = Vocabulary, PCn = Picture Concepts, SS = Symbol Search, WR = Word Reasoning, CD = Coding, CO = Comprehension, PCm = Picture Completion, SI = Similarities, RV = Receptive Vocabulary, OA = Object Assembly, PN = Picture Naming.
[a] Proportion of variance attributed to *g*.

Subtests as Measure of *g* at Ages 4-0 to 7-3

The loadings on the first unrotated factor provide information about *g*, or general intelligence. The WPPSI–III subtests form two *g*-related clusters at ages 4-0 to 7-3 (see Table 5-14):

- Word Reasoning, Information, Vocabulary, Similarities, and Comprehension are good measures of *g*.
- Picture Completion, Matrix Reasoning, Block Design, Symbol Search, Picture Concepts, Object Assembly, and Coding are fair measures of *g*.

The Verbal subtests have the highest *g* loadings in the test at ages 4-0 to 7-3. On average, the proportion of variance attributed to *g* is 62% for the Verbal subtests, 42% for the Performance subtests, and 33% for the Processing Speed subtests. Subtests with the highest proportion of variance attributed to *g* are Word Reasoning, Information, Vocabulary, Similarities, and Comprehension. None of the Performance or Processing Speed subtests are good measures of *g*.

Subtest Specificity

Subtest specificity refers to the proportion of a subtest's variance that is both reliable (i.e., not related to measurement error) and distinctive to the subtest (see Chapter 4 in Sattler, 2001, for further information about subtest specificity). Although the individual subtests on the WPPSI–III overlap in their measurement properties (i.e., the majority of the reliable variance for most subtests is common factor variance), many possess sufficient specificity at some ages to justify interpretation of specific subtest functions.

Matrix Reasoning, Picture Concepts, Picture Completion, Symbol Search, Receptive Vocabulary, and Object Assembly have ample specificity at all ages at which they are administered as core or supplemental subtests (see Table 5-15). In addition, Block Design, Coding, Comprehension, and Picture Naming have ample specificity at most of the ages at which they are administered as core or supplemental subtests. Each of the four remaining subtests—Information, Vocabulary, Word Reasoning, and Similarities—shows a unique pattern of specificity; that is, the ages at which each has ample, adequate, or inadequate specificity differ.

Converting Core Subtest Scaled Scores to Composite Scores and Full Scale IQs at Ages 2-6 to 3-11

At ages 2-6 to 3-11, the following tables in the Administration Manual are used to convert core subtest scores to IQs and one Composite score:

- Table A.2 (p. 231) for the Verbal IQ (Receptive Vocabulary and Information)
- Table A.3 (p. 232) for the Performance IQ (Block Design and Object Assembly)
- Table A.4 (p. 233) for the Full Scale (Receptive Vocabulary, Information, Block Design, and Object Assembly)
- Table A.5 (p. 234) for the General Language Composite (Receptive Vocabulary and Picture Naming)

There is no similar table in the Administration Manual that was derived using Picture Naming and Information (i.e., substituting Picture Naming for Receptive Vocabulary).

Converting Core Subtest Scaled Scores to Composite Scores and Full Scale IQs at Ages 4-0 to 7-3

At ages 4-0 to 7-3, the following tables in the Administration Manual are used to convert core subtest scores to IQs, one Quotient, and one Composite score:

- Table A.6 (p. 235) for the Verbal IQ (Information, Vocabulary, and Word Reasoning)

Table 5-15
Amount of Specificity in WPPSI–III Subtests for Nine Ages and Total Group

Subtest	Ages for which subtest has ample specificity	Ages for which subtest has adequate specificity	Ages for which subtest has inadequate specificity
Block Design	2-6–4-11, 5-6–7-3, Total[a,b]	5-0–5-5	—
Information	2-6–3-11, Total[a]	4-0–4-5, 5-0–6-11, Total[b]	4-6–4-11, 7-0–7-3
Matrix Reasoning	4-0–7-3, Total[b]	—	—
Vocabulary	4-0–4-11	6-0–7-3, Total[b]	5-0–5-11
Picture Concepts	4-0–7-3, Total[b]	—	—
Symbol Search	4-0–7-3, Total[b]	—	—
Word Reasoning	4-6–4-11, 6-0–6-11	4-0–4-5, 5-0–5-11, 7-0–7-3, Total[b]	—
Coding	4-0–5-11, 7-0–7-3, Total[b]	6-0–6-11	—
Comprehension	4-0–6-11, Total[b]	7-0–7-3	—
Picture Completion	4-0–7-3, Total[b]	—	—
Similarities	4-6–4-11, 6-0–7-3, Total[b]	4-0–4-5, 5-0–5-11	—
Receptive Vocabulary	2-6–3-11, Total[a]	—	—
Object Assembly	2-6–7-3, Total[a,b]	—	—
Picture Naming	2-6–3-5, Total[a]	3-6–3-11	—

Note. Kaufman's (1975) rule of thumb was used to classify the amount of specificity in each subtest. Subtests with ample specificity have specific variance that (a) reflects 25% or more of the subtest's total variance (100%) and (b) exceeds the subtest's error variance. Subtests with adequate specificity have specific variance that (a) reflects between 15% and 24% of the subtest's total variance and (b) exceeds the subtest's error variance. Subtests with inadequate specificity have specific variance that either (a) is less than 15% of the subtest's total variance or (b) is equal to or less than the subtest's error variance.

Specific variance is obtained by subtracting the squared multiple correlation (from the maximum-likelihood factor analysis with varimax rotation) from the subtest's reliability (r_{xx} – SMC) (A. Silverstein, personal communication, October 1991). Error variance is obtained by subtracting the subtest's reliability from 1.00 ($1 - r_{xx}$).

[a]For ages 2-6 to 3-11.
[b]For ages 4-0 to 7-3.

- Table A.7 (p. 236) for the Performance IQ (Block Design, Matrix Reasoning, and Picture Concepts)
- Table A.8 (p. 237) for the Processing Speed Quotient (Coding and Symbol Search)
- Table A.9 (pp. 238–239) for the Full Scale (Block Design, Information, Matrix Reasoning, Vocabulary, Picture Concepts, Word Reasoning, and Coding)
- Table A.10 (p. 240) for the General Language Composite (Receptive Vocabulary and Picture Naming)

There are no similar tables in the Administration Manual that were derived using core and supplemental subtests.

RANGE OF SUBTEST SCALED SCORES

Ages 2-6 to 3-11

The range of scaled scores from 1 to 19 is available for four of the five subtests, but not at each age level from 2-6 to 3-11 (see Table 5-16). For example, Block Design, Information, and Receptive Vocabulary have a range of scaled scores from 1 to 19 only at ages 3-0 to 3-11; they have a range of 2 to 19 at the other ages. Picture Naming has a range of scaled scores from 1 to 19 at ages 3-6 to 3-11 and a range of 2 to 19 at the other ages, while Object Assembly has a range of scaled scores from 2 to 19 at the three age levels from 2-6 to 3-11. Children receive credit even when they obtain a raw score of 0 on all items of a subtest. The generally uniform subtest scaled-score range helps in the interpretation process.

Ages 4-0 to 7-3

The range of scaled scores from 1 to 19 is available for 7 of the 14 subtests (Information, Vocabulary, Receptive Vocabulary, Block Design, Matrix Reasoning, Object Assembly, and Picture Naming; see Table 5-16). The seven other subtests (Word Reasoning, Comprehension, Similarities, Picture Naming, Picture Completion, Coding, and Symbol Search) have variable ranges. For some subtests at certain ages, the lowest possible subtest scaled score is 6 points (Similarities at ages 4-0 to 4-11; Symbol Search at ages 4-0 to 4-5), 5 points (Comprehension and Coding at ages 4-0 to 4-5), 4 points (Word

Table 5-16
WPPSI–III Subtest and Scaled-Score Ranges by Age

Subtest	Scaled-score range	Age
Verbal		
Information	2–19	2-6 to 2-11
	1–19	3-0 to 7-3
Vocabulary	1–19	4-0 to 7-3
Word Reasoning	4–19	4-0 to 4-5
	3–19	4-6 to 5-5
	2–19	5-6 to 5-11
	1–19	6-0 to 7-3
Receptive Vocabulary	2–19	2-6 to 2-11
	1–19	3-0 to 7-3
Comprehension	5–19	4-0 to 4-5
	4–19	4-6 to 4-11
	3–19	5-0 to 5-11
	2–19	6-0 to 6-11
	1–19	7-0 to 7-3
Similarities	6–19	4-0 to 4-11
	5–19	5-0 to 5-2
	4–19	5-3 to 5-11
	3–19	6-0 to 6-3
	2–19	6-4 to 7-3
Performance		
Block Design	2–19	2-6 to 2-11
	1–19	3-0 to 7-3
Matrix Reasoning	1–19	4-0 to 7-3
Picture Concepts	3–19	4-0 to 4-5
	2–19	4-6 to 5-5
	1–19	5-6 to 7-3
Object Assembly	2–19	2-6 to 3-11
	1–19	4-0 to 7-3
Picture Completion	2–19	4-0 to 4-5
	1–19	4-6 to 7-3
Processing Speed		
Coding	5–19	4-0 to 4-5
	4–19	4-6 to 4-8
	3–19	4-9 to 4-11
	2–19	5-0 to 5-5
	1–19	5-6 to 7-3
Symbol Search	6–19	4-0 to 4-5
	5–19	4-6 to 4-11
	4–19	5-0 to 5-2
	3–19	5-3 to 5-11
	2–19	6-0 to 6-11
	1–19	7-0 to 7-3
General Language		
Picture Naming	2–19	2-6 to 3-5
	1–19	3-6 to 7-3

Source: Adapted from Wechsler (2002a).

Reasoning at ages 4-0 to 4-5), or 3 points (Picture Concepts at ages 4-0 to 4-5). Children receive credit even when they obtain a raw score of 0 on all items of a subtest. The nonuniform subtest scaled-score range hinders the interpretation process.

RANGE OF FULL SCALE IQS

Ages 2-6 to 3-11

The range of WPPSI–III Full Scale IQs is 45 to 155 at ages 2-6 to 3-11 (see Table 5-17). This range is insufficient for children who are extremely low functioning or extremely high functioning. Even the lowest possible score on the test does not reflect the extent of a child's cognitive ability because, as noted previously, standard-score points are awarded even when a child receives 0 points on every item on a subtest. For example, a child who is 2-6 years old and who obtains scores of 0 on the four core subtests receives 8 scaled-score points and a corresponding Full Scale IQ of 44. However, as noted below, the Full Scale IQ of 44 should not be computed.

Recognizing that awarding scaled-score points for no successes might be a problem, the Administration Manual provides the following guidelines for computing scores in the event that a child has raw scores of 0.

- The Verbal IQ should be computed *only* when the child obtains a raw score greater than 0 on at least *one of the two subtests* in the Composite.
- The Performance IQ should be computed *only* when the child obtains a raw score greater than 0 on at least *one of the two subtests* in the Composite.
- The Full Scale IQ should be computed *only* when the child obtains raw scores greater than 0 on at least (a) *one of the two subtests* in the Verbal Composite and (b) *one of the two subtests* in the Performance Composite.
- The General Language Composite should be computed *only* when the child obtains a raw score greater than 0 on at least *one of the two subtests* in the Composite.

Neither the Administration Manual nor the Technical Manual provides any empirical basis (e.g., psychometric or research evidence) for these rules. Although they appear to have some merit, we need research to determine whether these rules are valid or whether other rules would be equally or more valid for computing Composite scores and IQs.

If The Psychological Corporation's recommended procedure is followed, the lowest possible IQ that a child who is 2 years, 6 months old can receive is 52, arrived at in the following way: The child obtains raw scores of 1 on Information and Object Assembly and raw scores of 0 on Receptive Vocabulary and Block Design. The resulting IQs are as follows: Verbal IQ = 58 (5 scaled-score points), Performance IQ = 60 (7 scaled-score points), and Full Scale IQ = 52 (12 scaled-score points). Two 1-point raw scores thus yield a Full Scale IQ of 52. Therefore, the WPPSI–III does not provide accurate IQs for children between ages 2-6 and 3-11 who are functioning at three or more standard deviations below the mean of the test. In other words, the WPPSI–III does not appear to sample a sufficient range of cognitive abilities for children in this age group who are extremely low functioning.

Table A.5 (FSIQ Equivalents of Sums of Scaled Scores) in the Administration Manual does not give any Full Scale IQs for sums of scaled scores below 5.

Ages 4-0 to 7-3

The range of WPPSI–III Full Scale IQs is 45 to 160 but not at all ages from 4-0 to 7-3 (see Table 5-17). The range is 56 to 160 at ages 4-0 to 4-2, 55 to 160 at ages 4-3 to 4-5, 53 to 160 at ages 4-6 to 4-8, 52 to 160 at ages 4-9 to 4-11, 51 to 160 at ages 5-0 to 5-5, 47 to 160 at ages 5-6 to 5-11, and 45 to 160 at ages 6-0 to 7-3. This range is insufficient for children who are extremely low functioning or extremely high functioning. Even the lowest possible score on the test does not reflect the extent of a child's cognitive ability because, as noted previously, standard-score points are awarded even when a child receives 0 points on every item on a subtest. For example, a child who is 4-0 years old and who obtains scores of 0 on the seven core subtests receives 15 scaled-score points and a corresponding Full Scale IQ of 58.

Recognizing that awarding scaled-score points for no successes might be a problem, the Administration Manual provides the following guidelines for computing scores in the event that a child has raw scores of 0.

- The Verbal IQ should be computed *only* when the child obtains a raw score greater than 0 on at least *two of the three subtests* in the Composite.
- The Performance IQ should be computed *only* when the child obtains a raw score greater than 0 on at least *two of the three subtests* in the Composite.

Table 5-17
WPPSI–III IQ Ranges for Verbal, Performance, Full Scale, and Processing Speed Composites, for Ages 2-6 to 3-11 and 4-0 to 7-3

	Composite			
Age	Verbal[a, b]	Performance[c, d]	Full Scale[e, f]	Processing Speed[g]
2-6 to 2-8	59–150	56–150	45–155	—
2-9 to 2-11	59–150	56–150	45–155	—
3-0 to 3-2	50–150	53–150	45–155	—
3-3 to 3-5	50–150	53–150	45–155	—
3-6 to 3-8	50–150	53–150	45–155	—
3-9 to 3-11	50–150	53–150	45–155	—
4-0 to 4-2	58–155	54–155	56–160	75–150
4-3 to 4-5	56–155	54–155	55–160	75–150
4-6 to 4-8	56–155	52–155	53–160	71–150
4-9 to 4-11	56–155	52–155	52–160	68–150
5-0 to 5-2	56–155	52–155	51–160	63–150
5-3 to 5-5	56–155	52–155	51–160	60–150
5-6 to 5-8	53–155	50–155	47–160	57–150
5-9 to 5-11	53–155	50–155	47–160	57–150
6-0 to 6-3	50–155	50–155	45–160	53–150
6-4 to 6-7	50–155	50–155	45–160	53–150
6-8 to 6-11	50–155	50–155	45–160	53–150
7-0 to 7-3	50–155	50–155	45–160	50–150

[a]Consists of Receptive Vocabulary and Information for ages 2-6 to 3-11 years.
[b]Consists of Information, Vocabulary, and Word Reasoning for ages 4-0 to 7-3 years.
[c]Consists of Block Design and Object Assembly for ages 2-6 to 3-11 years.
[d]Consists of Block Design, Matrix Reasoning, and Picture Concepts for ages 4-0 to 7-3 years.
[e]Consists of Receptive Vocabulary, Information, Block Design, and Object Assembly for ages 2-6 to 3-11 years.
[f]Consists of Information, Vocabulary, Word Reasoning, Block Design, Matrix Reasoning, Picture Concepts, and Coding for ages 4-0 to 7-3 years.
[g]Consists of Coding and Symbol Search for ages 4-0 to 7-3 years.
Source: Adapted from Wechsler (2002a).

- The Processing Speed Quotient should be computed *only* when the child obtains a raw score greater than 0 on at least *one of the two subtests* in the Composite.
- The Full Scale IQ should be computed *only* when the child obtains a raw score greater than 0 on at least (a) *two of the three subtests* in the Verbal Composite and (b) *two of the three subtests* in the Performance Composite.

- The General Language Composite should be computed *only* when the child obtains a raw score greater than 0 on at least *one of the two subtests* in the Composite.

Neither the Administration Manual nor the Technical Manual provides any empirical basis (e.g., psychometric or research evidence) for these rules. Although they appear to have some merit, we need research to determine whether these rules are valid or whether other rules would be equally or more valid for computing Composite scores and IQs.

If The Psychological Corporation's recommended procedure is followed, the lowest possible IQ that a 4-year-old child can receive is 50, arrived at in the following way: The child obtains raw scores of 1 on Block Design, Matrix Reasoning, Information, and Vocabulary and raw scores of 0 on Picture Concepts, Word Reasoning, and Coding. The resulting IQs are as follows: Verbal IQ = 51 (5 scaled-score points), Performance IQ = 53 (7 scaled-score points), Processing Speed Quotient = 56 (5 scaled-score points), and Full Scale IQ = 50 (17 scaled-score points). Four 1-point raw scores thus yield a Full Scale IQ of 50. Therefore, the WPPSI–III does not provide accurate IQs for children between ages 4-0 and 7-3 who are functioning at three or more standard deviations below the mean of the test. In other words, the WPPSI–III does not appear to sample a sufficient range of cognitive abilities for children in this age group who are extremely low functioning.

Table A.5 (FSIQ Equivalents of Sums of Scaled Scores) in the Administration Manual does not give any Full Scale IQs for sums of scaled scores below 7.

COMPARISON OF THE WPPSI–III AND WPPSI–R

The WPPSI–III and WPPSI–R have considerably different structures. Among the differences are variations in the composition of the test for younger and older children, the composition of the Full Scale in each broad age group, the composition of the individual Composites, and the number of supplemental subtests (see Tables 5-18, 5-19, and 5-20).

The numerous modifications that have been made in the third edition change the structure of the test. For example, the two age bands do not have the same subtests. Therefore, there is little continuity between the subtests given to children between ages 2-6 and 3-11 and to children between ages 4-0 and 7-3. Second, the latest revision covers a broader age range: The former age range of 3-0 to 7-3 has been extended to an age range of 2-6 to 7-3. Third, five subtests have been dropped—namely, Arithmetic, Sentences, Mazes, Animal Pegs, and Geometric Design. Finally, seven subtests have been added: Receptive Vocabulary, Picture Naming, Word Reasoning, Matrix Reasoning, Picture Concepts, Coding, and Symbol Search.

Composition of the Core Subtests on the Full Scale

At ages 2-6 to 3-11, the WPPSI–III Full Scale is composed of two core subtests assessing verbal ability (Receptive Vocabulary and Information) and two core subtests assessing nonverbal perceptual reasoning (Block Design and Object Assembly).

At ages 4-0 to 7-3, the WPPSI–III Full Scale is composed of three core subtests assessing verbal ability (Information, Vocabulary, and Word Reasoning), three core subtests assessing nonverbal perceptual reasoning (Block Design, Matrix Reasoning, and Picture Concepts), and one core subtest assessing visuomotor processing speed (Coding).

Composition of the Individual Composites

Verbal. At ages 2-6 to 3-11, the WPPSI–III Verbal Composite has two core subtests, while the WPPSI–R Verbal Scale has five core subtests. Information is a core subtest in both tests. The four other WPPSI–R Verbal Scale core subtests are not included in the WPPSI–III at ages 2-6 to 3-11 (Comprehension, Arithmetic, Vocabulary, and Similarities). The other WPPSI–III core Verbal subtest at ages 2-6 to 3-11 is new (Receptive Vocabulary). On the WPPSI–R, Sentences is a supplemental subtest on the Verbal Scale; On the WPPSI–III, Picture Naming, which is new, is a supplemental subtest.

At ages 4-0 to 7-3, the WPPSI–III Verbal Composite has three core subtests, while the WPPSI–R Verbal Scale has five core subtests. Information and Vocabulary are core subtests in both tests. The three other WPPSI–R Verbal Scale core subtests are not included in the WPPSI–III (Comprehension, Arithmetic, and Similarities). On the WPPSI–III Verbal Composite at ages 4-0 to 7-3, Comprehension and Similarities are supplemental subtests, while Receptive Vocabulary and Picture Naming are optional subtests. There are no optional subtests on the WPPSI–R.

Performance. At ages 2-6 to 3-11, the WPPSI–III Performance Composite has two core subtests, while the WPPSI–R Performance Composite has five core subtests. Block Design and Object Assembly are core subtests in both tests. The three other WPPSI–R core subtests are not included in the WPPSI–III at ages 2-6 to 3-

Table 5-18
Comparison of Numbers of Items on the WPPSI–III and the WPPSI–R

| | Number of items | | % increase in items | WPPSI–III | | | |
| | | | | Items retained[c] | | New items[d] | |
Subtest/Composite	WPPSI–R	WPPSI–III		N	%	N	%
Verbal							
Information	27	34	25.9	19	55.9	15	44.1
Vocabulary	25	25	0.0	16	64.0	9	36.0
Word Reasoning[a]	—	28	100.0	—	—	28	100.0
Comprehension	15	20	33.3	5	25.0	15	75.0
Similarities	20	24	20.0	2	8.3	22	91.7
Receptive Vocabulary[a]	—	38	100.0	—	—	38	100.0
Picture Naming[a]	—	30	100.0	—	—	30	100.0
Arithmetic[b]	23	—	—	—	—	—	—
Sentences[b]	12	—	—	—	—	—	—
Performance							
Block Design	14	20	42.9	7	35.0	13	65.0
Matrix Reasoning[a]	—	29	100.0	—	—	29	100.0
Picture Concepts[a]	—	28	100.0	—	—	28	100.0
Picture Completion	28	32	14.3	16	50.0	16	50.0
Object Assembly	6	14	133.3	3	21.4	11	78.6
Animal Pegs[b]	20	—	—	—	—	—	—
Geometric Designs[b]	16	—	—	—	—	—	—
Mazes[b]	11	—	—	—	—	—	—
Processing Speed							
Symbol Search[a]	—	50	100.0	—	—	50	100.0
Coding[a]	—	59	100.0	—	—	59	100.0
Composite							
Verbal	122	199	63.1	43	21.6	156	78.4
Performance	95	123	29.5	29	23.6	94	76.4
Processing Speed	—	109	100.0	—	—	109	100.0
Full Scale	217	431	98.6	72	16.7	359	83.3

[a] Not in WPPSI–R.
[b] Not in WPPSI–III.
[c] Essentially the same as they were in the WPPSI–R.
[d] Newly written or worded differently than in the WPPSI–R.

11 (Geometric Design, Mazes, and Picture Completion). On the WPPSI–R, Animal Pegs is a supplemental subtest on the Performance Scale; it is not included on the WPPSI–III, which has no supplemental subtests on the Performance Composite at ages 2-6 to 3-11.

At ages 4-0 to 7-3, the WPPSI–III Performance Composite has three core subtests, while the WPPSI–R Performance Composite has five core subtests. Block Design is a core subtest in both tests. The four other WPPSI–R Performance Scale core subtests are not core subtests in the WPPSI–III (Object Assembly, Geometric Design, Mazes, and Picture Completion). Picture Completion and Object Assembly are supplemental subtests on the WPPSI–III at ages 4-0 to 7-3.

Processing Speed. At ages 4-0 to 7-3, Coding is a core subtest on the WPPSI–III that is not included in either the Verbal or the Performance Composite. However, it can be used in the Processing Speed Composite if Symbol Search (a supplemental subtest) is also administered. There are no Processing Speed subtests at ages 2-6 to 3-11.

Table 5-19
Highlights of Characteristics of the WPPSI–III

Area	Characteristics of the WPPSI–III
Age range	Expanded by 6 months and covers ages 2-6 to 7-3.
Standardization	2000 U.S. Census data used to stratify a sample of 1,700 children (200 children at each 6-month interval from ages 2-6 to 6-11 and 100 children at ages 7-0 to 7-3).
Stratification variables	Generally similar to those of the WPPSI–R.
Structure of test	Two broad age bands instead of one (as on the WPPSI–R): ages 2-6 to 3-11 and ages 4-0 to 7-3, with different combinations of subtests in each broad age band.

Number of subtests
  Ages 2-6 to 3-11
  Ages 4-0 to 7-3
	5 instead of 12 (as on the WPPSI–R at ages 3-0 to 3-11).
	14 instead of 12 (as on the WPPSI–R).

Number of items	More than on comparable WPPSI–R subtests (e.g., 34 vs. 27 on Information, 24 vs. 20 on Similarities, 20 vs. 15 on Comprehension, 20 vs. 14 on Block Design, 32 vs. 28 on Picture Completion, and 14 vs. 6 on Object Assembly).
New subtests	Receptive Vocabulary, Picture Naming, Word Reasoning, Matrix Reasoning, Picture Concepts, Coding, and Symbol Search.
Deleted subtests	Arithmetic, Animal Pegs, Geometric Design, Mazes, and Sentences.
Manipulative materials	Fewer than on the WPPSI–R (e.g., Animal Pegs, Geometric Design, and Mazes are deleted).

Core subtests
  Ages 2-6 to 3-11
  Ages 4-0 to 7-3
	Receptive Vocabulary, Information, Block Design, and Object Assembly.
	Information, Vocabulary, Word Reasoning, Block Design, Matrix Reasoning, Picture Concepts, and Coding.

Supplemental subtests
  Ages 2-6 to 3-11
  Ages 4-0 to 7-3
	Picture Naming.
	Symbol Search, Comprehension, Picture Completion, Similarities, and Object Assembly.

Optional subtests
  Ages 2-6 to 3-11
  Ages 4-0 to 7-3
	None.
	Receptive Vocabulary and Picture Naming.

Reliability	Generally similar to that of the WPPSI–R.
Validity	Generally similar to that of the WPPSI–R.
Scoring examples	Generally similar to those of the WPPSI–R.
General administration	Changes in order of administering subtests, item order, start-point items, discontinue criteria, instructions, scoring criteria, bonus-point allotment, number of teaching examples, queries, and prompts. Sample items, easier items, and more difficult items added.

Administration time
  Ages 2-6 to 3-11
  Ages 4-0 to 7-3
	Shorter than that of the WPPSI–R (e.g., 29 to 49 minutes vs. 60 to 90 minutes, estimated).
	Shorter than that of the WPPSI–R (e.g., 41 to 67 minutes vs. 60 to 90 minutes, estimated).

Time to respond	Longer than that of the WPPSI–R (suggests that examiners wait 10 to 30 seconds for the child to respond before going to the next item vs. 15 to 20 seconds for the WPPSI–R).

(Continued)

Table 5-19 (*Continued*)

Area	*Characteristics of the WPPSI–III*
Time bonuses	Fewer than on the WPPSI–R (e.g., Coding provides time bonuses but Object Assembly and Block Design have no time bonuses).
Discontinue criteria	Generally similar to those of the WPPSI–R.
Computation of IQ Ages 2-6 to 3-11 Ages 4-0 to 7-3	Based on 4 core subtests (2 Verbal and 2 Performance). Two individual Composite scores computed with the following restrictions: (a) at least one raw score greater than 0 on Verbal and (b) at least one raw score greater than 0 on Performance. Full Scale IQ computed only when the Verbal IQ and Performance IQ can be computed (minimum of 2 raw scores of more than 0). Based on 7 core subtests (3 Verbal, 3 Performance, and Coding). Three individual Composite scores computed with the following restrictions: (a) at least two raw scores greater than 0 on Verbal, (b) at least two raw scores greater than 0 on Performance, and (c) at least one raw score greater than 0 on Processing Speed. Full Scale IQ computed only when the Verbal IQ and Performance IQ can be computed (minimum of 4 raw scores of more than 0).
Intelligence classification	IQs below 70 classified as "Extremely Low" instead of "Intellectually Deficient" (as on the WPPSI–R).
Record Form	Two Record Forms instead of one (as on the WPPSI–R): one for ages 2-6 to 3-11 and one for ages 4-0 to 7-3. Greatly expanded. First page contains sections for profiles for subtests and Composites, identifying information, raw score to scaled score conversions, scaled score to Composite score conversions. Second page is a discrepancy analysis page with sections for determining subtest strengths and weaknesses. Information about start points, reversals, time limits, prompts, and discontinue criteria is included on subtest pages. Last page contains sections for behavioral observations. More space is provided to write responses.
Record Booklet	One for Symbol Search and Coding, with the Mazes Record Booklet eliminated.
Types of scores	Provides a FSIQ ($M = 100$, $SD = 15$), two individual Composite scores for ages 2-6 to 3-11 and three individual Composite scores for ages 4-0 to 7-3 ($M = 100$, $SD = 15$), percentile ranks, and subtest scaled scores ($M = 10$, $SD = 3$).
Confidence intervals	Based on the estimated true score.
Factor structure Ages 2-6 to 3-11 Ages 4-0 to 7-3	A two-factor model, consisting of Verbal and Performance, that is similar to that of the WPPSI–R. A three-factor model, consisting of Verbal, Performance, and Processing Speed, that differs from the two-factor model on the WPPSI–R.
g loading	About the same as that of the WPPSI–R.
Art work	Updated to look more attractive and more contemporary, with color used instead of black and white for Picture Completion; some visual stimuli redrawn and enlarged.
Test-retest changes	Generally comparable to those of the WPPSI–R.
Range of Full Scale IQs Ages 2-6 to 3-11 Ages 4-0 to 7-3	Narrower than on the WPPSI–R (41 to 155 vs. 41 to 160). Wider than on the WPPSI–R (40 to 160 vs. 41 to 160).
Ranges of subtest scaled scores	More subtests have a range of 1 to 19 scaled-score points than on the WPPSI–R.

Table 5-20
Highlights of Changes in the WPPSI–III Subtests

Subtest	Changes from the WPPSI–III
Block Design	Contains 20 instead of 14 items, with 4 retained and 16 new items. Changes in number of trials administered and time limits, and bonus points have been eliminated.
Information	Contains 34 instead of 27 items, with 19 retained and 15 new items. Changes in start points.
Matrix Reasoning	New subtest with 29 items.
Vocabulary	Contains 25 items, with 16 retained and 9 new items. Changes in number of picture items and start points.
Picture Concepts	New subtest with 28 items.
Symbol Search	New subtest with 50 items.
Word Reasoning	New subtest with 28 items.
Coding	New subtest with 59 items.
Comprehension	Contains 20 instead of 15 items, with 5 retained and 15 new items. Now a supplemental subtest. Changes in start points and discontinue criterion.
Picture Completion	Contains 32 instead of 28 items, with 20 retained and 12 new items. Now a supplemental subtest. Changes in start points and time limit, and bonus points have been eliminated.
Similarities	Contains 24 instead of 20 items, with 5 retained and 19 new items. Now a supplemental subtest. Changes in type of items and discontinue criterion.
Receptive Vocabulary	New subtest with 38 items.
Object Assembly	Contains 14 instead of 6 items, with 3 retained and 11 new items.
Picture Naming	New subtest with 30 items.

Supplemental and Optional Subtests

The WPPSI–III has six supplemental subtests, whereas the WPPSI–R has no supplemental subtests. At ages 2-6 to 3-11, Picture Naming is a supplemental subtest on the WPPSI–III, and at ages 4-0 to 7-3, Symbol Search, Comprehension, Picture Completion, Similarities, and Object Assembly are supplemental subtests. Sentences and Animal Pegs, which are optional subtests on the WPPSI–R, are not included in the WPPSI–III. Receptive Vocabulary and Picture Naming are optional subtests on the WPPSI–III at ages 4-0 to 7-3 but are not used as substitute subtests. In contrast, even though Sentences and Animal Pegs are referred to as optional subtests in the WPPSI–R, Sentences can be used as an alternative for a Verbal Scale subtest and Animal Pegs can be used as an alternative for a Performance Scale subtest.

Other Differences

Other differences between the WPPSI–III and WPPSI–R include the following. The WPPSI–III eliminates the terms "Verbal Scale" and "Performance Scale" and, as noted previously, refers to these as "Composites." Scoring guidelines and administrative procedures have been modified. For example, changes have been made in item content, the order in which subtests are administered, the order of items, start points, discontinue criteria, timing, allotment of bonus points, and querying and scoring guidelines. The WPPSI–III deemphasizes speed of performance on tasks outside of Processing Speed. Finally, the number of items has been increased on most subtests.

Comment on Comparison of the WPPSI–III and WPPSI–R

The cumulative effects of these changes are particularly evident in both age groups. At ages 2-6 to 3-11, the WPPSI–III Full Scale is composed of only four core subtests, and at ages 4-0 to 7-3, the WPPSI–III Full Scale is composed of seven subtests. Thus, there are 60% fewer core subtests at ages 2-6 to 3-11 and 30% fewer core subtests at ages 4-0 to 7-3. In addition, of the four core subtests in the WPPSI–III at ages 2-6 to 3-11, Receptive Vocabulary is not a core subtest in the WPPSI–R. And, of the seven core subtests in the WPPSI–III at ages 4-0 to 7-3, Word Reasoning, Matrix Reasoning, Picture Concepts, and Coding are not core subtests in the WPPSI–R. Only 16.7% of the WPPSI–R items are retained in the WPPSI–III.

You will need to take into account the different structures of the WPPSI–III and WPPSI–R when comparing test-retest scores from the two tests. In addition, you also will need to consider other factors, such as practice effects, changes in the child's health, changes in the child's home environment, changes in the school setting, and changes in examiners (see Sattler, 2001, for further information about test-test changes). As noted previously, Full Scale IQs are likely to be lower on the WPPSI–III than on the WPPSI–R by about 1 point. A study of the pattern of subtest scores on the two tests, taking into account the different structures of the two tests, and the case history will guide you in interpreting test-retest changes from the WPPSI–R to the WPPSI–III.

ADMINISTERING THE WPPSI–III

To become proficient in administering the WPPSI–III, you must master the procedures described in the Administration Manual. Be careful not to confuse the administration procedures for the WPPSI–R, WISC–IV, or WAIS–III with those for the WPPSI–III. Confusion could occur because some subtests with the same name have different instructions and time limits. The administration guidelines discussed in the next two chapters (Chapter 6 for the core subtests and Chapter 7 for the supplemental subtests) complement those in the Administration Manual. Table C-8 in Appendix C presents special procedures for administering the WPPSI–III Performance subtests to children with hearing impairments. Chapters 6 and 7, along with the suggestions in Exhibit 5-1 and the checklist in Table D-2 in Appendix D, will help you become proficient in administering the WPPSI–III. By mastering the administrative procedures early in your testing career, you will be better able to focus on the equally important tasks of learning how to establish rapport, observe the child, and interpret the test results. (The procedures for administering psychological tests, discussed in Chapter 7 of Sattler, 2001, also are helpful in administering the WPPSI–III.)

General Guidelines for Test Administration

As you read about the subtests in Chapters 6 and 7, you will find questions to guide you in your test administration and in your evaluation and interpretation of the child's performance. The quality of the child's responses and the pattern of successes and failures, along with the child's scores and behavior, are important parts of the evaluation. Recording the child's responses verbatim, along with pertinent behavioral observations, will help you evaluate the test results, especially when you review your scoring, testify at an administrative hearing or in court, share the evaluation with other professionals, or reevaluate the child. Make an entry on the Record Form for every item that you administer.

As you administer the test, use the exact wording of the directions, questions, or items. Do not add explanations, use synonyms, or ad lib. Sometimes, however, you can use your own wording, except for the subtest questions, and these instances are noted in the Administration Manual. Common sense may dictate that you occasionally say something that is not in the Administration Manual, such as "Tell me when you're finished." Overall, the aim is to administer the test in a standardized manner.

When you compute the Full Scale IQ or Composite scores, never include scores from spoiled subtests (e.g., subtests spoiled through improper timing, interruptions, or mistakes in administration) or from supplemental subtests that were administered in addition to the core subtests.

When a child says "I don't know," consider what this response might mean and how you want to respond to it. It could mean, for example, that the child (a) does not know the answer, (b) is not confident of the answer and is unwilling to take a risk, (c) is being uncooperative and doesn't want to answer the question, or (d) has been inattentive and therefore doesn't know what the question is. If you decide that the response reflects a motivational

Exhibit 5-1
Supplementary Instructions for Administering the WPPSI–III

SUPPLEMENTARY INSTRUCTIONS FOR ADMINISTERING THE WPPSI–III

Preparing to Administer the WPPSI–III

1. Study the instructions in the Administration Manual, and practice administering the test before you give it to a child. It is a good idea to take the test yourself before you study it.
2. Organize your test materials before the child comes into the room. Make sure that all test materials—including the Stimulus Book, blocks, Record Forms, Response Booklet, stopwatch, and pencils—are in the kit. Have extra blank paper on which to take notes, if necessary.
3. Keep anything not needed for the test off the table (e.g., soda cans, pocketbook, keys).
4. Complete the top of the first page of the Record Form (child's name, sex, grade, handedness, school, parent/guardian, place of testing, and examiner's name).
5. Complete the "Calculation of Child's Age" section. Enter the date of testing and the child's date of birth and then compute the child's age at testing (i.e., chronological age). Months are considered to have 30 days for testing purposes. Check the child's chronological age by adding the child's chronological age to the date of birth to obtain the date of testing.

Administering the WPPSI–III

6. Administer the subtests in the order presented in the Administration Manual or on the Record Form, except in rare circumstances. Do not change the wording on any subtest. Read the directions exactly as shown in the Administration Manual. Do not ad lib.
7. Start with the appropriate item on each subtest and follow both the reverse rule and the discontinue criteria. You must be thoroughly familiar with the scoring criteria *before* you give the test.
8. Write down verbatim all of the child's responses that are pertinent to the test, the testing situation, and the referral question or that are otherwise helpful in understanding the child. Write clearly, and do not use unusual abbreviations. Record time accurately in the spaces provided on the Record Form. Use a stopwatch (or a wristwatch with a digital timer) to administer the timed WPPSI–III subtests.
9. Clearly and accurately complete the Record Form. A clearly written and accurate Record Form will (a) give you an opportunity to review your scoring after the test is completed, (b) provide a record for qualitative analysis, and (c) provide a document in case of litigation.
10. Question all incomplete, vague, or unclear responses, writing "(Q)" after each questionable response. Question all responses followed by "(Q)" in the Administration Manual.
11. Introduce the test by using the introduction on page 52 of the Administration Manual. Make eye contact with the child from time to time, and use the child's first name when possible. Watch for signs that the child needs a break

(e.g., a stretch, a drink, or a trip to the bathroom). If needed, between subtests say something like "Now we'll do something different." At the end of the test, thank the child for coming and for being cooperative (if appropriate).
12. Complete the first page of the Response Booklet by entering the child's name, the date, and the examiner's name.

Scoring

13. Be prepared to spend more time scoring the subtests in the Verbal Composite because they are generally more difficult to score than subtests in the other Composites.
14. Recheck your scoring when the test is finished. If you failed to question a response when you should have and the response is obviously not a 0-point response, give the child the most appropriate score based on the child's actual response.
15. If a subtest was spoiled, write "spoiled" by the subtest total score and on the first page of the Record Form next to the name of the subtest. If the subtest was not administered, write "NA" in the margin of the Record Form next to the subtest name and on the first page of the Record Form.
16. Add the raw scores for each subtest carefully.
17. Make sure that you give credit for all items below the first two items with perfect scores (even those with 0 points).
18. Make sure that you do not give credit for items above the last discontinue-point item (even those with perfect scores).

Specific Guidelines for Completing the Record Form for Ages 2-6 to 3-11

19. Transfer subtest scores from the inside pages of the Record Form to the first page of the Record Form in the section labeled "Total Raw Score to Scaled Score Conversions." After transferring the raw scores to the first page of the Record Form, check to see that you copied them correctly.
20. Transform raw scores into scaled scores by using Table A.1 on pages 216 to 218 of the Administration Manual. Be sure to use the page of Table A.1 that is appropriate for the child's age and the correct column for each transformation. For example, to convert a raw score on Receptive Vocabulary (the first subtest administered at ages 2-6 to 3-11) to a scaled score, you must use the column labeled RV in Table A.1. Find the entry for your raw score and the corresponding scaled score in the first column (labeled "Scaled Score").
21. Add the scaled scores for the two core Verbal subtests to compute the sum of the scaled scores. Do not use Picture Naming unless you have substituted it for another Verbal subtest. Compute the Verbal IQ only when the child has a raw score greater than 0 on at least one of the two subtests in the Composite.

(Continued)

Exhibit 5-1 (*Continued*)

22. Add the scaled scores for the two core Performance subtests. At these ages, there is no supplemental subtest. Compute the Performance IQ only when the child has a raw score greater than 0 on at least one of the two subtests in the Composite.

23. Add the scaled scores for the two General Language Composite subtests—one core and one supplemental—if you have administered both subtests. Compute the General Language Composite only when the child has a raw score greater than 0 on at least one of the two subtests in the Composite.

24. Add the Verbal and Performance subtest scaled scores to obtain the sum for the Full Scale. Double check all of your additions. Compute the Full Scale IQ only when the child has raw scores greater than 0 on at least two of the four subtests.

25. Convert the sums of scaled scores for the Verbal and Performance Composites and for the Full Scale by using the appropriate conversion tables in Appendix A in the Administration Manual. Use Table A.2 for the Verbal Composite (p. 231), Table A.3 for the Performance Composite (p. 232), Table A.4 for the Full Scale (p. 233), and Table A.5 for the General Language Composite (p. 234). Be sure to use the correct table for the appropriate Composite. Record the Composite scores and Full Scale IQ in the appropriate boxes on the first page of the Record Form.

Specific Guidelines for Completing the Record Form for Ages 4-0 to 7-3

26. Transfer subtest scores from the inside pages of the Record Form to the first page of the Record Form in the section labeled "Total Raw Score to Scaled Score Conversions." After transferring the raw scores to the first page of the Record Form, check to see that you copied them correctly.

27. Transform raw scores into scaled scores by using Table A.1 on pages 219 to 230 of the Administration Manual. Be sure to use the page of Table A.1 that is appropriate for the child's age and the correct column for each transformation. For example, to convert a raw score on Block Design (the first subtest administered at ages 4-0 to 7-3) to a scaled score, you must use the column labeled BD in Table A.1. Find the entry for your raw score and the corresponding scaled score in the first column (labeled "Scaled Score").

28. Add the scaled scores for the three core Verbal subtests to compute the sum of the scaled scores. Do not use Comprehension or Similarities unless you have substituted one for another Verbal subtest. Compute the Verbal IQ only when the child has raw scores greater than 0 on at least two of the three subtests in the Composite.

29. Add the scaled scores for the three core Performance subtests to compute the sum of the scaled scores. Do not use Picture Completion or Object Assembly unless you have substituted one for another Performance subtest.

Compute the Performance IQ only when the child has raw scores greater than 0 on at least two of the three subtests in the Composite.

30. Add the scaled scores for the two Processing Speed subtests—one core and one supplemental—if you have administered both subtests. Compute the Processing Speed Quotient only when the child has a raw score greater than 0 on at least one of the two subtests in the Composite.

31. Add the scaled scores for the two General Language Composite subtests—both optional—if you have administered both subtests. Compute the General Language Composite only when the child has a raw score greater than 0 on at least one of the two subtests in the Composite.

32. Add the Verbal, Performance, and Processing Speed subtest scaled scores to obtain the sum for the Full Scale. Double check all of your additions. Compute the Full Scale IQ only when the child has raw scores greater than 0 on at least (a) two of the three Verbal subtests and (b) two of the three Performance subtests.

33. Convert the sums of scaled scores for the Verbal, Performance, and Processing Speed Composites and for the Full Scale by using the appropriate conversion tables in Appendix A in the Administration Manual. Use Table A.6 for the Verbal IQ (p. 235), Table A.7 for the Performance IQ (p. 236), Table A.8 for the Processing Speed Quotient (p. 237), Table A.9 for the Full Scale IQ (p. 238), and Table A.10 for the General Language Composite (p. 240). Be sure to use the correct table for the appropriate Composite. Record the Composite scores and Full Scale IQ in the appropriate boxes on the first page of the Record Form.

General Guidelines for Completing the Record Form for All Ages

34. We recommend that you not compute either Composite scores or the Full Scale IQ if a supplementary subtest has been substituted for a core subtest because the norms were derived from the core subtests only. This recommendation is especially important in situations in which precise scores will be used for decision-making purposes (i.e., diagnostic classifications, eligibility decisions, etc.).

35. Recheck all of your work. If the IQ was obtained by use of a short form, write "SF" beside the appropriate IQ. If IQs were prorated, write "PRO" beside each appropriate IQ.

36. Make a profile of the child's scaled scores on the first page of the Record Form by plotting the scores on the graph provided.

37. Look up the confidence intervals for the Full Scale IQ in Table B-1 in Appendix B of this text. Use the confidence intervals appropriate for the child's age. Write the confidence intervals on the first page of the Record Form in the space provided. It is not necessary to obtain the confidence interval for any other Composite.

(Continued)

Exhibit 5-1 (*Continued*)

38. Look up the percentile ranks for the Verbal IQ, Performance IQ, Processing Speed Quotient, General Language Composite, and Full Scale IQ by using Table C-10 in Appendix C in this text or Tables A.2 to A.5 (pp. 231–234) for ages 2-6 to 3-11 or Tables A.6 to A.10 (pp. 235–240) for ages 4-0 to 7-3 in the Administration Manual. Use Table C-11 in Appendix C in this text or Table 6.3 (p. 133) in the Technical Manual to obtain the classification of the IQ.
39. If you want to obtain test-age equivalents, use Table A.12 (p. 242) in the Administration Manual. The equivalents can be placed (in parentheses) in the right margin of the box that contains the scaled scores on the first page of the Record Form. For test-age equivalents *above* those in the table, use the highest test-age equivalent and a plus sign. For test-age equivalents *below* those in the table, use the lowest test-age equivalent and a minus sign.
40. If you want to, complete the Discrepancy Analysis Page, which is page 2 of the Record Form.
41. Complete the last page of the Record Form.

Miscellaneous Information and Suggestions
42. Appendix B in the Administration Manual (pp. 245–256) contains six tables that provide statistical information about the Composites and subtest comparisons, including base rates and critical differences.
43. Appendixes B and C in this text contain several tables to assist you in interpreting the WPPSI–III and in obtaining IQs associated with short forms.
44. Be sure to check the scores you enter into any computer program you use to assist you in writing a report.

Summary
45. In summary, read the directions verbatim, pronounce words clearly, query and prompt at the appropriate times, start with the appropriate item, place items properly before the child, use correct timing, score appropriately, discontinue at the proper place, follow the specific guidelines in the Administration Manual for administering the test, and complete the Record Form appropriately.

issue, encourage the child to answer. If the subtest directions permit you to do so, consider repeating the question or asking it again at some later point, especially if the child says "I don't know" to easy questions.

Better yet, the first time a child says "I don't know," say something like "I want you to try your hardest on each question. Try your best to answer each question. If you are not sure, go ahead and take your best guess." You can also say, "It is OK to answer even if you are not sure." Give the child credit if the question is answered correctly.

Estimating the Time Required to Administer the WPPSI–III Core Battery

According to the Administration Manual, the times required to administer the WPPSI–III core battery were as follows:

- At ages 2-6 to 3-11, 50% of the standardization sample completed the core battery in 29 minutes or less, 70% in 35 minutes or less, 90% in 45 minutes or less, and 95% in 49 minutes or less.
- At ages 4-0 to 7-3, 50% of the standardization sample completed the core battery in 41 minutes or less, 70% in 48 minutes or less, 90% in 61 minutes or less, and 95% in 67 minutes or less.

Thus, at ages 2-6 to 3-11, the core battery can usually be administered in approximately 30 to 50 minutes, while at ages 4-0 to 7-3, the core battery can usually be administered in approximately 40 minutes to 1 hour. The time to administer the core battery tends to increase with increasing intellectual levels.

At the Beginning

At the beginning of a testing session, make sure that the room is well lit, has comfortable size-appropriate furniture for the child, and is free from distractions. Unlike on the WISC–IV, no subtests on the Record Form are printed in light blue ink. Position the child away from any windows and sit directly across from the child. If a parent is present, ask the parent to remain in the background and sit quietly out of the child's view. (Some of the material in this section is adapted from Wechsler, 2002a.)

Prepare for the session by making sure that the test materials are in order. During testing, keep the test kit out of the child's view. As you establish rapport, tell the child that breaks are OK and to let you know if a break is needed. Position the Administration Manual and the Record Form so that the child cannot read the questions or answers. After you establish rapport, begin the test. Do not prolong the getting-acquainted period, overstimulate the child, or entertain the child excessively. Introduce the test by following the instructions on page 20 in the Administration Manual; avoid using the term "test" during the introduction. Respond truthfully to any questions that the child has about the purpose of testing.

Subtest Sequence

Administer the subtests in the order specified in the Administration Manual for each age group (see p. 23) unless you have a compelling reason to use another order, such as to motivate a bored or frustrated child or to administer subtests that are appropriate for the child's disability (e.g., verbal subtests for a child with a visual impairment). By following the standard sequence of administration you use an order that (a) can serve as a baseline for evaluating children whom you may test in the future, (b) is comparable to that used by other examiners, and (c) alternates nonverbal and verbal subtests.

The subtest order was designed to increase the child's interest in the test, to maintain a variety of activities throughout the session, and to minimize fatigue effects. Each age group has a different order of subtest administration. Core subtests are usually administered first and are followed by supplemental and optional subtests, if any are administered. The exception is Symbol Search, a supplemental subtest. If administered, Symbol Search is given as the sixth subtest (after Picture Concepts). *Deviations from the specified subtest order should be based on clinical considerations and not on your own personal preference.* Note the reasons for any deviations from the specified subtest order on the Record Form and in the psychological report.

Attend to the child's behavior throughout the test, but especially at the beginning of the session. Do not assume that the order of the subtests will automatically reduce a child's level of anxiety or help a child feel relaxed. We need research on how the order of the subtests affects children's anxiety level and performance in general.

Queries

The rules that cover queries vary among subtests (see p. 34 of the Administration Manual for a general discussion of queries). Queries allow you to evaluate more thoroughly the extent of the child's knowledge. You will need to query any responses followed by a "(Q)" in the Administration Manual, as well as any other responses that you judge to be unclear, vague, or incomplete. However, you should not query a clear 0-point or 1-point answer in order to elicit a better answer unless the answer is listed in the Administration Manual. You also should not query obviously wrong answers or obviously

right answers. Excessive queries prolong the test unnecessarily and may invalidate the test results.

Prompts

Prompts are used to help the child follow the subtest instructions. For example, if the child says that there are two correct answers for a Picture Concepts item, you should tell the child to give only the one best answer. The General Directions in the Administration Manual for each subtest discuss the use of prompts. Record a "P" on the Record Form for each prompt that you give.

Start Point

At ages 2-6 to 3-11, all children start with item 1. At ages 4-0 to 7-3, the item with which you start depends on the child's age and ability level. For example, on the Comprehension subtest you start with item 1 for children 4 to 5 years of age and item 4 for children 6 to 7 years of age. In the Administration Manual, in the Record Form, and in this text, any ages expressed only in years are inclusive ages—that is, 4 to 5 years of age means 4-0 to 5-11 and 6 to 7 years of age means 6-0 to 7-3.

At ages 4-0 to 7-3, if you suspect that a child has an intellectual deficiency, regardless of the child's chronological age, begin at the start point for a 4-year-old child on all subtests, with the exception of Similarities, Coding, and Symbol Search. On these three subtests, all children are given the same items regardless of their chronological age or estimated level of intellectual ability.

Reverse Sequence

At ages 4-0 to 7-3, Block Design, Information, Matrix Reasoning, Vocabulary, Picture Concepts, Word Reasoning, Comprehension, Picture Completion, Receptive Vocabulary, Object Assembly, and Picture Naming have a reverse sequence, whereas Similarities, Coding, and Symbol Search do not. Thus, one Verbal subtest and the two Processing Speed subtests do not have a reverse sequence.

Use a reverse sequence when the child (a) does not obtain a perfect score on the first start-point item (except when item 1 is the start-point item) or (b) obtains a perfect score on the first start-point item but not on the subsequent item (again, except when item 1 is the start-point item). Sometimes you may reach item 1 and the child still does not have (a) two consecutive items with perfect scores or (b) the number of consecutive scores of 0 specified in the discontinue criterion (i.e., three, four, or five scores of 0 or four scores of 0 on five consecutive items). In either case, continue to administer items after the start-point item or subsequent item until the discontinue criterion has been met. If the discontinue criterion is met during a reversal, continue administering items in reverse order until the child has two consecutive perfect scores or until item 1 has been administered before discontinuing the subtest.

Let's look at some examples of how the reverse sequence is carried out on the Matrix Reasoning subtest.

No Perfect Score on Item 6
If you start with samples A, B, and C and then item 6 and the child does not obtain a perfect score on item 6, administer items 5, 4, 3, 2, and 1 in reverse sequence, as needed. If the child obtains two consecutive perfect scores, stop the reverse sequence and continue with item 7. If you reach item 1 and the child has neither two consecutive perfect scores nor four consecutive scores of 0, continue with item 7 and discontinue when the child meets the discontinue criterion for the Matrix Reasoning subtest.

A Perfect Score on Item 6 but Not on Item 7
If you start with samples A, B, and C and then item 6 and the child obtains a perfect score on item 6 but not on item 7, administer items 5, 4, 3, 2, and 1 in reverse sequence, as needed. If the child obtains two consecutive perfect scores, stop the reverse sequence and continue with item 8. If you reach item 1 and the child has neither two consecutive perfect scores nor four consecutive scores of 0, continue with item 8 and discontinue when the child meets the discontinue criterion for the Matrix Reasoning subtest.

Start-Point Scoring Rule

The start-point scoring rule states that the child receives full credit for all items located below the start-point item and subsequent item on which perfect scores were obtained. This rule applies to both administered and unadministered items, regardless of the child's scores on any items that were administered. The start-point scoring rule also applies in a reverse sequence to any items below two consecutive perfect scores.

Here is an example of the application of the start-point scoring rule. You administer items 8 and 9 on the Picture Concepts subtest to a 6-year-old child who obtains a perfect score on item 8 and a score of 0 on item 9. You then reverse the order of administration and give items 7 and 6, on each of which the child clearly obtains 0 points. You administer items 5 and 4, on each of which the child clearly obtains a perfect score. You then continue the subtest with item 10 because the discontinue criterion was not reached. After the examination, you review your scoring and decide that the child did indeed obtain a perfect score on item 9. The start-point scoring rule requires that you give full credit for items 6 and 7, even though the child obtained 0 points on these items, because items 6 and 7 are below the start-point item and subsequent item on which perfect scores were obtained.

The start-point scoring rule ensures that you do not penalize the child for obtaining 0 points on items that, as it turned out, you did not have to administer. The start-point scoring rule is an attempt to maintain standardized scoring procedures.

Discontinue-Point Scoring Rule

The discontinue-point scoring rule states that the child does not receive credit for any items above the last discontinue-point item. This rule applies to both administered and unadministered items, regardless of the child's scores on any items that were administered.

Here is an example of the application of the discontinue-point scoring rule. You administer the first 10 items of the Word Reasoning subtest, but are uncertain about how to score the child's responses to items 5 to 10. You then administer additional items. The child receives perfect scores on items 11 and 12 and 0 points on items 13 to 17. You therefore discontinue the subtest after item 17. After the test is over, you check your scoring and decide that the child should receive 0 points for items 5 to 10. The discontinue-point scoring rule requires that you not give credit for items 11 and 12, even though the child's answers were correct, because these items were administered after the discontinue criterion was met.

The discontinue-point scoring rule ensures that you do not give credit for items that, as it turned out, you did not have to administer. The rule is another attempt to maintain standardized scoring procedures.

Perfect Scores

Perfect scores are not the same on all subtests, and even within the same subtest items may have different perfect scores. Table 5-21 shows that Information, Matrix Reasoning, Picture Concepts, Symbol Search, Word Reasoning, Coding, Picture Completion, Receptive Vocabulary, and Picture Naming have a perfect score of 1 on all items. Block Design has a perfect score of 2 on all items. Vocabulary, Comprehension, Similarities, and Object Assembly have variable perfect scores.

Points for Unadministered Items

As you have recently read, the child receives points for unadministered items that *precede* perfect scores on (a) the age-appropriate start-point item and subsequent item or (b) the first two consecutive items below the age-appropriate start-point item if a reverse sequence was used. The number of additional points you award for the unadministered items depends on the subtest. For example, if you start with item 6 on Block Design and the child receives a perfect score on items 6 and 7, you award 10 points (2 points each for items 1 to 5). If you start with item 6 on Matrix Reasoning and the child obtains a score of 0 on items 6 and 5 but obtains a perfect score on items 4 and 3, you award 2 points (1 point each for items 1 and 2). The Administration Manual (see p. 28) recommends that you record the points for the unadministered items by putting a slash mark in the Score column on the Record Form over the item preceding the first two perfect scores and writing below the slash mark the number of points awarded.

Consider another example in which a reverse sequence is used. If you begin a subtest with item 7 and the child obtains 0 points on the item, administer item 6 and then items 5, 4, 3, 2, and 1, as needed. If the child obtains 0 points on item 6 but obtains a perfect score on items 5 and 4, do not administer items 3, 2, and 1; however, give the child full credit for these three items. If the perfect score on each item is 1 point, you would initially give, in this example, 5 points—1 point each for passing items 5 and 4 and 1 point for each of the three unadministered items (3, 2, and 1)—in addition to any points obtained on later items.

Table 5-21
Perfect Scores on WPPSI–III Subtests

Subtest	Perfect score
Block Design	2 points on all items
Information	1 point on all items
Matrix Reasoning	1 point on all items
Vocabulary	1 point on items 1 to 7 and 2 points on items 8 to 25
Picture Concepts	1 point on all items
Symbol Search	1 point on all items (reverse sequence does not apply)
Word Reasoning	1 point on all items
Coding	1 point on all items (reverse sequence does not apply)
Comprehension	1 point on items 1 and 2 and 2 points on items 3 to 20
Picture Completion	1 point on all items
Similarities	1 point on items 1 and 2 and 2 points on items 3 to 24 (reverse sequence does not apply)
Receptive Vocabulary	1 point on all items
Object Assembly	1 point on items 1 to 3; 2 points on items 5, 6, and 8; 3 points on items 4, 7, 9, 11, 12, and 13; 5 points on items 10 and 14
Picture Naming	1 point on all items

Source: Adapted from Wechsler (2002a).

Repeating Instructions

An introductory statement is used to begin Block Design, Vocabulary, and Comprehension. The introductory statement can be repeated as often as requested by the child or whenever you think that repetition is needed. In contrast, Matrix Reasoning, Picture Concepts, Symbol Search, Word Reasoning, Coding, and Picture Completion begin with a sample item. Finally, Information, Similarities, Receptive Vocabulary, Object Assembly, and Picture Naming begin directly with an item.

Repeating Items

On Information, Matrix Reasoning, Vocabulary, Picture Concepts, Comprehension, Similarities, Receptive Vocabulary, and Picture Naming, you are permitted to repeat items if (a) the child requests repetition, (b) you believe that the child misheard, misunderstood, or forgot the item, or (c) you need to administer the item again (e.g., if the child has not responded within 5 to 10 seconds, you will need to repeat the item unless it is clear that the child is thinking about a response). Record the repetition with an "R" on the Record Form. Additionally, on these eight subtests, if a child responds to one or more earlier items with "I don't know" but then receives points on more difficult items, readminister the earlier items if you believe the child might pass them (see p. 35 of the Administration Manual).

You are not permitted to repeat items on Block Design, Symbol Search, Coding, Picture Completion, and Object Assembly. On Word Reasoning you need to follow the specific directions for repeating items.

Additional Help

For each subtest, do not give additional help beyond that noted in the Administration Manual. This means that you should not spell, define, or explain any words that are in the directions, questions, or items or give any other kind of help unless it is specified in the Administration Manual. If a child asks for the meaning of a word, simply say, "Do the best you can" or something similar.

Waiting Time

For the Information, Matrix Reasoning, Vocabulary, Picture Concepts, Comprehension, Receptive Vocabulary, and Picture Naming subtests, wait about 30 seconds before going to the next item if the child makes no response, except when the child has been doing well and seems to need the additional time to solve a difficult item. However, use your judgment about when to move to the next item. For children who are clearly beyond their ability, 30 seconds may be a long time to wait, especially if it is the third or fourth 30-second wait. This might be the case for children who seem bored, who shrug their shoulders, or who look around the room after a few seconds and do not look at the items. On all subtests, when you proceed to another item, you may say, "Let's try another one."

Discontinue Criterion

Every subtest has a discontinue criterion—either a specific number of consecutive scores of 0 or a time limit. The discontinue criterion is noted in the Administration Manual as well as on the Record Form. Carefully study the discontinue criterion for each subtest. Coding and Symbol Search are discontinued after a specified time limit, unless the child finishes before the time limit is reached.

The discontinue criterion has one exception: *In a reverse sequence, continue to administer items even after the discontinue criterion has been met until you reach item 1 or until the child has perfect scores on two consecutive items.* This exception is illustrated in Figure 2.5 on page 30 of the Administration Manual. Figure 2.5 shows that Picture Concepts was started with item 8 and then a reverse sequence was followed because the child obtained a score of 0 on item 8. The child then obtained scores of 0 on items 7, 6, and 5 and therefore met the discontinue criterion (4 consecutive scores of 0 points). However, items 4 and 3 were still administered, and the child obtained perfect scores on these two items. The child received full credit for items 1 and 2 even though they were not administered, and the subtest was discontinued because the discontinue criterion had been met.

Scoring

Scoring the Vocabulary, Word Reasoning, Comprehension, and Similarities subtests may be especially challenging. Carefully study the scoring criteria, scoring guidelines, and scoring examples in the Administration Manual. Recognize that the scoring guidelines and sample responses for these four subtests do not cover all possible responses that children may give or cover every response contingency. For this reason, you must use judgment in scoring responses. As you study the scoring guidelines and the sample responses, try to understand the rationale underlying the guidelines.

Score the best response when a child gives multiple acceptable responses. If a child gives both a correct and an incorrect response and it is not clear which is the intended answer, ask, "Now, which one is it?" and then base your score on the answer. Do the best job possible with the scoring guidelines given in the Administration Manual. However, whenever you have any doubt about the scoring of a response, consult a colleague. In scoring queried responses, either those followed by a "(Q)" in the Administration Manual or those in response to your own queries, consider the child's entire response—the initial answer plus the answer to the query—in arriving at a score.

Some examiners are more lenient than others in giving credit, and even the same examiner may not consistently follow his or her own (relative) standards. For example, the examiner may be strict on some occasions and lenient on others or strict with some children and lenient with others. Studies with other Wechsler tests have reported differences in the scoring standards of examiners (see Sattler, 2001). We need research about how examiners score WPPSI–III responses.

Spoiled Responses

A spoiled response is one that was on the right path to obtain credit but was spoiled by the child's incorrect elaboration on the initial response—the elaboration revealed a fundamental misconception. A response may be spoiled when it contains multiple elements, some of which are correct and others incorrect. For example, if a child says that *clock* means "Goes tick-tock" and then spontaneously or in response to your query says, "It's the engine on a motorcycle," he or she has spoiled the response. The child's elaboration reveals a misconception about the meaning of the word *clock*, and hence the response receives a score of 0.

If a child adds additional irrelevant information that is not contrary to fact, the correct initial response is not spoiled, despite the fact that the information by itself might be given 0 points. For example, suppose a child defines *cow* as "an animal" and adds "My aunt has cows on her farm. Some cows have spots. I like cows; they have ears." The response is given a perfect score because the elaboration does not reveal a fundamental misconception about the word *cow*. Sometimes it may be difficult to distinguish a spoiled response from a poor

response.

Testing-of-Limits

Testing-of-limits is an informal, nonstandardized procedure designed to provide additional information about a child's cognitive abilities and processing skills. *Conduct testing-of-limits only after you have administered the entire test following standard procedures.* If you conduct testing-of-limits before you have administered the entire test, you will violate standard procedures, and the cues you give the child may lead to higher scores and to an invalid assessment. Research with previous editions of the Wechsler tests has shown that children may obtain higher scores when they receive extra help during the test (see Sattler, 2001).

Testing-of-limits is useful for (a) following up leads about the child's abilities, (b) testing clinical hypotheses, and (c) evaluating whether additional cues, strategies, or extra time helps the child solve problems. *Testing-of-limits may invalidate repeated evaluations and should be used cautiously.* In school settings, you may not want to use testing-of-limits if you think that the child may be reevaluated within a 3-year period. Any procedures used to test limits should be clearly described in the report. Scores derived from testing-of-limits procedures should be clearly differentiated from scores obtained under standardized conditions.

A multiple-choice testing-of-limits procedure may provide information about whether the child has a word retrieval deficit or a word knowledge deficit (see, for example, the discussion of testing-of-limits for the Similarities subtest in Chapter 2). Testing-of-limits allows you to generate hypotheses. However, you should not draw conclusions about a child's abilities or processing skills based on a few testing-of-limits multiple-choice questions. Follow up any hypotheses by testing the child with a psychometrically sound instrument.

Subtest Substitution

According to the Administration Manual, the following substitutions are acceptable:

Ages 2-6 to 3-11
- Picture Naming for Receptive Vocabulary
- Comprehension or Similarities for Information

Ages 4-0 to 7-3
- Comprehension or Similarities for Information

- Comprehension or Similarities for Vocabulary
- Comprehension or Similarities for Word Reasoning
- Picture Completion or Object Assembly for Block Design
- Picture Completion or Object Assembly for Matrix Reasoning
- Picture Completion or Object Assembly for Picture Concepts
- Symbol Search for Coding

Note that at ages 4-0 to 7-3 Comprehension and Similarities serve as substitutes for the three core Verbal subtests, while Picture Completion and Object Assembly serve as substitutes for the three Performance subtests.

Substitutions should be based on clinical need or a similar appropriate reason, not your own preferences or convenience. For example, you may substitute Picture Completion for Block Design for a child with fine-motor difficulties, or you may substitute Comprehension for Word Reasoning when Comprehension is invalidated (e.g., interrupted by a fire drill or because the child had a seizure).

Further, only one substitution is allowed for each Composite. For example, at ages 4-0 to 7-3, if Picture Completion is substituted for one of the three Performance core subtests, Object Assembly cannot be substituted for another Performance subtest. Thus, *two* substitutions are allowed for the Full Scale. Maintain the standard order of administration (described on the first page of the Record Form) when you substitute a supplemental subtest for a core subtest or when you administer a supplemental subtest in addition to the seven core subtests.

Neither the Administration Manual nor the Technical Manual discusses how the previous guidelines were developed or presents descriptive statistics for Composites composed of both core and supplemental subtests. Consider the following questions:

1. How can the norms based only on the core subtests be used when supplemental subtests, which have psychometric properties that differ from those of the core subtests, are substituted for core subtests?
2. What are the reliability and validity of the Composite scores and Full Scale IQ when a substitution is made?
3. What confidence intervals can be used for the Composite scores and Full Scale IQ when a substitution is made?

4. Why are only two substitutions permitted for the Full Scale?
5. Why is only one substitution permitted for each Composite?
6. What evidence is there that Full Scale IQs are less reliable and valid when three, four, or five substitutions are made?

We advise that substitutions be avoided whenever a specific IQ or Composite score needs to be used for decision-making purposes. Our reasons follow. At ages 4-0 to 7-3, there are a total of 12 Verbal subtest combinations and 12 Performance subtest combinations. These possible combinations allow for some latitude in deriving Composite scores and Full Scale IQs. There are, in fact, at least 24 different possible subtest combinations when supplemental subtests are substituted for core subtests. *Because the Full Scale IQ tables are based on the core subtests only, scores derived using one or two supplemental subtests have an unknown degree of additional measurement error.* Even a difference of 1 point may be critical for some decision-making purposes. If you do report Composite scores or IQs based on the substitution of one or more supplemental subtests, write "Estimated" before the scores.

The supplemental and core subtests differ with regard to their reliability, correlations with the Composite and with the Full Scale, and *g* loadings. Let's compare the supplemental subtests with the core subtests on one of these dimensions—correlations with the Composite score at ages 4-0 to 7-3. First, with the Verbal Composite, Comprehension and Similarities have correlations of .71 and .73, respectively, whereas Information, Vocabulary, and Word Reasoning have correlations of .82, .78, and .81, respectively. Second, with the Performance Composite, Picture Completion and Object Assembly have correlations of .66 and .55, respectively, whereas Block Design, Matrix Reasoning, and Picture Concepts have correlations of .72, .74, and .71, respectively.

Potential Problems in Administering the WPPSI–III

For a discussion of potential problems in administering the Wechsler tests (including the WPPSI–III) and ways to prevent these problems from occurring, please read pages 43 to 45 in Chapter 1.

Overall Guidelines for Test Administration

Maintain good rapport by being friendly and courteous, showing a reasonable amount of flexibility, being alert to the child's moods, and never badgering the child. Handle behavior problems appropriately as they arise.

Administer the test in a professional, unhurried manner; be well organized; and follow the recommended order for administering the subtests, altering it only on the basis of clinical need. Maintain a steady pace, and make smooth transitions from subtest to subtest. Place the test materials not currently in use out of the child's sight but within your easy reach. Avoid conspicuous efforts to conceal the materials. However, shield from the child's view the Record Form and the pages in the Administration Manual that have the correct answers. Also shield your writing because children may monitor it (particularly the scores you enter on the Record Form).

Take short breaks at the end of subtests, as needed, and not in the middle of subtests. Allow a fidgety child to take a break at the end of a subtest and walk around the room, if necessary. A hesitant child needs to be encouraged to try to answer the questions. Praise the child's effort (but not successes) by saying, for example, "I appreciate your efforts" or "You are working hard and that is good." Do not say "good" or "right" after a correct response unless these words are part of the instructions. Show empathy when the child is aware of performing poorly. Some children may need additional assurance if they are anxious about how they might perform. Encourage them to try their best, and remind them that some items will be easy and others hard. However, do not provide additional help beyond the instructions, such as by giving additional practice items, asking leading questions, spelling words, or defining words.

Record a "Q" for queried responses and a "P" for prompted responses. Repeat the instructions upon request, unless the directions prohibit repetition. On untimed subtests, when the child says "I don't know" to easy items but then responds correctly to more difficult items, readminister the early items. Also, on untimed subtests, use good judgment in deciding how much time to give the child to solve each item. Score each item after the child answers so that you know when to use a reverse procedure and when to discontinue the subtest. Be careful in scoring responses. Also, recheck your scoring when the test is finished. Make an entry in the Record Form for every item administered.

Always award full credit for all items preceding the first two items with perfect scores, regardless of the child's performance on the preceding items. Do this by putting a slash mark in the Score column over the item preceding the two items with perfect scores and writing the additional points. Never give credit for items passed above the last discontinue item or after the time limit. Record any deviations from the standard order for administering the subtests. The standard order is shown on the Record Form and on page 25 of the Administration Manual. Make every effort to administer the entire test in one session. If you cannot, try to complete the test within a 1-week period.

Overall, administer the subtests in the recommended order, start each subtest with the appropriate item, follow the instructions in the Administration Manual for administering each subtest, score each item, follow the reverse procedure if needed, follow the discontinue criterion, add the item scores for each subtest, complete the Record Form, and check all of your work.

It is valuable during training to make a videotape of one or more of your test administrations. Review the tape yourself, and have a fellow student review it as well. Making a videotape might also be a class assignment. Complete the Administrative Checklist for the WPPSI–III (see Table D-2 in Appendix D) after each administration, and have a fellow student also complete it after reviewing your tape. Your teacher or teaching assistant also might review your videotape or observe your test administration through a one-way mirror and then complete the Administrative Checklist. In order to administer the WPPSI–III efficiently and correctly, become thoroughly familiar with the administrative and scoring guidelines in the Administration Manual and in this text, be alert to any covert and overt sources of error in your test administration, and learn from your own mistakes and from the feedback you receive from others.

SHORT FORMS

Short forms of the WPPSI–III may be used for (a) screening purposes, when the short form may be followed by administration of the rest of the test, (b) research purposes, or (c) obtaining an estimate of the child's intellectual status when a precise IQ is not required. Ideally, the short form you select should (a) have acceptable reliability and validity, (b) be able to answer the referral question and provide clinically useful information, (c) be suited to the child's physical capabilities, and (d) be administered when the full battery of core subtests cannot be administered or is not needed. Short forms greatly magnify the effect of any administrative errors and give much weight to each subtest used in the short form. *If you need a classification for a clinical or psychoeducational purpose or need information for programming decisions, do not use a short form.* In addition, whenever you report IQs based on short forms, write "Estimated" by the IQ on the Record Form and in the psychological report.

For ages 2-6 to 3-11, Table B-7 in Appendix B lists the 10 most valid short-form combinations of two and three WPPSI–III subtests, and the four most valid subtest combinations of four WPPSI–III subtests. For ages 4-0 to 7-3, Table B-8 in Appendix B lists the 10 most valid short-form combinations of two, three, four, and five WPPSI–III subtests plus other short forms that may serve various purposes (e.g., to evaluate a child with a hearing impairment). The reliability and validity coefficients shown in Tables B-7 and B-8 were calculated using the standardization data and the Tellegen and Briggs (1967) procedure, which takes into account the reliabilities of the subtests used in the short form. Exhibit 8-4 (pp. 256–257) in *Assessment of Children: Cognitive Applications* (Sattler, 2001) shows the formulas used to compute the reliability and validity of the short-form combinations.

An inspection of the coefficients in Table B-7 in Appendix B indicates that the four best four-subtest short-form combinations have validity coefficients of .78. The 10 best three-subtest short-form combinations have validity coefficients of .74 to .76, while the 10 best two-subtest short-form combinations have validity coefficients of .63 to .73. Overall, for the combinations shown in Table B-7, the more subtests used in the short form, the higher the reliability and validity of the estimated IQ.

An inspection of the coefficients in Table B-8 in Appendix B indicates that the 10 best four- and five-subtest short-form combinations have validity coefficients of .92 or higher, the 10 best three-subtest short-form combinations have validity coefficients of .90 or higher, and the 10 best two-subtest short-form combinations have validity coefficients of .85 to .86. Overall, for the combinations shown in Table B-8, the more subtests used in the short form, the higher the reliability and validity of the estimated IQ.

Because the reliabilities and validities of the various short forms are high at ages 4-0 to 7-3, clinical considerations also should guide you in selecting a short form.

For example, at ages 4-0 to 7-3, if you want to use a three-subtest short form, consider selecting a combination that includes one subtest from each Composite (e.g., Information, Picture Completion, and Symbol Search) so that each area measured by the test (verbal, performance, and processing speed) is represented. At ages 2-6 to 3-11, the validity coefficients suggest that the short forms should be used only when time is at a premium.

A child's physical capabilities also may guide you in selecting a short form. Children with marked visual impairment or severe motor dysfunction of the upper extremities will have difficulty with some Performance or Processing Speed subtests. In such cases, the core Verbal subtests serve as a useful short form. For children with hearing impairments, the core Performance subtests alone comprise a useful short form. Administer these short forms by using the child's preferred mode of communication and, if possible, supplement your evaluation by using other tests designed to accommodate the special physical abilities of the child (see Sattler, 2001).

CHOOSING BETWEEN THE WPPSI–III AND THE WISC–IV AND BETWEEN THE WPPSI–III AND THE BSID–II

The WPPSI–III and WISC–IV and the WPPSI–III and BSID–II (Bayley Scales of Infant Development–II) overlap at ages 6-0 to 7-3 and ages 2-6 to 3-11, respectively. At the overlapping ages you have a choice about which test to administer, and you also have an alternative test to administer in retest situations. In order to determine which test to recommend at the overlapping ages, we compared the WPPSI–III and WISC–IV on several criteria, including mean subtest reliability, Full Scale reliability, mean subtest floor (mean number of raw-score points needed to obtain a scaled score of 1), mean subtest ceiling (mean number of raw-score points needed to obtain the highest scaled score), item gradients (number of raw-score points needed to go from the floor to the mean and from the mean to the ceiling and the relationship of raw-score points to scaled-score points), Full Scale floor, Full Scale ceiling, and breadth of coverage. Our recommendations for selecting either the WPPSI–III or the BSID–II generally follow those presented in the Administration Manual.

WPPSI–III vs. WISC–IV

The WPPSI–III and WISC–IV generally have similar psychometric properties at the overlapping ages. The primary advantage of the WISC–IV over the WPPSI–III is in its breadth of coverage. The WISC–IV has in its core battery 10 subtests that fall into four Composite areas, while the WPPSI–III has in its core battery seven subtests that fall into two Composite areas.

Because of its breadth of coverage, we recommend the following:

• *The WISC–IV should be used with children ages 6-0 to 7-3 at all ability levels.*

This recommendation differs somewhat from those in the WISC–IV Administration Manual, which advises that (a) the WPPSI–III be used for children suspected of below-average cognitive ability, (b) the WISC–IV be used for children suspected of above-average cognitive ability, and (c) clinical judgment be used to select the test for children suspected of average cognitive ability.

WPPSI–III vs. BSID–II

The Administration Manual suggests that young children suspected of having below-average cognitive ability be administered the BSID–II, while young children suspected of having high ability be administered the WPPSI–III. We also recommend that children suspected of having average cognitive ability be administered the WPPSI–III.

ADMINISTERING THE WPPSI–III TO CHILDREN WITH DISABILITIES

You will need to evaluate the sensory-motor abilities of children with disabilities before you administer the WPPSI–III. If you find that a child has a visual, hearing, attentional, or motor problem that may interfere with his or her ability to take one or more of the subtests, do not use these subtests in computing Composite scores or a Full Scale IQ. Examine closely the supplemental subtests and evaluate whether or not they offer the type of task that is most relevant to your evaluation. For example, you will not be able to administer any subtests requiring vision to children who are seriously visually impaired. Verbal subtests usually are extremely difficult

to administer to children with hearing impairments; obviously, if you give the directions aloud, the child must be able to hear what you say. Table C-8 in Appendix C shows modified instructions for administering the Performance subtests to children with hearing impairments. Table C-9 in Appendix C shows the physical abilities needed for subtests on the Wechsler tests.

If you administer the WPPSI–III to a child with a physical disability, you should not provide special cues. If your modifications go beyond simply permitting the child to respond in his or her preferred mode of communication or using alternative procedures to present the items, the results may be invalid.

Verbal Subtests

You can administer all of the Verbal subtests to a child whose hearing is intact. If the child cannot hear but can read, you can type the Information, Vocabulary, Word Reasoning, Comprehension, Similarities, and Picture Naming questions on cards and show the cards to the child one at a time. If the child cannot speak, you can accept written replies, replies typed on a keyboard, or replies made by pointing to letters on an alphabet sheet. Administering the test in American Sign Language may provide unintended cues, but it may be the only alternative for assessing the child's verbal abilities.

Performance Subtests

Adaptations of the Performance subtests center on the child's method of responding. You can give Matrix Reasoning, Picture Concepts, and Picture Completion to a child who has adequate vision and who can say, write, or type the answer or point to the answer, if appropriate. On subtests where a pointing response is acceptable, provide the child with a small, pointed stick that is soft and dull enough not to mar the pictures. You cannot easily adapt Block Design or Object Assembly for a child whose arm-hand use is severely impaired. The Performance subtests can be administered with few, if any, modifications to a child with a hearing impairment. However, because you will still need to convey the instructions in some manner, a child with a hearing impairment may be at a disadvantage. When you are reading the directions and items or giving prompts and queries, the child cannot look at the sample items or subtest items at the same time that he or she attends to your signs, cues, or lips.

Processing Speed Subtests

You can adapt the Coding and Symbol Search subtests by pointing to each item and having the child say, type, point to, or indicate by head movements the response (e.g., which symbol goes in the empty box or whether the symbol is or is not in the array).

Advantages of Separate Composites

The division of the WPPSI–III into the two or three individual Composites and the availability of supplemental subtests are helpful in testing children with disabilities. You can usually administer the Verbal subtests to a child with a visual impairment or to a child with severe motor disabilities. And you can administer the Performance and Processing Speed subtests to a child with a hearing impairment or to a child with little or no speech. If you also administer the Verbal subtests to a child with a hearing impairment, you can compare the child's performance on the Verbal Composite with that on the Performance Composite to evaluate whether there are any verbal deficits.

Unknown Effects of Modifications

Without empirical findings, there is no way of knowing whether modifications affect the reliability and validity of the test scores. Yet, when you cannot follow standard procedures because disabilities prevent the child from comprehending the instructions or manipulating the test materials, modifications are needed. *When you use modifications, consider the resulting score only as a rough estimate of the score that the child might obtain under standardized procedures.* Be sure to note any modifications on the Record Form and in the psychological report. You might want to consider a test other than the WPPSI–III for evaluating a child with a disability. Examples include the Leiter International Performance Scale–R, the Universal Nonverbal Intelligence Test, and the Test of Nonverbal Intelligence. (See Chapter 16 in Sattler 2001, *Assessment of Children: Cognitive Applications*, for reviews of these and other tests.)

ASSETS

The WPPSI–III has several assets.

1. *Excellent standardization.* The standardization procedures were excellent, sampling four geographical regions, both sexes, the four major ethnic groups (Euro American, African American, Hispanic American, and Asian American), and the entire socioeconomic status range. The standardization group well represents the nation as a whole for the age groups covered by the test.

2. *Good overall psychometric properties.* The Verbal, Performance, and Processing Speed Composites and the Full Scale have good reliability, and the Full Scale has adequate validity.

3. *Somewhat useful diagnostic information.* At ages 4-0 to 7-3, the WPPSI–III provides diagnostic information somewhat useful for the assessment of cognitive abilities of preschool and early elementary-school children who are functioning within three standard deviations from the mean (± 3 *SD*). It also provides data likely to be helpful in planning special school programs, perhaps tapping important developmental or maturational factors needed for school success, especially in the lower grades. The Verbal, Performance, and Processing Speed Composites are helpful in clinical and psychoeducational evaluations and aid in the assessment of brain-behavior relationships. However, at ages 2-6 to 3-11, the WPPSI–III provides limited diagnostic information.

4. *Generally good administrative procedures.* The examiner actively probes the child's responses to evaluate the breadth of the child's knowledge and to determine whether the child really knows the answer. The emphasis on probing questions and queries is extremely desirable.

5. *Good manuals and interesting test materials.* The Administration Manual is relatively easy to use, with clear directions and tables in most cases. Examiners are aided by instructions printed in a color that differs from that of other test materials. The Technical Manual presents useful information about the test and is well written. The test materials are interesting to children.

6. *Generally helpful scoring criteria.* Scoring guidelines for the Vocabulary and Similarities subtests detail the rationale for 2-, 1-, and 0-point scores. Several examples demonstrate the application of the scoring principles for items on the Vocabulary, Similarities, and Comprehension subtests. In addition, the guidelines for each Comprehension item provide the general rationale for the correct answer.

7. *Usefulness for children with some disabilities.* You can administer subtests on the Verbal Composite to children who have visual or motor impairments and sub-

tests on the Performance and Processing Speed Composites to children who are hearing impaired if they can understand the directions.

LIMITATIONS

The WPPSI–III also has several limitations.

1. *Severely limited breadth of coverage at ages 2-6 to 3-11.* With only four subtests in the core battery at these ages, the WPPSI–III is essentially a screening instrument, not a comprehensive measure of intellectual ability. The WPPSI–III at these ages does not include measures of memory or quantitative reasoning, which are important components of cognitive development.

2. *Limited breadth of coverage at ages 4-0 to 7-3.* With only seven subtests in the core battery at these ages, the WPPSI–III provides a broader range of coverage than at the younger age levels, but the coverage is still limited. The WPPSI–III at these ages also does not include measures of memory or quantitative reasoning, which are important components of cognitive development.

3. *Failure to provide conversion tables for computing Composite scores and Full Scale IQs when supplemental subtests are substituted for core subtests.* Not only are these conversion tables absent, but the Technical Manual does not give any descriptive statistics for distributions using substitute subtests. (Thus, you should substitute a supplemental subtest for a core subtest only in unusual circumstances and label the results "Estimated" when you report the test results.)

4. *Failure to provide the psychometric basis for the requirement that a child must obtain a certain number of raw scores of 1 in order for a Full Scale IQ to be computed.* What is the justification for the requirement that a child must obtain raw scores of 1 on at least two of the four subtests at ages 2-6 to 3-11 and on at least two Verbal and two Performance subtests at ages 4-0 to 7-3 in order for a Full Scale IQ to be computed? How do we know that other rules would not be equally valid or that this rule provides valid IQs? Although we advise you to follow these rules, it would have been helpful had The Psychological Corporation provided the psychometric justification for these rules.

5. *Limited range of scores for children who are extremely low functioning or children who are extremely high functioning.* The cognitive ability of children who

are functioning below or above three standard deviations from the mean is not adequately assessed by the WPPSI–III.

6. *Variable ranges of subtest scaled scores at ages 4-0 to 7-3.* The extremely variable ranges of from 1 to 19 to 6 to 19 hinder the interpretation process.

7. *Limited criterion validity studies.* We believe that it is poor practice to base information about the criterion validity of the WPPSI–III only on tests published by The Psychological Corporation. The failure to provide information about the relationship between the WPPSI–III and tests of cognitive ability and achievement available from other publishers limits our understanding of the WPPSI–III.

8. *Possible difficulties in scoring responses.* Work with previous editions indicated that Vocabulary, Similarities, and Comprehension may be difficult to score. The Technical Manual presents a study indicating high agreement among four examiners' scores. Although these results are encouraging, additional studies are needed, particularly with diversified samples of children and both student and professional examiners. We recommend that you consult a colleague whenever you are uncertain about scoring responses.

9. *Somewhat large practice effects.* The Performance and Processing Speed Composites have practice effects of about 5 and 6 points, respectively, for retest intervals of less than 9 weeks. Research is needed to determine practice effects over a longer period of time and with special populations. (See Chapter 4 in Sattler, 2001, *Assessment of Children: Cognitive Applications*, for more information about practice effects or repeated evaluations.) Because of the potentially confounding practice effects, carefully consider whether you want to use the WPPSI–III for a retest when you have previously given the test to the child.

10. *Poor quality of some test materials.* The templates on the Coding and Symbol Search subtests are poorly constructed and may rip.

11. *Occasional confusing guidelines.* The directions for subtests that have sample items fail to mention that all children should be given the sample items. Placing several different sample responses on one line separated by semicolons hinders scanning. Directions for scoring multiple responses could be improved. The Administration Manual fails to give the rationale for the correct answers on Picture Concepts, although it does do so for the Comprehension subtest. In addition, some subtests have correct answers not acknowledged in the Administration Manual.

CONCLUDING COMMENT

The WPPSI–III has good standardization, reliability, and concurrent and construct validity and generally useful administrative and scoring guidelines. The Administration Manual and Technical Manual are good, and much thought and preparation have gone into the revision. However, we do not know how well the test will be received. We also need research to evaluate how the changed structure of the WPPSI–III will affect how children are classified, particularly children who are intellectually gifted, children with learning disabilities, and children with mental retardation.

THINKING THROUGH THE ISSUES

1. Why do you think previous editions of the Wechsler tests were so successful?
2. Under what circumstances would you use a supplemental subtest as a substitute for a core subtest?
3. How does having at least 24 different combinations of subtests for computing Full Scale IQs create the potential for abuse? Discuss your answer.
4. Why do you think the Verbal subtests are better measures of *g* than are the Performance and Processing Speed subtests?
5. What can you do to develop skill at properly administering the WPPSI–III?
6. What limitations of the WPPSI–III might affect its clinical and psychoeducational usefulness?
7. Do you believe that the WPPSI–III is a good measure of intelligence? Discuss your answer.
8. What other kinds of subtests would you like to see in the WPPSI–IV?
9. Is the WPPSI–III culturally biased or culturally fair? Discuss your answer.

SUMMARY

1. The WPPSI–III was published in 2002, 13 years after the previous edition, called the WPPSI–R.
2. The WPPSI–III is divided into two broad age groups: ages 2-6 to 3-11 and ages 4-0 to 7-3.
3. Subtests are designated as one of three types.
4. *Core subtests* are used in the computation of the Verbal, Performance, and Full Scale IQ.
5. *Supplemental subtests* are used as replacements for the core subtests or to obtain additional information about cognitive functioning.
6. *Optional subtests* are used to obtain additional useful information about cognitive functioning, but are not used as replacements for core subtests.
7. The age group from 2-6 to 3-11 has the following four core subtests: (a) Receptive Vocabulary and Information form the Verbal Composite, and (b) Block Design and Object Assembly form the Performance Composite.
8. There is also one supplemental subtest, Picture Naming, which can be substituted for Receptive Vocabulary and, if administered, forms, with Receptive Vocabulary, the General Language Composite.
9. The age group from 4-0 to 7-3 has the following seven core subtests: (a) Information, Vocabulary, and Word Reasoning, which form the Verbal Composite, (b) Block Design, Matrix Reasoning, and Picture Concepts, which form the Performance Composite, and (c) Coding, which is in neither the Verbal nor the Performance Composite.
10. There are also five supplemental subtests: Similarities, Comprehension, Object Assembly, Picture Completion, and Symbol Search. Symbol Search, if administered, combines with Coding to form the Processing Speed Composite.
11. The optional subtests, Receptive Vocabulary and Picture Naming, cannot be used as substitutes for any subtests at ages 4-0 to 7-3; however, if administered, they form the General Language Composite.

Standardization

12. The WPPSI–III was standardized on 1,700 children who were selected to represent children in the United States.

Standard Scores, Scaled Scores, and Test-Age Equivalents

13. The WPPSI–III, like the WISC–IV and WAIS–III, uses standard scores ($M = 100$, $SD = 15$) for the Verbal IQ, Performance IQ, Full Scale IQ, Processing Speed Quotient, and General Language Composite, and scaled scores ($M = 10$, $SD = 3$) for the 14 subtests.
14. Proration should be avoided whenever possible because it introduces unknown measurement error.
15. Test-age equivalents are obtained directly from the raw scores on each subtest.

Reliability

16. The WPPSI–III has good reliability. For example, the three Composites and the Full Scale have internal consistency reliability coefficients of .86 or above over the entire age range covered in the standardization group.

17. Average internal consistency reliabilities are .95 for the Verbal IQ, .93 for the Performance IQ, .89 for the Processing Speed Quotient, and .96 for the Full Scale IQ.

18. Average internal consistency reliabilities range from .83 for Symbol Search to .95 for Similarities.

19. The average SEMs in standard-score points are 3.35 for the Verbal IQ, 4.15 for the Performance IQ, 4.94 for the Processing Speed Quotient, and 2.92 for the Full Scale IQ.

20. The average SEMs for the subtests in scaled-score points range from .69 for Similarities to 1.23 for Symbol Search.

21. Test-retest reliability coefficients indicate that the WPPSI–III generally provides stable Composite scores and Full Scale IQs.

22. In the total test-retest sample, average stability coefficients for the subtests ranged from a low of .61 for Picture Concepts to a high of .85 for Picture Naming. The subtests are less stable than the three individual Composites and the Full Scale.

23. Mean increases from the first to the second testing were 2.8 points for the Verbal IQ, 5.0 points for the Performance IQ, 6.2 points for the Processing Speed Quotient, and 5.2 points for the Full Scale IQ.

24. When tested a second time, children are likely to have greater gains on the Performance and Processing Speed Composites than on the Verbal Composite.

25. From first to second administration, Picture Completion showed the largest increase (1.4 points), while Vocabulary showed the smallest increase (.3 point).

26. Use the child's specific age group—not the average of the 11 age groups—to obtain the most accurate confidence interval.

Validity

27. Studies correlating the WPPSI–III with the WPPSI–R, WISC–III, WISC–IV, and other measures of intelligence, achievement, memory, emotional intelligence, and adaptive behavior indicate that the WPPSI–III has satisfactory criterion validity.

28. The mean WPPSI–III FSIQ was .6 point lower than the mean WPPSI–R FSIQ.

29. The mean WPPSI–III FSIQ was 4.9 points lower than the mean WISC–III FSIQ.

30. The mean WPPSI–III FSIQ and mean WISC–IV FSIQ differed by .2 point.

31. The mean WPPSI–III FSIQ was .9 point lower than the mean BSID–II Mental Composite.

32. The mean WPPSI–III FSIQ was 1.6 points lower than the mean DAS GCA.

Intercorrelations for Subtests and Composites

33. At ages 2-6 to 3-11, intercorrelations between the five subtests range from a low of .36 (Block Design and Receptive Vocabulary) to a high of .74 (Information and Picture Naming). The Verbal subtests have higher intercorrelations than do the Performance subtests. Information has the highest correlation with the Full Scale (.83), while Block Design has the lowest correlation with the Full Scale (.71).

34. At ages 4-0 to 7-3, intercorrelations between the 14 subtests range from a low of .27 (Coding and Picture Naming) to a high of .74 (Information and Word Reasoning). The Verbal subtests have higher intercorrelations than do the Performance subtests. Information has the highest correlation with the Full Scale (.82), while Object Assembly has the lowest correlation with the Full Scale (.55).

Demographic Variables

35. The mean Full Scale IQ was 3.22 points higher for girls than for boys. The most pronounced difference was on Processing Speed, where the mean Quotient was 6.38 points higher for girls than for boys.

36. The mean Full Scale IQ of Euro American children was about 10.33 points higher than that of African American children and 11.72 points higher than that of Hispanic American children. However, the mean Full Scale IQ of Asian American children was 1.86 points higher than that of Euro American children.

37. The mean Full Scale IQ of children whose parents had graduated from college was about 22 points higher than that of children whose parents had an eighth-grade education or less.

38. The mean Full Scale IQ of children from the Northeast was about 1 to 5 points higher than that of children from other regions.

Factor Analysis

39. At ages 2-6 to 3-11, the results of a factor analysis indicated that a two-factor model best describes the WPPSI–III: Verbal (Information, Receptive Vocabulary, and Picture Naming) and Performance (Block Design and Object Assembly).
40. The Verbal factor describes a hypothesized verbal-related ability underlying the Composite. The Verbal factor measures verbal knowledge and understanding obtained primarily through informal education and reflects the application of verbal skills to new situations. Information, Receptive Vocabulary, and Picture Naming have high loadings on the Verbal factor.
41. The Performance factor describes a hypothesized performance-related ability underlying the Composite. The Performance factor measures the ability to interpret and organize visually perceived material and to generate and test hypotheses related to problem solutions. Block Design and Object Assembly have high loadings on the Performance factor.
42. At ages 4-0 to 7-3, the results of a factor analysis indicated that a three-factor model best describes the WPPSI–III: Verbal (Information, Vocabulary, Word Reasoning, Similarities, and Comprehension), Performance (Block Design, Matrix Reasoning, Picture Completion, and Object Assembly), and Processing Speed (Coding and Symbol Search).
43. The Verbal factor describes a hypothesized verbal-related ability underlying the Composite. The Verbal factor measures verbal knowledge and understanding obtained primarily through informal education and reflects the application of verbal skills to new situations. Information, Vocabulary, Word Reasoning, Similarities, and Comprehension have high loadings on the Verbal factor, followed by Picture Concepts, which has a moderate loading (but only at four age levels and for the total group). Verbal mediation, perhaps, may be involved in performance on Picture Concepts.
44. The Performance factor describes a hypothesized performance-related ability underlying the Composite. The Performance factor measures the ability to interpret and organize visually perceived material and to generate and test hypotheses related to problem solutions. Block Design, Matrix Reasoning, Picture Completion, and Object Assembly have high loadings on the Performance factor. Coding and Symbol Search also have moderate to high loadings on the Performance factor at ages 4-6 to 4-

11. Picture Concepts, which is placed in the Performance Composite, has loadings below .30 at three age levels (4-0 to 4-5, 5-0 to 5-5, and 7-0 to 7-3) and for the total group.
45. The Processing Speed factor describes a hypothesized processing speed ability underlying the Composite. Processing Speed measures the ability to process visually perceived nonverbal information quickly, with concentration and rapid eye-hand coordination being important components. Coding and Symbol Search have high loadings on Processing Speed at every age and for the total group, except at ages 4-6 to 4-11, where the loadings are negative.
46. The factor analytic findings show different patterns of loadings at different ages.
47. At ages 2-6 to 3-11, the WPPSI–III subtests form two clusters with respect to the measurement of g: Information, Picture Naming, and Receptive Vocabulary are good measures of g, while Object Assembly and Block Design are fair measures of g.
48. At ages 4-0 to 7-3, the WPPSI–III subtests form two clusters with respect to the measurement of g: Word Reasoning, Information, Vocabulary, Similarities, and Comprehension are good measures of g, while Picture Completion, Matrix Reasoning, Block Design, Symbol Search, Picture Concepts, Object Assembly, and Coding are fair measures of g.
49. Many subtests possess sufficient specificity at some ages to justify interpretation of specific subtest functions.

Range of Subtest and Process Score Scaled Scores

50. At ages 2-6 to 3-11, the range of scaled scores from 1 to 19 is available for most subtests at each age group.
51. At ages 4-0 to 7-3, the range of scaled scores from 1 to 19 is available for 7 of the 14 subtests.

Range of Full Scale IQS

52. At ages 2-6 to 3-11, the range of WPPSI–III Full Scale IQs is 45 to 155. Compute the Full Scale IQ only when the child obtains raw scores greater than 0 on at least two of the four core subtests.
53. At ages 4-0 to 7-3, the range of WPPSI–III Full Scale IQs is 45 to 160. Compute the Full Scale IQ only when the child obtains raw scores greater than 0 on at least (a) two of the three subtests in the Verbal Composite and (b) two of the three subtests in the Performance Composite.

Comparison of the WPPSI–III and WPPSI–R

54. The WPPSI–III and WPPSI–R have considerably different structures.

55. The WPPSI–III has four core subtests at ages 2-6 to 3-11 and seven core subtests at ages 4-0 to 7-3. In contrast, the WPPSI–R has 10 core subtests at ages 3-0 to 7-3.

56. Only 16.7% of the WPPSI–R items are retained in the WPPSI–III.

57. A study of the pattern of subtest scores on the two tests, taking into account the different structures of the two tests, and the case history will guide you in interpreting test-retest changes from the WPPSI–R to the WPPSI–III.

Administering the WPPSI–III

58. To become proficient in administering the WPPSI–III, you must master the procedures described in the Administration Manual.

59. Areas on which you will need to focus are preparing for the session, following the subtest sequence, using queries and prompts, starting at the appropriate place, using a reverse sequence, following the start-point scoring rule, following the discontinue-point scoring rule, awarding perfect scores, awarding points for unadministered items, repeating instructions and items, giving additional help, determining how long to wait for a child's response, following discontinue criteria, following appropriate scoring procedures, scoring spoiled responses, using testing-of-limits, and making subtest substitutions.

60. The start-point scoring rule states that the child receives full credit for all items located below the start-point item and subsequent item on which perfect scores were obtained.

61. The discontinue-point scoring rule states that the child does not receive credit for any items above the last discontinue-point item.

62. In a reverse sequence, continue to administer items even after the discontinue criterion has been met until you reach item 1 or until the child has perfect scores on two consecutive items.

63. Conduct testing-of-limits only after you have administered the entire test following standard procedures.

64. Testing-of-limits may invalidate repeated evaluations and should be used cautiously.

65. Substitutions should be based on clinical need or a similar appropriate reason, not your own preferences or convenience.

66. We advise that substitutions be avoided whenever a specific IQ or Composite score needs to be used for decision-making purposes.

67. Because the Full Scale IQ tables are based on the core subtests only, scores derived using one or two supplemental subtests have an unknown degree of additional measurement error.

68. Overall, administer the subtests in the recommended order, start each subtest with the appropriate item, follow the instructions in the Administration Manual for administering each subtest, score each item, follow the reverse procedure if needed, follow the discontinue criterion, add the item scores for each subtest, complete the Record Form, and check all of your work.

Short Forms

69. Short forms of the WPPSI–III may be used for (a) screening purposes, when the short form may be followed by administration of the rest of the test, (b) research purposes, or (c) obtaining an estimate of the child's intellectual status when a precise IQ is not required.

70. If you need a classification for a clinical or psychoeducational purpose or need information for programming decisions, do not use a short form.

Choosing Between the WPPSI–III and the WISC–IV and Between the WPPSI–III and the BSID–II

71. Because of its breadth of coverage, we recommend that at the overlapping ages (6-0 to 7-3), the WISC–IV be used instead of the WPPSI–III with children at all ability levels.

72. We recommend that at the overlapping ages, the BSID–II be used with children with below-average ability and that the WPPSI–III be used with children with average or above-average ability.

Administering the WPPSI–III to Children with Disabilities

73. You will need to evaluate the sensory-motor abilities of children with disabilities before you administer the WPPSI–III. If you find that a child has a visual, hearing, attentional, or motor problem that may interfere with his or her ability to take one or more of the subtests, do not use these subtests in computing Composite scores or a Full Scale IQ.

74. If you administer the WPPSI–III to a child with a physical disability, you should not provide special cues. If your modifications go beyond simply per-

mitting the child to respond in his or her preferred mode of communication or using alternative procedures to present the items, the results may be invalid.

75. When you use modifications, consider the resulting score only as a rough estimate of the score that the child might obtain under standardized procedures.

Assets

76. The assets of the WPPSI–III include its excellent standardization, good overall psychometric properties, somewhat useful diagnostic information, generally good administrative procedures, good manuals and interesting test materials, generally helpful scoring criteria, and usefulness for children with some disabilities.

Limitations

77. The limitations of the WPPSI–III include severely limited breadth or coverage at ages 2-6 to 3-11, limited breadth of coverage at ages 4-0 to 7-3, failure to provide conversion tables for computing Composite scores and Full Scale IQs when supplemental subtests are substituted for core subtests, failure to provide the psychometric basis for the requirement that a child must obtain a certain number of raw scores of 1 in order for a Full Scale IQ to be computed, limited range of scores for children who are extremely high or low functioning, variable ranges of subtest scaled scores at ages 4-0 to 7-3, limited criterion validity studies, possible difficulties in scoring responses, somewhat large practice effects, poor quality of some test materials, and occasional confusing guidelines.

Concluding Comment

78. The WPPSI–III has good standardization, reliability, and concurrent and construct validity and generally useful administrative and scoring guidelines. The Administration Manual and Technical Manual are good, and much thought and preparation have gone into the revision. However, we do not know how well the test will be received.

KEY TERMS, CONCEPTS, AND NAMES

Testing-of-limits on the WPPSI–III (p. 190)

Subtest substitution on the WPPSI–III (p. 190)

Potential problems in administering the WPPSI–III (p. 191)

Overall guidelines for administering the WPPSI–III (p. 192)

Short forms of the WPPSI–III (p. 192)

Choosing between the WPPSI–III and the WISC–IV (p. 193)

Choosing between the WPPSI–III and the BSID–II (p. 194)

Administering the WPPSI–III to children with disabilities (p. 194)

Assets of the WPPSI–III (p. 195)

Limitations of the WPPSI–III (p. 196)

STUDY QUESTIONS

1. Discuss the WPPSI–III. Include in your discussion the following issues: standardization, types of scores, test-age equivalents, reliability, and validity.

2. Describe and interpret the intercorrelations between WPPSI–III subtests and scales.

3. Discuss demographic characteristics of the WPPSI–III standardization sample.

4. Describe and interpret WPPSI–III factor analytic findings.

5. Discuss the range of subtest scaled scores and Full Scale IQs on the WPPSI–III.

6. Compare the WPPSI–III and the WPPSI–R.

7. Discuss administrative considerations for the WPPSI–III.

8. Identify common administrative and scoring errors on the WPPSI–III, and describe what measures you could take to minimize and avoid these errors.

9. Discuss the substitution of supplemental subtests for core subtests.

10. Discuss WPPSI–III short forms, including their value and limitations.

11. For the overlapping ages, explain how you would go about choosing between the WPPSI–III and the WISC–IV, and between the WPPSI–III and the BSID–II. What recommendations would you make regarding which test to choose?

12. Identify the most important factors to consider in administering the WPPSI–III to children with disabilities.

13. Discuss the assets and limitations of the WPPSI–III.

6

WPPSI–III CORE SUBTESTS

The quality of our thoughts is bordered on all sides by our facility with language.

—Michael Straczynski

Goals and Objectives

This chapter is designed to enable you to do the following:

- Critically evaluate the seven WPPSI–III core subtests

- Describe the rationales, factor analytic findings, reliability and correlational highlights, and administrative and interpretive considerations for the seven WPPSI–III core subtests

This is the first of two chapters that provide information to help you administer, score, and interpret the WPPSI–III subtests. This chapter covers the seven WPPSI–III core subtests for ages 4-0 to 7-3, while the next chapter covers the five supplemental subtests and two optional subtests for ages 4-0 to 7-3. For ages 2-6 to 3-11, two of the four core subtests (Block Design and Information) are also core subtests for ages 4-0 to 7-3, while one of the other two core subtests (Object Assembly) is a supplemental subtest at ages 4-0 to 7-3 and the other core subtest (Receptive Vocabulary) is an optional subtest at ages 4-0 to 7-3. The one supplemental subtest (Picture Naming) at ages 2-6 to 3-11 is also an optional subtest at ages 4-0 to 7-3.

Included in these two chapters are the rationale, factor analytic findings, reliability and correlational highlights, administrative guidelines, and interpretive suggestions for each subtest. The factor analytic findings discussed in the two chapters are based on a principal factor analysis that we conducted based on the data presented in the Technical Manual (also see Chapter 5). The reliability and correlational findings reported in the two chapters are also based on the Technical Manual. Reliabilities for the Coding and Symbol Search subtests are test-retest correlations, whereas those for the remaining 12 subtests are split-half correlations corrected by the Spearman-Brown formula. The suggestions for administration are based on the Administration Manual, while the interpretive suggestions are based on clinical considerations.

Table C-2 in Appendix C summarizes (a) the abilities purportedly measured by each WPPSI–III subtest (along with the abilities in the Cattell-Horn-Carroll [CHC] model), (b) background factors influencing performance, (c) implications of high and low subtest scaled scores, and (d) instructional implications. Table C-2 deserves careful study because it is especially useful for report writing. Also see Tables C-3 and C-4 in Appendix C, which describe the Wechsler subtests associated with the CHC model.

Recognize that the standard administration of all WPPSI–III subtests requires the child to hear, pay attention, listen, understand instructions, and retain the instructions while solving problems. In addition, several subtests also require the child to have adequate vision. In addition, Block Design, Coding, and Symbol Search require the child to have adequate fine-motor skills. Coding is the only subtest where additional points are awarded for speed. For example, a child who has a perfect performance and completes Coding in 85 seconds or less receives 6 additional raw-score points.

Many of the WPPSI–III subtests have enough subtest specificity (i.e., ample or adequate) at most ages (see Table 5-14 in Chapter 5) to provide reliable estimates of specific abilities—or at least to permit development of hypotheses about the underlying cognitive functions that the subtests may measure.

The best estimates of abilities are provided by the Full Scale, followed by the Verbal Composite and the Performance Composite. For example, the Full Scale IQ, derived from a combination of four subtests at ages 2-6 to 3-11 and seven subtests at ages 4-0 to 7-3, provides the best estimate of general ability. The Verbal IQ, derived from a combination of two Verbal subtests at ages 2-6 to 3-11 and three Verbal subtests at ages 4-0 to 7-3, yields more accurate information about a child's verbal skills than does a single Verbal subtest, such as Vocabulary. Similarly, the Performance IQ, derived from a combination of two Performance subtests at ages 2-6 to 3-11 and three Performance subtests at ages 4-0 to 7-3, yields more accurate information about a child's nonverbal skills than does a single Performance subtest, such as Block Design. Finally, the Processing Speed Quotient, composed of Coding and Symbol Search, provides more information about processing speed (which includes immediate short-term memory and encoding ability) than does either of the two Processing Speed component subtests.

As noted in Chapter 5, Table D-2 in Appendix D is a useful checklist that will help in learning to administer the WPPSI–III. The Administrative Guidelines provided for each subtest in this and the following chapter are related to Table D-2 in Appendix D. The Administrative Guidelines represent an extended version of the brief checklist in Table D-2 in Appendix D.

Note that the reverse sequence rule discussed in this and the following chapter applies only when the subtest is started with an item higher than item 1.

On the Record Form, record a "(Q)" when you query a response and record a "(P)" when you prompt for an additional response.

As you read about each subtest, you will encounter questions posed to guide you in your test administration. Answering these questions will help you evaluate and interpret the child's performance. In addition to the child's scores, consider the quality of the child's responses, style of responding, handling of frustration, problem-solving approach, fine-motor skills, and pattern of successes and failures.

If you conduct testing-of-limits, remember that the results are to be used to guide your understanding of the child's abilities, and not for computing scores obtained under standard administration. If there is a need to retest using the WPPSI–III within a 3-year period, testing-of-limits is not advisable.

BLOCK DESIGN

Block Design, a core Performance subtest at all ages of the test, requires the child to reproduce designs, using one-color blocks for items 1 to 10 (Part A) and two-color blocks for items 11 to 20 (Part B). The blocks for items 1 to 10 have either red or white surfaces. The blocks for items 11 to 20 have red surfaces, white surfaces, and surfaces divided diagonally into half red and half white. The subtest contains 20 items and is timed. The child uses blocks to assemble a design identical to a model constructed by the examiner (items 1 to 12) or to a picture of a two-dimensional, red-and-white design (items 13 to 20). The subtest is somewhat difficult to administer and score.

Rationale

Block Design requires that the child perceive and analyze forms by breaking down a whole (the design) into its parts and then assembling the components into a design identical to the one shown in the model or the picture. This process is called analysis and synthesis. To succeed, the child must use visual organization and visual-motor coordination. Success also involves the application of logic and reasoning to spatial relationship problems. Consequently, you can consider Block Design to be a nonverbal concept-formation task requiring perceptual organization, spatial visualization, and abstract conceptualization. It also can be viewed as a constructional task involving spatial relations and figure-ground separation.

Different strategies can be used to assemble the blocks (Rozencwajg, 1991; Rozencwajg & Corroyer, 2002). One is a *global strategy* in which the design is viewed as a whole and not differentiated into units. The child assembles blocks in a stepwise trial-and-error procedure; with this strategy, the child does not analyze the components of the model. The order of placing the blocks is independent of the pattern. Children look frequently at the design to make the pattern.

A second is an *analytical strategy* in which the child forms a representation of the model and then decomposes the design into the appropriate number of blocks. Once the blocks have been separated, the child selects and orients them before placing them in the design. The order of placing the blocks is independent of the pattern. Children look frequently at the design to make the pattern.

A third is a *synthetic strategy* in which the placement of the blocks is dependent on the pattern in the design. In this strategy, the gestalts in the block patterns govern the child's placement of blocks. "A gestalt is a form or structure that cannot be reduced to the mere juxtaposition of elements; it has a specific quality that is not found in any of its constituents" (Rozencwajg & Corroyer, 2002, p. 3). The blocks are placed in an order that reflects the gestalts in the design. Children may not need to look frequently at the design to make the pattern.

A child's performance on Block Design may be affected by motor skill and vision. Do not interpret inadequate performance as direct evidence of inadequate visual form and pattern perception, because the ability to discriminate block designs (i.e., to perceive the designs accurately at a recognition level) may be intact even when the ability to reproduce the designs is impaired.

Factor Analytic Findings

At ages 2-6 to 3-11, Block Design is a fair measure of g (26% of its variance can be attributed to g). It contributes moderately to the Performance factor (average loading = .61). Subtest specificity is ample at all age groups from 2-6 to 3-11.

At ages 4-0 to 7-3, Block Design is a fair measure of g (44% of its variance can be attributed to g). It contributes moderately to the Performance factor (average loading = .62). Subtest specificity is ample at ages 4-0 to 4-11 and 5-6 to 7-3 and adequate at ages 5-0 to 5-5.

Reliability and Correlational Highlights

Block Design is a reliable subtest (r_{xx} = .84), with reliability coefficients at or above .75 at each age (range of .75 to .91).

At ages 2-6 to 3-11, Block Design correlates better with Information (r = .42) and with Object Assembly (r = .41) than with any of the other subtests. It has a moderately high correlation with the Full Scale IQ (r = .71), a high correlation with the Performance IQ (r = .84), and a moderately low correlation with the Verbal IQ (r = .42).

At ages 4-0 to 7-3, Block Design correlates better with Object Assembly (r = .53) and with Matrix Reasoning (r = .51) than with any of the other subtests. It has a moderately high correlation with the Full Scale IQ

(r = .72), a high correlation with the Performance IQ (r = .80), and a moderate correlation with both the Verbal IQ (r = .52) and the Processing Speed Quotient (r = .50).

Administrative Guidelines

The following administrative guidelines for the Block Design subtest must be followed carefully.

Background Considerations

1. Clear the area on your desk that you use to administer Block Design.
2. Read the instructions verbatim.
3. Read the instructions clearly.
4. Use a stopwatch quietly, if possible.
5. Keep the stopwatch on the table, if needed, but out of the child's reach, and handle it unobtrusively.
6. Repeat the instructions if the child asks or has not responded within 5 to 10 seconds, unless it is clear that the child is considering a response.
7. When explaining the task, only clarify the instructions by pointing to the model or picture as you speak to the child. Do not explain the construction to the child.
8. Use the appropriate instructions for item 6 depending on whether the child starts the subtest with item 1 or 6 (e.g., do not say "Let's play with blocks" for item 6 when the child starts with item 1).
9. Make sure that the child is seated directly in front of the table.
10. Show the different sides of the red-and-white blocks as you read the instructions for Part B, which precedes items 11 to 20.
11. Place the appropriate number of blocks in front of the child for items 1 to 20 (item 1, two red blocks; items 2 and 3, three red blocks; item 4, two red blocks; item 5, one white block and one red block; item 6, one white block and two red blocks; item 7, one red block and one white block; item 8, three red blocks; items 9 and 10, two white blocks and two red blocks; items 11 and 12, two red-and-white blocks; items 13 to 20, four red-and-white blocks). You will also need the same number of blocks for each item to assemble the model. The Record Form shows the number of blocks needed for each item. Although the Administration Manual simply says, "Place the appropriate blocks in front of the child," we suggest that you randomly place the blocks for each item.

12. Disassemble the models as noted in the Administration Manual.
13. Place the intact model or Stimulus Book 1 and blocks properly.
   a. When demonstrating a design, place the intact model or Stimulus Book 1 about 7 inches from the edge of the table closest to the child.
   b. For a right-handed child, place the intact model or Stimulus Book 1 slightly to the left of the child's midline.
   c. For a left-handed child, place the intact model or Stimulus Book 1 slightly to the right of the child's midline.
   d. If unable to determine whether the child is right- or left-handed, place the intact model or Stimulus Book 1 directly in front of the child.
   e. Place the coil-bound edge of Stimulus Book 1 facing the child for items 13 to 20 so that the book is completely flat when it is opened, and then open it to the appropriate page.
   f. When placing or scrambling the blocks for items 11 to 20, be sure that only one block has a red-and-white side facing up.
14. Turn the pages of Stimulus Book 1 toward the child as you administer the items.
15. Use only blocks as models for items 1 to 12, use blocks *and* a picture as models on item 13, and use *only* pictures as models on items 14 to 20.
16. On items 1 to 12, leave the model intact as the child constructs the designs.
17. Follow the appropriate procedure for item 13. Place Stimulus Book 1 toward the child, with the item 13 picture exposed. After building the model for item 13, disassemble it, scramble the blocks, place the blocks in front of the child, and leave the picture facing the child.
18. Scramble the blocks between designs.
19. Remove all unnecessary blocks from the child's view.
20. Do not permit the child to rotate Stimulus Book 1.
21. Time correctly.
   a. Begin timing after the last word of the instructions.
   b. Use the following time limits: 30 seconds maximum for items 1 to 7; 60 seconds maximum for items 8 to 13; 90 seconds maximum for items 14 to 20.
   c. When in doubt as to whether the child is finished with the task, say, "Tell me when you have finished."
   d. Stop timing when the child is obviously finished with an item, when the child indicates with gestures

that the item is completed, or when the time limit is reached.

e. Allow a few additional seconds after the time limit if the child is nearing completion of the design.

f. Do not stop timing once timing has begun, even to clarify instructions.

22. Give appropriate prompts.

a. One time only for items on Part A and one time only for items on Part B, if the child rotates or reverses a design, say, "See, it goes this way" and correct the child's design.

b. If the child tries to duplicate the sides of the model on items 11 to 20, point to the top faces of the blocks and say something like "Only the tops of the blocks need to be the same."

23. Administer trials correctly.

a. When demonstrating trials 1 and 2 on items 1 to 6, put the blocks together slowly. Be careful not to cover the blocks with your hand; the child needs to see what you are doing. Make the designs so that they are in the appropriate direction for the child. This means that you will be making the designs upside down. Do not make a design right side up and then turn the whole thing around to face the child.

b. Administer a second trial on items 1 to 6 if the child makes an incorrect construction on the first trial.

c. Do not give a second trial on items 7 to 20.

Starting Considerations

24. Start with the appropriate item.

a. The ages listed under "Start" on pages 54 and 176 of the Administration Manual are always intended to be inclusive; thus, ages 2–3 means children 2-6 to 3-11 years of age and ages 4–7 means children 4-0 to 7-3 years of age.

b. The starting ages on the Record Form are also inclusive.

c. Children 2 to 3 years of age (and older children suspected of having intellectual deficiency) start with item 1.

d. Children 4 to 7 years of age (not suspected of having intellectual deficiency) start with item 6.

Reverse Sequence

25. If necessary, administer the items in reverse sequence as directed in the Administration Manual.

a. The instructions on page 54 of the Administration Manual under the heading "Reverse" pertain to children who begin the subtest with item 6.

b. If the child (a) does not obtain full credit on the start-point item or (b) obtains full credit on the start-point item and a score of 0 on the next item, administer the items in reverse sequence.

c. Continue the reverse sequence until the child has perfect scores on two consecutive items or until item 1 has been administered, even if the discontinue criterion is met.

d. When there is a reverse sequence, the discontinue criterion is not met, and either there are two consecutive items with perfect scores or item 1 is administered, continue administration with the item after the last start-point item.

e. The instructions for item 6, trial 2 on page 63 of the Administration Manual are *incorrect* in the first printing of the Administration Manual (personal communication, Diane Coalson, Senior Research Director, The Psychological Corporation, October 16, 2002). As you read earlier, you should administer items in reverse order if the child does not obtain a perfect score on the start-point item and the next item. A perfect score on item 6 of the Block Design subtest is 2 points. If the child starts with item 6 and fails trial 1 but passes trial 2, he or she receives 1 point. Because 1 point is not a perfect score, the reverse sequence rule comes into play. The Administration Manual says, however, that if the child—after failing trial 1—passes trial 2 of item 6, you should "proceed to the next item" (Wechsler, 2002a, p. 63). This statement is wrong. The instructions in the Administration Manual should state the following: "If the child started with Item 6, administer preceding items in reverse sequence until the child obtains perfect scores on two consecutive items."

Discontinue Considerations

26. Count items administered in reverse sequence toward the discontinue criterion.

27. Discontinue the subtest when three consecutive scores of 0 are obtained, unless the consecutive 0's are obtained during a reverse sequence and (a) item 1 has not been reached or (b) the child has not obtained perfect scores on two consecutive items.

28. Once the subtest is completed, remove Stimulus Book 1 and the blocks from the child's view.

Scoring Guidelines

29. Score the items using the following guidelines:

a. Items 1 to 6 are scored 0 (failure on trials 1 and 2), 1 (correct construction on trial 2), or 2 (correct construction on trial 1).

b. Items 7 to 20 are scored 0 or 2.

c. For items 1 to 10, give the child credit if there are rotations of 30° or more in the designs when the designs are assembled correctly.

d. For items 11 to 20, do not give the child credit if there are rotations of 30° or more in the designs when the designs are assembled correctly.

e. Give the child credit if the designs are assembled correctly and the gaps or misalignments are ¼" or less.

f. Do not give the child credit if the designs are assembled correctly and the gaps or misalignments are more than ¼".

g. When the child earns perfect scores on the first two items at the start point or in a reversal, award full credit for all preceding items, regardless of the child's performance on these items if they have been administered.

h. Award no points for any items beyond the last score of 0 required for the discontinue criterion to be met, regardless of the child's performance on these items if they have been administered.

i. Do not award credit for any items completed after the time limit has expired.

Record Form

30. For each item (and for each trial on items 1 to 6), record the completion time in seconds in the Completion Time column. To assist you in recording the times for the two trials on items 1 to 6, draw a horizontal line dividing the six Completion Time boxes in half. Label the upper half of the box "Trial 1" and the lower half "Trial 2."

31. Note or sketch the incorrect design arrangements in the Incorrect Design column, if desired.

32. When the design is correct, make a check mark over the picture of the blocks in the Constructed Design column, if desired.

33. Note rotations with an arrow and the amount of rotation (in degrees) in the Constructed Design column, if desired.

34. Circle Y or N in the Correct Design column. Circle Y for items that are correctly assembled, even if they are (a) correctly completed after the time limit or (b) rotated but completed within the time limit. Circle N for items that are incorrectly assembled.

35. Circle 0, 1, or 2 in the Score column.

a. For items 1 to 6, circle 0 in the Score column when the child makes incorrect constructions on both trials.

b. For items 1 to 6, circle 1 in the Score column when the child makes a correct construction on the second trial.

c. For items 1 to 6, circle 2 in the Score column when the child makes a correct construction on the first trial.

d. For items 7 to 20, circle 0 in the Score column when the child makes an incorrect construction.

e. For items 7 to 20, circle 2 in the Score column when the child makes a correct construction.

f. For all items, circle 0 in the Score column for a correct construction assembled after the time limit.

g. For items 11 to 20, circle 0 in the Score column for rotations of 30° or more.

h. For all items, circle 0 in the Score column for gaps or misalignments greater than ¼".

36. To note the points awarded for items not administered below the first two items with perfect scores, put a slash mark in the Score column over the item preceding the first two items with perfect scores and write the numerals for these points.

37. Add the points, including the points for correct answers and the points for items not administered before the first two perfect scores, but not for items administered after the last discontinue item or for items completed after the time limit.

38. Enter the Total Raw Score in the shaded box.

The instructions on pages 60 and 62 of the Administration Manual for an incorrect response on item 1, trial 2 or on item 2, trial 2 say, "Proceed to the next appropriate item if the discontinuance criterion has not been met." The discontinuance criterion cannot be reached for items 1 and 2 if item 1 is the start-point item.

The Administration Manual on page 58 says that in the Incorrect Design column you may place a check mark through the grid for correct constructions. *We advise you not to put a check mark for a correct assembly in the column labeled "Incorrect Design."* It would be difficult to defend this procedure if you were questioned about the Record Form in a legal proceeding because it appears contradictory to place a check mark signaling a correct construction in a column headed "Incorrect Design."

Interpretive Suggestions

The following questions are useful to guide your observation of the child's performance on the Block Design subtest.

• Is the child hasty and impulsive or deliberate and

careful?

- Does the child slowly and methodically check each block with the design or rarely check?
- Does the child quit easily or become frustrated when faced with possible failure, or does the child persist and keep on working even after the time limit is reached?
- Does the child use only one approach to make the designs, or does the child alter the approach as the need arises?
- Does the child use a slow approach or a rapid trial-and-error approach to make the designs?
- Is the child excessively concerned with aligning the blocks precisely?
- Does the child study the designs first, before attempting to construct them?
- Does the child appear to have a plan when assembling the blocks?
- Does the child understand the principle of using individual blocks to construct the designs?
- Does the child try to place the blocks on the picture of the design on items 13 to 20?
- Does the child express concerns about differences between blocks?
- Does the child interpret white portions of the design card as open spaces in the assembled designs?
- Does the child use a solid red or solid white block surface for a red-and-white surface?
- Does the child say that the constructed designs are correct when, in fact, they are not?
- Are the child's designs correct but rotated? If so, how much are the designs usually rotated?
- Does the child rotate single blocks? If so, how many degrees are the individual blocks usually rotated?
- Does the child rotate a row of blocks at the bottom when the blocks are in the wrong direction, or does the child start the entire design over again?
- Does the child show any indications of fine-motor difficulties such as tremor or clumsiness?
- Does the child tend to construct the designs using a sequential, block-by-block approach or a more random, haphazard approach?
- Does the child use a left-to-right approach or the less common right-to-left or bottom-to-top approach?
- Does the child make internal detail errors or loss of configuration errors?
- Does the child make errors when the grid lines are removed from the stimulus pictures? Note that items 13 and 14 have grid lines while items 15 to 20 do not.
- Does the child assist you by shuffling the blocks or turning the pages of Stimulus Book 1?
- Does the child describe what he or she is doing with the blocks?
- Is the child overly concerned with speed or accuracy?
- Is the child impulsive, trying to begin before being told to do so or changing blocks after saying that the designs are done?
- Does the child offer to put the blocks back in the box after the task is completed?

Excessive fumbling or failure to check the pattern may indicate anxiety. Visuosensory difficulties may be indicated if the child moves or twists to improve perspective on the design or if the child leaves space between the blocks in the assembled design. Try to differentiate between excessive cautiousness as a personality style and excessive slowness as a possible indication of depression or boredom. Children who continually recheck their work with the model may be revealing insecurities or obsessive tendencies.

High scores on the Block Design subtest may indicate good spatial orientation in conjunction with speed, accuracy, and persistence; good visual-motor-spatial integration; good conceptualizing, analyzing, and synthesizing skills; good nonverbal reasoning ability; good use of trial-and-error methods to solve problems; good hand-eye coordination; good ability to evaluate a problem quickly and accurately; good attention to detail; or good motivation.

Low scores on the Block Design subtest may indicate poor visual-motor-spatial integration, visual-perceptual problems, poor spatial orientation, poor analyzing and synthesizing ability, poor nonverbal reasoning ability, poor ability to evaluate a problem, poor attention to detail, poor hand-eye coordination, difficulty working under time pressure, slow performance, poor motivation, or impulsivity.

One useful testing-of-limits procedure is to select an item that the child has incorrectly constructed, assemble the incorrect reproduction, and ask the child if the reproduction is the same as or different from the original design. If the child recognizes that the design is incorrect and can relate the specific errors (e.g., "A red-and-white block goes here, not a white block"), the child may have a visual-motor execution problem rather than a visual-motor recognition problem. In such cases, it may be useful to ask the child to make the recognized correction or corrections by saying, "Go ahead and make it look the way it should look."

Another testing-of-limits procedure involves showing the child a design that the child failed. As you give the instructions again, place one row or block in its correct position. Say, "Let's try some of these again. I'm going to put together some of the blocks. I'll make the top row [or arrange the first block]. Now you go ahead and finish it. Make one like this. Tell me when you have finished." If the child fails with this first cue, arrange additional blocks. Record the amount of help the child needs to reproduce the design accurately. A child who needs many cues to reproduce the design may have weaker spatial reasoning ability than a child who needs only one or a few cues. In some cases, the additional cues may not help the child reproduce the design.

Other testing-of-limits procedures are also possible. One is to show the child three different arrangements, only one of which is correct. Then ask the child to point to the arrangement that is the same as the model. Be sure to vary the placement of the correct design. Another procedure is to ask the child to tell you how the designs were constructed.

The range of scaled scores from 1 to 19 at ages 3-0 to 5-11 aids in profile analysis. However, profile analysis is moderately to slightly restricted at ages 7-0 to 7-3, 2-6 to 2-11, and 6-0 to 6-11, where scaled scores range from 1 to 17, 2 to 19, and 1 to 18, respectively.

INFORMATION

Information, a core Verbal subtest at all ages of the test, requires the child to answer questions dealing with various types of content, including body parts, names of animals, uses of common objects, and calendar information. Children need only show that they know facts; they need not find relationships between these facts. The subtest has 34 items and is not timed. Children can answer items 1 to 6 by either pointing to or saying the number of their choice, while they can answer items 7 to 34 with a brief statement. The subtest is easy to administer and score.

Rationale

The amount of knowledge a child has acquired may depend on (a) natural endowment, (b) cultural opportunities, experiences, and interests, and (c) both formal and informal education. The Information subtest samples the knowledge that average children with average opportunities should have acquired through typical home and school experiences in the American culture. The child's

responses and comments provide clues about range of information, alertness to the environment, social or cultural background, and attitudes toward school and school-like tasks. For example, a 6-year-old child may say, "Those questions are hard, just like the ones my teacher asks."

High scores may not necessarily indicate cognitive competence; children may have acquired isolated facts but may not know how to use the facts appropriately or effectively. Additionally, intellectual drive may contribute to higher scores. Successful performance on the Information subtest requires memory for habitual, overlearned material (i.e., repeated exposure), especially in school-aged children. Thus, Information provides clues about the child's ability to store and retrieve acquired knowledge (i.e., long-term memory).

Factor Analytic Findings

At ages 2-6 to 3-11, Information is a good measure of g (72% of its variance can be attributed to g). It contributes substantially to the Verbal factor (average loading = .80). Subtest specificity is ample at ages 2-6 to 3-11. At ages 4-0 to 7-3, Information is a good measure of g (66% of its variance can be attributed to g). It contributes substantially to the Verbal factor (average loading = .76). Subtest specificity is adequate at ages 4-0 to 4-5 and 5-0 to 6-11, but inadequate at ages 4-6 to 4-11 and 7-0 to 7-3.

Reliability and Correlational Highlights

Information is a reliable subtest (r_{xx} = .88), with reliability coefficients at or above .83 at all of the age groups (range of .83 to .93).

At ages 2-6 to 3-11, Information correlates better with Picture Naming (r = .74) and Receptive Vocabulary (r = .71) than with any of the other subtests. It has a high correlation with the Full Scale IQ (r = .83) and the Verbal IQ (r = .92) and a moderate correlation with the Performance IQ (r = .52).

At ages 4-0 to 7-3, Information correlates better with Word Reasoning (r = .74) and Vocabulary (r = .69) than with any of the other subtests. It has a high correlation with the Full Scale IQ (r = .83) and the Verbal IQ (r = .90), a moderate correlation with the Performance IQ (r = .63), and a moderately low correlation with the Processing Speed Quotient (r = .41).

Administrative Guidelines

The following administrative guidelines for the Information subtest must be followed carefully.

Background Considerations

1. Read the items verbatim.
2. Read the items clearly.
3. Place the closed Stimulus Book 1 with the coil-bound edge facing and close to the child for items 1 to 6 so that the book is completely flat when it is opened, and then open it to the appropriate page.
4. Remove Stimulus Book 1 from the child's view after administering item 6.
5. You can repeat an item as often as necessary, but do not change the wording in any way.
6. Query unclear or vague responses, as well as the sample responses marked by a "(Q)" in the Administration Manual. *This includes all the responses separated by semicolons on a line that has a "(Q)" at the end.* Query specific responses noted by an asterisk (*) in the Administration Manual. (These are for items 11, 12, 16, 18, 22, 25, 28, 29, 31, 32, and 34.) However, do not query clearly wrong responses or responses that are clearly correct. If the child gives unclear responses, say, "Explain what you mean" or "Tell me more about it." If the child's response suggests that a word was misunderstood, repeat the item with emphasis on the particular word.
7. For item 1, give the correct answer if the child obtains a score of 0.
8. Do not give correct answers for items 2 to 34.
9. If the child fails to respond and has been performing poorly, wait about 30 seconds before going to the next item and say, "Let's try another one." However, use your judgment about moving to the next item sooner. For children who are clearly beyond their ability, 30 seconds may be a long time to wait, especially if it is the third or fourth 30-second wait. For example, this would be the case for children who seem to be bored, who are shrugging their shoulders, or who are looking around the room after a few seconds and not looking at the item.
10. If the child fails to respond but has been performing successfully and appears to be working on a response, give the child the necessary time to respond before going to the next item.

Starting Considerations

11. Start with the appropriate item.
   a. The ages listed under "Start" on pages 68 and 189 of the Administration Manual are always intended to be inclusive; thus, ages 2–3 means children 2-6 to 3-11 years of age, ages 4–5 means children 4-0 to 5-11 years of age, and ages 6–7 means children 6-0 to 7-3 years of age.
   b. The starting ages on the Record Form are also inclusive.
   c. Children 2 to 3 years of age (and older children suspected of having intellectual deficiency) start with item 1.
   d. Children 4 to 5 years of age (not suspected of having intellectual deficiency) start with item 11.
   e. Children 6 to 7 years of age (not suspected of having intellectual deficiency) start with item 17.

Reverse Sequence

12. If necessary, administer the items in reverse sequence as directed in the Administration Manual.
   a. The instructions on page 68 of the Administration Manual under the heading "Reverse" pertain to children 4-0 to 7-3 years of age who begin the subtest with item 11 or 17. There is no reverse sequence for children 2-6 to 3-11 years of age.
   b. If the child (a) does not obtain full credit on the start-point item or (b) obtains full credit on the start-point item and a score of 0 on the next item, administer the items in reverse sequence.
   c. Continue the reverse sequence until the child has perfect scores on two consecutive items or until item 1 has been administered, even if the discontinue criterion is met.
   d. When there is a reverse sequence, the discontinue criterion is not met, and either there are two consecutive items with perfect scores or item 1 is administered, continue administration with the item after the last start-point item.

Discontinue Considerations

13. Count items administered in reverse sequence toward the discontinue criterion.
14. Discontinue the subtest when five consecutive scores of 0 are obtained, unless the consecutive 0's are obtained during a reverse sequence and (a) item 1 has not been reached or (b) the child has not obtained perfect scores on two consecutive items.

Scoring Guidelines

15. Score the items using the following guidelines.
   a. Scoring is straightforward: A correct response receives 1 point, and an incorrect response, 0 points.

b. Give credit for responses that are of the same caliber as those listed in the Administration Manual.

c. Items 1 to 6 are multiple-choice picture items and require a pointing response only. The child must have adequate vision to respond to these items. If the child points to more than one picture on items 1 to 6, ask the child to point to one picture only.

d. When two or more answers to an item vary greatly in quality and none reflect a fundamental misconception (a spoiled response), score the best answer given.

e. When two or more answers are given to an item, one of which reflects a fundamental misconception (a spoiled response), give the response a score of 0.

f. Superfluous remarks, in addition to the answer, do not affect the score.

g. For items 1 to 6, give credit for a correct pointing or verbal response.

h. For items 7 and 8, give credit for a correct touching, pointing, or other nonverbal response.

i. For item 9, give credit for a correct verbal or nonverbal response.

j. For items 10 and 12, give credit for a correct verbal, pointing, or other nonverbal response.

k. For item 11, give credit for a correct verbal or pointing response.

l. When the child earns perfect scores on the first two items at the start point or in a reversal, award full credit for all preceding items, regardless of the child's performance on these items if they have been administered.

m. Award no points for any items beyond the last score of 0 required for the discontinue criterion to be met, regardless of the child's performance on these items if they have been administered.

Record Form

16. For items 1 to 6, circle the response number or DK.

17. For items 7 to 17, record the child's responses verbatim for each item administered.

18. Circle 0 or 1 in the Score column for each item administered.

19. To note the points awarded for items not administered below the first two items with perfect scores, put a slash mark in the Score column over the item preceding the first two items with perfect scores and write the numerals for these points.

20. Add the points, including the points for correct answers and the points for items not administered before the first two perfect scores, but not for items administered after the last discontinue item.

21. Enter the Total Raw Score in the shaded box.

There are some administrative issues that need to be considered with respect to the Information subtest. One is that because the correct answers are presented in two columns rather than one column, you must check each column as you score the child's answers. Another is that item 22 instructs the child about how many acceptable answers must be given, whereas items 18 and 32, which also require more than one acceptable answer, do *not* tell the child how many acceptable answers are needed to obtain credit (item 18 requires three acceptable answers, while item 32 requires two acceptable answers). These items should have included in the question the number of acceptable answers needed in order to receive credit. When the child does not give the required number of acceptable answers, you are required to ask for more answers.

Interpretive Suggestions

The following questions are useful to guide your observation of the child's performance on the Information subtest.

- Is the child thinking through the questions, responding impulsively, or simply guessing?
- When responding, does the child appear confident or hesitant?
- Does the child give peculiar responses? What does your inquiry reveal?
- Does the child frequently say, "I know this answer, but I can't think of it" or "I don't know"?
- Are the child's answers precise, imprecise, or vague?
- Are the child's answers close to the correct answer or completely wrong?
- Are the child's answers wordy?
- Does the child seem to be inhibited in making responses?
- What is the pattern of the child's successes and failures?
- Does the child point to more than one picture on items 1 to 6? If so, what does he or she say or do when asked to point to one picture only?

Failures on easy items, coupled with successes on more difficult ones, may suggest poor motivation, anxiety, temporary inefficiency, boredom, or an inconsistent environment. Alternatively, this pattern may indicate a problem with retrieval of information from long-term memory. When you suspect such a problem, analyze the content of the failed items. Content analysis may provide clues about the child's interests, areas about which you might want to inquire after you complete the WPPSI–III, or areas that need remediation.

Difficulty in giving precise answers, such as saying "When it is hot" instead of "Summer" or "When it is cold" instead of "Winter," may suggest word-retrieval difficulties. Overly long responses or responses filled with extraneous information may suggest an obsessive-compulsive orientation—a child with this orientation sometimes feels compelled to prove how much he or she knows. Alternatively, responses with excessive details may simply reflect the style of responding of a gifted child or the child's desire to impress you. Consider the child's entire test performance, plus other relevant information, when you interpret overly long responses.

Inability to recall an answer may suggest that the question is associated with conflict-laden material. For example, a child may not be able to recall the number of legs on a dog because of an earlier traumatic experience with dogs. If possible, explore hypotheses during an interview with the child and his or her parents (see Sattler, 2002).

High scores on the Information subtest may indicate a wide range of factual knowledge, knowledge of the cultural and educational environment, good memory, an enriched background, alertness and interest in the environment, intellectual ambitiousness, intellectual curiosity, an urge to collect knowledge, or interest in a school-type task.

Low scores on the Information subtest may indicate a limited range of factual knowledge, limited knowledge of the cultural and educational environment, poor memory, a limited background, limited alertness and interest in the environment, limited intellectual ambitiousness, limited intellectual curiosity, a limited urge to collect knowledge, hostility to a school-type task, or having English as a second language.

If you suspect word-retrieval problems, use a multiple-choice testing-of-limits procedure. This procedure may help you distinguish between deficits associated with word-retrieval difficulties and those associated with deficient knowledge. After completing the *entire test*, go back to the item (or items) with which the child had difficulty and give the child three answers from which to choose. For example, say, "How many ears does a cat have—one, three, or two? Which one is it?" Be sure to randomly vary the position of the correct answer in the series (i.e., put the correct answer sometimes in first, sometimes in second, and sometimes in third position). If the child answers the multiple-choice questions correctly, the child may have a word-retrieval difficulty and not deficient knowledge. However, scores from the multiple-choice procedure should not be used to calculate an IQ.

The range of scaled scores from 1 to 19 at ages 3-0 to 6-11 aids in profile analysis. However, profile analysis is slightly restricted at ages 2-6 to 2-11 and ages 7-0 to 7-3, where scaled scores range from 2 to 19 and 1 to 18, respectively.

MATRIX REASONING

Matrix Reasoning, which is a core Performance subtest at ages 4-0 to 7-3 and is not given at ages 2-6 to 3-11, consists of individually presented colored matrices, each of which has a part missing. The child is asked to select the one pattern from an array of four or five choices that best completes the matrix. The subtest is composed of 29 items and is not timed. The subtest is relatively easy to administer and score.

Rationale

The Matrix Reasoning subtest measures perceptual reasoning ability without a speed component. Perceptual matching, attention to detail, concentration, classification, analogic reasoning, and serial reasoning are required for successful performance; spatial ability also may be involved for some children. Matrix Reasoning can be considered a measure of nonverbal fluid reasoning ability. Experience with part-whole relationships and pattern completion may be helpful, as may a willingness to respond when uncertain. Matrix Reasoning may also have a verbal mediation component and visuosensory and visuospatial construction skill components, but research is needed to determine whether this hypothesis holds for young children (cf. Dugbartey, Sanchez, Rosenbaum, Mahurin, Davis, & Townes, 1999).

Factor Analytic Findings

At ages 4-0 to 7-3, Matrix Reasoning is a fair measure of g (45% of its variance can be attributed to g). It contributes minimally to the Performance factor (average loading = .38). Subtest specificity is ample at all ages from 4-0 to 7-3.

Reliability and Correlational Highlights

Matrix Reasoning is a reliable subtest (r_{xx} = .90), with reliability coefficients at or above .89 at ages 4-0 to 7-3 (range of .88 to .91). It correlates better with Block Design (r = .51) and Information (r = .51) than with any of the other subtests. It has a moderately high correlation with the Full Scale IQ (r = .72), a high correlation with the Performance IQ (r = .82), a moderate correlation with the Verbal IQ (r = .55), and a moderately low correlation with the Processing Speed Quotient (r = .48).

Administrative Guidelines

The following administrative guidelines for the Matrix Reasoning subtest must be followed carefully.

Background Considerations

1. Read the directions verbatim.
2. Read the directions clearly.
3. Place the closed Stimulus Book 1 with the coil-bound edge facing and close to the child so that the book is completely flat when it is opened, and then open it to the appropriate page.
4. Position Stimulus Book 1 close to the child so that pointing to a response is easily accomplished. Also, if children rotate their bodies around the table, ask them to remain in their chairs during the test administration, and note this behavior in "Other Notes" on the back page of the Record Form and in the report if appropriate (personal communication, November 2003, Diane Coalson, Senior Research Director, The Psychological Corporation).
5. Turn the pages of Stimulus Book 1 toward the child during the subtest administration. Allow the child to rotate the Stimulus Book if he or she wants to do so (personal communication, February 5, 2004, Lisa Drozdick, Research Director, The Psychological Corporation).
6. If necessary, clarify the instructions by pointing across the response options and to the box with the question mark as the instructions and items are read.
7. If any sample is failed, demonstrate the correct way to solve the problem.
8. Repeat the instructions if the child asks or has not responded within 5 to 10 seconds, unless it is clear that the child is considering a response.
9. For items 1 to 29, if the child clearly understands the task, shorten or eliminate the instructions, if desired.
10. If the child names the picture or says other types of things, other than pointing to the response option or saying the number of the response, say, "Show me which one." If the child points to or says the name of more than one box, say, "There is only one correct answer to each problem. Just choose the best one."
11. Provide feedback only on the three samples.
12. If the child fails to respond and has been performing poorly, wait about 30 seconds before going to the next item and say, "Let's try another one." However, use your judgment about moving to the next item sooner. For children who are clearly beyond their ability, 30 seconds may be a long time to wait, especially if it is the third or fourth 30-second wait. For example, this would be the case for children who seem to be bored, who are shrugging their shoulders, or who are looking around the room after a few seconds and not looking at the item.
13. If the child fails to respond but has been performing successfully and appears to be working on a response, give the child the necessary time to respond before going to the next item.

Starting Considerations

14. Start with the appropriate item.
   a. The ages listed under "Start" on page 81 of the Administration Manual are always intended to be inclusive; thus, age 4 means children 4-0 to 4-11 years of age, age 5 means children 5-0 to 5-11 years of age, and ages 6–7 means children 6-0 to 7-3 years of age.
   b. The starting ages on the Record Form are also inclusive.
   c. All children are given the three sample items. These items are intended to help them understand the instructions.
   d. Children 4 years of age (and older children suspected of having intellectual deficiency) start with the three sample items, A, B, and C, and then item 1.
   e. Children 5 years of age (not suspected of having intellectual deficiency) start with the three sample items, A, B, and C, and then item 4.
   f. Children 6 to 7 years of age (not suspected of having intellectual deficiency) start with the three sample items, A, B, and C, and then item 6.
   g. If the child fails the three samples, proceed to the appropriate start-point item.

Reverse Sequence

15. If necessary, administer the items in reverse sequence as directed in the Administration Manual.
   a. The instructions on page 81 of the Administration

Manual under the heading "Reverse" pertain to children who begin the subtest with an item higher than 1.

b. If the child (a) does not obtain full credit on the start-point item or (b) obtains full credit on the start-point item and a score of 0 on the next item, administer the items in reverse sequence.

c. Continue the reverse sequence until the child has perfect scores on two consecutive items or until item 1 has been administered, even if the discontinue criterion is met.

d. When there is a reverse sequence, the discontinue criterion is not met, and either there are two consecutive items with perfect scores or item 1 is administered, continue administration with the item after the last start-point item.

Discontinue Considerations

16. Count items administered in reverse sequence toward the discontinue criterion.

17. Discontinue the subtest when four or four of five consecutive scores of 0 are obtained, unless the consecutive 0's are obtained during a reverse sequence and (a) item 1 has not been reached or (b) the child has not obtained perfect scores on two consecutive items.

18. Once the subtest is completed, remove Stimulus Book 1 from the child's view.

Scoring Guidelines

19. Score the items using the following guidelines.

a. All responses are scored 0 or 1. The correct responses are on page 84 of the Administration Manual.

b. When the child earns perfect scores on the first two items at the start point or in a reversal, award full credit for all preceding items, regardless of the child's performance on these items if they have been administered.

c. Award no points for any items beyond the last score of 0 required for the discontinue criterion to be met, regardless of the child's performance on these items if they have been administered.

d. The Administration Manual lists only one correct answer for item 25. However, after the first printing of the Administration Manual, The Psychological Corporation recognized that there are two correct answers—the one shown in the Administration Manual plus the next highest choice (personal communication, January 22, 2003, Diane Coalson, Senior Research Director, The Psychological Corporation).

Record Form

20. Circle the response number or DK for all sample and subtest items administered.

21. Circle 0 or 1 in the Score column for each item administered.

22. To note the points awarded for items not administered below the first two items with perfect scores, put a slash mark in the Score column over the item preceding the first two items with perfect scores and write the numerals for these points.

23. Add the points, including the points for correct answers and the points for items not administered before the first two perfect scores, but not for items administered after the last discontinue item.

24. Enter the Total Raw Score in the shaded box.

Interpretive Suggestions

The following questions are useful to guide your observation of the child's performance on the Matrix Reasoning subtest.

• What is the tempo of the child's responses (e.g., fast, slow, deliberate, impulsive, careful)?

• Are there any signs of a response set (i.e., child points to the same numbered choice for each item)?

• If the child takes a long time to respond, what might the reasons be for the long response time (e.g., depression, thoughtfulness, inability to make a decision, anxiety, hope that the right answer will somehow come to her or him)?

• How does the pattern of responding on Matrix Reasoning compare with the child's pattern of responding on other subtests?

• Are there any indications of visual difficulties that might impede the child's performance (e.g., visual acuity difficulties, color blindness)?

• On what types of items does the child have difficulty (e.g., pattern recognition)?

• Does the child point or trace items to assist in responding?

• Are there signs of negativism or uncooperative behavior? If so, what are the signs?

• Does the child talk, sing, or hum while working?

After you administer the *entire test*, you can ask the child about strategies used to solve the problems. The reply may provide insight about the child's problem-solving strategies.

High scores on the Matrix Reasoning subtest may indicate good perceptual organization ability, good reasoning ability, good attention to detail, good concentration, good vision, and persistence.

Low scores on the Matrix Reasoning subtest may indicate poor perceptual organization ability, poor reasoning ability, poor attention to detail, poor concentration, visual problems, limited motivation, or impulsivity.

The range of scaled scores from 1 to 19 at ages 4-0 to 7-3 aids in profile analysis.

VOCABULARY

Vocabulary, which is a core Verbal subtest at ages 4-0 to 7-3 and is not given at ages 2-6 to 3-11, requires the child to look at pictures and give the names of the objects (items 1 to 5) or to define words you have read aloud (items 6 to 25). The subtest contains 25 items (5 picture items and 20 word items). The child is asked to give names (e.g., "What is this?") for items 1 to 5 and to explain the meaning of words ("What is a _____?" or "What does _____ mean?") for items 6 to 25. The two different item types—naming pictures and defining words—measure different types of lexical knowledge. In addition, the Vocabulary subtest is not a completely independent subtest, because the five picture items are identical to 5 of the 30 items on the Picture Naming subtest. The Vocabulary subtest is relatively easy to administer but difficult to score.

Rationale

Vocabulary, a test of word knowledge, assesses several cognitive factors—such as the child's learning ability, fund of information, richness of ideas, memory, concept formation, and language development—that may be closely related to the child's home environment and, to some extent, educational experiences. Since a well-developed vocabulary is a reflection of the child's ability to learn and to accumulate information, the subtest provides an excellent estimate of intellectual ability. Performance on the subtest is stable over time and relatively resistant to neurological deficit and psychological disturbance. Scores on the Vocabulary subtest provide a useful index of the child's general mental ability.

Factor Analytic Findings

At ages 4-0 to 7-3, Vocabulary is a good measure of g (61% of its variance can be attributed to g). It contributes substantially to the Verbal factor (average loading = .88). Subtest specificity is ample at ages 4-0 to 4-11, adequate at ages 6-0 to 7-3, and inadequate at ages 5-0 to 5-11 .

Reliability and Correlational Highlights

Vocabulary is a reliable subtest (r_{xx} = .89), with reliability coefficients at or above .86 at ages 4-0 to 7-3 (range of .86 to .92). It correlates better with Word Reasoning (r = .71) and Comprehension (r = .70) than with any of the other subtests. It has a moderately high correlation with the Full Scale IQ (r = .78), a high correlation with the Verbal IQ (r = .89), a moderate correlation with the Performance IQ (r = .57), and a moderately low correlation with the Processing Speed Quotient (r = .39).

Administrative Guidelines

The following administrative guidelines for the Vocabulary subtest must be followed carefully.

Background Considerations

1. Read the directions verbatim.
2. Read the directions clearly.
3. Pronounce each word clearly and correctly, because you are not allowed to show the words or to spell the words. Use the local pronunciation of each word or the pronunciation that might be familiar to the child.
4. Repeat the instructions if the child asks or has not responded within 5 to 10 seconds, unless it is clear that the child is considering a response.
5. You can repeat each item as often as necessary, but do not change the wording in any way. If the child's response suggests that a word was misunderstood, repeat the question with emphasis on the particular word.
6. If you suspect that the child has not heard a word correctly, say, "Listen carefully, what does _____ mean?" or use similar neutral wording.
7. Place the closed Stimulus Book 1 with the coil-bound edge facing and close to the child for items 1 to 5 so that the book is completely flat when it is opened, and then open it to the appropriate page.
8. For items 1 to 5, open Stimulus Book 1, point to the

picture, and say, "What is this?"

9. Turn the pages of Stimulus Book 1 toward the child.

10. On items 1 to 5 (the picture items), query marginal responses, generalized responses, functional responses, and hand gesture responses as often as necessary. The Administration Manual (see pp. 85 and 86) gives suggested wording for such queries. However, on all items, query unclear or vague responses, as well as the sample responses marked by a "(Q)" in the Administration Manual. *This includes all the responses separated by semicolons on a line that has a "(Q)" at the end.* Do not query clearly wrong responses, personalized responses, or responses that are clearly correct. When you have any doubt about the acceptability of a response, ask the child for further elaboration or another meaning of the word, using the queries on page 86 of the Administration Manual.

11. When a perfect score (1) is not obtained on item 1, 6, or 7, tell the child the correct answer.

12. On items 2 to 5 and 8 to 25, do not give the child the correct answer if he or she gives an incorrect answer.

13. If the child fails to respond and has been performing poorly, wait about 30 seconds before going to the next item and say, "Let's try another one." However, use your judgment about moving to the next item sooner. For children who are clearly beyond their ability, 30 seconds may be a long time to wait, especially if it is the third or fourth 30-second wait. For example, this would be the case for children who seem to be bored, who are shrugging their shoulders, or who are looking around the room after a few seconds and not looking at the item.

14. If the child fails to respond but has been performing successfully and appears to be working on a response, give the child the necessary time to respond before going to the next item.

Starting Considerations

15. Start with the appropriate item.
   a. The ages listed under "Start" on page 85 of the Administration Manual are always intended to be inclusive; thus, ages 4–7 means children 4-0 to 7-3 years of age.
   b. The starting ages on the Record Form are also inclusive.
   c. Children 4 to 7 years of age (not suspected of having intellectual deficiency) start with item 6.
   d. Children suspected of having intellectual deficiency start with item 1.

Reverse Sequence

16. If necessary, administer items in reverse sequence as directed in the Administration Manual.
   a. The instructions on page 85 of the Administration Manual under the heading "Reverse" pertain to children who begin the subtest with an item higher than 1.
   b. If the child (a) does not obtain full credit on the start-point item or (b) obtains full credit on the start-point item and a score of 0 on the next item, administer the items in reverse sequence.
   c. Continue the reverse sequence until the child has perfect scores on two consecutive items or until item 1 has been administered, even if the discontinue criterion is met.
   d. When there is a reverse sequence, the discontinue criterion is not met, and either there are two consecutive items with perfect scores or item 1 is administered, continue administration with the item after the last start-point item.

Discontinue Considerations

17. Count items administered in reverse sequence toward the discontinue criterion.

18. Discontinue the subtest after five consecutive scores of 0 are obtained, unless the consecutive 0's are obtained during a reverse sequence and (a) item 1 has not been reached or (b) the child has not obtained perfect scores on two consecutive items.

19. Once the subtest is completed or once the picture items have been administered, remove Stimulus Book 1 from the child's view.

Scoring Guidelines

20. Score the responses using the following guidelines.
   a. Study the General Scoring Principles on page 88 of the Administration Manual and use the sample responses as guidelines to help you score responses.
   b. Items 1 to 5 (the five picture items) are scored 0 or 1.
   c. Items 6 and 7 (the first two oral items) are scored 0 or 1.
   d. Items 8 to 25 are scored 0, 1, or 2.
   e. On all items, give 0 points for obviously wrong answers, vague or trivial responses, responses that show little understanding of the word, regionalisms, and slang not found in dictionaries. In addition, on items 6 to 25, give 0 points for pointing responses. Thus, on items 6 to 25, the child must give the responses verbally in order to receive credit. (This last

statement was confirmed by J. J. Zhu, Manager of Data Analysis Operations, The Psychological Corporation, personal communication, October 14, 2002).

f. Give 0 points for a multiple response that has both correct and incorrect definitions, with the incorrect portion of the answer revealing a fundamental misunderstanding of the item; this is a spoiled response.

g. On items 6 and 7, award 1 point (full credit) for responses that fulfill the guidelines shown in the General Scoring Principles for either a 2-point or a 1-point response.

h. On items 8 to 25, award 2 points for good synonyms, major uses, general classifications, a primary feature, several less definitive but correct descriptive features, or a definitive example of action or causal relations (for verbs).

i. On items 8 to 25, award 1 point for minimal content responses, vague responses, less pertinent synonyms, minor uses, a less definitive or distinguishing feature, an unelaborated example, a definition of a related word, or a demonstration not elaborated with words.

j. In scoring the responses, do not consider the child's elegance of expression.

k. Do not penalize the child for articulation problems or for faulty pronunciation. Use your judgment in deciding, based on the response, whether the child knows what the word means, despite an inability to pronounce the word.

l. Give credit for all meanings recognized by standard dictionaries.

m. Score the entire response, including the response to the query.

n. When parts of the response vary in quality but none spoil the entire response, score the best response.

o. Score the response without considering extraneous parts of the response.

p. Inquiring about borderline responses and carefully studying the scoring guidelines may help you resolve some scoring problems.

q. When you have any doubt about the acceptability of a response, ask the child for another meaning of the word.

r. When the child earns perfect scores on the first two items at the start point or in a reversal, award full credit for all preceding items, regardless of the child's performance on these items if they have been administered.

s. Award no points for any items beyond the last score of 0 required for the discontinue criterion to be met, regardless of the child's performance on these items if they have been administered.

Record Form

21. For each item administered, record the child's responses verbatim in the Response column.

22. Circle 0 or 1 in the Score column for items 1 to 7 and circle 0, 1, or 2 for items 8 to 25.

23. To note the points awarded for items not administered below the first two items with perfect scores, put a slash mark in the Score column over the item preceding the first two items with perfect scores and write the numerals for these points.

24. Add the points, including the points for correct answers and the points for items not administered before the first two perfect scores, but not for items administered after the last discontinue item.

25. Enter the Total Raw Score in the shaded box.

In the first printing of the Administration Manual, the 13th line on page 89, which begins with "Correct response ([name of object]): Proceed to the next appropriate item," implies that there is one correct response to item 1. This implication is wrong. The Administration Manual shows three correct answers, and other correct answers are also possible. The statement should be changed in the Administration Manual.

Vocabulary is a difficult subtest to score because the scoring criteria given in the Administration Manual are subtle. Here are some examples. First, the Administration Manual (p. 88) notes that "several less definitive but correct descriptive features that cumulatively indicate understanding of the word" receive 2 points. However, it is difficult to determine precisely what constitutes "several less definitive but correct descriptive features" for each stimulus word. Second, in the scoring examples, a response on item 7 that is given full credit (1 point) seems vague, a 1-point response on item 9 seems like a 2-point response because it reflects a general classification, and the difference between a specific 0-point and 1-point response on item 10 is not clear. Similar difficulties exist in scoring examples for other items. Note that in order to receive 2 points, some responses (e.g., to items 13 and 18) must have two separate elements (e.g., if the item was to define the word *plane,* a 2-point response might mention that planes are used for both moving people *and* moving freight).

Interpretive Suggestions

The following questions are useful to guide your observation of the child's performance on the Vocabulary subtest.

- Is the child definitely familiar with the word or only vaguely familiar with it?
- What is the quality of the child's definitions (e.g., precise and brief, indirect and vague, or verbose and lengthy)?
- Are the child's responses objective or subjective (i.e., do they relate to impersonal or personal experiences)?
- Does the child confuse the word with another one that sounds like it?
- Does the child guess if the meaning of a word is not known?
- Does the child readily say, "I don't know" and shake off further inquiries, or does the child pause, ponder, or think aloud about the item?
- Does the child show signs of a possible hearing difficulty? If so, what are the signs (e.g., hears words with some distortion)?
- Does the child easily express the meaning of a word, or does the child struggle to define the words?
- Does the child have mechanical difficulties with pronouncing words properly? If so, what are these difficulties?
- Does the child seem uncertain about how best to express thoughts?
- Does the child use gestures to illustrate responses or even depend on gestures exclusively?
- Are the child's responses synonyms for the stimulus word (e.g., thief: "A burglar"), or do they describe an action (e.g., thief: "Takes stuff")?
- Does the child describe a particular feature of the object (e.g., donkey: "It has four legs") or try to fit it into some category (e.g., donkey: "A living creature that is kept in a barn")?
- Does the child respond with any non-English words?
- Are 2-point responses given freely, or do they require query?
- Does the child's response pattern vary, or is it fairly consistent across items?
- Are there any emotional overtones or references to personal experiences in the child's responses (e.g., alphabet: "I hate to write")? If so, what are the emotional overtones?

Children's responses to the Vocabulary subtest may reveal something about their language skills, background, cultural milieu, social development, life experiences, responses to frustration, and thought processes. Try to determine the basis for incorrect responses, and distinguish among guesses, clang associations (i.e., responses that appear to be based on the sound of the stimulus word rather than on its meaning), and idiosyncratic associations or bizarre associations. Whenever a child gives peculiar responses, mispronounces words, or has peculiar inflections, inquire further. Occasionally, you can identify language disturbances in the word definitions of children with a pervasive developmental disorder.

High scores on the Vocabulary subtest may indicate good word knowledge, good verbal comprehension, good verbal skills, good language development, good ability to conceptualize, intellectual striving, an enriched family or cultural background, or meaningful preschooling or schooling.

Low scores on the Vocabulary subtest may indicate poor word knowledge, poor verbal comprehension, poor verbal skills, poor language development, or poor ability to conceptualize. Low scores may also reflect a limited educational background, a home environment in which verbalization was not encouraged, or that English is the child's second language.

If you suspect word-retrieval problems, use a multiple-choice testing-of-limits procedure. This procedure may help you differentiate deficits associated with word-retrieval difficulties from those associated with deficient knowledge. After completing the *entire test*, go back to the item (or items) with which the child had difficulty and give the child three answers from which to choose. You might ask, for example, "Which one of the following does *pen* mean—something to eat, something to take to bed, or something to write with? Which one is it?" Be sure to randomly vary the position of the correct answer in the series (i.e., put the correct answer sometimes in first, sometimes in second, and sometimes in third position). If the child answers the multiple-choice questions correctly, the child has a word-retrieval difficulty and not deficient knowledge. However, the multiple-choice procedure should not be used to calculate an IQ.

If the child gave any responses during the subtest that are possibly indicative of a thought disorder, you may want to inquire about these responses. You might say, "When I asked you to tell me the meaning of _____, you said _____. Tell me more about your answer."

The range of scaled scores from 1 to 19 at ages 4-0 to 6-11 aids in profile analysis. However, profile analysis is slightly restricted at ages 7-0 to 7-3, where the scaled scores range from 1 to 18.

PICTURE CONCEPTS

Picture Concepts, which is a core Performance subtest at ages 4-0 to 7-3 and is not given at ages 2-6 to 3-11, requires the child to look at two or three rows of pictures and then select from each row one picture that best goes together with the other selection(s) to form a concept. The task is to find a common element in the pictures that forms a category, concept, or classification. The subtest has 28 items and is not timed. It is relatively easy to administer and score.

Rationale

Picture Concepts measures abstract, categorical reasoning based on perceptual recognition processes. The task is to scan an array of pictures and determine which pictures have a common characteristic. The child first must recognize or identify each picture and then determine a quality that a picture in one row shares with a picture in another row. The quality might represent a category (e.g., animals), an appearance (e.g., round), a function (e.g., bounce), or a use (e.g., for eating).

Factor Analytic Findings

At ages 4-0 to 7-3, Picture Concepts is a fair measure of g (41% of its variance can be attributed to g). It contributes minimally to the Verbal factor (average loading = .34). Subtest specificity is ample at all ages from 4-0 to 7-3.

Reliability and Correlational Highlights

Picture Concepts is a reliable subtest ($r_{xx} = .91$), with reliability coefficients at or above .89 at ages 4-0 to 7-3 (range of .89 to .93). It correlates better with Word Reasoning ($r = .51$) and Similarities ($r = .51$) than with any of the other subtests. It has a moderately high correlation with the Full Scale IQ ($r = .71$), a moderate correlation with both the Performance IQ ($r = .59$) and the Verbal IQ ($r = .54$), and a moderately low correlation with the Processing Speed Quotient ($r = .44$).

Administrative Guidelines

The following administrative guidelines for the Picture Concepts subtest must be followed carefully.

Background Considerations

1. Read the directions verbatim.
2. Read the directions clearly.
3. Repeat the instructions if the child asks or has not responded within 5 to 10 seconds, unless it is clear that the child is considering a response.
4. Place the coil-bound edge of Stimulus Book 1 facing the child so that the book is completely flat when it is opened, and then open it to the appropriate page.
5. Position Stimulus Book 1 close enough so that the child can easily point to the desired response.
6. As the instructions are read, point across the first and second rows for items 1 to 26 and across the first, second, and third rows for items 27 and 28.
7. Turn the pages of Stimulus Book 1 toward the child and show the items one at a time.
8. For items 1 to 26, when the child understands the task, shorten or eliminate the instructions, if desired.
9. If the child fails to select a picture in each row or selects more than one picture in a single row, give the prompts noted on page 108 of the Administration Manual as often as necessary.
10. If you are asked, tell the child the name of any picture.
11. Ask the child to point to the picture if his or her verbal response is not clear. Say, "Point to the picture you mean."
12. If the child gives an incorrect answer to either sample A or sample B, give the correct answer, point to the correct objects, and then give the reason for the answer.
13. Do not give the child the correct answer or explain the correct answer on subtest items.
14. If the child fails to respond and has been performing poorly, wait about 30 seconds before going to the next item and say, "Let's try another one." However, use your judgment about moving to the next item sooner. For children who are clearly beyond their ability, 30 seconds may be a long time to wait, especially if it is the third or fourth 30-second wait. For example, this would be the case for children who seem to be bored, who are shrugging their shoulders, or who are looking around the room after a few seconds and not looking at the item.
15. If the child fails to respond but has been performing successfully and appears to be working on a re-

sponse, give the child the necessary time to respond before going to the next item.

Starting Considerations

16. Start with the appropriate item.
  a. The ages listed under "Start" on page 107 of the Administration Manual are always intended to be inclusive; thus, ages 4–5 mean children 4-0 to 5-11 years of age and ages 6–7 mean children 6-0 to 7-3 years of age.
  b. The starting ages on the Record Form are also inclusive.
  c. Children 4 to 5 years of age (and older children suspected of having intellectual deficiency) start with samples A and B and then item 1.
  d. Children 6 to 7 years of age (not suspected of having intellectual deficiency) start with samples A and B and then item 8.
  e. Even if the child fails the two sample items, proceed to the start-point item.

Reverse Sequence

17. If necessary, administer the items in reverse sequence as directed in the Administration Manual.
  a. The instructions on page 107 of the Administration Manual under the heading "Reverse" pertain to children who begin the subtest with the samples and then with item 8.
  b. If the child (a) does not obtain full credit on the start-point item or (b) obtains full credit on the start-point item and a score of 0 on the next item, administer the items in reverse sequence.
  c. Continue the reverse sequence until the child has perfect scores on two consecutive items or until item 1 has been administered, even if the discontinue criterion is met.
  d. When there is a reverse sequence, the discontinue criterion is not met, and either there are two consecutive items with perfect scores or item 1 is administered, continue administration with the item after the last start-point item.

Discontinue Considerations

18. Count items administered in reverse sequence toward the discontinue criterion.
19. Discontinue the subtest when four consecutive scores of 0 are obtained, unless the consecutive 0's are obtained during a reverse sequence and (a) item 1 has not been reached or (b) the child has not obtained perfect scores on two consecutive items.

20. Once the subtest is completed, remove Stimulus Book 1 from the child's view.

Scoring Guidelines

21. Score the items using the following guidelines.
  a. All responses are scored 0 or 1.
  b. To receive a score of 1 on an item, the child must select the one correct picture from each of two rows (items 1 to 26) or the one correct picture from each of three rows (items 27 and 28).
  c. Give credit if the child points to or names the pictures or says the numbers of the chosen pictures.
  d. When the child earns perfect scores on the first two items at the start point or in a reversal, award full credit for all preceding items, regardless of the child's performance on these items if they have been administered.
  e. Award no points for any items beyond the last score of 0 required for the discontinue criterion to be met, regardless of the child's performance on these items if they have been administered.

Record Form

22. Circle the response number or DK for each item administered.
23. Circle DK when the child does not respond or says that the answer is unknown.
24. Circle 0 or 1 in the Score column for each item administered.
25. To note the points awarded for items not administered below the first two items with perfect scores, put a slash mark in the Score column over the item preceding the first two items with perfect scores and write the numerals for these points.
26. Add the points, including the points for correct answers and the points for items not administered before the first two perfect scores, but not for items administered after the last discontinue item.
27. Enter the Total Raw Score in the shaded box.

The correct answers are limited in that they do not recognize all possible logical classifications. Because the child only has to point to the answer, there is no way of knowing the basis for the answer. If two animals were selected, there is no way to determine, for example, whether the child (a) knows the names of the animals, (b) knows that the pictures are of animals, or (c) knows that the pictures represent any category at all. The child's response could be based simply on the fact that the two pictures look similar (visual matching); have something in common, like four feet or a menacing look (conceptual reasoning); look different from the other pictures (visual discrimination); or look nice (a personal decision that may have no cognitive component). Items 1 to 12 can more easily be solved by visual matching than can items 13 to 28.

Interpretive Suggestions

The following questions are useful to guide your observation of the child's performance on the Picture Concepts subtest.

- What is the tempo of the child's responses (e.g., fast, slow, deliberate, impulsive, careful)?
- Are there any signs of a response set (e.g., child points to the same numbered choice or position on the page for each item)?
- What might the reasons be for any long response times?
- How does the child's pattern of responding on Picture Concepts compare with responses on other subtests?
- How does the child respond to prompts?
- Are there any indications of visual difficulties that might impede the child's performance (e.g., visual acuity difficulties, color blindness)?
- Are there any signs of negativism or uncooperative behavior? If so, what are the signs?

In the exploratory factor analysis of the core and supplemental subtests presented in the Technical Manual, Picture Concepts loads on different factors at different ages. At ages 4-0 to 4-11, Picture Concepts has moderate loadings (.33 and .34) on the Verbal *and* Processing Speed factors, respectively; at ages 5-0 to 5-11, it has a moderate loading (.46) on the Performance factor; and at ages 6-0 to 7-3, it has a moderate loading (.51) on the Verbal factor. In the combined age group from 4-0 to 7-3, its loadings on the Verbal and Performance factors are similar (.30 and .26, respectively). The Technical Manual notes, "It is likely that older children employ more verbal mediation than younger children in this subtest [Picture Concepts], as more difficult items were designed to require more abstract reasoning ability" (p. 83). Although this interpretation may have merit, the Technical Manual provides no data to support it.

In the exploratory factor analysis of the core subtests presented in the Technical Manual, Picture Concepts has a pattern of loadings that differs from the one found for the core and supplemental subtests. For example, at ages 4-0 to 4-11, Picture Concepts has a moderate loading (.54) on the Performance factor; at ages 5-0 to 5-11, it has a high loading (.63) on the Performance factor; and at ages 6-0 to 7-3, it has a moderate loading (.42) on the Verbal factor. In the combined age group from 4-0 to 7-3, it has a high loading (.52) on the Performance factor. The different patterns of loadings at the three age groups and in the two different factor analyses—and the fact that Picture Concepts seems to have Verbal, Performance, and possibly Processing Speed components—raise questions about what kind of cognitive processes are being measured by the subtest.

The principal factor analysis discussed in Chapter 5 also indicates that Picture Concepts contributes more to the Verbal factor than to the Performance factor. In fact, Picture Concepts overall has the same minimal loadings on both the Performance and Processing Speed factors. In addition, Picture Concepts has different loadings at different ages (see Table 5-12 in Chapter 5). For example, Picture Concepts has higher loadings on the Verbal factor at ages 4-0 to 4-5 (.51) than it does at ages 4-6 to 6-11 (.10). Caution is thus needed in interpreting this subtest.

A useful testing-of-limits procedure is to ask the child the reasons for the chosen responses: "Tell me the reason why these two [three] pictures go together."

High scores on the Picture Concepts subtest may indicate good conceptual thinking, good ability to see relationships, good logical and abstract thinking ability, good ability to discriminate fundamental from superficial relationships, good ability to select appropriate relationships between two objects or concepts, or flexibility of thought processes.

Low scores on the Picture Concepts subtest may indicate poor conceptual thinking, difficulty in seeing relationships, poor logical and abstract thinking ability, difficulty in discriminating fundamental from superficial relationships, difficulty in selecting appropriate relationships between two objects or concepts, or rigidity of thought processes.

In some cases, low scores might be associated with bright children whose categorizations differ from those of the test constructor. To explore this hypothesis, ask the child to give you the reasons for the chosen responses.

The range of scaled scores from 1 to 19 at ages 5-6 to 6-11 aids in profile analysis. However, profile analysis is moderately to slightly restricted at ages 4-0 to 4-5, 4-6 to 5-5, and 7-0 to 7-3, where scaled scores range from 3 to 19, 2 to 19, and 1 to 18, respectively.

WORD REASONING

Word Reasoning, which is a core Verbal subtest at ages 4-0 to 7-3 and is not given at ages 2-6 to 3-11, requires the child to identify the common object or concept described by an increasingly specific series of one to three clues. The subtest contains three samples and 28 items. It is not timed and is somewhat awkward to administer and difficult to score. Administration is awkward because both the Record Form and the Administration Manual are needed, as the items are listed in the Record Form but not in the Administration Manual.

Rationale

Word Reasoning measures verbal reasoning, deductive reasoning, verbal comprehension, verbal abstraction, synthesizing ability, and the ability to generate alternative concepts (Wechsler, 2002b).

Factor Analytic Findings

At ages 4-0 to 7-3, Word Reasoning is a good measure of g (67% of its variance can be attributed to g). It contributes substantially to the Verbal factor (average loading = .83). Subtest specificity is ample at ages 4-6 to 4-11 and 6-0 to 6-11 and adequate at ages 4-0 to 4-5, 5-0 to 5-11, and 7-0 to 7-3.

Reliability and Correlational Highlights

Word Reasoning is a reliable subtest (r_{xx} = .91), with reliability coefficients at or above .89 at ages 4-0 to 7-3 (range of .89 to .93). It correlates better with Information (r = .74) and Vocabulary (r = .71) than with any of the other subtests. It has a moderately high correlation with the Full Scale IQ (r = .71), a high correlation with the Verbal IQ (r = .91), a moderately high correlation with the Performance IQ (r = .60), and a moderately low correlation with the Processing Speed Quotient (r = .41).

Administrative Guidelines

The following administrative guidelines for the Word Reasoning subtest must be followed carefully.

Background Considerations

1. Read the items verbatim.
2. Read the items clearly.
3. Introduce each item by saying "Let's try another one."
4. After you give each clue, allow the child about 5 seconds to answer.
5. If requested by the child or if the child delays 5 seconds before responding, repeat each clue one time only.
6. After each repetition of the clues, allow the child an additional 5 seconds to make a response.
7. As you add more clues, restate the preceding clues. For example, for items with two clues, restate the first clue before giving the second clue. For items with three clues, restate the first and second clue before giving the third clue. The instruction to "restate the preceding clues" on page 117 of the Administration Manual means to *repeat* the clues, not to rephrase them.
8. If the child gets an item correct before all clues have been presented, administer the next item.

Starting Considerations

9. Start with the appropriate item.
   a. The ages listed under "Start" on page 116 of the Administration Manual are always intended to be inclusive; thus, ages 4–5 means children 4-0 to 5-11 years of age and ages 6–7 means children 6-0 to 7-3 years of age.
   b. The starting ages on the Record Form are also inclusive.
   c. All children 4 to 7 years of age begin with the two sample items.
   d. Children 4 to 5 years of age (and older children suspected of having intellectual deficiency) start with item 1.
   e. Children 6 to 7 years of age (not suspected of having intellectual deficiency) start with item 6.

Reverse Sequence

10. If necessary, administer the items in reverse sequence as directed in the Administration Manual.
    a. The instructions on page 116 of the Administration Manual under the heading "Reverse" pertain to children who begin the subtest with the sample and then with item 6.
    b. If the child (a) does not obtain full credit on the start-point item or (b) obtains full credit on the start-point item and a score of 0 on the next item, administer the items in reverse sequence.
    c. Continue the reverse sequence until the child has perfect scores on two consecutive items or until item

1 has been administered, even if the discontinue criterion is met.

d. When there is a reverse sequence, the discontinue criterion is not met, and either there are two consecutive items with perfect scores or item 1 is administered, continue administration with the item after the last start-point item.

Discontinue Considerations

11. Count items administered in reverse sequence toward the discontinue criterion.
12. Discontinue the subtest when five consecutive scores of 0 are obtained, unless the consecutive 0's are obtained during a reverse sequence and (a) item 1 has not been reached or (b) the child has not obtained perfect scores on two consecutive items.

Scoring Guidelines

13. Score responses using the following guidelines.
   a. A correct response on each item receives a score of 1, regardless of whether the child receives one, two, or three clues.
   b. An incorrect response receives a score of 0.
   c. Give credit for responses that are of the same caliber—such as synonyms, specific brands, or objects—as those listed on pages 121 to 122 in the Administration Manual.
   d. Although the subtest is not timed, the instructions in the Administration Manual say that, if you repeat a clue, you should allow another 5 seconds for the child to respond and then, if the child answers incorrectly or does not respond, give the next clue or item. The instructions also state that you give credit for correct responses made after 5 seconds.
   e. When the child earns perfect scores on the first two items at the start point or in a reversal, award full credit for all preceding items, regardless of the child's performance on these items if they have been administered.
   f. Award no points for any items beyond the last score of 0 required for the discontinue criterion to be met, regardless of the child's performance on these items if they have been administered.

Record Form

14. Record the child's responses verbatim in the Response column.

15. If a clue is repeated, record an R.
16. Circle Y or N for each clue administered.
17. Circle 0 or 1 for each item administered.
18. To note the points awarded for items not administered below the first two items with perfect scores, put a slash mark in the Score column over the item preceding the first two items with perfect scores and write the numerals for these points.
19. Add the points, including the points for unadministered items, but not for items administered after the last discontinue item.
20. Enter the Total Raw Score in the shaded box.

Interpretive Suggestions

The following questions are useful to guide your observation of the child's performance on the Word Reasoning subtest.

- Is the child thinking through the questions, responding impulsively, or simply guessing?
- When responding, does the child appear confident or hesitant?
- Does the child give peculiar responses? What does your inquiry reveal?
- Does the child frequently say, "I know this answer, but I can't think of it" or "I don't know"?
- Are the child's answers precise or imprecise?
- How many clues does the child need to solve items 10 to 28?
- Is there a pattern of needing fewer clues on some items and more clues on other ones? If so, what is the pattern? What might the pattern suggest?
- Does the child synthesize clues or give separate responses to each clue?
- Does the child have problems beginning with item 1 (first one-clue item), beginning with item 10 (first two-clue item), or beginning with item 24 (first three-clue item)?

High scores on the Word Reasoning subtest may indicate good analogic reasoning ability or deductive reasoning ability, good ability to integrate and synthesize, good ability to generate alternative concepts, good ability to see relationships, good short-term memory, good vocabulary, good attention, or good achievement orientation.

Low scores on the Word Reasoning subtest may indicate poor analogic reasoning ability or deductive reasoning ability, difficulty in integrating and synthesizing, difficulty in generating alternative concepts, difficulty in seeing relationships, poor short-term memory, poor vocabulary, attention difficulties, low achievement orientation, or having English as a second language.

If you suspect word-retrieval problems, use a multiple-choice testing-of-limits procedure. This procedure may help you distinguish between deficits associated with word-retrieval difficulties and those associated with deficient knowledge. After completing the *entire test*, go back to the item (or items) with which the child had difficulty and give the child three answers from which to choose. For example, for a sample-like item, say, "This is an animal that goes meow. Is it a dog, a cat, or a bird?" Be sure to randomly vary the position of the correct answer in the series (i.e., put the correct answer sometimes in first, sometimes in second, and sometimes in third position). If the child answers the multiple-choice questions correctly, the child may have a word-retrieval difficulty and not deficient knowledge. However, the multiple-choice procedure should not be used to calculate an IQ.

The range of scaled scores from 1 to 19 at ages 6-0 to 6-11 aids in profile analysis. However, profile analysis is severely to slightly restricted at ages 4-0 to 4-5, 4-6 to 5-5, 5-6 to 5-11, and 7-0 to 7-3, where the scaled scores range from 4 to 19, 3 to 19, 2 to 19, and 1 to 18, respectively.

CODING

Coding, which is a core subtest at ages 4-0 to 7-3 and is not given at ages 2-6 to 3-11, requires that the child copy symbols paired with other symbols. Coding, along with Symbol Search, is used to form the Processing Speed Quotient. A key is provided that consists of five shapes (e.g., star, circle). Within each sample shape, there is a special mark (e.g., a vertical line, two horizontal lines). The child must place within each test shape (which is empty) the mark that is within the sample shape. There are 5 practice shapes, followed by 59 shapes in the subtest proper. Follow the instructions on page 123 of the Administration Manual for children who are left-handed. The subtest is timed and easy to administer and score.

Rationale

Coding assesses the child's ability to learn an unfamiliar task. The subtest involves the speed and accuracy of vis-

ual-motor coordination (or processing speed), speed of mental operation (psychomotor speed), attentional skills, visual acuity, visual scanning and tracking (repeated visual scanning between the code key and answer spaces), short-term memory for new learning (paired-associate learning of an unfamiliar code), cognitive flexibility (in shifting rapidly from one pair to another), handwriting speed, and, possibly, motivation. Success depends not only on comprehension of the task but also on fine-motor pencil-and-paper skills. The subtest is sensitive to visuosensory difficulties.

Coding also may involve a verbal-encoding process if the child attaches verbal descriptions to the symbols. For example, a child may label the = symbol as an "equal sign" or the 0 as a "circle" or "zero." Performance may be improved if the child uses verbal labels to code the symbols. Consequently, Coding can be described in part as measuring the ability to learn combinations of symbols and shapes and the ability to make associations quickly and accurately. The task requires the child to identify the shape (either verbally or nonverbally), go to the proper shape in the key, code the information, and carry this information in short-term memory long enough to reproduce the symbol in the space. Thus, Coding can be conceptualized as an information-processing task involving the discrimination and memory of visual pattern symbols.

Factor Analytic Findings

At ages 4-0 to 7-3, Coding is a fair measure of g (25% of its variance can be attributed to g), but it contributes less to g than any other subtest. It contributes substantially to the Processing Speed factor (average loading = .76). Subtest specificity is ample at ages 4-0 to 5-11 and 7-0 to 7-3 and adequate at ages 6-0 to 6-11.

Reliability and Correlational Highlights

Coding is a reliable subtest (r_{tt} = .84), with reliability coefficients at or above .79 at ages 4-0 to 7-3 (range of .79 to .88). It correlates better with Symbol Search (r = .59) and Block Design (r = .40) than with any of the other subtests. It has a moderate correlation with the Full Scale IQ (r = .59), a moderately low correlation with the Performance IQ (r = .46) and the Verbal IQ (r = .34), and a high correlation with the Processing Speed Quotient (r = .89).

Administrative Guidelines

The following administrative guidelines for the Coding subtest must be followed carefully.

Background Considerations

1. Provide a smooth working surface by placing the Response Booklet over a piece of cardboard, if needed.
2. Read the instructions verbatim.
3. Read the instructions clearly.
4. Repeat the instructions if the child asks or has not responded within 5 to 10 seconds, unless it is clear that the child is considering a response.
5. Point to the key as you read the instructions.
6. Wait until the child understands the task before proceeding with the items.
7. Use a stopwatch quietly, if possible.
8. Keep the stopwatch on the table, if needed, but out of the child's reach, and handle it unobtrusively.
9. Coding has a 120-second time limit; however, practice items are not timed. Begin timing after the last word of instructions. Once timing has begun, do not stop timing to clarify instructions.
10. Coding may penalize a left-handed child if the way the child writes causes him or her to cover the key immediately above the line of writing. If this is the case, the child will have to lift her or his hand repeatedly during the task to view the key. If the child is left-handed, place a second Response Booklet to the right of the first Response Booklet so that the key in the second Response Booklet for the sample and subtest items is aligned with the key in the first Response Booklet.
11. Demonstrate the sample.
12. Give the child a number 2 pencil without an eraser. Both you and the child should use pencils without erasers.
13. Do not provide or allow for the use of an eraser.
14. Give instructions verbatim, including the word "Go," even if explanations are not necessary.
15. Give further explanations, if necessary, before saying "Go."
16. If the child asks about a mistake, say, "That's OK. Just keep working as fast as you can" (see p. 124 of the Administration Manual). If the child omits an item, begins to complete a row in reverse order, or skips a complete row, say, "Do them in order. Don't skip any," and then point to the first omitted item and say, "Do this one next." These are new instructions authorized by The Psychological Corporation

(personal communication, November 2003, Diane Coalson, Senior Research Director, The Psychological Corporation). Give this prompt as often as needed within the time limit, even though the Administration Manual says, "Give no further assistance . . . " (personal communication, November 2003, Diane Coalson, Senior Research Director, The Psychological Corporation). If the child stops prematurely, say, "Keep working until I tell you to stop" (or something similar).
17. Count the time taken to give prompts as part of the 120-second time limit.
18. Allow the child to make spontaneous corrections unless the corrections are done repeatedly or impede the child's performance. When the child does so repeatedly, say something like "Try not to make so many corrections" or "Work as fast as you can without making mistakes."

Starting Considerations

19. Start with the appropriate item.
  a. The ages listed under "Start" on page 123 of the Administration Manual are always intended to be inclusive; thus, ages 4–7 means children 4-0 to 7-3 years of age.
  b. The starting ages on the Record Form are also inclusive.
  c. The Coding subtest is located on the last page in the Response Booklet.
  d. When you administer the practice items, correct the child's mistakes immediately.
  e. Do not start the subtest until the child clearly understands the task.
  f. There is no reverse sequence on the Coding subtest.

Discontinue Considerations

20. Discontinue the subtest (a) if the child still does not understand the task after instructions have been given and further explanation provided, (b) after 120 seconds, or (c) when the child finishes before the time limit.
21. Stop timing if the child finishes before 120 seconds.
22. After 120 seconds, say, "Stop" and discontinue the subtest.
23. Once the subtest is completed, close the Response Booklet and remove it from the child's view.

Scoring Guidelines

24. Score the subtest using the following guidelines.
  a. Use the template to score the subtest and align it properly.

b. Score only items completed within the allotted 120 seconds. Do not give credit for any items completed after 120 seconds.

c. Give 1 point for each correct item, and give as many as 6 additional time-bonus points for a perfect score.

d. Do not include the responses to the five practice items in scoring the subtest.

e. Give credit for any symbol identifiable as a keyed symbol and distinguishable from other symbols; therefore, do not penalize the child for imperfectly drawn symbols.

f. Give credit for symbols that are spontaneously corrected within the time limit, including a spontaneously drawn correct symbol near an incorrectly drawn symbol.

g. Do not count any item that was *not* attempted (i.e., either skipped or not reached before the time elapsed).

h. To prolong the life of the Scoring Key, which has the cumulative number of symbols at the end of each row, you may want to laminate the template.

Response Booklet

25. Enter the child's name, the date, and your name at the top of the Response Booklet if this information has not been recorded previously.

Record Form

26. Record the time in seconds in the Completion Time box.

27. If the child has a perfect score (59 points) and finishes before 116 seconds, circle the appropriate time-bonus points.

28. Add the points.

29. Enter the Total Raw Score in the shaded box.

Interpretive Suggestions

The following questions are useful to guide your observation of the child's performance on the Coding subtest:

- Does the child understand the task?
- Does the child understand and proceed correctly after you give an explanation?
- Does the child use one hand to hold the paper in place and the other hand to draw the symbols?
- Is the child impulsive?
- Is the child meticulous?

- Does the child seem overly anxious?
- Does the child display tremor?
- Does the child's speed increase or decrease as the subtest proceeds?
- Are the child's symbol marks well executed, barely recognizable, or incorrect?
- Do the child's symbol marks show any distortions, such as reversals? If so, do the distortions appear only once, occasionally, or each time the child draws the symbol mark? How many different symbols are distorted?
- Are there any noticeable differences in the quality of symbols drawn early and late in the task?
- Does the child draw the same symbol repeatedly even though the shapes change (perseveration)?
- Is the child penalized for slowness, inaccuracy, or both?
- Are the child's failures associated with inadequate form perception or with poor attention?
- Does the child check each symbol with the sample, or does the child seem to remember the symbols (e.g., not look up at the code at the top of the page)?
- Does the child recheck every symbol before moving on to the next one?
- Does the child try to pick one shape only and skip the others?
- Is the child's work smooth and orderly, or does the child seem confused at times and have difficulty finding the place?
- Is the child aware of any errors?
- Do the child's errors occur in some regular manner?
- How does the child react to errors?
- Is the child persistent?
- Does the child need urging to continue the task?
- Does the child appear bored with the task?
- Does the child hold the pencil in an appropriate or inappropriate way?
- Is the child's hand steady or shaking?
- Does the child try to use an eraser from another pencil or another source? If so, does the child seem to realize that an eraser is not supposed to be used?
- Does the child stop in the middle of the task, stretch, sigh, look around, or talk?
- Does the child talk, sing, or hum while working?

Answers to the above questions will provide information about the child's attention span, method of working, and other behaviors. If the child makes many errors, consider whether the errors might be related to impulsivity, poor self-monitoring, poor self-correction, or visual-motor difficulties. An increase in speed, coupled with correct copying of symbols, suggests that the child is adjusting well to the task. A decrease in speed, coupled with incorrect copying of symbols, suggests that the child may be showing fatigue. And a decrease in speed, coupled with correct copying of symbols, suggests that the child may be bored, distracted, or fatigued.

Coding is particularly useful for evaluating a child's attention when you suspect attentional difficulties, such as in cases of attention-deficit/hyperactivity disorder, anxiety, or a traumatic brain injury. If other tests indicate that the child has adequate response speed and visual acuity, then poor scores on Coding are likely to be associated with attentional deficits and not visuosensory difficulties per se. A slow and deliberate approach may suggest depressive features.

Distortion of forms may mean that the child has perceptual difficulties. To discern whether the symbol has some symbolic meaning to the child, ask the child about any symbol that was written peculiarly. Perseveration may suggest neurological difficulties that should be investigated further. Boredom might be present with a bright child who is not challenged by the task.

High scores on the Coding subtest may indicate good visual sequential processing ability, good visual-motor dexterity, good attention and concentration, good ability to learn new material associatively and reproduce it with speed and accuracy, sustained energy or persistence, motivation, or desire for achievement.

Low scores on the Coding subtest may indicate poor visual sequential processing ability, poor visual-motor dexterity, poor attention and concentration, difficulty in learning new material associatively and reproducing it with speed and accuracy, lethargy or boredom, limited motivation, distractibility, anxiety, poor pencil control, perfectionism (e.g., excessive concern for detail in reproducing symbols), difficulty in working under time pressure, or impulsivity.

After the *entire test* is completed, you can go back to the Coding subtest and ask the child about how the symbol-shape combinations were remembered. This testing-of-limits procedure may give you insight about the strategies the child used on the task. You also may want to review each symbol that was copied incorrectly and ask the child to tell you whether it looks like the symbol in the key.

The range of scaled scores from 1 to 19 at ages 5-6 to 7-3 aids in profile analysis. However, profile analysis is severely to slightly restricted at ages 4-0 to 4-5, 4-6 to 4-8, 4-9 to 4-11, and 5-0 to 5-5, where the scaled scores range from 5 to 19, 4 to 19, 3 to 19, and 2 to 19, respectively.

THINKING THROUGH THE ISSUES

1. Which WPPSI–III core subtests are most useful for measuring the intelligence level of preschool children and young school-aged children?

2. Do you believe that four subtests provide an adequate measure of young children's intelligence level? What are the reasons for your answer?

3. Should young children be administered intelligence tests? If so, under what circumstances?

4. What do you think it means when a subtest has loadings of .30 or higher on more than one factor?

SUMMARY

1. This chapter provides information about the rationale, factor analytic findings, reliability and correlational highlights, administrative guidelines, and interpretive suggestions for the seven WPPSI–III core subtests.

2. Many of the WPPSI–III subtests have enough subtest specificity (i.c., ample or adequate) at most ages to provide reliable estimates of specific abilities—or at least to permit development of hypotheses about the underlying cognitive functions that the subtests may measure.

3. The best estimates of abilities are provided by the Full Scale IQ, followed by the Verbal IQ and the Performance IQ, the Processing Speed Quotient, other combinations of subtests, and, finally, individual subtests.

4. In addition to the child's scores, always consider the quality of the child's responses and the pattern of his or her successes and failures in evaluating and interpreting the child's performance.

Block Design

5. Block Design measures nonverbal concept formation and requires perceptual organization, spatial visualization, and abstract conceptualization. The subtest is a fair measure of *g* and contributes moderately to the Performance factor. Subtest specificity is ample or adequate at all ages. Block Design is a reliable subtest ($r_{xx} = .84$). Block Design is somewhat difficult to administer and score.

Information

6. Information measures the amount of knowledge the child has acquired as a result of natural endowment, cultural opportunities, experiences, interests, and education (both formal and informal). The subtest is a good measure of g and contributes substantially to the Verbal factor. Subtest specificity is ample or adequate at most ages, with the exception of ages 4-6 to 4-11 and 7-0 to 7-3, where it is inadequate. Information is a reliable subtest (r_{xx} = .88). It is easy to administer and score.

Matrix Reasoning

7. Matrix Reasoning measures perceptual reasoning ability without a speed component and requires perceptual matching, attention to detail, concentration, classification, analogic reasoning, and serial reasoning. Matrix Reasoning is a fair measure of g and contributes minimally to the Performance factor. Subtest specificity is ample at all ages at which the subtest is administered. Matrix Reasoning is a reliable subtest (r_{xx} = .90). It is relatively easy to administer and score.

Vocabulary

8. Vocabulary measures learning ability, fund of information, richness of ideas, memory, concept formation, and language development. The subtest is a good measure of g and contributes substantially to the Verbal factor. Subtest specificity is ample or adequate at the ages at which the subtest is administered, except at ages 5-0 to 5-11, where it is inadequate. Vocabulary is a reliable subtest (r_{xx} = .89). It is relatively easy to administer, but it can be difficult to score.

Picture Concepts

9. Picture Concepts measures abstract, categorical reasoning based on perceptual recognition processes. The subtest is a fair measure of g and contributes minimally to the Verbal factor. Subtest specificity is ample at the ages at which the subtest is administered. Picture Concepts is a reliable subtest (r_{xx} = .91). It is relatively easy to administer and score.

Word Reasoning

10. Word Reasoning measures verbal reasoning, deduc

tive reasoning, verbal comprehension, verbal abstraction, synthesizing ability, and the ability to generate alternative concepts. The subtest is a good measure of g and contributes substantially to the Verbal factor. Subtest specificity is ample or adequate at the ages at which the subtest is administered. Word Reasoning is a reliable subtest (r_{xx} = .91). It is somewhat awkward to administer and difficult to score.

Coding

11. Coding measures a child's ability to learn an unfamiliar task and involves visual-motor coordination, speed of mental operation, attentional skills, visual acuity, visual scanning and tracking, short-term memory, cognitive flexibility, handwriting speed, and, possibly, motivation. The subtest is a fair measure of g and contributes substantially to the Processing Speed factor. Subtest specificity is ample or adequate at the ages at which the subtest is administered. Coding is a reliable subtest (r_{tt} = .84). It is easy to administer and score.

KEY TERMS, CONCEPTS, AND NAMES

WPPSI–III Block Design (p. 205)
Global strategy (p. 205)
Analytical strategy (p. 205)
Synthetic strategy (p. 205)
WPPSI–III Information (p. 210)
WPPSI–III Matrix Reasoning (p. 213)
WPPSI–III Vocabulary (p. 216)
WPPSI–III Picture Concepts (p. 220)
WPPSI–III Word Reasoning (p. 223)
WPPSI–III Coding (p. 225)

STUDY QUESTIONS

1. Discuss the rationale for each of the seven WPPSI–III core subtests for ages 4-0 to 7-3.
2. Describe the factor analytic findings for each of the seven WPPSI–III core subtests for ages 4-0 to 7-3. In your description, compare and contrast the major factor analytic findings among the seven core subtests.
3. Discuss the reliability and correlational highlights for each of the seven WPPSI–III core subtests for

ages 4-0 to 7-3. In your discussion, compare and contrast the reliability and correlational highlights among the seven core subtests.

4. List some major administrative guidelines for each of the seven WPPSI–III core subtests for ages 4-0 to 7-3.

5. Describe the interpretive suggestions for each of the seven WPPSI–III core subtests for ages 4-0 to 7-3.

6. Which two of the seven WPPSI–III core subtests for ages 4-0 to 7-3 are the best measures of intelligence? Give the reasons for your answer.

7

WPPSI–III SUPPLEMENTAL AND OPTIONAL SUBTESTS

The term preschooler signals another change in our expectations of children. While toddler refers to physical development, preschooler refers to a social and intellectual activity: going to school. That shift in emphasis is tremendously important, for it is at this age that we think of children as social creatures who can begin to solve problems.

—Lawrence Kutner

Symbol Search

Comprehension

Picture Completion

Similarities

Receptive Vocabulary

Object Assembly

Picture Naming

Thinking Through the Issues

Summary

Key Terms, Concepts, and Names

Study Questions

Goals and Objectives

This chapter is designed to enable you to do the following:

- Critically evaluate the five WPPSI–III supplemental and two optional subtests

- Describe the rationales, factor analytic findings, reliability and correlational highlights, and administrative and interpretive considerations for the seven WPPSI–III supplemental and optional subtests

This chapter covers the five WPPSI–III supplemental subtests (Symbol Search, Comprehension, Picture Completion, Similarities, and Object Assembly) and two optional subtests (Receptive Vocabulary and Picture Naming) for ages 4-0 to 7-3. For ages 2-6 to 3-11, Receptive Vocabulary and Object Assembly are core subtests, while Picture Naming is a supplemental subtest. As noted in Chapter 5, (a) for ages 2-6 to 3-11, Picture Naming can substitute for Receptive Vocabulary or Information, and (b) for ages 4-0 to 7-3, Comprehension and Similarities can substitute for Information, Vocabulary, or Word Reasoning, and Picture Completion and Object Assembly can substitute for Block Design, Matrix Reasoning, or Picture Concepts. The optional subtests for ages 4-0 to 7-3 cannot be used as substitutes for any core subtests. Substitutions introduce unknown degrees of measurement error because the norm tables for the Composite scores and IQs do not take into account the substitution of supplemental subtests for core subtests.

SYMBOL SEARCH

Symbol Search, which is a supplemental subtest at ages 4-0 to 7-3 and is not given at ages 2-6 to 3-11, requires the child to look at a symbol and then decide whether the symbol is present in an array of symbols. Symbol Search, along with Coding, is used to form the Processing Speed Quotient. The child is required to draw a line through the matching symbol. The subtest has a 120-second time limit. It is easy to administer but somewhat difficult to score.

Rationale

On the Symbol Search subtest, the child looks at a stimulus figure (target stimulus), scans an array, and decides whether the stimulus figure appears in the array. The task involves perceptual discrimination, speed and accuracy, visual scanning, attention and concentration, short-term memory, and cognitive flexibility (in shifting rapidly from one array to the next). Visual-motor coordination plays a role, although a minor one, because the only motor movement is that of drawing a line.

Most of the symbols used in the Symbol Search subtest will be difficult to encode verbally. However, the child may verbally encode some symbols to which verbal descriptions can be attached. These include, for example, △ (tent) and ♡ (an arrow). We need research to learn whether children verbally encode these or other symbols and whether the encoding affects their performance.

As in the Coding subtest, the speed and accuracy with which the child performs the Symbol Search task are measures of the child's intellectual ability. For each item, the child must inspect the target stimulus, go to the array, view the array items and determine whether the target stimulus is present, and then mark the appropriate stimulus once the decision is made. You can thus conceptualize Symbol Search as a task involving visual discrimination and visuosensory scanning.

Factor Analytic Findings

At ages 4-0 to 7-3, Symbol Search is a fair measure of g (42% of its variance can be attributed to g). It contributes substantially to the Processing Speed factor (average loading = .71). Subtest specificity is ample at all ages from 4-0 to 7-3.

Reliability and Correlational Highlights

Symbol Search is a reliable subtest (r_{tt} = .83), with reliability coefficients at or above .80 at ages 4-0 to 7-3 (range of .80 to .86). It correlates better with Coding (r = .59) than with any of the other subtests. It has a moderate correlation with the Full Scale IQ (r = .64) and the Performance IQ (r = .60), a moderately low correlation with the Verbal IQ (r = .46), and a high correlation with the Processing Speed Quotient (r = .89).

Administrative Guidelines

The following administrative guidelines for the Symbol Search subtest must be followed carefully.

Background Considerations

1. Provide a smooth working surface by placing the Record Booklet over a piece of cardboard, if needed.
2. Read the directions verbatim.
3. Read the directions clearly.
4. Repeat the instructions if the child asks or has not responded within 5 to 10 seconds, unless it is clear that the child is considering a response.
5. Use a stopwatch quietly, if possible.
6. Keep the stopwatch on the table, if needed, but out of the child's reach, and handle it unobtrusively.
7. During the sample and practice items, make sure that the child sees only the sample page of the Response Booklet.

8. Give the child a number 2 pencil without an eraser. Both you and the child should use pencils without erasers.

9. Open the Response Booklet to the appropriate page.

10. Show the child the first page of the Response Booklet, and point to the target symbol and search groups for the samples as you read the instructions.

11. Draw a diagonal line through the matching symbol in the search group for the first sample item, and draw a diagonal line through the question mark in the search group for the second sample item.

12. Point to the target symbol and search group for the practice items as you read the instructions.

13. If the child makes the correct response on the first practice item, say, "That's right. Now you know how to do them."

14. If the child makes an error on the practice items, correct the error immediately by following the instructions on page 115 of the Administration Manual.

15. If the child does not understand the instructions or appears confused when doing the practice items, explain the instructions and demonstrate the task using the practice items. Then allow the child to complete the practice items.

16. Do not proceed to subtest items unless the child understands the task.

17. After the child understands the task and completes the practice items, open the Response Booklet to page 2.

18. Give the instructions verbatim, including the word "Go," even if explanations are not necessary.

19. If necessary, give further explanations before saying "Go."

20. After you say the last word of the instructions, begin timing immediately.

21. If the child reaches the end of the page and stops working, turn each page of the Response Booklet for the child.

22. Give the following appropriate prompts.

   a. If the child stops working after an item or after he or she reaches the end of a page before 120 seconds, say, "Keep working as fast as you can."

   b. If the child asks what to do about a mistake or asks for an eraser, say, "Keep working until I tell you to stop."

   c. If the child skips an item, omits an item, or begins to complete a page in reverse order, say, "Do them in order. Don't skip any." Point to the item that should be completed and say, "Do this one next."

23. Count the time taken to give prompts as part of the 120-second time limit.

24. Do not discourage the child from making spontaneous corrections unless the corrections impede performance. When the child does so repeatedly, say something like "Try not to make so many corrections" or "Work as fast as you can without making mistakes."

Starting Considerations

25. Start with the appropriate item.

   a. The ages listed under "Start" on page 111 of the Administration Manual are always intended to be inclusive; thus, ages 4–7 means children 4-0 to 7-3 years of age.

   b. The starting ages on the Record Form are also inclusive.

   c. There is no reverse sequence on the Symbol Search subtest.

Discontinue Considerations

26. Discontinue the subtest (a) if the child still does not understand the task after instructions have been given and further explanation provided, (b) after 120 seconds, or (c) when the child finishes before the time limit.

27. If the child finishes before 120 seconds, stop timing.

28. After 120 seconds, say, "Stop" and discontinue the subtest.

29. After the child completes the subtest, close the Response Booklet and remove it from the child's view.

Scoring Guidelines

30. Score the subtest using the following guidelines.

   a. Use the template to score the subtest.

   b. Score only items completed within the allotted 120 seconds. Do not give credit for any items completed after 120 seconds.

   c. Align the scoring template properly.

   d. Record a + (plus) or a – (minus) sign next to each item in the Response Booklet.

   e. If more than one symbol is marked and there is no clear indication of self-correction, count the item as incorrect.

   f. If there is a clear indication of self-correction, score the final response.

   g. Do not count skipped items, items that have not been reached, or sample and practice items.

   h. Do not count spoiled items. Consider an item spoiled when the child marks (a) a target symbol, (b) a vertical line through symbols on more than one line, or (c) a diagonal line through symbols on more than one line. However, as the discussion below indicates, it may difficult to decide whether an item is spoiled.

i. There are no time-bonus credits.

Response Booklet

31. Enter the child's name, the date, and your name.
32. Enter the number of correct responses in the appropriate space at the bottom of each page of the Response Booklet.
33. Enter the number of incorrect responses in the appropriate space at the bottom of each page of the Response Booklet.

Record Form

34. Record the completion time in seconds in the Completion Time box.
35. Add the number of correct items (C) from the bottom of each page of the Response Booklet, and enter the sum in the Number Correct box on the Record Form.
36. Add the number of incorrect items (I) from the bottom of each page of the Response Booklet, and enter the sum in the Number Incorrect box on the Record Form.
37. Subtract the number of incorrect items from the number of correct items (not from the total number of items completed), and enter the score in the Total Raw Score box on the Record Form.
38. If the total raw score is equal to or less than 0 points, enter a 0.

In some cases it may be difficult to distinguish an incorrect response from a spoiled response. The instructions on page 113 of the Administration Manual say that an item is incorrect "if the child draws a line across all four of the search symbols or if more than one search symbol is marked." It also says that items are spoiled if the child "draws a vertical or diagonal line through a series of item search symbols." According to Figure 3.4 on page 113 of the Administration Manual, this seems to mean marking at least two or more different items with a continuous line. What is the proper score when a child draws a horizontal line through two symbols on one item and continues the horizontal line to the next item and then draws a line through two symbols?

Take another example. A child draws a vertical line connecting three question marks on three items. She draws this continuous vertical line to show that her answers are the same for all three items. If you followed the scoring guidelines, you would mark this as a spoiled response. But is it? We simply do not know. You need to know whether the child was marking the symbols

randomly or deliberately.

In describing the child's response to the last three items in Figure 3.4, the Administration Manual says, "Child did not appear to respond to a single item." How does one know whether the child was or was not responding to a single item? What if the child was responding to three single items but connecting his or her responses, as noted in the example above? In such cases, would it not be more appropriate to ask the child about his or her responses before assuming that the pattern indicated spoiled items? Scoring guidelines need to be as objective as possible. This in part means that it should not be the examiner's responsibility to infer what the child meant by his or her responses. The Administration Manual needs to present more objective guidelines on how to distinguish *incorrect responses* from *spoiled responses*. In addition, the instructions might be improved by including a provision requiring examiners to tell children who mark more than one item at a time to mark only one item at a time.

Interpretive Suggestions

The following questions are useful to guide your observation of the child's performance on the Symbol Search subtest.

- Does the child use one hand to hold the paper in place and the other hand to draw the diagonal lines?
- How does the child approach the task (e.g., is the child impulsive, meticulous, overly anxious)?
- Does the child display tremor?
- As the subtest proceeds, does the child's speed increase or decrease?
- Are the child's diagonal lines (/) well executed, or are they barely recognizable?
- Does the child draw the diagonal lines slowly or quickly?
- Does the child make errors? If so, note the kinds of errors made, the manner in which they are made, the child's awareness of making errors, and the child's reaction to the errors. For example, does the child mark the question mark when there is a match for the stimulus figure or mark an incorrect symbol when there is not a match for the stimulus figure?
- How long does it take for the child to understand the task?
- Is there any pattern to the child's successes and failures? For example, does the child tend to succeed on items in which the target symbol is displayed in the search group but fail items in which the target symbol is not displayed in the search group?

- Does the child lose points for inaccuracy?
- Does the child recheck every item before moving on to the next one?
- Does the child frequently look back and forth between the target symbol or symbols and the search group?
- Is the child's work smooth and orderly, or does the child seem confused at times and have difficulty finding his or her place?
- Is the child persistent?
- Does the child need repeated urging to continue the task?
- Is the child bored with the task?
- Does the child hold the pencil in an appropriate way?
- Does the child try to use an eraser from another pencil or another source? If so, does the child seem to realize that an eraser is not supposed to be used?
- Does the child stop in the middle of the task, stretch, sigh, look around, or talk?
- Does the child talk, sing, or hum while working?
- Does the child work so slowly that the task is not completed within the allotted time? If so, what might account for this performance?
- Does the child put a premium on speed or accuracy (i.e., is the final score a result of the child's going too fast at the expense of making mistakes or going too slow at the expense of completing too few items)?

Answers to these questions (and similar ones) may give you information about the child's attention, persistence, impulsive tendencies, compulsive tendencies, and depressive tendencies. An increase in speed, coupled with success on items, suggests that the child is adjusting well to the task. A decrease in speed, coupled with failure on items, suggests that the child may be showing fatigue.

It may be of interest to compare children who obtain the same score in varying ways. For example, suppose two children each get a raw score of 25, but one child completes 25 items and has 25 correct and 0 incorrect items and the other child completes 45 items and has 35 correct and 10 incorrect items. These two children display different styles of working. The first child is slower than the second child but careful in approaching the task. Perhaps this first child is a meticulous worker who carries out tasks steadily and methodically. In contrast, the second child works faster, but makes errors. Perhaps this second child is somewhat careless and impulsive. To support your hypotheses, you will need to examine scores from other WPPSI–III subtests, scores from other tests, and information from observations, interviews, and the case history.

Children may be penalized on the Symbol Search subtest if they (a) respond extremely slowly and carefully, (b) are compulsive and constantly check the target symbol against those in the search group, (c) are impulsive and fail to check the search group symbols against the target symbol, or (d) have trouble discriminating symbols. Again, look at the child's entire performance on the subtest (and all other sources of information) for possible hypotheses that might account for the child's performance on the Symbol Search subtest.

High scores on the Symbol Search subtest may indicate good processing speed ability, good perceptual discrimination ability, good attention and concentration, good short-term visual memory, sustained energy or persistence, motivation, or desire for achievement.

Low scores on the Symbol Search subtest may indicate poor processing speed ability, poor perceptual discrimination ability, poor attention and concentration, poor short-term visual memory, lethargy or boredom, limited motivation, limited desire to achieve, anxiety, difficulty in working under time pressure, or impulsivity.

For children who make many errors, one testing-of-limits procedure that can be carried out after the *entire test* is completed is to go over each item on which an error occurred. You can point to the items on which an error occurred and say, "Tell me about your answer" or "Tell me about why you marked that one." Another testing-of-limits procedure for highly distractible children is to see whether their performance improves when they are provided with a ruler or a piece of paper with which to cover all the rows except the one to be completed.

Profile analysis is severely to slightly restricted at ages 4-0 to 4-5, 4-6 to 4-11, 5-0 to 5-2, 5-3 to 5-11, 6-0 to 6-11, and 7-0 to 7-3, where the scaled scores range from 6 to 19, 5 to 19, 4 to 19, 3 to 19, 2 to 19, and 1 to 18, respectively.

COMPREHENSION

Comprehension, which is a supplemental subtest at ages 4-0 to 7-3 and is not given at ages 2-6 to 3-11, requires the child to explain situations, actions, or activities that relate to events familiar to most children. The 28 items cover several content areas, including survival skills, health practices, knowledge of one's body, interpersonal relations, and social mores. The subtest is not timed. It is somewhat difficult to administer and score.

Rationale

On the Comprehension subtest, the child must understand given situations and provide answers to specific problems. Success depends on the child's possession of practical information, plus an ability to make use of previous experiences. Responses may reflect the child's knowledge of conventional societal customs and behaviors and the extensiveness of cultural opportunities, particularly exposure to middle-class mores and customs. Success suggests that the child has common sense, social judgment, and a grasp of social conventionality. These characteristics imply an ability to use facts in a pertinent, meaningful, and emotionally appropriate manner. Success is also based on the child's ability to verbalize acceptable reasons for why certain things are done in our culture.

Factor Analytic Findings

At ages 4-0 to 7-3, Comprehension is a good measure of g (56% of its variance can be attributed to g). It contributes substantially to the Verbal factor (average loading = .75). Subtest specificity is ample at ages 4-6 to 4-11 and 6-0 to 7-3 and adequate at ages 4-0 to 4-5 and 5-0 to 5-11.

Reliability and Correlational Highlights

Comprehension is a reliable subtest (r_{xx} = .88), with reliability coefficients at or above .86 at ages 4-0 to 7-3 (range of .86 to .90). It correlates better with Vocabulary (r = .70) and Word Reasoning (r = .70) than with any of the other subtests. It has a moderately high correlation with the Full Scale IQ (r = .71) and the Verbal IQ (r = .76), a moderate correlation with the Performance IQ (r = .55), and a moderately low correlation with the Processing Speed Quotient (r = .38).

Administrative Guidelines

The following administrative guidelines for the Comprehension subtest must be followed carefully.

Background Considerations

1. Read the instructions verbatim.
2. Read the instructions clearly.
3. Read the items verbatim.
4. Read the items clearly.

5. Repeat the instructions if the child asks or has not responded within 5 to 10 seconds, unless it is clear that the child is considering a response.
6. Repeat items correctly.
7. If the child is hesitant, say, "Yes" or "Go ahead" or another suitable statement. However, do not define words or give any other help not specifically indicated in the Administration Manual.
8. If the child gives a 0-point response to items 1 and 2, give the correct 1-point answer.
9. For items 3 to 20, do not give the child the correct answers.
10. Query unclear or vague responses, as well as the sample responses marked by a "(Q)" in the Administration Manual. *This includes all the responses separated by semicolons on a line that has a "(Q)" at the end.* Do not query clearly wrong responses or responses that are clearly correct. For item 20, if the child gives the specific response noted on page 147, give the child the prompt noted at the bottom of the page.
11. If the child fails to respond and has been performing poorly, wait about 30 seconds before going to the next item and say, "Let's try another one." However, use your judgment about moving to the next item sooner. For children who are clearly beyond their ability, 30 seconds may be a long time to wait, especially if it is the third or fourth 30-second wait. For example, this would be the case for children who seem to be bored, who are shrugging their shoulders, or who are looking around the room after a few seconds and not looking at the item.
12. If the child fails to respond but has been performing successfully and appears to be working on a response, give the child the necessary time to respond before going to the next item.

Starting Considerations

13. Start with the appropriate item.
 a. The ages listed under "Start" on page 127 of the Administration Manual are always intended to be inclusive; thus, ages 4–5 means children 4-0 to 5-11 years of age and ages 6–7 means children 6-0 to 7-3 years of age.
 b. The starting ages on the Record Form are also inclusive.
 c. Children 4-0 to 5-11 years of age (and older children suspected of having intellectual deficiency) start with item 1.
 d. Children 6-0 to 7-3 years of age (not suspected of having intellectual deficiency) start with item 4.

Reverse Sequence

14. If necessary, administer the items in reverse sequence as directed in the Administration Manual.

a. The instructions on page 127 of the Administration Manual under the heading "Reverse" pertain to children who begin the subtest with item 4.

b. If the child (a) does not obtain full credit on the start-point item or (b) obtains full credit on the start-point item and a score of 0 on the next item, administer the items in reverse sequence.

c. Continue the reverse sequence until the child has perfect scores on two consecutive items or until item 1 has been administered, even if the discontinue criterion is met.

d. When there is a reverse sequence, the discontinue criterion is not met, and either there are two consecutive items with perfect scores or item 1 is administered, continue administration with the item after the last start-point item.

Discontinue Considerations

15. Count items administered in reverse sequence toward the discontinue criterion.

16. Discontinue the subtest when five consecutive scores of 0 are obtained, unless the consecutive 0's are obtained during a reverse sequence and (a) item 1 has not been reached or (b) the child has not obtained perfect scores on two consecutive items.

Scoring Guidelines

17. Score the items using the following guidelines.

a. Study carefully the general scoring principle for each item. The Comprehension subtest is somewhat difficult to score, and children may give responses that differ from those provided in the Administration Manual.

b. To score the child's response, use the general rule noted for each item.

c. Items 1 and 2 are scored 0 or 1. The most complete or best response receives a score of 1, and an incorrect response receives a score of 0.

d. Items 3 to 20 are scored 0, 1, or 2. The most complete or best response receives a score of 2; a less adequate response, 1; and an incorrect response, 0.

e. For multiple responses, score the entire response given, rather than just the initial response.

f. Added remarks that do not spoil an answer do not affect the score.

g. If a child gives a response that has multiple parts, none of which spoils the entire response, and these parts could be scored separately as 0, 1, or 2, score the best response.

h. Give 0 points for a multiple response that has both correct and incorrect concepts, with the incorrect portion of the answer revealing a fundamental misunderstanding of the item; this is a spoiled response.

i. When the child earns perfect scores on the first two items at the start point or in a reversal, award full credit for all preceding items, regardless of the child's performance on these items if they have been administered.

j. Award no points for any items beyond the last score of 0 required for the discontinue criterion to be met, regardless of the child's performance on these items if they have been administered.

Record Form

18. Record the child's responses verbatim in the Response column.

19. For items 1 and 2, circle 0 or 1 in the Score column for each item administered; for items 3 to 20, circle 0, 1, or 2.

20. To note the points awarded for items not administered below the first two items with perfect scores, put a slash mark in the Score column over the item preceding the first two items with perfect scores and write the numerals for these points.

21. Add the points, including the points for correct answers and the points for items not administered before the first two perfect scores, but not for items administered after the last discontinue item.

22. Enter the Total Raw Score in the shaded box.

Interpretive Suggestions

The following questions are useful to guide your observation of the child's performance on the Comprehension subtest.

• Do the child's failures indicate misunderstanding of the meaning of a word or the implications of a particular phrase?

• Does the child provide a complete answer or just part of one?

• Does the child respond to the entire question or only to a part of it?

• Does the child seem to be objective, seeing various possibilities and choosing the best possible response?

• Is the child indecisive, unable to give firm answers?

• Are the child's responses too quick, indicating failure to consider the questions in their entirety?

• Does the child recognize when answers were sufficient or insufficient?

- How does the child respond when asked to explain his or her answer (e.g., becomes impatient, flustered, challenged by the request)?
- Are any of the child's responses unusual? If so, how?

Responses to the Comprehension questions may provide information about the child's personality style, ethical values, and social and cultural background. Unlike the Information questions, which usually elicit precise answers, the Comprehension questions may elicit more complex and idiosyncratic replies. Because the questions may involve judgment of social situations, the answers may reflect the child's social attitudes. Some responses may reveal understanding and acceptance of social mores, whereas others may reveal understanding but not acceptance of social mores. A child may know the right answers but not always act properly.

A child's replies may reveal initiative, self-reliance, independence, self-confidence, helplessness, indecisiveness, inflexibility, manipulative tendencies, naive perceptions of problems, cooperative solutions, hostility, aggression, or other traits. For example, a child with a dependent personality style might describe seeking help from others when faced with a problem situation.

Because Comprehension requires considerable verbal expression, the subtest may be sensitive to mild language impairments and to disordered thought processes. Be alert to language deficits (such as word-retrieval difficulties), circumstantial or tangential speech, or other expressive difficulties.

High scores on the Comprehension subtest may indicate skill in forming social judgments and in using common sense, skill in recognizing when practical judgment and common sense are necessary, skill in knowing the rules of conventional behavior, skill in organizing knowledge, skill in verbalizing, maturity, or having had wide experiences.

Low scores on the Comprehension subtest may indicate difficulty in forming social judgments and in using common sense, difficulty in recognizing when practical judgment and common sense are necessary, difficulty in knowing the rules of conventional behavior, difficulty in organizing knowledge, difficulty in verbalizing, immaturity, or having had limited experiences. In some cases, low scores may reflect creativity in looking for unusual solutions or negativism.

If you suspect word-retrieval problems, use a multiple-choice testing-of-limits procedure. This procedure may help you distinguish between deficits associated with word-retrieval difficulties and those associated with deficient knowledge. After completing the *entire test*, go back to the item (or items) with which the child had difficulty and give the child three answers from which to choose. For example, say, "Why do we wear shoes—because shoes are hard to find, because shoes keep our feet dry when it rains, or because the heels wear out? Which one is it?" Be sure to randomly vary the position of the correct answer in the series (i.e., put the correct answer sometimes in first, sometimes in second, and sometimes in third position). If the child answers the multiple-choice questions correctly, the child may have a word-retrieval difficulty and not deficient knowledge. However, the multiple-choice procedure should not be used to calculate an IQ. Another testing-of-limits procedure is to ask the child to explain any unusual responses after the test is completed.

The range of scaled scores from 1 to 19 at ages 7-0 to 7-3 aids in profile analysis. However, profile analysis is severely to slightly restricted at ages 4-0 to 4-5, 4-6 to 4-11, 5-0 to 5-11, and 6-0 to 6-11, where the scaled scores range from 5 to 19, 4 to 19, 3 to 19, and 2 to 19, respectively.

PICTURE COMPLETION

Picture Completion, which is a supplemental subtest at ages 4-0 to 7-3 and is not given at ages 2-6 to 3-11, requires the child to identify the single most important missing detail in 32 drawings of common objects, animals, and people—such as a chair, a clock, or a door. The child's task is to name or point to the essential missing portion of the incomplete picture within the 20-second time limit. The subtest is relatively easy to administer and score.

Rationale

On the Picture Completion subtest, the child must recognize the object depicted in the picture, appreciate its incompleteness, and determine the missing part. It is a test of visual discrimination—the ability to differentiate between essential and nonessential details. Picture Completion requires concentration, reasoning (or visual alertness), attention to detail, visual organization, and long-term visual memory (as many of the items require a child to have stored information from previous experience and to retrieve the information to determine what is incomplete about the figure).

Picture Completion also measures the perceptual and conceptual abilities involved in visual recognition and identification of familiar objects. Perception, cognition, judgment, and delay of impulse all may influence performance. The time limit on the subtest places additional demands on the child. The richness of the child's life experiences also may affect her or his performance on the subtest.

Factor Analytic Findings

At ages 4-0 to 7-3, Picture Completion is a fair measure of *g* (48% of its variance can be attributed to *g*). It contributes moderately to the Performance factor (average loading = .47). Subtest specificity is ample at all ages from 4-0 to 7-3.

Reliability and Correlational Highlights

Picture Completion is a reliable subtest (r_{xx} = .90), with reliability coefficients at or above .87 at ages 4-0 to 7-3 (range of .87 to .92). It correlates better with Information (r = .55) and Word Reasoning (r = .55) than with any of the other subtests. It has a moderate correlation with the Full Scale IQ (r = .66), the Performance IQ (r = .59), and the Verbal IQ (r = .59) and a moderately low correlation with the Processing Speed Quotient (r = .46).

Administrative Guidelines

The following administrative guidelines for the Picture Completion subtest must be followed carefully.

Background Considerations

1. Read the items verbatim.
2. Read the items clearly.
3. Repeat the instructions if the child asks or has not responded within 5 to 10 seconds.
4. Place the closed Stimulus Book 2 with the coil-bound edge facing and close to the child so that the book is completely flat when it is opened.
5. Open Stimulus Book 2 to the sample, and turn the pages one at a time to show consecutive pictures.
6. Allow 20 seconds for each item.
7. For items 3 to 32, if the child clearly understands the task, shorten the instructions, if desired.
8. Begin timing after the last word of the instructions. Count any prompts as part of the 20-second time limit.
9. Stop timing when the child answers or after 20 seconds. Allow the child additional time after the time limit to complete his or her answer, if needed, but do not score as correct any response after the 20-second time limit.

10. If the child gives an incorrect response (or no response) to the sample or to item 1 or 2, give the child the correct answer.
11. For items 3 to 32, if the child gives an incorrect response (or no response), do not give the child the correct answers.
12. Query the child as often as necessary during the subtest if the child (a) names the object instead of the missing part, (b) names a part that is off the picture, or (c) mentions an unessential missing part. Use the specific queries noted on page 149 of the Administration Manual.
13. If the child gives one of the responses noted in the right-hand column of pages 153 to 156 in the Administration Manual, say, "Show me where you mean."

Starting Considerations

14. Start with the appropriate item.
    a. The ages listed under "Start" on page 148 of the Administration Manual are always intended to be inclusive; thus, age 4 means children 4-0 to 4-11 years of age, age 5 means children 5-0 to 5-11 years of age, and ages 6–7 means children 6-0 to 7-3 years of age.
    b. The starting ages on the Record Form are also inclusive.
    c. Children 4 years of age (and older children suspected of having intellectual deficiency) start with the sample items and then item 1.
    d. Children 5 years of age (not suspected of having intellectual deficiency) start with the sample items and then item 4.
    e. Children 6 to 7 years of age (not suspected of having intellectual deficiency) start with the sample items and then item 7.

Reverse Sequence

15. If necessary, administer the items in reverse sequence as directed in the Administration Manual.
    a. The instructions on page 148 of the Administration Manual under the heading "Reverse" pertain to children who begin the subtest with the samples and then with item 4 or 7.
    b. If the child (a) does not obtain full credit on the start-point item or (b) obtains full credit on the start-point item and a score of 0 on the next item, administer the items in reverse sequence.
    c. Continue the reverse sequence until the child has perfect scores on two consecutive items or until item 1 has been administered, even if the discontinue criterion is met.

d. When there is a reverse sequence, the discontinue criterion is not met, and either there are two consecutive items with perfect scores or item 1 is administered, continue administration with the item after the last start-point item.

Discontinue Considerations

16. Count items administered in reverse sequence toward the discontinue criterion.
17. Discontinue the subtest when five consecutive scores of 0 are obtained, unless the consecutive 0's are obtained during a reverse sequence and (a) item 1 has not been reached or (b) the child has not obtained perfect scores on two consecutive items.
18. Once the subtest is completed, remove Stimulus Book 2 from the child's view.

Scoring Guidelines

19. Score the items using the following guidelines.
   a. Score all items 0 or 1.
   b. Give 0 points for an incorrect response, a spoiled response (e.g., a correct pointing response accompanied by an incorrect verbal response), or a correct response given after the 20-second time limit.
   c. Give 1 point for any reasonable response; the response does not have to be the exact name of the missing part. Therefore, give 1 point for a correct verbal *or* pointing response (including any verbal *or* pointing response listed in the *second column* on pages 153 to 156 of the Administration Manual), a synonym for the missing part, a description of the missing part, or a verbal response listed in the *third column* on pages 153 to 156 of the Administration Manual that is accompanied by a correct pointing response.
   d. After a query, score the best response.
   e. When the child earns perfect scores on the first two items at the start point or in a reversal, award full credit for all preceding items, regardless of the child's performance on these items if they have been administered.
   f. Award no points for any items beyond the last score of 0 required for the discontinue criterion to be met, regardless of the child's performance on these items if they have been administered.

Record Form

20. Record the child's responses verbatim in the Response column. As an optional procedure, you can also record the completion time in seconds in the Response column.

21. Use PC to record a correct pointing response.
22. Use PX to record an incorrect pointing response.
23. Circle 0 or 1 in the Score column for each item administered.
24. Record the completion time in seconds in the Completion Time column.
25. To note the points awarded for items not administered below the first two items with perfect scores, put a slash mark in the Score column over the item preceding the first two items with perfect scores and write the numerals for these points.
26. Add the points, including the points for correct answers and the points for items not administered before the first two perfect scores, but not for items administered after the last discontinue item.
27. Enter the Total Raw Score in the shaded box.

Interpretive Suggestions

The following questions are useful to guide your observation of the child's performance on the Picture Completion subtest.

* Does the child understand the task?
* Does the child respond with a word, with a description of the missing detail, or by pointing?
* Does the child give mainly verbal responses or pointing responses?
* Does the child respond impulsively, saying anything that comes to mind, or does the child search for the right answer?
* How does the child respond when the missing part is not identified (e.g., accepts the failure or finds fault with himself or herself or with the picture)?
* Does the child benefit from any queries listed on page 164 of the Administration Manual?
* What is the child's rate of response (e.g., quick and impulsive or slow and deliberate)?
* Is the child fearful of making an error, hesitant, or suspicious?
* Is the child aware of being timed? If so, does the timing make the child anxious or prompt the child to change the pace of responding?
* Does the child frequently use nondescriptive speech, such as "It's that thing there"?
* Does the child give roundabout descriptions of words (sometimes called *circumlocutions* or *paraphasic language*)?
* Does the child have trouble producing the right word?
* Does the child repeatedly say that nothing is missing?

- Does the child hold Stimulus Book 2 near or move close to it?
- Does the child make a story about the picture while forming or giving a response?
- Is the child's response pattern consistent?
- Does the child have problems identifying specific items (e.g., does he or she ask what the picture is)?
- Does the child consistently miss items in which the missing part is in a specific area of the page (e.g., visual neglect)?
- How frequently does the child give correct answers after the time limit?
- Does the child attempt to turn pages of Stimulus Book 2 (showing impatience or a desire to control the testing situation)?

If the child's performance leaves any doubt as to whether he or she has normal vision, request a visual examination.

The child who usually responds in less than 5 seconds may be more impulsive, more confident, and, if correct, more skilled than the child who takes more time. The child who responds correctly after the time limit (for which no credit is received) may be more skilled than the child who fails the item even with additional time. Because the pass-fail scoring does not make provisions for such qualitative factors, carefully evaluate individual variations in each case and discuss these qualitative factors in the written report. Correct responses made slightly before or slightly after 20 seconds may suggest temporary inefficiency, insecurity, depression, or simply a slow and diligent approach, whereas extremely quick but incorrect responses may reflect impulsivity.

Circumlocutions, as well as difficulty producing the right word, suggest that the child has word-retrieval difficulties. Word-retrieval difficulties may be related to dysnomia (i.e., nominal aphasia), a form of aphasia in which the child has difficulty naming objects. A child who repeatedly says that nothing is missing may be revealing negativism. A child who holds Stimulus Book 2 close to his or her face or puts his or her face close to Stimulus Book 2 may have visual difficulties.

High scores on the Picture Completion subtest may indicate good perception and concentration, good alertness to details, good ability to differentiate between essential and nonessential details, or good ability to establish a learning set quickly.

Low scores on the Picture Completion subtest may indicate poor perception and concentration, poor alertness to details, difficulty in differentiating between essential and nonessential details, difficulty in establishing a learning set quickly, preoccupation with irrelevant details, anxiety, or negativism.

After you administer the subtest, you can inquire about the child's perceptions of the task: "How did you go about coming up with the answer?" or "How did you decide when to give an answer?" Inquire about any noteworthy or unclear answers. Children's behavior during this subtest may provide insight into their reaction to time pressure. As a testing-of-limits procedure, ask the child to look again at the pictures that were missed. Say, "Look at this picture again. Before, you said that ____ was missing. That's not the part that's missing. Look for something else." In some cases, it may be appropriate to ask the child to describe or name the picture, especially when many items are missed.

The range of scaled scores from 1 to 19 at ages 4-6 to 6-11 aids in profile analysis. However, profile analysis is slightly restricted at ages 4-0 to 4-5 and 7-0 to 7-3, where scaled scores range from 2 to 19 and 1 to 18, respectively.

SIMILARITIES

Similarities, which is a supplemental subtest at ages 4-0 to 7-3 and is not given at ages 2-6 to 3-11, requires the child to answer questions about how two common objects or concepts are alike. The child is asked to state the similarity between the two items in each pair. The subtest contains 24 pairs of words and one sample and is not timed. The subtest is relatively easy to administer but difficult to score.

Rationale

On the Similarities subtest, the child must perceive the common elements of the paired terms and then bring the common elements together into a meaningful concept. Thus, the subtest measures verbal concept formation—the ability to place objects and events together into a meaningful group. To do this, the child may need to find relationships that are not at first obvious, a process of abstraction. Although concept formation can be a voluntary, effortful process, it also can reflect well-automatized verbal conventions. Performance on the subtest may be related to cultural opportunities and interest patterns. Memory may also be involved. Success initially depends on the child's ability to comprehend the meaning of the task—that is, to find the common element of the paired items even though some of the paired items may be opposites. If the child does understand the task, the child still needs to know the concept that reflects the common element in the paired items in order to receive credit.

Factor Analytic Findings

At ages 4-0 to 7-3, Similarities is a good measure of g (58% of its variance can be attributed to g). It contributes substantially to the Verbal factor (average loading = .84). Subtest specificity is ample at ages 4-6 to 4-11 and 6-0 to 7-3 and adequate at ages 4-0 to 4-5 and 5-0 to 5-11.

Reliability and Correlational Highlights

Similarities is a reliable subtest (r_{xx} = .95), with reliability coefficients at or above .91 at ages 4-0 to 7-3 (range of .91 to .96). It correlates better with Vocabulary (r = .69), Information (r = .67), and Word Reasoning (r = .67) than with any of the other subtests. It has a moderately high correlation with the Full Scale IQ (r = .73) and the Verbal IQ (r = .75), a moderate correlation with the Performance IQ (r = .60), and a moderately low correlation with the Processing Speed Quotient (r = .39).

Administrative Guidelines

The following administrative guidelines for the Similarities subtest must be followed carefully.

Background Considerations

1. Read the items verbatim.
2. Read the items clearly.
3. Repeat the instructions if the child asks or has not responded within 5 to 10 seconds, unless it is clear that the child is considering a response.
4. Repeat each item as often as necessary.
5. Emphasize the word *both* in reading each item.
6. Query unclear or vague responses, as well as the sample responses marked by a "(Q)" in the Administration Manual. *This includes all the responses separated by semicolons on a line that has a "(Q)" at the end*. Do not query responses that are clearly wrong or responses that are clearly correct.
7. For trials 1 and 2 of items 1 and 2, if the child makes an incorrect response, give him or her the correct answers.
8. For items 3 to 24, if the child makes an incorrect response, do not give him or her the correct answers.

9. If the child fails to respond and has been performing poorly, wait about 30 seconds before going to the next item and say, "Let's try another one." However, use your judgment about moving to the next item sooner. For children who are clearly beyond their ability, 30 seconds may be a long time to wait, especially if it is the third or fourth 30-second wait. For example, this would be the case for children who seem to be bored, who are shrugging their shoulders, or who are looking around the room after a few seconds and not looking at the item.
10. If the child fails to respond but has been performing successfully and appears to be working on a response, give the child the necessary time to respond before going to the next item.

Starting Considerations

11. Start with the appropriate item.
   a. The ages listed under "Start" on page 157 of the Administration Manual are always intended to be inclusive; thus, ages 4–7 means children 4-0 to 7-3 years of age.
   b. The starting ages on the Record Form are also inclusive.
   c. All children begin with item 1.
   d. There is no reverse sequence on the Similarities subtest.

Discontinue Considerations

12. Discontinue the subtest when four consecutive scores of 0 are obtained.

Scoring Guidelines

13. Score the responses using the following guidelines.
   a. When a child gives multiple acceptable responses for an item, score the best response.
   b. The scoring examples are not an exhaustive list of correct and incorrect responses.
   c. A careful study of the sample responses will help you become more proficient in scoring Similarities responses.
   d. Study—and master—the General Principles, which clarify the rationales for scores of 0, 1, and 2.
   e. Note that the General Principles do not literally pertain to items 1 and 2. This is because items 1 and 2 can be scored only 0 or 1.
   f. When parts of the response vary in quality but none spoil the entire response, score the best response.
   g. Score the response without considering extraneous parts of the response.
   h. Give a score of 0 to the entire response if it has been spoiled or if it is not pertinent to both objects (or

terms), is too general, or reflects a difference in the objects (or terms).

i. Give a score of 1 on items 1 and 2 for any response that reflects a major classification, a minor classification, or a specific property of the objects (or terms) or on items 3 to 24 for any response that reflects a concrete response (i.e., a specific property common to both objects or terms) or that reflects a less major classification.

j. Give a score of 2 on items 3 to 24 for any response that reflects a conceptual response, such as a major classification.

k. Award no points for any items beyond the last score of 0 required for the discontinue criterion to be met, regardless of the child's performance on these items if they have been administered.

Record Form

14. Record the child's responses verbatim in the Response column. For items 1 and 2, use the appropriate spaces to record the child's responses for trial 1 and trial 2 (if needed).

15. Circle 0 or 1 in the Score column for items 1 and 2 and circle 0, 1, or 2 in the Score column for items 3 to 24.

16. Add the points correctly.

17. Enter the Total Raw Score in the shaded box.

Interpretive Suggestions

The following questions are useful to guide your observation of the child's performance on the Similarities subtest.

- Does the child seem to understand the task?
- How many 0-point, 1-point, and 2-point responses does the child have on items 3 to 24?
- Is the pattern of scores consistent or variable?
- Is the child thinking through the questions, responding impulsively, or simply guessing?
- Does the child appear confident or hesitant when responding?
- Does the child give peculiar responses? If so, in what way? What might these responses suggest?
- Does the child frequently say, "I know this answer, but I can't think of it" or "I don't know"?
- Are the child's answers precise, imprecise, or vague?
- Are the child's answers close to the correct answer or completely wrong?
- Are the child's answers overinclusive (see below)?
- Does the child give overly verbose responses or short, succinct responses?

- Does the child frequently give phonetic similarities between the words (e.g., says that both words end in *ing* or both words start with *p*)?
- Are there frequent self-corrections?
- Does the child seem to be inhibited in making responses?
- What is the pattern of the child's successes and failures?

The subtest requires knowing what the two words in each pair mean; therefore, a child who does not know the meaning of each word in the pair is likely to fail that item. If several items are failed because of vocabulary difficulties, the child's performance probably is related to vocabulary deficiency rather than to categorization ability deficiency.

Observing the child's typical level of conceptualization will help you understand the child's thinking style. Consider whether the answers are concrete, functional, or abstract. *Concrete answers* typically refer to qualities of the objects (or stimuli) that can be seen or touched (apple-banana: "Both have a skin"). *Functional answers* typically concern a function or use of the objects (apple-banana: "You eat them"). Finally, *abstract answers* typically refer to a more universal property or to a common classification of the objects (apple-banana: "Both are fruits").

You can tell, in part, whether the child's response style is concrete, functional, or abstract by the numbers of 0-, 1-, and 2-point responses. Responses that receive 0 or 1 suggest a more concrete and functional conceptualization style, while responses that receive 2 suggest a more abstract conceptualization style. However, a 2-point response does not necessarily reflect abstract thinking ability and may simply be an overlearned response. For example, there may be a difference between the 2-point response "Both fruits" for apple-banana and the 2-point response "Artistic expressions" for painting-statue. Although "Both fruits" receives 2 points, it may be an overlearned response, whereas "Artistic expressions" may reflect a more abstract level of conceptual ability.

Furthermore, if the child earns 1 point on several items but has few 2-point scores, the child may have a good breadth of knowledge but not depth. If the child earns 2 points on several items but has few 1-point scores, the child may have a good depth of knowledge but less breadth.

Failures on easy items coupled with successes on more difficult ones may suggest poor motivation, anxiety, temporary inefficiency, boredom, or an inconsistent environment. Alternatively, this pattern may indicate a problem with lower-level conceptual responses.

Overinclusive responses are so general that several objects are included in the concept. For example, the reply "Both contain molecules" to a question asking for the similarity between an apple and a banana is overinclusive because it does not delimit the particular characteristics of these two objects. A pattern of either overinclusive responses or responses filled with numerous similarities may suggest perfectionistic tendencies. Alternatively, responses with an excessive number of similarities may simply reflect the child's desire to impress you. Consider the child's entire test performance, plus other relevant information, when you interpret responses that may be overinclusive. Excessive overinclusive responses may be a subtle indication of unusual thinking.

Observe how the child handles any frustration induced by the subtest questions. For example, when the child has difficulty answering the questions, does the child become negativistic and uncooperative or continue to try to answer the questions? A child who responds with "They are not alike" may be displaying negativism, avoidance of the task demands, suspiciousness, a coping mechanism, or deficient knowledge. To determine which of these may account for the child's response, compare the child's style of responding to the Similarities questions with the style of responding to questions on other subtests; also refer to the interview and to other sources of information to develop and confirm hypotheses.

High scores on the Similarities subtest may indicate good conceptual thinking, good ability to see relationships, good ability to use logical and abstract thinking, good ability to discriminate fundamental from superficial relationships, good ability to select and verbalize appropriate relationships between two objects or concepts, or flexibility of thought processes.

Low scores on the Similarities subtest may indicate poor conceptual thinking, difficulty in seeing relationships, difficulty in selecting and verbalizing appropriate relationships between two objects or concepts, an overly concrete mode of thinking, poor vocabulary knowledge, rigidity of thought processes, or negativism.

If you suspect word-retrieval problems, use a multiple-choice testing-of-limits procedure. This procedure may help distinguish deficits associated with word-retrieval difficulties from those associated with deficient knowledge. After completing the *entire test*, go back to the item (or items) with which the child had difficulty and give the child three answers from which to choose. For example, follow an item like "In what way are radio and television alike?" with "Choose one of the following: Because you read them, listen to news on them, or watch cartoons on them. What is your answer?" Be sure to randomly vary the position of the correct answer in the series (i.e., put the correct answer sometimes in first, sometimes in second, and sometimes in third position). If the child answers the multiple-choice questions correctly, the child may have a word-retrieval difficulty rather than deficient knowledge. However, the multiple-choice procedure should not be used to calculate an IQ.

Profile analysis is severely to slightly restricted at ages 4-0 to 4-11, 5-0 to 5-2, 5-3 to 5-11, 6-0 to 6-3, and 6-4 to 7-3, where the scaled scores range from 6 to 19, 5 to 19, 4 to 19, 3 to 19, and 2 to 19, respectively.

RECEPTIVE VOCABULARY

Receptive Vocabulary, a core Verbal subtest at ages 2-6 to 3-11 and an optional subtest at ages 4-0 to 7-3, requires the child to point to one of four pictures that best represents the word spoken by the examiner. It contains 38 items and is untimed. At all ages, it combines with Picture Naming to form the General Language Composite. The subtest is easy to administer and score.

Rationale

The Receptive Vocabulary subtest, like the Vocabulary and Picture Naming subtests, is a test of word knowledge. It measures language development, memory, fund of information, perceptual recognition ability, and exposure to the culture. Scores on the subtest may be closely related to the child's home environment and, to some extent, educational experiences. Performance on the subtest is likely stable over time.

Factor Analytic Findings

At ages 2-6 to 3-11, Receptive Vocabulary is a good measure of g (66% of its variance can be attributed to g). It contributes substantially to the Verbal factor (average loading = .85). Subtest specificity is ample at all ages from 2-6 to 3-11.

Reliability and Correlational Highlights

Receptive Vocabulary is a reliable subtest ($r_{xx} = .88$), with reliability coefficients at or above .82 at all of the age groups (range of .82 to .91).

At ages 2-6 to 3-11, Receptive Vocabulary correlates better with Picture Naming ($r = .71$) and Information ($r = .71$) than with any of the other subtests. It has a high correlation with the Full Scale IQ ($r = .81$) and Verbal IQ ($r = .92$) and a moderately low correlation with the Performance IQ ($r = .46$).

At ages 4-0 to 7-3, Receptive Vocabulary correlates better with Picture Naming ($r = .67$), Word Reasoning ($r = .65$), and Information ($r = .65$) than with any of the other subtests. It has a moderate correlation with the Full Scale IQ ($r = .69$) and the Performance IQ ($r = .58$), a moderately high correlation with the Verbal IQ ($r = .70$), and a moderately low correlation with the Processing Speed Quotient ($r = .40$).

Administrative Guidelines

The following administrative guidelines for the Receptive Vocabulary subtest must be followed carefully.

Background Considerations

1. Read the items verbatim.
2. Read the items clearly.
3. Place the closed Stimulus Book 1 with the coil-bound edge facing and close to the child so that the book is completely flat when it is opened.
4. Open Stimulus Book 1 to item 1, and turn the pages one at a time to show consecutive pictures.
5. Repeat each item as often as necessary.
6. For item 1, if the child gives an incorrect response (or no response), give the child the correct answer.
7. For items 2 to 38, if the child gives an incorrect response (or no response), do not give the child the correct answers.

Starting Considerations

8. Start with the appropriate item.
   a. The ages listed under "Start" on page 173 of the Administration Manual are always intended to be inclusive; thus, ages 2–3 means children 2-6 to 3-11 years of age, ages 4–5 means children 4-0 to 5-11 years of age, and ages 6–7 means children 6-0 to 7-3 years of age.
   b. The starting ages on the Record Form are also inclusive.
   c. Children 2 to 3 years of age (and older children suspected of having intellectual deficiency) start with item 1.
   d. Children 4 to 5 years of age (not suspected of having intellectual deficiency) start with item 6.
   e. Children 6 to 7 years of age (not suspected of having intellectual deficiency) start with item 16.

Reverse Sequence

9. If necessary, administer the items in reverse sequence as directed in the Administration Manual.
   a. The instructions on page 173 of the Administration Manual under the heading "Reverse" pertain to children who begin the subtest with item 6 or 16.
   b. If the child (a) does not obtain full credit on the start-point item or (b) obtains full credit on the start-point item and a score of 0 on the next item, administer the items in reverse sequence.
   c. Continue the reverse sequence until the child has perfect scores on two consecutive items or until item 1 has been administered, even if the discontinue criterion is met.
   d. When there is a reverse sequence, the discontinue criterion is not met, and either there are two consecutive items with perfect scores or item 1 is administered, continue administration with the item after the last start-point item.

Discontinue Considerations

10. Count items administered in reverse sequence toward the discontinue criterion.
11. Discontinue the subtest after five consecutive scores of 0 are obtained, unless the consecutive 0's are obtained during a reverse sequence and (a) item 1 has not been reached or (b) the child has not obtained perfect scores on two consecutive items.
12. Once the subtest is completed, remove Stimulus Book 1 from the child's view.

Scoring Guidelines

13. Score the items using the following guidelines.
   a. Score all items 0 or 1. The correct responses are in the Record Booklet and on page 175 of the Administration Manual.
   b. When the child earns perfect scores on the first two items at the start point or in a reversal, award full credit for all preceding items, regardless of the child's performance on these items if they have been administered.
   c. Award no points for any items beyond the last score of 0 required for the discontinue criterion to be met, regardless of the child's performance on these items if they have been administered.

Record Form

14. For each item administered except for item 23, circle the response number or DK in the Response column.

15. For item 23, circle one of the four colors listed or DK.
16. Circle 0 or 1 in the Score column for each item administered.
17. To note the points awarded for items not administered below the first two items with perfect scores, put a slash mark in the Score column over the item preceding the first two items with perfect scores and write the numerals for these points.
18. Add the points, including the points for correct answers and the points for items not administered before the first two perfect scores, but not for items administered after the last discontinue item.
19. Enter the Total Raw Score in the shaded box.

Interpretive Suggestions

The following questions are useful to guide your observation of the child's performance on the Receptive Vocabulary subtest.

- How quickly does the child point to a picture?
- Does the child seem confident or uncertain in making his or her choices?
- Does the child have difficulty making a choice (e.g., points to several pictures)?
- Does the child confuse the stimulus word with another one that sounds like it?
- If the child does not know the meaning of a word, does he or she guess?
- Does the child readily say, "I don't know" and shake off further inquiries, or does the child pause, ponder, or think aloud about the item?
- Does the child say the name of the picture instead of pointing to the picture?
- Does the child show signs of a possible hearing difficulty? If so, what are the signs?
- Does the child have a response set, such as always pointing to the same place on the page?
- Does the child have any visual problems that may interfere with his or her ability to see the pictures?
- Does seeing the printed word during testing-of-limits help the child define the word?

The child's responses to the Receptive Vocabulary subtest may reveal something about her or his language skills, perceptual ability, background, cultural milieu, social development, life experiences, and responses to frustration. Try to determine the basis for incorrect responses.

High scores on the Receptive Vocabulary subtest may indicate good word knowledge, good verbal comprehension, good verbal skills and language development, good perceptual ability, extensive educational background, or a home environment in which language development was encouraged.

Low scores on the Receptive Vocabulary subtest may indicate poor word knowledge, poor verbal comprehension, poor verbal skills and language development, poor perceptual ability, limited educational background, or a home environment in which language development was not encouraged. Low scores may also occur with children who speak English as a second language or have a developmental delay.

At the end of the *entire test*, if you want to learn whether the child can define each word, you can ask him or her to do so. If you think the child may have perceptual difficulties, you can ask the child to describe the picture that he or she selected for those items that were missed. If the child can read, you can also show the child a printed version of each word to see if this additional cue helps the child point to the correct picture.

The range of scaled scores from 1 to 19 at ages 3-0 to 7-3 aids in profile analysis. However, profile analysis is slightly restricted at ages 2-6 to 2-11, where scaled scores range from 2 to 19.

OBJECT ASSEMBLY

Object Assembly, a core Performance subtest at ages 2-6 to 3-11 and a supplemental subtest at ages 4-0 to 7-3, requires a child to put jigsaw puzzle pieces together to form 14 common objects. The objects are a ball (two pieces), a hot dog (two pieces), a bird (two pieces), a clock (three pieces), a car (three pieces), a fish (three pieces), a bear (four pieces), a hand (three pieces), a house (four pieces), an apple (four pieces), a dog (four pieces), a star (three pieces), a calf (seven pieces), and a tree (six pieces). The subtest is relatively easy to administer but difficult to score.

Rationale

The Object Assembly subtest is mainly a test of the child's skill at synthesis—putting things together to form familiar objects. It requires visual-motor coordination, with motor activity guided by visual perception and sensorimotor feedback. Object Assembly also is a test of visual organizational ability, for the child needs visual organization to produce an object out of parts that may not be immediately recognizable. To solve the jigsaw puzzles, the child must be able to grasp an entire pattern by anticipating the relationships among its individual parts. The tasks require some constructive ability, as well as perceptual skill—the child must recognize individual parts and place them correctly in the incomplete figure. The child's performance also may be related to her or his rate and precision of motor activity; persistence, especially when much trial and error is required; and long-term visual memory (having stored information about the object to be formed).

Factor Analytic Findings

At ages 2-6 to 3-11, Object Assembly is a fair measure of g (31% of its variance can be attributed to g). It contributes moderately to the Performance factor (average loading = .59). Subtest specificity is ample at all ages from 2-6 to 3-11.

At ages 4-0 to 7-3, Object Assembly is a fair measure of g (34% of its variance can be attributed to g). It contributes substantially to the Performance factor (average loading = .72). Subtest specificity is ample at all ages from 4-0 and 7-3.

Reliability and Correlational Highlights

Object Assembly is a reliable subtest (r_{xx} = .85), with reliability coefficients at or above .78 at all of the age groups (range of .78 to .90).

At ages 2-6 to 3-11, Object Assembly correlates better with Picture Naming (r = .45) and Information (r = .44) than with any of the other subtests. It has a moderately high correlation with the Full Scale IQ (r = .73), a high correlation with the Performance IQ (r = .84), and a moderately low correlation with the Verbal IQ (r = .46).

At ages 4-0 to 7-3, Object Assembly correlates better with Block Design (r = .53) and Picture Completion (r = .48) than with any of the other subtests. It has a moderate correlation with the Full Scale IQ (r = .55) and the Performance IQ (r = .56) and a moderately low correlation with the Verbal IQ (r = .43) and the Processing Speed Quotient (r = .42).

Administrative Guidelines

The following administrative guidelines for the Object Assembly subtest must be followed carefully.

Background Considerations

1. Read the directions verbatim.

2. Read the directions clearly.
3. Seat the child directly opposite you.
4. Before administering each item, sequentially sort the pieces of each puzzle and stack the pieces face-down in order from highest to lowest.
5. Place the pieces of each puzzle on the table correctly.
   a. Place the pieces in sequential order from your left to right, with the number side shown and upright from your perspective.
   b. Place the pieces parallel to the edge of the table nearest the child.
   c. Place the pieces with one underline in the first row, closest to child. Place the pieces with two underlines in the second row.
   d. Place the pieces so that they are a comfortable distance from the child.
   e. Align the pieces so that the underlines beneath the numbers are in a row.
   f. After aligning the pieces, rotate them by flipping them from top to bottom, beginning with the piece numbered 1.
6. Time correctly.
   a. Begin timing after you read the last word of the instructions.
   b. Each item has a time limit of 90 seconds.
   c. When in doubt as to whether the child is finished with the task, say something like "Tell me when you have finished." Note that this instruction is not in the Administration Manual.
   d. Stop timing when the child is obviously finished with an item, when the child indicates with gestures that the item is completed, or when the time limit is reached.
   e. Allow a few additional seconds after the time limit if the child is nearing completion of an item.
   f. Do not stop timing once timing has begun, even to clarify instructions.
7. If the child hesitates or seems merely to be playing with the pieces, say, "Work as fast as you can."
8. For trials 1 and 2 of items 1 and 2, slowly put the pieces together and allow the child to look at the assembled puzzle for about 3 seconds.
9. For items 3 to 14, introduce the items by saying the specific sentences noted on page 207 of the Administration Manual.

Starting Considerations

10. Start with the appropriate item.
    a. The ages listed under "Start" on page 201 of the Administration Manual are always intended to be inclusive; thus, ages 2–3 means children 2-6 to 3-11 years of age, ages 4–5 means children 4-0 to 5-11

years of age, and ages 6–7 means children 6-0 to 7-3 years of age.

b. The starting ages on the Record Form are also inclusive.

c. Children 2 to 3 years of age (and older children suspected of having intellectual deficiency) start with item 1.

d. Children 4 to 5 years of age (not suspected of having intellectual deficiency) start with item 3.

e. Children 6 to 7 years of age (not suspected of having intellectual deficiency) start with item 8.

Reverse Sequence

11. If necessary, administer the items in reverse sequence as directed in the Administration Manual.

a. The instructions on page 201 of the Administration Manual under the heading "Reverse" pertain to children who begin the subtest with item 3 or 8.

b. If the child (a) does not obtain full credit on the start-point item or (b) obtains full credit on the start-point item and a score of 0 on the next item, administer the items in reverse sequence.

c. Continue the reverse sequence until the child has perfect scores on two consecutive items or until item 1 has been administered, even if the discontinue criterion is met.

d. When there is a reverse sequence, the discontinue criterion is not met, and either there are two consecutive items with perfect scores or item 1 is administered, continue administration with the item after the last start-point item.

Discontinue Considerations

12. Count items administered in reverse sequence toward the discontinue criterion.

13. Discontinue the subtest when three consecutive scores of 0 are obtained, unless the consecutive 0's are obtained during a reverse sequence and (a) item 1 has not been reached or (b) the child has not obtained perfect scores on two consecutive items.

14. Once the subtest is completed, remove the puzzle pieces from the child's view.

Scoring Guidelines

15. Score the responses using the following guidelines.

a. Items 1, 2, and 3 are scored 0 or 1.

b. Items 5, 6, and 8 are scored 0, 1, or 2.

c. Items 4, 7, 9, 11, 12, and 13 are scored 0, 1, 2, or 3.

d. Items 10 and 14 are scored 0, 1, 2, 3, 4, or 5.

e. For items 1 to 12, award 1 point for every correct juncture.

f. For items 13 and 14, award ½ point for every correct juncture.

g. Do not penalize for gaps and/or misalignments of ¼" or less between adjacent pieces.

h. Record the number of junctures completed within the time limit.

i. Do not award credit for any junctures completed after the time limit has expired.

j. On items 4 to 14, count the number of junctures correctly joined, and give credit for partially correct assemblies.

k. When the child earns perfect scores on the first two items at the start point or in a reversal, award full credit for all preceding items, regardless of the child's performance on these items if they have been administered.

l. Award no points for any items beyond the last score of 0 required for the discontinue criterion to be met, regardless of the child's performance on these items if they have been administered.

Record Form

16. For each trial and item, record the completion time in seconds in the Completion Time column.

17. Record the correct number of junctures in the Number of Correct Junctures column.

a. For items 1 to 12, multiply the number of correct junctures by 1.

b. For items 13 and 14, multiply the number of correct junctures by ½. When multiplying by ½, round the score upward. This procedure means that the child may get the maximum score on an item even though the assembly is imperfect (e.g., five of six correct junctures on item 13 receives an initial score of 2½ points, which is rounded to 3 points).

18. Circle the appropriate number in the Score column.

a. For items 1, 2, and 3, circle 0 or 1.

b. For items 5, 6, and 8, circle 0, 1, or 2.

c. For items 4, 7, 9, 11, 12, and 13, circle 0, 1, 2, or 3.

d. For items 10 and 14, circle 0, 1, 2, 3, 4, or 5.

19. To note the points awarded for items not administered below the first two items with perfect scores, put a slash mark in the Score column over the item preceding the first two items with perfect scores and write the numerals for these points.

20. Add the points, including the points for correct answers and the points for items not administered before the first two perfect scores, but not for items administered after the last discontinue item or for items completed after the time limit.

21. Enter the Total Raw Score in the shaded box.

Object Assembly is the only subtest in the WPPSI–III in which some items contribute as much as five times more to the final subtest score than other items. The maximum score on items 1, 2, and 3 is 1 point, whereas the maximum score on items 10 and 14 is 5 points. It is also the only subtest in which items later in the series count less in the final score than items earlier in the series. For example, item 10 has a maximum score of 5 points, whereas items 11, 12, and 13 have maximum scores of 3 points. Similarly, item 4 has a maximum score of 3 points, whereas items 5, 6, and 8 have maximum scores of 2 points. It is difficult to know the rationale for this pattern of awarding points.

There also appears to be an inconsistency in scoring. For each item, with the exception of item 13, every correct juncture receives 1 point. The definition of a juncture on page 202 of the Administration Manual is "the place where two adjacent pieces meet." The discussion on page 202 seems to imply that all correct junctures should be counted. However, on item 13, the juncture connecting the tail and rear leg of the calf is not counted. We don't know whether this was an oversight or part of the design of scoring the subtest. Because of rounding, the child can obtain a perfect score on item 13 even though he or she leaves off the calf's head, one of the two leg pieces, or the tail. For example, a headless calf has 5 correct junctures, but still receives 3 points ($5 \times \frac{1}{2} = 2\frac{1}{2} = 3$ when rounded up). If the juncture connecting the tail to the rear leg on item 13 were given credit, the maximum score would be 4 instead of 3 and the child would not obtain the maximum score if the head or one leg or the tail were left off. On the Object Assembly subtest of the WISC–III and WAIS–III, all correct junctures are counted. Item 13 on the WPPSI–III is the only Object Assembly item among these three Wechsler tests that does not count all correct junctures.

Interpretive Suggestions

The following questions are useful to guide your observation of the child's performance on the Object Assembly subtest.

- Does the child approach the task eagerly or with hesitation?
- Does the child insist that pieces are missing or say that the pieces don't make sense?
- Does the child say aloud the name of the object while he or she is working?
- Does the child have difficulty with certain types of connections (e.g., straight edge, curved, no visual cues across pieces)?

- Does the child have frequent failures due to misalignments or gaps that are associated with poor fine motor control?
- Does the child neglect one side of the puzzle or consistently have difficulty with one side of the pieces?
- Is the child easily overwhelmed and inclined to give up?
- Does the child demonstrate persistence, continuing to try to solve the puzzle until time runs out?
- Does the child verbalize while doing the task?
- Does the child misidentify any of the completed objects or misidentify an incomplete object and then attempt to make it conform to his or her identification?
- What is the child's problem-solving approach to the task (e.g., trial and error, a systematic and apparently planned process, random placement of pieces)?
- What is the tempo of the child's performance (e.g., slow, deliberate, fast, impulsive)?
- Does the child spend a long time with one piece, trying to position it in an incorrect location?
- Which hand does the child use to assemble the puzzles?
- What is the quality of the child's motor coordination (e.g., smooth, jerky, uncoordinated)?
- If the child earns low scores, are they due to, for example, temporary inefficiency (such as reversal of two parts) or spending too much time lining up the pieces?
- Does the child complete the puzzles if given additional time?
- Does the child offer to put the pieces back in the box after the task is completed?

Object Assembly is an especially good subtest for observing the child's thinking style and work habits. Some children envision the complete object almost from the start and either recognize or have an imperfect understanding of the relations of the individual parts to the whole. Other children merely try to fit the pieces together by trial-and-error methods. Still others experience initial failure, move on to using trial and error, and then have a sudden insight about how the pieces fit together.

High scores on the Object Assembly subtest may indicate good visual-motor abilities, good visuoperceptual processes, good planning ability, ability to perceive a whole, experience with construction tasks, interest in assembly tasks, persistence, ability to work under time pressure, or good planning ability.

Low scores on the Object Assembly subtest may indicate visual-motor difficulties, visuoperceptual problems, poor planning ability, difficulty in perceiving a whole, minimal experience with construction tasks, limited interest in assembly tasks, limited persistence, difficulty working under time pressure, or poor planning ability or impulsivity.

After you administer the subtest, ask the child about any constructions that may be peculiar or unusual (such as pieces placed on top of each other). A testing-of-limits procedure that you can use after the *entire test* has been administered is to introduce a series of graduated cues, such as placing one or more pieces in the correct location. Note the amount of help the child needs to complete the task successfully. The child who needs only a few cues to complete the object may have better underlying perceptual organization skills, not evident during the standard administration of the subtest, than the child who needs many cues.

Another testing-of-limits approach is to ask the child to visualize the object in her or his mind before you lay out the puzzle pieces. For example, say, "Think of how a dog looks" and then give the child the dog puzzle. See if this instruction helps the child assemble the puzzle. An additional procedure is to show the child a picture of the completed object and see whether the child is able to put the pieces together correctly with the aid of a picture. Still another procedure is to ask the child to tell you how he or she assembled each object.

The range of scaled scores from 1 to 19 at ages 4-0 to 6-5 aids in profile analysis. However, profile analysis is severely to slightly restricted at ages 7-0 to 7-3, 6-0 to 6-11, 5-6 to 5-11, 5-0 to 5-5, 4-6 to 4-11, and 2-6 to 2-11, where scaled scores range from 1 to 14, 1 to 15, 1 to 16, 1 to 17, 1 to 18, and 2 to 19, respectively.

PICTURE NAMING

Picture Naming, a supplemental subtest at ages 2-6 to 3-11 and an optional subtest at ages 4-0 to 7-3, requires the child to provide the name of the item depicted in a picture that is shown to him or her. The subtest combines with Receptive Vocabulary to form the General Language Composite at all ages. The subtest contains 30 items and is untimed. The subtest is easy to administer and score. Note that Picture Naming is not a completely independent subtest because five of the first 10 items are identical to the first five picture items on the Vocabulary subtest.

Rationale

The Picture Naming subtest, like the Vocabulary and Receptive Vocabulary subtests, is a test of word knowledge. It measures language development, memory, fund of information, perceptual recognition ability, and exposure to the culture. Scores on the subtest may be closely related to the child's home environment. Performance on the subtest is likely stable over time. On the Picture Naming subtest, the child must look at a picture and decide what word best names the picture. The task involves visual discrimination, memory, and language ability. It is a measure of expressive vocabulary associated with a visual stimulus. It is likely affected by the child's schooling and exposure to language stimulation, as well as the child's home environment. Children may perform poorly on the subtest if they have language problems, visual problems, long-term memory problems, or difficulty synthesizing visual perceptual stimuli with word knowledge.

Factor Analytic Findings

At ages 2-6 to 3-11, Picture Naming is a good measure of g (71% of its variance can be attributed to g). It contributes substantially to the Verbal factor (average loading = .85). Subtest specificity is ample at all ages from 2-6 to 3-5 and adequate at ages 3-6 to 3-11.

Reliability and Correlational Highlights

Picture Naming is a reliable subtest (r_{xx} = .88), with reliability coefficients at or above .84 at all of the age groups (range of .84 to .90).

At ages 2-6 to 3-11, Picture Naming correlates better with Information (r = .74) and Receptive Vocabulary (r = .71) than with any of the other subtests. It has a moderately high correlation with the Full Scale IQ (r = .74) and the Verbal IQ (r = .78) and a moderately low correlation with the Performance IQ (r = .48).

At ages 4-0 to 7-3, Picture Naming correlates better with Information (r = .73) and Word Reasoning (r = .70) than with any of the other subtests. It has a moderately high correlation with the Full Scale IQ (r = .70) and the Verbal IQ (r = .76), a moderate correlation with the Performance IQ (r = .53), and a moderately low correlation with the Processing Speed Quotient (r = .34).

Administrative Guidelines

The following administrative guidelines for the Picture Naming subtest must be followed carefully.

Background Considerations

1. Read the items verbatim.

2. Read the items clearly.

3. Place the closed Stimulus Book 2 with the coil-bound edge facing the child so that the book is completely flat when it is opened and approximately 7 inches from the edge of the table nearest the child.

4. Open Stimulus Book 2 to item 1, and turn the pages one at a time to show consecutive pictures.

5. If the child gives an incorrect response (or no response) to item 1, give the child the correct answer.

6. For items 2 to 30, do not give the child the correct answers.

7. Point to the picture of each item and say, "What is this?" This statement is optional after the first few items.

8. Query marginal responses, generalized responses, functional responses, and hand gesture responses as often as necessary. The Administration Manual (see p. 211) gives suggested wording for such queries. However, on all items, query unclear or vague responses, as well as the sample responses marked by a "(Q)" in the Administration Manual. *This includes all the responses separated by semicolons on a line that has a "(Q)" at the end.* Do not query a clearly wrong response or a clearly correct response. For item 9, use the specific query given for a response noted by an asterisk (*) in the Administration Manual.

Starting Considerations

9. Start with the appropriate item.

a. The ages listed under "Start" on page 210 of the Administration Manual are always intended to be inclusive; thus, ages 2–3 means children 2-6 to 3-11 years of age, ages 4–5 means children 4-0 to 5-11 years of age, ages 6–7 means children 6-0 to 7-3 years of age.

b. The starting ages on the Record Form are also inclusive.

c. Children 2 to 3 years of age (and older children suspected of having intellectual deficiency) start with item 1.

d. Children 4 to 5 years of age (not suspected of having intellectual deficiency) start with item 7.

e. Children 6 to 7 years of age (not suspected of having intellectual deficiency) start with item 11.

Reverse Sequence

10. If necessary, administer the items in reverse sequence as directed in the Administration Manual.

a. The instructions on page 210 of the Administration Manual under the heading "Reverse" pertain to children who begin the subtest with item 7 or 11.

b. If the child (a) does not obtain full credit on the start-point item or (b) obtains full credit on the start-point item and a score of 0 on the next item, administer the items in reverse sequence.

c. Continue the reverse sequence until the child has perfect scores on two consecutive items or until item 1 has been administered, even if the discontinue criterion is met.

d. When there is a reverse sequence, the discontinue criterion is not met, and either there are two consecutive items with perfect scores or item 1 is administered, continue administration with the item after the last start-point item.

Discontinue Considerations

11. Count items administered in reverse sequence toward the discontinue criterion.

12. Discontinue the subtest after five consecutive scores of 0, unless the consecutive 0's are obtained during a reverse sequence and (a) item 1 has not been reached or (b) the child does not have perfect scores on two consecutive items.

13. Once the subtest is completed, remove Stimulus Book 2 from the child's view.

Scoring Guidelines

14. Score the responses using the following guidelines.

a. All items are scored 0 or 1.

b. The sample responses are not an exhaustive list of correct answers and incorrect answers.

c. Give credit for any responses that are of the same caliber as those listed in the Administration Manual.

d. Give a score of 0 to inappropriate marginal responses, generalized responses, functional responses, hand gestures, and personalized responses.

e. When the child earns perfect scores on the first two items at the start point or in a reversal, award full credit for all preceding items, regardless of the child's performance on these items if they have been administered.

f. Award no points for any items beyond the last score of 0 required for the discontinue criterion to be met, regardless of the child's performance on these items if they have been administered.

Record Form

15. Record the child's responses verbatim in the Response column.

16. Circle 0 or 1 in the Score column for all items.

17. To note the points awarded for items not administered below the first two items with perfect scores, put a slash mark in the Score column over the item

preceding the first two items with perfect scores and write the numerals for these points.

18. Add the points, including the points for correct answers and the points for items not administered before the first two perfect scores, but not for items administered after the last discontinue item.

19. Enter the total raw score in the shaded box.

Interpretive Suggestions

The following questions are useful to guide your observation of the child's performance on the Picture Naming subtest.

- Does the child describe the picture rather than giving its name (e.g., "That is found in the bathroom" for *sink*)?
- What is the quality of the name the child gives to each picture (e.g., the precise name, a specific brand, an indirect and vague name, or several names, including synonyms)?
- Are the child's responses understandable, or do they relate primarily to his or her own personal experiences?
- Does the child confuse the word with another one that sounds like it?
- If the child does not know the name of the picture, does he or she guess?
- Does the child readily say, "I don't know" and shake off further inquiries, or does the child pause, ponder, or think aloud about the item?
- Does the child show signs of a possible hearing difficulty? If so, what are the signs?
- Does the child show signs of a possible visual difficulty? If so, what are the signs?
- Does the child say the word easily, or does the child struggle?
- Does the child have mechanical difficulties with pronouncing words properly? If so, what are these difficulties?
- Does the child describe a particular feature of the picture rather than give the name of the picture?
- Does the child make semantic or phonemic naming errors that may indicate particular problems?
- Are the errors reflective of any particular deficit in experience or in knowledge?
- Does the child use a foreign language to answer the items?
- Are there any emotional overtones or references to personal experiences in the child's responses (e.g., "I hate my bathroom")? If so, what are the emotional overtones?

- Does having three choices during testing-of-limits help the child arrive at the correct word?

The child's responses to the Picture Naming subtest may reveal something about her or his language skills, perceptual ability, background, cultural milieu, social development, life experiences, responses to frustration, and thought processes. Try to determine the basis for incorrect responses, and distinguish among guesses, idiosyncratic responses, and peculiar responses. Whenever a child gives peculiar responses, mispronounces words, or has peculiar inflections, inquire further. Also, if the child can describe the picture but not name it, you may want to inquire further about language problems. Occasionally, you can identify language disturbances in the responses given by children with a pervasive developmental disorder.

High scores on the Picture Naming subtest may indicate good word knowledge, good expressive language, good verbal comprehension, good verbal skills and language development, good long-term memory, good word retrieval ability, good perceptual abilities, enriched educational background, or a home environment in which language abilities were encouraged.

Low scores on the Picture Naming subtest may indicate poor word knowledge, expressive language problems, poor verbal comprehension, poor verbal skills and language development, poor long-term memory, word retrieval problems, poor perceptual abilities, limited educational background, or a home environment in which language abilities were not encouraged. Low scores may also occur with children who speak English as a second language or have a developmental delay.

If you suspect word-retrieval problems, use a multiple-choice testing-of-limits procedure. This procedure may help you distinguish between deficits associated with word-retrieval difficulties and those associated with deficient knowledge. After completing the *entire test*, go back to the item (or items) with which the child had difficulty and give the child three answers from which to choose. For example, say, "Is this picture called a fish, a bug, or a cat?" Be sure to randomly vary the position of the correct answer in the series (i.e., put the correct answer sometimes in first, sometimes in second, and sometimes in third position). If the child answers the multiple-choice questions correctly, the child may have a word-retrieval difficulty and not deficient knowledge. However, scores from the multiple-choice procedure should not be used to calculate an IQ.

The range of scaled scores from 1 to 19 at ages 3-6 to 7-3 aids in profile analysis. However, profile analysis is slightly restricted at ages 2-6 to 3-5, where scaled scores range from 2 to 19.

THINKING THROUGH THE ISSUES

1. Which WPPSI–III supplemental and optional subtests are most useful for measuring the intelligence level of preschool children and young school-aged children?
2. When do you think you would administer an optional or supplemental subtest?
3. When would you use a supplemental subtest to replace a core subtest?

SUMMARY

1. This chapter provides information about the rationale, factor analytic findings, reliability and correlational highlights, administrative guidelines, and interpretive suggestions for the five WPPSI–III supplemental and two optional subtests.

Symbol Search

2. Symbol Search measures perceptual discrimination, speed and accuracy, visual scanning, attention and concentration, short-term memory, and cognitive flexibility. The subtest is a fair measure of g and contributes substantially to the Processing Speed factor. Subtest specificity is ample at the ages at which the subtest is administered. Symbol Search is a reliable subtest ($r_{tt} = .83$). It is easy to administer but somewhat difficult to score.

Comprehension

3. Comprehension measures common sense, social judgment, and a grasp of social conventionality. The subtest is a good measure of g and contributes substantially to the Verbal factor. Subtest specificity is ample or adequate at the ages at which the subtest is administered. Comprehension is a reliable subtest ($r_{xx} = .88$). It is somewhat difficult to administer and score.

Picture Completion

4. Picture Completion measures visual discrimination (i.e., the ability to differentiate between essential and nonessential details) and requires concentration, reasoning, attention to detail, visual organization, and long-term visual memory. The subtest is a fair measure of g and contributes moderately to the Performance factor. Subtest specificity is ample at the ages at which the subtest is administered. Picture

Completion is a reliable subtest ($r_{xx} = .90$). It is relatively easy to administer and score.

Similarities

5. Similarities measures verbal concept formation. The subtest is a good measure of g and contributes substantially to the Verbal factor. Subtest specificity is ample or adequate at the ages at which the subtest is administered. Similarities is a reliable subtest ($r_{xx} = .95$). It is relatively easy to administer, but it can be difficult to score.

Receptive Vocabulary

6. Receptive Vocabulary measures language development, memory, fund of information, perceptual recognition ability, and exposure to the culture. The subtest is a good measure of g and contributes substantially to the Verbal factor. Subtest specificity is ample at ages 2-6 to 3-11. Receptive Vocabulary is a reliable subtest ($r_{xx} = .88$). It is easy to administer and score.

Object Assembly

7. Object Assembly measures skill at synthesis and requires visual-motor coordination and visual organizational ability. The subtest is a fair measure of g. At ages 2-6 to 3-11, it contributes moderately to the Performance factor. At ages 4-0 to 7-3, it contributes substantially to the Performance factor. Subtest specificity is ample at all ages. Object Assembly is a reliable subtest ($r_{xx} = .85$). It is relatively easy to administer but difficult to score.

Picture Naming

8. Picture Naming measures language development, memory, fund of information, perceptual recognition ability, and exposure to the culture. The subtest is a good measure of g and contributes substantially to the Verbal factor. Subtest specificity is ample or adequate at ages 2-6 to 3-11. Picture Naming is a reliable subtest ($r_{xx} = .88$). It is easy to administer and score.

KEY TERMS, CONCEPTS, AND NAMES

STUDY QUESTIONS

1. Discuss the rationale for each of the five WPPSI–III supplemental and two optional subtests for ages 4-0 to 7-3.
2. Describe the factor analytic findings for each of the five WPPSI–III supplemental and two optional subtests for ages 4-0 to 7-3. In your description, compare and contrast the major factor analytic findings among the five supplemental subtests.
3. Discuss the reliability and correlational highlights for each of the five WPPSI–III supplemental and two optional subtests for ages 4-0 to 7-3. In your discussion, compare and contrast the reliability and correlational highlights among the five supplemental and two optional subtests.
4. List some major administrative guidelines for each of the five WPPSI–III supplemental and two optional subtests for ages 4-0 to 7-3.
5. Describe the interpretive suggestions for each of the five WPPSI–III supplemental and two optional subtests for ages 4-0 to 7-3.
6. Which two of the five WPPSI–III supplemental and two optional subtests for ages 4-0 to 7-3 are the best measures of intelligence? Give the reasons for your answer.

8

INTERPRETING THE WPPSI–III

There's one basic rule you should remember about development charts that will save you countless hours of worry . . . . The fact that a child passes through a particular developmental stage is always more important than the age of that child when he or she does it. In the long run, it really doesn't matter whether you learn to walk at ten months or fifteen months—as long as you learn how to walk.

—Lawrence Kutner

Profile Analysis

A Successive-Level Approach to Test Interpretation

Steps in Analyzing a Protocol

The Composites

Estimated Percentile Ranks and Test-Age Equivalents for Raw Scores

Comment on Interpreting the WPPSI–III

Thinking Through the Issues

Summary

Key Terms, Concepts, and Names

Study Questions

Goals and Objectives

This chapter is designed to enable you to do the following:

- Describe profile analysis for the WPPSI–III

- Analyze and evaluate WPPSI–III scores from multiple perspectives

- Develop hypotheses about WPPSI–III scores and responses

This chapter will help you (a) perform a profile analysis, (b) determine whether the individual Composite scores (VIQ and PIQ at ages 2-6 to 3-11 and VIQ, PIQ, and PSQ at ages 4-0 to 7-3) differ significantly from each other, (c) determine whether the subtest scaled scores differ significantly from each other, (d) obtain the base rates for differences between Composite scores, (e) obtain the base rates for differences between some of the subtest scaled scores, (f) determine base rates for inter-subtest scatter, and (g) develop hypotheses and interpretations. Because the Full Scale IQ and Composite scores have a mean of 100 and standard deviation of 15 and because subtest scaled scores have a mean of 10 and standard deviation of 3, you can statistically evaluate profiles across the Composites and across the subtests.

After you statistically evaluate the Composite score discrepancies, subtest discrepancies, and the profile of subtest scaled scores, you will need to interpret the findings. This chapter, along with the information presented in Chapters 5, 6, and 7 and Appendixes B and C, will help you accomplish this goal. Table C-7 in Appendix C provides useful suggestions for describing the Composite scores and subtest scores to the referral source, to the parents, and in your report. In addition, your interpretation will benefit if you know about theories of intelligence and intellectual functioning (see Chapters 5 and 6 in Sattler, 2001), normal child development, and child psychopathology and exceptional children (see Sattler, 2002).

This chapter does not include a section on writing a psychological report. Instead we suggest that you read (or review) the following parts of Chapter 4 on pages 139 to 150: illustration of a portion of a psychological report, report writing guidelines, psychological evaluation, and test your skill. Also study Chapter 21 on report writing in Sattler (2001).

PROFILE ANALYSIS

Much of the discussion of profile analysis for the WISC–IV also pertains to the WPPSI–III. We, therefore, refer you to Chapter 4 (pp. 114 to 117) for the following topics: profile analysis (introduction), aim of profile analysis, interindividual comparisons, intraindividual comparisons, and establishing significant differences. We continue the discussion of profile analysis for the WPPSI–III with the topic of base rates.

Base Rates

One approach to profile analysis is to evaluate the scores in reference to the norm group (see Chapter 4). A second approach to profile analysis is to determine the frequency with which the differences between scores in the child's profile occurred in the standardization sample; this is called the *base rate approach* or the *probability-of-occurrence approach.* The following tables in the Administration Manual will give you base rate information:

- Table B.2 for differences between the three Composite scores
- Table B.4 for differences associated with five pairs of subtests
- Table B.5 for differences between individual subtest scaled scores and the mean subtest scaled score for the core Verbal subtests, the core Performance subtests, and the core Full Scale subtests
- Table B.6 for intersubtest scatter for core Verbal subtests, core Performance subtests, and core Full Scale subtests

Table B-4 in Appendix B in this text also provides information about the probabilities associated with differences between Composites.

Primary Methods of Profile Analysis

The primary methods of profile analysis are the following:

Method 1. Compare the Verbal IQ and the Performance IQ.

Method 2. Compare each Verbal subtest scaled score with the mean Verbal Composite scaled score.

Method 3. Compare each Performance subtest scaled score with the mean Performance Composite scaled score.

Method 4. Compare the two Processing Speed subtest scaled scores to each other.

Method 5. Compare each subtest scaled score with the mean subtest scaled score based on the core subtests and based on all subtests in each broad age group.

Method 6. Compare sets of individual subtest scaled scores.

Method 7. Compare the range of subtest scaled scores with that found in the standardization sample.

Method 1: Compare the Verbal IQ and the Performance IQ. Tables B-2 (ages 2-6 to 3-11) and B-3 (ages 4-0 to 7-3) in Appendix B provide the critical values for comparing the Verbal and Performance IQs for the nine WPPSI–III age groups and for the average. These values range from 10 to 12 at the .05 level and from 13 to 16 at the .01 level. You should not use an average critical value based on the entire standardization group, because this value may be misleading for some ages. Rather, use the values for a specific age group to evaluate differences between the Composites.

Exhibit 4-1 in Chapter 4 describes the procedure that was used to obtain the critical values shown in Tables B-2 and B-3 in Appendix B. You can use this procedure to determine the needed critical values for any comparison involving two Composites or two subtests. The values in Tables B-2 and B-3 in Appendix B differ in two ways from those in Table B.1 (p. 244) in the Administration Manual. First, the values in Tables B-2 and B-3 in Appendix B are whole numbers instead of decimals. A child's standard scores are always whole numbers without decimals. Second, the values in Tables B-2 and B-3 in Appendix B are for the .05 and .01 significance levels instead of the .15 and .05 significance levels. We recommend using either the .05 significance level or the .01 significance level; the .15 significance level is not traditionally used.

Table B-4 in Appendix B shows the probabilities associated with various differences between the Composites. This table provides an estimate of the probability of obtaining a given or greater discrepancy by chance. It shows probabilities from .001 (1 in 1,000) to .50 (50 in 100, or 1 out of 2). Thus, at 4 years of age, there is a 1 in 1,000 chance that a difference of 18.51 points will be found between the Verbal IQ and the Performance IQ. On the other hand, at this same age, there is a 50% chance that a difference of 3.79 points will be found between the Verbal IQ and the Performance IQ.

Table B.2 (p. 245) in the Administration Manual shows the cumulative percentages in the standardization sample that obtained various Composite discrepancies for the overall sample as well as for five ability levels (Full Scale IQs for 79 and below, 80 to 89, 90 to 109, 110 to 119, and 120 and above). In the segment of the overall sample that had a higher Verbal IQ than Performance IQ, the mean difference was 11.0 points, whereas in the segment that had a higher Performance IQ than Verbal IQ, the mean difference was 11.3 points. The Verbal IQ was higher than the Performance IQ by 15 points (one standard deviation) in 13.1% of the sample, whereas the Verbal IQ was lower than the Perform-

ance IQ by 15 points (one standard deviation) in 14.0% of the sample.

The cumulative percentages for the three Composite comparisons shown in Table B.2 in the Administration Manual differ at the five ability levels. For example, the base rate for a 15-point discrepancy for the Performance IQ > Processing Speed Quotient comparison is 14.2% in the overall sample, but it ranges from 3.7% to 24.1% at the five ability levels: 3.7% at FSIQ 79 and below, 6.9% at FSIQ 80 to 89, 12.4% at FSIQ 90 to 109, 23.5% at FSIQ 110 to 119, and 24.1% at FSIQ 120 and above. Use the child's Full Scale IQ to obtain the most accurate base rates for the VIQ–PIQ, VIQ–PSQ, and PIQ–PSQ comparisons.

Developing hypotheses based on a significant difference. A significant difference between any two IQs or an IQ and a Quotient score may indicate the following:

- Interest patterns
- Cognitive style
- Deficiencies or strengths in processing information
- Deficiencies or strengths in modes of expression
- Deficiencies or strengths in the ability to work under time pressure (such as the time constraints on Performance subtests)
- Sensory deficiencies
- Brain injury
- Psychopathology
- Behavioral problems, such as limited motivation or rebelliousness or anxiety
- A home or school environment in which language or materials differ from those commonly used in the wider culture

You will need to evaluate the child's entire performance, clinical history, and background information to arrive at the most reasonable hypothesis to account for a significant difference between Composite scores. Always formulate hypotheses about Composite score differences in relationship to the child's *absolute* score in each area and in relationship to the Full Scale IQ, and only when the differences are significant. This means, for example, that you would not say that a child with a Verbal IQ of 150 and a Performance IQ of 125 had a nonverbal deficit (or a performance deficit or perceptual reasoning deficit), even though the Performance IQ is significantly lower than the Verbal IQ. In this case, both abilities are well developed; verbal skills are simply better developed than nonverbal skills. Similarly, you should view a child with a Verbal IQ of 68 and a Performance IQ of 50 as having both a verbal deficit and a nonverbal deficit (or performance deficit or perceptual reasoning deficit), even though the Verbal IQ is significantly higher than the Performance IQ. As noted previously, the Verbal IQ of 68 may reflect a relative strength for this child, but it is not an absolute one.

Discrepancies between Composite scores may be used to generate hypotheses about a child's cognitive functioning but should not be used to diagnose or classify a child or to conclude that a child has a disability. *For example, a discrepancy between two or more Composite scores should never be used as the sole criterion for making a diagnosis of learning disability, brain injury, or mental retardation.* Table 8-1 shows suggested abilities and background factors associated with the individual Composites.

Examples of hypotheses for Composite scores.
Examples of hypotheses for Composite score comparisons follow.

ILLUSTRATIVE HYPOTHESES FOR
VERBAL > PERFORMANCE

1. Verbal skills are better developed than performance skills.
2. Verbal processing is better developed than visual-spatial processing.
3. Auditory-vocal processing is better developed than visual-discrimination processing.
4. Knowledge acquired through accumulated experience is better developed than knowledge needed to solve nonverbal problems.
5. Retrieval of verbal information from long-term memory is better developed than nonverbal problem solving.
6. Crystallized knowledge is better developed than fluid reasoning ability.

ILLUSTRATIVE HYPOTHESES FOR
PERFORMANCE > VERBAL

1. Performance skills are better developed than verbal skills.
2. Visual-spatial processing is better developed than verbal processing.
3. Visual-discrimination processing is better developed than auditory-vocal processing.
4. Knowledge needed to solve nonverbal problems is better developed than knowledge acquired through accumulated experience.

5. Nonverbal problem solving is better developed than retrieval of verbal information from long-term memory.
6. Fluid reasoning ability is better developed than crystallized knowledge.

ILLUSTRATIVE HYPOTHESES FOR
VERBAL > PROCESSING SPEED

1. Verbal skills are better developed than processing speed skills.
2. Verbal processing is better developed than speed of mental operation.
3. Auditory-vocal processing is better developed than visual-motor processing.
4. Processing of verbal stimuli is better developed than processing of nonverbal stimuli.
5. Long-term verbal memory is better developed than short-term visual memory.
6. Crystallized knowledge is better developed than processing speed.

ILLUSTRATIVE HYPOTHESES FOR
PROCESSING SPEED > VERBAL

1. Processing speed skills are better developed than verbal skills.
2. Speed of mental operation is better developed than verbal processing.
3. Visual-motor processing is better developed than auditory-vocal processing.
4. Processing of nonverbal stimuli is better developed than processing of verbal stimuli.
5. Short-term visual memory is better developed than long-term verbal memory.
6. Processing speed is better developed than crystallized knowledge.

ILLUSTRATIVE HYPOTHESES FOR
PERFORMANCE > PROCESSING SPEED

1. Performance skills are better developed than processing speed skills.
2. Visual-spatial processing is better developed than speed of mental operation.
3. Immediate problem solving is better developed than visual-motor coordination.
4. Interpretation or organization of visually perceived material is better developed than speed of processing nonverbal stimuli.
5. Fluid reasoning ability is better developed than processing speed.

1. Processing speed skills are better developed than performance skills.
2. Speed of mental operation is better developed than visual-spatial processing.
3. Visual-motor coordination is better developed than immediate problem solving.
4. Speed of processing nonverbal stimuli is better developed than interpretation or organization of visually perceived material.
5. Processing speed is better developed than fluid reasoning ability.

Table 8-1
Suggested Major Abilities and Background Factors Associated with WPPSI-III Composites

Verbal (V)	Performance (P)	Processing Speed (PS)	General Language (GL)	Full Scale (FS)	Major abilities and background factors
V	P	PS		FS	Attention
V				FS	Auditory-vocal processing
	P	PS		FS	Concentration
V			GL	FS	Crystallized knowledge
V			GL	FS	Cultural opportunity
V			GL	FS	Extent of outside reading
	P			FS	Fluid reasoning ability
	P			FS	Immediate problem solving
V			GL	FS	Interest and reading patterns
V			GL	FS	Language development
V			GL	FS	Lexical knowledge
V				FS	Long-term verbal memory
	P			FS	Nonverbal reasoning
	P			FS	Perceptual reasoning
		PS		FS	Processing speed
V			GL	FS	Retrieval of material from long-term memory
		PS		FS	Scanning ability
		PS		FS	Short-term memory
		PS		FS	Short-term visual memory
	P			FS	Spatial perception
		PS		FS	Speed of mental operation
V			GL	FS	Verbal comprehension
V				FS	Verbal processing
	P	PS		FS	Visual acuity and discrimination
		PS		FS	Visual-motor coordination
	P			FS	Visual-motor discrimination
	P	PS		FS	Visual-perceptual processing
	P			FS	Visual-perceptual reasoning
	P			FS	Visual-spatial processing
V			GL	FS	Vocabulary

Formulate hypotheses about Composite scores only when they are significantly different from each other (see Tables B-2 and B-3 in Appendix B). Table B-4 in Appendix B shows the estimates of the probability of obtaining designated differences between WPPSI–III Composite scores by chance. For example, for a 4-year-old child, the probability of obtaining a difference of 9.23 between Verbal IQ and Performance IQ is 10%. You can find a summary of interpretive rationales for Composite scores in Table C-5 in Appendix C. In all cases, to determine the best explanation of a child's Composite score, carefully analyze the child's entire performance on the WPPSI–III and on other tests and the child's case history information.

When the subtest scaled scores that comprise a Composite score are in a similar direction (e.g., all above average or all below average), you are on firm ground in interpreting the Composite score. However, when the subtest scaled scores that comprise a Composite differ in direction (e.g., some above average and some below average), the mean Composite score should be interpreted in light of the variability of its component subtest scores.

For example, let's consider two cases. In one case, the child has a Coding scaled score of 15 and a Symbol Search scaled score of 5. In the other case, the child has a Coding scaled score of 10 and a Symbol Search scaled score of 10. In both cases the mean scaled score is 10. However, in the first case, the mean reflects two discrepant subtest scaled scores—one high and one low. In the other case, the mean represents two similar subtest scaled scores—both average. In reporting on the first case, you must point out that the overall average score is based on above-average graphomotor ability for copying symbols and below-average mental scanning ability for symbols. The reader must be informed that the child's processing speed ability (as measured by these two WPPSI–III subtests) is variable. Apply this same rationale when you evaluate all of the Composite scores.

Method 2: Compare each Verbal subtest scaled score with the mean Verbal Composite scaled score.

Table B-5 in Appendix B provides the critical values for comparing each of the Verbal subtests with the mean of (a) the core Verbal subtests and (b) the core Verbal subtests plus the supplemental subtest(s) for each of the nine WPPSI–III age groups and the average for the two broad age groups. For example, critical values for children ages 4-0 to 4-5 on the three core Verbal subtests range from 1.80 to 2.07 at the .05 level and from 2.21 to 2.53 at the .01 level. We recom-

mend that you use each individual age group to get the most accurate critical value.

Table B.5 (p. 254) in the Administration Manual gives similar values, but only for (a) the two broad age groups, (b) the .15 and .05 significance levels, and (c) the core subtests. In contrast, Table B-5 in Appendix B in this text gives values for each individual age group as well as for the average of the two broad age groups, provides values at the .05 and .01 significance levels, and provides values for all core and supplemental subtest combinations for the Verbal Composite.

Table B.5 in the Administration Manual also gives the base rates for differences obtained by various percentages of the standardization sample between a subtest scaled score and the child's mean on the core subtests. The table shows, for example, that a difference of 3.33 points between the subtest scaled score on Information and the mean Verbal Composite subtest score at ages 4-0 to 7-3 (derived for the three core Verbal Composite subtests) was obtained by 1% of the standardization sample. The base rates are independent of the significance levels. Further, a significant difference of 2.11 for Information at the .05 level occurred in between 10% and 25% of the standardization sample.

Method 3: Compare each Performance subtest scaled score with the mean Performance Composite scaled score.

Table B-5 in Appendix B provides the critical values for comparing each of the Performance subtests with the mean of (a) the core Performance subtests and (b) the core Performance subtests plus the supplemental subtest for each of the nine WPPSI–III age groups and the average for the two broad age groups. For example, critical values for children ages 4-0 to 4-5 on the three core Performance subtests range from 2.08 to 2.63 at the .05 level and from 2.55 to 3.22 at the .01 level. We recommend that you use each individual age group to get the most accurate critical value.

Table B.5 (p. 254) in the Administration Manual gives similar values, but only for (a) the two broad age groups, (b) the .15 and .05 significance levels, and (c) the core subtests. In contrast, Table B-5 in Appendix B in this text gives values for each individual age group as well as for the average of the two broad age groups, provides values at the .05 and .01 significance levels, and provides values for all core and supplemental subtest combinations for the Performance Composite.

Table B.5 in the Administration Manual also gives the base rates for differences obtained by various percentages of the standardization sample between a subtest scaled score and the child's mean on the core subtests. The table shows, for example, that a difference of 5.00 points between the subtest scaled score on Block Design and the mean Performance IQ subtest score (derived for the three core Performance IQ subtests) was obtained by 1% of the standardization sample. The base rates are independent of the significance levels. Further, a significant difference of 2.22 for Block Design at the .05 level occurred in less than 25% of the standardization sample.

Method 4: Compare the two Processing Speed subtest scaled scores to each other.
Table B-5 in Appendix B provides the critical values for comparing each of the Processing Speed subtests with the mean of the two Processing Speed subtests for each of the six WPPSI–III age groups from 4-0 to 7-3 and the average for the broad age group. For example, critical values for 4-year-old children on the two Processing Speed subtests are 1.50 at the .05 level and 1.97 at the .01 level. We recommend that you use the values for each individual age group to get the most accurate results.

Table B.5 (p. 254) in the Administration Manual does not provide any values or base rates for Processing Speed. However, they are shown in Tables B.3 (for comparisons between Coding and Symbol Search) and B.4 (for base rate differences between Coding and Symbol Search). Table B.4 shows that the Coding score was 6 points lower than the Symbol Search score in 1.1% of the standardization sample. The base rates are independent of the significance levels. Further, a significant difference of 4 points between Coding and Symbol Search (in favor of Coding) occurred in 10.3% of the population.

Method 5: Compare each subtest scaled score with the mean subtest scaled score based on the core subtests and based on all subtests in each broad age group.
Table B-5 in Appendix B provides critical values for each of the 11 age groups and the average of each broad age group for the core subtests and for the core plus supplemental and optional subtests. For example, critical values for children ages 4-0 to 4-5 for the seven core subtests range from 2.22 to 3.58 at the .05 level and from 2.64 to 4.25 at the .01 level. We recommend that you use the values for each individual age group to get the most accurate values.

Table B.5 in the Administration Manual also gives the base rates for differences obtained by various percentages of the standardization sample between a subtest

scaled score and the child's mean on the seven core subtests (but not on the 14 subtests). The table shows, for example, that a difference of 5.64 points between the subtest scaled score on Block Design and the mean of the seven core subtests was obtained by 1% of the standardization sample. The base rates are independent of the significance levels. Further, a significant difference of 2.95 for Block Design at the .05 level occurred in between 10% and 25% of the standardization sample.

Method 6: Compare sets of individual subtest scaled scores.
Tables B-2 and B-3 in Appendix B provide critical values for comparing sets of subtest scaled scores for each of the nine age groups and for the average of each broad group. For example, for children who are 4 years of age, Table B-3 shows that the critical values for comparing Information and Vocabulary are 3 points at the .05 level and 4 points at the .01 level. The values in Tables B-2 and B-3 in Appendix B and Table B.3 in the Administration Manual are overly liberal (i.e., they often lead to significant differences that may not be true differences) when more than one comparison is made. They are most accurate when you plan to make specific comparisons before you administer the test—for example, when you plan to compare Similarities with Vocabulary or Matrix Reasoning with Picture Concepts.

Table B.3 in the Administration Manual gives similar values in decimal form, but only for the overall sample and the .15 and .05 significance levels. In contrast, Tables B-2 and B-3 in Appendix B in this text give values for each individual age group as well as for the total group, provide values at the .05 and .01 significance levels, and provide whole numbers instead of decimals (a child's subtest scaled scores are always whole numbers without decimals).

Before making multiple comparisons among the subtests, determine the difference between the highest and lowest subtest scaled scores. If this difference is 3 or more scaled-score points, a significant difference at the .05 level is indicated. Differences of 3 or more scaled-score points between subtests can then be interpreted. If the difference between the highest and lowest subtest scaled scores is less than 3 scaled-score points, multiple comparisons should not be made between individual subtest scaled scores. (The Note to Table B-3 in Appendix B in this text shows the formula that was used to compute the significant difference. The formula considers the average standard error of measurement for each of the seven core subtests and the Studentized range statistic.)

Comparisons between subtests. If you find significant differences between subtest scaled scores (see Tables B-2 and B-3 in Appendix B), you will need to interpret the findings. Several parts of this text will help you do so. First, study Table C-1 in Appendix C, which presents the percentile ranks and qualitative descriptions associated with subtest scaled scores. Second, study Table C-2 in Appendix C and Table 8-2 in this chapter, which show suggested abilities or background factors associated with the 14 WPPSI–III subtests. Third, review the three preceding chapters, because much of the material in these chapters is relevant to interpreting subtest scaled scores. Fourth, study the examples below, which are designed to help you make subtest comparisons.

Treat all hypotheses developed from subtest comparisons as tentative. Develop your hypotheses based on both significant differences between subtest scaled scores and the absolute values of the subtest scaled scores. Thus, remember that *subtest scaled scores of 10 or higher should be described as reflecting average or above-average ability and never as absolute weaknesses, whereas subtest scaled scores of 7 or lower should be described as reflecting below-average ability and never as absolute strengths. Any hypotheses about subtest scaled scores should be developed through study of the child's entire test performance and clinical history.*

Interpretation of subtest comparisons. Let's first compare subtests that are in the same Composite (core and supplemental) and then compare subtests across Composites.

COMPARISON OF VERBAL SUBTESTS

1. *Information (IN) and Word Reasoning (WR).* This comparison relates the amount of information retained (Information) to the ability to reason deductively (Word Reasoning).

- IN > WR: This pattern may suggest that the child's fund of information is better developed than his or her ability to reason deductively.
- WR > IN: This pattern may suggest that the child's ability to reason deductively is better developed than his or her fund of information.

2. *Vocabulary (VC) and Word Reasoning (WR).* Both Vocabulary and Word Reasoning measure abstract thinking ability and ability to form concepts, but Word Reasoning is a better measure of verbal reasoning and deductive reasoning.

- VC > WR: This pattern may suggest that the ability to understand or express the meaning of individual words is better developed than the ability to reason deductively.
- WR > VC: This pattern may suggest that the ability to reason deductively is better developed than the ability to understand or express the meaning of individual words.

3. *Similarities (SI) and Comprehension (CO).* Similarities and Comprehension both involve conceptualizing skills. Similarities usually requires a response expressing one primary idea, while Comprehension requires an extended response. In addition, Similarities also measures verbal concept formation, whereas Comprehension also measures factual knowledge and social judgment.

- SI > CO: This pattern may suggest that verbal concept formation is better developed than factual knowledge and social judgment.
- CO > SI: This pattern may suggest that factual knowledge and social judgment are better developed than verbal concept formation.

4. *Vocabulary (VC) and Similarities (SI).* Both Vocabulary and Similarities measure abstract thinking ability and ability to form concepts, but Similarities is a better measure of these abilities.

- SI > VC: This pattern may suggest that the ability to categorize is better developed than the ability to understand or express the meaning of individual words.
- VC > SI: This pattern may suggest that the ability to understand or express the meaning of individual words is better developed than the ability to categorize.

5. *Similarities (SI) and Word Reasoning (WR).* Both Similarities and Word Reasoning measure verbal comprehension and verbal abstraction. However, Similarities is a better measure of verbal concept formation, while Word Reasoning is a better measure of verbal reasoning and deductive reasoning.

- SI > WR: This pattern may suggest that the ability to categorize is better developed than the ability to reason deductively.
- WR > SI: This pattern may suggest that the ability to reason deductively is better developed than the ability to categorize.

Table 8-2
Suggested Abilities or Background Factors Associated with WPPSI–III Subtests

Block Design (BD)	Information (IN)	Matrix Reasoning (MR)	Vocabulary (VC)	Picture Concepts (PCn)	Symbol Search (SS)	Word Reasoning (WR)	Coding (CD)	Comprehension (CO)	Picture Completion (PCm)	Similarities (SI)	Receptive Vocabulary (RV)	Object Assembly (OA)	Picture Naming (PN)	M Abilities or background factors
		MR			SS		CD		PCm					___ Attention
				PCn	SS	WR	CD			SI				___ Cognitive flexibility
BD		MR			SS				PCm					___ Concentration
BD			VC	PCn		WR				SI				___ Conceptual thinking
	IN		VC					CO		SI	RV		PN	___ Crystallized knowledge
	IN		VC					CO			RV		PN	___ Cultural opportunities
	IN		VC	PCn						SI	RV		PN	___ Extent of outside reading
BD					SS		CD					OA		___ Fine-motor coordination
		MR		PCn		WR								___ Fluid reasoning ability
	IN		VC								RV		PN	___ Fund of information
	IN		VC	PCn		WR					RV		PN	___ Intellectual curiosity
	IN		VC	PCn		WR				SI	RV		PN	___ Interest and reading patterns
			VC					CO		SI	RV		PN	___ Language development
			VC							SI	RV		PN	___ Lexical knowledge
	IN		VC			WR		CO	PCm	SI	RV		PN	___ Long-term memory
BD		MR			SS		CD					OA		___ Motivation and persistence
BD		MR		PCn					PCm			OA		___ Nonverbal reasoning
				PCn					PCm		RV	OA	PN	___ Perception of meaningful stimuli
					SS		CD							___ Processing speed
	IN		VC	PCn		WR		CO		SI	RV		PN	___ Quality of schooling
BD		MR		PCn		WR		CO	PCm	SI				___ Reasoning
					SS		CD		PCm					___ Scanning ability
					SS		CD							___ Short-term memory
BD		MR							PCm			OA		___ Spatial perception
BD					SS				PCm					___ Speed of mental operation
	IN		VC			WR		CO		SI				___ Verbal comprehension
BD		MR		PCn	SS		CD		PCm			OA		___ Visual acuity
					SS		CD		PCm		RV		PN	___ Visual memory
BD					SS		CD					OA		___ Visual-motor coordination
BD		MR		PCn	SS		CD		PCm			OA		___ Visual-perceptual discrimination
BD		MR		PCn	SS				PCm			OA		___ Visual-perceptual organization
BD		MR		PCn	SS		CD		PCm		RV	OA	PN	___ Visual-perceptual processing
BD		MR		PCn					PCm			OA		___ Visual-perceptual reasoning
			VC			WR		CO		SI	RV		PN	___ Vocabulary

Note. M = mean of the subtest scaled scores for the ability or background factor.

6. *Information (IN) and Comprehension (CO).* This comparison relates the amount of information retained (Information) to the ability to use information (Comprehension). Information requires factual knowledge, while Comprehension requires both factual knowledge and social judgment.

- IN > CO: This pattern may suggest that the child's fund of information is better developed than his or her social judgment.
- CO > IN: This pattern may suggest that the child's social judgment is better developed than his or her fund of information.

7. *Information (IN) and Similarities (SI).* This comparison relates the amount of information retained (Information) to the ability to engage in conceptual thinking (Similarities).

- SI > IN: This pattern may suggest that the child's conceptual reasoning ability is better developed than his or her fund of information.
- IN > SI: This pattern may suggest that the child's fund of information is better developed than his or her conceptual reasoning ability.

8. *Receptive Vocabulary (RV) and Picture Naming (PN).* Both Receptive Vocabulary and Picture Naming measure language development. However, as their names imply, Receptive Vocabulary measures receptive vocabulary skills, whereas Picture Naming measures expressive vocabulary skills.

- RV > PN: This pattern may suggest that the child's receptive vocabulary is better developed than his or her expressive vocabulary.
- PN > RV: This pattern may suggest that the child's expressive vocabulary is better developed than his or her receptive vocabulary.

9. *Vocabulary (VC), Comprehension (CO), and Information (IN).* All three subtests involve verbal processing, but in different contexts.

- VC, IN > CO: This pattern may suggest that verbal ability and fund of information are better developed than social judgment.
- CO > VC, IN: This pattern may suggest that social judgment is better developed than verbal ability and fund of information.
- VC, CO > IN: This pattern may suggest that verbal ability and social judgment are better developed than fund of information.
- IN > VC, CO: This pattern may suggest that fund of information is better developed than verbal ability and social judgment.

10. *Receptive Vocabulary (RV), Picture Naming (PN), and Vocabulary (VC).* All three subtests involve language development, but in different contexts. Receptive Vocabulary measures receptive language ability, Picture Naming measures one-word expressive language ability, and Vocabulary measures complex expressive language ability.

- RV, PN > VC: This pattern may suggest that language development involving one-word receptive and expressive communications is better developed than language development involving use of phrases and sentences.
- VC > RV, PN: This pattern may suggest that language development involving use of phrases and sentences is better developed than language development involving one-word receptive and expressive communications.
- VC, PN > RV: This pattern may suggest that expressive vocabulary involving both complex language communications and one-word communications is better developed than receptive vocabulary.

COMPARISON OF PERFORMANCE SUBTESTS

1. *Matrix Reasoning (MR) and Block Design (BD).* This comparison relates two subtests that measure nonverbal reasoning ability. Matrix Reasoning requires analogic perceptual reasoning and has no time limits, whereas Block Design requires analysis and synthesis and has time limits.

- MR > BD: This pattern may suggest that analogic perceptual reasoning is better developed than perceptual analysis and synthesis skills when working under time pressure.
- BD > MR: This pattern may suggest that perceptual analysis and synthesis skills when working under time pressure are better developed than analogic perceptual reasoning.

2. *Matrix Reasoning (MR) and Picture Concepts (PCn).* This comparison relates two subtests that measure perceptual reasoning. However, Matrix Reasoning also measures spatial ability and perceptual organization, whereas Picture Concepts also measures conceptual thinking.

- MR > PCn: This pattern may suggest that analogic perceptual reasoning is better developed than conceptual thinking in a perceptual task.
- PCn > MR: This pattern may suggest that conceptual thinking in a perceptual task is better developed than analogic perceptual reasoning.

3. *Picture Completion (PCm) and Block Design (BD)*. This comparison relates nonspatial visual perceptual ability (Picture Completion) to spatial visualization ability (Block Design).

- PCm > BD: This pattern may suggest that nonspatial visual perceptual ability is better developed than spatial visualization ability.
- BD > PCm: This pattern may suggest that spatial visualization ability is better developed than nonspatial visual perceptual ability.

4. *Matrix Reasoning (MR) and Picture Completion (PCm)*. This comparison relates analogic nonverbal reasoning (Matrix Reasoning) to nonspatial visual perceptual ability (Picture Completion).

- MR > PCm: This pattern may suggest that analogic perceptual reasoning is better developed than nonspatial visual perceptual ability.
- PCm > MR: This pattern may suggest that nonspatial visual perceptual ability is better developed than analogic perceptual reasoning.

5. *Picture Completion (PCm) and Picture Concepts (PCn)*. This comparison relates two subtests that measure perceptual reasoning ability and perceptual recognition ability. However, Picture Completion also measures the ability to distinguish essential from nonessential details, whereas Picture Concepts also measures conceptual thinking.

- PCm > PCn: This pattern may suggest that the ability to distinguish essential from nonessential details is better developed than conceptual thinking in a perceptual task.
- PCn > PCm: This pattern may suggest that conceptual thinking in a perceptual task is better developed than the ability to distinguish essential from nonessential details.

6. *Block Design (BD) and Matrix Reasoning (MR) vs. Picture Concepts (PCn) and Picture Completion (PCm)*. Block Design, Matrix Reasoning, Picture Concepts, and Picture Completion all require perceptual

reasoning, attention to detail, and concentration. In addition, both Matrix Reasoning and Block Design may involve spatial ability.

- BD, MR > PCn, PCm: This pattern may suggest that spatial reasoning ability is better developed than nonspatial reasoning ability.
- PCn, PCm > MR, BD: This pattern may suggest that nonspatial reasoning ability is better developed than spatial reasoning ability.

COMPARISON OF PROCESSING SPEED SUBTESTS

1. *Coding (CD) and Symbol Search (SS)*. Both Coding and Symbol Search involve processing speed, perceptual discrimination, accuracy, attention, and concentration. However, Coding requires perceptual symbol-associative skills to a greater degree than Symbol Search, whereas Symbol Search requires perceptual discrimination skills to a greater extent than Coding.

- CD > SS: This pattern may suggest that perceptual symbol-associative skills are better developed than perceptual discrimination skills that do not involve association.
- SS > CD: This pattern may suggest that perceptual discrimination skills that do not involve association are better developed than perceptual symbol-associative skills.

COMPARISON OF VERBAL AND PERFORMANCE SUBTESTS

1. *Similarities (SI) and Block Design (BD)*. Similarities and Block Design both reflect abstract reasoning ability. The subtests require the abstraction of relations among stimulus items. However, Similarities involves verbal material and requires a verbal response, whereas Block Design involves nonverbal material and requires a motor response.

- SI > BD: This pattern may suggest that abstract reasoning ability with verbal stimuli is better developed than abstract reasoning ability with nonverbal stimuli.
- BD > SI: This pattern may suggest that abstract reasoning ability with nonverbal stimuli is better developed than abstract reasoning ability with verbal stimuli.

2. *Similarities (SI) and Picture Concepts (PCn)*. Similarities and Picture Concepts both reflect abstract reasoning ability involving conceptualization and categorization. They require the abstraction of relations

among stimulus items. However, Similarities involves verbal stimuli and requires a verbal response, whereas Picture Concepts involves visual stimuli and requires either a pointing or a verbal response. In addition, Picture Concepts does not require the child to express verbally the categorical concept.

- SI > PCn: This pattern may suggest that abstract reasoning ability with verbal stimuli is better developed than abstract reasoning ability with visual stimuli.
- PCn > SI: This pattern may suggest that abstract reasoning ability with visual stimuli is better developed than abstract reasoning ability with verbal stimuli.

3. *Similarities (SI) and Matrix Reasoning (MR).* This comparison relates the ability to engage in verbal conceptual reasoning (Similarities) to analogic nonverbal reasoning ability (Matrix Reasoning).

- SI > MR: This pattern may suggest that verbal conceptual reasoning is better developed than analogic nonverbal reasoning ability.
- MR > SI: This pattern may suggest that analogic nonverbal reasoning ability is better developed than verbal conceptual reasoning.

4. *Comprehension (CO) and Matrix Reasoning (MR).* This comparison relates social judgment (Comprehension) to analogic nonverbal reasoning ability (Matrix Reasoning).

- CO > MR: This pattern may suggest that social judgment is better developed than analogic nonverbal reasoning ability.
- MR > CO: This pattern may suggest that analogic nonverbal reasoning ability is better developed than social judgment.

5. *Vocabulary (VC) and Matrix Reasoning (MR).* This comparison relates the ability to understand or express the meanings of individual words (Vocabulary) to analogic nonverbal reasoning ability (Matrix Reasoning).

- VC > MR: This pattern may suggest that the ability to understand or express the meanings of individual words is better developed than analogic nonverbal reasoning ability.
- MR > VC: This pattern may suggest that analogic nonverbal reasoning ability is better developed than the ability to understand or express the meanings of individual words.

6. *Word Reasoning (WR) and Picture Concepts (PCn).* Word Reasoning and Picture Concepts both reflect abstract reasoning ability involving conceptualization and categorization. They require the abstraction of relations among stimulus items. However, Word Reasoning involves verbal stimuli and requires a verbal response, whereas Picture Concepts involves visual stimuli and requires either a pointing or a verbal response. In addition, Picture Concepts does not require the child to express verbally the categorical concept.

- WR > PCn: This pattern may suggest that abstract reasoning ability with verbal stimuli is better developed than abstract reasoning ability with visual stimuli.
- PCn > WR: This pattern may suggest that abstract reasoning ability with visual stimuli is better developed than abstract reasoning ability with verbal stimuli.

7. *Vocabulary (VC) and Information (IN) vs. Block Design (BD) and Matrix Reasoning (MR).* This is a comparison of two subtests that reflect the extent of previously learned and stored verbal material and crystallized knowledge (Vocabulary and Information) versus two subtests that reflect perceptual reasoning and fluid reasoning ability (Block Design and Matrix Reasoning).

- VC, IN > BD, MR: This pattern may suggest that abilities dependent on well-learned verbal facts and relationships are better developed than spatial reasoning ability and novel problem-solving ability.
- BD, MR > VC, IN: This pattern may suggest that spatial reasoning ability and novel problem-solving ability are better developed than abilities dependent on well-learned verbal facts and relationships.

COMPARISON OF PERFORMANCE AND PROCESSING SPEED SUBTESTS

1. *Matrix Reasoning (MR) and Coding (CD).* This comparison relates analogic nonverbal reasoning ability (Matrix Reasoning) to processing speed (Coding).

- MR > CD: This pattern may suggest that analogic perceptual reasoning is better developed than processing speed.
- CD > MR: This pattern may suggest that processing speed is better developed than analogic perceptual reasoning.

2. *Matrix Reasoning (MR) and Symbol Search (SS).* This comparison relates analogic nonverbal reasoning ability (Matrix Reasoning) to processing speed (Symbol Search).

- MR > SS: This pattern may suggest that analogic perceptual reasoning is better developed than processing speed.
- SS > MR: This pattern may suggest that processing speed is better developed than analogic perceptual reasoning.

3. *Block Design (BD), Matrix Reasoning (MR), and Picture Concepts (PCn) vs. Coding (CD) and Symbol Search (SS).* This is a comparison of sequential processing versus simultaneous processing.

- BD, MR, PCn > CD, SS: This pattern may suggest that sequential processing is better developed than simultaneous processing.
- CD, SS > BD, MR, PCn: This pattern may suggest that simultaneous processing is better developed than sequential processing.

Method 7: Compare the range of subtest scaled scores with that found in the standardization sample.

The subtest scaled-score range provides information about the variability (or scatter) in a child's WPPSI–III profile. The scaled-score range is the distance between the two most extreme subtest scaled scores. It is obtained by subtracting the lowest subtest scaled score from the highest subtest scaled score. For example, in a profile where the highest subtest scaled score is 15 and the lowest subtest scaled score is 3, the range is 12, since $15 - 3 = 12$. If the highest score in the profile is 10 and the lowest score is 5, the range is 5, since $10 - 5 = 5$.

Note that the scaled-score range is based on only two scores and therefore fails to take into account the variability among all subtest scaled scores used in the comparison. The base rate scaled-score range is still useful, however, because it provides information about what occurred in the standardization sample. It also is a relatively simple measure of variability that can be compared with more complex indices of variability, such as the standard deviation of the subtests. Let's look at two ways to evaluate intersubtest scatter by using data from the standardization sample.

1. *Overall scaled-score range.* One method is to compare the child's scaled-score range to the range found in the standardization sample for the seven core subtests. Table B.6 in the Administration Manual shows that the median scaled-score range was 6 points for the seven core subtests. Table B.6 also shows scatter for other combinations of subtests (3 core Verbal subtests, 3 core Performance subtests, and 4 or 7 Full Scale subtests).

2. *Scaled-score range based on specific subtest scaled scores.* Table B.6 in the Administration Manual shows that the median scaled-score range at ages 4-0 to 7-3 was 2 points for the three core Verbal subtests and 3 points for the three core Performance subtests. Table B.4 in the Administration Manual shows that the median scaled-score range at ages 4-0 to 7-3 was 2 points in either direction on Information vs. Receptive Vocabulary, Object Assembly vs. Block Design, Coding vs. Symbol Search, Receptive Vocabulary vs. Picture Naming, and Similarities vs. Picture Concepts. The median scaled-score range at ages 2-6 to 3-11 was 2 points in either direction on Information vs. Receptive Vocabulary and Receptive Vocabulary vs. Picture Naming and 3 points in either direction on Object Assembly vs. Block Design.

Statistically Reliable vs. Empirically Observed IQ Differences

We have seen that there are two types of complementary measures that can assist in profile analysis—statistically reliable differences and empirically observed base rates. Tables B-2 and B-3 in Appendix B present the differences required between the Composite scores for statistical significance. Table B.2 in the Administration Manual gives the actual (i.e., empirically observed) base rates of the frequencies of differences between the Composite scores for the standardization sample.

Whether an occurrence is "unusual" (i.e., low base rate) depends on how one defines the term. A difference that occurs in 15% or 20% of the population may be considered unusual by some, whereas others may consider a difference unusual only if it occurs in no more than 5% or 10% of the population. We believe that all statistically significant differences between scores are "unusual," regardless of the base rate, and deserve consideration in evaluating a child's profile of abilities. We also suggest that a low base rate is one that occurs in 10% to 15% or less of the standardization sample. In fact, all of the significant differences between the sets of Composite comparisons in Table B.2 in the Administration Manual (Verbal IQ vs. Performance IQ, Verbal IQ vs. Processing Speed Quotient, and Performance IQ vs. Processing Speed Quotient) also occur in less than 16% of the overall sample.

Let's look at an example. A 5-year-old child with a Full Scale IQ of 110 has a Verbal IQ that is 15 points higher than the Performance IQ. This difference is statistically significant at the .05 level. This is a reliable difference that is unlikely to be the result of measurement error (i.e., chance). Differences that are greater than chance may reflect differential functioning in the abilities measured by Verbal and Performance Composites. From Table B.2 in the Administration Manual (p. 245) we find that a difference of 15 points (VIQ > PIQ) occurred in 14.0% of the standardization sample. This 15-point difference, therefore, is statistically significant and occurs in less than 15% of the standardization sample. Whether the 15-point difference is clinically meaningful is, of course, an empirical question.

Clinical acumen, the child's medical history, behavioral observations, and the results of other tests that the child has taken will help you interpret differences between the Composite scores. The magnitude and direction of the Composite score discrepancies and subtest scaled-score discrepancies can be influenced by several variables, such as the child's educational level and cultural and linguistic background. For example, on average, children whose parents read to them or who are early readers may have higher scores on the Verbal Composite than on the Performance Composite, whereas children with a non-English or limited English linguistic background may have lower scores on the Verbal Composite than on the Performance Composite.

Procedure to Follow in Determining Whether Subtest Scaled Scores Are Significantly Different from the Mean

The following procedure will help you determine whether a subtest scaled score is significantly different from the mean of its respective Composite (based on 2, 3, 4, or 5 subtests) or the mean based on the Full Scale subtests.

Step 1. Write the names of the subtests and their respective scaled scores on a sheet of paper.

VERBAL

Step 2. Sum the two, three, four, or five Verbal subtest scaled scores.

Step 3. Compute the mean of the Verbal subtests by dividing the sum of the Verbal subtest scaled scores by the total number of Verbal subtests administered (2, 3, 4, or 5).

Step 4. Calculate the deviation from the mean for each Verbal subtest by subtracting the Verbal mean from each Verbal subtest scaled score. Enter these deviations, with a negative sign if appropriate (–), opposite the subtest scaled scores.

PERFORMANCE

Step 5. Sum the two, three, four, or five Performance subtest scaled scores.

Step 6. Compute the mean of the Performance subtests by dividing the sum of the Performance subtest scaled scores by the total number of Performance subtests administered (2, 3, 4, or 5).

Step 7. Calculate the deviation from the mean for each Performance subtest by subtracting the Performance mean from each Performance subtest scaled score. Enter these deviations, with a negative sign if appropriate (–), opposite the subtest scaled scores.

PROCESSING SPEED

Step 8. Sum the two Processing Speed subtest scaled scores.

Step 9. Compute the mean of the Processing Speed subtests by dividing the sum of the Processing Speed subtests by 2.

Step 10. Calculate the deviation from the mean for each Processing Speed subtest by subtracting the Processing Speed mean from each Processing Speed subtest scaled score. Enter these deviations, with a negative sign if appropriate (–), opposite the subtest scaled scores.

FULL SCALE

Step 11. Sum all of the subtest scaled scores.

Step 12. Compute the mean of the Full Scale by dividing the sum of the subtest scaled scores by the total number of subtests administered.

Step 13. Calculate the deviation from the Full Scale mean for each subtest scaled score by subtracting the Full Scale mean from each subtest scaled score. Enter these deviations, with a negative sign if appropriate (–), opposite the subtest scaled scores.

Step 14. Determine whether the deviations are significant by using Table B-5 in Appendix B. The values in Table B-5 reflect significant differences at the .05 and .01 levels of probability by age group. Be sure to use the appropriate column in Table B-5 to obtain the significant deviations.

Step 15. Place an asterisk next to each subtest deviation that is significant.

Step 16. After each asterisk, write S for a *strength* (interindividual comparison), RS for a *relative strength* (intraindividual comparison), W for a *weakness* (interindividual comparison), or RW for a *relative weakness* (intraindividual comparison).

Table 8-3 illustrates these steps and shows whether the subtest scaled scores differ significantly from the mean of (a) the Verbal scaled scores, (b) the Performance scaled scores, (c) the Processing Speed scaled scores, and (d) all Full Scale scaled scores for a 5 year, 0 month old child who was administered all 12 subtests. The comparisons in Table 8-3 show the following:

- Word Reasoning was the only subtest whose score was significantly higher than the Verbal mean.
- Comprehension was the only subtest whose score was significantly lower than the Verbal mean.
- Picture Concepts was the only subtest whose score was significantly lower than the Performance mean.
- No subtest score differed significantly from the Processing Speed mean.
- Word Reasoning was significantly higher and Picture Concepts was significantly lower than the Full Scale mean.

In determining whether a subtest scaled score is significantly different from the mean, disregard any minus signs in Table 8-3. You may now infer that the differences between the Word Reasoning, Comprehension, and Picture Concepts subtest scaled scores and the child's respective Composite mean scaled scores are not chance differences. The results suggest that, for this child, the abilities reflected by the Word Reasoning subtest scaled score are strengths, and the abilities reflected by the Comprehension and Picture Concepts subtest scaled scores are weaknesses.

The critical values used in the preparation of Table 8-3 are based on the assumption that the scores on all subtests in a scale are to be compared with the mean score for that scale. Therefore, use only one significance level (either .05 or .01) to determine the critical values. *Do not mix levels of significance for this type of comparison.*

As noted earlier, when evaluating the difference between Composite scores, you should determine whether the difference is likely to have occurred by chance—this is known as the *reliability-of-difference approach.* Differences that are not significant do not warrant your attention, because they are likely to have occurred by chance. Composite score differences may be significant yet occur with some frequency in the population. Thus, the discrepancy may be reliable but not occur infrequently. Whether a significant difference has practical significance is open to question. Statistically significant differences probably have diagnostic relevance (i.e., the difference tells you something about the child's abilities) even if they occur frequently in the population. Therefore, given a significant difference only, you can still formulate hypotheses about the child's cognitive strengths and weaknesses.

The standard error of measurement of each Composite is used in the reliability-of-difference approach, and the correlation between two Composites is used in the probability-of-occurrence approach. Both approaches assist in clinical judgment; however, neither should be used in a mechanical fashion or as a replacement for clinical judgment.

Comment on Profile Analysis

When a difference between two subtests or a difference between two Composites is statistically significant, it is large enough that it cannot be attributed to chance (i.e., measurement error). The Administration Manual lists the .15 level of significance as the minimum level for determining whether there are significant differences between subtest scaled scores or between Composite scores. In contrast, we recommend that you use the .05 level of significance as the minimum level because it is traditionally used.

Do not use scores on individual subtests to attempt precise descriptions of specific cognitive skills; rather, use them to generate hypotheses about the child's abilities. You can derive more reliable estimates of specific abilities from each Composite than from individual sub-

Table 8-3
An Example of Profile Analysis on the WPPSI–III:
Comparing Each Subtest Score to the Mean Individual Composite
Scaled Score and the Mean Full Scale Scaled Score

Composite	Subtest	Scaled score	Deviation from Individual Composite mean	Deviation from Full Scale mean
Verbal	Information	11	0.8	1.4
	Vocabulary	11	0.8	1.4
	Word Reasoning	13	2.8*S	3.4*S
	Comprehension	7	−3.2*W	−2.6
	Similarities	9	−1.2	−0.6
	Mean	10.2		
Performance	Block Design	11	1.8	1.4
	Matrix Reasoning	11	1.8	1.4
	Picture Concepts	5	−4.2*W	−4.6*W
	Picture Completion	10	0.8	0.4
	Object Assembly	9	-0.2	-0.6
	Mean	9.2		
Processing Speed	Coding	8	−1.5	−1.6
	Symbol Search	11	1.5	1.4
	Mean	9.5		
Overall	Mean	9.6		

Note. S = strength, W = weakness. See Table B-4 in Appendix B to obtain deviations that are significant.
* $p < .05$.

test scaled scores. The Composite scores also provide more reliable information about abilities than do individual subtest scaled scores. In fact, of the 99 separate reliability coefficients for the 14 subtests at the nine age groups of the test, 93% (93) are .80 or above. Of these, 39 are .90 or above. The remaining six reliability coefficients are below .80 and are not sufficiently reliable for decision-making or classification purposes (see Table 4.1 on page 53 of the Technical Manual). However, reliability coefficients of .70 or above on subtests are useful for generating hypotheses. Of the 42 separate reliabilities for the five Composites at the nine age groups of the test, all are greater than .85, and of these, only 12% (5) are below .90.

The difference between a child's subtest scaled score and the mean scaled score is a statistically more accurate measure than the difference between pairs of subtest scaled scores. Use of the mean scaled score has the additional advantage of reducing the accumulation of er-

rors associated with multiple comparisons.

What might account for a certain profile of scores? To attempt to answer this question, you must consider both stable factors (also referred to as trait characteristics or long-term factors) and transient conditions (also referred to as state characteristics or short-term factors). *Stable factors* include the child's cognitive skill development, age, sex, cultural group, socioeconomic status, education, special training, social and physical environment, family background, ethnicity, temperament, personality, and psychopathology. *Transient conditions* include the child's current health status (e.g., short-term illnesses), the amount of sleep the child had the previous night, the degree of tension in the home, any acute trauma that the child has faced (with possible post-traumatic stress disorder reactions), test anxiety, and adverse (or unexpected) drug reactions. Variability of subtest scores may even be simply a reflection of the unreliability of the subtest scaled scores, factors associated with the characteristics of the examiner, or factors associated with the assessment situation.

Profile analysis is a useful tool for evaluating intraindividual variability in various ability and achievement areas. Variability of scores, however, may represent only uneven skill development and is not a sufficient basis for making decisions about psychopathology. Again, you should view profile analysis as a clinical tool to be used *together with* other assessment strategies in developing hypotheses about the child's abilities.

A SUCCESSIVE-LEVEL APPROACH TO TEST INTERPRETATION

The following six-level approach to test interpretation can help you better understand a child's performance on the WPPSI–III (see Figure 8-1).

Level I: Full Scale IQ. The first level focuses on the Full Scale IQ. In most cases, the Full Scale IQ is the most reliable and valid estimate of the child's intellectual ability provided by the test. It is the primary numerical and quantitative index, providing information about the child's relative standing in the general population (as represented by the standardization group). The Full Scale IQ is a global estimate of the child's level of cognitive ability; it assesses verbal and performance (or nonverbal) reasoning. The Full Scale IQ is usually used to obtain the descriptive classification of the child's IQ level (e.g., Very Superior, Superior, High Average, Average, Low Average, Borderline, and Extremely Low). Converting the Full Scale IQ to a percentile rank will help you interpret this score for individuals who are not familiar with standard scores.

Level II: Individual Composite scores. The second level focuses on the individual Composite scores and the extent to which there is a significant difference between them. The Verbal Composite provides information about verbal skills and crystallized knowledge. The Performance Composite covers nonverbal reasoning skills and fluid reasoning ability. The Processing Speed Composite provides information about processing speed and rate of test taking.

Level III: Subtest deviations within Composites. The third level focuses on deviations of subtests from their respective Composite mean: (a) Verbal Composite subtest scaled scores from their mean, (b) Performance Composite subtest scaled scores from their mean, and (c) Processing Speed Composite subtest scaled scores from their mean. You can develop hypotheses about strengths and weaknesses from these analyses.

Level IV: Intersubtest comparisons. The fourth level focuses on comparisons between sets of subtest scaled scores or among clusters of subtest scaled scores. Although these comparisons are open to the errors associated with multiple comparisons, they are valuable for generating hypotheses about the child's intellectual abilities.

Level V: Intrasubtest patterns. The fifth level focuses on the pattern of raw scores within each subtest. Within a subtest, the items are presumably arranged in order of difficulty, which will help you to evaluate the pattern of successes and failures. Here are two examples:

1. A child who passes the first item, fails the next four, passes the next one, fails the next four, and overall passes a total of four items shows a different pattern from a child who passes the first four items and fails the remainder, although both children receive 4 raw-score points (assuming each item is worth 1 raw-score point). The child with the markedly un-

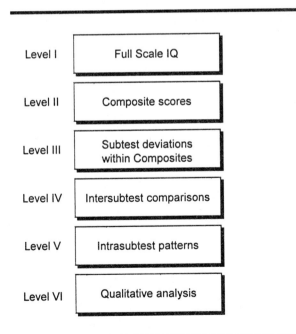

Figure 8-1. A successive-level approach to interpreting the WPPSI–III.

Level I	Full Scale IQ
Level II	Composite scores
Level III	Subtest deviations within Composites
Level IV	Intersubtest comparisons
Level V	Intrasubtest patterns
Level VI	Qualitative analysis

even pattern may have cognitive or attentional inefficiencies that need to be explored further.

2. A pattern of missing easy items and succeeding on more difficult items may occur among bright children who are bored by the easy items and thus give careless or even nonsense replies, only to become challenged by more difficult items that allow them to demonstrate their skills. This pattern may be evident, for example, on the Matrix Reasoning subtest, where a child may be observed to perform better on the more demanding later items. This pattern also may suggest inconsistent attention or effort resulting from anxiety or other factors.

Level VI: Qualitative analysis. The sixth level focuses on specific item failures and the content of the responses, or what is called "qualitative analysis." Inspecting responses to specific items can aid in understanding the child's knowledge of specific information. The child's unique or idiosyncratic responses also may help you in formulating hypotheses about his or her functioning. For example, querulous, distrustful, or legalistic responses (e.g., "I'm being tricked," "Why are you writing everything down?" "Are you going to use my answers against me?") will require further investigation, as will slow, hesitant, and blocked responses, interspersed with self-deprecatory remarks (e.g., "I'm worthless," "These things are tiring," "I've never been good at this," "Sure takes a lot of energy to do this puzzle"). Also consider nonverbal responses that accompany verbal responses, such as grimaces, laughter, crying, tone of voice, and motor movements.

STEPS IN ANALYZING A PROTOCOL

Use the following steps in analyzing a WPPSI–III protocol.

RELIABILITY AND VALIDITY

Step 1. Evaluate the reliability of the test scores.
Step 2. Evaluate the validity of the test scores.

COMPOSITES

Step 3. Examine the Full Scale IQ and its percentile rank, and evaluate the implications of this score.
Step 4. Examine the Verbal IQ and its percentile rank, and evaluate the implications of this score.

Step 5. Examine the Performance IQ and its percentile rank, and evaluate the implications of this score.
Step 6. Examine the Processing Speed Quotient and its percentile rank, and evaluate the implications of this score.

SIGNIFICANT DIFFERENCES

Step 7. Determine whether there are any significant discrepancies among the Composite scores. If so, which ones are discrepant? Note which Composite score is higher or lower than the others and the absolute level of each Composite score. What are the implications of any significant discrepancies?
Step 8. Determine whether any of the subtest scaled scores in a Composite differ significantly from the mean of that Composite. If there are significant differences, are these subtest scaled scores lower or higher than the mean? What are the base rates for the discrepancies? Note the absolute level of each subtest scaled score that differs significantly from its respective mean score. What are the implications of any significant discrepancies?
Step 9. Determine whether there are subtest scaled scores of interest that differ significantly from each other. If so, which ones? What are the implications of each discrepancy? Note which subtest scaled score is higher or lower than the other and the absolute level of each subtest scaled score. What are the implications of any significant discrepancies?

QUALITATIVE FEATURES

Step 10. Note any noteworthy qualitative features of the child's performance. What are the implications of any noteworthy features by themselves and in relation to the Full Scale IQ, the Composite scores, the subtest scaled scores, and the referral question and case history?

THE COMPOSITES

When you develop hypotheses about a child's performance on the Full Scale and the three individual Composites, the hypotheses are based primarily on the individual subtests that make up the respective Composite. However, some general observations about the Composites still can be made. To help guide your interpretations of the Full Scale IQ and three Composite scores, Table C-5 in Appendix C presents for each Composite a summary of (a) interpretive rationales, (b) possible implications of high scores, (c) possible implications of low scores, and (d) instructional implications.

Items on the Full Scale and the three individual Composites can be solved by the use of verbal strategies, nonverbal strategies, or a combination of the two. For example, items on Coding and Symbol Search in the Processing Speed Composite can be solved by either nonverbal strategies (e.g., primarily visual scanning) or verbal strategies (e.g., language activity in the form of overt verbal responses or mediating symbolic activity). Indeed, there may be no *pure* measures of verbal ability, performance ability, or processing speed on the WPPSI–III.

Verbal

Verbal tasks draw on the child's accumulated experience. The child is asked to respond verbally with what is likely learned information. The questions (input) are presented orally, and the child responds (output) orally. The Verbal Composite measures verbal ability, application of verbal skills and information to the solution of new problems, verbal comprehension, ability to process verbal information, ability to think with words, and crystallized knowledge.

Performance

Performance tasks require immediate problem-solving ability and perceptual reasoning. The child uses previously acquired skills to solve a novel set of problems. The stimuli (input) are nonverbal (aside from the directions), and most items are presented visually. The child's solutions (output) require motor responses and, to a lesser extent, verbal responses. The Performance Composite measures nonverbal reasoning skills; ability to think in terms of visual images and manipulate them with fluency, flexibility, and relative speed; ability to interpret or organize visually perceived material within a time limit; perceptual reasoning, ability to form relatively abstract concepts and relationships without the use of words; and fluid reasoning ability.

Let's examine more closely the subtests on the Performance Composite for possible influences of verbal abilities on the child's performance.

- Block Design depends on the ability to visualize configurations in space and therefore may not depend heavily on verbal processing. However, verbal strategies, such as thinking about the placement of the blocks or what the appropriate positions of the blocks should be, may accompany efforts to solve the problems.
- Matrix Reasoning depends on the ability to process information visually and may also involve verbal processing to solve the matrix.
- Picture Concepts depends on the ability to identify pictures, an ability that involves visual processing and may also involve verbal processing to categorize the pictures into logical groups.
- Picture Completion depends on the ability to know "the way the world is," and this knowledge may be imparted by verbal means.
- Object Assembly depends on the ability to visualize how the parts of an object might go together and may not depend heavily on verbal processing. However, verbal strategies, such as thinking about how the pieces fit together, may accompany efforts to solve the problems.

Processing Speed

Processing Speed tasks require the child to carry out instructions given by the examiner quickly and efficiently. The tasks rely heavily on visual processing and less on fine-motor skills. The Processing Speed Composite measures perceptual discrimination, speed of mental operation, psychomotor speed, attention, concentration, short-term visual memory, visual-motor coordination, and cognitive flexibility.

Let's examine more closely the subtests on Processing Speed for possible influences of verbal abilities on the child's performance.

- Coding depends on the ability to learn associations between simple geometric shapes and symbols that can be encoded verbally.
- Symbol Search depends on the ability to scan symbols rapidly, an ability that may be facilitated by attaching verbal descriptions to symbols.

ESTIMATED PERCENTILE RANKS AND TEST-AGE EQUIVALENTS FOR RAW SCORES

When you explain the test results to teachers, parents, physicians, attorneys, or other people involved in the assessment, it is helpful to use the percentile ranks associated with the Full Scale IQ, Composite scores, and subtest scaled scores. In the Administration Manual, Tables A.2, A.3, A.4, and A.5 show the percentile ranks for the Verbal IQ, Performance IQ, Full Scale IQ, and General Language Composite, respectively, for ages 2-3 to 3-11. Tables A.6, A.7, A.8, A.9, and A.10 show the percentile ranks for the Verbal IQ, Performance IQ, Processing Speed Quotient, Full Scale IQ, and General Language Composite, respectively, for ages 4-0 to 7-3. The qualitative descriptions for Composite score ranges are as follows (Wechsler, 2003b):

130 and above: Very Superior
120–129: Superior
110–119: High Average
90–109: Average
80–89: Low Average
70–79: Borderline
69 and below: Extremely Low

Table C-1 in Appendix C gives the estimated percentile ranks and qualitative descriptions for each WPPSI–III subtest scaled score. You should never estimate an IQ based on only one subtest scaled score.

Occasionally, you may want to use test-age equivalents. Table A.12 (p. 242) in the Administration Manual gives the test-age equivalents for raw scores on each subtest. The test-age equivalents provide approximate developmental levels for the child's achievement on a subtest. For example, a raw score of 23 on Block Design is roughly equivalent to a developmental age level of 4-10 years. Because test-age equivalents have several drawbacks, we do not recommend their routine use (see Chapter 4 in Sattler, 2001). The exception is for discussions with parents and others who may more easily understand test-age equivalents than standard scores.

COMMENT ON INTERPRETING THE WPPSI–III

Sometimes children have difficulty completing tasks. For example, tasks requiring speed and quick execution, such as Coding or Symbol Search, may be taxing for depressed children. Although depressed children's performance on these tasks may not reflect their level of cognitive ability, the tasks are still valuable because they provide information not readily obtained from interviews or observations conducted in natural settings. Coding, for example, can give you clues about the child's ability to follow a complex set of instructions, visual scanning processes, and learning ability. Symbol Search gives you clues about visual scanning and ability to shift rapidly. You may not want to report a score for these subtests for children who are depressed, but you can use the results to develop hypotheses to guide your clinical judgments.

When a significant split occurs between the Composite scores, the Full Scale IQ may be only a forced average of rather disparate primary skills. What meaning, for example, can we attach to a Full Scale IQ of 100 and a Verbal IQ of 130 and a Performance IQ of 70? Although the IQ of 100 may be the best overall estimate of the child's cognitive level, the child is not likely to be average in situations calling for both verbal and nonverbal reasoning. Unfortunately, there is little research that can help us understand how children with large Composite discrepancies function outside the test situation.

To a lesser extent, a similar problem exists in interpreting a Composite score when there is an exceptionally large amount of variability among the subtests within the Composite. Consider a 4-year-old child who obtains a score of 10 on each of the three core Verbal subtests and comes out with a Verbal IQ of 100. Then consider another 4-year-old child who obtains scores of 1, 10, and 19 on the three core Verbal subtests and a resulting Verbal IQ of 100. What is the meaning of the 100 IQ score in each case? Obviously, these two children differ in their pattern of ability. How should we interpret the Verbal IQ in each case? You will need to point out the variability and its possible implications (e.g., that the subtests comprising the Verbal Composite have variable scores and that the ability measured by the Verbal Composite is not pure).

In situations requiring the reporting of one number (e.g., in the determination of mental retardation or when a discrepancy formula is involved in cases of learning disability), we need to report a Full Scale IQ, regardless of whether it is obtained from a profile with minimal variability or one with extensive variability. Unfortunately, there is little research to guide us in determining whether the Full Scale IQ becomes invalid when the subtest scores are variable.

Subtest scaled scores, Composite scores, and Full Scale IQs are multidetermined. This means that any one subtest or Composite likely measures several abilities. Consequently, a high score or a low score does not indicate which particular functions measured by the subtest or Composite are well developed or not well developed. This information will come only from a sifting of all WPPSI–III scores, scores obtained on other tests, qualitative information, testing-of-limits, and the child's clinical history. As noted in Chapter 5, the WPPSI–III may not be the instrument of choice for evaluating the cognitive abilities of children who function at either an extremely low or an extremely high cognitive level. In both cases, there may be too few items on the test—that is, not enough easy items for low-functioning children and not enough challenging ones for high-functioning children.

Interpreting the WPPSI–III is a challenging activity. The WPPSI–III gives an estimate of the child's level of intellectual functioning. We need to emphasize the word *estimate*. The WPPSI–III provides useful—but not complete—information about the range, depth, and real-world applications of a child's intellectual ability.

The WPPSI–III should not be used to evaluate personality and temperament, to diagnose psychopathology, or to determine brain lateralization. Instead, the WPPSI–III should be used to learn about the child's intellectual ability and to generate hypotheses to account for the child's functioning on the test. There is a world of difference between reporting that the child performed in an impulsive manner and reporting that the WPPSI–III test results indicate that the child has ADHD. Once we go beyond the confines of the Full Scale IQ, Composite scores, and subtest scores, the ground becomes loose and wobbly. Interpretations become more impressionistic and less reliable and valid. When on this ground, step carefully, continually getting your bearings from research findings, other sources of information, and clinical experience. There are no WPPSI–III profiles that are known to reliably distinguish clinical groups from normal groups.

THINKING THROUGH THE ISSUES

1. In interpreting the WPPSI–III, you can use various procedures. How does profile analysis help in evaluating a child's WPPSI–III performance? What problems are associated with profile analysis?
2. The successive-level approach to test interpretation is based on a hierarchical model. What is the logic underlying the hierarchy?
3. How might a child function if he had a Verbal IQ of 120 and a Performance IQ of 80?
4. How might a child function if she had a Verbal IQ of 80 and a Performance IQ of 120?
5. How might a child function if he had a Verbal IQ of 120, a Performance IQ of 80, and a Processing

Speed Quotient of 80?
6. How might a child function if she had a Verbal IQ of 80, a Performance IQ of 120, and a Processing Speed Quotient of 120?
7. What would you do to improve the WPPSI–III?
8. How would you answer a parent who asked, "What is my child's potential?" after learning how the child did on the WPPSI–III?

SUMMARY

1. This chapter will help you (a) perform a profile analysis, (b) determine whether the individual Composite scores differ significantly from each other, (c) determine whether the subtest scaled scores differ significantly from each other, (d) obtain the base rates for differences between some Composite scores, (e) obtain the base rates for differences between some of the subtest scaled scores, (f) determine base rates for intersubtest scatter, and (g) develop hypotheses and interpretations.
2. After you statistically evaluate the Composite score discrepancies, subtest discrepancies, and the profile of subtest scaled scores, you will need to interpret the findings.

Profile Analysis

3. Much of the discussion of profile analysis for the WISC–IV also pertains to the WPPSI–III.
4. One approach to profile analysis is to evaluate the scores in reference to the norm group (see Chapter 4).
5. A second approach to profile analysis is to determine the frequency with which the differences between scores in the child's profile occurred in the standardization sample; this is called the base rate approach or the probability-of-occurrence approach.
6. The primary methods of profile analysis are evaluating the Composite scores, the subtest scaled scores, and the range of subtest scaled scores (or intersubtest scatter).
7. Both statistically reliable differences and empirically observed base rates can assist in profile analysis.
8. You will need to evaluate the child's entire performance, clinical history, and background information to arrive at the most reasonable hypothesis to account for a significant difference between Composite scores.

9. A discrepancy between two or more Composite scores should never be used as the sole criterion for making a diagnosis of learning disability, brain injury, or mental retardation.

10. Subtest scaled scores of 10 or higher should be described as reflecting average or above-average ability and never as absolute weaknesses, whereas subtest scaled scores of 7 or lower should be described as reflecting below-average ability and never as absolute strengths.

11. Any hypotheses about subtest scaled scores should be developed through study of the child's entire test performance and clinical history.

12. All statistically significant differences between scores are "unusual," regardless of the base rate, and deserve consideration in evaluating a child's profile of abilities.

13. We suggest that a low base rate is one that occurs in 10% to 15% or less of the standardization sample.

14. Clinical acumen, the child's medical history, behavioral observations, and the results of other tests that the child has taken will help you interpret differences between the Composite scores.

15. Neither the reliability-of-difference approach nor the probability-of-occurrence approach should be used in a mechanical fashion or as a replacement for clinical judgment.

16. When a difference between two subtests or a difference between two Composites is statistically significant, it is large enough that it cannot be attributed to chance (i.e., measurement error).

17. Do not use scores on individual subtests to attempt precise descriptions of specific cognitive skills; rather, use them to generate hypotheses about the child's abilities.

18. You can derive more reliable estimates of specific abilities from each Composite score than from individual subtest scaled scores.

19. Variability of scores may represent only uneven skill development and is not a sufficient basis for making decisions about psychopathology.

A Successive-Level Approach to Test Interpretation

20. A successive-level approach to test interpretation can help you better understand a child's performance. The six levels of the approach are (a) Full Scale IQ, (b) Composite scores, (c) subtests within each Composite, (d) subtest scaled score differences, (e) intrasubtest variability, and (f) qualitative analysis.

Steps in Analyzing a Protocol

21. A 10-step procedure is useful for analyzing a WPPSI–III protocol. The steps focus on evaluating the reliability and validity of the test scores, examining the Composite scores, determining significant differences between the scores, and evaluating qualitative features of the child's performance.

The Composites

22. When you develop hypotheses about a child's performance on the Full Scale and the individual Composites, the hypotheses are based primarily on the individual subtests that make up the respective Composite.

23. Verbal subtests draw on the child's accumulated experience, Performance subtests require immediate problem-solving ability, and Processing Speed subtests rely on visual processing.

Estimated Percentile Ranks and Test-Age Equivalents for Raw Scores

24. When you explain the test results to parents or others involved in the assessment, it is helpful to use the percentile ranks associated with the Full Scale IQ, Composite scores, and subtest scaled scores.

25. Occasionally, you may want to use test-age equivalents in your explanations.

Comment on Interpreting the WPPSI–III

26. You may not want to report a score for some subtests for children who are depressed, but you can use the results to develop hypotheses to guide your clinical judgments.

27. When a significant split occurs between the Composite scores, the Full Scale IQ may be only a forced average of rather disparate primary skills.

28. To a lesser extent, a similar problem exists in interpreting a Composite score when there is an exceptionally large amount of variability among the subtests within the Composite.

29. Subtest scaled scores, Composite scores, and Full Scale IQs are multidetermined.

30. The WPPSI–III gives an estimate of the child's level of intellectual functioning and provides useful—but not complete—information about the range, depth, and real-world applications of a child's intellectual ability.

31. The WPPSI–III should not be used to evaluate personality and temperament, to diagnose psychopathology, or to determine brain lateralization.

KEY TERMS, CONCEPTS, AND NAMES

Profile analysis (p. 256)
Base rate approach (p. 256)
Probability-of-occurrence approach (p. 256)
Primary methods of profile analysis (p. 256)
Reliability-of-difference approach (p. 269)
Successive-level approach to test interpretation (p. 271)
Steps in analyzing a protocol (p. 272)
Estimated percentile ranks (p. 273)
Test-age equivalents (p. 273)

STUDY QUESTIONS

1. Discuss approaches to profile analysis on the WPPSI–III beginning with base rates.
2. Describe the successive-level approach to interpreting the WPPSI–III.
3. Describe the steps used to analyze a WPPSI–III protocol.
4. Discuss how to interpret differences between the WPPSI–III Composite scores.
5. Discuss how to interpret differences between WPPSI–III subtests. Cite at least seven subtest comparisons in your presentation.
6. What are some general considerations in interpreting the WPPSI–III?

APPENDIX A

TABLES FOR THE WISC–IV

Table A-1
Confidence Intervals for WISC–IV Full Scale IQs and Composite Scores
Based on Obtained Score Only

Age	Index or Full Scale	Confidence level				
		68%	85%	90%	95%	99%
6 (6-0-0 through 6-11-30)	Verbal Comprehension	±5	±7	±8	±9	±12
	Perceptual Reasoning	±5	±7	±8	±9	±12
	Working Memory	±5	±7	±7	±9	±11
	Processing Speed	±7	±9	±11	±13	±16
	Full Scale	±3	±5	±5	±6	±8
7 (7-0-0 through 7-11-30)	Verbal Comprehension	±5	±7	±7	±9	±11
	Perceptual Reasoning	±5	±7	±7	±9	±11
	Working Memory	±5	±7	±8	±10	±13
	Processing Speed	±7	±10	±11	±13	±17
	Full Scale	±3	±5	±5	±6	±8
8 (8-0-0 through 8-11-30)	Verbal Comprehension	±5	±7	±7	±9	±11
	Perceptual Reasoning	±4	±6	±7	±8	±11
	Working Memory	±5	±7	±8	±9	±12
	Processing Speed	±6	±8	±9	±11	±14
	Full Scale	±3	±4	±5	±6	±7
9 (9-0-0 through 9-11-30)	Verbal Comprehension	±4	±6	±7	±8	±10
	Perceptual Reasoning	±4	±6	±7	±8	±11
	Working Memory	±5	±7	±7	±9	±11
	Processing Speed	±5	±8	±9	±10	±13
	Full Scale	±3	±4	±5	±6	±7
10 (10-0-0 through 10-11-30)	Verbal Comprehension	±4	±6	±7	±8	±10
	Perceptual Reasoning	±4	±6	±7	±8	±11
	Working Memory	±5	±7	±7	±9	±11
	Processing Speed	±5	±7	±8	±10	±13
	Full Scale	±3	±4	±5	±6	±7
11 (11-0-0 through 11-11-30)	Verbal Comprehension	±4	±6	±7	±8	±11
	Perceptual Reasoning	±4	±6	±7	±8	±11
	Working Memory	±5	±7	±7	±9	±11
	Processing Speed	±5	±7	±8	±10	±13
	Full Scale	±3	±4	±5	±6	±7
12 (12-0-0 through 12-11-30)	Verbal Comprehension	±4	±5	±6	±7	±9
	Perceptual Reasoning	±4	±6	±7	±8	±11
	Working Memory	±4	±6	±7	±8	±11
	Processing Speed	±5	±8	±9	±10	±13
	Full Scale	±3	±4	±5	±6	±7
13 (13-0-0 through 13-11-30)	Verbal Comprehension	±4	±6	±7	±8	±10
	Perceptual Reasoning	±4	±6	±7	±8	±11
	Working Memory	±5	±7	±8	±9	±12
	Processing Speed	±5	±8	±9	±10	±13
	Full Scale	±3	±4	±5	±6	±7

(Continued)

Table A-1 (*Continued*)

Age	Index or Full Scale	Confidence level				
		68%	85%	90%	95%	99%
14 (14-0-0 through 14-11-30)	Verbal Comprehension	±4	±5	±6	±7	±9
	Perceptual Reasoning	±5	±7	±7	±9	±11
	Working Memory	±4	±6	±7	±8	±11
	Processing Speed	±5	±8	±9	±10	±13
	Full Scale	±3	±4	±5	±6	±7
15 (15-0-0 through 15-11-30)	Verbal Comprehension	±4	±5	±6	±7	±9
	Perceptual Reasoning	±5	±7	±7	±9	±11
	Working Memory	±5	±7	±7	±9	±11
	Processing Speed	±5	±7	±8	±10	±13
	Full Scale	±3	±4	±5	±6	±7
16 (16-0-0 through 16-11-30)	Verbal Comprehension	±4	±5	±6	±7	±9
	Perceptual Reasoning	±5	±7	±8	±9	±12
	Working Memory	±4	±6	±7	±8	±11
	Processing Speed	±5	±8	±9	±10	±13
	Full Scale	±3	±4	±5	±6	±7
Average	Verbal Comprehension	±4	±6	±7	±8	±10
	Perceptual Reasoning	±5	±6	±7	±9	±11
	Working Memory	±5	±7	±8	±9	±12
	Processing Speed	±6	±8	±9	±11	±14
	Full Scale	±3	±4	±5	±6	±7

Note. Pages 109–110 in *Assessment of Children: Cognitive Applications* (Sattler, 2001) describe the procedure for computing confidence intervals. For the WISC–IV Verbal Comprehension Index, the confidence intervals are obtained by the following procedure: The appropriate SEM for the child's age is located in Table 4.3 of the Technical Manual. For example, for a 6-year-old child, the SEM = 4.50 for the Verbal Comprehension Index. This SEM is multiplied by the respective z values in order to obtain the confidence interval for the desired level. At the 68% confidence level, the SEM is multiplied by ±1 (±1 x 4.50 = ±5). At the 85% level, the SEM is multiplied by ±1.44 (±1.44 x 4.50 = ±7). At the 90% level, the SEM is multiplied by ±1.65 (±1.65 x 4.50 = ±8). At the 95% level, the SEM is multiplied by ±1.96 (±1.96 x 4.50 = ±9). At the 99% level, the SEM is multiplied by ±2.58 (±2.58 x 4.50 = ±12).

Table A-2
Differences Between WISC–IV Subtest Scaled Scores and Between Index Scores Required for Statistical Significance at the .05 and .01 Levels of Significance for the 11 Age Groups and the Total Group
(.05 significance level above diagonal, .01 significance level below diagonal)

Age 6

Subtest	BD	SI	DS	PCn	CD	VC	LN	MR	CO	SS	PCm	CA	IN	AR	WR	VCI	PRI	WMI	PSI
BD	—	4	4	4	4	4	3	4	4	4	4	4	4	4	4	—	—	—	—
SI	5	—	4	4	4	4	3	4	4	4	4	4	4	4	4	—	—	—	—
DS	5	5	—	4	4	4	3	3	4	4	4	4	4	4	4	—	—	—	—
PCn	5	5	5	—	4	4	3	4	4	4	4	4	4	4	4	—	—	—	—
CD	6	6	6	6	—	4	4	4	5	5	4	4	4	4	5	—	—	—	—
VC	5	5	5	5	6	—	3	4	4	4	4	4	4	4	4	—	—	—	—
LN	4	4	4	4	5	4	—	3	4	4	3	3	3	3	4	—	—	—	—
MR	5	5	4	5	5	5	4	—	4	4	4	4	4	3	4	—	—	—	—
CO	5	5	5	5	6	5	5	5	—	4	4	4	4	4	4	—	—	—	—
SS	5	5	5	5	6	5	5	5	5	—	4	4	4	4	4	—	—	—	—
PCm	5	5	5	5	6	5	4	5	5	5	—	4	4	4	4	—	—	—	—
CA	5	5	5	5	6	5	4	5	5	5	5	—	4	4	4	—	—	—	—
IN	5	5	5	5	6	5	4	5	5	5	5	5	—	4	4	—	—	—	—
AR	5	5	5	5	6	5	4	4	5	5	5	5	5	—	4	—	—	—	—
WR	5	5	5	5	6	5	5	5	5	6	5	5	5	5	—	—	—	—	—
VCI	—	—	—	—	—	—	—	—	—	—	—	—	—	—	—	—	13	13	15
PRI	—	—	—	—	—	—	—	—	—	—	—	—	—	—	—	17	—	13	15
WMI	—	—	—	—	—	—	—	—	—	—	—	—	—	—	—	16	16	—	15
PSI	—	—	—	—	—	—	—	—	—	—	—	—	—	—	—	20	20	20	—

Age 7

Subtest	BD	SI	DS	PCn	CD	VC	LN	MR	CO	SS	PCm	CA	IN	AR	WR	VCI	PRI	WMI	PSI
BD	—	4	4	4	4	4	3	4	4	4	4	4	4	3	4	—	—	—	—
SI	5	—	4	4	4	4	3	4	4	4	4	4	4	3	4	—	—	—	—
DS	5	5	—	4	5	4	4	4	4	4	4	4	4	4	4	—	—	—	—
PCn	5	5	5	—	4	4	3	4	4	4	4	4	4	3	4	—	—	—	—
CD	6	6	6	6	—	4	4	4	5	5	4	4	5	4	5	—	—	—	—
VC	5	5	5	5	6	—	3	4	4	4	4	4	4	3	4	—	—	—	—
LN	4	4	5	4	5	4	—	3	4	4	3	3	4	3	4	—	—	—	—
MR	5	5	5	5	5	5	4	—	4	4	4	4	4	3	4	—	—	—	—
CO	6	6	6	5	6	5	5	5	—	5	4	4	5	4	4	—	—	—	—
SS	5	5	5	5	6	5	5	5	6	—	4	4	4	4	4	—	—	—	—
PCm	5	5	5	5	6	5	4	5	5	5	—	4	4	3	4	—	—	—	—
CA	5	5	5	5	6	5	4	5	6	5	5	—	4	4	4	—	—	—	—
IN	5	5	5	5	6	5	5	5	6	6	5	5	—	4	4	—	—	—	—
AR	4	4	5	4	5	4	4	4	5	5	4	5	5	—	4	—	—	—	—
WR	5	5	5	5	6	5	5	5	6	5	5	5	5	5	—	—	—	—	—
VCI	—	—	—	—	—	—	—	—	—	—	—	—	—	—	—	—	12	13	16
PRI	—	—	—	—	—	—	—	—	—	—	—	—	—	—	—	16	—	13	16
WMI	—	—	—	—	—	—	—	—	—	—	—	—	—	—	—	17	17	—	16
PSI	—	—	—	—	—	—	—	—	—	—	—	—	—	—	—	21	21	21	—

(Continued)

Table A-2 (Continued)

Age 8

Subtest	BD	SI	DS	PCn	CD	VC	LN	MR	CO	SS	PCm	CA	IN	AR	WR	VCI	PRI	WMI	PSI
BD	—	4	4	4	4	4	3	3	4	4	4	4	4	4	4	—	—	—	—
SI	5	—	4	4	4	4	3	3	4	4	4	4	4	4	4	—	—	—	—
DS	5	5	—	4	4	4	3	3	4	4	4	4	4	4	4	—	—	—	—
PCn	5	5	5	—	4	4	4	4	4	4	4	4	4	4	4	—	—	—	—
CD	5	5	5	5	—	4	4	3	4	4	4	4	4	4	4	—	—	—	—
VC	5	5	5	5	5	—	3	3	4	4	4	4	4	4	4	—	—	—	—
LN	4	4	4	5	5	4	—	3	4	4	3	4	4	3	4	—	—	—	—
MR	4	4	4	5	4	4	4	—	4	3	3	4	3	3	3	—	—	—	—
CO	5	5	5	5	5	5	5	5	—	4	4	5	4	4	4	—	—	—	—
SS	5	5	5	5	5	5	5	4	5	—	4	4	4	4	4	—	—	—	—
PCm	5	5	5	5	5	5	4	4	5	5	—	4	4	4	4	—	—	—	—
CA	5	5	6	6	6	5	5	5	6	6	6	—	4	4	4	—	—	—	—
IN	5	5	5	5	5	5	5	4	5	5	5	6	—	4	4	—	—	—	—
AR	5	5	5	5	5	5	4	4	5	5	5	6	5	—	4	—	—	—	—
WR	5	5	5	5	5	5	5	4	5	5	5	6	5	5	—	—	—	—	—
VCI	—	—	—	—	—	—	—	—	—	—	—	—	—	—	—	—	12	13	14
PRI	—	—	—	—	—	—	—	—	—	—	—	—	—	—	—	15	—	12	13
WMI	—	—	—	—	—	—	—	—	—	—	—	—	—	—	—	16	16	—	14
PSI	—	—	—	—	—	—	—	—	—	—	—	—	—	—	—	18	17	18	—

Age 9

Subtest	BD	SI	DS	PCn	CD	VC	LN	MR	CO	SS	PCm	CA	IN	AR	WR	VCI	PRI	WMI	PSI
BD	—	4	4	4	4	4	3	3	4	4	4	4	4	3	4	—	—	—	—
SI	5	—	3	4	4	3	3	3	4	4	4	4	4	3	4	—	—	—	—
DS	5	4	—	4	4	3	3	3	4	4	4	4	4	3	4	—	—	—	—
PCn	5	5	5	—	4	4	3	3	4	4	4	4	4	4	4	—	—	—	—
CD	5	5	5	5	—	4	3	3	4	4	4	4	4	4	4	—	—	—	—
VC	5	4	4	5	5	—	3	3	4	4	4	4	4	3	4	—	—	—	—
LN	4	4	4	4	4	4	—	3	4	3	4	4	3	3	4	—	—	—	—
MR	4	4	4	4	4	4	4	—	4	3	4	4	3	3	4	—	—	—	—
CO	5	5	5	5	5	5	5	5	—	4	4	4	4	4	4	—	—	—	—
SS	5	5	5	5	5	5	4	4	5	—	4	4	4	4	4	—	—	—	—
PCm	5	5	5	5	5	5	5	5	5	5	—	4	4	4	4	—	—	—	—
CA	6	5	5	6	6	5	5	5	6	6	6	—	4	4	5	—	—	—	—
IN	5	5	5	5	5	5	4	4	5	5	5	6	—	3	4	—	—	—	—
AR	4	4	4	5	5	4	4	4	5	5	5	5	4	—	4	—	—	—	—
WR	5	5	5	5	5	5	5	5	5	5	5	6	5	5	—	—	—	—	—
VCI	—	—	—	—	—	—	—	—	—	—	—	—	—	—	—	—	11	12	13
PRI	—	—	—	—	—	—	—	—	—	—	—	—	—	—	—	14	—	12	13
WMI	—	—	—	—	—	—	—	—	—	—	—	—	—	—	—	15	15	—	13
PSI	—	—	—	—	—	—	—	—	—	—	—	—	—	—	—	16	17	17	—

(Continued)

Table A-2 (Continued)

Age 10

Subtest	BD	SI	DS	PCn	CD	VC	LN	MR	CO	SS	PCm	CA	IN	AR	WR	VCI	PRI	WMI	PSI
BD	—	4	4	4	4	3	4	4	4	4	4	4	4	3	4	—	—	—	—
SI	5	—	3	4	3	3	3	3	4	4	4	4	4	3	4	—	—	—	—
DS	5	4	—	4	3	3	3	3	4	4	3	4	4	3	4	—	—	—	—
PCn	5	5	5	—	4	3	4	4	4	4	4	4	4	3	4	—	—	—	—
CD	5	4	4	5	—	3	3	3	4	4	3	4	4	3	4	—	—	—	—
VC	4	4	4	4	4	—	3	3	4	4	3	3	4	3	4	—	—	—	—
LN	5	4	4	5	4	4	—	3	4	4	3	4	4	3	4	—	—	—	—
MR	5	4	4	5	4	4	4	—	4	4	3	4	4	3	4	—	—	—	—
CO	5	5	5	5	5	5	5	5	—	4	4	4	4	4	4	—	—	—	—
SS	5	5	5	5	5	5	5	5	5	—	4	4	4	4	4	—	—	—	—
PCm	5	5	4	5	4	4	4	4	5	5	—	4	4	3	4	—	—	—	—
CA	5	5	5	5	5	4	5	5	5	5	5	—	4	3	4	—	—	—	—
IN	5	5	5	5	5	5	5	5	5	5	5	5	—	3	4	—	—	—	—
AR	4	4	4	4	4	4	4	4	5	5	4	4	4	—	4	—	—	—	—
WR	5	5	5	5	5	5	5	5	5	5	5	5	5	5	—	—	—	—	—
VCI	—	—	—	—	—	—	—	—	—	—	—	—	—	—	—	—	11	12	12
PRI	—	—	—	—	—	—	—	—	—	—	—	—	—	—	—	14	—	12	13
WMI	—	—	—	—	—	—	—	—	—	—	—	—	—	—	—	15	15	—	13
PSI	—	—	—	—	—	—	—	—	—	—	—	—	—	—	—	16	16	17	—

Age 11

Subtest	BD	SI	DS	PCn	CD	VC	LN	MR	CO	SS	PCm	CA	IN	AR	WR	VCI	PRI	WMI	PSI
BD	—	4	4	4	3	3	3	3	4	4	3	4	4	4	4	—	—	—	—
SI	5	—	4	4	4	4	3	4	4	4	4	4	4	4	4	—	—	—	—
DS	5	5	—	4	3	4	3	3	4	4	4	4	4	4	4	—	—	—	—
PCn	5	5	5	—	4	4	3	4	4	4	4	4	4	4	4	—	—	—	—
CD	4	5	4	5	—	3	3	3	4	4	3	4	4	4	4	—	—	—	—
VC	4	5	5	5	4	—	3	3	4	4	3	4	4	4	4	—	—	—	—
LN	4	4	4	4	4	4	—	3	4	4	3	3	3	3	4	—	—	—	—
MR	4	5	4	5	4	4	4	—	4	4	3	4	4	4	4	—	—	—	—
CO	5	5	5	5	5	5	5	5	—	4	4	4	4	4	4	—	—	—	—
SS	5	5	5	5	5	5	5	5	5	—	4	4	4	4	4	—	—	—	—
PCm	4	5	5	5	4	4	4	4	5	5	—	4	4	4	4	—	—	—	—
CA	5	5	5	5	5	5	4	5	5	5	5	—	4	4	4	—	—	—	—
IN	5	5	5	5	5	5	4	5	5	5	5	5	—	4	4	—	—	—	—
AR	5	5	5	5	5	5	4	5	5	5	5	5	5	—	4	—	—	—	—
WR	5	5	5	5	5	5	5	5	5	6	5	5	5	5	—	—	—	—	—
VCI	—	—	—	—	—	—	—	—	—	—	—	—	—	—	—	—	12	12	13
PRI	—	—	—	—	—	—	—	—	—	—	—	—	—	—	—	15	—	12	13
WMI	—	—	—	—	—	—	—	—	—	—	—	—	—	—	—	15	15	—	13
PSI	—	—	—	—	—	—	—	—	—	—	—	—	—	—	—	16	16	17	—

(Continued)

Table A-2 (Continued)

Age 12

Subtest	BD	SI	DS	PCn	CD	VC	LN	MR	CO	SS	PCm	CA	IN	AR	WR	VCI	PRI	WMI	PSI
BD	—	3	3	4	3	3	3	3	4	4	4	4	3	3	4	—	—	—	—
SI	4	—	3	4	3	3	3	3	4	4	4	4	3	4	4	—	—	—	—
DS	4	4	—	4	3	3	3	3	3	4	4	4	3	3	4	—	—	—	—
PCn	5	5	5	—	4	4	4	4	4	4	4	4	4	4	4	—	—	—	—
CD	4	4	4	5	—	3	3	3	4	4	4	4	3	4	4	—	—	—	—
VC	4	4	4	5	4	—	3	3	3	4	3	4	3	3	4	—	—	—	—
LN	4	4	4	5	4	4	—	3	3	4	3	4	3	3	4	—	—	—	—
MR	4	4	4	5	4	4	4	—	3	4	3	4	3	3	4	—	—	—	—
CO	5	5	4	5	5	4	4	4	—	4	4	4	4	4	4	—	—	—	—
SS	5	5	5	5	5	5	5	5	5	—	4	4	4	4	4	—	—	—	—
PCm	5	5	5	5	5	4	4	4	5	5	—	4	4	4	4	—	—	—	—
CA	5	5	5	6	5	5	5	5	5	6	5	—	4	4	5	—	—	—	—
IN	4	4	4	5	4	4	4	4	5	5	5	5	—	4	4	—	—	—	—
AR	4	5	4	5	5	4	4	4	5	5	5	5	5	—	4	—	—	—	—
WR	5	5	5	6	5	5	5	5	5	6	5	6	5	5	—	—	—	—	—
VCI	—	—	—	—	—	—	—	—	—	—	—	—	—	—	—	—	11	11	12
PRI	—	—	—	—	—	—	—	—	—	—	—	—	—	—	—	14	—	12	13
WMI	—	—	—	—	—	—	—	—	—	—	—	—	—	—	—	14	15	—	13
PSI	—	—	—	—	—	—	—	—	—	—	—	—	—	—	—	16	17	17	—

Age 13

Subtest	BD	SI	DS	PCn	CD	VC	LN	MR	CO	SS	PCm	CA	IN	AR	WR	VCI	PRI	WMI	PSI
BD	—	4	3	4	3	3	4	3	4	4	4	4	3	4	4	—	—	—	—
SI	5	—	4	4	3	4	4	4	4	4	4	4	4	4	4	—	—	—	—
DS	4	5	—	4	3	3	4	3	4	4	4	4	3	4	4	—	—	—	—
PCn	5	5	5	—	4	4	4	4	4	4	4	4	4	4	4	—	—	—	—
CD	4	5	4	5	—	3	4	3	4	4	4	4	3	4	4	—	—	—	—
VC	4	4	4	5	4	—	3	3	4	4	4	4	3	3	4	—	—	—	—
LN	5	5	5	5	5	4	—	3	4	4	4	4	4	4	4	—	—	—	—
MR	4	5	4	5	4	4	4	—	4	4	4	4	3	3	4	—	—	—	—
CO	5	5	5	5	5	5	5	5	—	4	4	4	4	4	4	—	—	—	—
SS	5	5	5	5	5	5	5	5	5	—	4	4	4	4	4	—	—	—	—
PCm	5	5	5	5	5	5	5	5	5	5	—	4	4	4	4	—	—	—	—
CA	5	5	5	6	5	5	5	5	6	6	6	—	4	4	4	—	—	—	—
IN	4	5	4	5	4	4	5	4	5	5	5	5	—	4	4	—	—	—	—
AR	5	5	5	5	5	4	5	4	5	5	5	5	5	—	4	—	—	—	—
WR	5	5	5	5	5	5	5	5	5	5	5	6	5	5	—	—	—	—	—
VCI	—	—	—	—	—	—	—	—	—	—	—	—	—	—	—	—	11	12	13
PRI	—	—	—	—	—	—	—	—	—	—	—	—	—	—	—	14	—	12	13
WMI	—	—	—	—	—	—	—	—	—	—	—	—	—	—	—	15	16	—	14
PSI	—	—	—	—	—	—	—	—	—	—	—	—	—	—	—	16	17	18	—

(Continued)

Table A-2 (Continued)

Age 14

Subtest	BD	SI	DS	PCn	CD	VC	LN	MR	CO	SS	PCm	CA	IN	AR	WR	VCI	PRI	WMI	PSI
BD	—	3	3	4	4	3	3	4	4	4	4	4	4	4	4	—	—	—	—
SI	4	—	3	4	3	3	3	3	3	4	4	4	3	3	4	—	—	—	—
DS	4	4	—	4	3	3	3	3	3	4	4	4	3	3	4	—	—	—	—
PCn	5	5	5	—	4	3	3	4	4	4	4	4	4	4	4	—	—	—	—
CD	5	4	4	5	—	3	3	3	4	4	4	4	3	4	4	—	—	—	—
VC	4	4	4	4	4	—	3	3	3	4	4	4	3	3	3	—	—	—	—
LN	4	4	4	4	4	4	—	3	3	4	4	4	3	3	4	—	—	—	—
MR	5	4	4	5	4	4	4	—	4	4	4	4	3	4	4	—	—	—	—
CO	5	4	4	5	5	4	4	5	—	4	4	4	4	4	4	—	—	—	—
SS	5	5	5	5	5	5	5	5	5	—	4	4	4	4	4	—	—	—	—
PCm	5	5	5	5	5	5	5	5	5	5	—	4	4	4	4	—	—	—	—
CA	5	5	5	5	5	5	5	5	5	6	5	—	4	4	4	—	—	—	—
IN	5	4	4	5	4	4	4	4	5	5	5	5	—	4	4	—	—	—	—
AR	5	4	4	5	5	4	4	5	5	5	5	5	5	—	4	—	—	—	—
WR	5	5	5	5	5	4	5	5	5	5	5	5	5	5	—	—	—	—	—
VCI	—	—	—	—	—	—	—	—	—	—	—	—	—	—	—	—	11	11	12
PRI	—	—	—	—	—	—	—	—	—	—	—	—	—	—	—	14	—	12	13
WMI	—	—	—	—	—	—	—	—	—	—	—	—	—	—	—	14	15	—	13
PSI	—	—	—	—	—	—	—	—	—	—	—	—	—	—	—	16	17	17	—

Age 15

Subtest	BD	SI	DS	PCn	CD	VC	LN	MR	CO	SS	PCm	CA	IN	AR	WR	VCI	PRI	WMI	PSI
BD	—	3	3	4	3	3	3	3	4	4	4	4	3	3	4	—	—	—	—
SI	4	—	3	4	3	3	3	3	4	4	4	4	3	3	4	—	—	—	—
DS	4	4	—	4	3	3	3	3	4	4	4	4	3	3	4	—	—	—	—
PCn	5	5	5	—	4	4	4	4	4	4	4	4	4	4	4	—	—	—	—
CD	4	4	4	5	—	3	3	4	4	4	4	4	3	3	4	—	—	—	—
VC	4	4	4	5	4	—	3	3	3	4	3	4	3	3	3	—	—	—	—
LN	4	4	4	5	4	4	—	4	4	4	4	4	3	3	4	—	—	—	—
MR	4	4	4	5	5	4	5	—	4	4	4	4	3	3	4	—	—	—	—
CO	5	5	5	6	5	4	5	5	—	4	4	4	4	4	4	—	—	—	—
SS	5	5	5	6	5	5	5	5	6	—	4	4	4	4	4	—	—	—	—
PCm	5	5	5	6	5	4	5	5	5	5	—	4	3	3	4	—	—	—	—
CA	5	5	5	6	5	5	5	5	5	6	5	—	4	4	4	—	—	—	—
IN	4	4	4	5	4	3	4	4	5	5	4	5	—	3	3	—	—	—	—
AR	4	4	4	5	4	3	4	4	5	5	4	5	4	—	3	—	—	—	—
WR	5	5	5	5	5	4	5	5	5	5	5	5	4	4	—	—	—	—	—
VCI	—	—	—	—	—	—	—	—	—	—	—	—	—	—	—	—	11	11	12
PRI	—	—	—	—	—	—	—	—	—	—	—	—	—	—	—	14	—	12	13
WMI	—	—	—	—	—	—	—	—	—	—	—	—	—	—	—	14	16	—	13
PSI	—	—	—	—	—	—	—	—	—	—	—	—	—	—	—	15	17	17	—

(Continued)

Table A-2 (Continued)

Age 16

Subtest	BD	SI	DS	PCn	CD	VC	LN	MR	CO	SS	PCm	CA	IN	AR	WR	VCI	PRI	WMI	PSI
BD	—	4	3	4	3	3	3	3	4	4	4	4	3	3	4	—	—	—	—
SI	5	—	3	4	4	3	4	4	4	4	4	4	3	3	4	—	—	—	—
DS	4	4	—	4	3	3	3	3	3	4	3	4	3	3	4	—	—	—	—
PCn	5	5	5	—	4	4	4	4	4	4	4	4	4	4	5	—	—	—	—
CD	4	5	4	5	—	3	3	3	4	4	4	4	3	3	4	—	—	—	—
VC	4	4	4	5	4	—	3	3	3	4	3	4	3	3	4	—	—	—	—
LN	4	5	4	5	4	4	—	3	4	4	4	4	3	3	4	—	—	—	—
MR	4	5	4	5	4	4	4	—	4	4	4	4	3	3	4	—	—	—	—
CO	5	5	4	5	5	4	5	5	—	4	4	4	3	3	4	—	—	—	—
SS	5	5	5	6	5	5	5	5	5	—	4	4	4	4	4	—	—	—	—
PCm	5	5	4	5	5	4	5	5	5	5	—	4	3	3	4	—	—	—	—
CA	5	5	5	6	5	5	5	5	5	6	5	—	4	4	4	—	—	—	—
IN	4	4	4	5	4	4	4	4	4	5	4	5	—	3	4	—	—	—	—
AR	4	4	4	5	4	4	4	4	4	5	4	5	4	—	4	—	—	—	—
WR	5	5	5	6	5	5	5	5	5	6	5	6	5	5	—	—	—	—	—
VCI	—	—	—	—	—	—	—	—	—	—	—	—	—	—	—	—	12	11	12
PRI	—	—	—	—	—	—	—	—	—	—	—	—	—	—	—	15	—	12	14
WMI	—	—	—	—	—	—	—	—	—	—	—	—	—	—	—	14	16	—	13
PSI	—	—	—	—	—	—	—	—	—	—	—	—	—	—	—	16	18	17	—

Total Group

Subtest	BD	SI	DS	PCn	CD	VC	LN	MR	CO	SS	PCm	CA	IN	AR	WR	VCI	PRI	WMI	PSI
BD	—	4	4	4	4	3	3	3	4	4	4	4	4	3	4	—	—	—	—
SI	5	—	4	4	4	3	3	3	4	4	4	4	4	3	4	—	—	—	—
DS	5	5	—	4	4	3	3	3	4	4	4	4	4	3	4	—	—	—	—
PCn	5	5	5	—	4	4	4	4	4	4	4	4	4	4	4	—	—	—	—
CD	5	5	5	5	—	3	3	3	4	4	4	4	4	4	4	—	—	—	—
VC	4	4	4	5	4	—	3	3	4	4	4	4	3	3	4	—	—	—	—
LN	4	4	4	5	4	4	—	3	4	4	3	4	3	3	4	—	—	—	—
MR	4	4	4	5	4	4	4	—	4	4	4	4	3	3	4	—	—	—	—
CO	5	5	5	5	5	5	5	5	—	4	4	4	4	4	4	—	—	—	—
SS	5	5	5	5	5	5	5	5	5	—	4	4	4	4	4	—	—	—	—
PCm	5	5	5	5	5	5	4	5	5	5	—	4	4	4	4	—	—	—	—
CA	5	5	5	5	5	5	5	5	5	6	5	—	4	4	4	—	—	—	—
IN	5	5	5	5	5	4	4	4	5	5	5	5	—	3	4	—	—	—	—
AR	4	4	4	5	5	4	4	4	5	5	5	5	4	—	4	—	—	—	—
WR	5	5	5	5	5	5	5	5	5	5	5	5	5	5	—	—	—	—	—
VCI	—	—	—	—	—	—	—	—	—	—	—	—	—	—	—	—	12	12	13
PRI	—	—	—	—	—	—	—	—	—	—	—	—	—	—	—	15	—	12	14
WMI	—	—	—	—	—	—	—	—	—	—	—	—	—	—	—	15	16	—	14
PSI	—	—	—	—	—	—	—	—	—	—	—	—	—	—	—	17	18	18	—

(Continued)

Table A-2 (Continued)

Note. Abbreviations: BD = Block Design, SI = Similarities, DS = Digit Span, PCn = Picture Concepts, CD = Coding, VC = Vocabulary, LN = Letter–Number Sequencing, MR = Matrix Reasoning, CO = Comprehension, SS = Symbol Search, PCm = Picture Completion, CA = Cancellation, IN = Information, AR = Arithmetic, WR = Word Reasoning, VCI = Verbal Comprehension Index, PRI = Perceptual Reasoning Index, WMI = Working Memory Index, PSI = Processing Speed Index.

The critical values at the .05 level appear *above* the diagonal in the *shaded* area, while the critical values for the .01 level appear *below* the diagonal in the *unshaded* area.

Sample reading: At age 6 (6-0 to 6-11), a difference of 4 points between scaled scores on the Block Design and Similarities subtests is significant at the 5% level and a difference of 5 points is significant at the 1% level. Similarly, a difference of 13 points between the Verbal Comprehension Index and the Perceptual Reasoning Index is significant at the 5% level and a difference of 17 points is significant at the 1% level.

The values in this table for subtest comparisons are overly liberal when more than one comparison is made for a subtest. They are more accurate when a priori planned comparisons are made, such as Similarities vs. Vocabulary or Block Design vs. Matrix Reasoning.

All values in this table have been rounded up to the next higher number.

See Exhibit 4-1 in Chapter 4 for the procedure used to arrive at magnitudes of differences.

Silverstein (personal communication, February 1990) suggests that the following formula be used to obtain a value for the significant difference (at the .05 level) that must exist between the highest and lowest subtest scores on a profile before individual subtest comparisons can be made:

$$D = q\sqrt{\frac{\Sigma \text{SEM}^2}{k}}$$

where

D = significant difference
q = critical value of the Studentized range statistic
SEM = standard error of measurement of a particular subtest
k = number of subtests

For the WISC–IV, the q value is 4.47 at the .05 level for k = 10 (10 subtests) and ∞ degrees of freedom. The sum of the SEM^2 for the 10 subtests is 1.13 + 1.13 + 1.07 + 1.29 + 1.20 + 1.00 + 0.97 + 0.99 + 1.31 + 1.36 = 11.45 and

$$D = 4.47 \times \sqrt{\frac{11.45}{10}} = 4.47 \times \sqrt{1.145} = 4.47 \times 1.07 = 4.78$$

Thus, a difference of 5 points between the highest and lowest subtest scaled scores represents a significant difference at the .05 level.

Table A-3
Estimates of the Probability of Obtaining Designated Differences Between WISC–IV Composite Scores by Chance

Verbal Comprehension and Perceptual Reasoning

Probability of obtaining given or greater discrepancy by chance	Age (in years)											
	6	7	8	9	10	11	12	13	14	15	16	Total
.50	4.30	4.05	3.92	3.65	3.65	3.79	3.51	3.65	3.65	3.65	3.79	3.79
.25	7.32	6.90	6.68	6.22	6.22	6.46	5.97	6.22	6.21	6.21	6.45	6.46
.20	8.16	7.69	7.45	6.93	6.93	7.20	6.66	6.93	6.93	6.93	7.19	7.20
.10	10.47	9.86	9.55	8.89	8.89	9.24	8.55	8.89	8.89	8.89	9.23	9.23
.05	12.47	11.75	11.38	10.60	10.60	11.00	10.18	10.60	10.59	10.59	11.00	11.00
.02	14.81	13.95	13.52	12.58	12.58	13.06	12.09	12.58	12.57	12.57	13.05	13.06
.01	16.39	15.44	14.96	13.92	13.92	14.46	13.38	13.92	13.91	13.91	14.45	14.45
.001	21.00	19.79	19.17	17.84	17.84	18.53	17.14	17.84	17.83	17.83	18.51	18.52

Verbal Comprehension and Working Memory

Probability of obtaining given or greater discrepancy by chance	Age (in years)											
	6	7	8	9	10	11	12	13	14	15	16	Total
.50	4.17	4.29	4.17	3.79	3.79	3.92	3.51	3.92	3.51	3.65	3.51	3.85
.25	7.11	7.31	7.11	6.45	6.45	6.68	5.97	6.68	5.97	6.21	5.97	6.56
.20	7.93	8.15	7.93	7.19	7.19	7.45	6.66	7.44	6.66	6.93	6.66	7.31
.10	10.17	10.46	10.17	9.22	9.22	9.55	8.55	9.55	8.55	8.89	8.55	9.38
.05	12.12	12.46	12.12	10.99	10.99	11.38	10.18	11.38	10.18	10.59	10.18	11.18
.02	14.39	14.80	14.39	13.05	13.05	13.52	12.09	13.51	12.09	12.57	12.09	13.27
.01	15.92	16.38	15.92	14.44	14.44	14.96	13.38	14.95	13.38	13.91	13.38	14.68
.001	20.40	20.99	20.40	18.51	18.51	19.17	17.14	19.16	17.14	17.83	17.14	18.82

Verbal Comprehension and Processing Speed

Probability of obtaining given or greater discrepancy by chance	Age (in years)											
	6	7	8	9	10	11	12	13	14	15	16	Total
.50	5.16	5.26	4.53	4.17	4.05	4.17	4.05	4.17	4.05	3.92	4.05	4.34
.25	8.79	8.96	7.72	7.10	6.89	7.11	6.89	7.10	6.89	6.67	6.89	7.40
.20	9.80	9.99	8.60	7.92	7.69	7.93	7.68	7.92	7.68	7.44	7.68	8.25
.10	12.58	12.82	11.04	10.16	9.86	10.17	9.86	10.16	9.86	9.55	9.86	10.59
.05	14.98	15.28	13.15	12.11	11.75	12.12	11.75	12.11	11.75	11.38	11.75	12.62
.02	17.79	18.14	15.61	14.38	13.95	14.39	13.95	14.38	13.95	13.51	13.95	14.98
.01	19.69	20.07	17.28	15.91	15.44	15.92	15.43	15.91	15.43	14.95	15.43	16.57
.001	25.23	25.72	22.14	20.39	19.78	20.40	19.78	20.39	19.78	19.15	19.78	21.24

(Continued)

Table A-3 (Continued)

Perceptual Reasoning and Working Memory

Probability of obtaining given or greater discrepancy by chance	Age (in years)											
	6	7	8	9	10	11	12	13	14	15	16	Total
.50	4.17	4.29	4.05	3.92	3.92	3.92	3.79	4.05	3.92	4.05	4.05	4.02
.25	7.11	7.31	6.90	6.68	6.68	6.68	6.46	6.90	6.68	6.90	6.90	6.85
.20	7.93	8.15	7.69	7.45	7.45	7.45	7.20	7.69	7.45	7.69	7.69	7.63
.10	10.17	10.46	9.87	9.55	9.55	9.55	9.24	9.87	9.55	9.86	9.87	9.80
.05	12.12	12.46	11.76	11.38	11.38	11.38	11.00	11.76	11.38	11.75	11.76	11.67
.02	14.39	14.80	13.96	13.52	13.52	13.52	13.06	13.96	13.52	13.95	13.96	13.86
.01	15.92	16.38	15.45	14.96	14.96	14.96	14.46	15.45	14.96	15.44	15.45	15.33
.001	20.40	20.99	19.80	19.17	19.17	19.17	18.53	19.80	19.17	19.79	19.80	19.65

Perceptual Reasoning and Processing Speed

Probability of obtaining given or greater discrepancy by chance	Age (in years)											
	6	7	8	9	10	11	12	13	14	15	16	Total
.50	5.16	5.26	4.42	4.29	4.17	4.17	4.29	4.29	4.41	4.29	4.53	4.50
.25	8.79	8.96	7.52	7.32	7.11	7.11	7.32	7.32	7.51	7.31	7.71	7.66
.20	9.80	9.99	8.39	8.15	7.93	7.93	8.15	8.15	8.38	8.15	8.60	8.54
.10	12.58	12.82	10.76	10.46	10.17	10.17	10.46	10.46	10.75	10.46	11.03	10.96
.05	14.98	15.28	12.82	12.47	12.12	12.12	12.47	12.47	12.80	12.46	13.14	13.06
.02	17.79	18.14	15.22	14.80	14.39	14.39	14.80	14.80	15.20	14.80	15.60	15.50
.01	19.69	20.07	16.85	16.38	15.92	15.92	16.38	16.38	16.82	16.38	17.26	17.15
.001	25.23	25.72	21.59	20.99	20.40	20.40	20.99	20.99	21.56	20.99	22.12	21.98

Working Memory and Processing Speed

Probability of obtaining given or greater discrepancy by chance	Age (in years)											
	6	7	8	9	10	11	12	13	14	15	16	Total
.50	5.06	5.45	4.64	4.41	4.29	4.29	4.29	4.53	4.29	4.29	4.29	4.55
.25	8.62	9.29	7.91	7.51	7.31	7.31	7.32	7.71	7.32	7.31	7.32	7.75
.20	9.61	10.35	8.82	8.38	8.15	8.15	8.15	8.60	8.15	8.15	8.15	8.64
.10	12.33	13.29	11.31	10.75	10.46	10.46	10.46	11.03	10.46	10.46	10.46	11.08
.05	14.69	15.83	13.48	12.80	12.46	12.46	12.47	13.14	12.47	12.46	12.47	13.20
.02	17.44	18.80	16.00	15.20	14.80	14.80	14.80	15.60	14.80	14.80	14.80	15.68
.01	19.30	20.80	17.71	16.82	16.38	16.38	16.38	17.26	16.38	16.38	16.38	17.35
.001	24.73	26.65	22.69	21.56	20.99	20.99	20.99	22.12	20.99	20.99	20.99	22.23

Note. To use the table, find the column appropriate to the child's age. Locate the discrepancy that is just *less than* the discrepancy obtained by the child. The entry in the first column in that same row gives the probability of obtaining a given or greater discrepancy by chance. For example, the hypothesis that a 6-year-old child obtained a Verbal-Performance discrepancy of 17 by chance can be rejected at the .01 level of significance. The table is two-tailed.

See Exhibit 4-1 in Chapter 4 for an explanation of the method used to arrive at magnitudes of differences.

The following z values were used for the eight probability levels: $z = .675$ for .50, $z = 1.15$ for .25, $z = 1.282$ for .20, $z = 1.645$ for .10, $z = 1.96$ for .05, $z = 2.327$ for .02, $z = 2.575$ for .01, and $z = 3.30$ for .001.

Table A-4
Differences Required for Significance When Each WISC–IV Subtest Scaled Score Is Compared to the Mean Subtest Scaled Score for Any Individual Child for the 11 Age Groups and the Total Group

Age 6-0-0 through 6-11-30

Subtest	Mean of 2 subtests for WMI		Mean of 2 subtests for PSI		Mean of 3 subtests for VCI		Mean of 3 subtests for PRI	
	.05	.01	.05	.01	.05	.01	.05	.01
Block Design	—	—	—	—	—	—	2.33	2.86
Similarities	—	—	—	—	2.50	3.07	—	—
Digit Span	1.38	1.81	—	—	—	—	—	—
Picture Concepts	—	—	—	—	—	—	2.29	2.81
Coding	—	—	2.06	2.71	—	—	—	—
Vocabulary	—	—	—	—	2.50	3.07	—	—
Letter-Number Sequencing	1.38	1.81	—	—	—	—	—	—
Matrix Reasoning	—	—	—	—	—	—	2.09	2.57
Comprehension	—	—	—	—	2.57	3.15	—	—
Symbol Search	—	—	2.06	2.71	—	—	—	—
Picture Completion	—	—	—	—	—	—	—	—
Cancellation	—	—	—	—	—	—	—	—
Information	—	—	—	—	—	—	—	—
Arithmetic	—	—	—	—	—	—	—	—
Word Reasoning	—	—	—	—	—	—	—	—

Subtest	Mean of 3 subtests for WMI		Mean of 3 subtests for PSI		Mean of 4 subtests for VCI		Mean of 4 subtests for VCI	
	.05	.01	.05	.01	.05	.01	.05	.01
Block Design	—	—	—	—	—	—	—	—
Similarities	—	—	—	—	2.76	3.33	2.78	3.36
Digit Span	2.11	2.58	—	—	—	—	—	—
Picture Concepts	—	—	—	—	—	—	—	—
Coding	—	—	2.93	3.59	—	—	—	—
Vocabulary	—	—	—	—	2.76	3.33	2.78	3.36
Letter-Number Sequencing	1.85	2.27	—	—	—	—	—	—
Matrix Reasoning	—	—	—	—	—	—	—	—
Comprehension	—	—	—	—	2.86	3.45	2.88	3.48
Symbol Search	—	—	2.71	3.32	—	—	—	—
Picture Completion	—	—	—	—	—	—	—	—
Cancellation	—	—	2.59	3.17	—	—	—	—
Information	—	—	—	—	2.71	3.28	—	—
Arithmetic	2.11	2.58	—	—	—	—	—	—
Word Reasoning	—	—	—	—	—	—	2.93	3.53

Subtest	Mean of 4 subtests for PRI		Mean of 5 subtests for VCI		Mean of 10 subtests for FS		Mean of 15 subtests	
	.05	.01	.05	.01	.05	.01	.05	.01
Block Design	2.63	3.18	—	—	3.31	3.88	3.52	4.04
Similarities	—	—	2.95	3.54	3.38	3.97	3.60	4.13
Digit Span	—	—	—	—	3.02	3.55	3.21	3.68
Picture Concepts	2.57	3.11	—	—	3.21	3.77	3.42	3.92
Coding	—	—	—	—	4.15	4.87	4.45	5.10
Vocabulary	—	—	2.95	3.54	3.38	3.97	3.60	4.13
Letter-Number Sequencing	—	—	—	—	2.40	2.82	2.51	2.88
Matrix Reasoning	2.27	2.75	—	—	2.72	3.20	2.87	3.29
Comprehension	—	—	3.07	3.69	3.54	4.16	3.79	4.34
Symbol Search	—	—	—	—	3.62	4.25	3.87	4.43
Picture Completion	2.57	3.11	—	—	—	—	3.42	3.92
Cancellation	—	—	—	—	—	—	3.52	4.04
Information	—	—	2.90	3.48	—	—	3.52	4.04
Arithmetic	—	—	—	—	—	—	3.21	3.68
Word Reasoning	—	—	3.12	3.75	—	—	3.87	4.43

(Continued)

Table A-4 (Continued)

Age 7-0-0 through 7-11-30

Subtest	Mean of 2 subtests for WMI .05	.01	Mean of 2 subtests for PSI .05	.01	Mean of 3 subtests for VCI .05	.01	Mean of 3 subtests for PRI .05	.01
Block Design	—	—	—	—	—	—	2.28	2.79
Similarities	—	—	—	—	2.45	3.00	—	—
Digit Span	1.56	2.05	—	—	—	—	—	—
Picture Concepts	—	—	—	—	—	—	2.24	2.75
Coding	—	—	2.06	2.71	—	—	—	—
Vocabulary	—	—	—	—	2.41	2.96	—	—
Letter-Number Sequencing	1.56	2.05	—	—	—	—	—	—
Matrix Reasoning	—	—	—	—	—	—	2.12	2.60
Comprehension	—	—	—	—	2.78	3.40	—	—
Symbol Search	—	—	2.06	2.71	—	—	—	—
Picture Completion	—	—	—	—	—	—	—	—
Cancellation	—	—	—	—	—	—	—	—
Information	—	—	—	—	—	—	—	—
Arithmetic	—	—	—	—	—	—	—	—
Word Reasoning	—	—	—	—	—	—	—	—

Subtest	Mean of 3 subtests for WMI .05	.01	Mean of 3 subtests for PSI .05	.01	Mean of 4 subtests for VCI .05	.01	Mean of 4 subtests for VCI .05	.01
Block Design	—	—	—	—	—	—	—	—
Similarities	—	—	—	—	2.70	3.26	2.68	3.24
Digit Span	2.33	2.86	—	—	—	—	—	—
Picture Concepts	—	—	—	—	—	—	—	—
Coding	—	—	2.93	3.59	—	—	—	—
Vocabulary	—	—	—	—	2.64	3.19	2.62	3.17
Letter-Number Sequencing	1.93	2.36	—	—	—	—	—	—
Matrix Reasoning	—	—	—	—	—	—	—	—
Comprehension	—	—	—	—	3.18	3.84	3.16	3.82
Symbol Search	—	—	2.71	3.32	—	—	—	—
Picture Completion	—	—	—	—	—	—	—	—
Cancellation	—	—	2.59	3.17	—	—	—	—
Information	—	—	—	—	3.00	3.62	—	—
Arithmetic	1.97	2.42	—	—	—	—	—	—
Word Reasoning	—	—	—	—	—	—	2.83	3.42

Subtest	Mean of 4 subtests for PRI .05	.01	Mean of 5 subtests for VCI .05	.01	Mean of 10 subtests for FS .05	.01	Mean of 15 subtests .05	.01
Block Design	2.56	3.09	—	—	3.22	3.78	3.38	3.87
Similarities	—	—	2.85	3.42	3.22	3.78	3.38	3.87
Digit Span	—	—	—	—	3.48	4.08	3.67	4.21
Picture Concepts	2.50	3.02	—	—	3.12	3.67	3.27	3.75
Coding	—	—	—	—	4.15	4.87	4.42	5.07
Vocabulary	—	—	2.78	3.34	3.12	3.67	3.27	3.75
Letter-Number Sequencing	—	—	—	—	2.52	2.96	2.58	2.96
Matrix Reasoning	2.33	2.81	—	—	2.84	3.34	2.95	3.38
Comprehension	—	—	3.42	4.11	3.93	4.61	4.26	4.88
Symbol Search	—	—	—	—	3.62	4.25	3.83	4.39
Picture Completion	2.50	3.02	—	—	—	—	3.27	3.75
Cancellation	—	—	—	—	—	—	3.48	3.99
Information	—	—	3.21	3.85	—	—	3.94	4.51
Arithmetic	—	—	—	—	—	—	2.72	3.11
Word Reasoning	—	—	3.03	3.65	—	—	3.67	4.21

(Continued)

Table A-4 (*Continued*)

Age 8-0-0 through 8-11-30

Subtest	Mean of 2 subtests for WMI		Mean of 2 subtests for PSI		Mean of 3 subtests for VCI		Mean of 3 subtests for PRI	
	.05	.01	.05	.01	.05	.01	.05	.01
Block Design	—	—	—	—	—	—	2.18	2.67
Similarities	—	—	—	—	2.29	2.81	—	—
Digit Span	1.50	1.97	—	—	—	—	—	—
Picture Concepts	—	—	—	—	—	—	2.37	2.90
Coding	—	—	1.74	2.29	—	—	—	—
Vocabulary	—	—	—	—	2.29	2.81	—	—
Letter-Number Sequencing	1.50	1.97	—	—	—	—	—	—
Matrix Reasoning	—	—	—	—	—	—	1.93	2.36
Comprehension	—	—	—	—	2.58	3.16	—	—
Symbol Search	—	—	1.74	2.29	—	—	—	—
Picture Completion	—	—	—	—	—	—	—	—
Cancellation	—	—	—	—	—	—	—	—
Information	—	—	—	—	—	—	—	—
Arithmetic	—	—	—	—	—	—	—	—
Word Reasoning	—	—	—	—	—	—	—	—

Subtest	Mean of 3 subtests for WMI		Mean of 3 subtests for PSI		Mean of 4 subtests for VCI		Mean of 4 subtests for VCI	
	.05	.01	.05	.01	.05	.01	.05	.01
Block Design	—	—	—	—	—	—	—	—
Similarities	—	—	—	—	2.51	3.03	2.51	3.03
Digit Span	2.25	2.76	—	—	—	—	—	—
Picture Concepts	—	—	—	—	—	—	—	—
Coding	—	—	2.54	3.12	—	—	—	—
Vocabulary	—	—	—	—	2.51	3.03	2.51	3.03
Letter-Number Sequencing	2.01	2.47	—	—	—	—	—	—
Matrix Reasoning	—	—	—	—	—	—	—	—
Comprehension	—	—	—	—	2.93	3.54	2.93	3.54
Symbol Search	—	—	2.57	3.15	—	—	—	—
Picture Completion	—	—	—	—	—	—	—	—
Cancellation	—	—	2.86	3.51	—	—	—	—
Information	—	—	—	—	2.68	3.23	—	—
Arithmetic	2.21	2.71	—	—	—	—	—	—
Word Reasoning	—	—	—	—	—	—	2.68	3.23

Subtest	Mean of 4 subtests for PRI		Mean of 5 subtests for VCI		Mean of 10 subtests for FS		Mean of 15 subtests	
	.05	.01	.05	.01	.05	.01	.05	.01
Block Design	2.43	2.94	—	—	3.00	3.52	3.20	3.67
Similarities	—	—	2.65	3.18	3.00	3.52	3.20	3.67
Digit Span	—	—	—	—	3.19	3.75	3.41	3.91
Picture Concepts	2.71	3.28	—	—	3.45	4.05	3.70	4.24
Coding	—	—	—	—	3.29	3.86	3.52	4.03
Vocabulary	—	—	2.65	3.18	3.00	3.52	3.20	3.67
Letter-Number Sequencing	—	—	—	—	2.60	3.06	2.76	3.16
Matrix Reasoning	2.06	2.49	—	—	2.38	2.79	2.50	2.87
Comprehension	—	—	3.16	3.79	3.69	4.34	3.97	4.55
Symbol Search	—	—	—	—	3.36	3.94	3.60	4.12
Picture Completion	2.55	3.08	—	—	—	—	3.41	3.91
Cancellation	—	—	—	—	—	—	4.37	5.01
Information	—	—	2.86	3.43	—	—	3.52	4.03
Arithmetic	—	—	—	—	—	—	3.31	3.79
Word Reasoning	—	—	2.86	3.43	—	—	3.52	4.03

(*Continued*)

Table A-4 (*Continued*)

Age 9-0-0 through 9-11-30

Subtest	Mean of 2 subtests for WMI		Mean of 2 subtests for PSI		Mean of 3 subtests for VCI		Mean of 3 subtests for PRI	
	.05	.01	.05	.01	.05	.01	.05	.01
Block Design	—	—	—	—	—	—	2.26	2.77
Similarities	—	—	—	—	2.11	2.59	—	—
Digit Span	1.35	1.77	—	—	—	—	—	—
Picture Concepts	—	—	—	—	—	—	2.30	2.82
Coding	—	—	1.74	2.29	—	—	—	—
Vocabulary	—	—	—	—	2.06	2.53	—	—
Letter-Number Sequencing	1.35	1.77	—	—	—	—	—	—
Matrix Reasoning	—	—	—	—	—	—	1.93	2.37
Comprehension	—	—	—	—	2.38	2.92	—	—
Symbol Search	—	—	1.74	2.29	—	—	—	—
Picture Completion	—	—	—	—	—	—	—	—
Cancellation	—	—	—	—	—	—	—	—
Information	—	—	—	—	—	—	—	—
Arithmetic	—	—	—	—	—	—	—	—
Word Reasoning	—	—	—	—	—	—	—	—

Subtest	Mean of 3 subtests for WMI		Mean of 3 subtests for PSI		Mean of 4 subtests for VCI		Mean of 4 subtests for VCI	
	.05	.01	.05	.01	.05	.01	.05	.01
Block Design	—	—	—	—	—	—	—	—
Similarities	—	—	—	—	2.33	2.81	2.36	2.85
Digit Span	2.00	2.45	—	—	—	—	—	—
Picture Concepts	—	—	—	—	—	—	—	—
Coding	—	—	2.54	3.12	—	—	—	—
Vocabulary	—	—	—	—	2.26	2.73	2.29	2.77
Letter-Number Sequencing	1.77	2.17	—	—	—	—	—	—
Matrix Reasoning	—	—	—	—	—	—	—	—
Comprehension	—	—	—	—	2.72	3.29	2.75	3.32
Symbol Search	—	—	2.57	3.15	—	—	—	—
Picture Completion	—	—	—	—	—	—	—	—
Cancellation	—	—	2.86	3.51	—	—	—	—
Information	—	—	—	—	2.56	3.09	—	—
Arithmetic	1.87	2.29	—	—	—	—	—	—
Word Reasoning	—	—	—	—	—	—	2.79	3.37

Subtest	Mean of 4 subtests for PRI		Mean of 5 subtests for VCI		Mean of 10 subtests for FS		Mean of 15 subtests	
	.05	.01	.05	.01	.05	.01	.05	.01
Block Design	2.57	3.11	—	—	3.18	3.73	3.40	3.90
Similarities	—	—	2.49	2.99	2.80	3.28	2.98	3.42
Digit Span	—	—	—	—	2.89	3.39	3.09	3.54
Picture Concepts	2.63	3.18	—	—	3.27	3.84	3.51	4.02
Coding	—	—	—	—	3.27	3.84	3.51	4.02
Vocabulary	—	—	2.40	2.89	2.68	3.15	2.85	3.27
Letter-Number Sequencing	—	—	—	—	2.36	2.77	2.49	2.86
Matrix Reasoning	2.09	2.53	—	—	2.36	2.77	2.49	2.86
Comprehension	—	—	2.95	3.55	3.37	3.96	3.70	4.24
Symbol Search	—	—	—	—	3.34	3.93	3.59	4.11
Picture Completion	2.73	3.30	—	—	—	—	3.70	4.24
Cancellation	—	—	—	—	—	—	4.36	5.00
Information	—	—	2.76	3.32	—	—	3.40	3.90
Arithmetic	—	—	—	—	—	—	2.75	3.15
Word Reasoning	—	—	3.01	3.61	—	—	3.77	4.33

(*Continued*)

Table A-4 (Continued)

Age 10-0-0 through 10-11-30

Subtest	Mean of 2 subtests for WMI		Mean of 2 subtests for PSI		Mean of 3 subtests for VCI		Mean of 3 subtests for PRI	
	.05	.01	.05	.01	.05	.01	.05	.01
Block Design	—	—	—	—	—	—	2.28	2.79
Similarities	—	—	—	—	2.21	2.71	—	—
Digit Span	1.37	1.81	—	—	—	—	—	—
Picture Concepts	—	—	—	—	—	—	2.28	2.79
Coding	—	—	1.63	2.15	—	—	—	—
Vocabulary	—	—	—	—	2.06	2.52	—	—
Letter-Number Sequencing	1.37	1.81	—	—	—	—	—	—
Matrix Reasoning	—	—	—	—	—	—	2.08	2.55
Comprehension	—	—	—	—	2.43	2.98	—	—
Symbol Search	—	—	1.63	2.15	—	—	—	—
Picture Completion	—	—	—	—	—	—	—	—
Cancellation	—	—	—	—	—	—	—	—
Information	—	—	—	—	—	—	—	—
Arithmetic	—	—	—	—	—	—	—	—
Word Reasoning	—	—	—	—	—	—	—	—

Subtest	Mean of 3 subtests for WMI		Mean of 3 subtests for PSI		Mean of 4 subtests for VCI		Mean of 4 subtests for VCI	
	.05	.01	.05	.01	.05	.01	.05	.01
Block Design	—	—	—	—	—	—	—	—
Similarities	—	—	—	—	2.46	2.97	2.49	3.01
Digit Span	1.90	2.33	—	—	—	—	—	—
Picture Concepts	—	—	—	—	—	—	—	—
Coding	—	—	2.13	2.61	—	—	—	—
Vocabulary	—	—	—	—	2.23	2.69	2.26	2.73
Letter-Number Sequencing	1.90	2.33	—	—	—	—	—	—
Matrix Reasoning	—	—	—	—	—	—	—	—
Comprehension	—	—	—	—	2.78	3.36	2.81	3.39
Symbol Search	—	—	2.47	3.03	—	—	—	—
Picture Completion	—	—	—	—	—	—	—	—
Cancellation	—	—	2.33	2.85	—	—	—	—
Information	—	—	—	—	2.64	3.18	—	—
Arithmetic	1.82	2.23	—	—	—	—	—	—
Word Reasoning	—	—	—	—	—	—	2.85	3.45

Subtest	Mean of 4 subtests for PRI		Mean of 5 subtests for VCI		Mean of 10 subtests for FS		Mean of 15 subtests	
	.05	.01	.05	.01	.05	.01	.05	.01
Block Design	2.56	3.09	—	—	3.18	3.73	3.40	3.89
Similarities	—	—	2.64	3.17	2.99	3.51	3.19	3.65
Digit Span	—	—	—	—	2.68	3.15	2.84	3.26
Picture Concepts	2.56	3.09	—	—	3.18	3.73	3.40	3.89
Coding	—	—	—	—	2.68	3.15	2.84	3.26
Vocabulary	—	—	2.36	2.83	2.59	3.04	2.74	3.14
Letter-Number Sequencing	—	—	—	—	2.68	3.15	2.84	3.26
Matrix Reasoning	2.26	2.73	—	—	2.68	3.15	2.84	3.26
Comprehension	—	—	3.02	3.63	3.51	4.12	3.77	4.32
Symbol Search	—	—	—	—	3.51	4.12	3.77	4.32
Picture Completion	2.50	3.02	—	—	—	—	3.29	3.77
Cancellation	—	—	—	—	—	—	3.40	3.89
Information	—	—	2.85	3.42	—	—	3.50	4.02
Arithmetic	—	—	—	—	—	—	2.61	2.99
Word Reasoning	—	—	3.08	3.70	—	—	3.85	4.41

(Continued)

Table A-4 (*Continued*)

Age 11-0-0 through 11-11-30

Subtest	Mean of 2 subtests for WMI		Mean of 2 subtests for PSI		Mean of 3 subtests for VCI		Mean of 3 subtests for PRI	
	.05	.01	.05	.01	.05	.01	.05	.01
Block Design	—	—	—	—	—	—	2.14	2.62
Similarities	—	—	—	—	2.39	2.94	—	—
Digit Span	1.41	1.85	—	—	—	—	—	—
Picture Concepts	—	—	—	—	—	—	2.29	2.81
Coding	—	—	1.63	2.15	—	—	—	—
Vocabulary	—	—	—	—	2.24	2.75	—	—
Letter-Number Sequencing	1.41	1.85	—	—	—	—	—	—
Matrix Reasoning	—	—	—	—	—	—	2.05	2.51
Comprehension	—	—	—	—	2.46	3.02	—	—
Symbol Search	—	—	1.63	2.15	—	—	—	—
Picture Completion	—	—	—	—	—	—	—	—
Cancellation	—	—	—	—	—	—	—	—
Information	—	—	—	—	—	—	—	—
Arithmetic	—	—	—	—	—	—	—	—
Word Reasoning	—	—	—	—	—	—	—	—

Subtest	Mean of 3 subtests for WMI		Mean of 3 subtests for PSI		Mean of 4 subtests for VCI		Mean of 4 subtests for VCI	
	.05	.01	.05	.01	.05	.01	.05	.01
Block Design	—	—	—	—	—	—	—	—
Similarities	—	—	—	—	2.66	3.22	2.70	3.27
Digit Span	2.15	2.63	—	—	—	—	—	—
Picture Concepts	—	—	—	—	—	—	—	—
Coding	—	—	2.13	2.61	—	—	—	—
Vocabulary	—	—	—	—	2.44	2.94	2.48	3.00
Letter-Number Sequencing	1.94	2.38	—	—	—	—	—	—
Matrix Reasoning	—	—	—	—	—	—	—	—
Comprehension	—	—	—	—	2.77	3.34	2.80	3.39
Symbol Search	—	—	2.47	3.03	—	—	—	—
Picture Completion	—	—	—	—	—	—	—	—
Cancellation	—	—	3.03	2.85	—	—	—	—
Information	—	—	—	—	2.61	3.15	—	—
Arithmetic	2.23	2.73	—	—	—	—	—	—
Word Reasoning	—	—	—	—	—	—	2.95	3.57

Subtest	Mean of 4 subtests for PRI		Mean of 5 subtests for VCI		Mean of 10 subtests for FS		Mean of 15 subtests	
	.05	.01	.05	.01	.05	.01	.05	.01
Block Design	2.35	2.84	—	—	2.90	3.40	3.09	3.54
Similarities	—	—	2.87	3.45	3.28	3.85	3.51	4.02
Digit Span	—	—	—	—	2.99	3.51	3.19	3.66
Picture Concepts	2.59	3.13	—	—	3.28	3.85	3.51	4.02
Coding	—	—	—	—	2.69	3.15	2.85	3.27
Vocabulary	—	—	2.60	3.12	2.90	3.40	3.09	3.54
Letter-Number Sequencing	—	—	—	—	2.48	2.91	2.62	3.00
Matrix Reasoning	2.23	2.69	—	—	2.69	3.15	2.85	3.27
Comprehension	—	—	2.99	3.59	3.44	4.04	3.69	4.23
Symbol Search	—	—	—	—	3.52	4.13	3.77	4.32
Picture Completion	2.35	2.84	—	—	—	—	3.09	3.54
Cancellation	—	—	—	—	—	—	3.40	3.90
Information	—	—	2.80	3.36	—	—	3.40	3.90
Arithmetic	—	—	—	—	—	—	3.40	3.90
Word Reasoning	—	—	3.17	3.81	—	—	3.96	4.54

(Continued)

Table A-4 (Continued)

Age 12-0-0 through 12-11-30

Subtest	Mean of 2 subtests for WMI		Mean of 2 subtests for PSI		Mean of 3 subtests for VCI		Mean of 3 subtests for PRI	
	.05	.01	.05	.01	.05	.01	.05	.01
Block Design	—	—	—	—	—	—	2.08	2.56
Similarities	—	—	—	—	2.08	2.55	—	—
Digit Span	1.34	1.77	—	—	—	—	—	—
Picture Concepts	—	—	—	—	—	—	2.39	2.93
Coding	—	—	1.71	2.25	—	—	—	—
Vocabulary	—	—	—	—	1.91	2.34	—	—
Letter-Number Sequencing	1.63	2.15	—	—	—	—	—	—
Matrix Reasoning	—	—	—	—	—	—	1.91	2.35
Comprehension	—	—	—	—	2.16	2.65	—	—
Symbol Search	—	—	1.71	2.25	—	—	—	—
Picture Completion	—	—	—	—	—	—	—	—
Cancellation	—	—	—	—	—	—	—	—
Information	—	—	—	—	—	—	—	—
Arithmetic	—	—	—	—	—	—	—	—
Word Reasoning	—	—	—	—	—	—	—	—

Subtest	Mean of 3 subtests for WMI		Mean of 3 subtests for PSI		Mean of 4 subtests for VCI		Mean of 4 subtests for VCI	
	.05	.01	.05	.01	.05	.01	.05	.01
Block Design	—	—	—	—	—	—	—	—
Similarities	—	—	—	—	2.32	2.81	2.40	2.90
Digit Span	1.96	2.41	—	—	—	—	—	—
Picture Concepts	—	—	—	—	—	—	—	—
Coding	—	—	2.36	2.90	—	—	—	—
Vocabulary	—	—	—	—	2.07	2.50	2.15	2.60
Letter-Number Sequencing	1.93	2.36	—	—	—	—	—	—
Matrix Reasoning	—	—	—	—	—	—	—	—
Comprehension	—	—	—	—	2.44	2.95	2.51	3.04
Symbol Search	—	—	2.63	3.23	—	—	—	—
Picture Completion	—	—	—	—	—	—	—	—
Cancellation	—	—	2.76	3.39	—	—	—	—
Information	—	—	—	—	2.32	2.81	—	—
Arithmetic	2.09	2.57	—	—	—	—	—	—
Word Reasoning	—	—	—	—	—	—	2.93	3.54

Subtest	Mean of 4 subtests for PRI		Mean of 5 subtests for VCI		Mean of 10 subtests for FS		Mean of 15 subtests	
	.05	.01	.05	.01	.01	.01	.05	.01
Block Design	2.31	2.79	—	—	2.90	3.40	2.93	3.36
Similarities	—	—	2.53	3.04	3.28	3.85	3.04	3.49
Digit Span	—	—	—	—	2.99	3.51	2.80	3.21
Picture Concepts	2.75	3.33	—	—	3.28	3.85	3.74	4.28
Coding	—	—	—	—	2.69	3.15	3.04	3.49
Vocabulary	—	—	2.23	2.68	2.90	3.40	2.56	2.94
Letter-Number Sequencing	—	—	—	—	2.48	2.91	2.70	3.09
Matrix Reasoning	2.06	2.48	—	—	2.69	3.15	2.43	2.79
Comprehension	—	—	2.67	3.21	3.44	4.04	3.25	3.73
Symbol Search	—	—	—	—	3.52	4.13	3.82	4.38
Picture Completion	2.54	3.07	—	—	—	—	3.36	3.85
Cancellation	—	—	—	—	—	—	4.17	4.78
Information	—	—	2.53	3.04	—	—	3.04	3.49
Arithmetic	—	—	—	—	—	—	3.15	3.61
Word Reasoning	—	—	3.17	3.81	—	—	4.01	4.59

(Continued)

Table A-4 (*Continued*)

Age 13-0-0 through 13-11-30

Subtest	Mean of 2 subtests for WMI		Mean of 2 subtests for PSI		Mean of 3 subtests for VCI		Mean of 3 subtests for PRI	
	.05	.01	.05	.01	.05	.01	.05	.01
Block Design	—	—	—	—	—	—	2.12	2.60
Similarities	—	—	—	—	2.31	2.83	—	—
Digit Span	1.55	2.04	—	—	—	—	—	—
Picture Concepts	—	—	—	—	—	—	2.42	2.97
Coding	—	—	1.71	2.25	—	—	—	—
Vocabulary	—	—	—	—	2.07	2.54	—	—
Letter-Number Sequencing	1.55	2.04	—	—	—	—	—	—
Matrix Reasoning	—	—	—	—	—	—	2.08	2.55
Comprehension	—	—	—	—	2.42	2.96	—	—
Symbol Search	—	—	1.71	2.25	—	—	—	—
Picture Completion	—	—	—	—	—	—	—	—
Cancellation	—	—	—	—	—	—	—	—
Information	—	—	—	—	—	—	—	—
Arithmetic	—	—	—	—	—	—	—	—
Word Reasoning	—	—	—	—	—	—	—	—

Subtest	Mean of 3 subtests for WMI		Mean of 3 subtests for PSI		Mean of 4 subtests for VCI		Mean of 4 subtests for VCI	
	.05	.01	.05	.01	.05	.01	.05	.01
Block Design	—	—	—	—	—	—	—	—
Similarities	—	—	—	—	2.56	3.09	2.61	3.15
Digit Span	2.16	2.65	—	—	—	—	—	—
Picture Concepts	—	—	—	—	—	—	—	—
Coding	—	—	2.36	2.90	—	—	—	—
Vocabulary	—	—	—	—	2.20	2.66	2.26	2.73
Letter-Number Sequencing	2.24	2.74	—	—	—	—	—	—
Matrix Reasoning	—	—	—	—	—	—	—	—
Comprehension	—	—	—	—	2.72	3.29	2.77	3.34
Symbol Search	—	—	2.63	3.23	—	—	—	—
Picture Completion	—	—	—	—	—	—	—	—
Cancellation	—	—	2.76	3.39	—	—	—	—
Information	—	—	—	—	2.38	2.88	—	—
Arithmetic	2.24	2.74	—	—	—	—	—	—
Word Reasoning	—	—	—	—	—	—	2.81	3.39

Subtest	Mean of 4 subtests for PRI		Mean of 5 subtests for VCI		Mean of 10 subtests for FS		Mean of 15 subtests	
	.05	.01	.05	.01	.05	.01	.05	.01
Block Design	2.34	2.83	—	—	2.90	3.40	2.99	3.43
Similarities	—	—	2.76	3.32	3.28	3.85	3.41	3.91
Digit Span	—	—	—	—	2.99	3.51	3.09	3.55
Picture Concepts	2.78	3.36	—	—	3.28	3.85	3.78	4.33
Coding	—	—	—	—	2.69	3.15	3.09	3.55
Vocabulary	—	—	2.34	2.81	2.90	3.40	2.75	3.16
Letter-Number Sequencing	—	—	—	—	2.48	2.91	3.30	3.79
Matrix Reasoning	2.27	2.75	—	—	2.69	3.15	2.86	3.28
Comprehension	—	—	2.95	3.55	3.44	4.04	3.70	4.24
Symbol Search	—	—	—	—	3.52	4.13	3.86	4.42
Picture Completion	2.63	3.18	—	—	—	—	3.51	4.03
Cancellation	—	—	—	—	—	—	4.21	4.82
Information	—	—	2.55	3.07	—	—	3.09	3.55
Arithmetic	—	—	—	—	—	—	3.30	3.79
Word Reasoning	—	—	3.01	3.61	—	—	3.78	4.33

(Continued)

Table A-4 (*Continued*)

Age 14-0-0 through 14-11-30

Subtest	Mean of 2 subtests for WMI		Mean of 2 subtests for PSI		Mean of 3 subtests for VCI		Mean of 3 subtests for PRI	
	.05	.01	.05	.01	.05	.01	.05	.01
Block Design	—	—	—	—	—	—	2.25	2.76
Similarities	—	—	—	—	1.96	2.41	—	—
Digit Span	1.34	1.77	—	—	—	—	—	—
Picture Concepts	—	—	—	—	—	—	2.29	2.81
Coding	—	—	1.74	2.29	—	—	—	—
Vocabulary	—	—	—	—	1.88	2.30	—	—
Letter-Number Sequencing	1.34	1.77	—	—	—	—	—	—
Matrix Reasoning	—	—	—	—	—	—	2.17	2.67
Comprehension	—	—	—	—	2.13	2.62	—	—
Symbol Search	—	—	1.74	2.29	—	—	—	—
Picture Completion	—	—	—	—	—	—	—	—
Cancellation	—	—	—	—	—	—	—	—
Information	—	—	—	—	—	—	—	—
Arithmetic	—	—	—	—	—	—	—	—
Word Reasoning	—	—	—	—	—	—	—	—

Subtest	Mean of 3 subtests for WMI		Mean of 3 subtests for PSI		Mean of 4 subtests for VCI		Mean of 4 subtests for VCI	
	.05	.01	.05	.01	.05	.01	.05	.01
Block Design	—	—	—	—	—	—	—	—
Similarities	—	—	—	—	2.18	2.63	2.21	2.67
Digit Span	1.96	2.41	—	—	—	—	—	—
Picture Concepts	—	—	—	—	—	—	—	—
Coding	—	—	2.33	2.85	—	—	—	—
Vocabulary	—	—	—	—	2.05	2.48	2.09	2.52
Letter-Number Sequencing	1.93	2.36	—	—	—	—	—	—
Matrix Reasoning	—	—	—	—	—	—	—	—
Comprehension	—	—	—	—	2.43	2.93	2.46	2.97
Symbol Search	—	—	2.64	3.24	—	—	—	—
Picture Completion	—	—	—	—	—	—	—	—
Cancellation	—	—	2.60	3.19	—	—	—	—
Information	—	—	—	—	2.31	2.79	—	—
Arithmetic	2.09	2.57	—	—	—	—	—	—
Word Reasoning	—	—	—	—	—	—	2.57	3.11

Subtest	Mean of 4 subtests for PRI		Mean of 5 subtests for VCI		Mean of 10 subtests for FS		Mean of 15 subtests	
	.05	.01	.05	.01	.05	.01	.05	.01
Block Design	2.53	3.05	—	—	2.90	3.40	3.29	3.77
Similarities	—	—	2.34	2.81	3.28	3.85	2.84	3.26
Digit Span	—	—	—	—	2.99	3.51	2.84	3.26
Picture Concepts	2.58	3.12	—	—	3.28	3.85	3.40	3.89
Coding	—	—	—	—	2.69	3.15	3.08	3.53
Vocabulary	—	—	2.19	2.63	2.90	3.40	2.61	2.99
Letter-Number Sequencing	—	—	—	—	2.48	2.91	2.74	3.14
Matrix Reasoning	2.41	2.91	—	—	2.69	3.15	3.08	3.53
Comprehension	—	—	2.63	3.16	3.44	4.04	3.29	3.77
Symbol Search	—	—	—	—	3.52	4.13	3.96	4.53
Picture Completion	2.69	3.24	—	—	—	—	3.58	4.11
Cancellation	—	—	—	—	—	—	3.85	4.41
Information	—	—	2.49	3.00	—	—	3.08	3.53
Arithmetic	—	—	—	—	—	—	3.19	3.65
Word Reasoning	—	—	2.77	3.33	—	—	3.50	4.02

(*Continued*)

Table A-4 (Continued)

Age 15-0-0 through 15-11-30

Subtest	Mean of 2 subtests for WMI		Mean of 2 subtests for PSI		Mean of 3 subtests for VCI		Mean of 3 subtests for PRI	
	.05	.01	.05	.01	.05	.01	.05	.01
Block Design	—	—	—	—	—	—	2.20	2.70
Similarities	—	—	—	—	1.99	2.44	—	—
Digit Span	1.44	1.89	—	—	—	—	—	—
Picture Concepts	—	—	—	—	—	—	2.60	3.18
Coding	—	—	1.74	2.29	—	—	—	—
Vocabulary	—	—	—	—	1.76	2.16	—	—
Letter-Number Sequencing	1.44	1.89	—	—	—	—	—	—
Matrix Reasoning	—	—	—	—	—	—	2.28	2.79
Comprehension	—	—	—	—	2.35	2.88	—	—
Symbol Search	—	—	1.74	2.29	—	—	—	—
Picture Completion	—	—	—	—	—	—	—	—
Cancellation	—	—	—	—	—	—	—	—
Information	—	—	—	—	—	—	—	—
Arithmetic	—	—	—	—	—	—	—	—
Word Reasoning	—	—	—	—	—	—	—	—

Subtest	Mean of 3 subtests for WMI		Mean of 3 subtests for PSI		Mean of 4 subtests for VCI		Mean of 4 subtests for VCI	
	.05	.01	.05	.01	.05	.01	.05	.01
Block Design	—	—	—	—	—	—	—	—
Similarities	—	—	—	—	2.16	2.61	2.22	2.68
Digit Span	1.93	2.37	—	—	—	—	—	—
Picture Concepts	—	—	—	—	—	—	—	—
Coding	—	—	2.33	2.85	—	—	—	—
Vocabulary	—	—	—	—	1.81	2.19	1.88	2.27
Letter-Number Sequencing	2.02	2.48	—	—	—	—	—	—
Matrix Reasoning	—	—	—	—	—	—	—	—
Comprehension	—	—	—	—	2.69	3.25	2.73	3.30
Symbol Search	—	—	2.64	3.24	—	—	—	—
Picture Completion	—	—	—	—	—	—	—	—
Cancellation	—	—	2.60	3.19	—	—	—	—
Information	—	—	—	—	2.03	2.46	—	—
Arithmetic	1.85	2.27	—	—	—	—	—	—
Word Reasoning	—	—	—	—	—	—	2.52	3.05

Subtest	Mean of 4 subtests for PRI		Mean of 5 subtests for VCI		Mean of 10 subtests for FS		Mean of 15 subtests	
	.05	.01	.05	.01	.05	.01	.05	.01
Block Design	2.38	2.88	—	—	2.90	3.40	2.97	3.41
Similarities	—	—	2.32	2.79	3.28	3.85	2.84	3.26
Digit Span	—	—	—	—	2.99	3.51	2.84	3.26
Picture Concepts	2.96	3.58	—	—	3.28	3.85	4.03	4.62
Coding	—	—	—	—	2.69	3.15	3.08	3.53
Vocabulary	—	—	1.90	2.28	2.90	3.40	2.18	2.49
Letter-Number Sequencing	—	—	—	—	2.48	2.91	3.08	3.53
Matrix Reasoning	2.49	3.01	—	—	2.69	3.15	3.18	3.65
Comprehension	—	—	2.94	3.53	3.44	4.04	3.77	4.32
Symbol Search	—	—	—	—	3.52	4.13	3.95	4.53
Picture Completion	2.60	3.15	—	—	—	—	3.40	3.89
Cancellation	—	—	—	—	—	—	3.85	4.41
Information	—	—	2.17	2.61	—	—	2.61	2.99
Arithmetic	—	—	—	—	—	—	2.61	2.99
Word Reasoning	—	—	2.69	3.23	—	—	3.40	3.89

(Continued)

Table A-4 (*Continued*)

Age 16-0-0 through 16-11-30

Subtest	Mean of 2 subtests for WMI		Mean of 2 subtests for PSI		Mean of 3 subtests for VCI		Mean of 3 subtests for PRI	
	.05	.01	.05	.01	.05	.01	.05	.01
Block Design	—	—	—	—	—	—	2.25	2.76
Similarities	—	—	—	—	2.16	2.65	—	—
Digit Span	1.35	1.77	—	—	—	—	—	—
Picture Concepts	—	—	—	—	—	—	2.64	3.24
Coding	—	—	1.74	2.29	—	—	—	—
Vocabulary	—	—	—	—	1.87	2.29	—	—
Letter-Number Sequencing	1.35	1.77	—	—	—	—	—	—
Matrix Reasoning	—	—	—	—	—	—	2.25	2.76
Comprehension	—	—	—	—	2.12	2.60	—	—
Symbol Search	—	—	1.74	2.29	—	—	—	—
Picture Completion	—	—	—	—	—	—	—	—
Cancellation	—	—	—	—	—	—	—	—
Information	—	—	—	—	—	—	—	—
Arithmetic	—	—	—	—	—	—	—	—
Word Reasoning	—	—	—	—	—	—	—	—

Subtest	Mean of 3 subtests for WMI		Mean of 3 subtests for PSI		Mean of 4 subtests for VCI		Mean of 4 subtests for VCI	
	.05	.01	.05	.01	.05	.01	.05	.01
Block Design	—	—	—	—	—	—	—	—
Similarities	—	—	—	—	2.42	2.92	2.51	3.04
Digit Span	1.76	2.15	—	—	—	—	—	—
Picture Concepts	—	—	—	—	—	—	—	—
Coding	—	—	2.33	2.85	—	—	—	—
Vocabulary	—	—	—	—	1.98	2.39	2.09	2.52
Letter-Number Sequencing	1.98	2.43	—	—	—	—	—	—
Matrix Reasoning	—	—	—	—	—	—	—	—
Comprehension	—	—	—	—	2.36	2.85	2.46	2.97
Symbol Search	—	—	2.64	3.24	—	—	—	—
Picture Completion	—	—	—	—	—	—	—	—
Cancellation	—	—	2.60	3.19	—	—	—	—
Information	—	—	—	—	2.11	2.55	—	—
Arithmetic	1.80	2.21	—	—	—	—	—	—
Word Reasoning	—	—	—	—	—	—	2.93	3.54

Subtest	Mean of 4 subtests for PRI		Mean of 5 subtests for VCI		Mean of 10 subtests for FS		Mean of 15 subtests	
	.05	.01	.05	.01	.05	.01	.05	.01
Block Design	2.43	2.93	—	—	2.90	3.40	3.08	3.53
Similarities	—	—	2.66	3.19	3.28	3.85	3.29	3.77
Digit Span	—	—	—	—	2.99	3.51	2.48	2.85
Picture Concepts	3.00	3.62	—	—	3.28	3.85	4.12	4.72
Coding	—	—	—	—	2.69	3.15	3.08	3.53
Vocabulary	—	—	2.14	2.57	2.90	3.40	2.48	2.85
Letter-Number Sequencing	—	—	—	—	2.48	2.91	3.08	3.53
Matrix Reasoning	2.43	2.93	—	—	2.69	3.15	3.19	3.65
Comprehension	—	—	2.59	3.11	3.44	4.04	3.96	4.54
Symbol Search	—	—	—	—	3.52	4.13	3.19	3.65
Picture Completion	2.48	3.00	—	—	—	—	3.19	3.65
Cancellation	—	—	—	—	—	—	3.85	4.41
Information	—	—	2.30	2.76	—	—	2.74	3.14
Arithmetic	—	—	—	—	—	—	2.61	3.00
Word Reasoning	—	—	3.16	3.79	—	—	4.04	4.63

(*Continued*)

Table A-4 (Continued)

Total Group

Subtest	Mean of 2 subtests for WMI		Mean of 2 subtests for PSI		Mean of 3 subtests for VCI		Mean of 3 subtests for PRI	
	.05	.01	.05	.01	.05	.01	.05	.01
Block Design	—	—	—	—	—	—	2.22	2.72
Similarities	—	—	—	—	2.23	2.73	—	—
Digit Span	1.42	1.86	—	—	—	—	—	—
Picture Concepts	—	—	—	—	—	—	2.38	2.92
Coding	—	—	1.78	2.34	—	—	—	—
Vocabulary	—	—	—	—	2.11	2.58	—	—
Letter-Number Sequencing	1.42	1.86	—	—	—	—	—	—
Matrix Reasoning	—	—	—	—	—	—	2.09	2.56
Comprehension	—	—	—	—	2.41	2.95	—	—
Symbol Search	—	—	1.78	2.34	—	—	—	—
Picture Completion	—	—	—	—	—	—	—	—
Cancellation	—	—	—	—	—	—	—	—
Information	—	—	—	—	—	—	—	—
Arithmetic	—	—	—	—	—	—	—	—
Word Reasoning	—	—	—	—	—	—	—	—

Subtest	Mean of 3 subtests for WMI		Mean of 3 subtests for PSI		Mean of 4 subtests for VCI		Mean of 4 subtests for VCI	
	.05	.01	.05	.01	.05	.01	.05	.01
Block Design	—	—	—	—	—	—	—	—
Similarities	—	—	—	—	2.46	2.98	2.50	3.02
Digit Span	2.05	2.51	—	—	—	—	—	—
Picture Concepts	—	—	—	—	—	—	—	—
Coding	—	—	2.46	3.01	—	—	—	—
Vocabulary	—	—	—	—	2.28	2.76	2.32	2.80
Letter-Number Sequencing	1.95	2.39	—	—	—	—	—	—
Matrix Reasoning	—	—	—	—	—	—	—	—
Comprehension	—	—	—	—	2.73	3.30	2.76	3.34
Symbol Search	—	—	2.61	3.20	—	—	—	—
Picture Completion	—	—	—	—	—	—	—	—
Cancellation	—	—	2.63	3.23	—	—	—	—
Information	—	—	—	—	2.51	3.03	—	—
Arithmetic	2.03	2.49	—	—	—	—	—	—
Word Reasoning	—	—	—	—	—	—	2.81	3.39

Subtest	Mean of 4 subtests for PRI		Mean of 5 subtests for VCI		Mean of 10 subtests for FS		Mean of 15 subtests	
	.05	.01	.05	.01	.05	.01	.05	.01
Block Design	2.47	2.98	—	—	2.90	3.40	3.22	3.69
Similarities	—	—	2.65	3.18	3.28	3.85	3.22	3.69
Digit Span	—	—	—	—	2.99	3.51	3.06	3.51
Picture Concepts	2.70	3.26	—	—	3.28	3.85	3.64	4.18
Coding	—	—	—	—	2.69	3.15	3.40	3.60
Vocabulary	—	—	2.43	2.92	2.90	3.40	2.88	3.30
Letter-Number Sequencing	—	—	—	—	2.48	2.91	2.80	3.21
Matrix Reasoning	2.27	2.74	—	—	2.69	3.15	2.85	3.27
Comprehension	—	—	2.96	3.55	3.44	4.04	3.70	4.24
Symbol Search	—	—	—	—	3.52	4.13	3.83	4.39
Picture Completion	2.57	3.10	—	—	—	—	3.40	3.90
Cancellation	—	—	—	—	—	—	3.88	4.45
Information	—	—	2.70	3.24	—	—	3.30	3.78
Arithmetic	—	—	—	—	—	—	3.01	3.45
Word Reasoning	—	—	3.01	3.62	—	—	3.78	4.33

(Continued)

Table A-4 (*Continued*)

Note. Abbreviations: VCI = Verbal Comprehension Index, PRI = Perceptual Reasoning Index, WMI = Working Memory Index, PSI = Processing Speed Index, FS = Full Scale.

The table shows the minimum deviations from a child's average subtest scaled score that are significant at the .05 and .01 levels.

The following formula, obtained from Davis (1959), was used to compute the deviations from average that are significant at the desired significance level:

$$D = CR \times SEM_{((T/m)-Z_I)}$$

where

D = deviation from average
CR = critical ratio desired
$SEM_{((T/m)-Z_I)}$ = standard error of measurement of the difference between an average subtest scaled score and any one of the subtest scaled scores that entered into the average

The standard error of measurement can be obtained from the following formula:

$$SEM_{((T/m)-Z_I)} = \sqrt{\frac{SEM_T^2}{m^2} + \left(\frac{m-2}{m}\right)SEM_{Z_I}^2}$$

where

SEM_T^2 = sum of the squared standard errors of measurement of the m subtests
m = number of subtests included in the average
T/m = average of the subtest scaled scores
$SEM_{Z_I}^2$ = squared standard error of measurement of any one of the subtest scaled scores

The critical ratios used were based on the Bonferroni inequality, which controls the family-wise error rate at .05 (or .01) by setting the error rate per comparison at .05/m (or .01/m). The critical ratios at the .05 level are 2.39 for 3 subtests, 2.50 for 4 subtests, 2.58 for 5 sub-tests, 2.81 for 10 subtests, and 2.94 for 15 subtests. The critical ratios at the .01 level are 2.93 for 3 sub-tests, 3.02 for 4 subtests, 3.10 for 5 subtests, 3.30 for 10 subtests, and 3.37 for 15 subtests. For 6 and 7 subtests, the Bonferroni inequality critical ratios would be 2.64 and 2.69, respectively, at the .05 level and 3.14 and 3.19, respectively, at the .01 level.

The following example illustrates the procedure. We will determine the minimum deviaton required for a 6-year-old child's score on the WISC–IV Similarities subtest to be significantly different from his or her average score on the three standard Verbal Comprehension subtests (Similarities, Vocabulary, and Comprehension) at the 95% level of confidence. We calculate SEM_T^2 by first squaring the appropriate average standard error of measurement for each of the three subtests and then summing the squares. These standard errors of measurement are in Table 4.3 (p. 38) in the Technical Manual.

$$SEM_T^2 = (1.27)^2 + (1.27)^2 + (1.34)^2 = 5.02$$

We determine $SEM_{Z_I}^2$ by squaring the average standard error of measurement of the subtest of interest, the Information subtest:

$$SEM_{Z_I}^2 = (1.27)^2 = 1.6129$$

The number of subtests, m, equals 3. Substituting these values into the formula yields the following:

$$SEM_{((T/m)-Z_I)} = \sqrt{\frac{5.02}{(3)^2} + \left(\frac{3-2}{3}\right)1.6129} = 1.046$$

The value, 1.046, is then multiplied by the appropriate z value for the 95% confidence level to obtain the minimum significant deviation (D). Using the Bonferroni correction (.05/3 = .0167), we have a z value of 2.39.

$$D = 2.39 \times 1.046 = 2.499$$

The Bonferonni correction was not applied to the two-subtest mean comparisons.

Table A-5
Differences Between WISC–IV Process Scaled Scores Required for Statistical Significance at the .05 and .01 Levels of Significance for the 11 Age Groups and the Total Group

Comparison	Level	Age (in years)											Total
		6	7	8	9	10	11	12	13	14	15	16	
BD vs. BDN	.05	4	4	4	4	4	4	3	4	4	3	4	4
	.01	5	5	5	5	5	5	4	5	5	4	5	5
DSF vs. DSB	.05	4	5	5	4	4	4	4	4	4	4	4	4
	.01	5	6	6	5	5	5	5	5	5	5	5	5
CAR vs. CAS	.05	5	5	5	5	5	5	5	5	5	5	5	5
	.01	6	6	6	6	6	6	6	6	6	6	6	6

Note. Abbreviations: BD = Block Design, BDN = Block Design No Time Bonus, DSF = Digit Span Forward, DSB = Digit Span Backward, CAR = Cancellation Random, CAS = Cancellation Structured.

Sample reading: At age 6 (6-0 to 6-11), a difference of 4 points between scaled scores on the Block Design and Block Design No Time Bonus is significant at the 5% level and a difference of 5 points is significant at the 1% level.

All values in this table have been rounded up to the next higher number.

See Exhibit 4-1 in Chapter 4 for the procedure used to arrive at magnitudes of differences.

Table A-6
Estimates of the Differences Obtained by Various Percentages of the WISC–IV Standardization Sample When Each WISC–IV Subtest Scaled Score Is Compared to the Mean Scaled Score for Any Individual Child

| Subtest | Verbal Comprehension | | | | | | | | Perceptual Reasoning | | | |
| | Core subtests | | | | Core subtests plus Information | | | | Core subtests | | | |
	10%	5%	2%	1%	10%	5%	2%	1%	10%	5%	2%	1%
Block Design	—	—	—	—	—	—	—	—	2.90	3.45	4.11	4.53
Similarities	2.28	2.72	3.24	3.57	2.39	2.84	3.39	3.73	—	—	—	—
Digit Span	—	—	—	—	—	—	—	—	—	—	—	—
Picture Concepts	—	—	—	—	—	—	—	—	3.11	3.71	4.42	4.87
Coding	—	—	—	—	—	—	—	—	—	—	—	—
Vocabulary	2.05	2.45	2.92	3.22	2.09	2.49	2.96	3.27	—	—	—	—
Letter-Number Sequencing	—	—	—	—	—	—	—	—	—	—	—	—
Matrix Reasoning	—	—	—	—	—	—	—	—	2.72	3.24	3.87	4.26
Comprehension	2.48	2.96	3.53	3.89	2.72	3.24	3.86	4.26	—	—	—	—
Symbol Search	—	—	—	—	—	—	—	—	—	—	—	—
Picture Completion	—	—	—	—	—	—	—	—	—	—	—	—
Cancellation	—	—	—	—	—	—	—	—	—	—	—	—
Information	—	—	—	—	2.36	2.81	3.35	3.69	—	—	—	—
Arithmetic	—	—	—	—	—	—	—	—	—	—	—	—
Word Reasoning	—	—	—	—	—	—	—	—	—	—	—	—

| Subtest | Verbal Comprehension | | | | | | | | Perceptual Reasoning | | | |
| | Core subtests plus Word Reasoning | | | | Core subtests plus Information and Word Reasoning | | | | Core subtests plus Picture Completion | | | |
	10%	5%	2%	1%	10%	5%	2%	1%	10%	5%	2%	1%
Block Design	—	—	—	—	—	—	—	—	2.93	3.49	4.16	4.59
Similarities	2.46	2.93	3.49	3.84	2.49	2.97	3.54	3.90	—	—	—	—
Digit Span	—	—	—	—	—	—	—	—	—	—	—	—
Picture Concepts	—	—	—	—	—	—	—	—	3.37	4.02	4.79	5.28
Coding	—	—	—	—	—	—	—	—	—	—	—	—
Vocabulary	2.19	2.61	3.12	3.43	2.18	2.60	3.10	3.41	—	—	—	—
Letter-Number Sequencing	—	—	—	—	—	—	—	—	—	—	—	—
Matrix Reasoning	—	—	—	—	—	—	—	—	2.97	3.54	4.22	4.65
Comprehension	2.69	3.21	3.82	4.21	2.82	3.36	4.01	4.42	—	—	—	—
Symbol Search	—	—	—	—	—	—	—	—	—	—	—	—
Picture Completion	—	—	—	—	—	—	—	—	3.15	3.75	4.48	4.93
Cancellation	—	—	—	—	—	—	—	—	—	—	—	—
Information	—	—	—	—	2.47	2.95	3.51	3.87	—	—	—	—
Arithmetic	—	—	—	—	—	—	—	—	—	—	—	—
Word Reasoning	2.74	3.26	3.89	4.28	2.86	3.40	4.06	4.47	—	—	—	—

(Continued)

Table A-6 (Continued)

| | Working Memory | | | | | | | | Full Scale | | | |
| | Core subtests | | | | Core subtests plus Arithmetic | | | | Core subtests | | | |
Subtest	10%	5%	2%	1%	10%	5%	2%	1%	10%	5%	2%	1%
Block Design	—	—	—	—	—	—	—	—	3.52	4.20	5.00	5.51
Similarities	—	—	—	—	—	—	—	—	3.15	3.75	4.47	4.93
Digit Span	2.49	2.97	3.54	3.90	2.93	3.50	4.17	4.59	3.92	4.66	5.56	6.13
Picture Concepts	—	—	—	—	—	—	—	—	3.78	4.50	5.36	5.91
Coding	—	—	—	—	—	—	—	—	4.10	4.88	5.82	6.41
Vocabulary	—	—	—	—	—	—	—	—	3.08	3.67	4.37	4.82
Letter-Number Sequencing	2.49	2.97	3.54	3.90	2.82	3.36	4.01	4.42	3.57	4.25	5.07	5.59
Matrix Reasoning	—	—	—	—	—	—	—	—	3.41	4.06	4.84	5.34
Comprehension	—	—	—	—	—	—	—	—	3.46	4.12	4.91	5.42
Symbol Search	—	—	—	—	—	—	—	—	3.70	4.41	5.26	5.80
Picture Completion	—	—	—	—	—	—	—	—	—	—	—	—
Cancellation	—	—	—	—	—	—	—	—	—	—	—	—
Information	—	—	—	—	—	—	—	—	—	—	—	—
Arithmetic	—	—	—	—	2.88	3.43	4.09	4.50	—	—	—	—
Word Reasoning	—	—	—	—	—	—	—	—	—	—	—	—

| | Processing Speed | | | | | | | | Full Scale | | | |
| | Core subtests | | | | Core subtests plus Cancellation | | | | Core subtests plus Information, Word Reasoning, Picture Completion, Arithmetic, and Cancellation | | | |
Subtest	10%	5%	2%	1%	10%	5%	2%	1%	10%	5%	2%	1%
Block Design	—	—	—	—	—	—	—	—	3.52	4.20	5.01	5.52
Similarities	—	—	—	—	—	—	—	—	3.11	3.70	4.42	4.87
Digit Span	—	—	—	—	—	—	—	—	4.05	4.82	5.75	6.34
Picture Concepts	—	—	—	—	—	—	—	—	3.88	4.63	5.52	6.08
Coding	2.39	2.85	3.40	3.74	2.81	3.35	3.99	4.40	4.15	4.95	5.90	6.50
Vocabulary	—	—	—	—	—	—	—	—	3.00	3.58	4.27	4.70
Letter-Number Sequencing	—	—	—	—	—	—	—	—	3.71	4.42	5.27	5.81
Matrix Reasoning	—	—	—	—	—	—	—	—	3.52	4.19	5.00	5.51
Comprehension	—	—	—	—	—	—	—	—	3.45	4.11	4.90	5.40
Symbol Search	2.39	2.85	3.40	3.74	3.03	3.61	4.31	4.75	3.80	4.53	5.40	5.95
Picture Completion	—	—	—	—	—	—	—	—	3.70	4.41	5.26	5.80
Cancellation	—	—	—	—	3.36	4.01	4.78	5.26	4.93	5.87	7.00	7.72
Information	—	—	—	—	—	—	—	—	3.11	3.70	4.42	4.87
Arithmetic	—	—	—	—	—	—	—	—	3.23	3.85	4.59	5.06
Word Reasoning	—	—	—	—	—	—	—	—	3.45	4.11	4.89	5.39

Note. The formula used to obtain the values in this table was obtained from Silverstein (1984):

$$SD_{Da} = 3\sqrt{1 + \overline{G} - 2\overline{T}_a}$$

where

SD_{Da} = standard deviation of the difference for subtest a
3 = standard deviation of the scaled scores on each of the subtests
$\overline{G}$ = mean of all the elements in the matrix (including 1s in the diagonal)
$\overline{T}_a$ = mean of the elements in row or column a of the matrix (again including 1s in the diagonal)

Table A-7
Reliability and Validity Coefficients of WISC–IV Short Forms for 2-, 3-, 4-, and 5-Subtest Combinations

Short form				r_{ss}	r	Short form					r_{ss}	r
Two subtests						**Three subtests** (*Continued*)						
VC	AR			.928	.879	PCn	MR	PCm[c, e]			.920	.828
BD	VC			.916	.874	BD	PCn	PCm[e]			.915	.823
SI	AR			.917	.874	DS	LN	AR[f]			.941	.819
VC	MR			.926	.873	CD	SS	CA[c, g]			.896	.636
VC	SS			.884	.863	**Four subtests**						
BD	IN			.905	.861							
SI	MR			.916	.860	SI	VC	SS	AR		.943	.933
AR	WR			.926	.860	VC	SS	AR	WR		.945	.932
IN	AR			.920	.858	SI	CD	VC	AR		.946	.931
MR	IN			.917	.857	SI	CD	AR	WR		.944	.931
LN	AR[a]			.927	.818	SI	VC	MR	SS		.942	.931
DS	AR[a]			.915	.779	SI	CD	VC	MR		.945	.930
SS	CA[b, c]			.841	.583	SI	SS	AR	WR		.941	.930
CD	CA[b, c]			.871	.517	VC	MR	SS	IN		.942	.930
Three subtests						VC	MR	SS	AR		.943	.930
						VC	MR	SS	WR		.944	.930
VC	SS	AR		.924	.911	BD	SI	DS	CD[h]		.932	.909
VC	MR	AR		.946	.908	SI	VC	CO	IN[i]		.953	.882
BD	VC	AR		.941	.907	SI	VC	CO	WR[i]		.954	.878
VC	PCm	AR		.935	.906	BD	PCn	MR	PCm[c, j]		.939	.858
BD	VC	LN		.939	.905	DS	CD	LN	SS[k]		.931	.826
SI	SS	AR		.918	.905	**Five subtests**						
SI	VC	SS		.924	.904							
VC	MR	SS		.923	.904	SI	CD	MR	AR	WR	.955	.949
VC	SS	IN		.924	.904	CD	VC	MR	AR	WR	.957	.949
BD	VC	IN		.939	.903	VC	MR	SS	AR	WR	.955	.949
SI	VC	IN		.947	.874	SI	CD	VC	MR	AR	.956	.948
SI	VC	WR[d]		.950	.870	SI	VC	MR	SS	AR	.954	.948
SI	CO	IN[d]		.932	.867	BD	SI	CD	VC	LN	.953	.947
VC	CO	IN[d]		.938	.863	SI	MR	SS	AR	WR	.953	.947
SI	CO	WR[d]		.935	.858	BD	SI	CD	VC	AR	.954	.946
VC	CO	WR[d]		.942	.854	BD	CD	VC	AR	WR	.955	.946
BD	MR	PCm[e]		.933	.831	SI	CD	VC	PCm	AR	.952	.946
						SI	VC	CO	IN	WR[l]	.963	.891

(*Continued*)

Table A-7 (*Continued*)

Note. Abbreviations: BD = Block Design, SI = Similarities, DS = Digit Span, PCn = Picture Concepts, CD = Coding, VC = Vocabulary, LN = Letter–Number Sequencing, MR = Matrix Reasoning, CO = Comprehension, SS = Symbol Search, PCm = Picture Completion, CA = Cancellation, IN = Information, AR = Arithmetic, WR = Word Reasoning.

The estimated Full Scale IQs associated with each short form are shown in Tables A-9 to A-12.

The first 10 combinations represent the best ones, based on validity. See Exhibit 8-4 on pages 256–257 in *Assessment of Children: Cognitive Applications* (Sattler, 2001) for formulas used to obtain reliability and validity coefficients.

[a]This combination represents the subtests in the Working Memory Composite with the substitution of Arithmetic.

[b]This combination represents the subtests in the Processing Speed Composite with the substitution of Cancellation.

[c]This combination is useful for children who are hearing impaired.

[d]This combination represents the subtests in the Verbal Comprehension Composite with the substitution of a supplemental subtest.

[e]This combination represents the subtests in the Perceptual Reasoning Composite with the substitution of a supplemental subtest.

[f]This combination represents all core and supplemental subtests in the Processing Speed Composite.

[g]This combination represents all core and supplemental subtests in the Working Memory Composite.

[h]This combination represents one core subtest from each Composite.

[i]This combination represents three core subtests and one supplemental subtest (all with high *g* loadings) in the Verbal Comprehension Composite.

[j]This combination represents all core and supplemental subtests in the Perceptual Reasoning Composite.

[k]This combination represents all core subtests in both Working Memory and Processing Speed Composites.

[l]This combination represents all core and supplemental subtests in the Verbal Comprehension Composite.

Table A-8
Reliable and Unusual Scaled-Score Ranges for WISC–IV Selected Subtest Combinations

Composite or short form						Reliable scaled-score range	Unusual scaled-score range
Two subtests							
DS	LN					3	5
CD	SS					4	5
VC	AR					3	5
BD	VC					3	6
SI	AR					4	5
VC	MR					3	5
VC	SS					4	6
BD	IN					4	6
SI	MR					3	5
AR	WR					4	6
IN	AR					4	5
MR	IN					3	5
LN	AR					3	5
DS	AR					3	6
SS	CA					4	6
CD	CA					4	6
Three subtests							
SI	VC	CO				4	5
BD	PCn	MR				4	7
DS	LN	AR				4	7
CD	SS	CA				5	7
VC	SS	AR				4	7
VC	MR	AR				4	6
BD	VC	AR				4	6
VC	PCm	AR				4	7
BD	VC	LN				4	7
SI	SS	AR				4	7
SI	VC	SS				4	7
VC	MR	SS				4	7
VC	SS	IN				4	7
BD	VC	IN				4	6
SI	VC	IN				4	5
SI	VC	WR				4	5
SI	CO	IN				4	6
VC	CO	IN				4	5
SI	CO	WR				5	6
VC	CO	WR				5	6
BD	MR	PCm				4	7
PCn	MR	PCm				4	7
BD	PCn	PCm				4	7

Composite or short form						Reliable scaled-score range	Unusual scaled-score range
Four subtests							
SI	VC	CO	IN			5	6
SI	VC	CO	WR			5	6
BD	PCn	MR	PCm			5	8
SI	VC	SS	AR			5	7
VC	SS	AR	WR			5	8
SI	CD	VC	AR			5	8
SI	CD	AR	WR			5	8
SI	VC	MR	SS			5	7
SI	CD	VC	MR			4	8
SI	SS	AR	WR			5	8
VC	MR	SS	IN			5	7
VC	MR	SS	AR			4	7
VC	MR	SS	WR			5	8
BD	SI	DS	CD			5	8
DS	CD	LN	SS			5	8
Five subtests							
SI	VC	CO	IN	WR		6	7
SI	CD	MR	AR	WR		6	8
CD	VC	MR	AR	WR		5	8
VC	MR	SS	AR	WR		6	8
SI	CD	VC	MR	AR		5	8
SI	VC	MR	SS	AR		5	8
BD	SI	CD	VC	LN		5	8
SI	MR	SS	AR	WR		6	8
BD	SI	CD	VC	AR		5	8
BD	CD	VC	AR	WR		6	8
SI	CD	VC	PCm	AR		5	8
Six subtests							
BD	SI	PCn	VC	MR	CO	5	8
10 subtests (core only)							
10 subtests						6	10
15 subtests (core plus supplemental)							
15 subtests						6	12

(Continued)

Table A-8 (*Continued*)

Note. Abbreviations: BD = Block Design, SI = Similarities, DS = Digit Span, PCn = Picture Concepts, CD = Coding, VC = Vocabulary, LN = Letter–Number Sequencing, MR = Matrix Reasoning, CO = Comprehension, SS = Symbol Search, PCm = Picture Completion, CA = Cancellation, IN = Information, AR = Arithmetic, WR = Word Reasoning.

The formula used to obtain the reliable scaled-score range is as follows (Silverstein, 1989):

$$R = q \sqrt{\frac{\sum \text{SEM}_i^2}{k}}$$

where

q = critical value (n/v) of the Studentized range for a specified probability level (.05 in this case)

SEM = standard error of measurement of the scores on subtest i

k = number of subtests in the short form

The formula used to obtain the unusual scaled-score range is as follows (Silverstein, 1989):

$$R = q \cdot \sigma \sqrt{1 - \frac{2 \sum r_{ij}}{k(k-1)}}$$

where

q = critical value (n/v) of the Studentized range for a specified probability level (.10 in this case)

σ = standard deviation of the subtest scores

k = number of subtests in the short form

r_{ij} = correlation between subtests i and j

The following are the appropriate q values to use in the two formulas for ns (size of samples) ranging from 2 to 10 plus 15, with v (degrees of freedom) = ∞, at the .10 probability level and at the .05 probability level (.10 or .05): for 2, 2.33 or 2.77; for 3, 2.90 or 3.31; for 4, 3.24 or 3.63; for 5, 3.48 or 3.86; for 6, 3.66 or 4.03; for 7, 3.81 or 4.17; for 8, 3.93 or 4.29; for 9, 4.04 or 4.39, for 10, 4.13 or 4.47; and for 15, 4.47 or 4.80.

The table is read as follows: In the two-subtest short form composed of Digit Span and Letter–Number Sequencing, a range of 3 points between the two scores indicates a nonchance difference at the .05 level. A range of 5 occurs in less than 10% of the population and should be considered unusual, as should all ranges higher than 5 points. Less credence can be placed in a Composite score or short-form IQ when the scatter is larger than expected.

Table A-9
Estimated WISC–IV Full Scale IQs for Sum of Scaled Scores for 10 Best 2-Subtest Short Forms and Other Combinations

Sum of scaled scores	Combination C2	C3	C4	C5	C6	C7	C8	C9	C10	C11	C12
2	45	46	48	48	48	48	48	49	50	50	54
3	48	49	50	51	51	51	51	52	52	53	56
4	51	52	53	54	54	54	54	55	55	56	59
5	54	55	56	56	57	57	57	58	58	58	61
6	57	58	59	59	59	60	60	60	61	61	64
7	60	61	62	62	62	62	63	63	64	64	66
8	63	64	65	65	65	65	65	66	66	67	69
9	66	67	68	68	68	68	68	69	69	69	72
10	69	70	71	71	71	71	71	72	72	72	74
11	72	73	74	74	74	74	74	75	75	75	77
12	75	76	77	77	77	77	77	77	78	78	79
13	78	79	80	80	80	80	80	80	80	81	82
14	82	82	83	83	83	83	83	83	83	83	85
15	85	85	85	85	86	86	86	86	86	86	87
16	88	88	88	88	88	88	88	89	89	89	90
17	91	91	91	91	91	91	91	92	92	92	92
18	94	94	94	94	94	94	94	94	94	94	95
19	97	97	97	97	97	97	97	97	97	97	97
20	100	100	100	100	100	100	100	100	100	100	100
21	103	103	103	103	103	103	103	103	103	103	103
22	106	106	106	106	106	106	106	106	106	106	105
23	109	109	109	109	109	109	109	108	108	108	108
24	112	112	112	112	112	112	112	111	111	111	110
25	115	115	115	115	114	114	114	114	114	114	113
26	118	118	117	117	117	117	117	117	117	117	115
27	122	121	120	120	120	120	120	120	120	119	118
28	125	124	123	123	123	123	123	123	122	122	121
29	128	127	126	126	126	126	126	125	125	125	123
30	131	130	129	129	129	129	129	128	128	128	126
31	134	133	132	132	132	132	132	131	131	131	128
32	137	136	135	135	135	135	135	134	134	133	131
33	140	139	138	138	138	138	137	137	136	136	134
34	143	142	141	141	141	140	140	140	139	139	136
35	146	145	144	144	143	143	143	142	142	142	139
36	149	148	147	146	146	146	146	145	145	144	141
37	152	151	150	149	149	149	149	148	148	147	144
38	155	154	152	152	152	152	152	151	150	150	146

Note. The subtest combinations are as follows:

C2 = SS + CA[a, b]
C3 = VC + SS
    CD + CA[a, b]
C4 = DS + AR[c]
C5 = BD + IN
    BD + VC
C6 = SI + MR
    VC + MR
C7 = MR + IN
C8 = LN + AR[c]
C9 = SI + AR
C10 = VC + AR
C11 = IN + AR
C12 = AR + WR

Abbreviations: BD = Block Design, SI = Similarities, DS = Digit Span, PCn = Picture Concepts, CD = Coding, VC = Vocabulary, LN = Letter–Number Sequencing, MR = Matrix Reasoning, CO = Comprehension, SS = Symbol Search, PCm = Picture Completion, CA = Cancellation, IN = Information, AR = Arithmetic, WR = Word Reasoning.

Reliability and validity coefficients associated with each short-form combination are shown in Table A-7. See Exhibit 8-4 on pages 256–257 in *Assessment of Children: Cognitive Applications* (Sattler, 2001) for an explanation of the procedure used to obtain the estimated IQs.

[a]This combination represents the subtests in the Processing Speed Composite with the substitution of Cancellation.

[b]This combination is useful for examinees who are hearing impaired.

[c]This combination represents the subtests in the Working Memory Composite with the substitution of Arithmetic.

Table A-10
Estimated WISC–IV Full Scale IQs for Sum of Scaled Scores for 10 Best 3-Subtest Short Forms and Other Combinations

Sum of scaled scores	Combination																
	C2	C3	C4	C5	C6	C7	C8	C9	C10	C11	C12	C13	C14	C15	C16	C17	C18
3	42	43	43	44	44	44	45	45	45	46	47	47	47	48	49	49	50
4	45	45	45	46	46	46	47	47	47	48	49	49	49	50	50	51	52
5	47	48	47	48	48	48	49	49	49	50	51	51	51	52	52	53	54
6	49	50	49	50	50	50	51	51	51	52	53	53	53	54	54	55	56
7	51	52	51	52	52	52	53	53	53	54	55	55	55	56	56	57	58
8	53	54	53	54	54	54	55	55	55	56	57	57	57	58	58	59	60
9	55	56	56	56	56	56	57	57	57	58	58	59	59	60	60	61	61
10	57	58	58	58	58	58	59	59	60	60	60	61	61	62	62	62	63
11	59	60	60	60	60	61	61	61	62	62	62	63	63	64	64	64	65
12	62	62	62	62	62	63	63	63	64	64	64	64	65	65	66	66	67
13	64	64	64	64	65	65	65	65	66	66	66	66	67	67	68	68	69
14	66	66	66	67	67	67	67	67	68	68	68	68	69	69	70	70	71
15	68	69	68	69	69	69	69	69	70	70	70	70	71	71	71	72	72
16	70	71	70	71	71	71	71	71	72	72	72	72	73	73	73	74	74
17	72	73	72	73	73	73	73	74	74	74	74	74	75	75	75	76	76
18	74	75	75	75	75	75	75	76	76	76	76	76	77	77	77	77	78
19	77	77	77	77	77	77	77	78	78	78	78	78	79	79	79	79	80
20	79	79	79	79	79	79	79	80	80	80	80	80	81	81	81	81	82
21	81	81	81	81	81	81	82	82	82	82	82	82	82	83	83	83	83
22	83	83	83	83	83	83	84	84	84	84	84	84	84	85	85	85	85
23	85	85	85	85	85	85	86	86	86	86	86	86	86	87	87	87	87
24	87	87	87	87	88	88	88	88	88	88	88	88	88	88	89	89	89
25	89	90	89	90	90	90	90	90	90	90	90	90	90	90	90	91	91
26	91	92	92	92	92	92	92	92	92	92	92	92	92	92	92	92	93
27	94	94	94	94	94	94	94	94	94	94	94	94	94	94	94	94	94
28	96	96	96	96	96	96	96	96	96	96	96	96	96	96	96	96	96
29	98	98	98	98	98	98	98	98	98	98	98	98	98	98	98	98	98
30	100	100	100	100	100	100	100	100	100	100	100	100	100	100	100	100	100
31	102	102	102	102	102	102	102	102	102	102	102	102	102	102	102	102	102
32	104	104	104	104	104	104	104	104	104	104	104	104	104	104	104	104	104
33	106	106	106	106	106	106	106	106	106	106	106	106	106	106	106	106	106
34	109	108	108	108	108	108	108	108	108	108	108	108	108	108	108	108	107
35	111	110	111	110	110	110	110	110	110	110	110	110	110	110	110	109	109
36	113	113	113	113	113	112	112	112	112	112	112	112	112	112	111	111	111
37	115	115	115	115	115	115	114	114	114	114	114	114	114	113	113	113	113
38	117	117	117	117	117	117	116	116	116	116	116	116	116	115	115	115	115
39	119	119	119	119	119	119	118	118	118	118	118	118	118	117	117	117	117
40	121	121	121	121	121	121	121	120	120	120	120	120	119	119	119	119	118
41	123	123	123	123	123	123	123	122	122	122	122	122	121	121	121	121	120
42	126	125	125	125	125	125	125	124	124	124	124	124	123	123	123	123	122
43	128	127	128	127	127	127	127	126	126	126	126	126	125	125	125	124	124
44	130	129	130	129	129	129	129	129	128	128	128	128	127	127	127	126	126
45	132	131	132	131	131	131	131	131	130	130	130	130	129	129	129	128	128
46	134	134	134	133	133	133	133	133	132	132	132	132	131	131	130	130	129
47	136	136	136	136	135	135	135	135	134	134	134	134	133	133	132	132	131
48	138	138	138	138	138	137	137	137	136	136	136	136	135	135	134	134	133
49	141	140	140	140	140	139	139	139	138	138	138	137	137	136	136	136	135

(Continued)

Table A-10 (Continued)

Sum of scaled scores	Combination																	
	C2	C3	C4	C5	C6	C7	C8	C9	C10	C11	C12	C13	C14	C15	C16	C17	C18
50	143	142	142	142	142	142	141	141	140	140	140	139	139	138	138	138	137
51	145	144	144	144	144	144	143	143	143	142	142	141	141	140	140	139	139
52	147	146	147	146	146	146	145	145	145	144	143	143	143	142	142	141	140
53	149	148	149	148	148	148	147	147	147	146	145	145	145	144	144	143	142
54	151	150	151	150	150	150	149	149	149	148	147	147	147	146	146	145	144
55	153	152	153	152	152	152	151	151	151	150	149	149	149	148	148	147	146
56	155	155	155	154	154	154	153	153	153	152	151	151	151	150	150	149	148
57	158	157	157	156	156	156	155	155	155	154	153	153	153	152	151	151	150

Note. The subtest combinations are as follows:

C2 = CD + SS + CA[a, b]
C3 = BD + PCn + PCm[c]
     PCn + MR + PCm[c]
C4 = VC + MR + SS
C5 = BD + VC + LN
C6 = SI + SS + AR
C7 = VC + SS + AR
C8 = DS + LN + AR[d]
C9 = VC + PCm + AR
     SI + VC + SS
     VC + SS + IN

C10 = BD + MR + PCm[a, c]
C11 = VC + MR + AR
      BD + VC + AR
C12 = SI + CO + WR[e]
C13 = BD + VC + IN
C14 = VC + CO + WR[e]
C15 = SI + VC + WR[e]
C16 = SI + CO + IN[e]
C17 = VC + CO + IN[e]
C18 = SI + VC + IN[e]

Abbreviations: BD = Block Design, SI = Similarities, DS = Digit Span, PCn = Picture Concepts, CD = Coding, VC = Vocabulary, LN = Letter–Number Sequencing, MR = Matrix Reasoning, CO = Comprehension, SS = Symbol Search, PCm = Picture Completion, CA = Cancellation, IN = Information, AR = Arithmetic, WR = Word Reasoning.

Reliability and validity coefficients associated with each short-form combination are shown in Table A-7. See Exhibit 8-4 on pages 256–257 in *Assessment of Children: Cognitive Applications* (Sattler, 2001) for an explanation of the procedure used to obtain the estimated IQs.

[a]This combination is useful for examinees who are hearing impaired.
[b]This combination represents all core and supplemental subtests in the Working Memory Composite.
[c]This combination represents the subtests in the Perceptual Reasoning Composite with the substitution of a supplemental subtest.
[d]This combination represents all core and supplemental subtests in the Processing Speed Composite.
[e]This combination represents the subtests in the Verbal Comprehension Composite with the substitution of a supplemental subtest.

Table A-11
Estimated WISC–IV Full Scale IQs for Sum of Scaled Scores
for 10 Best 4-Subtest Short Forms and Other Combinations

Sum of scaled scores	Combination												
	C2	C3	C4	C5	C6	C7	C8	C9	C10	C11	C12	C13	C14
4	37	38	41	42	42	43	43	43	44	44	45	47	49
5	39	40	43	44	44	44	44	45	45	46	46	48	50
6	41	42	44	45	45	46	46	46	47	48	48	50	51
7	42	43	46	47	47	47	47	48	48	49	49	51	53
8	44	45	48	48	49	49	49	49	50	51	51	53	54
9	46	47	49	50	50	51	51	51	51	52	52	54	56
10	48	49	51	52	52	52	52	53	53	54	54	56	57
11	49	50	52	53	53	54	54	54	55	55	55	57	59
12	51	52	54	55	55	55	55	56	56	57	57	59	60
13	53	54	56	57	57	57	57	57	58	58	59	60	61
14	55	55	57	58	58	59	59	59	59	60	60	62	63
15	56	57	59	60	60	60	60	60	61	61	62	63	64
16	58	59	61	61	61	62	62	62	62	63	63	64	66
17	60	61	62	63	63	63	63	64	64	65	65	66	67
18	62	62	64	65	65	65	65	65	66	66	66	67	69
19	63	64	66	66	66	66	67	67	67	68	68	69	70
20	65	66	67	68	68	68	68	68	69	69	69	70	71
21	67	67	69	69	69	70	70	70	70	71	71	72	73
22	69	69	70	71	71	71	71	72	72	72	72	73	74
23	70	71	72	73	73	73	73	73	73	74	74	75	76
24	72	73	74	74	74	74	74	75	75	75	75	76	77
25	74	74	75	76	76	76	76	76	76	77	77	78	79
26	76	76	77	77	78	78	78	78	78	78	78	79	80
27	77	78	79	79	79	79	79	79	80	80	80	81	81
28	79	79	80	81	81	81	81	81	81	81	82	82	83
29	81	81	82	82	82	82	82	83	83	83	83	84	84
30	83	83	84	84	84	84	84	84	84	85	85	85	86
31	84	85	85	86	86	86	86	86	86	86	86	87	87
32	86	86	87	87	87	87	87	87	87	88	88	88	89
33	88	88	89	89	89	89	89	89	89	89	89	90	90
34	90	90	90	90	90	90	90	91	91	91	91	91	91
35	91	91	92	92	92	92	92	92	92	92	92	93	93
36	93	93	93	94	94	94	94	94	94	94	94	94	94
37	95	95	95	95	95	95	95	95	95	95	95	96	96
38	97	97	97	97	97	97	97	97	97	97	97	97	97
39	98	98	98	98	98	98	98	98	98	98	98	99	99
40	100	100	100	100	100	100	100	100	100	100	100	100	100
41	102	102	102	102	102	102	102	102	102	102	102	101	101
42	103	103	103	103	103	103	103	103	103	103	103	103	103
43	105	105	105	105	105	105	105	105	105	105	105	104	104
44	107	107	107	106	106	106	106	106	106	106	106	106	106
45	109	109	108	108	108	108	108	108	108	108	108	107	107
46	110	110	110	110	110	110	110	109	109	109	109	109	109
47	112	112	111	111	111	111	111	111	111	111	111	110	110
48	114	114	113	113	113	113	113	113	113	112	112	112	111
49	116	115	115	114	114	114	114	114	114	114	114	113	113

(Continued)

Table A-11 (*Continued*)

Sum of scaled scores	Combination												
	C2	C3	C4	C5	C6	C7	C8	C9	C10	C11	C12	C13	C14
50	117	117	116	116	116	116	116	116	116	115	115	114	114
51	119	119	118	118	118	118	118	117	117	117	117	116	116
52	121	121	120	119	119	119	119	119	119	119	118	117	117
53	123	122	121	121	121	121	121	121	120	120	120	119	119
54	124	124	123	123	122	122	122	122	122	122	122	120	120
55	126	126	125	124	124	124	124	124	124	123	123	121	121
56	128	127	126	126	126	126	126	125	125	125	125	123	123
57	130	129	128	127	127	127	127	127	127	126	126	124	124
58	131	131	130	129	129	129	129	128	128	128	128	126	126
59	133	133	131	131	131	130	130	130	130	129	129	127	127
60	135	134	133	132	132	132	132	132	131	131	131	129	129
61	137	136	134	134	134	134	133	133	133	132	132	130	130
62	138	138	136	135	135	135	135	135	134	134	134	131	131
63	140	139	138	137	137	137	137	136	136	135	135	133	133
64	142	141	139	139	139	138	138	138	138	137	137	134	134
65	144	143	141	140	140	140	140	140	139	139	138	136	136
66	145	145	143	142	142	141	141	141	141	140	140	137	137
67	147	146	144	143	143	143	143	143	142	142	141	139	139
68	149	148	146	145	145	145	145	144	144	143	143	140	140
69	151	150	148	147	147	146	146	146	145	145	145	141	141
70	152	151	149	148	148	148	148	147	147	146	146	143	143
71	154	153	151	150	150	149	149	149	149	148	148	144	144
72	156	155	152	152	151	151	151	151	150	149	149	146	146
73	158	157	154	153	153	153	153	152	152	151	151	147	147
74	159	158	156	155	155	154	154	154	153	152	152	149	149
75	161	160	157	156	156	156	156	155	155	154	154	150	150
76	163	162	159	158	158	157	157	157	156	156	155	151	151

Note. The subtest combinations are as follows:

C2 = BD + SI + DS + CD[a]
C3 = DS + LN + CD + SS[b]
C4 = SI + CD + VC + MR
C5 = BD + PCn + MR + PCm[c, d]

C6 = VC + MR + SS + WR
    SI + CD + VC + WR
    VC + MR + SS + AR
C7 = SI + VC + MR + SS
C8 = VC + MR + SS + IN

C9 = SI + CD + AR + WR
C10 = SI + VC + SS + AR
C11 = SI + SS + AR + WR
C12 = VC + SS + AR + WR
C13 = SI + VC + CO + WR[e]
C14 = SI + VC + CO + IN[e]

Abbreviations: BD = Block Design, SI = Similarities, DS = Digit Span, PCn = Picture Concepts, CD = Coding, VC = Vocabulary, LN = Letter–Number Sequencing, MR = Matrix Reasoning, CO = Comprehension, SS = Symbol Search, PCm = Picture Completion, CA = Cancellation, IN = Information, AR = Arithmetic, WR = Word Reasoning.

Reliability and validity coefficients associated with each short-form combination are shown in Table A-7. See Exhibit 8-4 on pages 256–257 in *Assessment of Children: Cognitive Applications* (Sattler, 2001) for an explanation of the procedure used to obtain the estimated IQs.

[a]This combination represents one core subtest from each Composite.
[b]This combination represents the core subtests in both the Working Memory and the Processing Speed Composite.
[c]This combination is useful for children who are hearing impaired.
[d]This combination represents all core and supplemental subtests in the Perceptual Reasoning Composite.
[e]This combination represents three core subtests and one supplemental subtest in the Verbal Comprehension Composite.

Table A-12
Estimated WISC–IV Full Scale IQs for Sum of Scaled Scores
for 10 Best 5-Subtest Short Forms and Other Combinations

Sum of scaled scores	Combination									
	C2	C3	C4	C5	C6	C7	C8	C9	C10	C11
5	39	40	41	42	42	42	42	43	43	47
6	40	41	42	43	43	43	43	44	44	48
7	42	43	43	44	44	45	45	45	46	49
8	43	44	45	45	46	46	46	47	47	50
9	44	45	46	47	47	47	47	48	48	51
10	46	47	47	48	48	48	48	49	49	53
11	47	48	49	49	50	50	50	50	51	54
12	48	49	50	51	51	51	51	52	52	55
13	50	51	51	52	52	52	52	53	53	56
14	51	52	53	53	54	54	54	54	54	57
15	53	53	54	55	55	55	55	56	56	59
16	54	55	55	56	56	56	56	57	57	60
17	55	56	57	57	57	57	57	58	58	61
18	57	57	58	58	59	59	59	59	59	62
19	58	59	59	60	60	60	60	61	61	63
20	59	60	60	61	61	61	61	62	62	64
21	61	61	62	62	63	63	63	63	63	66
22	62	63	63	64	64	64	64	64	65	67
23	63	64	64	65	65	65	65	66	66	68
24	65	65	66	66	66	66	67	67	67	69
25	66	67	67	68	68	68	68	68	68	70
26	67	68	68	69	69	69	69	70	70	72
27	69	69	70	70	70	70	70	71	71	73
28	70	71	71	71	72	72	72	72	72	74
29	72	72	72	73	73	73	73	73	73	75
30	73	73	74	74	74	74	74	75	75	76
31	74	75	75	75	75	75	76	76	76	77
32	76	76	76	77	77	77	77	77	77	79
33	77	77	78	78	78	78	78	78	78	80
34	78	79	79	79	79	79	79	80	80	81
35	80	80	80	81	81	81	81	81	81	82
36	81	81	82	82	82	82	82	82	82	83
37	82	83	83	83	83	83	83	83	84	85
38	84	84	84	84	85	85	85	85	85	86
39	85	85	86	86	86	86	86	86	86	87
40	86	87	87	87	87	87	87	87	87	88
41	88	88	88	88	88	88	88	89	89	89
42	89	89	89	90	90	90	90	90	90	91
43	91	91	91	91	91	91	91	91	91	92
44	92	92	92	92	92	92	92	92	92	93
45	93	93	93	94	94	94	94	94	94	94
46	95	95	95	95	95	95	95	95	95	95
47	96	96	96	96	96	96	96	96	96	96
48	97	97	97	97	97	97	97	97	97	98
49	99	99	99	99	99	99	99	99	99	99
50	100	100	100	100	100	100	100	100	100	100
51	101	101	101	101	101	101	101	101	101	101
52	103	103	103	103	103	103	103	103	103	102
53	104	104	104	104	104	104	104	104	104	104
54	105	105	105	105	105	105	105	105	105	105

(Continued)

Table A-12 (Continued)

Sum of scaled scores	Combination									
	C2	C3	C4	C5	C6	C7	C8	C9	C10	C11
55	107	107	107	106	106	106	106	106	106	106
56	108	108	108	108	108	108	108	108	108	107
57	109	109	109	109	109	109	109	109	109	108
58	111	111	111	110	110	110	110	110	110	109
59	112	112	112	112	112	112	112	111	111	111
60	114	113	113	113	113	113	113	113	113	112
61	115	115	114	114	114	114	114	114	114	113
62	116	116	116	116	115	115	115	115	115	114
63	118	117	117	117	117	117	117	117	116	115
64	119	119	118	118	118	118	118	118	118	117
65	120	120	120	119	119	119	119	119	119	118
66	122	121	121	121	121	121	121	120	120	119
67	123	123	122	122	122	122	122	122	122	120
68	124	124	124	123	123	123	123	123	123	121
69	126	125	125	125	125	125	124	124	124	123
70	127	127	126	126	126	126	126	125	125	124
71	128	128	128	127	127	127	127	127	127	125
72	130	129	129	129	128	128	128	128	128	126
73	131	131	130	130	130	130	130	129	129	127
74	133	132	132	131	131	131	131	130	130	128
75	134	133	133	132	132	132	132	132	132	130
76	135	135	134	134	134	134	133	133	133	131
77	137	136	136	135	135	135	135	134	134	132
78	138	137	137	136	136	136	136	136	135	133
79	139	139	138	138	137	137	137	137	137	134
80	141	140	140	139	139	139	139	138	138	136
81	142	141	141	140	140	140	140	139	139	137
82	143	143	142	142	141	141	141	141	141	138
83	145	144	143	143	143	143	143	142	142	139
84	146	145	145	144	144	144	144	143	143	140
85	147	147	146	145	145	145	145	144	144	141
86	149	148	147	147	146	146	146	146	146	143
87	150	149	149	148	148	148	148	147	147	144
88	152	151	150	149	149	149	149	148	148	145
89	153	152	151	151	150	150	150	150	149	146
90	154	153	153	152	152	152	152	151	151	147
91	156	155	154	153	153	153	153	152	152	149
92	157	156	155	155	154	154	154	153	153	150
93	158	157	157	156	156	155	155	155	154	151
94	160	159	158	157	157	157	157	156	156	152

Note. The subtest combinations are as follows:

C2 = BD + SI + CD + VC + LN   C5 = SI + CD + MR + AR + WR   C9 = SI + MR + SS + AR + WR
C3 = SI + CD + VC + PCm + AR   C6 = CD + VC + MR + AR + WR   C10 = VC+ MR + SS + AR + WR
C4 = BD + SI + CD + VC + AR   C7 = BD + CD + VC + AR + WR   C11 = SI + VC + CO + IN + WR[a]
    SI + CD + VC + MR + AR   C8 = SI + VC + MR + SS + AR

Abbreviations: BD = Block Design, SI = Similarities, DS = Digit Span, PCn = Picture Concepts, CD = Coding, VC = Vocabulary, LN = Letter–Number Sequencing, MR = Matrix Reasoning, CO = Comprehension, SS = Symbol Search, PCm = Picture Completion, CA = Cancellation, IN = Information, AR = Arithmetic, WR = Word Reasoning.

Reliability and validity coefficients associated with each short-form combination are shown in Table A-7. See Exhibit 8-4 on pages 256–257 in *Assessment of Children: Cognitive Applications* (Sattler, 2001) for an explanation of the procedure used to obtain the estimated IQs.

[a] This combination represents all core and supplemental subtests in the Verbal Comprehension Composite.

Table A-13
Estimated WISC–IV Full Scale IQs for Sum of Scaled Scores for One 6-Subtest Short-Form Combination (Block Design, Similarities, Picture Concepts, Vocabulary, Matrix Reasoning, and Comprehension)

Sum of scaled scores	FSIQ	Sum of scaled scores	FSIQ	Sum of scaled scores	FSIQ
6	41	46	85	86	128
7	42	47	86	87	129
8	43	48	87	88	131
9	44	49	88	89	132
10	45	50	89	90	133
11	46	51	90	91	134
12	48	52	91	92	135
13	49	53	92	93	136
14	50	54	93	94	137
15	51	55	95	95	138
16	52	56	96	96	139
17	53	57	97	97	140
18	54	58	98	98	142
19	55	59	99	99	143
20	56	60	100	100	144
21	57	61	101	101	145
22	58	62	102	102	146
23	60	63	103	103	147
24	61	64	104	104	148
25	62	65	105	105	149
26	63	66	107	106	150
27	64	67	108	107	151
28	65	68	109	108	152
29	66	69	110	109	154
30	67	70	111	110	155
31	68	71	112	111	156
32	69	72	113	112	157
33	71	73	114	113	158
34	72	74	115	114	159
35	73	75	116	115	160
36	74	76	117	116	161
37	75	77	119	117	162
38	76	78	120	118	163
39	77	79	121	119	164
40	78	80	122	120	166
41	79	81	123		
42	80	82	124		
43	81	83	125		
44	83	84	126		
45	84	85	127		

Note. See Exhibit 8-4 on pages 256–257 in *Assessment of Children: Cognitive Applications* (Sattler, 2001) for an explanation of the procedure used to obtain the estimated IQs.

The reliability and validity of this combination are r_{ss} = .958 and r = .941, respectively.

APPENDIX B

TABLES FOR THE WPPSI–III

Table B-1
Confidence Intervals for WPPSI–III Individual Composite Scores and Full Scale IQs Based on Obtained Score Only

Age level	Individual Composite or Full Scale	Confidence level				
		68%	85%	90%	95%	99%
2½ (2-6-0 through 2-11-30)	Verbal	±4	±5	±6	±7	±9
	Performance	±5	±7	±8	±10	±13
	Full Scale	±4	±5	±6	±7	±9
3 (3-0-0 through 3-5-30)	Verbal	±4	±5	±6	±7	±9
	Performance	±5	±8	±9	±10	±13
	Full Scale	±4	±5	±6	±7	±9
3½ (3-6-0 through 3-11-30)	Verbal	±4	±5	±6	±7	±9
	Performance	±5	±7	±8	±9	±12
	Full Scale	±3	±5	±5	±6	±8
Average (2-6-0 through 3-11-30)	Verbal	±4	±5	±6	±7	±9
	Performance	±5	±7	±8	±10	±13
	Full Scale	±4	±5	±6	±7	±9
4 (4-0-0 through 4-5-30)	Verbal	±4	±5	±6	±7	±9
	Performance	±5	±7	±8	±9	±12
	Processing Speed	±5	±7	±7	±9	±11
	Full Scale	±3	±5	±5	±6	±8
4½ (4-6-0 through 4-11-30)	Verbal	±4	±5	±6	±7	±9
	Performance	±4	±6	±7	±8	±10
	Processing Speed	±5	±7	±8	±9	±12
	Full Scale	±3	±4	±5	±6	±7
5 (5-0-0 through 5-5-30)	Verbal	±3	±5	±5	±6	±8
	Performance	±4	±6	±7	±8	±10
	Processing Speed	±5	±7	±7	±9	±11
	Full Scale	±3	±4	±5	±6	±7
5½ (5-6-0 through 5-11-30)	Verbal	±4	±5	±6	±7	±9
	Performance	±4	±6	±7	±8	±10
	Processing Speed	±6	±8	±9	±11	±14
	Full Scale	±3	±4	±5	±6	±7
6 (6-0-0 through 6-11-30)	Verbal	±4	±6	±7	±8	±10
	Performance	±4	±6	±7	±8	±10
	Processing Speed	±6	±8	±9	±11	±14
	Full Scale	±3	±5	±5	±6	±8
7 (7-0-0 through 7-3-30)	Verbal	±4	±5	±6	±7	±9
	Performance	±4	±5	±6	±7	±9
	Processing Speed	±6	±9	±10	±11	±15
	Full Scale	±3	±4	±5	±6	±7
Average (4-0-0 through 7-3-30)	Verbal	±4	±5	±6	±7	±9
	Performance	±4	±6	±7	±8	±10
	Processing Speed	±5	±8	±9	±10	±13
	Full Scale	±3	±4	±5	±6	±8

Note. Pages 109–110 in *Assessment of Children: Cognitive Applications* (Sattler, 2001) describe the procedure for computing confidence intervals. For the WPPSI–III Verbal Composite, the confidence intervals are obtained by the following procedure: The appropriate SEM for the child's age is located in Table 4.3 of the Technical Manual. For example, for a child who is 2 years, 6 months old, the SEM = 3.35 for the Verbal Composite. This SEM is multiplied by the respective z values in order to obtain the confidence interval for the desired level. At the 68% confidence level, the SEM is multiplied by ±1 (±1 x 3.35 = ±4). At the 85% level, the SEM is multiplied by ±1.44 (±1.44 x 3.35 = ±5). At the 90% level, the SEM is multiplied by ±1.65 (±1.65 x 3.35 = ±6). At the 95% level, the SEM is multiplied by ±1.96 (±1.96 x 3.35 = ±7). At the 99% level, the SEM is multiplied by ±2.58 (±2.58 x 3.35 = ±9).

Table B-2
Differences Between WPPSI–III Subtest Scaled Scores and Between Composite Scores Required for Statistical Significance at the .05 and .01 Levels of Significance for Ages 2-6 to 3-11 and Combined Ages (.05 significance level above diagonal, .01 significance level below diagonal)

Age 2-6 to 2-11

Subtest	RV	BD	IN	OA	PN	VIQ	PIQ
Receptive Vocabulary	—	3	3	3	3	—	—
Block Design	4	—	4	4	4	—	—
Information	4	3	—	3	3	—	—
Object Assembly	4	5	4	—	4	—	—
Picture Naming	4	5	4	5	—	—	—
Verbal IQ	—	—	—	—	—	—	12
Performance IQ	—	—	—	—	—	16	—

Age 3-0 to 3-5

Subtest	RV	BD	IN	OA	PN	VIQ	PIQ
Receptive Vocabulary	—	3	3	3	3	—	—
Block Design	4	—	4	4	3	—	—
Information	4	3	—	3	3	—	—
Object Assembly	4	5	4	—	3	—	—
Picture Naming	4	4	4	4	—	—	—
Verbal IQ	—	—	—	—	—	—	12
Performance IQ	—	—	—	—	—	16	—

Age 3-6 to 3-11

Subtest	RV	BD	IN	OA	PN	VIQ	PIQ
Receptive Vocabulary	—	3	3	3	3	—	—
Block Design	4	—	4	3	3	—	—
Information	4	3	—	3	3	—	—
Object Assembly	4	4	4	—	3	—	—
Picture Naming	4	4	4	4	—	—	—
Verbal IQ	—	—	—	—	—	—	11
Performance IQ	—	—	—	—	—	15	—

Average

Subtest	RV	BD	IN	OA	PN	VIQ	PIQ
Receptive Vocabulary	—	3	3	3	3	—	—
Block Design	4	—	4	3	3	—	—
Information	4	3	—	3	3	—	—
Object Assembly	4	4	4	—	3	—	—
Picture Naming	4	4	4	4	—	—	—
Verbal IQ	—	—	—	—	—	—	12
Performance IQ	—	—	—	—	—	15	—

(*Continued*)

Table B-2 (*Continued*)

Note. Abbreviations: RV = Receptive Vocabulary, BD = Block Design, IN = Information, OA = Object Assembly, PN = Picture Naming, VIQ = Verbal IQ, PIQ = Performance IQ.

The critical values at the .05 level appear *above* the diagonal in the *shaded area*, while the critical values for the .01 level appear *below* the diagonal in the *unshaded area*.

Sample reading: At age 2-6 to 2-11, a difference of 3 points between scaled scores on the Information and Receptive Vocabulary subtests is significant at the 5% level and a difference of 4 points is significant at the 1% level. Similarly, a difference of 12 points between the Verbal IQ and Performance IQ is significant at the 5% level and a difference of 16 points is significant at the 1% level.

The values in this table for subtest comparisons are overly liberal when more than one comparison is made for a subtest. They are more accurate when a priori planned comparisons are made, such as Receptive Vocabulary vs. Information or Block Design vs. Object Assembly.

All values in this table have been rounded up to the next higher number.

See Exhibit 4-1 in Chapter 4 for an explanation of the method used to arrive at magnitudes of differences.

Silverstein (personal communication, February 1990) suggests that the following formula be used to obtain a value for the significant difference (at the .05 level) that must exist between the highest and lowest subtest scores on a profile before individual subtest comparisons can be made:

$$D = q\sqrt{\frac{\sum \text{SEM}^2}{k}}$$

where

D = significant difference
q = critical value of the Studentized range statistic
SEM = standard error of measurement of a particular subtest
k = number of subtests

For the WPPSI–III, the q value is 3.86 at the .05 level for $k = 5$ (5 subtests) and ∞ degrees of freedom. The sum of the SEM^2 for the 5 subtests at age 2-6 to 2-11 is $1.44 + 0.72 + 0.81 + 1.44 + 1.17 = 5.58$ and

$$D = 3.86 \times \sqrt{\frac{5.58}{5}} = 3.86 \times \sqrt{1.16} = 3.86 \times 1.06 = 4.08$$

Thus, a difference of 4 points between the highest and lowest subtest scaled scores represents a significant difference at the .05 level.

Table B-3
Differences Between WPPSI–III Subtest Scaled Scores, IQs, and Composite Scores for Ages 4-0 to 7-3
(.05 significance level above diagonal, .01 significance level below diagonal)

Age 4-0 to 4-5

Subtest	BD	IN	MR	VC	PCn	SS	WR	CD	CO	PCm	SI	RV	OA	PN	VIQ	PIQ	PSQ
Block Design	—	4	4	4	4	4	4	4	4	4	4	4	4	4	—	—	—
Information	5	—	3	3	3	4	3	3	4	3	3	3	3	3	—	—	—
Matrix Reasoning	5	4	—	3	3	3	3	3	3	3	3	3	3	3	—	—	—
Vocabulary	5	4	4	—	3	3	3	3	3	3	3	3	3	3	—	—	—
Picture Concepts	5	4	4	4	—	3	3	3	3	3	3	3	3	3	—	—	—
Symbol Search	5	5	4	4	4	—	3	3	4	3	3	3	3	3	—	—	—
Word Reasoning	5	4	4	4	4	4	—	3	3	3	3	3	3	3	—	—	—
Coding	5	4	4	4	4	4	4	—	3	3	3	3	3	3	—	—	—
Comprehension	5	5	4	4	4	5	4	4	—	3	3	3	3	3	—	—	—
Picture Completion	5	4	4	4	4	4	4	4	4	—	3	3	3	3	—	—	—
Similarities	5	5	4	4	4	5	4	4	5	4	—	3	3	3	—	—	—
Receptive Vocabulary	5	4	4	4	4	4	4	4	4	4	3	—	3	3	—	—	—
Object Assembly	5	4	4	4	4	4	4	4	4	4	4	4	—	3	—	—	—
Picture Naming	5	4	4	4	4	4	4	4	4	4	3	4	4	—	—	—	—
Verbal IQ	—	—	—	—	—	—	—	—	—	—	—	—	—	—	—	11	11
Performance IQ	—	—	—	—	—	—	—	—	—	—	—	—	—	—	15	—	15
Processing Speed Q	—	—	—	—	—	—	—	—	—	—	—	—	—	—	14	16	—

Age 4-6 to 4-11

Subtest	BD	IN	MR	VC	PCn	SS	WR	CD	CO	PCm	SI	RV	OA	PN	VIQ	PIQ	PSQ
Block Design	—	4	4	4	3	4	3	4	3	3	3	4	4	4	—	—	—
Information	5	—	4	4	3	4	3	4	3	3	3	4	4	4	—	—	—
Matrix Reasoning	5	5	—	3	3	3	3	3	3	3	3	3	3	3	—	—	—
Vocabulary	5	5	4	—	3	3	3	3	3	3	3	3	3	3	—	—	—
Picture Concepts	4	4	4	4	—	3	3	3	3	3	3	3	3	3	—	—	—
Symbol Search	5	5	4	4	4	—	3	3	3	3	3	4	4	3	—	—	—
Word Reasoning	4	4	4	4	4	4	—	3	3	3	2	3	3	3	—	—	—
Coding	5	5	4	4	4	4	4	—	3	3	3	3	3	3	—	—	—
Comprehension	4	4	4	4	4	4	4	4	—	3	3	3	3	3	—	—	—
Picture Completion	4	4	4	4	4	4	3	4	4	—	3	3	3	3	—	—	—
Similarities	4	4	3	4	3	4	3	4	3	3	—	3	3	3	—	—	—
Receptive Vocabulary	5	5	4	4	4	5	4	4	4	4	4	—	4	3	—	—	—
Object Assembly	5	5	4	4	4	5	4	4	4	4	4	5	—	3	—	—	—
Picture Naming	5	5	4	4	4	4	4	4	4	4	4	4	4	—	—	—	—
Verbal IQ	—	—	—	—	—	—	—	—	—	—	—	—	—	—	—	10	11
Performance IQ	—	—	—	—	—	—	—	—	—	—	—	—	—	—	13	—	12
Processing Speed Q	—	—	—	—	—	—	—	—	—	—	—	—	—	—	15	15	—

(Continued)

Table B-3 (Continued)

Age 5-0 to 5-5

Subtest	BD	IN	MR	VC	PCn	SS	WR	CD	CO	PCm	SI	RV	OA	PN	VIQ	PIQ	PSQ
Block Design	—	4	4	4	3	4	3	4	4	4	3	4	4	4	—	—	—
Information	5	—	3	3	3	3	3	3	3	3	3	3	3	3	—	—	—
Matrix Reasoning	5	4	—	3	3	3	3	3	3	3	3	3	3	3	—	—	—
Vocabulary	5	4	4	—	3	3	3	3	3	3	3	3	3	3	—	—	—
Picture Concepts	4	4	4	4	—	3	3	3	3	3	3	3	3	3	—	—	—
Symbol Search	5	4	4	4	4	—	3	3	3	3	3	3	4	4	—	—	—
Word Reasoning	4	4	4	4	3	4	—	3	3	3	3	3	3	3	—	—	—
Coding	5	4	4	4	4	4	4	—	3	3	3	3	4	3	—	—	—
Comprehension	5	4	4	4	4	4	4	4	—	3	3	3	3	3	—	—	—
Picture Completion	5	4	4	4	4	4	4	4	4	—	3	3	3	3	—	—	—
Similarities	4	3	3	4	3	4	3	4	4	3	—	3	3	3	—	—	—
Receptive Vocabulary	5	4	4	4	4	4	4	4	4	4	4	—	3	3	—	—	—
Object Assembly	5	4	4	4	4	5	4	5	4	4	4	4	—	4	—	—	—
Picture Naming	5	4	4	4	4	5	4	4	4	4	4	4	5	—	—	—	—
Verbal IQ	—	—	—	—	—	—	—	—	—	—	—	—	—	—	—	10	11
Performance IQ	—	—	—	—	—	—	—	—	—	—	—	—	—	—	13	—	11
Processing Speed Q	—	—	—	—	—	—	—	—	—	—	—	—	—	—	14	15	—

Age 5-6 to 5-11

Subtest	BD	IN	MR	VC	PCn	SS	WR	CD	CO	PCm	SI	RV	OA	PN	VIQ	PIQ	PSQ
Block Design	—	4	3	4	3	4	3	4	4	4	3	4	4	4	—	—	—
Information	5	—	3	3	3	4	3	4	3	3	3	3	4	3	—	—	—
Matrix Reasoning	4	4	—	3	3	4	3	4	3	3	3	3	4	3	—	—	—
Vocabulary	5	4	4	—	3	4	3	4	3	3	3	4	4	3	—	—	—
Picture Concepts	4	4	4	4	—	4	3	4	3	3	3	3	3	3	—	—	—
Symbol Search	5	5	5	5	5	—	4	4	4	4	3	4	4	4	—	—	—
Word Reasoning	4	4	4	4	4	5	—	4	3	3	3	3	4	3	—	—	—
Coding	5	5	5	5	5	5	5	—	4	4	3	4	4	4	—	—	—
Comprehension	5	4	4	4	4	5	4	5	—	3	3	3	4	3	—	—	—
Picture Completion	5	4	4	4	4	5	4	5	4	—	3	3	4	3	—	—	—
Similarities	4	4	3	4	3	4	3	4	3	4	—	3	3	3	—	—	—
Receptive Vocabulary	5	4	4	5	4	5	4	5	4	4	4	—	4	3	—	—	—
Object Assembly	5	5	5	5	4	5	5	5	5	5	4	5	—	4	—	—	—
Picture Naming	5	4	4	4	4	5	4	5	4	4	3	4	5	—	—	—	—
Verbal IQ	—	—	—	—	—	—	—	—	—	—	—	—	—	—	—	10	13
Performance IQ	—	—	—	—	—	—	—	—	—	—	—	—	—	—	13	—	13
Processing Speed Q	—	—	—	—	—	—	—	—	—	—	—	—	—	—	17	17	—

(Continued)

Table B-3 (*Continued*)

Age 6-0 to 6-11

Subtest	BD	IN	MR	VC	PCn	SS	WR	CD	CO	PCm	SI	RV	OA	PN	VIQ	PIQ	PSQ
Block Design	—	4	3	3	3	4	3	4	4	3	3	4	4	4	—	—	—
Information	5	—	4	4	4	4	4	4	4	4	3	4	4	4	—	—	—
Matrix Reasoning	4	5	—	3	3	4	3	4	3	3	3	4	4	3	—	—	—
Vocabulary	4	5	4	—	3	4	3	4	3	3	3	4	4	4	—	—	—
Picture Concepts	4	5	4	4	—	4	3	4	3	3	3	4	4	4	—	—	—
Symbol Search	5	5	5	5	5	—	4	4	4	4	4	4	4	4	—	—	—
Word Reasoning	4	5	4	4	4	5	—	4	3	3	3	4	4	4	—	—	—
Coding	5	5	5	5	5	5	5	—	4	4	4	4	4	4	—	—	—
Comprehension	5	5	4	4	4	5	4	5	—	3	3	4	4	4	—	—	—
Picture Completion	4	5	4	4	4	5	4	5	4	—	3	4	4	4	—	—	—
Similarities	4	4	4	4	4	5	4	5	4	4	—	4	4	3	—	—	—
Receptive Vocabulary	5	5	5	5	5	5	5	5	5	5	5	—	4	4	—	—	—
Object Assembly	5	5	5	5	5	6	5	6	5	5	5	5	—	4	—	—	—
Picture Naming	5	5	4	5	5	5	5	5	5	5	4	5	5	—	—	—	—
Verbal IQ	—	—	—	—	—	—	—	—	—	—	—	—	—	—	—	11	13
Performance IQ	—	—	—	—	—	—	—	—	—	—	—	—	—	—	14	—	13
Processing Speed Q	—	—	—	—	—	—	—	—	—	—	—	—	—	—	17	17	—

Age 7-0 to 7-3

Subtest	BD	IN	MR	VC	PCn	SS	WR	CD	CO	PCm	SI	RV	OA	PN	VIQ	PIQ	PSQ
Block Design	—	3	3	3	3	4	3	4	3	3	3	3	4	3	—	—	—
Information	4	—	4	3	3	4	3	4	4	4	3	4	4	4	—	—	—
Matrix Reasoning	4	5	—	3	3	4	3	4	3	3	3	3	4	4	—	—	—
Vocabulary	4	4	4	—	3	4	3	4	3	3	3	3	4	3	—	—	—
Picture Concepts	4	4	4	4	—	4	3	4	3	3	3	3	4	3	—	—	—
Symbol Search	5	5	5	5	5	—	4	4	4	4	3	4	4	4	—	—	—
Word Reasoning	4	4	4	4	4	5	—	4	3	3	3	3	4	3	—	—	—
Coding	5	5	5	5	5	5	5	—	4	4	3	4	4	4	—	—	—
Comprehension	4	5	4	4	4	5	4	5	—	3	3	3	4	4	—	—	—
Picture Completion	4	5	4	4	4	5	4	5	4	—	3	4	4	4	—	—	—
Similarities	3	4	4	3	3	4	3	4	4	4	—	3	3	3	—	—	—
Receptive Vocabulary	4	5	4	4	4	5	4	5	4	5	4	—	4	4	—	—	—
Object Assembly	5	5	5	5	5	5	5	6	5	5	4	5	—	4	—	—	—
Picture Naming	4	5	5	4	4	5	4	5	5	5	4	5	5	—	—	—	—
Verbal IQ	—	—	—	—	—	—	—	—	—	—	—	—	—	—	—	10	13
Performance IQ	—	—	—	—	—	—	—	—	—	—	—	—	—	—	13	—	13
Processing Speed Q	—	—	—	—	—	—	—	—	—	—	—	—	—	—	17	17	—

(*Continued*)

Table B-3 (*Continued*)

							Average										
Subtest	BD	IN	MR	VC	PCn	SS	WR	CD	CO	PCm	SI	RV	OA	PN	VIQ	PIQ	PSQ
Block Design	—	4	3	4	3	4	3	4	4	3	3	4	4	4	—	—	—
Information	5	—	3	3	3	4	3	4	3	3	3	4	4	4	—	—	—
Matrix Reasoning	4	4	—	3	3	4	3	3	3	3	3	3	3	3	—	—	—
Vocabulary	5	4	4	—	3	4	3	4	3	3	3	3	4	3	—	—	—
Picture Concepts	4	4	4	4	—	3	3	3	3	3	3	3	3	3	—	—	—
Symbol Search	5	5	5	5	4	—	3	4	4	4	3	4	4	4	—	—	—
Word Reasoning	4	4	4	4	4	4	—	3	3	3	3	3	3	3	—	—	—
Coding	5	5	4	5	4	5	4	—	4	3	3	4	4	4	—	—	—
Comprehension	5	4	4	4	4	5	4	5	—	3	3	3	4	3	—	—	—
Picture Completion	4	4	4	4	4	5	4	4	4	—	3	3	3	3	—	—	—
Similarities	4	4	3	4	3	4	3	4	4	3	—	3	3	3	—	—	—
Receptive Vocabulary	5	5	4	4	4	5	4	5	4	4	4	—	4	3	—	—	—
Object Assembly	5	5	4	5	4	5	4	5	5	4	4	5	—	4	—	—	—
Picture Naming	5	5	4	4	4	5	4	5	4	4	4	4	5	—	—	—	—
Verbal IQ	—	—	—	—	—	—	—	—	—	—	—	—	—	—	—	10	12
Performance IQ	—	—	—	—	—	—	—	—	—	—	—	—	—	—	13	—	13
Processing Speed Q	—	—	—	—	—	—	—	—	—	—	—	—	—	—	16	16	—

Note. Abbreviations: BD = Block Design, IN = Information, MR = Matrix Reasoning, VC = Vocabulary, PCn = Picture Concepts, SS = Symbol Search, WR = Word Reasoning, CD = Coding, CO = Comprehension, PCm = Picture Completion, SI = Similarities, RV = Receptive Vocabulary, OA = Object Assembly, PN = Picture Naming, VIQ = Verbal IQ, PIQ = Performance IQ, PSQ = Performance Speed IQ.

The critical values at the .05 level appear *above* the diagonal in the *shaded* area, while the critical values for the .01 level appear *below* the diagonal in the *unshaded* area.

Sample reading: At age 4-0 to 4-5, a difference of 3 points between scaled scores on the Information and Vocabulary subtests is significant at the 5% level and a difference of 4 points is significant at the 1% level. Similarly, a difference of 11 points between the Verbal IQ and Performance IQ is significant at the 5% level and a difference of 15 points is significant at the 1% level.

The values in this table for subtest comparisons are overly liberal when more than one comparison is made for a subtest. They are more accurate when a priori planned comparisons are made, such as Information vs. Vocabulary or Block Design vs. Object Assembly.

All values in this table have been rounded up to the next higher number.

See Exhibit 4-1 in Chapter 4 for the procedure used to arrive at magnitudes of differences.

Silverstein (personal communication, February 1990) suggests that the following formula be used to obtain a value for the significant difference (at the .05 level) that must exist between the highest and lowest subtest scores on a profile before individual subtest comparisons can be made:

$$D = q\sqrt{\frac{\sum SEM^2}{k}}$$

where

D = significant difference
q = critical value of the Studentized range statistic
SEM = standard error of measurement of a particular subtest
k = number of subtests

For the WPPSI–III, the q value is 4.62 at the .05 level for k = 12 (12 subtests) and ∞ degrees of freedom. The sum of the SEM^2 for the 12 subtests is 1.30 + 1.02 + 0.77 + 1.46 + 0.192 + 0.83 + 1.49 + 1.51 + 1.06 + 0.92 + .48 + 1.49 = 13.26 and

$$D = 4.62 \times \sqrt{\frac{13.26}{12}} = 4.62 \times \sqrt{1.10} = 4.62 \times 1.05 = 4.85$$

Thus, at ages 4-0 to 7-3 a difference of 5 points between the highest and lowest subtest scaled scores represents a significant difference at the .05 level.

Table B-4
Estimates of the Probability of Obtaining Designated Differences Between WPPSI–III Composite Scores by Chance

Verbal and Performance

Probability of obtaining given or greater discrepancy by chance	Age											
	2-6	3-0	3-6	Total[a]	4-0	4-6	5-0	5-6	6-0	7-0	Total[b]	Ov.[c]
.50	4.05	4.05	3.79	3.96	3.79	3.35	3.20	3.35	3.50	3.20	3.40	3.60
.25	6.89	6.89	6.45	6.75	6.45	5.71	5.45	5.71	5.97	5.45	5.80	6.13
.20	7.68	7.68	7.19	7.53	7.19	6.37	6.08	6.37	6.65	6.07	6.47	6.84
.10	9.86	9.86	9.23	9.66	9.23	8.17	7.80	8.17	8.54	7.79	8.30	8.77
.05	11.75	11.75	11.00	11.50	11.00	9.74	9.29	9.74	10.17	9.29	9.88	10.45
.02	13.95	13.95	13.05	13.66	13.05	11.56	11.03	11.56	12.08	11.02	11.74	12.41
.01	15.43	15.43	14.45	15.11	14.45	12.80	12.21	12.80	13.36	12.20	12.99	13.73
.001	19.78	19.78	18.51	19.37	18.51	16.40	15.64	16.40	17.13	15.63	16.64	17.60

Verbal and Processing Speed

Probability of obtaining given or greater discrepancy by chance	Age											
	2-6	3-0	3-6	Total[a]	4-0	4-6	5-0	5-6	6-0	7-0	Total[b]	Ov.[d]
.50	—	—	—	—	3.65	3.79	3.51	4.37	4.41	4.41	4.03	4.03
.25	—	—	—	—	6.21	6.45	5.97	7.45	7.52	7.51	6.86	6.86
.20	—	—	—	—	6.93	7.19	6.66	8.30	8.38	8.38	7.65	7.65
.10	—	—	—	—	8.89	9.23	8.54	10.65	10.75	10.75	9.82	9.82
.05	—	—	—	—	10.59	11.00	10.18	12.69	12.81	12.81	11.70	11.70
.02	—	—	—	—	12.57	13.05	12.09	15.07	15.21	15.20	13.89	13.89
.01	—	—	—	—	13.91	14.45	13.37	16.67	16.83	16.83	15.37	15.37
.001	—	—	—	—	17.83	18.51	17.14	21.36	21.57	21.56	19.70	19.70

Performance and Processing Speed

Probability of obtaining given or greater discrepancy by chance	Age											
	2-6	3-0	3-6	Total[a]	4-0	4-6	5-0	5-6	6-0	7-0	Total[b]	Ov.[d]
.50	—	—	—	—	4.17	3.92	3.79	4.49	4.41	4.41	4.19	4.35
.25	—	—	—	—	7.11	6.68	6.45	7.64	7.52	7.51	7.15	7.42
.20	—	—	—	—	7.93	7.44	7.19	8.52	8.38	8.38	7.97	8.27
.10	—	—	—	—	10.17	9.55	9.22	10.93	10.75	10.75	10.22	10.61
.05	—	—	—	—	12.12	11.38	10.99	13.02	12.81	12.81	12.18	12.65
.02	—	—	—	—	14.39	13.51	13.05	15.46	15.21	15.20	14.46	15.01
.01	—	—	—	—	15.92	14.95	14.44	17.11	16.83	16.83	16.00	16.61
.001	—	—	—	—	20.40	19.16	18.51	21.93	21.57	21.56	20.51	21.29

Note. To use the table, find the column appropriate to the child's age. Locate the discrepancy that is just *less than* the discrepancy obtained by the child. The entry in the first column in that same row gives the probability of obtaining a given or greater discrepancy by chance. For example, the hypothesis that a 6-year-old child obtained a Verbal-Performance discrepancy of 17 by chance can be rejected at the .01 level of significance. The table is two-tailed.

See Exhibit 4-1 in Chapter 4 for an explanation of the method used to arrive at magnitudes of differences.

The following z values were used for the eight probability levels: $z = .675$ for .50, $z = 1.15$ for .25, $z = 1.282$ for .20, $z = 1.645$ for .10, $z = 1.96$ for .05, $z = 2.327$ for .02, $z = 2.575$ for .01, and $z = 3.30$ for .001.

[a] Total = Total for ages 2-6 to 3-11.
[b] Total = Total for ages 4-0 to 7-3.
[c] Ov. = Overall for ages 2-6 to 7-3.
[d] Ov. = Overall for ages 4-0 to 7-3.

Table B-5
Differences Required for Significance When Each WPPSI–III Subtest Scaled Score Is Compared to the Mean Subtest Scaled Score for Any Individual Child

Age 2-6 to 2-11

Subtest	Mean of 2 subtests[a]		Mean of 2 subtests		Mean of 3 subtests		Mean of 4 subtests		Mean of 5 subtests	
	.05	.01	.05	.01	.05	.01	.05	.01	.05	.01
Block Design	1.66	2.19	—	—	—	—	2.49	3.01	2.69	3.44
Information	1.21	1.60	—	—	1.76	2.15	2.00	2.41	2.09	2.67
Receptive Vocabulary	1.21	1.60	1.38	1.81	1.80	2.21	2.06	2.49	2.17	2.78
Object Assembly	1.66	2.19	—	—	—	—	2.49	3.01	2.69	3.44
Picture Naming	—	—	1.38	1.81	1.98	2.43	—	—	2.48	3.17

Age 3-0 to 3-5

Subtest	Mean of 2 subtests[a]		Mean of 2 subtests		Mean of 3 subtests		Mean of 4 subtests		Mean of 5 subtests	
	.05	.01	.05	.01	.05	.01	.05	.01	.05	.01
Block Design	1.58	2.08	—	—	—	—	2.42	2.92	2.60	3.32
Information	1.25	1.64	—	—	1.77	2.17	2.04	2.47	2.14	2.74
Receptive Vocabulary	1.25	1.64	1.28	1.69	1.77	2.17	2.04	2.47	2.14	2.74
Object Assembly	1.58	2.08	—	—	—	—	2.36	2.85	2.52	3.23
Picture Naming	—	—	1.28	1.69	1.82	2.23	—	—	2.23	2.85

Age 3-6 to 3-11

Subtest	Mean of 2 subtests[a]		Mean of 2 subtests		Mean of 3 subtests		Mean of 4 subtests		Mean of 5 subtests	
	.05	.01	.05	.01	.05	.01	.05	.01	.05	.01
Block Design	1.47	1.93	—	—	—	—	2.38	2.88	2.57	3.29
Information	1.21	1.59	—	—	1.65	2.03	1.85	2.24	1.93	2.47
Receptive Vocabulary	1.21	1.59	1.32	1.73	1.81	2.21	2.07	2.50	2.20	2.82
Object Assembly	1.47	1.93	—	—	—	—	2.07	2.50	2.20	2.82
Picture Naming	—	—	1.32	1.73	1.81	2.21	—	—	2.20	2.82

Average for Ages 2-6 to 3-11

Subtest	Mean of 2 subtests[a]		Mean of 2 subtests		Mean of 3 subtests		Mean of 4 subtests		Mean of 5 subtests	
	.05	.01	.05	.01	.05	.01	.05	.01	.05	.01
Block Design	1.57	2.06	—	—	—	—	2.43	2.93	2.61	3.34
Information	1.23	1.62	—	—	1.73	2.13	1.97	2.38	2.06	2.64
Receptive Vocabulary	1.23	1.62	1.33	1.75	1.80	2.21	2.06	2.49	2.18	2.79
Object Assembly	1.57	2.06	—	—	—	—	2.31	2.79	2.47	3.16
Picture Naming	—	—	1.33	1.75	1.88	2.30	—	—	2.31	2.96

(Continued)

Table B-5 (Continued)

Age 4-0 to 4-5

Subtest	Mean of 2 subtests[b]		Mean of 3 subtests[c]		Mean of 4 subtests		Mean of 4 subtests		Mean of 4 subtests	
	.05	.01	.05	.01	.05	.01	.05	.01	.05	.01
Block Design	—	—	2.63	3.22	3.00	3.63	2.99	3.61	—	—
Information	—	—	2.07	2.53	—	—	—	—	2.29	2.77
Matrix Reasoning	—	—	2.08	2.55	2.19	2.65	2.17	2.62	—	—
Vocabulary	—	—	1.93	2.37	—	—	—	—	2.10	2.53
Picture Concepts	—	—	2.12	2.60	2.25	2.72	2.23	2.69	—	—
Symbol Search	1.50	1.97	—	—	—	—	—	—	—	—
Word Reasoning	—	—	1.80	2.21	—	—	—	—	1.89	2.29
Coding	1.50	1.97	—	—	—	—	—	—	—	—
Comprehension	—	—	—	—	—	—	—	—	—	—
Picture Completion	—	—	—	—	—	—	2.04	2.46	—	—
Similarities	—	—	—	—	—	—	—	—	1.65	2.00
Receptive Vocabulary	1.32	1.73	—	—	—	—	—	—	—	—
Object Assembly	—	—	—	—	2.25	2.72	—	—	—	—
Picture Naming	1.32	1.73	—	—	—	—	—	—	—	—

Subtest	Mean of 4 subtests		Mean of 5 subtests		Mean of 5 subtests		Mean of 7 subtests		Mean of 12 subtests	
	.05	.01	.05	.01	.05	.01	.05	.01	.05	.01
Block Design	—	—	3.25	4.15	—	—	3.58	4.25	4.02	4.69
Information	2.35	2.84	—	—	2.50	3.19	2.77	3.29	3.06	3.57
Matrix Reasoning	—	—	2.27	2.90	—	—	2.42	2.87	2.63	3.07
Vocabulary	2.16	2.61	2.27	2.90	—	—	2.50	2.97	2.73	3.19
Picture Concepts	—	—	—	—	2.34	2.99	2.50	2.97	2.73	3.19
Symbol Search	—	—	—	—	—	—	—	—	3.06	3.57
Word Reasoning	1.97	2.38	—	—	2.03	2.59	2.22	2.64	2.39	2.78
Coding	—	—	—	—	—	—	2.61	3.09	2.86	3.33
Comprehension	2.29	2.77	—	—	2.42	3.10	—	—	2.96	3.45
Picture Completion	—	—	2.11	2.69	—	—	—	—	2.39	2.78
Similarities	—	—	—	—	1.74	2.22	—	—	1.95	2.28
Receptive Vocabulary	—	—	—	—	—	—	—	—	—	—
Object Assembly	—	—	2.34	2.99	—	—	—	—	2.73	3.19
Picture Naming	—	—	—	—	—	—	—	—	—	—

(Continued)

Table B-5 (*Continued*)

Age 4-6 to 4-11

Subtest	Mean of 2 subtests[b]		Mean of 3 subtests[c]		Mean of 4 subtests		Mean of 4 subtests		Mean of 4 subtests	
	.05	.01	.05	.01	.05	.01	.05	.01	.05	.01
Block Design	—	—	2.20	2.70	2.50	3.02	2.47	2.98	—	—
Information	—	—	2.18	2.67	—	—	—	—	2.42	2.93
Matrix Reasoning	—	—	1.99	2.44	2.19	2.65	2.15	2.60	—	—
Vocabulary	—	—	2.01	2.47	—	—	—	—	2.18	2.63
Picture Concepts	—	—	1.96	2.40	2.14	2.58	2.10	2.53	—	—
Symbol Search	1.50	1.97	—	—	—	—	—	—	—	—
Word Reasoning	—	—	1.78	2.19	—	—	—	—	1.82	2.20
Coding	1.50	1.97	—	—	—	—	—	—	—	—
Comprehension	—	—	—	—	—	—	—	—	—	—
Picture Completion	—	—	—	—	—	—	1.96	2.37	—	—
Similarities	—	—	—	—	—	—	—	—	1.58	1.91
Receptive Vocabulary	1.50	1.97	—	—	—	—	—	—	—	—
Object Assembly	—	—	—	—	2.32	2.81	—	—	—	—
Picture Naming	1.50	1.97	—	—	—	—	—	—	—	—

Subtest	Mean of 4 subtests		Mean of 5 subtests		Mean of 5 subtests		Mean of 7 subtests		Mean of 12 subtests	
	.05	.01	.05	.01	.05	.01	.05	.01	.05	.01
Block Design	—	—	2.67	3.42	—	—	2.93	3.47	3.25	3.79
Information	2.47	2.98	—	—	2.63	3.37	2.93	3.47	3.25	3.79
Matrix Reasoning	—	—	2.30	2.95	—	—	2.49	2.95	2.72	3.18
Vocabulary	2.23	2.69	3.34	3.00	—	—	2.59	3.07	2.85	3.32
Picture Concepts	—	—	—	—	2.23	2.86	2.40	2.85	2.62	3.06
Symbol Search	—	—	—	—	—	—	—	—	3.05	3.56
Word Reasoning	1.88	2.27	—	—	1.91	2.45	2.08	2.47	2.23	2.60
Coding	—	—	—	—	—	—	2.59	3.07	2.85	3.32
Comprehension	2.10	2.53	—	—	2.19	2.80	—	—	2.62	3.06
Picture Completion	—	—	2.07	2.64	—	—	—	—	2.38	2.77
Similarities	—	—	—	—	1.62	2.07	—	—	1.78	2.07
Receptive Vocabulary	—	—	—	—	—	—	—	—	—	—
Object Assembly	—	—	2.46	3.15	—	—	—	—	2.95	3.44
Picture Naming	—	—	—	—	—	—	—	—	—	—

(Continued)

Table B-5 (Continued)

Age 5-0 to 5-5

Subtest	Mean of 2 subtests[b]		Mean of 3 subtests[c]		Mean of 4 subtests		Mean of 4 subtests		Mean of 4 subtests	
	.05	.01	.05	.01	.05	.01	.05	.01	.05	.01
Block Design	—	—	2.24	2.74	2.60	3.14	2.56	3.09	—	—
Information	—	—	1.82	2.23	—	—	—	—	1.99	2.41
Matrix Reasoning	—	—	1.86	2.29	2.06	2.49	2.01	2.43	—	—
Vocabulary	—	—	1.86	2.28	—	—	—	—	2.05	2.48
Picture Concepts	—	—	1.77	2.17	1.91	2.31	1.86	2.25	—	—
Symbol Search	1.50	1.97	—	—	—	—	—	—	—	—
Word Reasoning			1.67	2.04	—	—	—	—	1.76	2.13
Coding	1.50	1.97	—	—	—	—	—	—	—	—
Comprehension	—	—	—	—	—	—	—	—	—	—
Picture Completion	—	—	—	—	—	—	2.01	2.43	—	—
Similarities	—	—	—	—	—	—	—	—	1.60	1.93
Receptive Vocabulary	1.44	1.89	—	—	—	—	—	—	—	—
Object Assembly	—	—	—	—	2.43	2.94	—	—	—	—
Picture Naming	1.44	1.89	—	—	—	—	—	—	—	—

Subtest	Mean of 4 subtests		Mean of 5 subtests		Mean of 5 subtests		Mean of 7 subtests		Mean of 12 subtests	
	.05	.01	.05	.01	.05	.01	.05	.01	.05	.01
Block Design	—	—	2.80	3.58	—	—	3.05	3.62	3.42	4.00
Information	2.05	2.47	—	—	2.16	2.76	2.38	2.82	2.62	3.06
Matrix Reasoning	—	—	2.15	2.75	—	—	2.27	2.70	2.49	2.91
Vocabulary	2.10	2.54	2.23	2.85	—	—	2.46	2.92	2.72	3.17
Picture Concepts	—	—	—	—	1.97	2.52	2.05	2.43	2.22	2.59
Symbol Search	—	—	—	—	—	—	—	—	3.04	3.55
Word Reasoning	1.82	2.20	—	—	1.88	2.41	2.05	2.43	2.22	2.59
Coding	2.10	2.54	—	—	—	—	2.56	3.04	2.84	3.32
Comprehension	—	—	—	—	2.23	2.85	—	—	2.72	3.17
Picture Completion	—	—	2.15	2.75	—	—	—	—	2.49	2.91
Similarities	—	—	—	—	1.69	2.16	—	—	1.93	2.26
Receptive Vocabulary	—	—	—	—	—	—	—	—	—	—
Object Assembly	—	—	2.60	3.33	—	—	—	—	3.15	3.67
Picture Naming	—	—	—	—	—	—	—	—	—	—

(Continued)

Table B-5 (Continued)

Age 5-6 to 5-11

Subtest	Mean of 2 subtests[b]		Mean of 3 subtests[c]		Mean of 4 subtests		Mean of 4 subtests		Mean of 4 subtests	
	.05	.01	.05	.01	.05	.01	.05	.01	.05	.01
Block Design	—	—	2.16	2.65	2.51	3.03	2.47	2.99	—	—
Information	—	—	2.03	2.49	2.15	2.60	—	—	2.19	2.64
Matrix Reasoning	—	—	1.91	2.35	—	—	2.11	2.55	—	—
Vocabulary	—	—	2.11	2.58	—	—	—	—	2.31	2.79
Picture Concepts	—	—	1.82	2.23	2.01	2.43	1.97	2.38	—	—
Symbol Search	1.88	2.47	—	—	—	—	—	—	—	—
Word Reasoning	—	—	1.94	2.38	—	—	—	—	2.06	2.48
Coding	1.88	2.47	—	—	—	—	—	—	—	—
Comprehension	—	—	—	—	—	—	—	—	—	—
Picture Completion	—	—	—	—	—	—	2.24	2.70	—	—
Similarities	—	—	—	—	—	—	—	—	1.59	1.92
Receptive Vocabulary	1.44	1.89	—	—	—	—	—	—	—	—
Object Assembly	—	—	—	—	2.57	3.10	—	—	—	—
Picture Naming	1.44	1.89	—	—	—	—	—	—	—	—

Subtest	Mean of 4 subtests		Mean of 5 subtests		Mean of 5 subtests		Mean of 7 subtests		Mean of 12 subtests	
	.05	.01	.05	.01	.05	.01	.05	.01	.05	.01
Block Design	—	—	2.70	3.45	—	—	2.94	3.49	3.27	3.81
Information	2.24	2.71	—	—	2.35	3.01	2.61	3.09	2.87	3.35
Matrix Reasoning	—	—	2.26	2.89	—	—	2.42	2.87	2.64	3.09
Vocabulary	2.36	2.85	2.50	3.19	—	—	2.77	3.29	3.07	3.58
Picture Concepts	—	—	—	—	2.10	2.68	2.22	2.64	2.40	2.80
Symbol Search	—	—	—	—	—	—	—	—	3.62	4.23
Word Reasoning	2.11	2.55	—	—	2.20	2.81	2.42	2.87	2.64	3.09
Coding	—	—	—	—	—	—	3.30	3.92	3.70	4.32
Comprehension	2.17	2.62	—	—	2.27	2.90	—	—	2.74	3.20
Picture Completion	—	—	2.42	3.09	—	—	—	—	2.87	3.35
Similarities	—	—	—	—	1.63	2.08	—	—	1.81	2.11
Receptive Vocabulary	—	—	—	—	—	—	—	—	—	—
Object Assembly	—	—	2.77	3.54	—	—	—	—	3.37	3.93
Picture Naming	—	—	—	—	—	—	—	—	—	—

(Continued)

Table B-5 (*Continued*)

Age 6-0 to 6-11

Subtest	Mean of 2 subtests[b]		Mean of 3 subtests[c]		Mean of 4 subtests		Mean of 4 subtests		Mean of 4 subtests	
	.05	.01	.05	.01	.05	.01	.05	.01	.05	.01
Block Design	—	—	2.09	2.57	2.43	2.94	2.36	2.85	—	—
Information	—	—	2.28	2.80	—	—	—	—	2.55	3.09
Matrix Reasoning	—	—	1.93	2.36	2.20	2.65	2.11	2.55	—	—
Vocabulary	—	—	2.08	2.56	—	—	—	—	2.26	2.73
Picture Concepts	—	—	1.96	2.41	2.25	2.72	2.17	2.62	—	—
Symbol Search	1.88	2.47	—	—	—	—	—	—	—	—
Word Reasoning	—	—	2.04	2.50	—	—	—	—	2.19	2.64
Coding	1.88	2.47	—	—	—	—	—	—	—	—
Comprehension	—	—	—	—	—	—	—	—	—	—
Picture Completion	—	—	—	—	—	—	2.24	2.71	—	—
Similarities	—	—	—	—	—	—	—	—	2.06	2.49
Receptive Vocabulary	1.71	2.25	—	—	—	—	—	—	—	—
Object Assembly	—	—	—	—	2.87	3.46	—	—	—	—
Picture Naming	1.71	2.25	—	—	—	—	—	—	—	—

Subtest	Mean of 4 subtests		Mean of 5 subtests		Mean of 5 subtests		Mean of 7 subtests		Mean of 12 subtests	
	.05	.01	.05	.01	.05	.01	.05	.01	.05	.01
Block Design	—	—	2.58	3.30	—	—	2.78	3.30	3.08	3.60
Information	2.59	3.13	—	—	2.77	3.54	3.04	3.60	3.38	3.95
Matrix Reasoning	—	—	2.29	2.93	—	—	2.44	2.89	2.66	3.11
Vocabulary	2.30	2.77	2.41	3.09	—	—	2.62	3.11	2.88	3.37
Picture Concepts	—	—	—	—	2.36	3.02	2.52	2.99	2.76	3.22
Symbol Search	—	—	—	—	—	—	—	—	3.64	4.24
Word Reasoning	2.23	2.69	—	—	2.33	2.98	2.52	2.99	2.76	3.22
Coding	—	—	—	—	—	—	3.31	3.93	3.71	4.33
Comprehension	2.41	2.91	—	—	2.55	3.27	—	—	3.08	3.60
Picture Completion	—	—	2.44	3.13	—	—	—	—	2.88	3.37
Similarities	—	—	—	—	2.18	2.79	—	—	2.54	2.96
Receptive Vocabulary	—	—	—	—	—	—	—	—	—	—
Object Assembly	—	—	3.10	3.96	—	—	—	—	3.81	4.45
Picture Naming	—	—	—	—	—	—	—	—	—	—

(*Continued*)

Table B-5 (*Continued***)**

Age 7-0 to 7-3

Subtest	Mean of 2 subtests[b]		Mean of 3 subtests[c]		Mean of 4 subtests		Mean of 4 subtests		Mean of 4 subtests	
	.05	.01	.05	.01	.05	.01	.05	.01	.05	.01
Block Design	—	—	1.80	2.21	2.08	2.51	2.01	2.43	—	—
Information	—	—	2.21	2.71	—	—	—	—	2.49	3.00
Matrix Reasoning	—	—	1.94	2.38	2.27	2.75	2.21	2.67	1.91	2.30
Vocabulary	—	—	1.82	2.24	—	—	—	—	—	—
Picture Concepts	—	—	1.80	2.21	2.08	2.51	2.01	2.43	—	—
Symbol Search	1.88	2.47	—	—	—	—	—	—	—	—
Word Reasoning	—	—	1.87	2.29	—	—	—	—	1.98	2.39
Coding	1.88	2.47	—	—	—	—	—	—	—	—
Comprehension	—	—	—	—	—	—	—	—	—	—
Picture Completion	—	—	—	—	—	—	2.27	2.74	—	—
Similarities	—	—	—	—	—	—	—	—	1.67	2.01
Receptive Vocabulary	1.58	2.08	—	—	—	—	—	—	—	—
Object Assembly	—	—	—	—	2.77	3.34	—	—	—	—
Picture Naming	1.58	2.08	—	—	—	—	—	—	—	—

Subtest	Mean of 4 subtests		Mean of 5 subtests		Mean of 5 subtests		Mean of 7 subtests		Mean of 12 subtests	
	.05	.01	.05	.01	.05	.01	.05	.01	.05	.01
Block Design	—	—	2.18	2.79	—	—	2.31	2.73	2.52	2.94
Information	2.54	3.06	—	—	2.71	3.47	3.01	3.57	3.37	3.93
Matrix Reasoning	—	—	2.42	3.09	—	—	2.59	3.07	2.87	3.35
Vocabulary	1.97	2.38	2.03	2.59	—	—	2.21	2.62	2.40	2.80
Picture Concepts	—	—	—	—	2.18	2.79	2.31	2.73	2.52	2.94
Symbol Search	—	—	—	—	—	—	—	—	3.62	4.23
Word Reasoning	2.04	2.46	—	—	2.11	2.70	2.31	2.73	2.52	2.94
Coding	—	—	—	—	—	—	3.29	3.90	3.70	4.32
Comprehension	2.24	2.70	—	—	2.35	3.01	—	—	2.87	3.35
Picture Completion	—	—	2.49	3.18	—	—	—	—	2.97	3.46
Similarities	—	—	—	—	1.74	2.22	—	—	1.97	2.30
Receptive Vocabulary	—	—	—	—	—	—	—	—	—	—
Object Assembly	—	—	3.00	3.84	—	—	—	—	3.70	4.32
Picture Naming	—	—	—	—	—	—	—	—	—	—

(Continued)

Table B-5 (Continued)

Average for Ages 4-0 to 7-3

Subtest	Mean of 2 subtests[b]		Mean of 3 subtests[c]		Mean of 4 subtests		Mean of 4 subtests		Mean of 4 subtests	
	.05	.01	.05	.01	.05	.01	.05	.01	.05	.01
Block Design	—	—	2.20	2.69	2.53	3.06	2.49	3.01	—	—
Information	—	—	2.11	2.58	—	—	—	—	2.34	2.82
Matrix Reasoning	—	—	1.95	2.39	2.17	2.62	2.12	2.56	—	—
Vocabulary	—	—	1.98	2.42	—	—	—	—	2.14	2.59
Picture Concepts	—	—	1.90	2.33	2.10	2.54	2.05	2.48	—	—
Symbol Search	1.70	2.23	—	—	—	—	—	—	—	—
Word Reasoning	—	—	1.85	2.27	—	—	—	—	1.95	2.36
Coding	1.70	2.23	—	—	—	—	—	—	—	—
Comprehension	—	—	—	—	—	—	—	—	—	—
Picture Completion	—	—	—	—	—	—	2.12	2.56	—	—
Similarities	—	—	—	—	—	—	—	—	1.70	2.05
Receptive Vocabulary	1.50	1.97	—	—	—	—	—	—	—	—
Object Assembly	—	—	—	—	2.55	3.08	—	—	—	—
Picture Naming	1.50	1.97	—	—	—	—	—	—	—	—

Subtest	Mean of 4 subtests		Mean of 5 subtests		Mean of 5 subtests		Mean of 7 subtests		Mean of 12 subtests	
	.05	.01	.05	.01	.05	.01	.05	.01	.05	.01
Block Design	—	—	2.71	3.47	—	—	2.95	3.50	3.29	3.84
Information	2.38	2.88	—	—	2.53	3.24	2.81	3.33	3.11	3.63
Matrix Reasoning	—	—	2.28	2.91	—	—	2.43	2.88	2.66	3.11
Vocabulary	2.19	2.65	2.30	2.95	—	—	2.53	3.01	2.79	3.25
Picture Concepts	—	—	—	—	2.19	2.80	2.33	2.76	2.54	2.96
Symbol Search	—	—	—	—	—	—	—	—	3.34	3.90
Word Reasoning	2.01	2.43	—	—	2.08	2.66	2.27	2.69	2.46	2.88
Coding	—	—	—	—	—	—	2.97	3.53	3.31	3.87
Comprehension	2.22	2.68	—	—	2.34	2.99	—	—	2.84	3.31
Picture Completion	—	—	2.28	2.91	—	—	—	—	2.66	3.11
Similarities	—	—	—	—	1.77	2.26	—	—	2.01	2.34
Receptive Vocabulary	—	—	—	—	—	—	—	—	—	—
Object Assembly	—	—	2.73	3.49	—	—	—	—	3.31	3.87
Picture Naming	—	—	—	—	—	—	—	—	—	—

(Continued)

Table B-5 (*Continued*)

[a]In this column, the entries for Block Design and Object Assembly are compared to the mean of these two subtests. Similarly, the entries for Information and Receptive Vocabulary are compared to the mean of these two subtests.

[b]In this column, the entries for Symbol Search and Coding are compared to the mean of these two subtests. Similarly, the entries for Receptive Vocabulary and Picture Naming are compared to the mean of these two subtests.

[c]In this column, the entries for Block Design, Matrix Reasoning, and Picture Concepts are compared to the mean of these three subtests. Similarly, the entries for Information, Vocabulary, and Word Reasoning are compared to the mean of these three subtests.

Note. The table shows the minimum deviations from a child's average subtest scaled score that are significant at the .05 and .01 levels.

The following formula, obtained from Davis (1959), was used to compute the deviations from average that are significant at the desired significance level:

$$D = \text{CR} \times \text{SEM}_{((T/m) - Z_I)}$$

where

D = deviation from average
CR = critical ratio desired
$\text{SEM}_{((T/m) - Z_I)}$ = standard error of measurement of the difference between an average subtest scaled score and any one of the subtest scaled scores that entered into the average

The standard error of measurement can be obtained from the following formula:

$$\text{SEM}_{((T/m) - Z_I)} = \sqrt{\frac{\text{SEM}_T^2}{m^2} + \left(\frac{m-2}{m}\right)\text{SEM}_{Z_I}^2}$$

where

SEM_T^2 = sum of the squared standard errors of measurement of the m subtests
m = number of subtests included in the average
T/m = average of the subtest scaled scores
$\text{SEM}_{Z_I}^2$ = squared standard error of measurement of any one of the subtest scaled scores

The critical ratios used were based on the Bonferroni inequality, which controls the family-wise error rate at .05 (or .01) by setting the error rate per comparison at .05/m (or .01/m). The critical ratios at the .05 level are 2.39 for 3 subtests, 2.50 for 4 subtests, 2.58 for 5 subtests, 2.81 for 10 subtests, and 2.94 for 15 subtests. The critical ratios at the .01 level are 2.93 for 3 subtests, 3.02 for 4 subtests, 3.10 for 5 subtests, 3.30 for 10 subtests, and 3.37 for 15 subtests. For 6 and 7 subtests, the Bonferroni inequality critical ratios would be 2.64 and 2.69, respectively, at the .05 level and 3.14 and 3.19, respectively, at the .01 level.

The following example illustrates the procedure. We will determine the minimum deviation required for a 6-year-old child's score on the WPPSI–III Information subtest to be significantly different from his or her average score on the three standard Verbal subtests (Information, Vocabulary, and Word Reasoning) at the 95% level of confidence. We calculate SEM_T^2 by first squaring the appropriate average standard error of measurement for each of the three subtests and then summing the squares. These standard errors of measurement are in Table 4.3 (p. 57) in the Technical Manual.

$$\text{SEM}_T^2 = (1.24)^2 + (1.04)^2 + (.99)^2 = 3.599$$

We determine $\text{SEM}_{Z_I}^2$ by squaring the average standard error of measurement of the subtest of interest, the Information subtest:

$$\text{SEM}_{Z_I}^2 = (1.24)^2 = 1.53$$

The number of subtests, m, equals 3. Substituting these values into the formula yields the following:

$$\text{SEM}_{((T/m) - Z_I)} = \sqrt{\frac{3.599}{(3)^2} + \left(\frac{3-2}{3}\right)1.53} = .953$$

The value, .953, is then multiplied by the appropriate z value for the 95% confidence level to obtain the minimum significant deviation (D). Using the Bonferroni correction (.05/3 = .0167), we have a z value of 2.39.

$$D = 2.39 \times .953 = 2.28$$

The Bonferonni correction was not applied to the two-subtest mean comparisons.

Table B-6
Estimates of the Differences Obtained by Various Percentages of the WPPSI–III Standardization Sample When Each WPPSI–III Subtest Scaled Score Is Compared to the Mean Scaled Score for Any Individual Child

Age 2-6 to 3-11

Subtest	Verbal (core subtests)				Performance (core subtests)				General Language (core plus supplemental subtests)			
	10%	5%	2%	1%	10%	5%	2%	1%	10%	5%	2%	1%
Block Design	—	—	—	—	2.68	3.19	3.81	4.20	—	—	—	—
Information	1.88	2.24	2.67	2.94	—	—	—	—	—	—	—	—
Receptive Vocabulary	1.88	2.24	2.67	2.94	—	—	—	—	1.88	2.24	2.67	2.94
Object Assembly	—	—	—	—	2.68	3.19	3.81	4.20	—	—	—	—
Picture Naming	—	—	—	—	—	—	—	—	1.88	2.24	2.67	2.94

Subtest	Verbal (core plus supplemental subtests)				Full Scale (core subtests)				Full Scale (core plus supplemental subtests)			
	10%	5%	2%	1%	10%	5%	2%	1%	10%	5%	2%	1%
Block Design	—	—	—	—	3.49	4.15	4.95	5.46	3.75	4.47	5.33	5.87
Information	2.09	2.49	2.97	3.28	2.74	3.27	3.90	4.29	2.60	3.10	3.69	4.07
Receptive Vocabulary	2.21	2.63	3.14	3.45	2.94	3.50	4.17	4.59	2.82	3.36	4.00	4.41
Object Assembly	—	—	—	—	3.36	4.00	4.77	5.26	3.55	4.23	5.04	5.56
Picture Naming	2.09	2.49	2.97	3.28	—	—	—	—	2.67	3.19	3.80	4.19

Age 4-0 to 7-3

Subtest	Processing Speed (core plus supplemental subtests)				General Language (optional subtests)				Verbal (core subtests)			
	10%	5%	2%	1%	10%	5%	2%	1%	10%	5%	2%	1%
Block Design	—	—	—	—	—	—	—	—	2.14	2.56	3.05	3.36
Information	—	—	—	—	—	—	—	—	—	—	—	—
Matrix Reasoning	—	—	—	—	—	—	—	—	2.26	2.69	3.20	3.53
Vocabulary	—	—	—	—	—	—	—	—	—	—	—	—
Picture Concepts	—	—	—	—	—	—	—	—	—	—	—	—
Symbol Search	2.23	2.66	3.17	3.50	—	—	—	—	—	—	—	—
Word Reasoning	—	—	—	—	—	—	—	—	2.07	2.46	2.94	3.24
Coding	2.23	2.66	3.17	3.50	—	—	—	—	—	—	—	—
Receptive Vocabulary	—	—	—	—	2.00	2.39	2.85	3.14	—	—	—	—
Picture Naming	—	—	—	—	2.00	2.39	2.85	3.14	—	—	—	—

Subtest	Performance (core subtests)				Verbal (core subtests plus Comprehension)				Verbal (core subtests plus Similarities)			
	10%	5%	2%	1%	10%	5%	2%	1%	10%	5%	2%	1%
Block Design	2.98	3.55	4.23	4.66	—	—	—	—	—	—	—	—
Information	—	—	—	—	2.37	2.82	3.36	3.70	2.32	2.77	3.30	3.63
Matrix Reasoning	2.78	3.31	3.95	4.35	—	—	—	—	—	—	—	—
Vocabulary	—	—	—	—	2.34	2.79	3.33	3.66	2.35	2.80	3.33	3.67
Picture Concepts	3.06	3.65	4.35	4.79	—	—	—	—	—	—	—	—
Word Reasoning	—	—	—	—	2.21	2.63	3.14	3.45	2.27	2.70	3.22	3.55
Comprehension	—	—	—	—	2.44	2.91	3.47	3.82	—	—	—	—
Similarities	—	—	—	—	—	—	—	—	2.50	2.98	3.55	3.91
Object Assembly	—	—	—	—	—	—	—	—	—	—	—	—

(Continued)

Table B-6 (Continued)

Subtest	Performance (core subtests plus Object Assembly)				Performance (core subtests plus Picture Completion)				Verbal (core plus supplemental subtests)			
	10%	5%	2%	1%	10%	5%	2%	1%	10%	5%	2%	1%
Block Design	3.00	3.58	4.26	4.70	3.10	3.69	4.40	4.85	—	—	—	—
Information	—	—	—	—	—	—	—	—	2.43	2.90	3.46	3.81
Matrix Reasoning	3.04	3.62	4.32	4.76	3.02	3.59	4.29	4.72	—	—	—	—
Vocabulary	—	—	—	—	—	—	—	—	2.37	2.83	3.37	3.71
Picture Concepts	3.33	3.97	4.73	5.21	3.23	3.85	4.59	5.06	—	—	—	—
Symbol Search	—	—	—	—	—	—	—	—	—	—	—	—
Word Reasoning	—	—	—	—	—	—	—	—	2.31	2.75	3.28	3.62
Coding	—	—	—	—	—	—	—	—	2.61	3.11	3.70	4.08
Comprehension	—	—	—	—	—	—	—	—	—	—	—	—
Picture Completion	—	—	—	—	3.08	3.67	4.37	4.82	—	—	—	—
Similarities	—	—	—	—	—	—	—	—	2.66	3.17	3.78	4.17
Object Assembly	3.18	3.79	4.52	4.98	—	—	—	—	—	—	—	—

Subtest	Performance (core plus supplemental subtests)				Full scale (core subtests)				Full scale (core plus supplemental subtests)			
	10%	5%	2%	1%	10%	5%	2%	1%	10%	5%	2%	1%
Block Design	3.10	3.69	4.40	4.85	3.44	4.10	4.88	5.38	3.50	4.17	4.97	5.47
Information	—	—	—	—	2.84	3.38	4.03	4.44	2.96	3.53	4.21	4.64
Matrix Reasoning	3.17	3.78	4.51	3.97	3.32	3.96	4.72	5.20	3.45	4.11	4.90	5.40
Vocabulary	—	—	—	—	3.06	3.65	4.35	4.80	3.12	3.72	4.44	4.89
Picture Concepts	3.41	4.06	4.85	5.34	3.48	4.14	4.94	5.44	3.58	4.26	5.08	5.60
Symbol Search	—	—	—	—	—	—	—	—	3.58	4.27	5.09	5.61
Word Reasoning	—	—	—	—	2.89	3.44	4.10	4.52	2.96	3.52	4.20	4.63
Coding	—	—	—	—	4.09	4.88	5.82	6.41	4.14	4.93	5.88	6.48
Comprehension	—	—	—	—	—	—	—	—	3.26	3.88	4.63	5.10
Picture Completion	3.16	3.76	4.49	4.94	—	—	—	—	3.39	4.04	4.82	5.31
Similarities	—	—	—	—	—	—	—	—	3.17	3.78	4.51	4.97
Object Assembly	3.26	3.89	4.64	5.11	—	—	—	—	3.86	4.59	5.48	6.03

Note. The formula used to obtain the values in this table was obtained from Silverstein (1984):

$$SD_{Da} = 3\sqrt{1 + \overline{G} - 2\overline{T}_a}$$

where

SD_{Da} = standard deviation of the difference for subtest a
3 = standard deviation of the scaled scores on each of the subtests
$\overline{G}$ = mean of all the elements in the matrix (including 1s in the diagonal)
$\overline{T}_a$ = mean of the elements in row or column a of the matrix (again including 1s in the diagonal)

Table B-7
Reliability and Validity Coefficients of WPPSI–III Short Forms for 2-, 3-, and 4-Subtest Combinations for Ages 2-6 to 3-11

Two subtests				Three subtests					Four subtests					
Short form		r_{ss}	r	Short form			r_{ss}	r	Short form				r_{ss}	r
IN	PN[a]	.945	.730	IN	RV	OA	.951	.767	BD	RV	OA	PN	.949	.781
IN	RV[b]	.950	.729	IN	OA	PN	.949	.764	BD	IN	OA	PN	.951	.780
IN	OA	.927	.729	BD	RV	PN	.940	.762	BD	IN	RV	PN	.960	.778
RV	PN[b]	.942	.721	BD	IN	RV	.946	.761	IN	RV	OA	PN	.962	.778
RV	OA	.922	.720	BD	IN	PN	.944	.761						
OA	PN	.917	.718	RV	OA	PN	.946	.760						
BD	PN	.905	.717	IN	RV	PN[b]	.962	.747						
BD	IN	.919	.713	BD	IN	OA	.935	.744						
BD	RV	.912	.712	BD	RV	OA	.931	.744						
BD	OA[c]	.901	.633	BD	OA	PN	.929	.743						

Note. Abbreviations: BD = Block Design, IN = Information, RV = Receptive Vocabulary, OA = Object Assembly, PN = Picture Naming. The estimated Full Scale IQs associated with each short form are shown in Tables B-12, B-13, and B-14.
[a]This combination is useful for a rapid screening; it also has the highest *g* loadings.
[b]This combination is useful for a rapid screening.
[c] This combination is useful for examinees who are hearing impaired.

Table B-8
Reliability and Validity Coefficients of WPPSI–III Short Forms for 2-, 3-, 4-, and 5-Subtest Combinations for Ages 4-0 to 7-3

Combination								
Two subtests				Three subtests				
Short form		r_{xx}	r	Short form			r_{xx}	r
SS	WR	.908	.869	IN	SS	WR	.935	.909
IN	SS	.890	.868	SS	WR	SI	.949	.907
MR	WR	.936	.868	IN	SS	SI	.940	.906
PCm	SI	.949	.864	IN	VC	SS	.930	.905
IN	MR[a]	.921	.858	VC	SS	WR	.939	.903
WR	PCm	.939	.858	SS	WR	PCm	.938	.903
VC	PCm	.930	.857	SS	PCm	SI	.943	.903
MR	VC	.929	.856	BD	MR	VC	.942	.902
BD	VC	.906	.855	IN	SS	PCm[a]	.929	.902
IN	PCm	.923	.854	MR	VC	PCm	.947	.902
IN	CD[a]	.866	.822	IN	MR	SS[a]	.930	.896
BD	MR[b]	.914	.771	IN	MR	CD[a]	.926	.879
BD	PCn[b]	.911	.789	IN	MR	PCm[a]	.944	.896
BD	SS[b]	.890	.753	IN	CD	PCm[a]	.927	.876
BD	CD[b]	.886	.707	BD	MR	CD[a]	.924	.802
MR	PCn[b]	.936	.804	BD	SS	CD[b]	.918	.757
MR	SS[b]	.909	.795	BD	CD	PCm[a]	.924	.807
PCn	CD[b]	.905	.755	BD	SS	PCm[b]	.927	.833
IN	WR[c]	.934	.849	BD	PCm	OA[b]	.930	.800
				BD	PCn	SS[a, b]	.927	.828
				BD	PCn	CD[a, b]	.922	.812
				BD	PCn	PCm[a, b]	.939	.848
				BD	PCn	OA[a, b]	.928	.810
				MR	CD	PCm[a, b]	.933	.846
				PCn	SS	CD[a, b]	.927	.791
				PCn	SS	PCm[a, b]	.937	.863
				PCn	PCm	OA[a, b]	.938	.843
				BD	MR	PCm[d]	.940	.842
				MR	PCn	PCm[e]	.950	.870
				VC	WR	SI[f]	.965	.868

(Continued)

Table B-8 (*Continued*)

Combination										
Four subtests						Five subtests				
Short form				r_{xx}	r	Short form				r_{xx}	r
SS WR PCm SI				.959	.934	MR SS WR PCm SI				.966	.947
IN SS PCm SI				.954	.932	MR VC SS WR PCm				.962	.945
IN MR SS WR				.951	.929	IN MR VC SS PCm				.958	.944
IN VC SS PCm				.948	.929	IN MR SS PCm SI				.962	.944
VC SS WR PCm				.953	.929	MR WR CD PCm SI				.964	.944
BD VC SS WR				.946	.928	BD VC PCn SS WR				.957	.943
IN VC SS OA				.938	.928	BD VC SS WR PCm				.957	.943
IN SS WR PCm				.951	.928	IN MR SS WR PCm				.960	.943
MR VC SS WR				.953	.928	IN SS CO SI OA				.955	.943
MR WR PCm SI				.967	.928	MR VC SS PCm SI				.964	.943
IN MR SS PCm[a]				.948	.921	IN MR SS CD PCm[a]				.952	.914
IN MR SS CD[a]				.939	.885	BD MR PCn SS CD[b]				.952	.863
IN MR CD PCm[a]				.955	.919	BD MR PCn SS PCm[b]				.957	.896
BD MR SS CD[b]				.939	.821	BD MR PCn CD PCm[b]				.955	.891
BD MR SS PCm[b]				.946	.869	BD MR SS CD PCm[b]				.952	.866
BD MR PCn SS[b]				.946	.863	MR PCn SS CD PCm[b]				.960	.931
BD MR CD PCm[b]				.944	.857	BD PCn SS CD PCm[a, b]				.951	.871
BD PCn SS CD[b]				.938	.827	IN VC WR CO SI[h]				.973	.890
BD MR PCn CD[a, b]				.943	.857						
BD PCn CD PCm[a, b]				.943	.863						
MR PCn CD PCm[a, b]				.950	.886						
IN VC WR SI[g]				.968	.885						

Note. Abbreviations: BD = Block Design, IN = Information, MR = Matrix Reasoning, V = Vocabulary, PCn = Picture Concepts, SS = Symbol Search, WR = Word Reasoning, CD = Coding, CO = Comprehension, PCm = Picture Completion, SI = Similarities, OA = Object Assembly. The estimated Full Scale IQs associated with each short form are shown in Tables B-14, B-15, B-16, and B-17.

The highest *g* loadings on three Verbal subtests are for Word Reasoning, Information, and Vocabulary—the three subtests that form the Verbal IQ.

[a] Useful for a rapid screening.
[b] Useful for examinees who are hearing impaired.
[c] Highest *g* loadings on two Verbal subtests.
[d] Highest *g* loadings on three Performance subtests.
[e] Highest reliability on three Performance subtests.
[f] Highest reliability on three Verbal subtests.
[g] Highest *g* loadings on four subtests.
[h] Highest *g* loadings on five subtests.

Table B-9
Reliable and Unusual Scaled-Score Ranges for WPPSI–III Selected Subtest Combinations for Ages 2-6 to 3-11

Composite or short form			Reliable scaled-score range	Unusual scaled-score range	Composite or short form			Reliable scaled-score range	Unusual scaled-score range
Two subtests					**Three subtests (Continued)**				
IN	PN		3	4	BD	IN	RV	4	7
IN	RV		3	4	BD	IN	PN	4	7
IN	OA		3	6	RV	OA	PN	4	7
RV	PN		3	4	IN	RV	PN	4	5
RV	OA		3	6	BD	IN	OA	4	7
OA	PN		3	6	BD	RV	OA	4	7
BD	PN		3	6	BD	OA	PN	4	7
BD	IN		3	6					
BD	RV		3	6	**Four subtests**				
BD	OA		4	6	BD	RV	OA	PN	4	8
Three subtests					BD	IN	OA	PN	4	8
IN	RV	OA	4	7	BD	IN	RV	PN	4	7
IN	OA	PN	4	6	IN	RV	OA	PN	4	7
BD	RV	PN	4	7					

Note. Abbreviations: BD = Block Design, IN = Information, RV = Receptive Vocabulary, OA = Object Assembly, PN = Picture Naming.

The formula used to obtain the reliable scaled-score range is as follows (Silverstein, 1989):

$$R = q\sqrt{\frac{\sum \text{SEM}_i^2}{k}}$$

where

q = critical value (n/v) of the Studentized range for a specified probability level (.05 in this case)
SEM = standard error of measurement of the scores on subtest i
k = number of subtests in the short form

The formula used to obtain the unusual scaled-score range is as follows (Silverstein, 1989):

$$R = q \cdot \sigma \sqrt{1 - \frac{2\sum r_{ij}}{k(k-1)}}$$

where

q = critical value (n/v) of the Studentized range for a specified probability level (.10 in this case)
σ = standard deviation of the subtest scores
k = number of subtests in the short form
r_{ij} = correlation between subtests i and j

The following are the appropriate q values to use in the two formulas for ns (size of samples) ranging from 2 to 10 plus 15, with v (degrees of freedom) = ∞, at the .10 probability level and at the .05 probability level (.10 or .05): for 2, 2.33 or 2.77; for 3, 2.90 or 3.31; for 4, 3.24 or 3.63; for 5, 3.48 or 3.86; for 6, 3.66 or 4.03; for 7, 3.81 or 4.17; for 8, 3.93 or 4.29; for 9, 4.04 or 4.39, for 10, 4.13 or 4.47; and for 15, 4.47 or 4.80.

The table is read as follows: In the two-subtest short form composed of Information and Receptive Vocabulary, a range of 3 points between the two scores indicates a nonchance difference at the .05 level. A range of 4 occurs in less than 10% of the population and should be considered unusual, as should all ranges higher than 4 points. Less credence can be placed in a Composite score or short-form IQ when the scatter is larger than expected.

Table B-10
Reliable and Unusual Scaled-Score Ranges for WPPSI–III Selected Subtest Combinations for Ages 4-0 to 7-3

Composite or short form			Reliable scaled-score range	Unusual scaled-score range	Composite or short form			Reliable scaled-score range	Unusual scaled-score range
Two subtests					**Three subtests (Continued)**				
SS	WR		3	6	BD	SS	PCm	4	7
IN	SS		4	6	BD	PCm	OA	4	7
MR	WR		3	5	BD	PCn	SS	4	7
PCm	SI		3	6	BD	PCn	CD	4	7
IN	MR		3	5	BD	PCn	PCm	4	7
WR	PCm		3	5	BD	PCn	OA	4	7
VC	PCm		3	5	MR	CD	PCm	4	7
MR	VC		3	6	PCn	SS	CD	4	7
BD	VC		4	6	PCn	SS	PCm	4	7
IN	PCm		3	5	PCn	PCm	OA	4	7
IN	CD		4	6	BD	MR	PCm	4	7
BD	MR		4	5	MR	PCn	PCm	4	7
BD	PCn		3	6	VC	WR	SI	3	5
BD	SS		4	5					
BD	CD		4	6	**Four subtests**				
MR	PCn		3	6	SS	WR	PCm	SI	4	7
MR	SS		4	5	IN	SS	PCm	SI	4	7
PCn	CD		3	6	IN	MR	SS	WR	4	7
IN	WR		3	4	IN	VC	SS	PCm	4	7
Three subtests					VC	SS	WR	PCm	4	7
IN	SS	WR	4	7	BD	VC	SS	WR	5	7
SS	WR	SI	4	7	IN	VC	SS	OA	5	8
IN	SS	SI	4	7	IN	SS	WR	PCm	4	7
IN	VC	SS	4	7	MR	VC	SS	WR	4	7
VC	SS	WR	4	7	MR	WR	PCm	SI	4	7
SS	WR	PCm	4	7	IN	MR	SS	PCm	4	8
SS	PCm	SI	4	7	IN	MR	SS	CD	5	8
BD	MR	VC	4	7	IN	MR	CD	PCm	4	8
IN	SS	PCm	4	7	BD	MR	SS	CD	5	8
MR	VC	PCm	4	7	BD	MR	SS	PCm	4	7
IN	MR	SS	4	7	BD	MR	PCn	SS	4	8
IN	MR	CD	4	7	BD	MR	CD	PCm	4	8
IN	MR	PCm	4	7	BD	PCn	SS	CD	5	8
IN	CD	PCm	4	7	BD	MR	PCn	CD	4	8
BD	MR	CD	4	7	BD	PCn	CD	PCm	4	8
BD	SS	CD	5	7	MR	PCn	CD	PCm	4	8
BD	CD	PCm	4	7	IN	VC	WR	SI	4	6

(Continued)

Table B-10 (*Continued*)

Composite or short form					Reliable scaled-score range	Unusual scaled-score range
Five subtests						
MR	SS	WR	PCm	SI	4	8
MR	VC	SS	WR	PCm	4	8
IN	MR	VC	SS	PCm	5	8
IN	MR	SS	PCm	SI	4	8
MR	WR	CD	PCm	SI	4	8
BD	VC	PCn	SS	WR	5	8
BD	VC	SS	WR	PCm	5	8
IN	MR	SS	WR	PCm	5	8
IN	SS	CO	SI	OA	5	8
MR	VC	SS	PCm	SI	4	8
IN	MR	SS	CD	PCm	5	8
BD	MR	PCn	SS	CD	5	8
BD	MR	PCn	SS	PCm	5	8
BD	MR	PCn	CD	PCm	5	8
BD	MR	SS	CD	PCm	5	8

Composite or short form					Reliable scaled-score range	Unusual scaled-score range
Five subtests (Continued)						
MR	PCn	SS	CD	PCm	5	8
BD	PCn	SS	CD	PCm	5	8
IN	VC	WR	CO	SI	4	6
Six subtests						
MR VC PCn	WR	PCm	SI		4	8
BD IN MR	VC	PCn	WR		5	8
BD IN MR	VC	WR	PCm		4	8
Seven subtests						
MR VC PCn WR CD PCm SI					4	9
BD IN MR VC PCn SS WR					5	9
BD IN MR VC SS WR PCm					5	8

Note. Abbreviations: BD = Block Design, IN = Information, MR = Matrix Reasoning, VC = Vocabulary, PCn = Picture Concepts, SS = Symbol Search, WR = Word Reasoning, CD = Coding, CO = Comprehension, PCm = Picture Completion, SI = Similarities, OA = Object Assembly.

The formula used to obtain the reliable scaled-score range is as follows (Silverstein, 1989):

$$R = q \sqrt{\frac{\sum \mathrm{SEM}_i^2}{k}}$$

where

q = critical value (n/v) of the Studentized range for a specified probability level (.05 in this case)
SEM = standard error of measurement of the scores on subtest i
k = number of subtests in the short form

The formula used to obtain the unusual scaled-score range is as follows (Silverstein, 1989):

$$R = q \cdot \sigma \sqrt{1 - \frac{2\sum r_{ij}}{k(k-1)}}$$

where

q = critical value (n/v) of the Studentized range for a specified probability level (.10 in this case)
σ = standard deviation of the subtest scores
k = number of subtests in the short form
r_{ij} = correlation between subtests i and j

The following are the appropriate q values to use in the two formulas for ns (size of samples) ranging from 2 to 10 plus 15, with v (degrees of freedom) = ∞, at the .10 probability level and at the .05 probability level (.10 or .05): for 2, 2.33 or 2.77; for 3, 2.90 or 3.31; for 4, 3.24 or 3.63; for 5, 3.48 or 3.86; for 6, 3.66 or 4.03; for 7, 3.81 or 4.17; for 8, 3.93 or 4.29; for 9, 4.04 or 4.39; for 10, 4.13 or 4.47; and for 15, 4.47 or 4.80.

The table is read as follows: In the two-subtest short form composed of Information and Word Reasoning, a range of 3 points between the two scores indicates a nonchance difference at the .05 level. A range of 4 occurs in less than 10% of the population and should be considered unusual, as should all ranges higher than 4 points. Less credence can be placed in a Composite score or short-form IQ when the scatter is larger than expected.

Table B-11
Estimated WPPSI–III Full Scale IQs for Sum of Scaled Scores for 10 Best 2-Subtest Short Forms for Ages 2-6 to 3-11

Sum of scaled scores	Combination						
	C2	C3	C4	C5	C6	C7	C8
2	45	46	47	47	47	51	52
3	48	49	50	50	50	54	54
4	51	52	53	53	53	57	57
5	55	55	55	56	56	59	60
6	58	58	58	59	59	62	62
7	61	61	61	62	62	65	65
8	64	64	64	65	65	68	68
9	67	67	67	68	68	70	71
10	70	70	70	71	71	73	73
11	73	73	73	73	74	76	76
12	76	76	76	76	77	78	79
13	79	79	79	79	79	81	81
14	82	82	82	82	82	84	84
15	85	85	85	85	85	86	87
16	88	88	88	88	88	89	89
17	91	91	91	91	91	92	92
18	94	94	94	94	94	95	95
19	97	97	97	97	97	97	97
20	100	100	100	100	100	100	100
21	103	103	103	103	103	103	103
22	106	106	106	106	106	105	105
23	109	109	109	109	109	108	108
24	112	112	112	112	112	111	111
25	115	115	115	115	115	114	113
26	118	118	118	118	118	116	116
27	121	121	121	121	121	119	119
28	124	124	124	124	123	122	121
29	127	127	127	127	126	124	124
30	130	130	130	129	129	127	127
31	133	133	133	132	132	130	129
32	136	136	136	135	135	132	132
33	139	139	139	138	138	135	135
34	142	142	142	141	141	138	138
35	145	145	145	144	144	141	140
36	149	148	147	147	147	143	143
37	152	151	150	150	150	146	146
38	155	154	153	153	153	149	148

Note. The subtest combinations are as follows:

C2 = BD + RV	C4 = BD + IN	C7 = RV + PN[b]
C3 = RV + OA	C5 = IN + OA	IN + RV[b]
BD + PN	C6 = OA + PN	C8 = IN + PN[b]
BD + OA[a]		

Abbreviations: BD = Block Design, IN = Information, RV = Receptive Vocabulary, OA = Object Assembly, PN = Picture Naming.

Reliability and validity coefficients associated with each short-form combination are shown in Table B-7. See Exhibit 8-4 on pages 256–257, in *Assessment of Children: Cognitive Applications, Fourth Edition* (Sattler, 2001) for an explanation of the procedure used to obtain the estimated IQs.
[a]This combination is useful for examinees who are hearing impaired.
[b]This combination is useful for a rapid screening.

Table B-12
Estimated WPPSI–III Full Scale IQs for Sum of Scaled Scores for 10 Best 3-Subtest Short Forms for Ages 2-6 to 3-11

Sum of scaled scores	Combination								
	C2	C3	C4	C5	C6	C7	C8	C9	C10
3	42	42	43	44	45	45	45	46	50
4	44	44	45	46	47	47	47	48	52
5	46	47	47	48	49	49	49	50	54
6	48	49	49	51	51	51	51	52	56
7	50	51	51	53	53	53	54	54	57
8	52	53	53	55	55	55	56	56	59
9	55	55	55	57	57	57	58	58	61
10	57	57	58	59	59	59	60	60	63
11	59	59	60	61	61	61	62	62	65
12	61	61	62	63	63	63	64	64	67
13	63	64	64	65	65	65	66	66	69
14	65	66	66	67	67	68	68	68	70
15	68	68	68	69	69	70	70	70	72
16	70	70	70	71	71	72	72	72	74
17	72	72	72	73	73	74	74	74	76
18	74	74	75	75	75	76	76	76	78
19	76	76	77	77	78	78	78	78	80
20	78	79	79	79	80	80	80	80	82
21	81	81	81	81	82	82	82	82	83
22	83	83	83	84	84	84	84	84	85
23	85	85	85	86	86	86	86	86	87
24	87	87	87	88	88	88	88	88	89
25	89	89	89	90	90	90	90	90	91
26	91	91	92	92	92	92	92	92	93
27	94	94	94	94	94	94	94	94	94
28	96	96	96	96	96	96	96	96	96
29	98	98	98	98	98	98	98	98	98
30	100	100	100	100	100	100	100	100	100
31	102	102	102	102	102	102	102	102	102
32	104	104	104	104	104	104	104	104	104
33	106	106	106	106	106	106	106	106	106
34	109	109	108	108	108	108	108	108	107
35	111	111	111	110	110	110	110	110	109
36	113	113	113	112	112	112	112	112	111
37	115	115	115	114	114	114	114	114	113
38	117	117	117	116	116	116	116	116	115
39	119	119	119	119	118	118	118	118	117
40	122	121	121	121	120	120	120	120	118
41	124	124	123	123	122	122	122	122	120
42	126	126	125	125	125	124	124	124	122
43	128	128	128	127	127	126	126	126	124
44	130	130	130	129	129	128	128	128	126
45	132	132	132	131	131	130	130	130	128
46	135	134	134	133	133	132	132	132	130
47	137	136	136	135	135	135	134	134	131
48	139	139	138	137	137	137	136	136	133
49	141	141	140	139	139	139	138	138	135

(Continued)

Table B-12 (*Continued*)

Sum of scaled scores	Combination								
	C2	C3	C4	C5	C6	C7	C8	C9	C10
50	143	143	142	141	141	141	140	140	137
51	145	145	145	143	143	143	142	142	139
52	148	147	147	145	145	145	144	144	141
53	150	149	149	147	147	147	146	146	143
54	152	151	151	149	149	149	149	148	144
55	154	153	153	152	151	151	151	150	146
56	156	156	155	154	153	153	153	152	148
57	158	158	157	156	155	155	155	154	150

Note. The subtest combinations are as follows:

C2 = BD + RV + OA	C7 = BD + IN + PN
C3 = BD + OA + PN	C8 = IN + RV + OA
C4 = BD + IN + OA	C9 = IN + OA + PN
C5 = BD + RV + PN	RV + OA + PN
C6 = BD + IN + RV	C10 = IN + RV + PN[a]

Abbreviations: BD = Block Design, IN = Information, RV = Receptive Vocabulary, OA = Object Assembly, PN = Picture Naming.

Reliability and validity coefficients associated with each short-form combination are shown in Table B-7. See Exhibit 8-4 on pages 256–257 in *Assessment of Children: Cognitive Applications, Fourth Edition* (Sattler, 2001) for an explanation of the procedure used to obtain the estimated IQs.

[a]This combination is useful for a rapid screening.

Table B-13
Estimated WPPSI–III Full Scale IQs for Sum of Scaled Scores
for 4-Subtest Short Forms for Ages 2-6 to 3-11

Sum of scaled scores	Combination				Sum of scaled scores	Combination			
	C2	C3	C4	C5		C2	C3	C4	C5
4	41	42	45	46	43	105	105	105	105
5	43	44	46	47	44	107	106	106	106
6	45	45	48	49	45	108	108	108	108
7	46	47	49	50	46	110	110	109	109
8	48	49	51	52	47	111	111	111	111
9	49	50	52	53	48	113	113	112	112
10	51	52	54	55	49	115	114	114	114
11	53	53	56	56	50	116	116	115	115
12	54	55	57	58	51	118	118	117	117
13	56	57	59	59	52	120	119	118	118
14	58	58	60	61	53	121	121	120	120
15	59	60	62	62	54	123	123	121	121
16	61	61	63	64	55	124	124	123	123
17	63	63	65	65	56	126	126	125	124
18	64	65	66	67	57	128	127	126	126
19	66	66	68	68	58	129	129	128	127
20	67	68	69	70	59	131	131	129	129
21	69	69	71	71	60	133	132	131	130
22	71	71	72	73	61	134	134	132	132
23	72	73	74	74	62	136	135	134	133
24	74	74	75	76	63	137	137	135	135
25	76	76	77	77	64	139	139	137	136
26	77	77	79	79	65	141	140	138	138
27	79	79	80	80	66	142	142	140	139
28	80	81	82	82	67	144	143	141	141
29	82	82	83	83	68	146	145	143	142
30	84	84	85	85	69	147	147	144	144
31	85	86	86	86	70	149	148	146	145
32	87	87	88	88	71	151	150	148	147
33	89	89	89	89	72	152	151	149	148
34	90	90	91	91	73	154	153	151	150
35	92	92	92	92	74	155	155	152	151
36	93	94	94	94	75	157	156	154	153
37	95	95	95	95	76	159	158	155	154
38	97	97	97	97					
39	98	98	98	98					
40	100	100	100	100					
41	102	102	102	102					
42	103	103	103	103					

Note. The subtest combinations are as follows:

C2 = BD + RV + OA + PN   C4 = BD + IN + RV + PN
C3 = BD + IN + PN + OA   C5 = IN + RV + OA + PN

Abbreviations: BD = Block Design, IN = Information, RV = Receptive Vocabulary, OA = Object Assembly, PN = Picture Naming.

Reliability and validity coefficients associated with each short-form combination are shown in Table B-7. See Exhibit 8-4 on pages 256–257 in *Assessment of Children: Cognitive Applications, Fourth Edition* (Sattler, 2001) for an explanation of the procedure used to obtain the estimated IQs.

Table B-14
Estimated WPPSI–III Full Scale IQs for Sum of Scaled Scores
for 10 Best 2-Subtest Short Forms and Other Combinations for Ages 4-0 to 7-3

Sum of scaled scores	Combination										
	C2	C3	C4	C5	C6	C7	C8	C9	C10	C11	C12
2	45	46	47	47	47	48	48	48	48	49	52
3	48	49	50	50	50	50	51	51	51	52	54
4	51	52	53	53	53	53	54	54	54	55	57
5	54	55	55	56	56	56	56	57	57	57	60
6	57	58	58	59	59	59	59	59	60	60	62
7	60	61	61	62	62	62	62	62	63	63	65
8	63	64	64	65	65	65	65	65	65	66	68
9	66	67	67	68	68	68	68	68	68	69	71
10	69	70	70	71	71	71	71	71	71	72	73
11	72	73	73	74	73	74	74	74	74	74	76
12	75	76	76	77	76	77	77	77	77	77	79
13	78	79	79	80	79	80	80	80	80	80	81
14	82	82	82	82	82	83	83	83	83	83	84
15	85	85	85	85	85	85	85	86	86	86	87
16	88	88	88	88	88	88	88	88	88	89	89
17	91	91	91	91	91	91	91	91	91	91	92
18	94	94	94	94	94	94	94	94	94	94	95
19	97	97	97	97	97	97	97	97	97	97	97
20	100	100	100	100	100	100	100	100	100	100	100
21	103	103	103	103	103	103	103	103	103	103	103
22	106	106	106	106	106	106	106	106	106	106	105
23	109	109	109	109	109	109	109	109	109	109	108
24	112	112	112	112	112	112	112	112	112	111	111
25	115	115	115	115	115	115	115	114	114	114	113
26	118	118	118	118	118	117	117	117	117	117	116
27	122	121	121	120	121	120	120	120	120	120	119
28	125	124	124	123	124	123	123	123	123	123	121
29	128	127	127	126	127	126	126	126	126	126	124
30	131	130	130	129	129	129	129	129	129	128	127
31	134	133	133	132	132	132	132	132	132	131	129
32	137	136	136	135	135	135	135	135	135	134	132
33	140	139	139	138	138	138	138	138	137	137	135
34	143	142	142	141	141	141	141	141	140	140	138
35	146	145	145	144	144	144	144	143	143	143	140
36	149	148	147	147	147	147	146	146	146	145	143
37	152	151	150	150	150	150	149	149	149	148	146
38	155	154	153	153	153	152	152	152	152	151	148

Note. The subtest combinations are as follows:

C2 = IN + CD[a]	C4 = SS + WR	C8 = MR + PCn[b]	C10 = IN + MR[a]
PCn + CD[b]	C5 = PCm + SI	C9 = MR + WR	BD + MR[b]
C3 = IN + SS	C6 = BD + VC	VC + PCm	C11 = WR + PCm
BD + PCn[b]	C7 = MR + VC	BD + SS[b]	IN + PCm
BD + CD[b]		MR + SS[b]	C12 = IN + WR[c]

Abbreviations: BD = Block Design, IN = Information, MR = Matrix Reasoning, VC = Vocabulary, PCn = Picture Concepts, SS = Symbol Search, WR = Word Reasoning, CD = Coding, CO = Comprehension, PCm = Picture Completion, SI = Similarities, OA = Object Assembly.

Reliability and validity coefficients associated with each short-form combination are shown in Table B-8. See Exhibit 8-4 on pages 256–257 in *Assessment of Children: Cognitive Applications, Fourth Edition* (Sattler, 2001) for an explanation of the procedure used to obtain the estimated IQs.
[a] Useful for a rapid screening.
[b] Useful for examinees who are hearing impaired.
[c] Highest *g* loadings on two subtests.

Table B-15
Estimated WPPSI–III Full Scale IQs for Sum of Scaled Scores
for 10 Best 3-Subtest Short Forms and Other Combinations for Ages 4-0 to 7-3

Sum of scaled scores	Combination										
	C2	C3	C4	C5	C6	C7	C8	C9	C10	C11	C12
3	41	42	42	42	43	43	43	44	44	44	44
4	43	44	44	44	45	45	45	46	46	46	46
5	45	46	46	47	47	47	47	48	48	48	48
6	48	48	48	49	49	49	50	50	50	50	50
7	50	50	51	51	51	52	52	52	52	52	52
8	52	53	53	53	53	54	54	54	54	54	54
9	54	55	55	55	55	56	56	56	56	56	56
10	56	57	57	57	58	58	58	58	58	58	59
11	59	59	59	59	60	60	60	60	60	61	61
12	61	61	61	62	62	62	62	62	62	63	63
13	63	63	63	64	64	64	64	64	65	65	65
14	65	66	66	66	66	66	66	67	67	67	67
15	67	68	68	68	68	68	68	69	69	69	69
16	69	70	70	70	70	71	71	71	71	71	71
17	72	72	72	72	72	73	73	73	73	73	73
18	74	74	74	74	75	75	75	75	75	75	75
19	76	76	76	77	77	77	77	77	77	77	77
20	78	78	78	79	79	79	79	79	79	79	79
21	80	81	81	81	81	81	81	81	81	81	81
22	83	83	83	83	83	83	83	83	83	83	83
23	85	85	85	85	85	85	85	85	85	85	85
24	87	87	87	87	87	87	87	87	87	88	88
25	89	89	89	89	89	89	89	90	90	90	90
26	91	91	91	91	92	92	92	92	92	92	92
27	93	94	94	94	94	94	94	94	94	94	94
28	96	96	96	96	96	96	96	96	96	96	96
29	98	98	98	98	98	98	98	98	98	98	98
30	100	100	100	100	100	100	100	100	100	100	100
31	102	102	102	102	102	102	102	102	102	102	102
32	104	104	104	104	104	104	104	104	104	104	104
33	107	106	106	106	106	106	106	106	106	106	106
34	109	109	109	109	108	108	108	108	108	108	108
35	111	111	111	111	111	111	111	110	110	110	110
36	113	113	113	113	113	113	113	113	113	112	112
37	115	115	115	115	115	115	115	115	115	115	115
38	117	117	117	117	117	117	117	117	117	117	117
39	120	119	119	119	119	119	119	119	119	119	119
40	122	122	122	121	121	121	121	121	121	121	121
41	124	124	124	123	123	123	123	123	123	123	123
42	126	126	126	126	125	125	125	125	125	125	125
43	128	128	128	128	128	127	127	127	127	127	127
44	131	130	130	130	130	129	129	129	129	129	129
45	133	132	132	132	132	132	132	131	131	131	131
46	135	134	134	134	134	134	134	133	133	133	133
47	137	137	137	136	136	136	136	136	135	135	135
48	139	139	139	138	138	138	138	138	138	137	137
49	141	141	141	141	140	140	140	140	140	139	139

(Continued)

Table B-15 (*Continued*)

Sum of scaled scores	Combination										
	C2	C3	C4	C5	C6	C7	C8	C9	C10	C11	C12
50	144	143	143	143	142	142	142	142	142	142	141
51	146	145	145	145	145	144	144	144	144	144	144
52	148	147	147	147	147	146	146	146	146	146	146
53	150	150	149	149	149	148	148	148	148	148	148
54	152	152	152	151	151	151	150	150	150	150	150
55	155	154	154	153	153	153	153	152	152	152	152
56	157	156	156	156	155	155	155	154	154	154	154
57	159	158	158	158	157	157	157	156	156	156	156

(Continued)

Table B-15 (*Continued*)

Sum of scaled scores	Combination										
	C13	C14	C15	C16	C17	C18	C19	C20	C21	C22	C23
3	44	44	44	45	45	45	45	45	45	46	49
4	46	46	46	47	47	47	47	47	47	48	51
5	48	48	48	49	49	49	49	49	49	50	53
6	50	50	51	51	51	51	51	51	51	52	55
7	52	52	53	53	53	53	53	53	53	54	57
8	54	55	55	55	55	55	55	55	55	56	59
9	57	57	57	57	57	57	57	57	57	58	61
10	59	59	59	59	59	59	59	59	59	60	63
11	61	61	61	61	61	61	61	61	61	62	64
12	63	63	63	63	63	63	63	64	63	64	66
13	65	65	65	65	65	65	65	66	65	66	68
14	67	67	67	67	67	67	68	68	67	68	70
15	69	69	69	69	69	69	70	70	69	70	72
16	71	71	71	71	71	71	72	72	71	72	74
17	73	73	73	73	73	73	74	74	74	74	76
18	75	75	75	75	75	76	76	76	76	76	78
19	77	77	77	77	78	78	78	78	78	78	79
20	79	79	79	80	80	80	80	80	80	80	81
21	81	81	81	82	82	82	82	82	82	82	83
22	83	83	84	84	84	84	84	84	84	84	85
23	86	86	86	86	86	86	86	86	86	86	87
24	88	88	88	88	88	88	88	88	88	88	89
25	90	90	90	90	90	90	90	90	90	90	91
26	92	92	92	92	92	92	92	92	92	92	93
27	94	94	94	94	94	94	94	94	94	94	94
28	96	96	96	96	96	96	96	96	96	96	96
29	98	98	98	98	98	98	98	98	98	98	98
30	100	100	100	100	100	100	100	100	100	100	100
31	102	102	102	102	102	102	102	102	102	102	102
32	104	104	104	104	104	104	104	104	104	104	104
33	106	106	106	106	106	106	106	106	106	106	106
34	108	108	108	108	108	108	108	108	108	108	107
35	110	110	110	110	110	110	110	110	110	110	109
36	112	112	112	112	112	112	112	112	112	112	111
37	114	114	114	114	114	114	114	114	114	114	113
38	117	117	116	116	116	116	116	116	116	116	115
39	119	119	119	118	118	118	118	118	118	118	117
40	121	121	121	120	120	120	120	120	120	120	119
41	123	123	123	123	122	122	122	122	122	122	121
42	125	125	125	125	125	124	124	124	124	124	122
43	127	127	127	127	127	127	126	126	126	126	124
44	129	129	129	129	129	129	128	128	129	128	126
45	131	131	131	131	131	131	130	130	131	130	128
46	133	133	133	133	133	133	132	132	133	132	130
47	135	135	135	135	135	135	135	134	135	134	132
48	137	137	137	137	137	137	137	136	137	136	134
49	139	139	139	139	139	139	139	139	139	138	136

(*Continued*)

Table B-15 (Continued)

Sum of scaled scores	Combination										
	C13	C14	C15	C16	C17	C18	C19	C20	C21	C22	C23
50	141	141	141	141	141	141	141	141	141	140	137
51	143	143	143	143	143	143	143	143	143	142	139
52	146	145	145	145	145	145	145	145	145	144	141
53	148	148	147	147	147	147	147	147	147	146	143
54	150	150	149	149	149	149	149	149	149	148	145
55	152	152	152	151	151	151	151	151	151	150	147
56	154	154	154	153	153	153	153	153	153	152	149
57	156	156	156	155	155	155	155	155	155	154	151

Note. The subtest combinations are as follows:

C2 = BD + PCn + CD[a, b]
C3 = IN + MR + CD[a]
C4 = MR + CD + PCm[a, b]
C5 = IN + CD + PCm[a]
C6 = BD + MR + CD[a]
    BD + CD + PCm[a]
C7 = SS + PCm + SI
C8 = BD + PCn + OA[a, b]
    PCn + PCm + OA[a, b]
C9 = PCn + SS + PCm[a, b]

C10 = BD + PCn + SS[b]
    BD + PCn + PCm[a, b]
    PCn + SS + CD[a, b]
C11 = IN + SS + PCm[a]
C12 = SS + WR + PCm
    IN + MR + SS[a]
    MR + PCn + PCm[c]
C13 = BD + MR + VC
C14 = MR + VC + PCm
C15 = BD + SS + PCm[b]

C16 = BD + MR + PCm[d]
C17 = BD + SS + CD[b]
C18 = IN + SS + SI
C19 = IN + MR + PCm[a]
C20 = V + SS + WR
C21 = SS + WR + SI
    IN + VC + SS
    BD + PCm + OA[b]
C22 = IN + SS + WR
C23 = VC + WR + SI[e]

Abbreviations: BD = Block Design, IN = Information, MR = Matrix Reasoning, VC = Vocabulary, PCn = Picture Concepts, SS = Symbol Search, WR = Word Reasoning, CD = Coding, CO = Comprehension, PCm = Picture Completion, SI = Similarities, OA = Object Assembly.

Reliability and validity coefficients associated with each short-form combination are shown in Table B-8. See Exhibit 8-4 on pages 256–257 in *Assessment of Children: Cognitive Applications, Fourth Edition* (Sattler, 2001) for an explanation of the procedure used to obtain the estimated IQs.

The three Verbal subtests with the highest *g* loadings are the core Verbal subtests—Information, Vocabulary, and Word Reasoning.

[a] Useful for a rapid screening.
[b] Useful for examinees who are hearing impaired.
[c] Highest reliability on three Performance subtests.
[d] Highest *g* loadings on three Performance subtests.
[e] Highest reliability on three Verbal subtests.

Table B-16
Estimated WPPSI–III Full Scale IQs for Sum of Scaled Scores
for 10 Best 4-Subtest Short Forms and Other Combinations for Ages 4-0 to 7-3

Sum of scaled scores	Combination																
	C2	C3	C4	C5	C6	C7	C8	C9	C10	C11	C12	C13	C14	C15	C16	C17	C18
4	40	40	41	41	41	41	42	42	43	43	43	43	43	43	44	44	49
5	41	42	42	42	43	43	44	44	44	44	44	45	45	45	45	45	50
6	43	43	44	44	44	44	45	46	46	46	46	46	46	47	47	47	52
7	45	45	45	46	46	46	47	47	47	47	48	48	48	48	48	49	53
8	46	47	47	47	48	48	49	49	49	49	49	49	50	50	50	50	54
9	48	48	49	49	49	49	50	50	51	51	51	51	51	51	52	52	56
10	50	50	50	51	51	51	52	52	52	52	52	53	53	53	53	53	57
11	51	52	52	52	53	53	53	54	54	54	54	54	54	54	55	55	59
12	53	53	54	54	54	54	55	55	55	55	56	56	56	56	56	56	60
13	55	55	55	56	56	56	57	57	57	57	57	57	57	58	58	58	62
14	56	57	57	57	57	58	58	58	59	59	59	59	59	59	59	59	63
15	58	58	59	59	59	59	60	60	60	60	60	60	61	61	61	61	64
16	60	60	60	60	61	61	61	62	62	62	62	62	62	62	62	63	66
17	61	62	62	62	62	62	63	63	63	63	63	64	64	64	64	64	67
18	63	63	64	64	64	64	65	65	65	65	65	65	65	65	66	66	69
19	65	65	65	65	66	66	66	66	67	66	67	67	67	67	67	67	70
20	67	67	67	67	67	67	68	68	68	68	68	68	68	69	69	69	72
21	68	68	69	69	69	69	69	70	70	70	70	70	70	70	70	70	73
22	70	70	70	70	71	71	71	71	71	71	71	72	72	72	72	72	74
23	72	72	72	72	72	72	73	73	73	73	73	73	73	73	73	73	76
24	73	73	74	74	74	74	74	74	75	74	75	75	75	75	75	75	77
25	75	75	75	75	75	75	76	76	76	76	76	76	76	76	77	77	79
26	77	77	77	77	77	77	78	78	78	78	78	78	78	78	78	78	80
27	78	78	79	79	79	79	79	79	79	79	79	79	79	80	80	80	81
28	80	80	80	80	80	80	81	81	81	81	81	81	81	81	81	81	83
29	82	82	82	82	82	82	82	82	82	82	83	83	83	83	83	83	84
30	83	83	83	84	84	84	84	84	84	84	84	84	84	84	84	84	86
31	85	85	85	85	85	85	86	86	86	86	86	86	86	86	86	86	87
32	87	87	87	87	87	87	87	87	87	87	87	87	87	87	87	88	89
33	88	88	88	88	89	89	89	89	89	89	89	89	89	89	89	89	90
34	90	90	90	90	90	90	90	90	90	90	90	91	91	91	91	91	91
35	92	92	92	92	92	92	92	92	92	92	92	92	92	92	92	92	93
36	93	93	93	93	93	93	94	94	94	94	94	94	94	94	94	94	94
37	95	95	95	95	95	95	95	95	95	95	95	95	95	95	95	95	96
38	97	97	97	97	97	97	97	97	97	97	97	97	97	97	97	97	97
39	98	98	98	98	98	98	98	98	98	98	98	98	98	98	98	98	99
40	100	100	100	100	100	100	100	100	100	100	100	100	100	100	100	100	100
41	102	102	102	102	102	102	102	102	102	102	102	102	102	102	102	102	101
42	103	103	103	103	103	103	103	103	103	103	103	103	103	103	103	103	103
43	105	105	105	105	105	105	105	105	105	105	105	105	105	105	105	105	104
44	107	107	107	107	107	107	106	106	106	106	106	106	106	106	106	106	106
45	108	108	108	108	108	108	108	108	108	108	108	108	108	108	108	108	107
46	110	110	110	110	110	110	110	110	110	110	110	109	109	109	109	109	109
47	112	112	112	112	111	111	111	111	111	111	111	111	111	111	111	111	110
48	113	113	113	113	113	113	113	113	113	113	113	113	113	113	113	112	111
49	115	115	115	115	115	115	114	114	114	114	114	114	114	114	114	114	113

(Continued)

Table B-16 (*Continued*)

Sum of scaled scores	Combination																
	C2	C3	C4	C5	C6	C7	C8	C9	C10	C11	C12	C13	C14	C15	C16	C17	C18
50	117	117	117	116	116	116	116	116	116	116	116	116	116	116	116	116	114
51	118	118	118	118	118	118	118	118	118	118	117	117	117	117	117	117	116
52	120	120	120	120	120	120	119	119	119	119	119	119	119	119	119	119	117
53	122	122	121	121	121	121	121	121	121	121	121	121	121	120	120	120	119
54	123	123	123	123	123	123	122	122	122	122	122	122	122	122	122	122	120
55	125	125	125	125	125	125	124	124	124	124	124	124	124	124	123	123	121
56	127	127	126	126	126	126	126	126	125	126	125	125	125	125	125	125	123
57	128	128	128	128	128	128	127	127	127	127	127	127	127	127	127	127	124
58	130	130	130	130	129	129	129	129	129	129	129	128	128	128	128	128	126
59	132	132	131	131	131	131	131	130	130	130	130	130	130	130	130	130	127
60	133	133	133	133	133	133	132	132	132	132	132	132	132	131	131	131	128
61	135	135	135	135	134	134	134	134	133	134	133	133	133	133	133	133	130
62	137	137	136	136	136	136	135	135	135	135	135	135	135	135	134	134	131
63	139	138	138	138	138	138	137	137	137	137	137	136	136	136	136	136	133
64	140	140	140	140	139	139	139	138	138	138	138	138	138	138	138	137	134
65	142	142	141	141	141	141	140	140	140	140	140	140	139	139	139	139	136
66	144	143	143	143	143	142	142	142	141	141	141	141	141	141	141	141	137
67	145	145	145	144	144	144	143	143	143	143	143	143	143	142	142	142	138
68	147	147	146	146	146	146	145	145	145	145	144	144	144	144	144	144	140
69	149	148	148	148	147	147	147	146	146	146	146	146	146	146	145	145	141
70	150	150	150	149	149	149	148	148	148	148	148	147	147	147	147	147	143
71	152	152	151	151	151	151	150	150	149	149	149	149	149	149	148	148	144
72	154	153	153	153	152	152	151	151	151	151	151	151	150	150	150	150	146
73	155	155	155	154	154	154	153	153	153	153	152	152	152	152	152	151	147
74	157	157	156	156	156	156	155	154	154	154	154	154	154	153	153	153	148
75	159	158	158	158	157	157	156	156	156	156	156	155	155	155	155	155	150
76	160	160	159	159	159	159	158	158	157	157	157	157	157	157	156	156	151

Note. The subtest combinations are as follows:

C2 = BD + PCn + CD + PCm[a, b]
  MR + PCn + CD + PCm[a, b]
C3 = BD + MR + PCn + CD[a, b]
C4 = IN + MR + CD + PCm[a]
C5 = BD + MR + CD + PCm[b]
C6 = IN + VC + SS + OA
C7 = IN + MR + SS + CD[a]
  BD + PCn + SS + CD[b]
C8 = BD + MR + SS + CD[b]
  BD + MR + PCn + SS[b]
C9 = IN + MR + SS + PCm[a]

C10 = BD + VC + SS + WR
C11 = BD + MR + SS + PCm[b]
C12 = SS + WR + PCm + SI
  IN + SS + PCm + SI
C13 = IN + VC + SS + PCm
  MR + VC + SS + WR
C14 = VC + SS + WR + PCm
C15 = IN + MR + SS + WR
C16 = IN + SS + WR + PCm
C17 = MR + WR + PCm + SI
C18 = IN + VC + WR + SI[c]

Abbreviations: BD = Block Design, IN = Information, MR = Matrix Reasoning, VC = Vocabulary, PCn = Picture Concepts, SS = Symbol Search, WR = Word Reasoning, CD = Coding, CO = Comprehension, PCm = Picture Completion, SI = Similarities, OA = Object Assembly.

Reliability and validity coefficients associated with each short-form combination are shown in Table B-9. See Exhibit 8-4 on pages 256–257 in *Assessment of Children: Cognitive Applications, Fourth Edition* (Sattler, 2001) for an explanation of the procedure used to obtain the estimated IQs.
[a]This combination is useful for a rapid screening.
[b]This combination is useful for examinees who are hearing impaired.
[c]Highest *g* loadings on four subtests.

Table B-17
Estimated WPPSI–III Full Scale IQs for Sum of Scaled Scores
for 10 Best 5-Subtest Short Forms and Other Combinations for Ages 4-0 to 7-3

Sum of scaled scores	Combination													
	C2	C3	C4	C5	C6	C7	C8	C9	C10	C11	C12	CI3	C14	C15
5	39	40	40	40	40	41	41	41	41	42	42	42	42	48
6	40	41	41	41	42	42	42	42	43	43	43	43	43	49
7	42	42	42	43	43	43	43	44	44	44	44	44	45	50
8	43	44	44	44	44	45	45	45	45	45	46	46	46	51
9	44	45	45	45	46	46	46	46	46	47	47	47	47	53
10	46	46	46	47	47	47	47	48	48	48	48	48	49	54
11	47	48	48	48	48	48	49	49	49	49	49	49	50	55
12	48	49	49	49	50	50	50	50	50	51	51	51	51	56
13	50	50	50	51	51	51	51	51	52	52	52	52	52	57
14	51	52	52	52	52	52	53	53	53	53	53	53	54	58
15	52	53	53	53	54	54	54	54	54	55	55	55	55	60
16	54	54	54	55	55	55	55	55	56	56	56	56	56	61
17	55	56	56	56	56	56	57	57	57	57	57	57	58	62
18	57	57	57	57	58	58	58	58	58	58	58	59	59	63
19	58	58	58	59	59	59	59	59	60	60	60	60	60	64
20	59	60	60	60	60	60	61	61	61	61	61	61	61	65
21	61	61	61	61	62	62	62	62	62	62	62	62	63	66
22	62	62	62	63	63	63	63	63	63	64	64	64	64	68
23	63	64	64	64	64	64	64	65	65	65	65	65	65	69
24	65	65	65	65	66	66	66	66	66	66	66	66	67	70
25	66	66	66	67	67	67	67	67	67	68	68	68	68	71
26	67	68	68	68	68	68	68	69	69	69	69	69	69	72
27	69	69	69	69	70	70	70	70	70	70	70	70	70	73
28	70	70	71	71	71	71	71	71	71	71	71	71	72	75
29	71	72	72	72	72	72	72	72	73	73	73	73	73	76
30	73	73	73	73	74	74	74	74	74	74	74	74	74	77
31	74	75	75	75	75	75	75	75	75	75	75	75	76	78
32	76	76	76	76	76	76	76	76	77	77	77	77	77	79
33	77	77	77	77	77	78	78	78	78	78	78	78	78	80
34	78	79	79	79	79	79	79	79	79	79	79	79	79	81
35	80	80	80	80	80	80	80	80	80	81	81	81	81	83
36	81	81	81	81	81	82	82	82	82	82	82	82	82	84
37	82	83	83	83	83	83	83	83	83	83	83	83	83	85
38	84	84	84	84	84	84	84	84	84	84	84	84	85	86
39	85	85	85	85	85	85	86	86	86	86	86	86	86	87
40	86	87	87	87	87	87	87	87	87	87	87	87	87	88
41	88	88	88	88	88	88	88	88	88	88	88	88	88	90
42	89	89	89	89	89	89	89	90	90	90	90	90	90	91
43	90	91	91	91	91	91	91	91	91	91	91	91	91	92
44	92	92	92	92	92	92	92	92	92	92	92	92	92	93
45	93	93	93	93	93	93	93	93	93	94	94	94	94	94
46	95	95	95	95	95	95	95	95	95	95	95	95	95	95
47	96	96	96	96	96	96	96	96	96	96	96	96	96	97
48	97	97	97	97	97	97	97	97	97	97	97	97	97	98
49	99	99	99	99	99	99	99	99	99	99	99	99	99	99
50	100	100	100	100	100	100	100	100	100	100	100	100	100	100
51	101	101	101	101	101	101	101	101	101	101	101	101	101	101
52	103	103	103	103	103	103	103	103	103	103	103	103	103	102
53	104	104	104	104	104	104	104	104	104	104	104	104	104	103
54	105	105	105	105	105	105	105	105	105	105	105	105	105	105

(Continued)

Table B-17 (*Continued*)

Sum of scaled scores	C2	C3	C4	C5	C6	C7	C8	C9	C10	C11	C12	CI3	C14	C15
55	107	107	107	107	107	107	107	107	107	106	106	106	106	106
56	108	108	108	108	108	108	108	108	108	108	108	108	108	107
57	110	109	109	109	109	109	109	109	109	109	109	109	109	108
58	111	111	111	111	111	111	111	110	110	110	110	110	110	109
59	112	112	112	112	112	112	112	112	112	112	112	112	112	110
60	114	113	113	113	113	113	113	113	113	113	113	113	113	112
61	115	115	115	115	115	115	114	114	114	114	114	114	114	113
62	116	116	116	116	116	116	116	116	116	116	116	116	115	114
63	118	117	117	117	117	117	117	117	117	117	117	117	117	115
64	119	119	119	119	119	118	118	118	118	118	118	118	118	116
65	120	120	120	120	120	120	120	120	120	119	119	119	119	117
66	122	121	121	121	121	121	121	121	121	121	121	121	121	119
67	123	123	123	123	123	122	122	122	122	122	122	122	122	120
68	124	124	124	124	124	124	124	124	123	123	123	123	123	121
69	126	125	125	125	125	125	125	125	125	125	125	125	124	122
70	127	127	127	127	126	126	126	126	126	126	126	126	126	123
71	129	128	128	128	128	128	128	128	127	127	127	127	127	124
72	130	130	129	129	129	129	129	129	129	129	129	129	128	125
73	131	131	131	131	130	130	130	130	130	130	130	130	130	127
74	133	132	132	132	132	132	132	131	131	131	131	131	131	128
75	134	134	134	133	133	133	133	133	133	132	132	132	132	129
76	135	135	135	135	134	134	134	134	134	134	134	134	133	130
77	137	136	136	136	136	136	136	135	135	135	135	135	135	131
78	138	138	138	137	137	137	137	137	137	136	136	136	136	132
79	139	139	139	139	138	138	138	138	138	138	138	138	137	134
80	141	140	140	140	140	140	139	139	139	139	139	139	139	135
81	142	142	142	141	141	141	141	141	140	140	140	140	140	136
82	143	143	143	143	142	142	142	142	142	142	142	141	141	137
83	145	144	144	144	144	144	143	143	143	143	143	143	142	138
84	146	146	146	145	145	145	145	145	144	144	144	144	144	139
85	148	147	147	147	146	146	146	146	146	145	145	145	145	140
86	149	148	148	148	148	148	147	147	147	147	147	147	146	142
87	150	150	150	149	149	149	149	149	148	148	148	148	148	143
88	152	151	151	151	150	150	150	150	150	149	149	149	149	144
89	153	152	152	152	152	152	151	151	151	151	151	151	150	145

(Continued)

Table B-17 (Continued)

Sum of scaled scores	Combination													
	C2	C3	C4	C5	C6	C7	C8	C9	C10	C11	C12	CI3	C14	C15
90	154	154	154	153	153	153	153	152	152	152	152	152	151	146
91	156	155	155	155	154	154	154	154	154	153	153	153	153	147
92	157	156	156	156	156	155	155	155	155	155	154	154	154	149
93	158	158	158	157	157	157	157	156	156	156	156	156	155	150
94	160	159	159	159	158	158	158	158	157	157	157	157	157	151
95	161	160	160	160	160	159	159	159	159	158	158	158	158	152

Note. The subtest combinations are as follows:

C2 = BD + MR + PCn + CD + PCm[a]
C3 = MR + PCn + SS + CD + PCm[a]
    BD + PCn + SS + CD + PCm[a, b]
C4 = MR + WR + CD + PCm + SI
C5 = IN + MR + SS + CD + PCm[b]
    BD + MR + PCn + SS + CD[a]
C6 = BD + MR + SS + CD + PCm[b]
C7 = IN + SS + CO + SI + OA
C8 = BD + MR + PCn + SS + PCm[a]
C9 = BD + VC + PCn + SS + WR
C10 = MR + VC + SS + PCm + SI
C11 = MR + SS + WR + PCm + SI
    IN + MR + SS + PCm + SI
    BD + VC + SS + WR + PCm
C12 = IN + MR + VC + SS + PCm
C13 = MR + VC + SS + WR + PCm
C14 = IN + MR + SS + WR + PCm
C15 = IN + VC + WR + CO + SI[c]

Abbreviations: BD = Block Design, IN = Information, MR = Matrix Reasoning, VC = Vocabulary, PCn = Picture Concepts, SS = Symbol Search, WR = Word Reasoning, CD = Coding, CO = Comprehension, PCm = Picture Completion, SI = Similarities, OA = Object Assembly.

Reliability and validity coefficients associated with each short-form combination are shown in Table B-9. See Exhibit 8-4 on pages 256–257 in *Assessment of Children: Cognitive Applications, Fourth Edition* (Sattler, 2001) for an explanation of the procedure used to obtain the estimated IQs.

[a]This combination is useful for examinees who are hearing impaired.
[b]This combination is useful for a rapid screening.
[c]Highest *g* loadings on five subtests.

Table B-18
Estimated WPPSI–III Full Scale IQs for Sum of Scaled Scores
for Three 6-Subtest Short-Form Combinations for Ages 4-0 to 7-3

Sum of scaled scores	Combination			Sum of scaled scores	Combination			Sum of scaled scores	Combination			Sum of scaled scores	Combination		
	C2	C3	C4		C2	C3	C4		C2	C3	C4		C2	C3	C4
6	42	42	43	36	74	74	74	66	106	106	106	96	139	139	138
7	43	43	44	37	75	75	76	67	107	108	107	97	140	140	139
8	44	44	45	38	76	76	77	68	109	109	109	98	141	141	140
9	45	45	46	39	78	77	78	69	110	110	110	99	142	142	141
10	47	46	47	40	79	79	79	70	111	111	111	100	143	143	143
11	48	47	48	41	80	80	80	71	112	112	112	101	144	144	144
12	49	49	49	42	81	81	81	72	113	113	113	102	145	145	145
13	50	50	50	43	82	82	82	73	114	114	114	103	146	146	146
14	51	51	51	44	83	83	83	74	115	115	115	104	147	147	147
15	52	52	52	45	84	84	84	75	116	116	116	105	148	148	148
16	53	53	53	46	85	85	85	76	117	117	117	106	149	149	149
17	54	54	54	47	86	86	86	77	118	118	118	107	150	150	150
18	55	55	55	48	87	87	87	78	119	119	119	108	151	151	151
19	56	56	56	49	88	88	88	79	120	120	120	109	152	153	152
20	57	57	57	50	89	89	89	80	121	121	121	110	153	154	153
21	58	58	59	51	90	90	90	81	122	123	122	111	155	155	154
22	59	59	60	52	91	91	91	82	124	124	123	112	156	156	155
23	60	60	61	53	93	92	93	83	125	125	124	113	157	157	156
24	61	61	62	54	94	94	94	84	126	126	126	114	158	158	157
25	63	62	63	55	95	95	95	85	127	127	127	115	159	159	158
26	64	64	64	56	96	96	96	86	128	128	128				
27	65	65	65	57	97	97	97	87	129	129	129				
28	66	66	66	58	98	98	98	88	130	130	130				
29	67	67	67	59	99	99	99	89	131	131	131				
30	68	68	68	60	100	100	100	90	132	132	132				
31	69	69	69	61	101	101	101	91	133	133	133				
32	70	70	70	62	102	102	102	92	134	134	134				
33	71	71	71	63	103	103	103	93	135	135	135				
34	72	72	72	64	104	104	104	94	136	136	136				
35	73	73	73	65	105	105	105	95	137	138	137				

Note. The subtest combinations are as follows:

C2 = MR + VC + PCn + WR + PCm + SI[a]
C3 = BD + IN + MR + VC + PCn + WR[b]
C4 = BD + IN + MR + VC + WR + PCm[c]

Abbreviations: BD = Block Design, IN = Information, MR = Matrix Reasoning, VC = Vocabulary, PCn = Picture Concepts, SS = Symbol Search, WR = Word Reasoning, CD = Coding, CO = Comprehension, PCm = Picture Completion, SI = Similarities, OA = Object Assembly.

See Exhibit 8-4 on pages 256–257 in *Assessment of Children: Cognitive Applications, Fourth Edition* (Sattler, 2001) for an explanation of the procedure used to obtain the estimated IQs.
[a]The reliability and validity of this combination are r_{ss} = .975 and r = .945, respectively.
[b]The reliability and validity of this combination are r_{ss} = .968 and r = .948, respectively.
[c]The reliability and validity of this combination are r_{ss} = .968 and r = .946, respectively.

Table B-19
Estimated WPPSI–III Full Scale IQs for Sum of Scaled Scores
for Three 7-Subtest Short-Form Combinations for Ages 4-0 to 7-3

Sum of scaled scores	C2	C3	C4	Sum of scaled scores	C2	C3	C4	Sum of scaled scores	C2	C3	C4	Sum of scaled scores	C2	C3	C4
6	38	40	40	41	72	73	73	76	106	106	106	111	140	139	138
7	39	41	41	42	73	74	74	77	107	107	107	112	141	140	139
8	40	42	42	43	74	75	75	78	108	108	107	113	142	141	140
9	41	42	43	44	75	75	76	79	109	108	108	114	143	142	141
10	42	43	44	45	76	76	77	80	110	109	109	115	144	142	142
11	43	44	45	46	77	77	78	81	111	110	110	116	145	143	143
12	44	45	46	47	78	78	78	82	112	111	111	117	145	144	144
13	45	46	47	48	79	79	79	83	113	112	112	118	146	145	145
14	46	47	48	49	80	80	80	84	114	113	113	119	147	146	146
15	47	48	48	50	81	81	81	85	115	114	114	120	148	147	147
16	48	49	49	51	82	82	82	86	115	115	115	121	149	148	148
17	49	50	50	52	83	83	83	87	116	116	116	122	150	149	149
18	50	51	51	53	84	84	84	88	117	117	117	123	151	150	150
19	51	52	52	54	85	85	85	89	118	118	118	124	152	151	151
20	52	53	53	55	85	86	86	90	119	119	119	125	153	152	152
21	53	54	54	56	86	87	87	91	120	120	120	126	154	153	152
22	54	55	55	57	87	88	88	92	121	121	121	127	155	154	153
23	55	56	56	58	88	89	89	93	122	122	122	128	156	155	154
24	55	57	57	59	89	90	90	94	123	123	122	129	157	156	155
25	56	58	58	60	90	91	91	95	124	124	123	130	158	157	156
26	57	58	59	61	91	92	92	96	125	125	124	131	159	158	157
27	58	59	60	62	92	92	93	97	126	125	125	132	160	158	158
28	59	60	61	63	93	93	93	98	127	126	126	133	161	159	159
29	60	61	62	64	94	94	94	99	128	127	127				
30	61	62	63	65	95	95	95	100	129	128	128				
31	62	63	63	66	96	96	96	101	130	129	129				
32	63	64	64	67	97	97	97	102	131	130	130				
33	64	65	65	68	98	98	98	103	132	131	131				
34	65	66	66	69	99	99	99	104	133	132	132				
35	66	67	67	70	100	100	100	105	134	133	133				
36	67	68	68	71	101	101	101	106	135	134	134				
37	68	69	69	72	102	102	102	107	136	135	135				
38	69	70	70	73	103	103	103	108	137	136	136				
39	70	71	71	74	104	104	104	109	138	137	137				
40	71	72	72	75	105	105	105	110	139	138	137				

Note. The subtest combinations are as follows:

C2 = MR + VC + PCn + WR + CD + PCm + SI[a]
C3 = BD + IN + MR + VC + PCn + SS + WR[b]
C4 = BD + IN + MR + VC + SS + WR + PCm[c]

Abbreviations: BD = Block Design, IN = Information, MR = Matrix Reasoning, VC = Vocabulary, PCn = Picture Concepts, SS = Symbol Search, WR = Word Reasoning, CD = Coding, CO = Comprehension, PCm = Picture Completion, SI = Similarities, OA = Object Assembly.

See Exhibit 8-4 on pages 256–257 in *Assessment of Children: Cognitive Applications, Fourth Edition* (Sattler, 2001) for an explanation of the procedure used to obtain the estimated IQs.
[a]The reliability and validity of this combination are r_{ss} = .974 and r = .955, respectively.
[b]The reliability and validity of this combination are r_{ss} = .969 and r = .953, respectively.
[c]The reliability and validity of this combination are r_{ss} = .969 and r = .953, respectively.

APPENDIX C

TABLES FOR THE WECHSLER TESTS

Table C-1
Percentile Ranks and Suggested Qualitative Descriptions for Scaled Scores on the Wechsler Tests

Scaled score	Percentile rank	Three-category qualitative descriptions	Five-category qualitative descriptions
19	99		Exceptional strength or Very well developed or Superior or Excellent
18	99		
17	99		
16	98	Strength or Above average	
15	95		Strength or Well developed or Above average or Good
14	91		
13	84		
12	75		
11	63		
10	50	Average	Average
9	37		
8	25		
7	16		Weakness or Poorly developed or Below average or Poor
6	9		
5	5	Weakness or Below average	
4	2		Exceptional weakness or Very poorly developed or Far below average or Very poor
3	1		
2	1		
1	1		

TABLE C-2   **363**

Table C-2
Interpretive Rationales, Implications of High and Low Scores, and Instructional Implications for Wechsler Subtests

Ability	Background factors	Possible implications of high scores	Possible implications of low scores	Instructional implications
Arithmetic (AR)				
Quantitative knowledge (Gq) Short-term memory (Gsm) Fluid reasoning ability (Gf) Mathematical achievement (A3) Working memory (MW) Quantitative reasoning (RQ) Long-term memory Numerical reasoning ability Mental computation Application of basic arithmetical processes Concentration Attention Mental alertness Auditory sequential processing	Opportunity to acquire fundamental arithmetical processes Quality of preschooling or schooling Ability to attend to stimuli Ability to self-monitor	Good working memory Good ability in mental arithmetic Good ability to apply reasoning skills in the solution of mathematical problems Good ability to apply arithmetical skills in personal and social problem-solving situations Good concentration Good attention Good short-term memory Good ability to convert word problems into mathematical calculations Good ability to engage in complex thought patterns, mainly for upper-level items Good interest in school achievement	Poor working memory Poor ability in mental arithmetic Poor ability to apply reasoning skills in the solution of mathematical problems Poor ability to apply arithmetical skills in personal and social problem-solving situations Poor concentration Poor attention Poor short-term memory Poor ability to convert word problems into mathematical calculations Poor ability to engage in complex thought patterns, mainly for upper-level items Poor interest in school achievement Anxiety, blocking, or fear	Develop arithmetical skills Develop concentration skills Use concrete objects to introduce concepts Drill in basic skills Provide interesting "real" problems to solve Use exercises involving analyzing arithmetical word problems Increase attention span
Block Design (BD)				
Visual processing (Gv) Visualization (VZ) Spatial relations (SR) Visual-perceptual reasoning Visual-perceptual organization Visual-motor coordination Spatial perception Abstract conceptualizing ability Analysis and synthesis Speed of mental processing Nonverbal reasoning Planning ability Concentration Fine-motor coordination Visual-perceptual discrimination	Rate of motor activity Color vision Ability to work under time pressure Visual acuity Trial-and-error learning Motivation and persistence	Good perceptual reasoning Good perceptual organization Good spatial orientation Good visual-motor-spatial integration Good conceptualizing, analyzing, and synthesizing ability Good ability to evaluate a problem quickly and accurately Good speed and accuracy Good nonverbal reasoning ability Good trial-and-error methods Good vision Good hand-eye coordination Good attention to detail Good motivation and persistence	Poor perceptual reasoning Poor perceptual organization Poor spatial orientation Poor visual-motor-spatial integration Poor conceptualizing, analyzing, and synthesizing ability Poor ability to evaluate a problem quickly and accurately Poor speed and accuracy Poor nonverbal reasoning ability Poor trial-and-error methods Poor vision Poor hand-eye coordination Poor attention to detail Poor motivation and persistence	Use puzzles, blocks, Legos, spatial-visual tasks, perceptual tasks involving breaking down an object and building it up again, and art work with geometric forms and flannel board Focus on part-whole relationships and working with a model or a key Focus on activities involving recognition of visual details Increase motivation

(Continued)

Table C-2 (*Continued*)

Ability	Background factors	Possible implications of high scores	Possible implications of low scores	Instructional implications
Cancellation (CA)				
Processing speed (Gs) Perceptual speed (P) Rate of test taking (R9) Visual-motor coordination or dexterity Visual processing Speed of mental operation Scanning ability Psychomotor speed Short-term visual memory Visual recall Attention Concentration Fine-motor coordination Visual-perceptual discrimination	Rate of motor activity Motivation and persistence Visual acuity Ability to work under time pressure Cognitive flexibility	Good processing speed Good perceptual scanning ability Good perceptual recognition ability Good vision Good attention and concentration Good short-term memory Good cognitive flexibility Good ability to work under time pressure Good motivation and persistence	Poor processing speed Poor perceptual scanning ability Poor perceptual recognition ability Poor vision Poor attention and concentration Poor short-term memory Poor cognitive flexibility Poor ability to work under time pressure Poor motivation and persistence	Use scanning exercises, such as looking at two or more objects and deciding if they are the same or different Increase attention span Reinforce persistence Increase motivation Reduce stress of working under time pressure
Coding (CD)				
Processing speed (Gs) Rate of test taking (R9) Visual-motor coordination or dexterity Speed of mental operation Scanning ability Psychomotor speed Short-term visual memory Visual recall Attention Concentration Symbol-associative skills Visual processing Fine-motor coordination Numerical ability Visual-perceptual discrimination	Rate of motor activity Motivation and persistence Visual acuity Attention span Ability to work under time pressure Cognitive flexibility	Good processing speed Good visual sequential processing ability Good visual-motor dexterity Good vision Good attention and concentration Good ability to learn new material associatively and reproduce it with speed and accuracy Good scanning ability Good cognitive flexibility Good motivation and persistence Good pencil control Good ability to work under time pressure	Poor processing speed Poor visual sequential processing ability Poor visual-motor dexterity Poor vision Poor attention and concentration Difficulty in learning new material associatively and reproducing it with speed and accuracy Poor scanning ability Poor cognitive flexibility Poor motivation and persistence Poor pencil control Poor ability to work under time pressure	Use visual-motor learning exercises, such as developing a code for matching geometric figures and numbers, learning Morse Code, and working on tracing activities Improve scanning techniques aimed at identifying things that go together Reinforce persistence Reduce stress of working under time pressure Increase attention span Increase motivation

(*Continued*)

TABLE C-2   365

Table C-2 (*Continued*)

Ability	Background factors	Possible implications of high scores	Possible implications of low scores	Instructional implications
Comprehension (CO)				
Crystallized knowledge (Gc) Language development (LD) General information (KO) Verbal comprehension Social judgment Common sense Logical reasoning Application of practical knowledge and judgment in social situations Knowledge of conventional standards of behavior (fund of information) Reasoning Ability to evaluate past experience Moral and ethical judgment Long-term memory	Cultural opportunities Quality of preschooling or schooling Development of conscience or moral sense Alertness to environment	Good verbal comprehension Good social judgment Good common sense Good knowledge of rules of conventional behavior Good ability to organize knowledge Good ability to verbalize Social maturity Wide experience	Poor verbal comprehension Poor social judgment Poor common sense Poor knowledge of rules of conventional behavior Poor ability to organize knowledge Poor ability to verbalize Immaturity Limited experience	Help child understand social mores, customs, and societal activities, such as how other children react to things, how the government works, and how banks operate Discuss the actions of others to help child develop an awareness of social relationships and what others expect Encourage child to take others' points of view Role-play situations, such as reporting fires, calling police, and calling the plumber
Digit Span (DS)				
Short-term memory (Gsm) Working memory (MW) Memory span (MS) Rote memory Immediate auditory memory Attention Concentration Auditory sequential processing Numerical ability	Ability to passively receive stimuli Auditory acuity Ability to self-monitor Ability to use encoding strategies Ability to use rehearsal strategies	Good auditory sequential processing Good short-term auditory memory Good rote memory Good immediate recall Good attention and concentration Good encoding ability Good rehearsal strategies Good ability to self-monitor	Poor auditory sequential processing Poor short-term auditory memory Poor rote memory Poor immediate recall Poor attention and concentration Poor encoding ability Poor rehearsal strategies Poor ability to self-monitor	Emphasize listening skills by using sequencing activities, reading a short story and asking the child to recall details, and seeing whether the child can follow directions Develop visualization skills Use short and simple directions and repeat when necessary Use other memory exercises and memory games Decrease anxiety

(*Continued*)

Table C-2 (Continued)

Ability	Background factors	Possible implications of high scores	Possible implications of low scores	Instructional implications
Information (IN)				
Crystallized knowledge (Gc) General information (KO) Verbal comprehension Range of factual knowledge Fund of information Long-term memory	Natural endowment Richness of early environment Quality of preschooling or schooling Cultural opportunities Interests and reading patterns Alertness to environment Intellectual curiosity	Good range of factual knowledge Good knowledge of the cultural and educational environment Good long-term memory Enriched background Alertness and interest in the environment Intellectual ambitiousness Intellectual curiosity Urge to collect knowledge	Poor range of factual knowledge Poor knowledge of the cultural and educational environment Poor long-term memory Limited background Limited alertness and interest in the environment Limited intellectual ambitiousness Limited intellectual curiosity Limited urge to collect knowledge	Stress factual material by having child read newspaper articles, listen to television news broadcasts, discuss current events, and do memory exercises Use other enrichment activities, including activities centering on national holidays, science and social studies projects, and projects involving animals and their function in society
Letter–Number Sequencing (LN)				
Short-term memory (Gsm) Working memory (MW) Memory span (MS) Rote memory Immediate auditory memory Attention Concentration Auditory sequential processing Numerical ability	Ability to passively receive stimuli Auditory acuity Ability to self-monitor Ability to use encoding strategies Ability to use rehearsal strategies	Good auditory sequential processing Good short-term auditory memory Good rote memory Good attention and concentration Good encoding ability Good rehearsal strategies Good ability to self-monitor	Poor auditory sequential processing Poor short-term auditory memory Poor rote memory Poor attention and concentration Poor encoding ability Poor rehearsal strategies Poor ability to self-monitor	Emphasize listening skills by using sequencing activities, reading a short story and asking the child to recall details, and seeing whether the child can follow directions Develop visualization skills Use short and simple directions and repeat when necessary Use other memory exercises and memory games

(Continued)

TABLE C-2   **367**

Table C-2 (*Continued*)

Ability	Background factors	Possible implications of high scores	Possible implications of low scores	Instructional implications
Matrix Reasoning (MR)				
Fluid reasoning ability (Gf) Visual processing (Gv) Induction (I) Visualization (VZ) Visual-perceptual reasoning Visual-perceptual organization Reasoning ability Nonverbal reasoning Analogic reasoning Classification ability Ability to form analogies Attention to detail Concentration Spatial ability Visual-perceptual discrimination	Motivation and persistence Ability to work toward a goal Ability to use trial and error Visual acuity	Good visual-perceptual reasoning ability Good perceptual organization ability Good reasoning ability Good attention to detail Good concentration Good vision Good motivation and persistence	Poor visual-perceptual reasoning ability Poor perceptual organization ability Poor reasoning ability Poor attention to detail Poor concentration Poor vision Poor motivation and persistence	Use puzzles, blocks, Legos, spatial-visual tasks, perceptual tasks involving breaking down an object and building it up again, and art work with geometric forms and flannel board Focus on part-whole relationships Use sequencing tasks
Object Assembly (OA)				
Visual processing (Gv) Spatial relations (SR) Closure speed (CS) Visual-perceptual organization Visual-perceptual discrimination Visual-motor coordination Ability to synthesize concrete parts into meaningful wholes Speed of mental processing Fine-motor coordination Nonverbal reasoning Perception of meaningful stimuli Analysis and synthesis Psychomotor speed	Rate of motor activity Familiarity with figures and puzzles Motivation and persistence Experience with part-whole relationships Ability to work toward an unknown goal Ability to work under time pressure Trial-and-error learning Visual acuity	Good visual-perceptual organization Good visual-motor coordination Good ability to visualize a whole from its parts Good ability to perceive a whole, with critical understanding of the relationships of the individual parts Good trial and error ability Experience in assembling puzzles Good motivation and persistence Good ability to work under time pressure	Poor visual-perceptual organization Poor visual-motor coordination Poor ability to visualize a whole from its parts Poor ability to perceive a whole, with critical understanding of the relationships of the individual parts Poor trial and error ability Limited experience in assembling puzzles Poor motivation and persistence Poor ability to work under time pressure	Develop perceptual and psychomotor skills through guided practice in assembling parts into familiar configurations Encourage trial-and-error activities Reinforce persistence Work with puzzles and activities centering on recognition of missing body parts Employ construction, cutting, and pasting activities Focus on interpretation of wholes from minimal cues

(Continued)

Table C-2 (*Continued*)

Ability	Background factors	Possible implications of high scores	Possible implications of low scores	Instructional implications
Picture Arrangement (PA)				
Visual processing (Gv) Crystallized knowledge (Gc) General information (KO) Visualization (VZ) Visual-perceptual organization Planning ability Interpretation of social situations Nonverbal reasoning ability Attention to details Alertness Common sense Anticipation of consequences	Cultural opportunities Ability to work under time pressure Ability to infer cause-and-effect relationships Visual acuity	Good visual-perceptual organization Good planning ability Good ability to interpret social situations Good nonverbal reasoning ability Attentive to detail Good ability to synthesize parts into intelligible wholes Good ability to work under time pressure	Poor visual-perceptual organization Poor planning ability Poor ability to interpret social situations Poor nonverbal reasoning ability Inattentive to detail Poor ability to synthesize parts into intelligible wholes Poor ability to work under time pressure	Focus on cause-and-effect relationships, logical sequential presentations, and part-whole relationships Use story completion exercises Discuss alternative behaviors and endings in stories and events
Picture Completion (PCm)				
Crystallized knowledge (Gc) Visual processing (Gv) Flexibility of closure (CF) General information (KO) Visual-perceptual reasoning Visual-perceptual organization Visual-perceptual discrimination Visual long-term memory Ability to differentiate essential from nonessential details Identification of familiar objects (visual recognition) Concentration on visually perceived material Alertness to detail Reasoning Speed of mental processing Scanning ability Attention Nonverbal reasoning Spatial perception Perception of meaningful stimuli	Experiences Alertness to environment Concentration Ability to work under time pressure Visual acuity Willingness to guess when uncertain	Good visual-perceptual reasoning Good perception and concentration Good alertness to details Good ability to differentiate between essential and nonessential details Good vision	Poor visual-perceptual reasoning Poor perception and concentration Poor alertness to details Poor ability to differentiate between essential and nonessential details Poor vision Preoccupation with irrelevant details Anxiety Negativism	Focus on visual learning techniques stressing individual parts that make up the whole Use perceptual activities that focus on recognizing objects, describing objects, and attention to details (e.g., maps and art work) Improve scanning techniques aimed at identifying missing elements in pictures

(Continued)

TABLE C-2   **369**

Table C-2 (Continued)

Ability	Background factors	Possible implications of high scores	Possible implications of low scores	Instructional implications
Picture Concepts (PCn)				
Fluid reasoning ability (Gf) Crystallized knowledge (Gc) Induction (I) Lexical knowledge (VL) Visual-perceptual reasoning Conceptual thinking Language ability Ability to separate essential from nonessential details Nonverbal reasoning Visual-perceptual organization Visual-perceptual discrimination Visual processing Perception of meaningful stimuli Reasoning	Education Cultural opportunities Interests and reading patterns Extent of outside reading Cognitive flexibility Intellectual curiosity Quality of preschooling or schooling Visual acuity	Good perceptual reasoning Good conceptual thinking Good ability to see relationships Good ability to use logical and abstract thinking Good ability to discriminate fundamental from superficial relationships Good ability to select appropriate relationships between two objects or concepts Good vision Flexibility of thought processes	Poor perceptual reasoning Poor conceptual thinking Poor ability to see relationships Poor ability to use logical and abstract thinking Poor ability to discriminate fundamental from superficial relationships Poor ability to select appropriate relationships between two objects or concepts Poor vision Rigidity of thought processes	Focus on describing the parts of objects Focus on describing recognition of differences and likenesses in shapes, textures, and daily surroundings Use exercises involving classifications and generalizations
Picture Naming (PN)				
Crystallized knowledge (Gc) Language development (LD) Lexical knowledge (VL) Word knowledge Verbal comprehension Acquired knowledge Fund of information Long-term memory Perception of meaningful stimuli Visual memory Visual processing Visual-perceptual discrimination	Education Cultural opportunities at home Interests and reading patterns Extent of outside reading Richness of early environment Quality of preschooling or schooling Visual acuity	Good word knowledge Good verbal comprehension Good verbal skills and language development Good family or cultural background Good preschooling or schooling Good ability to conceptualize Intellectual striving	Poor word knowledge Poor verbal comprehension Poor verbal skills and language development Limited family or cultural background Limited preschooling or schooling Poor ability to conceptualize Limited intellectual striving English as a second language	Develop working vocabulary Encourage child to discuss experiences, ask questions, and make a dictionary Use other verbal enrichment exercises, including Scrabble, analogy, and other word games

(Continued)

Table C-2 (*Continued*)

Ability	Background factors	Possible implications of high scores	Possible implications of low scores	Instructional implications
Receptive Vocabulary (RV)				
Crystallized knowledge (Gc) Language development (LD) Lexical knowledge (VL) Word knowledge Verbal comprehension Fund of information Long-term memory Perception of meaningful stimuli Visual memory Visual processing Visual-perceptual discrimination	Education Cultural opportunities at home Interests and reading patterns Richness of early environment Quality of preschooling or schooling Extent of outside reading School learning Intellectual curiosity Visual acuity	Good word knowledge Good verbal comprehension Good verbal skills and language development Good family or cultural background Good preschooling or schooling Good ability to conceptualize Intellectual striving	Poor word knowledge Poor verbal comprehension Poor verbal skills and language development Limited family or cultural background Limited preschooling or schooling Poor ability to conceptualize Limited intellectual striving English as a second language	Develop working vocabulary Encourage child to discuss experiences, ask questions, and make a dictionary Use other verbal enrichment exercises, including Scrabble, analogy, and other word games
Similarities (SI)				
Crystallized knowledge (Gc) Language development (LD) Lexical knowledge (VL) Verbal comprehension Verbal concept formation Abstract thinking ability Reasoning ability Capacity for associative thinking Ability to separate essential from nonessential details Long-term memory Vocabulary	Education Cultural opportunities Richness of early environment Interests and reading patterns Extent of outside reading Cognitive flexibility	Good verbal comprehension Good conceptual thinking Good ability to see relationships Good ability to use logical and abstract thinking Good ability to discriminate fundamental from superficial relationships Good ability to select and verbalize appropriate relationships between two objects or concepts Flexibility of thought processes	Poor verbal comprehension Poor conceptual thinking Poor ability to see relationships Poor ability to use logical and abstract thinking Poor ability to discriminate fundamental from superficial relationships Poor ability to select and verbalize appropriate relationships between two objects or concepts Rigidity of thought processes	Focus on recognition of differences and likenesses in shapes, textures, and daily surroundings Provide activities involving sorting objects or pictures Stress language development, synonyms and antonyms, and exercises involving abstract words, classifications, and generalizations

(*Continued*)

TABLE C-2   **371**

Table C-2 (*Continued*)

Ability	Background factors	Possible implications of high scores	Possible implications of low scores	Instructional implications
Symbol Search (SS)				
Processing speed (Gs) Perceptual speed (P) Rate of test taking (R9) Visual-perceptual discrimination Speed of mental processing Scanning ability Psychomotor speed Attention Concentration Short-term visual memory Visual-motor coordination or dexterity Fine-motor coordination	Rate of motor activity Motivation and persistence Ability to work under time pressure Visual acuity Cognitive flexibility	Good processing speed Good perceptual discrimination ability Good attention and concentration Good short-term visual memory Good cognitive flexibility Good vision Good motivation and persistence Good ability to work under time pressure	Poor processing speed Poor perceptual discrimination ability Poor attention and concentration Poor short-term visual memory Poor cognitive flexibility Poor vision Poor motivation and persistence Poor ability to work under time pressure	Use scanning exercises, such as looking at two or more objects and deciding if they are the same or different Reinforce persistence Reduce stress of working under time pressure Increase attention span Increase motivation
Vocabulary (VC)				
Crystallized knowledge (Gc) Language development (LD) Lexical knowledge (VL) Verbal comprehension Vocabulary Word knowledge Fund of information Richness of ideas Long-term memory Verbal fluency Conceptual thinking	Education Cultural opportunities Interests and reading patterns Extent of outside reading Richness of early environment Quality of preschooling or schooling Intellectual curiosity	Good word knowledge Good verbal comprehension Good verbal skills Good language development Good ability to conceptualize Good intellectual striving Good family or cultural background Good preschooling or schooling Good encouragement of verbalization in family	Poor word knowledge Poor verbal comprehension Poor verbal skills Poor language development Poor ability to conceptualize Limited intellectual striving Limited family or cultural background Limited preschooling or schooling Limited encouragement of verbalization in family English as a second language	Develop working vocabulary Encourage child to discuss experiences, ask questions, and make a working vocabulary with cards and definitions Use other verbal enrichment exercises, including Scrabble, analogy, and other word games Encourage child to write about his or her activities and to keep a diary

(*Continued*)

Table C-2 (Continued)

Ability	Background factors	Possible implications of high scores	Possible implications of low scores	Instructional implications
Word Reasoning (WR)				
Crystallized knowledge (Gc) Fluid reasoning ability (Gf) Language development (LD) Lexical knowledge (VL) Induction (I) Verbal comprehension Verbal reasoning Analogic reasoning Capacity for associative thinking Integration and synthesizing ability Ability to generate alternative concepts Long-term memory Attention Conceptual thinking Short-term memory Vocabulary Reasoning	Education Cultural opportunities Interests and reading patterns Extent of outside reading Cognitive flexibility Attention Intellectual curiosity Achievement orientation	Good verbal comprehension Good analogic reasoning ability Good integration and synthesizing ability Good ability to generate alternative concepts Good ability to see relationships Good long-term memory Good vocabulary Good attention Good cognitive flexibility Good achievement orientation	Poor verbal comprehension Poor analogic reasoning ability Poor integration and synthesizing ability Poor ability to generate alternative concepts Poor ability to see relationships Poor long-term memory Poor vocabulary Poor attention Poor cognitive flexibility Poor achievement orientation	Focus on reasoning tasks Develop understanding of how to use information in a logical manner Use guessing games such as "20 Questions"

Note. Abbreviations for the broad and narrow abilities in the Cattell-Horn-Carroll (CHC) model are shown within the parentheses. Table C-3 defines the CHC broad and narrow abilities associated with the Wechsler subtests, and Table C-4 shows the CHC broad and narrow abilities associated with the Wechsler subtests in grid form.

Crystallized knowledge is also referred to as crystallized intelligence or crystallized ability. Fluid reasoning ability is also referred to as fluid reasoning or fluid intelligence.

Select the appropriate implication(s) based on the entire test protocol and background information.

Source: The CHC broad and narrow abilities adapted, in part, from Flanagan, McGrew, and Ortiz (2000) and Horn (1987, 1998).

TABLE C-3   **373**

Table C-3
Definitions of Broad and Narrow Abilities in the Cattell-Horn-Carroll (CHC) Model Associated with Wechsler Subtests

Broad and narrow abilities	*Subtests*
Crystallized Knowledge (Gc): The ability to use the knowledge base accumulated over time in the process of acculturation.	Comprehension, Information, Picture Arrangement, Picture Completion, Picture Concepts, Picture Naming, Receptive Vocabulary, Similarities, Vocabulary, Word Reasoning
General Information (KO): The ability to use a range of general knowledge.	Comprehension, Information, Picture Arrangement, Picture Completion
Language Development (LD): The ability to understand spoken native language.	Comprehension, Picture Naming, Receptive Vocabulary, Similarities, Vocabulary, Word Reasoning
Lexical Knowledge (VL): The ability to use and understand words.	Picture Concepts, Picture Naming, Receptive Vocabulary, Similarities, Vocabulary, Word Reasoning
Fluid reasoning ability (Gf): The ability to solve relatively novel tasks by forming and recognizing concepts, identifying and perceiving relationships, drawing inferences, and reorganizing and transforming information.	Arithmetic, Matrix Reasoning, Picture Concepts, Word Reasoning
Induction (I): The ability to find a principle of relationships among elements.	Matrix Reasoning, Picture Concepts, Word Reasoning
Quantitative Reasoning (RQ): The ability to inductively and deductively reason with mathematical concepts.	Arithmetic
Quantitative Knowledge (Gq): The ability to use acquired mathematical knowledge.	Arithmetic
Mathematical Achievement (A3): The ability to demonstrate mathematical ability on an achievement test.	Arithmetic
Processing Speed (Gs): The ability to perform clerical-type tasks quickly and efficiently using sustained attention and concentration.	Cancellation, Coding, Symbol Search
Perceptual Speed (P): The ability to distinguish similar visual patterns and to find instances of a particular pattern under highly speeded conditions.	Cancellation, Symbol Search
Rate of Test Taking (R9): The ability to perform relatively simple tasks quickly.	Cancellation, Coding, Symbol Search
Short-Term Memory (Gsm): The ability to hold information in immediate memory and then use it within a few seconds.	Arithmetic, Digit Span, Letter–Number Sequencing
Memory Span (MS): The ability to immediately recall a series of randomly related elements (letters, numbers) after a few seconds.	Digit Span (primarily Digit Span Forward), Letter–Number Sequencing
Working Memory (MW): The ability to perform cognitive operations on information stored in short-term memory.	Arithmetic, Digit Span (primarily Digit Span Backward), Letter–Number Sequencing
Visual Processing (Gv): The ability to solve simple and complex visual problems.	Block Design, Matrix Reasoning, Object Assembly, Picture Arrangement, Picture Completion
Closure Speed (CS): The ability to rapidly organize separate visual stimuli into a meaningful whole.	Object Assembly
Flexibility of Closure (CF): The ability to identify a particular figure in a complex visual array.	Picture Completion
Spatial Relations (SR): The ability to solve problems involving spatial relations.	Block Design, Object Assembly
Visualization (VZ): The ability to mentally manipulate objects or visual patterns.	Block Design, Matrix Reasoning, Picture Arrangement

Note. Crystallized knowledge is also referred to as crystallized intelligence or crystallized ability. Fluid reasoning ability is also referred to as fluid ability, fluid reasoning, or fluid intelligence.
Source: Adapted, in part, from Flanagan, McGrew, and Ortiz (2000) and Horn (1987, 1998).

Table C-4

Broad and Narrow Abilities in the Cattell-Horn-Carroll (CHC) Model Associated with Wechsler Subtests

CHC broad and narrow abilities	Arithmetic (AR)	Block Design (BD)	Cancellation (CA)	Coding (CD)	Comprehension (CO)	Digit Span (DS)	Information (IN)	Letter–Number Sequencing (LN)	Matrix Reasoning (MR)
Crystallized Knowledge (Gc)					CO		IN		
General Information (KO)					CO		IN		
Language Development (LD)					CO				
Lexical Knowledge (VL)									
Fluid Reasoning Ability (Gf)	AR								MR
Induction (I)									MR
Quantitative Reasoning (RQ)	AR								
Quantitative Knowledge (Gq)	AR								
Mathematical Achievement (A3)	AR								
Processing Speed (Gs)			CA	CD					
Perceptual Speed (P)			CA						
Rate of Test Taking (R9)			CA	CD					
Short-Term Memory (Gsm)	AR					DS		LN	
Memory Span (MS)						DS		LN	
Working Memory (MW)	AR					DS		LN	
Visual Processing (Gv)		BD							MR
Closure Speed (CS)									
Flexibility of Closure (CF)									
Spatial Relations (SR)		BD							
Visualization (VZ)		BD							MR

(Continued)

Table C-4 (Continued)

Object Assembly (OA)	Picture Arrangement (PA)	Picture Completion (PCm)	Picture Concepts (PCn)	Picture Naming (PN)	Receptive Vocabulary (RV)	Similarities (SI)	Symbol Search (SS)	Vocabulary (VC)	Word Reasoning (WR)	CHC broad and narrow abilities
	PA	PCm	PCn	PN	RV	SI		VC	WR	**Crystallized Knowledge (Gc)**
	PA	PCm								General Information (KO)
				PN	RV	SI		VC	WR	Language Development (LD)
			PCn	PN	RV	SI		VC	WR	Lexical Knowledge (VL)
			PCn						WR	**Fluid Reasoning Ability (Gf)**
			PCn						WR	Induction (I)
										Quantitative Reasoning (RQ)
										Quantitative Knowledge (Gq)
										Mathematical Achievement (A3)
							SS			**Processing Speed (Gs)**
							SS			Perceptual Speed (P)
							SS			Rate of Test Taking (R9)
										Short-Term Memory (Gsm)
										Memory Span (MS)
										Working Memory (MW)
OA	PA	PCm								**Visual Processing (Gv)**
OA										Closure Speed (CS)
		PCm								Flexibility of Closure (CF)
OA										Spatial Relations (SR)
	PA									Visualization (VZ)

Note. Crystallized knowledge is also referred to as crystallized intelligence or crystallized ability. Fluid reasoning ability is also referred to as fluid ability, fluid reasoning, or fluid intelligence.

TABLE C-4   375

Table C-5
Interpretive Rationales, Implications of High and Low Scores, and Instructional Implications for Wechsler Composites

Ability	Background factors	Possible implications of high scores	Possible implications of low scores	Instructional implications
Full Scale				
Crystallized knowledge (Gc) Fluid reasoning ability (Gf) General intelligence Scholastic aptitude Academic aptitude Readiness to master a school curriculum Verbal skills Nonverbal skills Retrieval of material from long-term memory Attention Concentration	Natural endowment Richness of early environment Extent and quality of schooling Cultural opportunities Interests and reading patterns Rate of motor activity Persistence and motivation Alertness Ability to self-monitor Visual and auditory acuity Cognitive flexibility	Good general intelligence Good scholastic aptitude Good verbal and nonverbal skills Good readiness to master school curriculum	Poor general intelligence Poor scholastic aptitude Poor verbal and nonverbal skills Poor readiness to master school curriculum	Focus on language development activities Focus on visual learning activities Use spatial-visual activities Develop concept formation skills Reinforce persistence and motivation Reduce stress
Verbal Comprehension/Verbal Composite				
Crystallized knowledge (Gc) Fluid reasoning ability (Gf) Language development (LD) Lexical knowledge (VL) Verbal comprehension Application of verbal skills and information to the solution of new problems Verbal ability Ability to process verbal information Ability to think with words Auditory-vocal processing Retrieval of material from long-term memory Attention	Natural endowment Richness of early environment Extent and quality of schooling Cultural opportunities Interests and reading patterns Achievement orientation	Good verbal comprehension Good language development Good scholastic aptitude Good knowledge of the cultural milieu Good concept formation Good readiness to master school curriculum Good achievement orientation	Poor verbal comprehension Poor language development Poor scholastic aptitude Poor knowledge of the cultural milieu Poor concept formation Poor readiness to master school curriculum Poor achievement orientation	Stress language development activities Use verbal enrichment activities Focus on current events Use exercises involving concept formation

(Continued)

TABLE C-5   **377**

Table C-5 (*Continued*)

Ability	Background factors	Possible implications of high scores	Possible implications of low scores	Instructional implications
Perceptual Reasoning/Performance Composite				
Fluid reasoning ability (Gf) Visual processing (Gv) Spatial relations (SR) Perceptual reasoning Perceptual organization Ability to think in terms of visual images and manipulate them with fluency, flexibility, and relative speed Ability to interpret or organize visually perceived material within a time limit Nonverbal reasoning Visual-perceptual discrimination Ability to form relatively abstract concepts and relationships without the use of words Immediate problem-solving ability Attention Concentration	Natural endowment Motivation and persistence Ability to use trial and error Alertness Cultural opportunities Interests Visual acuity	Good perceptual reasoning Good perceptual organization Good alertness to detail Good nonverbal reasoning ability Good motivation and persistence Good ability to work quickly and efficiently Good spatial ability	Poor perceptual reasoning Poor perceptual organization Poor alertness to detail Poor nonverbal reasoning ability Poor motivation and persistence Poor ability to work quickly and efficiently Poor spatial ability	Focus on visual learning activities Focus on part-whole relationships Use spatial-visual tasks Encourage trial-and-error activities Reinforce persistence Focus on visual planning activities
Working Memory				
Short-term auditory memory (Gsm) Working memory (MW) Memory span (MS) Rote memory Immediate auditory memory Attention Concentration Numerical ability	Natural endowment Ability to passively receive stimuli Ability to self-monitor Auditory acuity and discrimination Ability to use encoding strategies Ability to use rehearsal strategies	Good short-term auditory memory Good working memory Good rote memory Good ability to sustain attention and concentrate Good encoding ability Good rehearsal strategies Good ability to self-monitor	Poor short-term auditory memory Poor working memory Poor rote memory Poor ability to sustain attention and concentrate Poor encoding ability Poor rehearsal strategies Poor ability to self-monitor	Develop short-term auditory memory skills Emphasize listening skills Develop attention skills Develop concentration skills Develop visualization skills Focus on small, meaningful units of instruction Develop basic arithmetical skills Reduce stress

(Continued)

Table C-5 (*Continued*)

Ability	Background factors	Possible implications of high scores	Possible implications of low scores	Instructional implications
Processing Speed				
Processing speed (Gs) Perceptual speed (P) Rate of test taking (R9) Visual-motor coordination and dexterity Speed of mental operation Scanning ability Psychomotor speed Attention Concentration Short-term visual memory Fine-motor coordination Visual-perceptual discrimination	Rate of motor activity Motivation and persistence Visual acuity Attention span Ability to work under time pressure Cognitive flexibility	Good processing speed Good perceptual speed Good attention and concentration Good short-term visual memory Good sustained energy or persistence Good cognitive flexibility Good visual processes Good motivation and persistence Good ability to work under time pressure Good perceptual discrimination ability	Poor processing speed Poor perceptual speed Poor attention and concentration Poor short-term visual memory Poor sustained energy or persistence Poor cognitive flexibility Poor visual processes Poor motivation and persistence Poor ability to work under time pressure Poor perceptual discrimination ability	Develop visual-motor skills Develop concentration skills Focus on learning codes Focus on selecting numbers that match Improve scanning techniques

Note. Abbreviations for the broad and narrow abilities in the Cattell-Horn-Carroll (CHC) model are shown within the parentheses. Table C-3 defines the CHC broad and narrow abilities associated with the Wechsler subtests, and Table C-4 shows the CHC broad and narrow abilities associated with the Wechsler subtests in grid form.

Crystallized knowledge is also referred to as crystallized intelligence or crystallized ability. Fluid reasoning ability is also referred to as fluid ability, fluid reasoning, or fluid intelligence.
Source: The CHC broad and narrow abilities adapted, in part, from Flanagan, McGrew, and Ortiz (2000) and Horn (1987, 1998).

TABLE C-6　　**379**

Table C-6
Suggested Remediation Activities for Combinations of Wechsler Subtests

Subtests	Ability	Instructional implications
Comprehension, Information, Picture Naming, Receptive Vocabulary, Vocabulary	Crystallized knowledge (Gc) Language development (LD) Lexical knowledge (VL) General knowledge Verbal fluency	(1) Review basic concepts, such as days of the week, months, time, distances, and directions; (2) have children report major current events by referring to pictures and articles from magazines and newspapers; (3) have children use a dictionary; (4) have children learn new words; (5) have children repeat simple stories; (6) have children explain how story characters are feeling and thinking.
Picture Concepts, Similarities, Vocabulary, Word Reasoning	Verbal conceptual ability	(1) Teach similarities and differences in designs, topography, transportation, etc.; (2) use show-and-tell games; (3) have children make scrapbooks of classifications such as animals, vehicles, or utensils; (4) have children match abstract concepts; (5) have children find commonality in dissimilar objects; (6) review basic concepts such as days of the week, months, time, directions, and distances.
Arithmetic, Digit Span, Letter–Number Sequencing	Short-term memory (Gsm) Memory span (MS) Working memory (MW) Attention Concentration	(1) Have children arrange cards in a meaningful sequence; (2) have children learn their telephone number, address, etc.; (3) use spelling word games; (4) use memory games; (5) have children learn days of the week and months of the year; (6) use mathematical word problems; (7) use dot-to-dot exercises; (8) have children describe details in pictures; (9) use tracing activities; (10) use Tinker Toys.
Block Design, Matrix Reasoning, Object Assembly	Visual processing (Gv) Spatial relations (SR) Visualization (VZ)	(1) Have children identify common objects and discuss details; (2) use guessing games involving description of a person, place, or thing; (3) have children match letters, shapes, numbers, etc.; (4) use jigsaw puzzles; (5) use block-building activities.
Block Design, Coding, Cancellation, Object Assembly, Symbol Search	Processing speed (Gs) Perceptual speed (P) Visual-motor ability	(1) Use paper-folding activities; (2) use finger-painting activities; (3) use dot-to-dot exercises; (4) use scissor-cutting exercises; (5) use skywriting exercises; (6) have children string beads in patterns; (7) use pegboard designs; (8) use puzzles (large jigsaw pieces); (9) have children solve a maze; (10) have children follow a moving object with coordinated eye movements; (11) use tracing exercises (e.g., trace hand, geometric forms, and letters); (12) have children make large circles and lines on the chalkboard; (13) have children copy from patterns; (14) have children draw from memory; (15) use scanning exercises.

Note. Abbreviations for the broad and narrow abilities in the Cattell-Horn-Carroll (CHC) model are shown within the parentheses. Table C-3 defines the CHC broad and narrow abilities associated with the Wechsler subtests, and Table C-4 shows the CHC broad and narrow abilities associated with the Wechsler subtests in grid form.

Crystallized knowledge is also referred to as crystallized intelligence or crystallized ability. Fluid reasoning ability is also referred to as fluid ability, fluid reasoning, or fluid intelligence.
Source: The CHC broad and narrow abilities adapted, in part, from Flanagan, McGrew, and Ortiz (2000) and Horn (1987, 1998).

Table C-7
Reporting on Wechsler Composites and Subtests

REPORTING ON WECHSLER COMPOSITES AND SUBTESTS

Following are summaries of the essential features of the WISC–IV, WPPSI–III, and WAIS–III Composites and subtests. You can use this material to discuss the assessment results with parents and the referral source, as well as to write your report.

COMPOSITES

Full Scale Composite
Usually, the Full Scale IQ is the best measure of cognitive ability. It measures general intelligence, scholastic aptitude, and readiness to master a school curriculum. The examinee's scores may be affected by motivation, interests, cultural opportunities, natural endowment, neurological integrity, attention span, ability to process verbal information, ability to process visual information, psychomotor ability, and capacity of short-term memory.

Perceptual Reasoning Composite, Performance Composite, or Perceptual Organization Composite
The Perceptual Reasoning Composite, Performance Composite, or Perceptual Organization Composite measures nonverbal skills, perceptual reasoning, and perceptual organization. These skills involve the ability to think in visual images and to manipulate these images with fluency and relative speed, to reason without the use of words (in some cases), and to interpret visual material quickly. The three Composites provide information about visual processing, planning and organizational ability, nonverbal learning, and memory. The examinee's scores may be affected by motivation, interests, cultural opportunities, natural endowment, long-term memory, attention span, ability to process visual information, and psychomotor ability.

Processing Speed Composite
The Processing Speed Composite measures such skills as psychomotor speed and mental speed. These skills include the ability to copy visual images with relative speed, to scan, and to evaluate visual material quickly. The Processing Speed Composite provides information about visual processing, planning and organizational ability, cognitive flexibility, visual memory, visual-motor coordination, visual selective attention, and vigilance. The examinee's scores may be affected by motivation, short-term memory, attention span, ability to process visual information, and psychomotor ability.

Verbal Comprehension Composite or Verbal Composite
The Verbal Comprehension Composite or Verbal Composite measures verbal skills and verbal comprehension. These skills include the application of verbal skills and information to the solution of new problems, the ability to process verbal information, and the ability to think with words. The two Composites provide information about language processing, verbal conceptualization, and verbal learning. The examinee's score may be affected by motivation, interests, cultural opportunities, natural endowment, long-term memory, attention span, and ability to process verbal information.

Working Memory Composite
The Working Memory Composite measures such skills as attention, concentration, and working memory. These skills include mental alertness, rote learning and attention, sequencing, and cognitive flexibility. The Working Memory Composite provides information about mental alertness, short-term auditory memory, mental manipulation, number facility, and concentration. The examinee's scores may be affected by motivation, interests, cultural opportunities, natural endowment, attention span, anxiety, and ability to process auditory information.

SUBTESTS

Arithmetic
The Arithmetic subtest provides a measure of the examinee's facility in mental arithmetic. The examinee is asked to solve several types of arithmetic problems involving addition, subtraction, multiplication, division, and problem solving. The subtest provides valuable information about the examinee's numerical reasoning ability, concentration, attention, short-term memory, and long-term memory. Performance may be influenced by the examinee's attitude toward school and level of anxiety.

Block Design
The Block Design subtest provides a measure of the examinee's spatial visualization and nonverbal reasoning ability. The examinee is asked to use blocks to assemble a design identical to one made by the examiner or one pictured on a card. The subtest provides valuable information about the examinee's ability to analyze and synthesize visual-spatial material and the examinee's visual-motor coordination. Performance may be influenced by rate of motor activity.

Cancellation
The Cancellation subtest provides a measure of the examinee's visual alertness and visual scanning ability. The task is to mark only the pictures of animals. First the examinee is asked to scan a page on which the pictures are arranged in random order. Then the examinee is asked to scan a page on which the pictures are placed in rows. The subtest provides valuable information about the examinee's perceptual discrimination, speed and accuracy, attention and concentration, and vigilance. Performance may be influenced by speed of motor activity, visual perceptive ability, and motivation.

Coding
The Coding subtest provides a measure of the examinee's ability to learn a code rapidly. The examinee is shown a key in which several symbols are matched with other symbols. Then the examinee is shown one symbol and is asked to put the matching symbol in the blank space on a preprinted form. The subtest provides valuable information about speed and accuracy of eye-hand coordination, short-term visual memory, and attentional skills. Performance may be influenced by rate of motor activity and by motivation.

(Continued)

TABLE C-7   **381**

Table C-7 (*Continued*)

Comprehension

The Comprehension subtest provides a measure of the examinee's social judgment and common sense. The examinee is asked to answer questions dealing with various problem situations that, in part, involve interpersonal relations and social mores. The subtest provides valuable information about the examinee's knowledge of conventional standards of behavior. Performance may be influenced by cultural opportunities, ability to evaluate and draw from experiences, and moral sense.

Digit Span

The Digit Span subtest provides a measure of the examinee's short-term memory. In this two-part subtest, the examinee is asked to repeat series of digits given orally by the examiner. Each series in the first part is to be repeated as given by the examiner, and each series in the second part is to be repeated in reverse order. The subtest provides valuable information about the examinee's rote short-term memory, attention, and concentration. Performance may be influenced by level of anxiety.

Information

The Information subtest provides a measure of how much general factual knowledge the examinee has acquired from his or her environment. The examinee is asked to answer questions that cover a range of material. The subtest provides valuable information about the examinee's range of factual knowledge and long-term memory. Performance may be influenced by cultural opportunities, outside interests, richness of early environment, reading, and school learning.

Letter–Number Sequencing

The Letter–Number Sequencing subtest provides a measure of the examinee's short-term memory, including the ability to attend and concentrate. The examinee is asked to repeat a series of letters and numbers in ascending and alphabetic order. The subtest provides valuable information about the examinee's concentration, attention, short-term memory, and mental manipulation. Performance may be influenced by the examinee's attention, anxiety, and numerical facility.

Matrix Reasoning

The Matrix Reasoning subtest provides a measure of the examinee's nonverbal problem-solving ability. The examinee looks at an incomplete matrix and must choose the missing portion from a selection of five options. The subtest provides valuable information about the examinee's inductive reasoning, visual processing, and problem-solving abilities. Performance may be influenced by alertness to the visual aspects of the environment and reasoning ability.

Object Assembly

The Object Assembly subtest provides a measure of the examinee's visual-spatial organization, understanding of part-to-whole relationships, nonverbal reasoning, and trial and error learning. The examinee is presented with specific puzzle pieces and asked to assemble them into a meaningful whole. The subtest provides valuable information about the examinee's spatial abilities, visual-motor coordination, and motivation and persistence.

Picture Arrangement

The Picture Arrangement subtest provides a measure of the examinee's ability to comprehend and evaluate social situations. The examinee is presented with pictures in a mixed-up order and is asked to rearrange them in a logical sequence. The pictures are similar to those seen in short comic strips. The subtest provides valuable information about the examinee's ability to attend to details, alertness, planning ability, and visual sequencing. Performance may be influenced by cultural opportunities.

Picture Completion

The Picture Completion subtest provides a measure of the examinee's ability to distinguish between essential and nonessential details. The examinee is shown pictures of objects from everyday life and is asked to indicate the single most important part missing from each picture. The subtest provides valuable information about the examinee's ability to concentrate on visually perceived material and alertness to details. Performance may be influenced by cultural experiences and alertness to the visual aspects of the environment.

Picture Concepts

The Picture Concepts subtest provides a measure of the examinee's abstract, categorical reasoning based on perceptual recognition processes. The examinee is asked to scan an array of pictures and determine what pictures have a common characteristic. The subtest provides valuable information about the examinee's categorical nonverbal reasoning ability. Performance also may be influenced by the examinee's language and reasoning skills.

Picture Naming

The Picture Naming subtest provides a measure of the examinee's expressive word knowledge. The examinee is asked to give the name of the picture. The subtest provides valuable information about the examinee's language development. Performance may be influenced by cultural opportunities, education, reading habits, and familiarity with English.

Receptive Vocabulary

The Receptive Vocabulary subtest provides a measure of the examinee's receptive word knowledge. The examinee is asked to look at four pictures and point to the one picture that matches what the examiner said. The subtest provides valuable information about the examinee's verbal skills, language development, and long-term memory. Performance may be influenced by cultural opportunities, education, reading habits, and familiarity with English.

Similarities

The Similarities subtest provides a measure of the examinee's ability to select and verbalize appropriate relationships between two objects or concepts. The examinee is asked to state how two things are alike. A response indicating an abstract classification receives more credit than a response indicating a concrete classification. The subtest provides valuable information about the examinee's verbal concept formation and long-term memory. Performance may be influenced by cultural opportunities, interests, reading habits, and school learning.

(Continued)

Table C-7 (*Continued*)

Symbol Search

The Symbol Search subtest provides a measure of the examinee's visual discrimination and visual-perceptual scanning ability. In one part of the subtest, after looking at a target symbol, the examinee looks at another group of symbols and indicates whether the target symbol is in the group of symbols. In the other part of the subtest, after looking at two target symbols, the examinee looks at another group of symbols and indicates whether the two target symbols are in the group of symbols. The subtest provides valuable information about the examinee's perceptual discrimination, speed and accuracy, attention and concentration, and short-term memory. Performance may be influenced by rate of motor activity and motivation and perhaps by cognitive flexibility. Cognitive flexibility refers to an ability to shift between the target symbols and the other groups of symbols as they change for each item.

Vocabulary

The Vocabulary subtest provides a measure of the examinee's word knowledge. The examinee is asked to define individual words of increasing difficulty. The subtest provides valuable information about the examinee's verbal skills, language development, and long-term memory. Performance may be influenced by cultural opportunities, education, reading habits, and familiarity with English.

Word Reasoning

The Word Reasoning subtest provides a measure of verbal reasoning. The examinee is asked to identify the common concept being described in a series of clues. The subtest provides valuable information about the examinee's verbal comprehension, analogic and general reasoning abilities, and ability to analyze and integrate different types of information. Performance may be influenced by cultural opportunities, outside interests, richness of early environment, reading, and school learning.

TABLE C-8   **383**

Table C-8
Modified Instructions for Administering Subtests on the Wechsler Perceptual Reasoning Composite, Performance Composite, or Perceptual Organization Composite to Examinees with Hearing Impairments

Examinees with hearing impairments should be administered the Wechsler tests in their native language or preferred mode of communication, such as American Sign Language. If this is not possible, use the modified instructions below for the subtests on the WISC–IV Perceptual Reasoning Composite, WPPSI–III Performance Composite, or WAIS–III Perceptual Organization Composite, recognizing that modifications introduce an unknown source of error. Write the word "Estimate" next to any scores obtained through modified procedures.

Before administering the test, you should prepare an instruction sheet for each subtest in the Perceptual Reasoning Composite, the Performance Composite, or the Perceptual Organization Composite. The instruction sheet will be used for examinees who can read. During the test, you must make sure that the examinee is looking at you each time you speak, shake your head "yes" or "no," or nod your head for any other purpose. Also make sure that the examinee is looking at the model, the Response Booklet, the supplemental instruction sheet, or any materials that you point to. Finally, do not speak, nod, or gesture when the examinee is looking at any materials.

It is difficult to communicate the need to work as quickly as possible nonverbally. Suggestions include pointing to those words on the supplemental instruction sheet, emphasizing those words if the examinee can hear or read your speech, conveying a sense of urgency with body language, and displaying the stopwatch. Also consider finger spelling or signing the word *fast* if the examinee knows either of these methods. Do this by making a fist with your thumb tucked under your forefinger, then quickly lowering the fist and snapping out the thumb as if shooting a marble.

BLOCK DESIGN

Additional Materials
Three instruction sheets prepared by the examiner. For each test, the instruction sheet should contain the information printed in color on (a) pages 65 to 68 of the WISC–IV Administration Manual, (b) pages 59 to 67 of the WPPSI–III Administration Manual, or (c) pages 116 to 122 of the WAIS–III Administration Manual.

Procedure
If the examinee can read, show her or him the instruction sheet and wait until the examinee has finished reading it. For all examinees, motion for the examinee to assemble the design. Point to the examinee, point to the examinee's blocks, and point to the model or the card with the designs. Follow the instructions in the WISC–IV Administration Manual, in the WPPSI–III Administration Manual, or in the WAIS–III Administration Manual for the Block Design subtest.

CANCELLATION

Additional Materials
One instruction sheet prepared by the examiner. This sheet should contain the information printed in color on pages 173 and 174 of the WISC–IV Administration Manual.

Procedure
If the examinee can read, show him or her the instruction sheet and wait until the examinee has finished reading it. For all examinees, demonstrate the sample item. Open Response Booklet 2 to the first page. Show the first page to the examinee. Move your finger in a sweeping motion, from the examinee's left to right, across the first row of animals (the row below the word "Animals"). Then go to the second row. Point to each object individually. As you point to each object, let the examinee look at it, make sure that you catch the examinee's eye, and then shake your head "no" for nonanimal objects. As you point to each animal, make sure that you catch the examinee's eye and shake your head "yes" before drawing a line through the animal. Motion to the examinee to do the same on the practice items: Move your finger in a sweeping motion across the practice items. Give the examinee a red pencil, point to the animals in the first row, and draw a line through the baby chick. Then, point to the remaining items and motion for the examinee to proceed.

CODING or DIGIT SYMBOL–CODING

Additional Materials
Four instruction sheets prepared by the examiner. For each test, the instruction sheet should contain the information printed in color on (a) pages 97 and 98 of the WISC–IV Administration Manual for Coding A, (b) pages 98 and 99 of the WISC–IV Administration Manual for Coding B, (c) pages 125 and 126 of the WPPSI–III Administration Manual, or (d) pages 93 to 95 of the WAIS–III Administration Manual.

Two additional practice Coding items prepared by the examiner. The practice items are item CD-1 and item CD-2. Item CD-1 is used for the WISC–IV Coding A (for examinees ages 6 to 7 years) and for the WPPSI–III. Item CD-2 is used for the WISC–IV Coding B (for examinees ages 8 to 16 years) and for the WAIS–III. Each item consists of a key and two practice trials. Photocopy these items and attach each one to a sheet of paper.

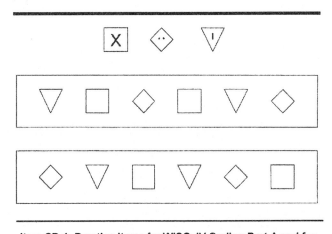

Item CD-1. Practice items for WISC–IV Coding Part A and for WPPSI–III Coding for children who are hearing impaired.

(Continued)

Table C-8 (Continued)

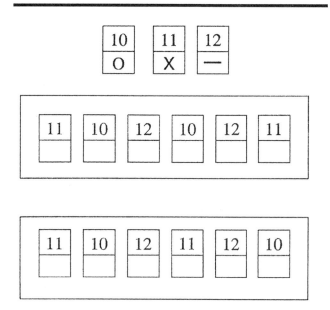

Item CD-2. Practice items for WISC–IV Coding Part B and for WAIS–III Digit Symbol–Coding for children who are hearing impaired.

Procedure for WISC–IV Coding A (examinees ages 6 to 7) and for WPPSI–III

Show the examinee item CD-I. Point to the key (the geometric shape and then the symbol inside the shape). Then go to trial 1 (the first row), which contains six practice items. Point to the empty geometric shape in the first practice box. Draw the symbol inside the triangle. Follow the same procedure for the second and third geometric shapes. Then point to the examinee and motion for him or her to complete the remaining three shapes. Demonstrate how to complete the first three shapes of trial 2 (the second row), following the same procedure as on trial 1. Have the examinee complete the last three shapes of trial 2.

If the examinee can read, show him or her the instruction sheet and wait until the examinee has finished reading it. For the WISC–IV, take out Response Booklet 1 and open it to Coding A. For the WPPSI–III, take out the Response Booklet and open it to Coding. Point to the examinee, point to the sample box, and motion for the examinee to begin. After the sample items have been completed, point to the examinee, point to the first box of the subtest proper, and then with a sweeping motion indicate that the examinee should begin the task. Follow the instructions in the WISC–IV Administration Manual or in the WPPSI–III Administration Manual for the Coding subtest. It is important to communicate the need for speed on Coding A.

Procedure for WISC–IV Coding B (examinees ages 8 to 16) and for WAIS–III Digit Symbol–Coding

Show the examinee item CD-2. Point to the key (the boxes that have a number in the upper half and a symbol in the lower half). Then go to trial 1 (the first row), which contains six practice items. Draw the symbol in the first empty box under the number 11. Follow the same procedure for the second and third boxes. Then point to the examinee and motion for her or him to complete the remaining three boxes. Demonstrate how to complete the first three boxes of trial 2 (the second row), following the same procedure as on trial 1. Have the examinee complete the last three boxes of trial 2.

If the examinee can read, show her or him the instruction sheet and wait until the examinee has finished reading it. For the WISC–IV, open Response Booklet 1 to Coding B. For the WAIS–III, open the Response Booklet to the Digit Symbol–Coding page. Point to the examinee, point to the sample box, and motion for the examinee to begin. After the sample items have been completed, point to the examinee, point to the first box of the subtest proper, and then with a sweeping motion indicate that the examinee should begin the task. Follow the instructions in the WISC–IV Administration Manual for the Coding subtest or in the WAIS–III Administration Manual for the Digit Symbol–Coding subtest. It is important to communicate the need for speed on Coding B and Digit Symbol–Coding.

MATRIX REASONING

Additional Materials

Three instruction sheets prepared by the examiner. The sheets should contain the information printed in color on (a) pages 132 to 133 of the WISC–IV Administration Manual, (b) pages 82 and 83 of the WPPSI–III Administration Manual, or (c) pages 130 and 131 of the WAIS–III Administration Manual.

Two additional practice items prepared by the examiner. The practice items are item MR-1 and item MR-2. Photocopy these items and attach each one to a 3" x 5" card.

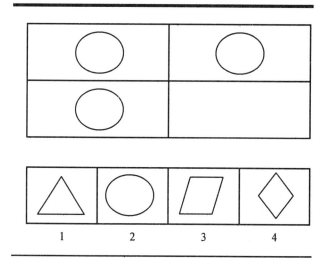

Item MR-1. Practice item for WISC–IV and WAIS–III Matrix Reasoning for children who are hearing impaired.

(Continued)

TABLE C-8   **385**

Table C-8 (*Continued*)

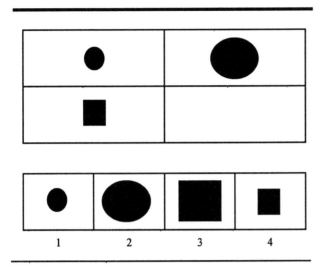

Item MR-2. Practice item for WISC–IV and WAIS–III Matrix Reasoning for children who are hearing impaired.

Procedure
Show the examinee item MR-1. Point to each large box with a circle (i.e., upper right, upper left, lower right). Next point to the four choices below the boxes by moving your finger in a sweeping motion, from the examinee's left to right. Then point to the blank box. Point to the four choices again in a sweeping motion, stop at the circle (2), and make sure you catch the examinee's eye before shaking your head "yes."

Show the examinee item MR-2. Point to each large box with a figure (i.e., upper right, lower right, lower left). Then point to the four choices below the boxes by moving your finger in a sweeping motion, from the examinee's left to right. Then point to the blank box. Motion for the examinee to begin. If the examinee points to the correct choice (3), shake your head "yes." If the examinee points to the incorrect choice, shake your head "no," then point to the correct choice, and shake your head "yes."

If the examinee can read, show him or her the instruction sheet and wait until the examinee has finished reading it. Open the Stimulus Book to the Matrix Reasoning subtest. Point to the examinee, point to the first sample item, and motion for the examinee to begin. After the sample items have been completed, point to the examinee, point to the start-point item of the subtest proper, and then with a sweeping motion indicate that the examinee should begin the task. Follow the instructions in the WISC–IV Administration Manual, in the WPPSI–III Administration Manual, or in the WAIS–III Administration Manual for the Matrix Reasoning subtest.

OBJECT ASSEMBLY

Additional Materials
Two instruction sheets prepared by the examiner. For each test, the instruction sheet should contain the information printed in color on pages 205 to 207 of the WPPSI–III Administration Manual or on pages 173 to 174 of the WAIS–III Administration Manual.

One additional practice item prepared by the examiner. Before you begin the assessment, select a picture from a magazine and put it with the other materials.

Procedure
Show the picture from the magazine to the examinee. Then cut the picture into three pieces. Place the three pieces randomly on the table. Then put the pieces together. Present the pieces to the examinee in a random arrangement. Motion to indicate that the examinee should put the pieces together.

If the examinee can read, show him or her the instruction sheet and wait until the examinee has finished reading it. For all examinees, place the first item before the examinee and motion for the examinee to assemble the sample puzzle. Point to the examinee, point to the puzzle pieces, and motion to indicate that the pieces must be put together. Follow the instructions in the WPPSI–III Administration Manual or in the WAIS–III Administration Manual for the Object Assembly subtest.

PICTURE ARRANGEMENT

Additional Materials
One instruction sheet prepared by the examiner. This sheet should contain the information printed in color on pages 143 and 144 of the WAIS–III Administration Manual.

Two additional practice items prepared by the examiner. The practice items are item PA-1 and item PA-2, each of which is made from three white 3" x 5" cards, as follows:

1. Item PA-1: Print the number 1 on one card, the number 2 on one card, and the number 3 on one card. On the back of each card, print the word NUMBERS and the appropriate number.
2. Item PA-2: Print the letter A on one card, the letter B on one card, and the letter C on one card. On the back of each card, print the word LETTERS and the appropriate letter.

Procedure
For all examinees, present the cards in item PA-1 (NUMBERS) in the order 2, 3, 1, from the examinee's left to right. Then arrange the cards in correct numerical sequence. Allow the examinee to view the arrangement for 10 seconds. Rearrange the cards in the original order. By pointing to the examinee and the cards with a general sweeping motion, indicate to the examinee to arrange the cards. If the examinee does not respond or arranges the cards incorrectly, arrange the cards in their correct sequence. Then rearrange the cards in the original administration order and again motion to the examinee to arrange the cards. Follow the same procedure for item PA-2 (LETTERS).

If the examinee can read, show him or her the instruction sheet and wait until the examinee has finished reading it. Follow the instructions in the WAIS–III Administration Manual for the Picture Arrangement subtest.

(*Continued*)

Table C-8 (*Continued*)

PICTURE COMPLETION

Additional Materials
Three instruction sheets prepared by the examiner. For each test, the instruction sheet should contain the information printed in color on (a) pages 164 to 166 of the WISC–IV Administration Manual, (b) pages 150 to 152 of the WPPSI–III Administration Manual, or (c) pages 64 and 65 of the WAIS–III Administration Manual.

Three additional practice items prepared by the examiner. The practice items are PCm-1, PCm-2, and PCm-3. Item PCm-1 has a picture of a bird missing a wing on one side of a card and a picture of the complete bird on the other side (BIRD). Item PCm-2 has a picture of a bow and arrow missing part of the arrow on one side of a card and a picture of the complete bow and arrow on the other side (BOW & ARROW). Item PCm-3 has a picture of a pair of scissors missing part of the handle on one side of a card and a picture of the complete pair of scissors on the other side (SCISSORS). To make the three cards, photocopy the pictures and attach them to 3" x 5" cards.

Item PCm-1. Practice item for WISC–IV, WPPSI–III, and WAIS–IV Picture Completion for children who are hearing impaired.

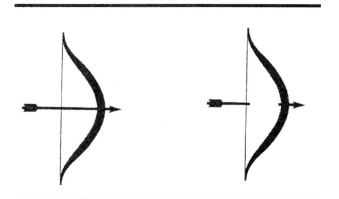

Item PCm-2. Practice item for WISC–IV, WPPSI–III, and WAIS–IV Picture Completion for children who are hearing impaired.

Item PCm-3. Practice item for WISC–IV, WPPSI–III, and WAIS–IV Picture Completion for children who are hearing impaired.

Procedure
First show the examinee the side of item PCm-1 (BIRD) with the picture of the complete bird. Then turn the card over and show the bird with the missing wing. Point to the missing wing.

Show the examinee the side of item PCm-2 (BOW & ARROW) with the picture of the complete bow and arrow. Then turn the card over and show the bow and arrow with a part of the arrow missing. Point to the missing part of the arrow.

Show the examinee the side of item PCm-3 (SCISSORS) with part of the handle missing. Motion for the examinee to point. If the examinee points to the missing detail, shake your head to indicate "yes." If the examinee points to a part of the picture that is not missing or does not point, point to the missing part of the picture. Then turn the card over and show the complete pair of scissors. Present the sample item from the Picture Completion subtest in the Stimulus Book.

If the examinee can read, show her or him the instruction sheet and wait until the examinee has finished reading it. Follow the instructions in the WISC–IV Administration Manual, in the WPPSI–III Administration Manual, or in the WAIS–III Administration Manual for the Picture Completion subtest.

PICTURE CONCEPTS

Additional Materials
Two instruction sheets prepared by the examiner. For each test, the instruction sheet should contain the information printed in color on pages 91 and 92 of the WISC–IV Administration Manual or on pages 108 and 109 of the WPPSI–III Administration Manual.

Three additional practice items prepared by the examiner. The practice items are PCn-1, PCn-2, and PCn-3. Photocopy the items and attach each one to a 3" x 5" card.

Procedure
Show the examinee item PCn-1. Move your finger in a sweeping motion, from the examinee's left to right, across the top row and then across the bottom row. Next point to the strawberry in the top row and then make a sweeping motion across the bottom row. Point to the giraffe in the bottom row. Shake your head from side to side to indicate "no." Point to the airplane in the bottom row and shake your head from side to side to indicate "no." Point to the deer in the top row. Then point to the giraffe in the bottom row and shake your head to indicate "yes."

(*Continued*)

TABLE C-8   387

Table C-8 (*Continued*)

Item PCn-1. Practice item for WISC–IV and WPPSI–III Picture Concepts for children who are hearing impaired.

Item PCn-3. Practice item for WISC–IV and WPPSI–III Picture Concepts for children who are hearing impaired.

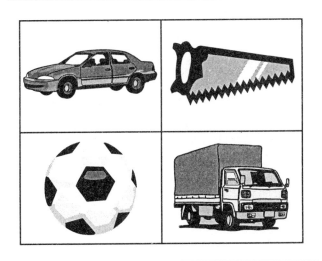

Item PCn-2. Practice item for WISC–IV and WPPSI–III Picture Concepts for children who are hearing impaired.

Show the examinee item PCn-2. Move your finger in a sweeping motion, from the examinee's left to right, across the top row and then across the bottom row. Motion for the examinee to begin. If the examinee points to the two correct choices (car and truck), shake your head to indicate "yes." If the examinee points to two incorrect choices, shake your head to indicate "no." Then point to the car and truck and shake your head to indicate "yes."

If the examinee can read, show him or her the instruction sheet and wait until the examinee has finished reading it. Follow the instructions in the WPPSI–III Administration Manual or in the WISC–IV Administration Manual for the Picture Concepts subtest.

If the examinee reaches item 13 on the WISC–III or item 27 on the WPPSI–III, show the examinee item PCn-3. Move your finger in a sweeping motion, from the examinee's left to right, across the top row of the sample, then across the middle row, and then across the bottom row. Next point to the guitar in the first row, then the saxophone in the second row, and then the trumpet in the third row. Let the examinee study the pictures. Make sure that you have the examinee's eye and shake your head "yes" when you point to the designated picture in each row.

SYMBOL SEARCH

Additional Materials
Four instruction sheets prepared by the examiner. For each test, the instruction sheet should contain the information printed in color on (a) pages 145 to 147 of the WISC–IV Administration Manual for Symbol Search A, (b) pages 147 to 149 of the WISC–IV Administration Manual for Symbol Search B, (c) pages 114 to 115 of the WPPSI–III Administration Manual, or (d) pages 166 to 168 of the WAIS–III Administration Manual.

Procedure for WISC–IV Symbol Search A (examinees ages 6 to 7)
The following instructions cover the sample items, practice items, and subtest items.

(*Continued*)

Table C-8 (*Continued*)

Sample items. Open Response Booklet 1 to Symbol Search A on page 3. Move your finger in a sweeping motion, from the examinee's left to right, across the entire row of the first sample item. Then point to the single target symbol in the first column. Next point to the first symbol in the search group. Then make sure you catch the examinee's eye and shake your head "no" to indicate that the first search symbol does not match the target symbol.

Repeat this procedure two more times for the first sample item. Point to the single target symbol and then to the second search symbol. Shake your head "no." Again point to the single target symbol and then to the third search symbol. This time shake your head "yes" to indicate that the search symbol matches the target symbol. With a no. 2 pencil, draw a diagonal line through the YES box. Be sure that the examinee is looking at the Response Booklet or at you at the appropriate times.

For the second sample item, generally follow the same procedure. However, for this item, shake your head "no" for each search symbol. After demonstrating the third search symbol, draw a diagonal line through the NO box.

Practice items. Give the examinee a no. 2 pencil. Point to the first row of the practice items and move your finger in a sweeping motion, from the examinee's left to right, along the entire row. Nod your head to indicate to the examinee to begin. If the examinee draws a diagonal line through the YES box, nod your head to indicate "good" and go to the second practice item.

If the examinee draws a diagonal line through the NO box on the first practice item, correct the examinee. Point to the target symbol and then to the second search symbol. Shake your head to indicate "yes." Then draw a diagonal line through the YES box. Do not demonstrate the third symbol.

Point to the second practice item and, by nodding your head, encourage the examinee to do it. If the examinee draws a diagonal line through the NO box, nod your head to indicate "good" and proceed to the regular subtest items (see below).

If the examinee draws a diagonal line through the YES box, correct the examinee. Point to the target symbol and each of the three search symbols in turn, shaking your head each time to indicate "no." Then draw a diagonal line through the NO box.

Do not go on to the regular subtest items until the examinee understands the task. You may have to erase your marks and the examinee's marks and ask the examinee to do the sample and/or practice items again.

Subtest items. When the examinee understands the task, open the Symbol Search Booklet to page 4 and fold the page over. If the examinee can read, show her or him the first instruction sheet and wait until the examinee has finished reading it. After the examinee reads the directions, point to the first row to indicate that the examinee should begin the task.

If the examinee cannot read, run your finger down the entire page 4. Then turn to page 5, and again run your finger down the entire page. Then turn to page 6, and again run your finger down the entire page. After showing the examinee the three pages of items, turn back to page 3. Point to the pencil and then to the first row, run your finger down the page, and then nod your head to indicate to the examinee to begin. It is important to communicate the need for speed on Symbol Search A.

If the examinee ceases to work after completing the first row, direct the examinee's attention to the second row by pointing to the entire second row with a sweeping motion and encourage the examinee to continue. If the examinee stops at the end of page 3, turn to page 4 and encourage the examinee to continue. If the examinee stops at the end of page 4, turn to page 5 and encourage the examinee to continue. Allow 120 seconds.

Procedure for WISC–IV Symbol Search B (examinees ages 8 to 16)
The following instructions cover the sample items, practice items, and subtest items.

Sample items. Open Response Booklet 1 to page 7. Move your finger in a sweeping motion, from the examinee's left to right, across the entire row of the first sample item in Part B. Then point to the two target symbols in the first column. Next point to the first symbol in the search group. Then make sure you catch the examinee's eye and shake your head "yes" to indicate that the first search symbol matches the target symbol. With a no. 2 pencil, draw a diagonal line through the YES box. Go to the second sample item, without demonstrating the remaining symbols in the first sample item.

For the second sample item, point to the two target symbols and then to the first search symbol. Shake your head "no" to indicate that the search symbol does not match either of the target symbols. Repeat this procedure four more times. In each case, point to the two target symbols and then to the search symbol. Shake your head "no" each time. After demonstrating the last search symbol, draw a diagonal line through the NO box. Make sure that the examinee is looking at the Response Booklet and at you at the appropriate times.

Practice items. Give the examinee a no. 2 pencil. Point to the first row of the practice items and move your finger in a sweeping motion, from the examinee's left to right, along the entire row. Nod your head to indicate to the examinee to begin. If the examinee draws a diagonal line through the YES box, nod your head to indicate "good" and go to the second practice item.

If the examinee draws a diagonal line through the NO box on the first practice item, correct the examinee. Point to the two target symbols and then to the second search symbol. Shake your head to indicate "yes." Then draw a diagonal line through the YES box. Do not demonstrate the remaining three symbols.

Point to the second practice item and, by nodding your head, encourage the examinee to do it. If the examinee draws a diagonal line through the NO box, nod your head to indicate "good" and proceed to the regular subtest items (see below).

If the examinee draws a diagonal line through the YES box, correct the examinee. Point to the two target symbols and each of the five search symbols in turn, shaking your head each time to indicate "no." Then draw a diagonal line through the NO box.

Do not go on to the regular subtest items until the examinee understands the task. You may have to erase your marks and the examinee's marks and ask the examinee to do the sample and/or practice items again. It is important to communicate the need for speed on Symbol Search B.

(Continued)

TABLE C-8   **389**

Table C-8 (*Continued*)

Subtest items. When the examinee understands the task, open Response Booklet 1 to page 8 and fold the page over. If the examinee can read, show him or her the second instruction sheet and wait until the examinee has finished reading it. After the examinee reads the directions, point to the first row to indicate that the examinee should begin the task.

If the examinee cannot read, run your finger down the entire page 8. Then turn to page 9, and again run your finger down the entire page. Follow the same procedure for pages 10 and 11. After showing the examinee the four pages of items, turn back to page 8. Point to the pencil and then to the first row, then run your finger down the page, and then nod your head to indicate to the examinee to begin.

If the examinee ceases to work after completing the first row, direct the examinee's attention to the second row by pointing to the entire second row with a sweeping motion and encourage the examinee to continue. If the examinee stops at the end of page 8, turn to page 9. If the examinee stops at the end of page 9, turn to page 10. If the examinee stops at the end of page 10, turn to page 11. Allow 120 seconds.

Procedure for WPPSI–III
The following instructions cover the sample items, practice items, and subtest items.

Sample items. Open the Response Booklet to page 1. Move your finger in a sweeping motion, from the examinee's left to right, across the entire row of the first sample item. Then point to the single target symbol in the first column. Next point to the first symbol in the search group. Then make sure you catch the examinee's eye and shake your head "no" to indicate that the first search symbol does not match the target symbol.

Point to the single target symbol and then to the second search symbol. This time shake your head "yes" to indicate that the search symbol matches the target symbol. With a no. 2 pencil, draw a diagonal line through the matching symbol.

Point to the single target symbol and then to the third search symbol. Shake your head "no" to indicate that the third search symbol does not match the target symbol.

Repeat this procedure one more time. Point to the single target symbol and then to the fourth search symbol. Shake your head "no."

For the second sample item, generally follow the same procedure. However, for this item, shake your head "no" for each search symbol. After demonstrating the third search symbol, draw a diagonal line through the question mark. Be sure that the examinee is looking at the Response Booklet and at you at the appropriate times.

Practice items. Give the examinee a no. 2 pencil. Point to the first row of the practice items and move your finger in a sweeping motion, from the examinee's left to right, along the entire row. Nod your head to indicate to the examinee to begin. If the examinee draws a diagonal line through the second search symbol, nod your head to indicate "good" and go to the second practice item.

If the examinee draws a diagonal line through the question mark on the first practice item, correct the examinee. Point to the target symbol and then to the second search symbol. Shake your head to indicate "yes." Then draw a diagonal line through the second search symbol.

Point to the second practice item and, by nodding your head, encourage the examinee to do it. If the examinee draws a diagonal line through the question mark, nod your head to indicate "good" and proceed to the third practice item.

If the examinee draws a diagonal line through a nonmatching symbol, correct the examinee. Point to the target symbol and each of the three search symbols in turn, shaking your head each time to indicate "no." Then draw a diagonal line through the question mark.

Follow the same procedure for the third and fourth practice items.

Do not go on to the regular subtest items until the examinee understands the task. You may have to erase your marks and the examinee's marks and ask the examinee to do the sample and/or practice items again. It is important to communicate the need for speed on Symbol Search.

Subtest items. When the examinee understands the task, open the Response Booklet to page 2 and fold the page over. If the examinee can read, show her or him the instruction sheet and wait until the examinee has finished reading it. After the examinee reads the directions, point to the first row to indicate that the examinee should begin the task.

If the examinee cannot read, run your finger down the entire page 2. Then turn to page 3, and again run your finger down the entire page. Then turn to page 4, and again run your finger down the entire page. Do the same for pages 5 and 6. After showing the examinee the five pages of items, turn back to page 2. Point to the pencil and then to the first row, run your finger down the page, and then nod your head to indicate to the examinee to begin.

If the examinee ceases to work after completing the first row, direct the examinee's attention to the second row by pointing to the entire second row with a sweeping motion and encourage the examinee to continue. If the examinee stops at the end of page 2, turn to page 3 and encourage the examinee to continue. If the examinee stops at the end of page 3, turn to page 4 and encourage the examinee to continue. Follow the same procedure for pages 4 and 5. Allow 120 seconds.

Procedure for WAIS–III
The following instructions cover the sample items, practice items, and subtest items.

Sample items. Open the Response Booklet to the Symbol Search opening page. Move your finger in a sweeping motion, from the examinee's left to right, across the entire row of the first sample item. Then point to the two target symbols in the first column. Next point to the first symbol in the search group. Then make sure you catch the examinee's eye and shake your head "yes" to indicate that the first search symbol matches the target symbol. With a no. 2 pencil, draw a diagonal line through the YES box. Go to the second sample item, without demonstrating the remaining symbols in the first sample item.

For the second sample item, point to the two target symbols in the first column. Next point to the first symbol in the search group. Then make sure you catch the examinee's eye and shake your head "no" to indicate that the second search symbol does not match the target symbol. Next point to the second symbol in the search group and shake your head "yes" to indicate that the second search symbol matches the target symbol.

Table C-8 (Continued)

With a no. 2 pencil, draw a diagonal line through the YES box. Go to the third sample item, without demonstrating the remaining symbols in the second sample item.

For the third sample item, point to the two target symbols and then to the first search symbol. Shake your head "no" to indicate that the search symbol does not match either of the target symbols. Repeat this procedure four more times. In each case, point to the two target symbols and then to the search symbol. Shake your head "no" each time. After demonstrating the last search symbol, draw a diagonal line through the NO box. Be sure that the examinee is looking at the Response Booklet and at you at the appropriate times.

Practice items. Give the examinee a no. 2 pencil. Point to the first row of the practice items and move your finger in a sweeping motion, from the examinee's left to right, along the entire row. Nod your head to indicate to the examinee to begin. If the examinee draws a diagonal line through the YES box, nod your head to indicate "good" and go to the second practice item.

If the examinee marks NO on the first practice item, correct the examinee. Point to the two target symbols and then to the second search symbol. Shake your head to indicate "yes." Then draw a diagonal line through the YES box. Do not demonstrate the remaining three symbols.

Point to the second practice item and, by nodding your head, encourage the examinee to do it. If the examinee marks NO, nod your head to indicate "good" and go to the third practice item.

If the examinee marks YES, correct the examinee. Point to the two target symbols and each of the five search symbols in turn, shaking your head each time to indicate "no." Then draw a diagonal line through the NO box.

Point to the third practice item and, by nodding your head, encourage the examinee to do it. If the examinee marks NO,

nod your head to indicate "good" and proceed to the regular subtest items (see below).

If the examinee marks YES, correct the examinee. Point to the two target symbols and each of the five search symbols in turn, shaking your head each time to indicate "no." Then draw a diagonal line through the NO box.

Do not go on to the regular subtest items until the examinee understands the task. You may have to erase your marks and the examinee's marks and ask the examinee to do the sample and/or practice items again. It is important to communicate the need for speed on Symbol Search.

Subtest items. When the examinee understands the task, open the Response Booklet to page 1 and fold the page over. If the examinee can read, show him or her the instruction sheet and wait until the examinee has finished reading it. After the examinee reads the directions, point to the first row to indicate that the examinee should begin the task

If the examinee cannot read, run your finger down the entire page 1. Then turn to page 2, and again run your finger down the entire page. Then turn to page 3, and again run your finger down the entire page. Then turn to page 4, and again run your finger down the entire page. After showing the examinee the four pages of items, turn back to page 1. Point to the pencil and then to the first row, then run your finger down the page, and then nod your head to indicate to the examinee to begin.

If the examinee ceases to work after completing the first row, direct the examinee's attention to the second row by pointing to the entire second row with a sweeping motion and encourage the examinee to continue. If the examinee stops at the end of page 1, turn to page 2. If the examinee stops at the end of page 2, turn to page 3. If the examinee stops at the end of page 3, turn to page 4. Allow 120 seconds.

TABLE C-9   **391**

Table C-9
Physical Abilities Necessary for the Wechsler Tests or Their Adaptation

Subtest	Physical ability			
	Vision	Hearing	Oral-speech	Arm-hand use
Arithmetic	R[a] or S[b]	A[b]	A	N, W
Block Design	R	A	N	R
Cancellation	R	N	N	P or W
Coding	R	N	N	R
Comprehension	S	A	A	N, W
Digit Span	N	R	A	N, W
Information	S	A	A	N, W
Letter–Number Sequencing	N	R	A	N, W
Matrix Reasoning	R	A	O	P or W
Object Assembly	R	A	N	R
Picture Arrangement	R	A	N	A
Picture Completion	R	A	O	P or W
Picture Concepts	R	A	O	P or W
Picture Naming	R	A	A	W
Receptive Vocabulary	R	A	N	P or W
Similarities	S	A	A	N, W
Symbol Search	R	N	N	P or W
Vocabulary	S	A	A	N, W
Word Reasoning	S	A	A	N, W

Note. The codes below refer to how a child responds to the subtest, not how the subtest is presented to the child. All subtests, when presented in standardized fashion, require the child to hear and understand the verbal instructions.

The codes are as follows:

A—This ability is required for standard administration, but the subtest is adaptable.
N—This ability is not required.
O—Children who are able to speak can say their answers.
P—Children who are able to point can point to their answers.
R—This ability is required. Adaptation is not feasible if this function is absent or more than mildly impaired.
S—Children who are able to read can be shown the questions. If the examinee cannot read, he or she must be able to hear. If the child can neither read nor hear, the subtest should not be administered.
W—Children who are able to write can write their answers.

[a] Items 1 to 5 on WISC–IV.
[b] Items 6 to 34 on WISC–IV and all items on WAIS–III.

Table C-10
Percentile Ranks for IQs and Composite Scores with a Mean = 100 and SD = 15

IQ	Percentile rank	IQ	Percentile rank	IQ	Percentile rank
155	99.99	118	88	81	10
154	99.98	117	87	80	9
153	99.98	116	86	79	8
152	99.97	115	84	78	7
151	99.97	114	82	77	6
150	99.96	113	81	76	5
149	99.95	112	79	75	5
148	99.93	111	77	74	4
147	99.91	110	75	73	4
146	99.89	109	73	72	3
145	99.87	108	70	71	3
144	99.83	107	68	70	2
143	99.79	106	66	69	2
142	99.74	105	63	68	2
141	99.69	104	61	67	1
140	99.62	103	58	66	1
139	99.53	102	55	65	1
138	99	101	53	64	1
137	99	100	50	63	1
136	99	99	47	62	1
135	99	98	45	61	.47
134	99	97	42	60	.38
133	99	96	39	59	.31
132	98	95	37	58	.26
131	98	94	34	57	.21
130	98	93	32	56	.17
129	97	92	30	55	.13
128	97	91	27	54	.11
127	96	90	25	53	.09
126	96	89	23	52	.07
125	95	88	21	51	.05
124	95	87	19	50	.04
123	94	86	18	49	.03
122	93	85	16	48	.03
121	92	84	14	47	.02
120	91	83	13	46	.02
119	90	82	12	45	.01

Table C-11
Classification Ratings for IQs on the Wechsler Tests

IQ	Classification
130 and above	Very Superior
120–129	Superior
110–119	High Average
90–109	Average
80–89	Low Average
70–79	Borderline
69 and below	Extremely Low

Source: Adapted from Wechsler (1997, 2002b, 2003b).

APPENDIX D

ADMINISTRATIVE CHECKLISTS

Table D-1
Administrative Checklist for WISC–IV

ADMINISTRATIVE CHECKLIST FOR WISC–IV

Name of examiner: _____   Date: _____

Name of child: _____   Name of observer: _____

(Note: If an item is not appropriate, mark NA next to number.)

At the Beginning

	Circle One	
1. Room is well lit	Yes	No
2. Furniture is comfortable and size appropriate for child	Yes	No
3. Room is free from distractions	Yes	No
4. Asks parent, if present, to remain in background and sit quietly out of child's view	Yes	No
5. Positions child correctly	Yes	No
6. Sits directly across from child	Yes	No
7. Attempts to establish rapport	Yes	No
8. Tells child that breaks are OK and to let examiner know when he or she needs a break	Yes	No
9. Does not prolong getting-acquainted period	Yes	No
10. Does not overstimulate child or entertain child excessively before administering test	Yes	No
11. Avoids use of term *intelligence* when introducing test	Yes	No
12. Responds in truthful manner to child's questions (if any) about purpose of testing	Yes	No
13. Test materials are in order	Yes	No
14. Test kit is out of child's vision	Yes	No
15. Begins test when rapport has been established	Yes	No
16. Positions Record Form and Administration Manual so that child cannot read questions or answers	Yes	No
17. Introduces test by reading precisely instructions noted in Administration Manual	Yes	No

Comments

_____

_____

_____

Block Design

(See pp. 59–62 for detailed information.)

Background Considerations

	Circle One	
1. Clears desk	Yes	No
2. Reads instructions verbatim	Yes	No
3. Reads instructions clearly	Yes	No
4. Uses stopwatch quietly, if possible	Yes	No
5. Places stopwatch correctly	Yes	No
6. Repeats instructions correctly	Yes	No
7. On items 5 to 10, shortens instructions appropriately	Yes	No

Block Design (*Continued*)

	Circle One	
8. Clarifies instructions appropriately	Yes	No
9. Positions child correctly	Yes	No
10. As instructions are read, shows different sides of block correctly	Yes	No
11. Gives child only appropriate number of blocks needed for each item	Yes	No
12. Disassembles models as noted in Administration Manual	Yes	No
13. Places intact model, Stimulus Book, and blocks properly	Yes	No
14. Turns pages of Stimulus Book appropriately	Yes	No
15. Use blocks and pictures as models appropriately	Yes	No
16. For items 1 and 2, leaves model intact	Yes	No
17. For items 1 and 2, gives appropriate caution if child attempts to duplicate sides of model	Yes	No
18. For item 3, follows appropriate procedure	Yes	No
19. Scrambles blocks between designs	Yes	No
20. Removes all unnecessary blocks from child's view	Yes	No
21. Does not permit child to rotate Stimulus Book	Yes	No
22. Times correctly	Yes	No
23. Gives appropriate prompts	Yes	No
24. Administers trials correctly	Yes	No

Starting Considerations

	Circle One	
25. Starts with appropriate item	Yes	No

Reverse Sequence

26. Administers items in reverse sequence correctly	Yes	No

Discontinue Considerations

27. Counts items administered in reverse sequence toward discontinue criterion	Yes	No
28. Discontinues appropriately	Yes	No
29. Removes Stimulus Book and blocks from child's view	Yes	No

Scoring Guidelines

30. Scores items correctly	Yes	No

(*Continued*)

Table D-1 (*Continued*)

Block Design (*Continued*)	Circle One	
Record Form		
31. Records completion time correctly	Yes	No
32. Notes or sketches incorrect design appropriately	Yes	No
33. Makes check mark appropriately	Yes	No
34. Notes rotation correctly	Yes	No
35. Circles Y or N correctly	Yes	No
36. Circles 0, 1, 2, 4, 5, 6, or 7 correctly	Yes	No
37. Notes additional points correctly	Yes	No
38. Adds points correctly	Yes	No
39. Enters Total Raw Score in shaded box correctly	Yes	No
40. Enters Block Design No Time-Bonus Total Raw Score in shaded box correctly	Yes	No

Comments

_____

_____

_____

Similarities

(See pp. 64–65 for detailed information.)

Background Considerations		
1. Reads instructions verbatim	Yes	No
2. Reads instructions clearly	Yes	No
3. Reads items verbatim	Yes	No
4. Reads items clearly	Yes	No
5. Repeats instructions correctly	Yes	No
6. Repeats items correctly	Yes	No
7. Queries appropriately	Yes	No
8. For sample and items 1 and 2, gives child correct answers, if needed	Yes	No
9. For items 3 to 23, does not give child correct answers	Yes	No
10. If child fails to respond and has been performing poorly, follows appropriate procedure	Yes	No
11. Grants additional time appropriately	Yes	No

Starting Considerations		
12. Starts with appropriate item	Yes	No

Reverse Sequence		
13. Administers items in reverse sequence correctly	Yes	No

Discontinue Considerations		
14. Counts items administered in reverse sequence toward discontinue criterion	Yes	No
15. Discontinues appropriately	Yes	No

Scoring Guidelines		
16. Scores responses correctly	Yes	No

Record Form		
17. Records child's responses	Yes	No
18. Circles 0, 1, or 2 correctly	Yes	No

Similarities (*Continued*)	Circle One	
19. Notes additional points correctly	Yes	No
20. Adds points correctly	Yes	No
21. Enters Total Raw Score in shaded box correctly	Yes	No

Comments

_____

_____

_____

Digit Span

(See p. 68 for detailed information.)

Background Considerations		
1. Reads instructions verbatim	Yes	No
2. Reads instructions clearly	Yes	No
3. Repeats instructions correctly	Yes	No
4. Shields digits in Record Form and Administration Manual	Yes	No
5. Reads digits clearly at one digit per second, without chunking, and drops voice slightly on last digit	Yes	No
6. Administers items correctly	Yes	No
7. If asked to repeat an item, makes appropriate response	Yes	No

Starting Considerations		
8. Starts with appropriate item	Yes	No

Discontinue Considerations		
9. Discontinues appropriately	Yes	No

Scoring Guidelines		
10. Scores items correctly	Yes	No

Record Form		
11. Records child's responses	Yes	No
12. Circles 0 or 1 in Trial Score column	Yes	No
13. Circles 0, 1, or 2 in Item Score column	Yes	No
14. Enters Total Raw Scores in appropriate boxes correctly	Yes	No
15. Enters Longest Digit Span Forward score correctly	Yes	No
16. Enters Longest Digit Span Backward score correctly	Yes	No

Comments

_____

_____

_____

Picture Concepts

(See pp. 70–72 for detailed information.)

Background Considerations		
1. Reads instructions verbatim	Yes	No
2. Reads instructions clearly	Yes	No
3. Repeats instructions correctly	Yes	No
4. Places Stimulus Book correctly	Yes	No

(Continued)

Table D-1 (Continued)

Picture Concepts (Continued)	Circle One
5. Positions Stimulus Book correctly	Yes No
6. Points across rows as instructions are read	Yes No
7. Turns pages of Stimulus Book correctly	Yes No
8. For items 2 to 12 and 14 to 28, shortens or eliminates instructions appropriately	Yes No
9. Gives appropriate prompts	Yes No
10. If asked, tells child only name of picture	Yes No
11. If response is not clear, asks child to point to picture	Yes No
12. If child gives correct answer to sample A or B, asks appropriate question	Yes No
13. Gives reason for correct answer to samples, if needed	Yes No
14. If child does not give correct answer to either sample A or B, gives correct answers and reasons for correct answers	Yes No
15. Does not give correct answers and reasons for correct answers on test items	Yes No
16. If child fails to respond and has been performing poorly, follows appropriate procedure	Yes No
17. Grants additional time appropriately	Yes No

Starting Considerations

18. Starts with appropriate item	Yes No

Reverse Sequence

19. Administers items in reverse sequence correctly	Yes No

Discontinue Considerations

20. Counts items administered in reverse sequence toward discontinue criterion	Yes No
21. Discontinues appropriately	Yes No
22. Removes Stimulus Book from child's view	Yes No

Scoring Guidelines

23. Scores items correctly	Yes No

Record Form

24. Circles number of each response	Yes No
25. Circles DK appropriately	Yes No
26. Circles 0 or 1 correctly	Yes No
27. Notes additional points correctly	Yes No
28. Adds points correctly	Yes No
29. Enters Total Raw Score in shaded box correctly	Yes No

Comments

_____

_____

_____

Coding	Circle One
(See pp. 73–75 for detailed information.)	Yes No
Background Considerations	Yes No
1. Provides smooth working surface	Yes No
2. Reads instructions verbatim	Yes No
3. Reads instructions clearly	Yes No
4. Repeats instructions correctly	Yes No
5. Points to key as instructions are read	Yes No
6. Waits until child understands task before proceeding with items	Yes No
7. Uses stopwatch quietly, if possible	Yes No
8. Places stopwatch appropriately	Yes No
9. Times appropriately	Yes No
10. Notes child's handedness on Record Form	Yes No
11. Places second Response Booklet properly, if needed	Yes No
12. Demonstrates sample correctly	Yes No
13. Gives child number 2 pencil without eraser	Yes No
14. Does not provide or allow eraser	Yes No
15. Gives instructions verbatim, including word "Go," even if explanations are not necessary	Yes No
16. Before saying "Go," gives further explanations, if necessary	Yes No
17. Gives appropriate prompts	Yes No
18. Counts prompts as part of 120-second time limit	Yes No
19. Allows spontaneous corrections, unless corrections impede performance	Yes No

Starting Considerations

20. Starts with appropriate item	Yes No

Discontinue Considerations

21. Discontinues appropriately	Yes No
22. Stops timing if child finishes before 120 seconds	Yes No
23. Says, "Stop" after 120 seconds and discontinues subtest	Yes No
24. Closes Response Booklet and removes it from child's view	Yes No

Scoring Guidelines

25. Scores subtest correctly	Yes No

Response Booklet

26. Enters child's name, examiner's name, date, and child's age on Response Booklet 1	Yes No

Record Form

27. Records completion time correctly	Yes No
28. For Coding A, circles appropriate time-bonus points correctly	Yes No
29. Add points correctly	Yes No
30. Enters Total Raw Score in shaded box correctly	Yes No

(Continued)

Table D-1 (*Continued*)

Coding (*Continued*)	Circle One		Vocabulary (*Continued*)	Circle One	
Comments			*Comments*		

_____
_____
_____
_____

| | | | | | |

Vocabulary
(See pp. 76–78 for detailed information.)
Background Considerations

1. Reads instructions verbatim	Yes	No
2. Reads instructions clearly	Yes	No
3. Pronounces words clearly	Yes	No
4. Repeats instructions correctly	Yes	No
5. Repeats items correctly	Yes	No
6. In cases of suspected hearing deficit, asks child to repeat word	Yes	No
7. Places closed Stimulus Book properly and then opens it to appropriate page	Yes	No
8. On items 1 to 4, points to the picture	Yes	No
9. On items 5 to 36, points to each word in Stimulus Book as it is pronounced	Yes	No
10. Turns pages of Stimulus Book toward child	Yes	No
11. Queries appropriately	Yes	No
12. Gives correct 2-point answers, as needed	Yes	No
13. For items 1 to 4 and items 7 to 36, does not give correct answers	Yes	No
14. If child fails to respond and has been performing poorly, follows correct procedure	Yes	No
15. Grants additional time appropriately	Yes	No

Starting Considerations

16. Starts with appropriate item	Yes	No

Reverse Sequence

17. Administers items in reverse sequence correctly	Yes	No

Discontinue Considerations

18. Counts items administered in reverse sequence toward discontinue criterion	Yes	No
19. Discontinues appropriately	Yes	No
20. Removes Stimulus Book appropriately	Yes	No

Scoring Guidelines

21. Scores responses correctly	Yes	No

Record Form

22. Records each response	Yes	No
23. Circles 0, 1, or 2 correctly	Yes	No
24. Notes additional points correctly	Yes	No
25. Adds points correctly	Yes	No
26. Enters Total Raw Score in shaded box correctly	Yes	No

Letter–Number Sequencing
(See pp. 80–81 for detailed information.)
Background Considerations

1. Reads instructions verbatim	Yes	No
2. Reads instructions clearly	Yes	No
3. Repeats instructions correctly	Yes	No
4. Shields digits and letters in Administration Manual and on Record Form	Yes	No
5. Administers qualifying item correctly	Yes	No
6. Administers both trials of sample, regardless of child's response on first trial	Yes	No
7. Corrects child and readministers trial 1 of sample if child makes an incorrect response	Yes	No
8. Corrects child and readministers trial 2 of sample if child makes an incorrect response	Yes	No
9. Proceeds with subtest even if child makes incorrect responses on both trials of sample	Yes	No
10. Administers item 1 after samples	Yes	No
11. Reads digits and letters at rate of one digit or letter per second without chunking	Yes	No
12. Drops voice slightly on last digit or letter in sequence	Yes	No
13. Gives all three trials of each item	Yes	No
14. Pauses after each sequence to allow child to respond	Yes	No
15. Never repeats any digits or letters during subtest proper	Yes	No
16. If asked to repeat a trial of an item, gives appropriate response	Yes	No
17. Uses appropriate wording to correct child, as needed	Yes	No
18. Says nothing if child makes a mistake on certain items	Yes	No

Starting Considerations

19. Starts with appropriate item	Yes	No

Discontinue Considerations

20. Discontinues appropriately	Yes	No

Scoring Guidelines

21. Scores items correctly	Yes	No

Record Form

22. Circles Y or N correctly	Yes	No
23. Records responses correctly	Yes	No
24. Circles 0 or 1 in Trial Score column correctly	Yes	No

(*Continued*)

Table D-1 (*Continued*)

Letter–Number Sequencing (*Continued*)	Circle One	
25. Circles 0, 1, 2, or 3 in Item Score column correctly	Yes	No
26. Adds points correctly	Yes	No
27. Enters Total Raw Score in shaded box correctly	Yes	No

Comments

_____

_____

_____

Matrix Reasoning
(See pp. 83–84 for detailed information.)
Background Considerations

	Circle One	
1. Reads instructions verbatim	Yes	No
2. Reads instructions clearly	Yes	No
3. Places Stimulus Book properly	Yes	No
4. Positions Stimulus Book correctly	Yes	No
5. Turns pages of Stimulus Book correctly	Yes	No
6. Clarifies instructions correctly	Yes	No
7. If any sample is failed, demonstrates correct way to solve problem	Yes	No
8. Repeats instructions correctly	Yes	No
9. Gives appropriate prompts	Yes	No
10. Provides feedback only on three samples	Yes	No
11. If child fails to respond and has been performing poorly, follows appropriate procedure	Yes	No
12. Grants additional time appropriately	Yes	No

Starting Considerations

13. Starts with appropriate item	Yes	No

Reverse Sequence

14. Administers items in reverse sequence correctly	Yes	No

Discontinue Considerations

15. Counts items administered in reverse sequence toward discontinue criterion appropriately	Yes	No
16. Discontinues appropriately	Yes	No
17. Removes Stimulus Book from child's view	Yes	No

Scoring Guidelines

18. Scores items correctly	Yes	No

Record Form

19. Circles response number or DK correctly	Yes	No
20. Circles 0 or 1 correctly	Yes	No
21. Notes additional points correctly	Yes	No
22. Adds points correctly	Yes	No
23. Enters Total Raw Score in shaded box correctly	Yes	No

Matrix Reasoning (*Continued*)	Circle One	
Comments		

_____

_____

_____

Comprehension
(See pp. 85–87 for detailed information.)
Background Considerations

	Circle One	
1. Reads instructions verbatim	Yes	No
2. Reads instructions clearly	Yes	No
3. Reads items verbatim	Yes	No
4. Reads items clearly	Yes	No
5. Repeats instructions correctly	Yes	No
6. Repeats items correctly	Yes	No
7. If child is hesitant, gives appropriate prompts	Yes	No
8. If child gives 0- or 1-point response to item 1, tells child correct 2-point answer	Yes	No
9. For items 2 to 21, does not tell child correct answer	Yes	No
10. Queries appropriately	Yes	No
11. If child fails to respond and has been performing poorly, follows appropriate procedure	Yes	No
12. Grants additional time appropriately	Yes	No

Starting Considerations

13. Starts with appropriate item	Yes	No

Reverse Sequence

14. Administers items in reverse sequence correctly	Yes	No

Discontinue Considerations

15. Counts items administered in reverse sequence toward discontinue criterion	Yes	No
16. Discontinues appropriately	Yes	No

Scoring Guidelines

17. Scores items correctly	Yes	No

Record Form

18. Records responses correctly	Yes	No
19. Circles 0, 1, or 2 correctly	Yes	No
20. Notes additional points correctly	Yes	No
21. Adds points correctly	Yes	No
22. Enters Total Raw Score in shaded box correctly	Yes	No

Comments

_____

_____

_____

(*Continued*)

Table D-1 (*Continued*)

Symbol Search	Circle One	
(See pp. 88–90 for detailed information.)		
Background Considerations		
1. Provides smooth working surface	Yes	No
2. Reads instructions verbatim	Yes	No
3. Reads instructions clearly	Yes	No
4. Repeats instructions correctly	Yes	No
5. Uses stopwatch quietly, if possible	Yes	No
6. Places stopwatch appropriately	Yes	No
7. During sample and practice items, makes sure that child sees only sample page of Response Booklet 1	Yes	No
8. Provides child with number 2 pencil without eraser	Yes	No
9. Opens Response Booklet 1 to appropriate page	Yes	No
10. For samples, points to target symbol and search groups	Yes	No
11. For samples, draws diagonal line through correct YES or NO box	Yes	No
12. For practice items, points to target symbol and search groups and gives appropriate instructions	Yes	No
13. Gives appropriate feedback	Yes	No
14. If child makes an error on practice items, follows correct procedure	Yes	No
15. Explains instructions using practice items, if needed	Yes	No
16. Does not proceed to test items unless child understands task	Yes	No
17. Opens Response Booklet 1 to page 4 or 8, as appropriate	Yes	No
18. Gives instructions verbatim, including word "Go," even if explanations are not necessary	Yes	No
19. Before saying "Go," gives further explanations, if necessary	Yes	No
20. Begins timing appropriately	Yes	No
21. Turns pages of Response Booklet 1, if needed	Yes	No
22. Gives appropriate prompts	Yes	No
23. Counts prompts as part of 120-second time limit	Yes	No
24. Does not discourage child from making spontaneous corrections, unless corrections impede performance	Yes	No

Starting Considerations

	Circle One	
25. Starts with appropriate item	Yes	No

Discontinue Considerations

	Circle One	
26. Discontinues appropriately	Yes	No
27. Stops timing if child finishes before 120 seconds	Yes	No
28. Says, "Stop" after 120 seconds and discontinues subtest	Yes	No
29. Closes Response Booklet 1 and removes it from child's view	Yes	No

Symbol Search (*Continued*)	Circle One	
Scoring Guidelines		
30. Scores subtest correctly	Yes	No

Response Booklet

	Circle One	
31. If Coding was not administered, enters child's name, examiner's name, date, and child's age	Yes	No
32. Enters number of correct items correctly	Yes	No
33. Enters number of incorrect items correctly	Yes	No

Record Form

	Circle One	
34. Records completion time correctly	Yes	No
35. Correctly enters total number of C's in Number Correct box	Yes	No
36. Correctly enters total number of I's in Number Incorrect box	Yes	No
37. Enters Total Raw Score in shaded box correctly	Yes	No
38. Enters 0 if Total Raw Score is equal to or less than 0	Yes	No

Comments

_____

_____

_____

Picture Completion

(See pp. 96–98 for detailed information.)

Background Considerations

	Circle One	
1. Reads instructions verbatim	Yes	No
2. Reads instructions clearly	Yes	No
3. Reads items verbatim	Yes	No
4. Reads items clearly	Yes	No
5. Repeats instructions correctly	Yes	No
6. Places Stimulus Book properly	Yes	No
7. Turns pages of Stimulus Book correctly	Yes	No
8. Allows 20 seconds for each item	Yes	No
9. For items 3 to 38, shortens or eliminates instructions correctly	Yes	No
10. Begins timing correctly	Yes	No
11. Stops timing correctly	Yes	No
12. On sample, repeats child's correct answer	Yes	No
13. For sample and items 1 and 2, gives child correct answers, if needed	Yes	No
14. For items 3 to 38, does not give child correct answers	Yes	No
15. Queries only once during subtest for specific responses	Yes	No
16. Correctly queries ambiguous or incomplete responses	Yes	No
17. Correctly queries responses noted in right-hand column of pages 166 to 169 in Administration Manual	Yes	No

(*Continued*)

Table D-1 (*Continued*)

Picture Completion (*Continued*)	Circle One	
Starting Considerations		
18. Starts with appropriate item	Yes	No
Reverse Sequence		
19. Administers items in reverse sequence correctly	Yes	No
Discontinue Considerations		
20. Counts items administered in reverse sequence toward discontinue criterion	Yes	No
21. Discontinues appropriately	Yes	No
22. Removes Stimulus Book from child's view	Yes	No
Scoring Guidelines		
23. Scores items correctly	Yes	No
Record Form		
24. Records child's responses	Yes	No
25. Records PC for correct pointing responses	Yes	No
26. Records PX for incorrect pointing responses	Yes	No
27. Circles 0 or 1 correctly	Yes	No
28. Notes additional points correctly	Yes	No
29. Adds points correctly	Yes	No
30. Enters Total Raw Score in shaded box correctly	Yes	No

Comments

_____

_____

_____

Cancellation
(See pp. 99–101 for detailed information.)

Background Considerations		
1. Reads instructions verbatim	Yes	No
2. Reads instructions clearly	Yes	No
3. Repeats instructions correctly	Yes	No
4. Provides smooth working surface	Yes	No
5. At beginning, shows only cover page of Response Booklet 2 to child	Yes	No
6. Provides red pencil without eraser	Yes	No
7. Uses stopwatch quietly, if possible	Yes	No
8. Places stopwatch appropriately	Yes	No
9. When administering sample, directs child's attention to animals at top of page	Yes	No
10. Points to row of animals in sweeping motion, left to right from child's perspective	Yes	No
11. Draws line through two animal pictures of samples	Yes	No
12. Points to practice items while reading instructions	Yes	No
13. Gives appropriate feedback	Yes	No
14. If child makes an error on practice items, follows correct procedure	Yes	No
15. Gives appropriate prompts	Yes	No

Cancellation (*Continued*)	Circle One	
16. Counts prompts as part of 120-second time limit	Yes	No
17. Allows spontaneous corrections, unless corrections impede performance	Yes	No
18. Proceeds to test items when child understands task	Yes	No
19. Opens Response Booklet 2 to appropriate page for item 1	Yes	No
20. Gives instructions verbatim for item 1, including word "Go," even if explanations are not necessary	Yes	No
21. Before saying "Go," gives further explanations for item 1, if necessary	Yes	No
22. Begins timing item 1 appropriately	Yes	No
23. Administers item 2 if child finishes item 1 early	Yes	No
24. Says, "Stop" after 45 seconds on item 1 and administers item 2	Yes	No
25. Opens Response Booklet 2 to appropriate page for item 2	Yes	No
26. Gives instructions verbatim for item 2, including word "Go," even if explanations are not necessary	Yes	No
27. Before saying "Go," gives further explanations for item 2, if necessary	Yes	No
28. Begins timing item 2 appropriately	Yes	No
Starting Considerations		
29. Starts with appropriate item	Yes	No
Discontinue Considerations		
30. Discontinues appropriately	Yes	No
31. Records time and discontinues subtest if child completes item 2 early	Yes	No
32. Says, "Stop" after 45 seconds on item 2 and discontinues subtest	Yes	No
33. Closes Response Booklet 2 and removes it from child's view	Yes	No
Scoring Guidelines		
34. Scores subtest correctly	Yes	No
Response Booklet		
35. Enters child's name, examiner's name, date, and child's age	Yes	No
Record Form		
36. Enters completion time correctly	Yes	No
37. Correctly enters total number of correct objects marked	Yes	No
38. Correctly enters total number of incorrect objects marked	Yes	No
39. For each item, subtracts Number Incorrect from Number Correct and records result in Difference column	Yes	No
40. Enters time-bonus points for each item correctly	Yes	No

(*Continued*)

Table D-1 (*Continued*)

Cancellation (*Continued*)	Circle One	
41. For items 1 and 2, correctly enters sum of Difference *plus* Bonus Points (if any) in Total Raw Score column	Yes	No
42. Correctly enters Total Raw Score for item 1 *plus* item 2 in shaded box	Yes	No

Comments

_____

_____

_____

Information | **Circle One** | |
(See pp. 103–104 for detailed information.)

Background Considerations

	Circle One	
1. Reads instructions verbatim	Yes	No
2. Reads instructions clearly	Yes	No
3. Reads items verbatim	Yes	No
4. Reads items clearly	Yes	No
5. Repeats items correctly	Yes	No
6. Repeats instructions correctly	Yes	No
7. Queries and prompts appropriately	Yes	No
8. Gives correct answers appropriately	Yes	No
9. For items 3 to 33, does not give correct answers	Yes	No
10. If child fails to respond and has been performing poorly, follows appropriate procedure	Yes	No
11. Grants additional time appropriately	Yes	No

Starting Considerations

12. Starts with appropriate item	Yes	No

Reverse Sequence

13. Administers items in reverse sequence correctly	Yes	No

Discontinue Considerations

14. Counts items administered in reverse sequence toward discontinue criterion	Yes	No
15. Discontinues appropriately	Yes	No

Scoring Guidelines

16. Scores items correctly	Yes	No

Record Form

17. Records child's responses correctly	Yes	No
18. Circles 0 or 1 correctly	Yes	No
19. Notes additional points correctly	Yes	No
20. Adds points correctly	Yes	No
21. Enters Total Raw Score in shaded box correctly	Yes	No

Comments

_____

_____

_____

Arithmetic | **Circle One** | |
(See pp. 106–107 for detailed information.)

Background Considerations

	Circle One	
1. Reads items verbatim	Yes	No
2. Reads items clearly	Yes	No
3. Repeats instructions correctly	Yes	No
4. Repeats items correctly	Yes	No
5. Places closed Stimulus Book properly and then opens it to correct page	Yes	No
6. Turns pages of Stimulus Book toward child during subtest administration	Yes	No
7. Times correctly	Yes	No
8. For items 1, 2, and 3, provides appropriate feedback for incorrect responses	Yes	No
9. Does not give answers for items 4 to 34	Yes	No
10. Does not allow child to use pencil and paper	Yes	No
11. Allows child to use finger to "write" on table	Yes	No
12. When it is not clear which of two responses is final choice, gives appropriate prompt	Yes	No

Starting Considerations

13. Starts with appropriate item	Yes	No

Reverse Sequence

14. Administers items in reverse sequence correctly	Yes	No

Discontinue Considerations

15. Counts items administered in reverse sequence toward discontinue criterion	Yes	No
16. Discontinues appropriately	Yes	No
17. Removes Stimulus Book from child's view	Yes	No

Scoring Guidelines

18. Scores items correctly	Yes	No

Record Form

19. Records child's responses correctly	Yes	No
20. Circles 0 or 1 correctly	Yes	No
21. Notes additional points correctly	Yes	No
22. Adds points correctly	Yes	No
23. Enters Total Raw Score in shaded box correctly	Yes	No

Comments

_____

_____

_____

Word Reasoning
(See pp. 109–110 for detailed information.)

Background Considerations

	Circle One	
1. Reads items verbatim	Yes	No
2. Reads items clearly	Yes	No
3. Introduces each item appropriately	Yes	No

(*Continued*)

Table D-1 (Continued)

Word Reasoning (Continued)	Circle One	
4. After giving each clue, allows child about 5 seconds to answer	Yes	No
5. Repeats each clue correctly	Yes	No
6. Allows child additional time appropriately	Yes	No
7. Restates previous clues correctly	Yes	No
8. Stops giving additional clues correctly	Yes	No

Starting Considerations

9. Starts with appropriate item	Yes	No

Reverse Sequence

10. Administers items in reverse sequence correctly	Yes	No

Discontinue Considerations

11. Counts items administered in reverse sequence toward discontinue criterion	Yes	No
12. Discontinues appropriately	Yes	No

Scoring Guidelines

13. Scores responses correctly	Yes	No

Record Form

14. Records responses verbatim in Response column	Yes	No
15. Records R if clue is repeated	Yes	No
16. Circles Y or N correctly	Yes	No
17. Circles 0 or 1 correctly	Yes	No
18. Notes additional points correctly	Yes	No
19. Adds points correctly	Yes	No
20. Enters Total Raw Score in shaded box correctly	Yes	No

Comments

_____

_____

_____

Front Page of Record Form

1. Completes child's full name and examiner's full name correctly	Yes	No

Calculation of Child's Age

2. Records date of testing correctly (Y, M, D)	Yes	No
3. Records child's date of birth correctly (Y, M, D)	Yes	No
4. Computes child's age of testing correctly (Y, M, D)	Yes	No

Total Raw Score to Scaled Score Conversions

5. For each subtest administered, transfers Total Raw Score to front of Record Form correctly	Yes	No
6. Enters correct scaled score in appropriate unshaded box	Yes	No

Front Page of Record Form (Continued)	Circle One	
7. For Verbal Comprehension Index, sums three scaled scores correctly and enters sum in appropriate shaded box	Yes	No
8. For Perceptual Reasoning Index, sums three scaled scores correctly and enters sum in appropriate shaded box	Yes	No
9. For Working Memory Index, sums two scaled scores correctly and enters sum in appropriate shaded box	Yes	No
10. For Processing Speed Index, sums two scaled scores correctly and enters sum in appropriate shaded box	Yes	No
11. For Full Scale IQ, sums 10 scaled scores correctly and enters sum in appropriate shaded box	Yes	No

Sum of Scaled Scores to Composite Score Conversions

12. Transfers sums of scaled scores to appropriate shaded boxes	Yes	No
13. Enters correct Verbal Comprehension Composite score	Yes	No
14. Enters correct Perceptual Reasoning Composite score	Yes	No
15. Enters correct Working Memory Composite score	Yes	No
16. Enters correct Processing Speed Composite score	Yes	No
17. Enters correct Full Scale IQ	Yes	No
18. Enters correct Verbal Comprehension percentile rank	Yes	No
19. Enters correct Perceptual Reasoning percentile rank	Yes	No
20. Enters correct Working Memory percentile rank	Yes	No
21. Enters correct Processing Speed percentile rank	Yes	No
22. Enters correct Full Scale IQ percentile rank	Yes	No
23. Enters selected confidence interval	Yes	No
24. Enters correct Verbal Comprehension Composite confidence interval	Yes	No
25. Enters correct Perceptual Reasoning Composite confidence interval	Yes	No
26. Enters correct Working Memory Composite confidence interval	Yes	No
27. Enters correct Processing Speed Composite confidence interval	Yes	No
28. Enters correct Full Scale IQ confidence interval	Yes	No

Subtest Scaled Score Profile

29. Completes Subtest Scaled Score Profile (if desired) correctly	Yes	No

(Continued)

Table D-1 (*Continued*)

Front Page of Record Form (*Continued*)	Circle One	
Composite Score Profile		
30. Completes Composite Score Profile (if desired) correctly	Yes	No
31. Notes order of administering subtests on Record Form, if different from standard order	Yes	No

Comments

_____

_____

_____

Analysis Page
Discrepancy Comparisons

	Circle One	
1. Correctly enters scaled scores in Scaled Score 1 and Scaled Score 2 columns	Yes	No
2. Calculates difference scores correctly	Yes	No
3. Enters critical values correctly	Yes	No
4. Enters significant differences (Y or N) correctly	Yes	No
5. Enters base rate in standardization sample correctly	Yes	No
6. Checks one of two basis-for-comparison boxes	Yes	No
7. Checks one of two basis-for-statistical-significance boxes	Yes	No

Determining Strengths and Weaknesses

8. Enters subtest scaled scores correctly	Yes	No
9. Enters mean scaled scores correctly	Yes	No
10. Calculates differences from mean scaled scores correctly	Yes	No
11. Enters critical values correctly	Yes	No
12. Enters significant strengths or weaknesses (S or W) correctly, if needed	Yes	No
13. Correctly enters base rate in standardization sample for strengths and weaknesses, if needed	Yes	No
14. Checks one of two basis-for-comparison boxes	Yes	No
15. Checks one of two basis-for-statistical-significance boxes	Yes	No
16. Correctly enters sums of scaled scores for 10 subtests, 3 Verbal Comprehension subtests, and 3 Perceptual Reasoning subtests	Yes	No

Process Analysis

17. Enters raw scores for process scores correctly	Yes	No
18. Enters scaled scores for process scores correctly	Yes	No
19. Enters raw score for LDSF and LDSB correctly	Yes	No
20. Enters base rate for LDSF and LDSB correctly	Yes	No

Analysis Page (*Continued*)	Circle One	
21. Enters raw score 1 and raw score 2 for LDSF–LDSB discrepancy comparison correctly	Yes	No
22. Computes difference score for LDSF–LDSB discrepancy comparison correctly	Yes	No
23. Enters base rate for LDSF–LDSB discrepancy comparison correctly	Yes	No
24. Enters scaled score 1 and scaled score 2 for three subtest/process score discrepancy comparisons correctly	Yes	No
25. Computes difference score for three subtest/process score discrepancy comparisons correctly	Yes	No
26. Enters critical value for three subtest/process score discrepancy comparisons correctly	Yes	No
27. Enters base rate for three subtest/process score discrepancy comparisons correctly, if needed	Yes	No
28. Checks one of two statistical significance levels for three subtest/process score discrepancy comparisons	Yes	No

Comments

_____

_____

_____

Last Page of Record Form

	Circle One	
1. Completes last page, if desired	Yes	No

General Evaluation

1. Maintains rapport throughout testing	Yes	No
2. Shows reasonable amount of flexibility in maintaining rapport	Yes	No
3. Is alert to child's moods	Yes	No
4. Does not badger child	Yes	No
5. Handles behavior problems appropriately	Yes	No
6. Administers test in professional, unhurried manner	Yes	No
7. Is well organized	Yes	No
8. Administers subtests in order noted on page 25 of Administration Manual, altering order based only on clinical need	Yes	No
9. Maintains steady pace	Yes	No
10. Makes smooth transition from subtest to subtest	Yes	No
11. Places test materials not currently in use out of child's sight but within easy reach of examiner	Yes	No
12. Avoids conspicuous efforts to conceal materials	Yes	No
13. Takes short break, as needed, at end of a subtest	Yes	No
14. Does not take any breaks in middle of a subtest	Yes	No

(*Continued*)

Table D-1 (*Continued*)

General Evaluation (*Continued*)	Circle One	
15. Allows fidgety child to take break at end of a subtest	Yes	No
16. Allows child to walk around room, if needed	Yes	No
17. Encourages child who expresses inability to perform a task	Yes	No
18. Praises child's effort	Yes	No
19. Does not say "Good" or "Right" after correct response, unless these words are part of instructions	Yes	No
20. If child is aware of poor performance, shows empathy	Yes	No
21. Does not provide additional help beyond instructions (e.g., giving additional items to practice, asking leading questions, spelling words on any subtest, using Vocabulary words in a sentence, etc.)	Yes	No
22. Gives credit for correct responses given at any time during test, except on timed items and items passed above discontinue criterion	Yes	No
23. Does not give credit on timed subtests for any correct responses or correct completions *after* time limit	Yes	No
24. Records Q for queried responses	Yes	No
25. Records P for prompted responses	Yes	No
26. Records on Record Form any deviations from standard order of administering subtests	Yes	No
27. Repeats instructions on request, unless prohibited by subtest instructions	Yes	No
28. On untimed subtests, repeats early item(s) if child says, "I don't know" to early item(s) but then responds correctly to more difficult items	Yes	No
29. On untimed subtests, uses good judgment overall in deciding how much time to give child to solve each item	Yes	No
30. Scores each item after child answers	Yes	No
31. Uses good judgment overall in scoring responses	Yes	No
32. Rechecks scoring after test is administered	Yes	No

General Evaluation (*Continued*)	Circle One	
33. Makes entry in Record Form for every item administered	Yes	No
34. Awards full credit for all items preceding first two items with perfect scores, regardless of child's performance on preceding items, by putting slash mark in Score column over item preceding two items with perfect scores and writing the numerals for these points	Yes	No
35. Does not give credit for any item(s) beyond last score of 0 required for discontinue criterion, regardless of child's performance on these items if they have been administered	Yes	No
36. Records on Record Form any deviation from procedure	Yes	No
37. Makes every effort to administer entire test in one session	Yes	No

Qualitative Feedback

_____
_____
_____

Overall Strengths

_____
_____
_____

Areas Needing Improvement

_____
_____
_____

Other Comments

_____
_____
_____

Overall Evaluation
Circle One: Excellent   Good   Average   Poor   Failing

Table D-2
Administrative Checklist for WPPSI–III

ADMINISTRATIVE CHECKLIST FOR WPPSI–III

Name of examiner: _____   Date: _____

Name of child: _____   Name of observer: _____

(Note: If an item is not appropriate, mark NA next to the number.)

At the Beginning   Circle One

1. Room is well lit   Yes   No
2. Furniture is comfortable and size appropriate
    for child   Yes   No
3. Room is free from distractions   Yes   No
4. Asks parent, if present, to remain in back-
    ground and sit quietly out of child's view   Yes   No
5. Positions child correctly   Yes   No
6. Sits directly across from child   Yes   No
7. Attempts to establish rapport   Yes   No
8. Tells child that breaks are OK and to let
    examiner know when he or she needs a
    break   Yes   No
9. Does not prolong getting-acquainted period   Yes   No
10. Does not overstimulate child or entertain
    child excessively before administering test   Yes   No
11. Avoids use of term *test* when introducing test   Yes   No
12. Responds in truthful manner to child's
    questions (if any) about purpose of testing   Yes   No
13. Test materials are in order   Yes   No
14. Test kit is out of child's vision   Yes   No
15. Begins test when rapport has been
    established   Yes   No
16. Positions Record Form and Administration
    Manual so that child cannot read questions
    or answers   Yes   No
17. Introduces test by following instructions
    noted in Administration Manual   Yes   No

Comments

_____
_____
_____

Block Design
(See pp. 205–210 for detailed information.)
Background Considerations

1. Clears desk   Yes   No
2. Reads instructions verbatim   Yes   No
3. Reads instructions clearly   Yes   No
4. Uses stopwatch quietly, if possible   Yes   No
5. Places stopwatch correctly   Yes   No
6. Repeats instructions correctly   Yes   No
7. Clarifies instructions appropriately   Yes   No
8. Uses appropriate instructions for item 6   Yes   No
9. Positions child correctly   Yes   No
10. As instructions are read for Part B, shows
    different sides of block correctly   Yes   No

Block Design (*Continued*)   Circle One

11. Gives child only appropriate number of
    blocks needed for each item   Yes   No
12. Disassembles models as noted in
    Administration Manual   Yes   No
13. Places intact model, Stimulus Book 1, and
    blocks properly   Yes   No
14. Turns pages of Stimulus Book 1
    appropriately   Yes   No
15. Uses blocks and pictures as models
    appropriately   Yes   No
16. For items 1 to 12, leaves model intact   Yes   No
17. For item 13, follows appropriate procedure   Yes   No
18. Scrambles blocks between designs   Yes   No
19. Removes all unnecessary blocks from child's
    view   Yes   No
20. Does not permit child to rotate Stimulus
    Book 1   Yes   No
21. Times correctly   Yes   No
22. Gives appropriate prompts   Yes   No
23. Administers trials correctly   Yes   No

Starting Considerations
24. Starts with appropriate item   Yes   No

Reverse Sequence
25. Administers items in reverse sequence
    correctly   Yes   No

Discontinue Considerations
26. Counts items administered in reverse
    sequence toward discontinue criterion   Yes   No
27. Discontinues appropriately   Yes   No
28. Removes Stimulus Book 1 and blocks from
    child's view   Yes   No

Scoring Guidelines
29. Scores items correctly   Yes   No

Record Form
30. Records completion time correctly   Yes   No
31. Notes or sketches incorrect design
    appropriately   Yes   No
32. Makes check mark appropriately   Yes   No
33. Notes rotation correctly   Yes   No
34. Circles Y or N correctly   Yes   No

(Continued)

Table D-2 (*Continued*)

Block Design (*Continued*)	Circle One
35. Circles 0, 1, or 2 correctly	Yes No
36. Notes additional points correctly	Yes No
37. Adds points correctly	Yes No
38. Enters Total Raw Score in shaded box correctly	Yes No

Comments

_____

_____

_____

Information
(See pp. 210–213 for detailed information.)
Background Considerations

	Circle One
1. Reads items verbatim	Yes No
2. Reads items clearly	Yes No
3. Places Stimulus Book 1 properly and then opens it to correct page	Yes No
4. Removes Stimulus Book 1 from child's view after item 6	Yes No
5. Repeats items correctly	Yes No
6. Queries and prompts appropriately	Yes No
7. For item 1, gives correct answer appropriately	Yes No
8. For items 2 to 34, does not give correct answers	Yes No
9. If child fails to respond and has been performing poorly, follows appropriate procedure	Yes No
10. Grants additional time appropriately	Yes No

Starting Considerations

11. Starts with appropriate item	Yes No

Reverse Sequence

12. Administers items in reverse sequence correctly	Yes No

Discontinue Considerations

13. Counts items administered in reverse sequence toward discontinue criterion	Yes No
14. Discontinues appropriately	Yes No

Scoring Guidelines

15. Scores items correctly	Yes No

Record Form

16. For items 1 to 6, circles response number or DK correctly	Yes No
17. For items 7 to 17, records child's responses correctly	Yes No
18. Circles 0 or 1 correctly	Yes No
19. Notes additional points correctly	Yes No
20. Adds points correctly	Yes No
21. Enters Total Raw Score in shaded box correctly	Yes No

Information (*Continued*)	Circle One
Comments	

_____

_____

_____

Matrix Reasoning
(See pp. 213–216 for detailed information.)
Background Considerations

	Circle One
1. Reads instructions verbatim	Yes No
2. Reads instructions clearly	Yes No
3. Places Stimulus Book 1 properly	Yes No
4. Positions Stimulus Book 1 correctly	Yes No
5. Turns pages of Stimulus Book 1 correctly	Yes No
6. Clarifies instructions correctly	Yes No
7. If any sample is failed, demonstrates correct way to solve problem	Yes No
8. Repeats instructions correctly	Yes No
9. For items 1 to 29, shortens or eliminates instructions appropriately	Yes No
10. Gives appropriate prompts	Yes No
11. Provides feedback only on three samples	Yes No
12. If child fails to respond and has been performing poorly, follows appropriate procedure	Yes No
13. Grants additional time appropriately	Yes No

Starting Considerations

14. Starts with appropriate item	Yes No

Reverse Sequence

15. Administers items in reverse sequence correctly	Yes No

Discontinue Considerations

16. Counts items administered in reverse sequence toward discontinue criterion appropriately	Yes No
17. Discontinues appropriately	Yes No
18. Removes Stimulus Book 1 from child's view	Yes No

Scoring Guidelines

19. Scores items correctly	Yes No

Record Form

20. Circles response number or DK correctly	Yes No
21. Circles 0 or 1 correctly	Yes No
22. Notes additional points correctly	Yes No
23. Adds points correctly	Yes No
24. Enters Total Raw Score in shaded box correctly	Yes No

Comments

_____

_____

_____

(*Continued*)

Table D-2 (*Continued*)

Vocabulary	Circle One	
(See pp. 216–219 for detailed information.)		
Background Considerations		
1. Reads instructions verbatim	Yes	No
2. Reads instructions clearly	Yes	No
3. Pronounces words clearly	Yes	No
4. Repeats instructions correctly	Yes	No
5. Repeats items correctly	Yes	No
6. In cases of suspected hearing deficit, asks child to repeat word	Yes	No
7. Places closed Stimulus Book 1 properly and then opens it to appropriate page	Yes	No
8. On items 1 to 5, points to the picture	Yes	No
9. Turns pages of Stimulus Book 1 toward child	Yes	No
10. Queries appropriately	Yes	No
11. Gives correct 1-point answers as needed	Yes	No
12. For items 2 to 5 and items 8 to 25, does not give correct answers	Yes	No
13. If child fails to respond and has been performing poorly, follows correct procedure	Yes	No
14. Grants additional time appropriately	Yes	No
Starting Considerations		
15. Starts with appropriate item	Yes	No
Reverse Sequence		
16. Administers items in reverse sequence correctly	Yes	No
Discontinue Consideration		
17. Counts items administered in reverse sequence toward discontinue criterion	Yes	No
18. Discontinues appropriately	Yes	No
19. Removes Stimulus Book 1 appropriately	Yes	No
Scoring Guidelines		
20. Scores responses correctly	Yes	No
Record Form		
21. Records each response	Yes	No
22. Circles 0, 1, or 2 correctly	Yes	No
23. Notes additional points correctly	Yes	No
24. Adds points correctly	Yes	No
25. Enters Total Raw Score in shaded box correctly	Yes	No

Comments

_____

_____

_____

Picture Concepts

	Circle One	
(See pp. 220–222 for detailed information.)		
Background Considerations		
1. Reads instructions verbatim	Yes	No
2. Reads instructions clearly	Yes	No
3. Repeats instructions correctly	Yes	No
4. Places Stimulus Book 1 correctly	Yes	No

Picture Concepts (*Continued*)	Circle One	
5. Positions Stimulus Book 1 correctly	Yes	No
6. Points across rows as instructions are read	Yes	No
7. Turns pages of Stimulus Book 1 correctly	Yes	No
8. For items 1 to 26, shortens or eliminates instructions appropriately	Yes	No
9. Gives appropriate prompts	Yes	No
10. If asked, tells child only name of picture	Yes	No
11. If response is not clear, asks child to point to picture	Yes	No
12. If child does not give correct answer to sample A or B, gives correct answer and reason for correct answer	Yes	No
13. Does not give correct answers and reasons for correct answers on subtest items	Yes	No
14. If child fails to respond and has been performing poorly, follows appropriate procedure	Yes	No
15. Grants additional time appropriately	Yes	No
Starting Considerations		
16. Starts with appropriate item	Yes	No
Reverse Sequence		
17. Administers items in reverse sequence correctly	Yes	No
Discontinue Considerations		
18. Counts items administered in reverse sequence toward discontinue criterion	Yes	No
19. Discontinues appropriately	Yes	No
20. Removes Stimulus Book 1 from child's view	Yes	No
Scoring Guidelines		
21. Scores items correctly	Yes	No
Record Form		
22. Circles number of each response	Yes	No
23. Circles DK appropriately	Yes	No
24. Circles 0 or 1 correctly	Yes	No
25. Notes additional points correctly	Yes	No
26. Adds points correctly	Yes	No
27. Enters Total Raw Score in shaded box correctly	Yes	No

Comments

_____

_____

Word Reasoning

	Circle One	
(See pp. 223–225 for detailed information.)		
Background Considerations		
1. Reads items verbatim	Yes	No
2. Reads items clearly	Yes	No
3. Introduces each item appropriately	Yes	No
4. After giving each clue, allows child about 5 seconds to answer	Yes	No

(*Continued*)

Table D-2 (*Continued*)

Word Reasoning (*Continued*)	Circle One	
5. Repeats each clue correctly	Yes	No
6. Allows child additional time appropriately	Yes	No
7. Restates previous clues correctly	Yes	No
8. Stops giving additional clues correctly	Yes	No

Starting Considerations

9. Starts with appropriate item	Yes	No

Reverse Sequence

10. Administers items in reverse sequence correctly	Yes	No

Discontinue Considerations

11. Counts items administered in reverse sequence toward discontinue criterion	Yes	No
12. Discontinues appropriately	Yes	No

Scoring Guidelines

13. Scores responses correctly	Yes	No

Record Form

14. Records responses verbatim in Response column	Yes	No
15. Records R if clue is repeated	Yes	No
16. Circles 0 or 1 correctly	Yes	No
17. Notes additional points correctly	Yes	No
18. Adds points correctly	Yes	No
19. Circles Y or N correctly	Yes	No
20. Enters Total Raw Score in shaded box correctly	Yes	No

Comments

_____

_____

_____

Coding
(See pp. 225–228 for detailed information.)
Background Considerations

1. Provides smooth working surface	Yes	No
2. Reads instructions verbatim	Yes	No
3. Reads instructions clearly	Yes	No
4. Repeats instructions correctly	Yes	No
5. Points to key as instructions are read	Yes	No
6. Waits until child understands task before proceeding with items	Yes	No
7. Uses stopwatch quietly, if possible	Yes	No
8. Places stopwatch appropriately	Yes	No
9. Times appropriately	Yes	No
10. Places second Response Booklet properly, if needed	Yes	No
11. Demonstrates sample correctly	Yes	No
12. Gives child number 2 pencil without eraser	Yes	No
13. Does not provide or allow eraser	Yes	No
14. Gives instructions verbatim, including word "Go," even if explanations are not necessary	Yes	No

Coding (*Continued*)	Circle One	
15. Before saying "Go," gives further explanations, if necessary	Yes	No
16. Gives appropriate prompts	Yes	No
17. Counts prompts as part of 120-second time limit	Yes	No
18. Allows spontaneous corrections, unless corrections impede performance	Yes	No

Starting Considerations

19. Starts with appropriate item	Yes	No

Discontinue Considerations

20. Discontinues appropriately	Yes	No
21. Stops timing if child finishes before 120 seconds	Yes	No
22. Says, "Stop" after 120 seconds and discontinues subtest	Yes	No
23. Closes Response Booklet and removes it from child's view	Yes	No

Scoring Guidelines

24. Scores subtest correctly	Yes	No

Response Booklet

25. Enters child's name, examiner's name, date, and child's age on Response Booklet	Yes	No

Record Form

26. Records completion time correctly	Yes	No
27. Circles appropriate time-bonus points correctly	Yes	No
28. Add points correctly	Yes	No
29. Enters Total Raw Score in shaded box correctly	Yes	No

Comments

_____

_____

_____

Symbol Search
(See pp. 232–235 for detailed information.)
Background Considerations

1. Provides smooth working surface	Yes	No
2. Reads instructions verbatim	Yes	No
3. Reads instructions clearly	Yes	No
4. Repeats instructions correctly	Yes	No
5. Uses stopwatch quietly, if possible	Yes	No
6. Places stopwatch appropriately	Yes	No
7. During sample and practice items, makes sure that child sees only sample page of Response Booklet	Yes	No
8. Provides child with number 2 pencil without eraser	Yes	No
9. Opens Response Booklet to appropriate page	Yes	No

(*Continued*)

Table D-2 (*Continued*)

Symbol Search (*Continued*)	Circle One
10. For samples, points to target symbol and search groups	Yes No
11. For samples, draws diagonal line through matching symbol	Yes No
12. For practice items, points to target symbol and search groups and gives appropriate instructions	Yes No
13. Gives appropriate feedback	Yes No
14. If child makes an error on practice items, follows correct procedure	Yes No
15. Explains instructions using sample items, if needed	Yes No
16. Does not proceed to test items unless child understands task	Yes No
17. Opens Response Booklet to page 2	Yes No
18. Gives instructions verbatim, including word "Go," even if explanations are not necessary	Yes No
19. Before saying "Go," gives further explanations, if necessary	Yes No
20. Begins timing appropriately	Yes No
21. Turns pages of Response Booklet, if needed	Yes No
22. Gives appropriate prompts	Yes No
23. Counts prompts as part of 120-second time limit	Yes No
24. Does not discourage child from making spontaneous corrections, unless corrections impede performance	Yes No

Starting Considerations
25. Starts with appropriate item	Yes No

Discontinue Considerations
26. Discontinues appropriately	Yes No
27. Stops timing if child finishes before 120 seconds	Yes No
28. Says, "Stop" after 120 seconds and discontinues subtest	Yes No
29. Closes Response Booklet and removes it from child's view	Yes No

Scoring Guidelines
30. Scores subtest correctly	Yes No

Response Booklet
31. Enters child's name, date, and examiner's name	Yes No
32. Enters number of correct items correctly	Yes No
33. Enters number of incorrect items correctly	Yes No

Record Form
34. Records completion time correctly	Yes No
35. Correctly enters total number of C's in Number Correct box	Yes No
36. Correctly enters total number of I's in Number Incorrect box	Yes No
37. Enters Total Raw Score in shaded box correctly	Yes No

Symbol Search (*Continued*)	Circle One
38. Enters a 0 if Total Raw Score is equal to or less than 0	Yes No

Comments

_____

_____

_____

Comprehension
(See pp. 235–238 for detailed information.)

Background Considerations
1. Reads instructions verbatim	Yes No
2. Reads instructions clearly	Yes No
3. Reads items verbatim	Yes No
4. Reads items clearly	Yes No
5. Repeats instructions correctly	Yes No
6. Repeats items correctly	Yes No
7. If child is hesitant, gives appropriate prompts	Yes No
8. If child gives 0-point response to item 1 or 2, tells child correct 1-point answer	Yes No
9. For items 3 to 20, does not tell child correct answers	Yes No
10. Queries appropriately	Yes No
11. If child fails to respond and has been performing poorly, follows appropriate procedure	Yes No
12. Grants additional time appropriately	Yes No

Starting Considerations
13. Starts with appropriate item	Yes No

Reverse Sequence
14. Administers items in reverse sequence correctly	Yes No

Discontinue Considerations
15. Counts items administered in reverse sequence toward discontinue criterion	Yes No
16. Discontinues appropriately	Yes No

Scoring Guidelines
17. Scores items correctly	Yes No

Record Form
18. Records responses correctly	Yes No
19. Circles 0, 1, or 2 correctly	Yes No
20. Notes additional points correctly	Yes No
21. Adds points correctly	Yes No
22. Enters Total Raw Score in shaded box correctly	Yes No

Comments

_____

_____

_____

(Continued)

Table D-2 (*Continued*)

Picture Completion	Circle One
(See pp. 238–241 for detailed information.)	

Background Considerations

1. Reads items verbatim	Yes	No
2. Reads items clearly	Yes	No
3. Repeats instructions correctly	Yes	No
4. Places Stimulus Book 2 properly	Yes	No
5. Turns pages of Stimulus Book 2 correctly	Yes	No
6. Allows 20 seconds for each item	Yes	No
7. For items 3 to 32, shortens or eliminates instructions correctly	Yes	No
8. Begins timing correctly	Yes	No
9. Stops timing correctly	Yes	No
10. For sample and items 1 and 2, gives child correct answers, if needed	Yes	No
11. For items 3 to 32, does not give child correct answers	Yes	No
12. Queries appropriately	Yes	No
13. Correctly queries responses noted in right-hand column of pages 153 to 156 in Administration Manual	Yes	No

Starting Considerations

14. Starts with appropriate item	Yes	No

Reverse Sequence

15. Administers items in reverse sequence correctly	Yes	No

Discontinue Considerations

16. Counts items administered in reverse sequence toward discontinue criterion	Yes	No
17. Discontinues appropriately	Yes	No
18. Removes Stimulus Book 2 from child's view	Yes	No

Scoring Guidelines

19. Scores items correctly	Yes	No

Record Form

20. Records child's responses	Yes	No
21. Records PC for correct pointing responses	Yes	No
22. Records PX for incorrect pointing responses	Yes	No
23. Circles 0 or 1 correctly	Yes	No
24. Records completion time correctly	Yes	No
25. Notes additional points correctly	Yes	No
26. Adds points correctly	Yes	No
27. Enters Total Raw Score in shaded box correctly	Yes	No

Comments

_____

_____

_____

Similarities

(See pp. 241–244 for detailed information.)

Background Considerations

1. Reads items verbatim	Yes	No

Similarities (*Continued*)	Circle One

2. Reads items clearly	Yes	No
3. Repeats instructions correctly	Yes	No
4. Repeats items correctly	Yes	No
5. Emphasizes word *both* in reading each item	Yes	No
6. Queries appropriately	Yes	No
7. For trials 1 and 2 of items 1 and 2, gives child correct answers appropriately	Yes	No
8. For items 3 to 24, does not give child correct answers	Yes	No
9. If child fails to respond and has been performing poorly, follows appropriate procedure	Yes	No
10. Grants additional time appropriately	Yes	No

Starting Considerations

11. Starts with appropriate item	Yes	No

Discontinue Considerations

12. Discontinues appropriately	Yes	No

Scoring Guidelines

13. Scores responses correctly	Yes	No

Record Form

14. Records child's responses	Yes	No
15. Circles 0, 1, or 2 correctly	Yes	No
16. Adds points correctly	Yes	No
17. Enters Total Raw Score in shaded box correctly	Yes	No

Comments

_____

_____

_____

Receptive Vocabulary

(See pp. 244–246 for detailed information.)

Background Considerations

1. Reads items verbatim	Yes	No
2. Reads items clearly	Yes	No
3. Positions Stimulus Book 1 properly	Yes	No
4. Turns pages of Stimulus Book 1 correctly	Yes	No
5. Repeats items correctly	Yes	No
6. For item 1, gives correct answer appropriately	Yes	No
7. For items 2 to 38, does not give correct answers	Yes	No

Starting Considerations

8. Starts with appropriate item	Yes	No

Reverse Sequence

9. Administers items in reverse sequence correctly	Yes	No

(*Continued*)

Table D-2 (*Continued*)

Receptive Vocabulary (*Continued*)	Circle One
Discontinue Considerations	
10. Counts items administered in reverse sequence toward discontinue criterion	Yes No
11. Discontinues appropriately	Yes No
12. Removes Stimulus Book 1 from child's view	Yes No
Scoring Guidelines	
13. Scores items correctly	Yes No
Record Form	
14. For items 1 to 22 and for items 24 to 38, circles response number or DK	Yes No
15. For item 23, circles one of four colors or DK	Yes No
16. Circles 0 or 1 for each item	Yes No
17. Notes additional points correctly	Yes No
18. Adds points correctly	Yes No
19. Enters Total Raw Score in shaded box correctly	Yes No

Comments

_____

_____

_____

Object Assembly
(See pp. 246–250 for detailed information.)

Background Considerations	
1. Reads items verbatim	Yes No
2. Reads items clearly	Yes No
3. Positions child correctly	Yes No
4. Sequentially sorts and stacks pieces of each puzzle	Yes No
5. Places pieces of each puzzle on table correctly	Yes No
6. Times correctly	Yes No
7. If child is hesitant, gives appropriate prompts	Yes No
8. For trials 1 and 2 of items 1 and 2, allows child to look at assembled puzzle for about 3 seconds	Yes No
9. For items 3 to 14, introduces items correctly	Yes No
Starting Considerations	
10. Starts with appropriate item	Yes No
Reverse Sequence	
11. Administers items in reverse sequence correctly	Yes No
Discontinue Considerations	
12. Counts items administered in reverse sequence toward discontinue criterion	Yes No
13. Discontinues appropriately	Yes No
14. Removes puzzle pieces from child's view	Yes No
Scoring Guidelines	
15. Scores items correctly	Yes No

Object Assembly (*Continued*)	Circle One
Record Form	
16. Records completion time correctly	Yes No
17. Records correct number of junctures in Number of Correct Junctures column	Yes No
18. Circles 0, 1, 2, 3, 4, or 5 correctly	Yes No
19. Notes additional points correctly	Yes No
20. Adds points correctly	Yes No
21. Enters Total Raw Score in shaded box correctly	Yes No

Comments

_____

_____

_____

Picture Naming
(See pp. 250–252 for detailed information.)

Background Considerations	
1. Reads items verbatim	Yes No
2. Reads items clearly	Yes No
3. Positions Stimulus Book 2 correctly	Yes No
4. Turns pages of Stimulus Book 2 correctly	Yes No
5. For item 1, gives correct answer appropriately	Yes No
6. For items 2 to 30, does not give correct answers	Yes No
7. Points to pictures correctly	Yes No
8. Queries appropriately	Yes No
Starting Considerations	
9. Starts with appropriate item	Yes No
Reverse Sequence	
10. Administers items in reverse sequence correctly	Yes No
Discontinue Considerations	
11. Counts items administered in reverse sequence toward discontinue criterion	Yes No
12. Discontinues appropriately	Yes No
13. Removes Stimulus Book 2 from child's view	Yes No
Scoring guidelines	
14. Scores items correctly	Yes No
Record Form	
15. Records child's responses verbatim	Yes No
16. Circles 0 or 1 correctly	Yes No
17. Notes additional points correctly	Yes No
18. Adds points correctly	Yes No
19. Enters Total Raw Score in shaded box correctly	Yes No

Comments

_____

_____

_____

Table D-2 (Continued)

Front Page of Record Form	Circle One
1. Completes child's full name, sex, grade, handedness, school, parent's/guardian's full name, place of testing, and examiner's full name correctly	Yes No
Calculation of Child's Age	
2. Records date of testing correctly (Y, M, D)	Yes No
3. Records child's date of birth correctly (Y, M, D)	Yes No
4. Computes child's age of testing correctly (Y, M, D)	Yes No
Total Raw Score to Scaled Score Conversion	
5. For each subtest administered, transfers Total Raw Score to front of Record Form correctly	Yes No
6. Enters correct scaled score in appropriate unshaded box	Yes No
7. For Verbal subtests, sums two or three scaled scores correctly and enters sum in appropriate shaded box	Yes No
8. For Performance subtests, sums two or three scaled scores correctly and enters sum in appropriate shaded box	Yes No
9. For Processing Speed subtests, sums two scaled scores correctly and enters sum in appropriate shaded box	Yes No
10. For Full Scale IQ, sums four or seven scaled scores correctly and enters sum in appropriate shaded box	Yes No
11. For General Language Composite, sums two scaled scores correctly and enters sum in appropriate shaded box	Yes No
Sum of Scaled Scores to Composite Score Conversions	
12. Transfers sums of scaled scores to appropriate boxes	Yes No
13. Enters correct Verbal IQ	Yes No
14. Enters correct Performance IQ	Yes No
15. Enters correct Processing Speed Quotient	Yes No
16. Enters correct Full Scale IQ	Yes No
17. Enters correct General Language Composite	Yes No
18. Enters correct Verbal IQ percentile rank	Yes No
19. Enters correct Performance IQ percentile rank	Yes No
20. Enters correct Processing Speed Quotient percentile rank	Yes No
21. Enters correct Full Scale IQ percentile rank	Yes No
22. Enters correct General Language Composite percentile rank	Yes No
23. Enters selected confidence interval	Yes No
24. Enters correct Verbal IQ confidence interval	Yes No
25. Enters correct Performance IQ confidence interval	Yes No
26. Enters correct Processing Speed Quotient confidence interval	Yes No

Front Page of Record Form (*Continued*)	Circle One
27. Enters correct Full Scale IQ confidence interval	Yes No
28. Enters correct General Language Composite confidence interval	Yes No
Subtest Scaled Score Profile	
29. Completes Subtest Scaled Score Profile (if desired) correctly	Yes No
Composite Score Profile	
30. Completes Composite Score Profile (if desired) correctly	Yes No
31. Notes order of administering subtests on Record Form, if different from standard order	Yes No

Comments

_____

_____

_____

Analysis Page

Discrepancy Comparisons

	Circle One
1. Correctly enters scaled scores in Scaled Score 1 and Scaled Score 2 columns	Yes No
2. Calculates difference scores correctly	Yes No
3. Enters critical value correctly	Yes No
4. Enters significant difference (Y or N) correctly	Yes No
5. Enters base rate in standardization sample correctly	Yes No
6. Checks one of two basis-for-comparison boxes	Yes No
7. Checks one of two basis-for-statistical-significance boxes	Yes No

Determining Strengths and Weaknesses

	Circle One
8. Enters subtest scaled scores correctly	Yes No
9. Enters mean scaled scores correctly	Yes No
10. Calculates differences from mean scaled scores correctly	Yes No
11. Enters critical values correctly	Yes No
12. Enters strengths and weaknesses (S or W) correctly, if needed	Yes No
13. Correctly enters base rate in standardization sample for strengths and weaknesses, if needed	Yes No
14. Checks one of two basis-for-comparison boxes	Yes No
15. Checks one of two basis-for-statistical-significance boxes	Yes No
16. Correctly enters sums of scaled scores for 7 subtests, 3 Verbal subtests, and 3 Performance subtests (ages 4-0 to 7-3) or sum of scaled scores for 4 subtests (ages 2-6 to 3-11)	Yes No

(*Continued*)

Table D-2 (*Continued*)

Analysis Page (*Continued*)	Circle One
17. Correctly enters mean scores for 7 subtests, 3 Verbal subtests, and 3 Performance subtests (ages 4-0 to 7-3) or sum of scaled scores for 4 subtests (ages 2-6 to 3-11)	Yes No

Last Page of Record Form
1. Completes last page, if desired — Yes No

General Evaluation
1. Maintains rapport throughout testing — Yes No
2. Shows reasonable amount of flexibility in maintaining rapport — Yes No
3. Is alert to child's moods — Yes No
4. Does not badger child — Yes No
5. Handles behavior problems appropriately — Yes No
6. Administers test in professional, unhurried manner — Yes No
7. Is well organized — Yes No
8. Administers subtests in order noted on page 22 of Administration Manual, altering order based only on clinical need — Yes No
9. Maintains steady pace — Yes No
10. Makes smooth transition from subtest to subtest — Yes No
11. Places test materials not currently in use out of child's sight but within easy reach of examiner — Yes No
12. Avoids conspicuous efforts to conceal materials — Yes No
13. Takes short break, as needed, at end of a subtest — Yes No
14. Does not take any breaks in middle of a subtest — Yes No
15. Allows fidgety child to take break at end of a subtest — Yes No
16. Allows child to walk around room, if needed — Yes No
17. Encourages child who expresses inability to perform a task — Yes No
18. Praises child's effort — Yes No
19. Does not say "Good" or "Right" after correct response, unless these words are part of instructions — Yes No
20. If child is aware of poor performance, shows empathy — Yes No
21. Does not provide additional help beyond instructions (e.g., giving additional items to practice, asking leading questions, spelling words on any subtest, using Vocabulary words in a sentence, etc.) — Yes No
22. Gives credit for correct responses given at any time during test, except on timed items and items passed above discontinue criterion — Yes No
23. Does not give credit on timed subtests for any correct responses or correct completions *after* time limit — Yes No
24. Records Q for queried responses — Yes No

General Evaluation (*Continued*)	Circle One
25. Records P for prompted responses	Yes No
26. Records on Record Form any deviations from standard order of administering subtests	Yes No
27. Repeats instructions on request, unless prohibited by subtest instructions	Yes No
28. On untimed subtests, repeats early item(s) if child says, "I don't know" to early item(s) but then responds correctly to more difficult items	Yes No
29. On untimed subtests, uses good judgment overall in deciding how much time to give child to solve each item	Yes No
30. Scores each item after child answers	Yes No
31. Uses good judgment overall in scoring responses	Yes No
32. Rechecks scoring after test is administered	Yes No
33. Makes entry in Record Form for every item administered	Yes No
34. Awards full credit for all items preceding first two items with perfect scores, regardless of child's performance on preceding items, by putting slash mark in Score column over item preceding two items with perfect scores and writing the numerals for these points	Yes No
35. Does not give credit for any item(s) beyond last score of 0 required for discontinue criterion, regardless of child's performance on these items if they have been administered	Yes No
36. Records on Record Form any deviation from procedure	Yes No
37. Makes every effort to administer entire test in one session	Yes No

Qualitative Feedback

_____
_____
_____

Overall Strengths

_____
_____
_____

Areas Needing Improvement

_____
_____
_____

Other Comments

_____
_____
_____

Overall Evaluation
Circle one: Excellent   Good   Average   Poor   Failing

REFERENCES

Alfonso, V. C., Johnson, A., Patinella, L., & Rader, D. E. (1998). Common WISC–III examiner errors: Evidence from graduate students in training. *Psychology in the Schools, 35,* 119–125.

American Association on Mental Retardation. (2002). *Mental retardation: Definition, classification, and systems of support* (10th ed.). Washington, DC: Author.

American Psychiatric Association. (2000). *Diagnostic and statistical manual of mental disorders: Text revision (DSM-IV-TR)* (4th ed.). Washington, DC: Author.

Cohen, J. (1988). *Statistical power analysis for the behavioral sciences.* Hillsdale, NJ: Erlbaum.

Davis, F. B. (1959). Interpretation of differences among averages and individual test scores. *Journal of Educational Psychology, 50,* 162–170.

Dugbartey, A. T., Sanchez, P. N., Rosenbaum, J. G., Mahurin, R. K., Davis, J. M., & Townes, B. D. (1999). WAIS–III Matrix Reasoning test performance in a mixed clinical sample. *Clinical Neuropsychologist, 13,* 396–404.

Flanagan, D. P., McGrew, K. S., & Ortiz, S. O. (2000). *The Wechsler Intelligence Scales and Gf-Gc theory.* Needham Heights, MA: Allyn & Bacon.

Glutting, J. J., Youngstrom, E. A., Ward, T., Ward, S., & Hale, R. L. (1997). Incremental efficacy of WISC–III factor scores in predicting achievement: What do they tell us? *Psychological Assessment, 9,* 295–301.

Horn, J. L. (1987). A context for understanding information processing studies of human abilities. In P. A. Vernon (Ed.), *Speed of information-processing and intelligence* (pp. 201–238). Norwood, NJ: Ablex.

Horn, J. L. (1988). A basis for research on age differences in cognitive capabilities. In J. J. McArdle & R. W. Woodcock (Eds.), *Human cognitive abilities in theory and practice* (pp. 57–87). Mahwah, NJ: Erlbaum.

Kaufman, A. S. (1975). Factor analysis of the WISC–R at 11 age levels between 6½ and 16½ years. *Journal of Consulting and Clinical Psychology, 43,* 135–147.

Klassen, R. M., & Kishor, N. (1996). A comparative analysis of practitioners' errors on WISC–R and WISC–III. *Canadian Journal of School Psychology, 12,* 35–43.

Levenson, R. L., Jr., Golden-Scaduto, C. J., Aiosa-Karpas, C. J., & Ward, A. W. (1988). Effects of examiners' education and sex on presence and type of clerical errors made on WISC–R protocols. *Psychological Reports, 62,* 659–664.

Rozencwajg, P. (1991). Analysis of problem solving strategies on the Kohs Block Design Test. *European Journal of Psychology of Education, 6,* 73–88.

Rozencwajg, P., & Corroyer, D. (2002). Strategy development in a block design task. *Intelligence, 30,* 1–25.

Sattler, J. M. (2001). *Assessment of children: Cognitive applications* (4th ed.). La Mesa, CA: Author.

Sattler, J. M. (2002). *Assessment of children: Behavioral and clinical applications* (4th ed.). La Mesa, CA: Author.

Slate, J. R., & Hunnicutt, L. C., Jr. (1988). Examiner errors on the Wechsler scales. *Journal of Psychoeducational Assessment, 6,* 280–288.

Slate, J. R., Jones, C. H., Coulter, C., & Covert, T. L. (1992). Practitioners' administration and scoring of the WISC–R: Evidence that we do err. *Journal of School Psychology, 30,* 77–82.

Teglasi, H., & Freeman, R. W. (1983). Rapport pitfalls of beginning testers. *Journal of School Psychology, 21,* 229–240.

Tellegen, A., & Briggs, P. F. (1967). Old wine in new skins: Grouping Wechsler subtests into new scales. *Journal of Consulting Psychology, 31,* 499–506.

Wagoner, R. (1988). *Scoring errors made by practicing psychologists on the WISC–R.* Unpublished masters thesis, Western Carolina University at Cullowhee, North Carolina.

Wechsler, D. (1939). *The measurement of adult intelligence.* Baltimore: Williams & Wilkins.

Wechsler, D. (1949). *Wechsler Intelligence Scale for Children.* San Antonio: The Psychological Corporation.

Wechsler, D. (1997). *WAIS–III and WMS–III: Technical manual.* San Antonio: The Psychological Corporation.

Wechsler, D. (2002a).*WPPSI–III: Administration and scoring manual.* San Antonio: The Psychological Corporation.

Wechsler, D. (2002b). *WPPSI–III: Technical and interpretive manual.* San Antonio: The Psychological Corporation.

Wechsler, D. (2003a). *Wechsler Intelligence Scale for Children–Fourth Edition: Administration and scoring manual.* San Antonio: The Psychological Corporation.

Wechsler, D. (2003b). *Wechsler Intelligence Scale for Children–Fourth Edition: Technical and interpretive manual.* San Antonio: The Psychological Corporation.

INDEX